In Combat

Historical Materialism Book Series

The Historical Materialism Book Series is a major publishing initiative of the radical left. The capitalist crisis of the twenty-first century has been met by a resurgence of interest in critical Marxist theory. At the same time, the publishing institutions committed to Marxism have contracted markedly since the high point of the 1970s. The Historical Materialism Book Series is dedicated to addressing this situation by making available important works of Marxist theory. The aim of the series is to publish important theoretical contributions as the basis for vigorous intellectual debate and exchange on the left.

The peer-reviewed series publishes original monographs, translated texts, and reprints of classics across the bounds of academic disciplinary agendas and across the divisions of the left. The series is particularly concerned to encourage the internationalization of Marxist debate and aims to translate significant studies from beyond the English-speaking world.

For a full list of titles in the Historical Materialism Book Series available in paperback from Haymarket Books, visit:
https://www.haymarketbooks.org/series_collections/1-historical-materialism

In Combat

The Life of Lombardo Toledano

Daniela Spenser

Haymarket Books
Chicago, IL

First published in 2019 by Brill Academic Publishers, The Netherlands
© 2019 Koninklijke Brill NV, Leiden, The Netherlands

Published in paperback in 2020 by
Haymarket Books
P.O. Box 180165
Chicago, IL 60618
773-583-7884
www.haymarketbooks.org

ISBN: 978-1-64259-334-1

Distributed to the trade in the US through Consortium Book Sales and Distribution (www.cbsd.com) and internationally through Ingram Publisher Services International (www.ingramcontent.com).

This book was published with the generous support of Lannan Foundation and Wallace Action Fund.

Special discounts are available for bulk purchases by organizations and institutions. Please call 773-583-7884 or email info@haymarketbooks.org for more information.

Cover design by Jamie Kerry and Ragina Johnson.

Printed in the United States.

10 9 8 7 6 5 4 3 2 1

Library of Congress Cataloging-in-Publication data is available.

Contents

Acknowledgements IX
List of Illustrations XI
Abbreviations XIII

Introduction 1

PART 1
Changing Times and Ideas

1 **Family** 8
   1 The Village 9
   2 Children 10
   3 Vicente Lombardo Toledano 18
   4 The Wise Man 21
   5 The Family 25

2 **Knowledge and Power** 29
   1 Renewal 29
   2 The Break 33
   3 On the Campaign Trail 35
   4 From the Government Palace 37
   5 On the Road to the Chamber of Deputies 40
   6 The Trip 48
   7 The Polemical Dispute 50
   8 Ideological Passion 53

3 **Exodus** 56
   1 In the CROM 57
   2 Collapse 63
   3 The Labour Law 65
   4 The Road to the Left 73

PART 2
Crusades

4 A Journey into the World of the Future   84
  1   The Preparations   84
  2   The Trip   87
  3   Different Perspectives   93
  4   Back in Mexico   97
  5   The President and the Leader   100
  6   The Gide Case   102

5 The Foundations of the Nation   107
  1   The Preparations   107
  2   The First Pillar   110
  3   Into Action   114
  4   The Schism   118
  5   Disunity   122
  6   The President and the Leader   127

6 A Continental Feat   131
  1   In Santiago de Chile   131
  2   The Planning   134
  3   In the United States   137
  4   In Europe   140
  5   The Founding Congress   142
  6   To the Attack   149

PART 3
War: Threshold of a Better World?

7 Fight Fascism!   156
  1   The Defeat of the Spanish Republic   157
  2   Exile   159
  3   Face to Face with Leon Trotsky   163
  4   The Pact and Its Violation   169
  5   In Soviet Intelligence   170
  6   The Undesirable Anti-fascists   173

CONTENTS

8   **The Illusory Unity**   176
    1   On the Campaign Trail   176
    2   The Victory   182
    3   The Farewell   185
    4   The Re-election   188
    5   The Elusive Unity   191

9   **The Fragile Harmony**   197
    1   The Latin American Panorama   198
    2   The Congress   201
    3   The Celebrated Trip   202
    4   The Catavi Massacre   210
    5   Coups and Blows   212
    6   From Montevideo to Caracas   216
    7   From Philadelphia to Cali   218
    8   The Elusive Harmony   221

PART 4
Animosities and Confrontations

10 **For the Renewal of the Nation**   226
    1   The Future   227
    2   On the Campaign Trail   230
    3   The Roundtable   234
    4   Elections in the CTM   240
    5   The Expulsion   244
    6   The Crisis of the Nation   247

11 **For the Spilled Blood**   250
    1   The Postwar Map   250
    2   In London   252
    3   In Paris   254
    4   In the Other Europe   258
    5   Confrontations   261
    6   In People's China   267

12 **Emancipation**   274
    1   Removing Obstacles   274
    2   On an Inspection Tour   277

3   In Lima   283
4   The Third Congress   285
5   The Oil Workers   290
6   Failed Emancipation   292

PART 5
On the Fronts of the Cold Peace

13 **Rearmament**   300
    1   The People's Party   300
    2   UGOCM   308
    3   Back on the Campaign Trail   312
    4   Aftermath of Defeat   316
    5   The Succession   321
    6   The Cold Peace   325

14 **Mission Completed**   330
    1   Anti-communist Liberalism   330
    2   Liberal Internationalism   333
    3   In Decline   342
    4   The CTAL Dies in Bucharest   346
    5   The CTAL Completed Its Historic Mission   350

15 **The Road to 1968**   356
    1   PPS   356
    2   Against the Current   361
    3   On the Final Campaign Trail   365
    4   Schism in the Party   374
    5   1968   378

Epilogue: Testament and Testimonies   383

Bibliography and Works Cited   387
Index   411
Illustrations   423

Acknowledgements

It is mandatory, but no less satisfactory, to acknowledge once again the institutional scaffolding of the Centre for Research and Advanced Studies in Social Anthropology (CIESAS), which for more than 35 years has been my oasis for the optimal development of research and academic dialogue. Both the directors in charge of CIESAS as well as its administrative services facilitated the unhindered development of this study. The CIESAS library and its staff displayed exemplary dedication in providing me with the necessary and timely material to prepare this book.

I would like to thank the family of Vicente Lombardo Toledano for their willingness to talk and help me understand the world in which the family lived with its father, uncle, father-in-law and grandfather. Among its members who shared their recollections were Adriana Lombardo Otero and Marcela Lombardo Otero, Raúl Gutiérrez Lombardo, Federico Silva, Vicente Silva Lombardo, Laura Noriega, Sonia Lombardo, Sonia Henríquez Ureña, María Elena Lombardo, Rosa María and Lili Soto Lombardo, Emiliano and Natalia Silva, and Andrés Caso Lombardo. I would like to also thank Martín Tavira Uriostegui and Adolfo Mejía, Lombardo's comrades, for a pleasant afternoon chat in Morelia, Michoacán. Thanks to the support of Luis Monter and Emiliano Silva, I had privileged access to the Lombardo Toledano Historical Archives at the Workers' University.

This book would not have existed if between 2007 and 2008 the John Simon Guggenheim Memorial Foundation had not financially supported the necessary travel to archives in search of materials on Lombardo Toledano. Funding obtained through the short grant from the Diplomatic Archive of the Mexican Foreign Affairs Ministry allowed me to conduct research in the Nettie Lee Benson Library at the University of Texas in Austin and the Lyndon B. Johnson Archives. My stay at Columbia University in 2012 under the O'Gorman Visiting Scholars Programme was as unforgettable as it was helpful. The knowledge, experience and imagination of a great many archivists were indispensable in enabling me to scrutinise their collections in search of data on a figure with whose name they were totally unfamiliar. The documents of the Russian State Archive of Socio-Political History come from research conducted by Rina Ortiz of the Department of Historical Studies of the National Institute of Anthropology and History and the joint research, funded by the basic science programme of the National Council of Science and Technology (CONACYT) between 1999–2001.

It was a privilege not to have experienced any pressure from CIESAS or the National Researchers System (SNI) to finish the book by a specific deadline, as opposed to when I felt it was ready. Albert Einstein once said 'An academic career in which a person is forced to produce scientific writings in great amounts creates a danger of intellectual superficiality'.[1]

Several research assistants within the generous programme of the CONACYT's National Researchers System helped, with grinding work, in the search for data in archives and libraries. Each and every one of them has become a professional in their own right. In chronological order, I received collaborative support from María Cristina Tamariz, Alejandro Peña García, Anahí Parra, Alberto Torrentera, Isaac Rosas, Jerónimo Palomares, Nadia Zempoaltecatl Cantero, Serena Chew Plascencia, Julio Navarro Vilches, Mizraim Garnica and Raúl Téllez Farfán.

The support, friendship and solidarity of many people were indispensable. In Austin, Texas, Robin Moore; in Moscow, Svetlana Rosenthal, her daughter Mila and Emma Ancelevich; in Geneva, Peter Huber; in Washington, D.C., Ana Serra and Mary Kay Vaughan; in London and Prague, Ruth Tosek, my mother, who did not live to see this book.

There were many people with whom I engaged in discussions during the preparation of this book, and others to whom I listened even though I might have appeared driven by a singleminded concern. Some offered pointed questions and suggestions, still others contributed materials for the production of this book. Among them are Ignacio Almada Bay, William Booth, John Burstein, Claudia Caretta, Barry Carr, Margarita Estrada, Olivia Gall, María Antonieta Hernández Rojas, Michael Hoare, Patrick Iber, Gilbert Joseph, Friedrich Katz, Renata Keller, Dan La Botz, John Lear, Sergio Mastretta, Lorenzo Meyer, Magaly Rodríguez García, Mario Vázquez Olivera, Juan Pedro Viqueira, Daniel Yanes, María Antonia Yanes, Pablo Yanes, and Pablo Yankelevich.

Peter Gellert, knowledgeable of the background and motivations that inspired this study, translated the text from Spanish into English.

Enrique Krauze, unwittingly, pointed me to where to start the book; Adolfo Gilly, knowingly, on where to continue the study. From Arturo Alcalde Justiniani's articles published on Saturdays in *La Jornada*, I learned the meaning of trade-union democracy and what corrupts it. I was inspired by many historical novels; the one that taught me most on how best to tell a story was *The Man Who Loved Dogs* by Leonardo Padura.

---

1 Isaacson 2007, p. 79.

Illustrations

All illustrations can be found in the separate Illustration Section following the Index.

1. Vicente Lombardo Toledano. Archive of the International Labour Organisation
2. Vincenzo Lombardo Catti. Archivo Fotográfico del Centro de Estudios Filosóficos, Políticos y Sociales 'Vicente Lombardo Toledano'
3. Vicente Lombardo and Isabel Toledano. Archivo Fotográfico del Centro de Estudios Filosóficos, Políticos y Sociales 'Vicente Lombardo Toledano'
4. Vicente Lombardo Toledano hunting in the Sierra de Puebla. Ca. 1911. Archivo Fotográfico del Centro de Estudios Filosóficos, Políticos y Sociales 'Vicente Lombardo Toledano'
5. Bridal photography of Vicente Lombardo Toledano and Rosa María Otero. 22 April 1921. Archivo Fotográfico del Centro de Estudios Filosóficos, Políticos y Sociales 'Vicente Lombardo Toledano'
6. Vicente Lombardo Toledano and family. Ca. 1930. Archivo Fotográfico del Centro de Estudios Filosóficos, Políticos y Sociales 'Vicente Lombardo Toledano'
7. Vicente Lombardo Toledano sitting on the steps of an archaeological site in Yucatán. 1941. Archivo Fotográfico del Centro de Estudios Filosóficos, Políticos y Sociales 'Vicente Lombardo Toledano'
8. Vicente Lombardo Toledano and Marcela Lombardo Otero. Ca. 1946. Archivo Fotográfico del Centro de Estudios Filosóficos, Políticos y Sociales 'Vicente Lombardo Toledano'
9. Vicente Lombardo Toledano portrayed during his trip from New York to Liverpool. 1938. Archivo Fotográfico del Centro de Estudios Filosóficos, Políticos y Sociales 'Vicente Lombardo Toledano'
10. Vicente Lombardo Toledano and Fidel Velázquez in the farewell to the direction of the CTM. 1941. Archivo Fotográfico del Centro de Estudios Filosóficos, Políticos y Sociales 'Vicente Lombardo Toledano'
11. Vicente Lombardo Toledano in Yugoslavia. June–July 1947. Archivo Fotográfico del Centro de Estudios Filosóficos, Políticos y Sociales 'Vicente Lombardo Toledano'
12. María Teresa Puente delivering a speech during an assembly of the Partido Popular. Archivo Fotográfico del Centro de Estudios Filosóficos, Políticos y Sociales 'Vicente Lombardo Toledano'
13. Vicente Lombardo Toledano with the children of the workers. Ca. 1951. Archivo Fotográfico del Centro de Estudios Filosóficos, Políticos y Sociales 'Vicente Lombardo Toledano'

14 Vicente Lombardo Toledano and Cuban leader Jesús Menéndez. Archivo Fotográfico del Centro de Estudios Filosóficos, Políticos y Sociales 'Vicente Lombardo Toledano'
15 Vicente Lombardo Toledano portrayed with indigenous women from Juchitán, Oaxaca. 1952. Archivo Fotográfico del Centro de Estudios Filosóficos, Políticos y Sociales 'Vicente Lombardo Toledano'
16 Vicente Lombardo Toledano in Chihuahua, Chihuahua during his presidential campaign. 1952. Archivo Fotográfico del Centro de Estudios Filosóficos, Políticos y Sociales 'Vicente Lombardo Toledano'
17 Vicente Lombardo Toledano in the capital Zócalo. 1952. Archivo Fotográfico del Centro de Estudios Filosóficos, Políticos y Sociales 'Vicente Lombardo Toledano'
18 Vicente Lombardo Toledano leading a PPS march through the streets of Teziutlán, Puebla. 1964. Archivo Fotográfico del Centro de Estudios Filosóficos, Políticos y Sociales 'Vicente Lombardo Toledano'
19 Lázaro Cárdenas, Vicente Lombardo Toledano and Gustavo Díaz Ordaz. 1968. Archivo Fotográfico del Centro de Estudios Filosóficos, Políticos y Sociales 'Vicente Lombardo Toledano'
20 'Leon Trotsky, as he really is', *Futuro*, no. 34, December 1938, p. 16
21 'Not even for free', *Excélsior*, 17 June 1952, p. 6-A
22 'I am a communist and a Marxist by conviction and as in all parts, Mexico will be completely socialist!' – Oh wow! ... He wants to be a president and a Soviet secretary?, *Novedades*, 1 July 1952, p. 4
23 'The greasy electoral pole. Yesterday's conflict', *Excélsior* by Freyre, 7 July 1952, p. 6-A
24 'Mourning on the left', *Excélsior* by Marino, 18 November 1968, p. 6-A
25 'And now what?' *Excélsior* by Marino, 19 November 1968, p. 6-A

Abbreviations

AFL	American Federation of Labor
APRA	American Popular Revolutionary Alliance
ATLAS	Association of Unionised Latin American Workers
BBC	British Broadcasting Corporation
CCI	Independent Peasant Confederation
CGOCM	General Confederation of Workers and Peasants of Mexico
CGT	General Confederation of Workers
CIA	Central Intelligence Agency
CIO	Congress of Industrial Organizations
CIOSL	International Confederation of Free Trade Unions
CIT	Inter-American Confederation of Workers
CNC	National Peasant Confederation
CNOP	National Confederation of Popular Organisations
CPUSTAL	Permanent Congress of Trade Union Unity of Latin American Workers
CROM	Mexican Regional Workers Confederation
CSLA	Latin American Trade Union Confederation
CTAL	Latin American Workers Confederation
CTC	Cuban Workers Confederation
CTM	Mexican Workers Confederation
CUT	United Trade Union Confederation of Mexico
DF	Federal District
DFS	Federal Security Directorate
DT	Labour Department
FBI	Federal Bureau of Investigation
FSM	World Federation of Trade Unions
ICFTU	International Confederation of Free Trade Unions
IFTU	International Federation of Trade Unions
ILO	International Labour Organization
KGB	Komitet Gosudárstvennoy Gezopásnosti (Committee for State Security, before GPU and NKVD)
MLN	National Liberation Movement
NATO	North Atlantic Treaty Organisation
NSDAP	Nationalsozialistische Deutsche Arbeiter Partei (National Socialist German Workers Party)
OAS	Organisation of American States
ORIT	Inter-American Regional Organisation of Workers
PAN	National Action Party

PARM	Authentic Party of the Mexican Revolution
PCM	Mexican Communist Party
PEMEX	Mexican Oil
PIR	Party of the Revolutionary Left
PLM	Mexican Labor Party
PNA	National Agrarian Party
PNR	National Revolutionary Party
PP	People's Party
PPS	People's Socialist Party
POCM	Mexican Workers and Peasants Party
POUM	Workers' Party of Marxist Unification
PRI	Institutional Revolutionary Party
PRM	Party of the Mexican Revolution
SNTE	National Teachers' Union
TUC	Trades Union Congress
UFCO	United Fruit Company
UGOCM	Union of Workers and Peasants of Mexico
UNAM	National Autonomous University of Mexico
UO	Workers' University
URSS	Union of Soviet Socialist Republics
WFTU	World Federation of Trade Unions

Introduction

> History is incorruptible. In its time, it will inflexibly judge our generation, each of the men and women who are conscious of the role they fulfilled in national life. (1957)¹

⋯

> My work, however modest it might have been, cannot be judged superficially, especially now that I'm still fully alive and fighting. Perhaps after my death it would be worthwhile to consider this matter. (1961)²

⋮

On the hundredth anniversary of the birth of Vicente Lombardo Toledano in 1994, the government of Carlos Salinas de Gortari paid him the ultimate tribute as if he were a hero who gave Mexico its sense of nationhood. On 16 July, he was exhumed from the Jardin Cemetery and to the beat of Ludwig van Beethoven's funeral march, his ashes were buried in the Rotunda of Illustrious Men in the Pantheon of Dolores, opposite the cauldron with the eternal flame, adorned by white daisies.³ As in life, 20 years after his death, the honour that the state bestowed on Lombardo provoked controversy, this time on whether or not he was worthy of occupying such a venue.

Lombardo Toledano was born with a silver spoon in his mouth in 1894 in Teziutlán, in the mountains of Puebla, and died in Mexico City in 1968, following the massacre of the students in the Plaza de las Tres Culturas in Tlatelolco and the jubilant sports competition of the Olympic Games. In life, he aroused feelings of love and hate; he was the object of royal welcomes and the target of several attacks; national and international espionage agencies did not let him

---

1   Vicente Lombardo Toledano (henceforth VLT), 'La sucesión presidencial 1958', in *Obra Histórico-Cronológica* (henceforth *Obra*), book V, vol. 26 (Mexico City: Centro de Estudios Filosóficos, Políticos y Sociales 'Vicente Lombardo Toledano', 2007), p. 77.
2   Answer to questionnaire of Jack Altshul, editor of *Newsday*, Mexico City, 16 January 1961, in Fondo Histórico Lombardo Toledano (henceforth FHLT), file 1128.
3   Renato Dávalos, 'VLT antepuso el interés nacional al partidista', *Excélsior*, 17 July 1994; Julieta Medina, 'Viven los mexicanos en una nación plural', *Reforma*, 17 July 1994.

out of their sights. He was detained in and expelled from several countries and prevented from visiting others.[4] Those who knew him still evoke his incendiary oratorical style, which others remember as soporific. His admirers praise him as the helmsman of Mexican and Latin American workers; others scorn the means he used to achieve his goals as opportunist.

Lombardo Toledano's life is a window into the history of the twentieth century: the rise and fall of the old regime; the Mexican Revolution and the transformations that it introduced into society; the intellectual and social reconstruction of the country under new parameters that included the rise of the labour movement to political prominence, as well as the intervention of trade unions in the construction and consolidation of the state; of the dispute over the course of the nation in the tumultuous 1930s, and the configuration of the political and ideological left in Mexico. Lombardo Toledano's life and work reveal Mexico's connections with the world during the Second World War and the Cold War.

Lombardo Toledano belonged to the intellectual elite of men and women who considered themselves progressives, Marxists and socialists and who believed in a bright future for humanity. He viewed himself as the conscious reflection of the unconscious movement of the masses. With unbridled energy and ideological fervour, he founded unions, parties, and newspapers. During the course of his life, he adhered to various beliefs, from Christianity to Marxism, raising dialectical materialism to the level of a theory of knowledge that validated absolute certainties in the way that idealism had previously. He conceived of the relationship of intellectuals with workers as a metaphysical one, since intellectuals 'spring directly from the masses and developing in a broader field, they dissolve into them'.[5]

He believed that the Soviet Union had achieved a future that Mexico should aspire to imitate. Mexico was a semi-feudal and semi-colonial country, hindered by imperialism in its economic development and the creation of a national bourgeoisie, without which it could not pass on to the next stage in the evolution of humankind and without which the working class and peasantry were doomed to underdevelopment. In his interpretation of history, the autonomy of the subordinate classes did not enter into the picture, rather it was the intellectual elites allied with the state who had the task of instilling class consciousness in them. His life's fortunes ordained him to lead the way. The book explores Lombardo Toledano's political journey from being a Chris-

---

4 VLT to J. Natividad Rosales, Mexico City, 3 July 1964, FHLT, file 1188.
5 VLT, 'La ampliación de la democracia soviética', 9 October 1935, VLT, FHLT, file 267.

tian well-wisher concerned with social issues under the influence of the tenets of the Mexican Revolution, to becoming a dominant public figure who contributed to shaping the national and international labour movement under the influence of his Stalinist convictions.

The studies on Lombardo Toledano and his work fill several shelves.[6] The books devoted to extolling his life have created the myth of the hero and perpetuated the belief in the validity of his thought to illuminate the problems of the present. His writings, speeches, and public acts, which number in the thousands, have been published in dozens of tomes by the 'Vicente Lombardo Toledano' Centre for Philosophical, Political and Social Studies, located in the street that bears his name, under the editorship of Marcela Lombardo Otero, his daughter, and Raúl Gutiérrez Lombardo, his grandson. The dour Workers' University in the historic centre of the capital, houses his personal archives. Overlooking the beautiful courtyard adorned with shrubs with lilies of the valley and geraniums, with the dome of the Church of Loreto at a discreet distance projecting its majesty, the archive comprising more than 1,300 boxes arranged chronologically,[7] full of speeches, lectures, corridos, odes, poems, drawings, notebooks with their respective annotations, drafts of unwritten books, thousands of letters between him and his comrades the world over and with figures from the world of high politics, barely touches the intimate moments of his life. Personal letters do not allow the reader to rebuild his private life, but they do reveal that he conducted himself like a poker player who did not show his cards.

Writing the biography of Lombardo Toledano has not been easy. In the 1960s the American historian James Wilkie and his Guatemalan wife Edna Monzon, who came to Mexico to consult with several leading figures who played an active role in the Mexican Revolution and the political life of the country, interviewed him. Since the result of this research, *México visto en el siglo xx, entrevistas de historia oral*, was first published in 1969, historians have based their narratives on what the interviewee told the Wilkies without questioning his intent.[8] It was hardly noticeable that Lombardo Toledano had airbrushed some episodes of his life to project them, not as they actually happened, but as he would have wanted them to occur and how he would have wanted history to remember them. He denied that subjectivity and personal relationships

---

6 Millon 1964; Unzueta 1966; Krauze 1976; Chassen de López 1977; Quintanilla Obregón 1982; Ramírez Cuéllar 1992; Tavira Urióstegui 1999; Bolívar Meza 2005; Hernández Beltrán 2007; Gutiérrez Lombardo 2010; Amezcua Dromundo 2012.
7 The archives have recently been digitalised.
8 Wilkie and Monzón 1969; Wilkie and Monzón 2005.

had importance. When Wilkie touched on the subject, he replied that 'I do not want to deal with things that have absolutely no value whatsoever for me'.[9] He considered such facets of his life as accidental, because history progressed according to the inexorable laws of which he was an incarnation. History was also one of his instruments of struggle to win followers to adopt his ideas and directives. Ideas were part of his arsenal against his opponents, who, lacking the breadth of his knowledge and information about the world, resorted to using diatribes that he demolished with subtleties, rhetorical twists and turns, historical references and egocentricities.

No matter how prominent a personality he was in his time, today few remember the *maestro* Vicente Lombardo Toledano, despite the many streets and schools named after him. The story of his life is significant because it reveals the vivid and contradictory history of the twentieth century, with traces that remain in contemporary Mexico, even after the shock of 11 September 2001, which superimposed the spectre of terrorism over the dominant ideologies of the past century, postponing the rebuilding of democracy, whose realisation such ideas hindered, to a nebulous future.

---

9 Wilkie 1969, p. 231.

PART 1
Changing Times and Ideas

Mexico needs foreign capital that will surely not be willing to invest in our land if not given extensive guarantees of freedom. (1919)[1]

∴

The social revolution launched in 1910 returned the ethics of Christ to the Mexican nation, to fight for the advent of a new social order based on love for mankind. (1923)[2]

∴

Twenty years ago, the Mexican proletariat rose up to conquer Mexico. Our deep desire is to contribute, along with the international proletariat, to the conquest of the planet. (1929)[3]

∴

On numerous occasions I have stated that the true government of a country lies in its educated minority. (1931)[4]

∴

On behalf of the Federal District Federation of Labour Unions, members of the CROM, I wish to strongly protest the survival of the bourgeois regime in the world and in Mexico. (1932)[5]

∴

Be modest in all pleasures. Instincts are like dogs: you can educate them to bite or to remain quiet. Revolutionaries must live constantly garrisoned on the inside, like soldiers ready for the unexpected action. (1934)[6]

∴

---

1 VLT, *El derecho público y las corrientes filosóficas*, thesis for law degree in the National School of Jurisprudence, 15 March 1919 in *Obra*, I/1, 1917–1923, pp. 107–8.
2 VLT, 'La moral de la revolución mexicana', *El Heraldo*, 13 July 1923, FHLT, file 39.
3 VLT, 'Mensaje del frente obrero al pueblo de la república', Mexico City, 22 September 1929, FHLT, file 160.
4 VLT, 'Del patrimonio de la universidad', October 1931, FHLT, file 188.
5 VLT, 'Discurso del 1 de mayo de 1932', Mexico City, in *Obra*, II/3, 1932, p. 103.
6 VLT, 'Máximas para los revolucionarios mexicanos', 7 June 1934, FHLT, file 241.

CHAPTER 1

Family

Vicente Lombardo Toledano was the third in a lineage carrying the same first name on the paternal side of the family. Three men from three generations, whose fortune began when the grandfather saw the Veracruz coast for the first time in 1858. The legendary Vincenzo Lombardo Catti was born in 1836 in Settimo Torinese, seven Roman leagues from the industrial centre of Turin in northern Italy. Due to a spirit of adventure, or perhaps out of necessity, the twenty-something Vincenzo was one of the more than two hundred emigrants from the Piedmont, Genoa and Lombardy regions who, upon arrival, were disillusioned by Mexican government promises to colonise lands in Veracruz. They were unaware that they had arrived in a country immersed in civil war and that the land that they were offered was barren and infested with malaria.[1]

The young Vincenzo was not to be disheartened by the inclement weather of the tropics or by the country's adversities. Along with his companions Montessoro, Gaia, Montini, Palavicini, Ricciardi, and many others who used their meagre wealth to pay for a one-way trip, he tried his luck in Papantla as a farmer and manufacturer of tiles and bricks; laying cobblestones in the streets of the country's capital, and back in Veracruz, in the newly founded village of Gutiérrez Zamora in rubber extraction and agriculture. There he met Marcelina Carpio, a Totonaca indigenous woman from Tianguistengo, Hidalgo, with whom he buried two children outside of marriage and baptised two others before moving to Teziutlán in the mountains of Puebla in 1881. Although the family's departure was seen as an attempt to seek better opportunities, it was rumoured that Vincenzo fled from the wrath of the Gutiérrez Zamora caciques, rural bosses, who had put a price on his head when he challenged their abuses and corruption. People also wondered if the family was leaving because Luis Costa, Vincenzo's nephew, in the confusion of the night and thinking he was stalking thieves, had killed a neighbour in his vanilla fields.[2]

---

1   Tommasi and Zilli Mánica 1924, in http://www.oocities.org/trentinimessico/ponenciaMontevideo.doc. Accessed 20 December 2012.
2   Biographical data of Vicente Lombardo, 1921, FHLT, vol. 15; Tibón 1946, pp. 133–5; Krauze 1976, pp. 21–4.

1   The Village

Whatever the cause of the family's departure, Teziutlán was the beginning of the true promised land. Nestled in the foothills of the Sierra Norte de Puebla, which descend from the forest to the hot plains of Veracruz, it was well-known for its rough terrain and stormy weather. The mountain range was prodigious in the wood of its forests, inhabited by indigenous plant life such as oyameles, chicozapotes, ojanchos, arbutus, sweetgum, chijoles and jamalcuahuitles, which produced natural ceilings with their generous foliage. Artisans produced useful objects that they sold when the rains didn't make the roads unusable. Peasant farmers grew vanilla, achotillo, sugar cane and indigo on the land; they also raised corn and beans together with pasture for sheep, goats or cattle. Nostalgically, the Teziutecos who migrated to the capital city evoked the murmur of streams and the rivers snaking the hillsides.[3]

Inhabited by about 11,000 souls consisting of pious traders, herdsmen, peasant farmers, mestizo and Totonac indigenous artisans, Teziutlán was a land of patriarchs, small-town gatherings, balconies and Sunday Masses, 'where women with large hats adorned with feathers and ribbons, left High Mass and headed to the village square going round and round, wearing flowing robes of bright and intensely coloured silk'.[4]

Vincenzo Lombardo arrived in Teziutlán in peacetime before the emergence of mining and railroad capital changed the sleepy nature of the village. A man of labour and who enjoyed life, he used to walk through the mountains as a hunter and prospector until the local residents would show him the place with the shiny rocks. There he found the mother lode of what would be the Aurora mine and the Ceres, Venus and Saturno mines. He found the source of his wealth, but lacking capital and the knowledge to exploit it, he partnered up with American entrepreneur George Barron, who had technical and financial support from another countryman, Robert Safford Towne, to convert the riches that lay beneath the land into a source of wealth to provide his family with financial means and the good life.

Originally from Ohio, Safford was an engineer and owner of mining emporiums in the Mexican states of San Luis Potosí, Chihuahua, Zacatecas and Nuevo León. Along with Lombardo and Barron they founded the Teziutlán Copper and Smelting Company in 1898. On suit, they wanted to ensure the quality of their products, sending three boxcars of the mineral to Colorado to be smelted.

---

3   García Cubas 1959, p. 94.
4   Ramos de Guzmán 1978, manuscript. I would like to thank Sergio Mastretta for the manuscript written by his maternal grandmother.

The samples taken proved that the Aurora mineral was of good quality. It contained silver, zinc, copper, although no gold. Even so, it was worth further investment. They installed a one horsepower modern device for the extraction of the mineral and water, built cabins for workers and a solid house for the mine manager and visitors, and acquired an electricity-powered smelter. The railway, which was two leagues from Teziutlán, transported the products from the mine to Tecolutla on the coast close to the port of Veracruz. The business was promising and this encouraged investors to continue injecting capital into the company. Vincenzo Lombardo, in addition to being a shareholder, was appointed to the company board of directors and to be its legal representative in Teziutlán. Over time, the upstart Lombardo earned the reputation of being wealthy to the point of being regarded as perhaps the richest man in Teziutlán. Vincenzo was happy, because the future was promising, judging by the juicy dividends being paid at the time and due to the widespread idea that with the wealth hidden beneath the surface of the earth, cities and empires could be built. Even with the death of the aging President Porfirio Díaz, the investments seemed to be safe.[5]

Vincenzo Lombardo and Marcelina Carpio were married four years after their arrival in Teziutlán and after the birth of their sons Luis, Vicente, Alejandro and Pedro, and daughters Emilia, Marcelina and María. In a photograph of the couple, Vincenzo has an Emperor Victor Emmanuel II-style beard. Next to him is Marcelina, who looks petite but strong, with thick braided hair, wearing a dress and an apron covering her breast as if they were the crossed cartridge belts of a female soldier in the Mexican Revolution.

2 Children

Perhaps the most dynamic and the one with an inclination to be a merchant was Vicente, his father's favourite, to whom he entrusted the management of his business in Teziutlán when he decided to return to his hometown. Vicente Lombardo Carpio, the second of the surviving children, was born in 1870 in Papantla, Veracruz. Like the others, he grew up surrounded by abundance,

---

5 Interview with Edgar Ulibarry, former employee of the Aurora, Teziutlán metallurgical plant, 20 November 2005; 'Informe que rinde el gerente sobre la Cía. minera beneficiadora de Teziutlán S.A. a la asamblea general extraordinaria del 28 de noviembre de 1898', FHLT, vol. 1; Pletcher 1948, pp. 19–26; Reginald Tower to Sir Edward Grey, 'Report on the political situation in Mexico during 1907', Mexico City, 4 January 1908, The National Archives, Great Britain, Foreign Office 371 (henceforth FO 371)/ 881/9162.

to which he was accustomed thanks to the wealth of his father. Pragmatic and with a simple view of the world, he tried his hand as a bookkeeper, a commission agent for products of the region such as zacaton root, purge de Xalapa, rubber, vanilla, coffee, tobacco, in addition to the sale of products of Waters Pierce oil company like naphtha, paraffin wax, cottonseed oils and lubricants. When Vicente Lombardo accumulated his own capital, he purchased real estate, which he later sold or rented.[6]

When he was 20 years old, Vicente married Isabel Toledano, of Sephardic Jewish decent. They had ten children: Vicente, Luis, María, Margarita, Isabel (the second daughter carrying the name, following the death of the first), Humberto, Guillermo, Elena and Aida. When he reached 30 years of age, Vicente Lombardo felt the urge to leave the hometown in order to discover the outside world. He entrusted the responsibility of tending to his business in Teziutlán to Luis Lombardo, his older brother, and took the train 'with the taste of Jesus in my mouth due to the often terrifying vomiting and even though I left Puebla clean like a dove, I arrived at night in Veracruz dirtier and more irritated than a packhorse in August'. The heat was infernal. He bathed in the hotel 'and I was so shocked at the dirt and grime that I decided to send the dirty clothes in a basket and in fact sent it by express, though I'm sure you thought it was something new and pleasant'.[7] This was the first of several letters that Vicente would write to his wife Isabel, before setting sail in the steamboat that would take him to New York.

The steamship left its mooring and crossed the Gulf of Mexico heading toward the Yucatán Peninsula. It landed at Progreso and went on to Havana. Lombardo went ashore. US-occupied Cuba was recovering from the fighting during the War of Independence from Spain, although Havana, with a quarter of a million inhabitants, was spared. The Americans launched their modernisation efforts, providing running water, sewage systems, telephone service and tram transportation.[8] Lombardo's impressions of Havana in letters to Isabel noted 'a large amount of commercial activity and everything being very expensive' and beautiful; he noted well-fed mules, shops more attractive than in Mexico City and 'charming and very nice women ... with the most beautiful eyes anywhere, not painted as in Mexico, but with the natural purity, and really

---

6 Tibón 1946, p. 133; VLT to María Lombardo Treviño y Morton, Mexico City, 19 September 1929, FHLT, file 160.
7 Vicente Lombardo to Isabel Toledano (henceforth VL to IT), New York, 22 April 1901, FHLT, file 2.
8 Estrada 2007, pp. 145–6.

charming girls. Many of them graceful and nice just like you, but not as you are now, but as you were *when I fell in love with you*'.[9]

New York overwhelmed him. He contrasted it to Mexico, writing, 'ah! It's sad to say, but it [Mexico] is horrible', while in New York 'one sees intellect developed in all its grandeur not only in people, but even in animals'. And the Brooklyn Bridge, what a 'colossal work of construction' with the traffic in trams, horses, and carts.[10] Chicago, with more than a million and a half inhabitants, impressed Lombardo with its 'feverish traffic' and for being 'a city only for work'. He was irritated by Waukesha, a town in Wisconsin known for its medicinal hot springs that was recommended to him by his brother Luis, as he 'saw so many invalids and so many on crutches in this village and it's so very hot!' New Orleans, a 'beautiful and friendly city', was his last stop before he crossed the border into Mexico in mid-June, wandering the roads to Puebla through major cities that were on his route back home. There is no record of these travels as it was his last letter.[11]

On his return to Teziutlán, Vicente Lombardo resumed control of his businesses and management of his father's properties. Unlike silver, copper experienced a spectacular rise in price between 1900 and 1905 and the extraction and export of this mineral from the mines increased. The family enjoyed the economic boom. Considered a man of wealth, Lombardo was elected mayor of Teziutlán in 1905. Seen from Settimo Torinese, the land of his father, the Mexican panorama seemed indomitable. Vincenzo Lombardo beamed with optimism about the future of the country and the family's economic status. Not wanting to leave anything left unturned in his patriarchal legacy, he went to an art academy to commission a bust, first of clay, then plaster; he had it sculptured in marble and forged in bronze. As was his desire, the bust has survived to this day.

Vincenzo was lenient with Vicente and applauded the businesses he launched, even though they might not have been the best investment, and tolerated his extravagant spending. When Lombardo purchased a new sailboat in the exclusive summer resort of the Mexican elite at Lake Chapala, a few miles from Guadalajara, the father applauded the move. 'I'm glad that you're enjoying things while you can. That's what life is'.[12] Father and son exchanged

---

9   VL to IT, New York, 22 April 1901, FHLT, file 2.
10 VL to IT, New York, 25 April 1901, FHLT, file 2.
11 VL to IT, Chicago, 25 May 1901; VL to IT, Waukesha, Wisconsin, 9 and 10 June 1901; VL to IT, New Orleans, 15 June 1901, FHLT, file 2.
12 Vincenzo Lombardo to his son Lombardo junior, Settimo Torinese, 14 April 1905, FHLT, file 2; Vincenzo Lombardo to his son Lombardo junior, Settimo Torinese, 28 February 1906 and 5 February 1907, FHLT, file 3.

letters about business, money transfers or properties acquired, leased or sold. Rarely did they mention Marcelina, his wife who stayed behind in Teziutlán, daughters, sons or grandchildren. There was no need to bring back the funds deposited in New York. 'I think there will be no revolutions in Mexico, but it is always good to be cautious just in case. The gains and losses can be total'.[13]

The other children were a disaster, especially Pedro and Alejandro. The same could be said of the daughters, because they failed to choose their husbands well. Pedro, the youngest, selected Cornell University in Ithaca to study civil engineering. The father thought that Pedro was wasting his time and spending the wealth produced by the mine. His business partner Barron stringently handled the money for Pedro's room and board and other expenses. 'The truth be told, Dad, is that I don't know if you told him not to give me what I need in my academic career here or if he got this idea on his own', Pedro complained to the distrustful Vincenzo who sided with Barron.

The 24-year-old Pedro did not really want to study engineering; he would have preferred to try his luck in California without saying in what field or to return home or to do business. He had no money and no clear idea what to do with his life. He sent instructions to have new suits made without the money to pay for them and asked his brother Vicente for a loan until his father finally had had enough: 'I do not want to use my children as a toy or be a toy for them'.[14]

Alejandro was another lost cause. Younger than Vicente, he was not entrusted with family businesses. He teamed up with John or Juan Barron, son of Vincenzo's partner, who lacked the intelligence of his father. Don Vincenzo lent Alejandro money so as not to be idle. Juan Barron became his son-in-law when he married his daughter Emilia, but in the father-in-law's opinion Juan did not know how to be a provider. His daughter Marcelina also did not satisfy her father; she married James Mister, who lacked the capacity to work and tenacity, the yardstick by which Don Vincenzo measured men.[15]

Don Vincenzo returned to Mexico for the penultimate time in 1908 to provide his inheritance to his children while he was still alive so as to feel good about himself and for them to feel good about him. The assets would be divided by merit and not by the number of heirs. He left Luis and Vicente the shares of

---

13 Vincenzo Lombardo to his son Lombardo Jr., Settimo Torinese, 19 December 1906, FHLT, file 3.
14 Pedro Lombardo to Vicente Lombardo, Ithaca, New York, 30 September 1905, FHLT, file 2; Pedro Lombardo to Vicente Lombardo, Ithaca, New York, 9 and 16 March 1909; Vincenzo Lombardo to his son Lombardo Jr., Settimo Torinese, 27 March 1909, 7 May 1909, FHLT, file 4; Vincenzo Lombardo to Vicente Lombardo, Settimo Torinese, 2 August 1910, FHLT, file 5.
15 Vincenzo Lombardo to Vicente Lombardo, Settimo Torinese, 17 March 1907, FHLT, file 3.

the Aurora mine, 'now that this business is already well developed and on track and wishing to get my affairs definitively in order'. He instructed Oil Fuels of Mexico, of which he was a shareholder, to provide fifty shares to each of his heirs: 'I do want my promise made years ago to you to be fulfilled, with me feeling calm and satisfied'.[16]

The last will and testament of the septuagenarian Vincenzo, a naturalised Mexican citizen, revealed that he was the father of Delfina de Jesús Lombardo, the natural daughter of an unknown mother, married, to whom he did not leave money because she had enough assets and he had helped her in the past. The testament also revealed that Vincenzo owned four homes acquired during his marriage to Marcelina on Avenida Juárez in Teziutlán, one next to the other. Two houses were passed on to his wife and two to his sons and daughters, including Delfina. The male children received more than the daughters. Luis, Vicente and Pedro were the main heirs, although they received unequal parts of the inheritance.[17] Vincenzo returned to Italy in December 1908, optimistic that the family's strong economic situation would be long-lasting.

Vicente Lombardo Carpio, then 38 years old, was now at the helm of the family businesses, not suspecting that the boom would be short-lived. Late in 1908 the price of copper began to fall and the company suspended smelting ore as uneconomical. The dividends were irregularly deposited in the Lombardo family account in New York. Had the company invested elsewhere, Vincenzo asked. Uncertainty began to emerge. Juan Barron, his brother-in-law, to whom Vicente Lombardo had rented the hotel owned by his father for him to manage, stopped paying rent. In fact, 1909 was the last year of peace and comfort for the family. Without anticipating the collapse of his world, Vicente took the family to spend New Year's Eve at his home on the shores of Lake Chapala where they went duck hunting.[18]

In mid-1911, the Teziutlán mining company sent Luis and Vicente 3,500 and 3,400 dollars to their father from New York, at the time a huge sum of money and perhaps one of the last, if not the last such payment. US mining companies adopted a cautious approach to the industry in Mexico and had their mines working at 50% capacity, given the revolt in Puebla due to the revolution that erupted against the government of the aging Porfirio Díaz and the ills of the country that soon would become nationwide. The railroad lines were cut in some sections and shipments of metal had to be transported to the port of Ver-

---

16   Vincenzo Lombardo to Luis and Vicente Lombardo, Puebla, 10 August 1908, FHLT, file 4.
17   Last will and testament of Vicente Lombardo Catti, 18 September 1908, FHLT, file 4.
18   Vincenzo Lombardo to his son Lombardo junior, Settimo Torinese, 1 September 1909, FHLT, file 4.

acruz by alternative routes. The low price of the metal and taxes imposed by the United States were coupled with shortages of dynamite, which the government had withheld. Between 1912 and 1916 copper production dropped drastically, while ownership and export taxes mushroomed. The mine owners complained that instead of working, the miners, whose right to unionise had been recognised by the newly created Department of Labour, were arguing about the revolution. Some miners deserted their places of employment to enlist as soldiers. Robberies, kidnappings and murders increased as chaos ensued following the assassination of the antiporfirista President Francisco I. Madero in February 1913; the railways stopped running and several mines were forced to close. Given the lack of maintenance, some mines flooded or collapsed or were destroyed by vengeful rebels when the managers refused to reach an agreement on the demanded price. For Vicente Lombardo, who did not care which revolutionary faction interrupted the peaceful life of the family, businesses and hunting, the outlook became sombre.[19]

For reasons unknown, Vincenzo arrived in Mexico in January 1912 to a country immersed in convulsions and political conspiracies, to which he gave no importance. He stayed in Teziutlán for just a few weeks, because in March he wrote from Settimo Torinese, pleased because the price of copper had risen slightly and the revolution in Mexico was an opportunity to get rid of 'rogues' that hindered the smooth development of the business. He was not concerned about which side the revolutionaries belonged to and seemed to view the military skirmishes that Teziutlán and Mexico were experiencing as not being an impediment to a normal life. From Settimo Torinese Vincenzo was about to send to his son Luis two Saint Bernard puppies, to Vicente clothing from the fabrics that he had selected and a catalogue of Fiat cars for him to choose the model that he would like the most. The revolution was not an impediment for Vicente Lombardo, who moved the family to Mexico City, to plan the purchase of hunting rifles in a London armoury.[20] He still could provide for the family with perhaps the last round of dividends.

Vicente Lombardo's great despair was the lack of 'security for going to the countryside' to hunt wild boars and deer in Teziutlán. Instead, he had to go

---

19   Bortz 2008, pp. 113–32; Pletcher 1948, p. 21; LaFrance 2003, pp. 25–41; Knight 1990, vol. 1, p. 217; Paxman 2008, p. 57.
20   Vincenzo Lombardo to his son Lombardo junior, Settimo Torinese, 4 November 1910, FHLT, file 5; Vicente Lombardo to Vincenzo Lombardo, Teziutlán, 29 August, 13 September, 12 October 1911, file 5; 'A los habitantes de la nación', Tlatlauqui, 14 February 1912, FHLT, file 6; Vincenzo Lombardo to his son Lombardo junior, Settimo Torinese, 1 May 1912, FHLT, file 6.

hunting in a nearby Tulancingo, where he shot a tiger without killing it: 'I haven't slept in three days just thinking that I could let such a beautiful animal escape'.[21] When there was no way to reach Teziutlán due to the existing insecurity of the roads, when the Zapatista and the Carrancista revolutionary armies pursued each other and demanded ransom to allow travellers to pass through their territory, Vicente Lombardo's concern were the dogs that were left idle. 'Don't fail to keep the dogs in shape so that they don't deteriorate', he wrote to Julio, the servant at his home.[22]

On 1 August 1914 war broke out in Europe. This time Vincenzo felt the effects close to home without losing his usual optimism. His business partner Barron was not sending him any money and although it appeared that he forgot about him, he did not care, he wrote in his last letter. The children sent him money instead; he had enough to spend the next winter comfortably and by then the situation both in Mexico and in Europe would surely improve.[23] The day after writing this letter, on 1 November 1914 Vincenzo Lombardo passed away.

The Sierra de Puebla mountain range continued to be the scene of repeated incursions by the Zapatista forces, accompanied by other local indigenous groups, and displaced by the Carrancistas. The homes that the neighbours left abandoned, when fleeing to the capital, were occupied by the armies which, when they left, tended to take what they wanted. The haciendas, the large rural estates, in the hands of managers, were emptied of livestock. Juan Barron saw the hotel he managed turned into an army barracks. With up to five hundred male and female soldiers on hand, with the exception of one honourable general, no one else paid rent. The rooms occupied by officers and soldiers suffered the effects of theft and destruction, and sentries stationed at the front door chased away the clientele.[24]

At the dawn of 1916, Vicente Lombardo confided in his eldest son:

> I am writing my first letter today in the early hours of the new day of the newest year. For me, this entire past year has been blacker than all the 300,000 hells [and] for the 1,001 penalties that we have had to face, separ-

---

21 Vicente Lombardo to Julio, Mexico City, 10 December 1913, FHLT, file 6; Vicente Lombardo to Julio, Mexico City, 25 October 1914, FHLT, file 7.
22 Vicente Lombardo to Julio, Mexico City, 2 August 1914, FHLT, file 7; LaFrance 2003, p. 41.
23 Vincenzo Lombardo to Vicente and Luis Lombardo, Settimo Torinese, 30 October 1914, FHLT, file 7.
24 Knight 1990, vol. 1, p. 205; LaFrance 2003, pp. 41–4; Juan Barron to the Governor of the State of Puebla, Teziutlán, 25 March 1919, FHLT, file 9; Ramos de Guzmán 1978, p. 19.

ated, and with the road to life or road to the preparation for life cut off for all of you who urgently need to get on board for the struggle for this life that we so arduously defend and I don't know up to what point you can say that such an effort is worth it.[25]

Without any hope remaining, the chairman of the mining company gave it the axe. 'Nobody is willing to invest a single dollar in Mexico at this time'. With no other alternative, Lombardo began selling his properties in order to keep the family afloat, until there was nothing left to sell. With Don Vincenzo dead, it came to light that for at least the last years of his life, the children financially maintained their father in Settimo Torinese not with company dividends as they led him to believe, but with loans. Without anything left to sell, Lombardo used the depreciated shares from the mining companies as a swap to purchase a home in Mexico City's Colonia Roma neighbourhood. The home's 153 square metres was a tight squeeze for the family, who longed for their house in Teziutlán, famous for being the most modern in the village, with a large terrace overlooking the Xoloco canyon and a large ballroom. The last disgrace and humiliation inflicted on the 50-year-old Vicente Lombardo was having to accept employment as a second-level bureaucrat in the Mexico City government which, he confided in his son now in his twenties, irritated him so much that when he left the office he said 'I no longer want to speak a single word'.[26]

Since 1911 the family had sought refuge in the capital as protection from the revolution in Puebla. Even though the shots appeared to be far away, the echoes of the revolution in northern Mexico and in the closer-to-home south were threatening the capital, until the city was occupied in mid-1914. The troops of Venustiano Carranza, of Álvaro Obregon, the Zapatistas and the Villistas, conquered, lost, abandoned and reconquered positions in the capital and surrounding cities. The ravages of the war caused an endless anxiety in the population. When in December 1914 Emiliano Zapata and Francisco Villa stood on the balcony of the National Palace to watch the parade of their troops from the Liberation Army of the South and the Northern Division, the capital's society trembled. Lacking water and food, prices rose in response to shortages. Horses and cars were confiscated. All kinds of rumours circulated. Among many other horror stories of the revolution it was reported that French national Justin

---

25 Vicente Lombardo to Vicente Lombardo Toledano (henceforth VLT), 1 January 1916, FHLT, file 7; Safford Towne to Vicente Lombardo, New York, 28 March 1916, FHLT, file 7.

26 Bernstein 1964, pp. 60–1; Vicente Lombardo to VLT, Mexico City, 15 June 1924, FHLT, file 58.

Morin, who was taking care of the La Hormiga factory in one corner of the city, was killed by soldiers in General Álvaro Obregon's forces. It was said that not only did they steal his possessions, but they broke a finger to take off his ring and disfigured his jaw to remove the gold fillings from his teeth, and then they killed him.[27]

Less drastically, Lombardo could have been affected by the inconveniences caused by strikes that had become endemic and which for periods of time led to a suspension of the services offered by hairdressers, waiters, printers and garbage collectors. Communications in the city became difficult. The different banknotes in circulation were part of the economic chaos. In addition to banknotes issued by the Carrancistas and Villistas, counterfeit bills also circulated, hindering commercial transactions. Businesses and companies of all types were subject to extortion, which made their functioning unviable. It was impossible to obtain raw materials and transportation to move them without paying bribes to pass through unsafe roads. Beggars and vagrants were everywhere, and the lack of hygiene and hot water caused diseases. An epidemic of typhoid and influenza hit the city, 'which beyond taking its toll in terms of a considerable number of victims, spawned the superstitious fear that this was another calamity that heaven wanted to inflict on Mexicans for being irrational and wild'.[28] Due to the uncertainty and the high cost of living in the city, Vicente Lombardo moved the family back to Teziutlán in 1917.

3 Vicente Lombardo Toledano

The third in the generation of Vicentes was born in 1894 in Teziutlán, the mountain village that was part of his mindset for his entire life: its plants, trees and animals as well as their hunting, local politics, but also its provincialism, ignorance and folklore.[29] Teziutlán gave him several life skills. In the secular Liceo Teziuteco school he learned discipline, 'moral judgements', patriotic poetry in addition to shorthand that later would serve him in annotating the letters he received so that others would not be able to understand them. Mexican history classes were a delight because the teacher, ignoring the texts in use, taught from

---

27   Gilly 1977, pp. 139–45; T.B. Hohler to Sir Edward Grey, Mexico City, 8 January 1915 and 5 April 1915, FO 371/ 12509 and 12746; Ulloa 1988, pp. 206–27; Rodríguez Kuri 2010, pp. 100–15.
28   T.B. Hohler to Sir Edward Grey, 'The Political Situation in Mexico', Mexico City, 6 December 1915, FO371/ 13197.
29   VLT, 'Recuerdos de mi infancia. El primer astronauta', in *Obra*, VI/6, 1961, pp. 69–73.

memory what his father, who had immigrated to Mexico during the nineteenth-century French intervention, had recalled of the battles of the time as if he had been an eyewitness. His fellow students remembered Vicente as an outstanding pupil.[30]

At the age of 15 in 1909, Lombardo Toledano's father sent him to the capital and enrolled him in the exclusive French Business School, founded in 1907 by the progenitor of Mexican national education, Justo Sierra. Students from wealthy provincial families studied there, while the rich sons of Mexico City attended the Jesuit-run Mascarones College, which had better facilities. The following year, Lombardo entered the prestigious National Preparatory School, an 'anarchic and even sinful', nationalist and xenophobic high school, according to one student. The school was housed in a beautiful baroque building of the Colegio de San Ildefonso, adjacent to the Porrúa bookstore, which became its extension for students who liked books.[31]

Lombardo Toledano was a student at the National Preparatory School when Victoriano Huerta, the conspirator against President Madero, militarised the campus. Although opposition to the usurper of the presidency on the part of high-school students, teachers and authorities was weak, outside its walls the violence committed by Huerta's minions reigned and the crossfire between the revolutionaries and their opponents produced a frightening echo within the school where new ideals were brewing; where the teacher Antonio Caso, 'a brilliant, masterful speaker, and a well-liked individual ... molded our ideas in the main branches of knowledge, almost without realising the consequences that the idealist-spiritualist philosophy he advocated would have on our lives as soon we left the classroom'.[32]

It was also there that Pedro Henríquez Ureña, the Socrates of the Dominican Republic, taught the latest trends in Spanish and Latin American literature in the deepest humanist tradition, as opposed to the mildewed recipes for studying the subject, thus 'sparking our interest for contact with the main sources of culture and the development and prospects of knowledge'. In the library of the eminent engineer Agustin Aragón, Lombardo Toledano discovered a world of erudition that he had not known in the home of his father.[33]

---

30 Uhthoff 1959, pp. 23–40.
31 Krauze 1976, p. 34; Alberto Vásquez del Mercado in Calderón Vega 1961, pp. 57–8; Cosío Villegas 1977, pp. 40–1. I would like to thank Luz Elena Galván for the information.
32 Cosío Villegas 1977, pp. 40–1.
33 Garciadiego 2000, pp. 221–30; Cosío Villegas 1977, pp. 40–1; Krauze 1999, pp. 18–19; Henríquez Ureña 2013, pp. 140–50; VLT, 'Contestación al cuestionario del periódico de la Confederación de Estudiantes, Reforma Universitaria', June 1958, FHLT, file 1065.

On the last day of school in October 1913, then 19-years-old Lombardo Toledano was designated to lead the graduating ceremony ... He chose to address his fellow students of the National Preparatory School as if he were delivering the Sermon on the Mount. He predicted that they would be the wise and great men of the future, perfect or supermen, who would occupy a privileged place in the future society. In the bombastic style that would characterise his entire life, Lombardo preached to them about courage and hope, about sacrifice for the redemption of society and the deification of man, and incited these soldiers of humanity, strong and great, to embrace life and acclaim liberty. It was a time of celebration of change, innovation of ideas and faith in spiritual regeneration. 'TODAY'S YOUTH IS A CORPSE', he boldly proclaimed and emphasised that it had to be resurrected.[34]

At about the same time that the widely hated dictator Huerta went into exile in 1914, Lombardo Toledano enrolled at the Law School and the School of Higher Education at the National University of Mexico. The Huertistas were expelled and the Maderistas, turned into Carrancistas, returned to the university. The new academic model tended to eliminate the elitist nature of higher education, assumed the welfare of the poor as a goal and worked with the new judicial authorities. The university was closed and reopened in accordance with disputes among the revolutionary factions for control of the government in the capital, which interrupted the process of renewal and often suspending courses and exams.[35]

'The culture of the humanities' was how Pedro Henríquez Ureña titled his 1914 influential address at the opening of the school year, a few months before he left the country. Lacking Lombardo Toledano's fresh outlook on Mexico's future, Henríquez Ureña was discouraged by 'the dreadful Mexico', whose government 'has ceased to exist' along with private property, individual rights, courts and civil registry and the destruction wrought by the revolution. He felt rejected for being a foreigner, different in his habits and teaching methods, in addition to being an upstart vis-à-vis the old positivists with ingrained practices. 'What will emerge from this strange disaster? Will there once again be civilization in Mexico', he asked. He recalled the School of Higher Education and its dilettantish launching in 1909, which despite 'these convoluted times was able to provide an example of harmony and respite', because the effort

---

34   VLT, 'Discurso pronunciado el último día de clases a mis queridos compañeros de la Escuela Nacional Preparatoria', 30 October 1913, FHLT, file 6.
35   Krauze 1976, pp, 61–2; Cosío Villegas 1977, pp. 43–4; Knight 1990, vol. 2, pp. 403–22; Alfonso Caso in Calderón Vega 1961, pp. 26–8, and Alberto Vásquez del Mercado in Calderón Vega 1961, p. 61; Garciadiego 2000, pp. 276–327.

undertaken was altruistic and dedicated to culture as 'the only saviour of the peoples'.[36] Lombardo Toledano was one of the attentive listeners of his address.

4   The Wise Man

It was not until the enactment of the 1917 Constitution that Mexico gave the appearance of order and the new state assumed its functions, when Lombardo Toledano began to reflect on the revolution and his own role in the 'reconstruction of the homeland'.[37] In his thinking, the lessons on public morals of Antonio Caso and the teachings of Henríquez Ureña on high culture as the universal social adhesive were combined. Neither then nor later did he speak about the armed revolution that he had witnessed. He detested the anarchy personified by Zapata and Villa. After all, those were the times of the economic decline of his family that affected the mood of his father, ill-prepared to live impoverished and as a second-level employee.

Culture was a supreme value and spreading it to the less blessed was an obligation for men of good will and fortune. The other lesson Vicente received from his teacher Antonio Caso was that spiritualism was the moral antidote to government corruption and selfish interests. Inspired by Christian morality, Lombardo Toledano and his friends from the Law School and the School of Higher Education – the 'seven wise men', as Manuel Gómez Morín, Alberto Vázquez del Mercado, Antonio Castro Leal, Alfonso Caso, Theophilus Olea y Leyva, Jesús Moreno Vaca and Lombardo were known – founded the Society for Conferences and Concerts on the occasion of Mexican Independence Day in September 1916. It was to be an updated version of the organisation created in 1907 by intellectuals who coalesced into the Ateneo de México.[38] Its purpose was to spread culture among students, workers and the general public with lectures about socialist doctrine and its possibilities in Mexico, justice, democracy, education and trade unions, along with concerts of classical music, which among those sectors was new and amateur. With meagre resources, the Society organised lectures on art, aesthetics and social morality, one on 'The art of travelling', given by Gómez Morín, courses on sexual hygiene by Dr Alfonso Pruneda and history lessons for workers, which included

---

36   Henríquez Ureña 2013, p. 77 and in FHLT, file 7; Cosío Villegas 1977, pp. 56–7; Quintanilla 2009, p. 271.
37   VLT, 'La Universidad Nacional', speech delivered in the School of Higher Education, 22 September 1917, in *Obra*, I/1, 1917–1923, pp. 12–13.
38   Krauze 1976, pp. 72–4; Quintanilla 2008, pp. 63–72; Garciadiego 2000, pp. 341–2.

'Bolshevism and the Russian Revolution' presented by Lombardo Toledano, who still did not believe in its virtues. The Society was an economic failure, 'but it certainly was an example of a failure with an abundant fruit for cultural stimulation and university orientation that was much needed ... when the impact of the Revolution raised so many new questions for Mexico and its youth'.[39]

Creating culture was a way to help the government, which had 'daunting' problems to resolve in moralising the people and 'saving' it. With the same fervour, Lombardo Toledano took part in the revitalisation of the People's University, which was founded in 1912 by the Ateneo de México, although it went downhill in subsequent years due to lack of resources. With an orderly and methodical life, he explained on one occasion, 'I am at home from 2 to 4pm or at night, as usual',[40] he assumed its tasks and accepted an austere salary. The economic situation of the People's University did not return to its heyday and by 1920 it closed its doors, although that did not mean the end of the goals that had given rise to the project, namely, to 'make individuals into useful citizens for themselves and the country'.[41]

Lombardo Toledano felt bound to the fate of Mexico and the world and with the duty to participate in public affairs, even though he finished his university years with an abstract and bookish vision. When speaking before a group of railway workers in 1918, he did not have a practical message to communicate: 'to achieve optimum results in life you have to have your soul burning with faith', not religious faith, but faith in the institutions 'that represent our tradition and our blood', he preached. His speech, peppered with names such as Hegel, Carlyle, Taine, Emerson, Spencer, Schiller, perhaps was far from the reality and concerns of the workers, but Mexico, which was experiencing a 'spiritual night' of an uneducated people and 'with no visible remedy for now', had hopes for the future based on sacrifice, goodness and optimism.[42]

In 1919 Vicente graduated from the National School of Law with a thesis entitled 'Public law and the new philosophical currents', a kaleidoscopic jour-

---

39 Cosío Villegas 1977, pp. 57–8; Quintanilla 2009, p. 148; Calderón Vega 1961, pp. 28–9, p. 46, pp. 68 and 77; Garciadiego 2007, p. 336; Azuela 2005, p. 64.
40 VLT to Gustavo Robirosa, Mexico City, 23 October 1917, FHLT, file 8.
41 'Carta constitutiva de la Sociedad de Conferencias y Conciertos', 11 September 1916, FHLT, file 7; Carretta Beltrán 2002; Alberto J. Pani and Dr Alfonso Pruneda, Mexico City, 20 September 1917, FHLT, file 8; *Programa de trabajos de la Universidad Popular Mexicana en el año de 1920*, p. 13; Garciadiego 2007, p. 408.
42 VLT, 'La influencia de los héroes en el progreso social', speech delivered to the Railway Workers Alliance, 5 May 1918, in *Obra*, I/1, 1917–1923, pp. 15–22.

ney into ideas of philosophers of the past two centuries and recent sociologists. He pointed to the Communist Manifesto of Karl Marx and Friedrich Engels as the most important document of the nineteenth century, because Antonio Caso had indicated so without inviting the students to read it. Based on a confusing array of ideas that Lombardo Toledano studied, he put forward a still idealistic synthesis of the world. Ideas gave rise to social movements and social movements sparked new ideas that explained such movements and foresaw their consequences. His nodal idea, which he was never to abandon, was the centrality of the state, which in his moralising vision he conceived of as a school of virtue with therapeutic functions for the historical evils of Mexico.[43] Mexico had a new juridical system, which was to ensure that foreign capital received good treatment. He quoted Cicero's refrain that the more laws, the less justice, as the application of the law to the letter could become a major form of injustice.[44]

In accordance with his worldview, Lombardo Toledano railed against Marxism, which he said engendered 'a false concept of the value of human labour, the consequences of which are collectivism without restraint, false trade unionism and ambition without limits'.[45] He expected the emergence of a state in the tradition of ancient Greece as a 'school of virtue', seeking the common good that is not in opposition to the individual, nor the latter to the state.[46]

Lombardo Toledano had not read Karl Marx's *Capital* when he wrote his thesis. Influenced by humanism, liberalism and the anti-Marxism of his teacher Caso, he regarded it as 'colossal absurdity', 'truly puerile reasoning' and considered the theory of surplus value – work for which payment was less than the value of goods produced by the same labour which would enrich the bourgeoisie and alienate the proletariat from its labour and from its humanity – as 'gratuitous assumptions'. Marx's mistake, according to Lombardo, was not taking into account the intellectual work represented by managing the productive work of a company. He could not imagine that there might be a conflict of interest between the employer and the employee, but rather saw the need

---

43   VLT, 'El derecho público y las nuevas corrientes filosóficas', thesis presented to obtain his law degree at the National School of Law of the National University of Mexico, 15 March 1919, in *Obra*, I/1, 1917–1923, pp. 55–109.
44   Ibid, p. 82 and p. 108.
45   Ibid, p. 77; Chassen de López 1977, pp. 51–2.
46   VLT, 'El derecho público y las nuevas corrientes filosóficas', thesis presented to obtain his law degree at the National School of Law of the National University of Mexico, 15 March 1919, in *Obra*, I/1, 1917–1923, p. 82.

for maximising production, combining capital and labour, intelligent leadership and physical strength. This central tenet of Marxist theory, 'this false theory of unpaid work ... which has stirred up and overheated workers' passions', deserved his scorn.⁴⁷

Those who knew Lombardo Toledano in those years recalled his 'frolicking conversation peppered with witty jokes ... jokes that tended to lower a person's status and the importance of a fact'. Alberto Vásquez del Mercado, the other 'wise' friend, characterised Lombardo as clever, witty, sharp, friendly, and incisive, a person who 'liked to find the weak side in people and attack on that level, but with cordiality'. Another acquaintance, Daniel Cosío Villegas, recalled Lombardo Toledano as an admirer of nature, a fan of hunting and archeology.⁴⁸

After graduating as a lawyer and obtaining another degree from the School of Higher Education, with diploma, cap and gown in hand, Lombardo Toledano did what any newly anointed lawyer would have done. On Avenida 5 de Mayo in downtown Mexico City, he opened a law firm. Even though he knew that being a litigant was not his vocation, he had to economise. He had plans to marry the 20-year-old Rosa María Otero Gama, a native of the state of San Luis Potosí, hailing from a distinguished family of medical doctors and his girlfriend at the School of Higher Education, where she studied geography without graduating. Lombardo rented a house in San Angel for 80 pesos a month and in April 1921 they were married in the parish church of the Sacred Heart of Jesus in Mexico City's Colonia Juárez neighbourhood, standing before an altar with a priest and cassock, and cherubs and virgins as heavenly witnesses.⁴⁹ In the wedding photo, probably choreographed, the newlyweds looked in different directions without making any contact; she was dressed in gauzy white, standing, with a headdress in her hair; he was seated, wearing a dark suit, white shirt with a raised collar and sporting a tie and a handkerchief peeking discreetly from the elegant coat pocket.

In choosing a wife, Lombardo revealed his idea of what a woman in society and in the home should be: educated in order to achieve a level of economic independence with respect to the husband, and with the ability and imagination to organise the household beyond the hearth. In the eyes of others, Rosa María would meet Lombardo Toledano's expectations to a T. She did not lock herself in the cage of domesticity, but neither did she forge her own destiny.

---

47 Ibid.
48 Cosío Villegas 1977, pp. 51–2; Alberto Vásquez del Mercado in Calderón Vega 1961, p. 61.
49 Isabel de Lombardo, 'Parte del matrimonio de Lombardo Toledano con Rosa María Otero y Gama', Mexico City, April 1921, FHLT, file 11.

She devoted her life to her husband, living his vocation. She took care of him, fed him, protected him and was his inseparable companion in almost all his travels because she also served as his secretary. Rosa María was the mother of his three daughters and when the family economy failed, she supplemented the budget with small businesses such as raising rabbits, knitting sweaters or binding books. He was the thinking part of the marriage; she was the operational end of the household team to the point of appearing to be his extension. Several legends survived the death of Vicente and Rosa María: that she saved his life from the imminent attack of a man at a rally in Tamaulipas when she stopped the attacker; or at a banquet when she served herself her husband's meal because she suspected it might be poisoned by changing plates and 'she almost could have died'.[50]

5   The Family

The history of the family in these years is hazy. In 1917 they returned to Teziutlán to save money, given the cost of living in the capital. The price of copper had not recovered after the revolution; the company sold what it had stored along with the shares to keep the mines running without production and without distributing dividends. The older Vicente Lombardo wanted to sell his shares, but found no buyers.[51]

Although no longer living with them, Lombardo Toledano felt responsible for his sisters – María, Margarita, Isabel, Elena and Aida, beautiful women and some of them talented as well – possibly because his father was mired in sadness and Isabel, their mother, never displayed the qualities of being their confidant. If someone wanted to be one of their boyfriends, he had to seek the approval of the elder brother. To his sisters María, Margarita and Isabel, Lombardo Toledano wrote:

> I am not an idiot moron brother suffering from irrational jealousy or a clumsy individual opposing the just desires that you may well have. My desire is to make you happy. But the dire situation that we are facing,

---

50   Interview with Adriana Lombardo Otero, Mexico City, 17 August 2005; interview with Marcela Lombardo Otero and with Raúl Gutiérrez Lombardo, Mexico City, 1 September 2005.
51   'To the stockholders', Teziutlán Copper and Mining Company, New York, 31 March 1919; Teziutlán Copper Mining and Smelting Company, San Diego, California, 28 June 1919 and 1 October 1919, FHLT, file 9; Ernest Smith and Company investments securities to LT, 8 September 1920 and 2 December 1920, FHLT, file 10.

which has divided the family, has brought many setbacks for all of us, including tremendous bitterness.[52]

Why would Lombardo Toledano have written that letter on good moral behaviour to his sisters, as if they had transgressed certain norms? He was cryptic in his complaint, exclaiming that 'unfortunately we have not been in the habit due to heredity and education to tell each other everything we're thinking'. He did not mention anyone by name, but he must have been referring to his sisters' choice of boyfriends that probably caused rifts, which the parents did not know how to deal with. It was necessary to 'make others notice your unfortunate actions' without grudges or prejudice, with affection, 'as I am doing for the first time in my life'. The sisters knew what he meant: María, the girlfriend of Alfonso Caso, Lombardo's friend and fellow student at the School of Law who thought it was right to advise him of his crush on the 20-year-old María, and Margarita who was about to marry Sidney Kilroe, an English doctor almost 20 years her senior and who ultimately proved to be a scoundrel. Despite the brother's admonition, the sisters married the boyfriends they had chosen.[53]

Lombardo Toledano never reproached his father for the way in which he managed money or property; he supported him and listened to his advice, even though he went his own way. From his brothers and sisters he demanded that they honour their father, even if his father's mistress and three half-brothers became an embarrassment that separated his parents forever. Perhaps due to an obligation to their father, Vicente and Humberto took on the responsibility for their half-brothers when in 1927, at only 57 years of age, Vicente Lombardo died unexpectedly.

In the eyes of the sisters, brothers and parents, Lombardo Toledano was an exceptional man in terms of ambition, talent and success. What a contrast this was with his younger brother Guillermo, who reached adulthood with the fear of living it due to 'my intellectual incapacity'. On one occasion, Guillermo shared reminiscences of family life with his brother Humberto:

> if you remember the education that we received since our childhood, you will undoubtedly recall the eminently selfish principles that we received. Our family never was and never has been bound by ties of love as you cite in your letter. On the contrary, the spiritual bond was non-existent among

---

52   VLT to María, Margarita and Isabel, Mexico City, 10 February 1919, FHLT, file 9; Interview with Laura Navarro, 4 August 2011.
53   Alfonso Caso to VLT, 11 April, 1918, FHLT, file 8; Hernández Soto, 'Descendientes de Vincenzo Lombardo Catti', http://gw5.geneanet.org/sanchiz. Accessed 20 November 2010.

us, because in all my years that I've been alive, I cannot remember a kiss or a caress or any other detail that would imply affection, from my parents or my brothers.

The family was united by blood and convenience. Its socialisation was 'like the savage hordes of Tierra del Fuego'. With pain, Guillermo recalled his father, an intelligent but uneducated man, whose lesson to his children was that 'each of us puts on the crown of his own making'. He extolled the value of the individual and

> boasted that he despised humanity. What could you expect from us? ... All of us grew up lonely, sad, devoid of ideals and goals and hating humanity because we were taught that every man was an enemy ... Our brother Vicente, totally different from us due to his culture and talents, went his own way without reaching out to us, and we continued to be disorientated.

It was not until Guillermo married that he could vent his anguish, because 'being sentimental, crying, suffering and communicating our sorrows, was an unforgivable crime that was cruelly condemned with ridicule'.[54]

Humberto resolved his comparison with Vicente by emulating him and collaborating on his brother's projects. In the 1920s when Humberto was a labour inspector in Puebla, he provided his brother with valuable information on the conditions of workers in the state. He also collaborated with Vicente in politics and ideological propaganda. Unlike his brother, Humberto did not have the doors of opportunity open for him. After each episode, which Vicente considered a victory even though he may have lost, the other brother was poorer and sadder than before. In Vicente's 1952 presidential campaign, which Humberto assumed as his own, he pawned and lost his home to subsidise his brother's crusade.[55]

The sisters were the wives of so and so, with the exception of María, who made a career as a novelist alongside the archaeologist Alfonso Caso, and Margarita, who devoted herself to diplomacy after being left alone raising her child. The other brothers did not attempt to emulate their older brother, and like the uncles and sisters, sought in Vicente an avenue for obtaining employment and a better life than they would have achieved on their own merits.

---

54   Guillermo Lombardo Toledano to Humberto Lombardo Toledano, Jalapa, 17 September 1933, FHLT, file 226.
55   Interview with María Elena Lombardo, Mexico City, 1 April 2013.

Unlike his brothers and sisters, Lombardo Toledano had the virtue of never falling into despair, since he had a mission to fulfil in life. Sometimes he was in a blind alley, and to pull himself out he would write verses that gave him peace of mind even though they lacked poetic quality; he read books, engaged in study, in conversation, in hunting, which sparked his inquisitiveness for the names of things, colours and smells of plants and trees; he visited archaeological sites, travelled around the country and abroad in an infinite curiosity to get to know the world. Only the dream of hunting elephants in Africa was not fulfilled. Field trips served to cement family life with his wife and later with his three daughters. Occasionally a brother or sister with their families joined him. More than friends, Lombardo Toledano had admirers, followers, comrades, a life-long chauffer, collaborators and numerous secretaries. He tended to be the axis around which the lives of others revolved.

Vicente Lombardo Toledano was an attractive man. He was thin, of taller than average height, with wavy hair on an oval head, expressive eyes with a hint of languor on an always cleanly shaven face, fine hands, meticulous in his selection of good quality and well-cut suits. He had exquisite taste and sported an inseparable gold ring on his fourth finger. He emerged from his teenage years with a trove of intangible assets that, even in the economic hardship of the post-revolutionary years, opened up the world to him. He had immense faith in himself and a willingness to put his assets to the service of an idea, namely to build a new world and the new man who would be its reflection.

CHAPTER 2

Knowledge and Power

Lombardo Toledano liked lofty phrases. He declared that 'for me, the 1920s were perhaps the most important period in the contemporary life of Mexico. As occurs with the dying of storms, following the popular armed movement, great euphoria gripped the people of Mexico, the unspeakable joy of living'.[1] But this idyllic vision had little to do with his experience of permanent personal and political turbulence or with the endless anguish of the Mexican people. The country was emerging from the ravages of the revolution; its future was being shaped in the context of marked small town and national violent struggles for the conquest of power, which the new mandarins seized from the old regime to seize it later from each other.

1 Renewal

The euphoria and joy was a vision, not of the imagined people, but of painters, writers and intellectuals, as well as of 'missionary' teachers, for whom post-revolutionary Mexico opened up endless possibilities for cultural and educational development. Even the severe critic of the revolution, Pedro Henríquez Ureña, was on their side. After seven years of living in the United States, he returned to Mexico in June 1921 and warmed up to the country he encountered: 'everything is *mexicanismo*'; he liked the national revival.[2]

Lombardo Toledano was his model of that renewed creative spirit. In search of his own place in the new world, serious, and with a deep sense of responsibility, he plunged into the whirlwind of the events of the day. His reputation for being prudent and honest earned him several simultaneous positions in a city suffering from chronic unemployment. For a brief period of time, he was department head in the Interior Ministry; an official in the Mexico City government, which enabled him to take his first steps in land distribution to peasant farmers in Iztapalapa, Xochimilco and other villages near the capital; a teacher at the National Preparatory School, where he taught classes in ethics

---

1 Interview with VLT by Paco Malgesto on TV canal 2, Mexico City, 18 January 1967, FHLT, file 1246.
2 Pedro Henríquez Ureña to Alfonso Reyes (henceforth PHU to AR), Mexico City, 29 July 1921, in Jacobo de Lara 1983, vol. 3, pp. 196–7; Vaughan 1982, pp. 142–4.

that allowed him to pontificate on the eternal problem of good and evil and which motivated him to develop a manual of moral pedagogy.³ With legendary painter Diego Rivera and other friends with whom he had worked together at the People's University and the ephemeral Society of Conferences and Concerts, they founded the Group in Solidarity with the Labour Movement to further encourage popular education.

Between 1919, when Lombardo Toledano graduated with a law degree, and 1921 when he had the opportunity to exercise power in the government of the country's capital city, barely two years had transpired. But this was enough time for him to evolve from questioning the 1917 Constitution to its adoption and application. Studying jurisprudence taught him that the state's mission was to make laws that 'did not tilt to one side or the other' and that the law protected the personality of men, uniting them in a social interdependence. But he was concerned that the law as a set of rules was not necessarily ethical and that the social and political reality of post-revolutionary Mexico was so variegated that the mere fulfilment of the law did not ensure an acceptable life standard.⁴

In November 1921 Lombardo Toledano resigned from the city government to take charge of the department of libraries of the Public Education Ministry and participate in the literacy crusade conducted in isolated rural areas, in need of 'civilisation'. Minister José Vasconcelos had called on the generation of young intellectuals to take part in the effort.⁵ Vasconcelos wanted to flood the country with works of classical literature and brochures on practical crafts; sometimes he himself distributed such books in villages. As with everything else he undertook, Lombardo Toledano took it upon himself and arranged with a manifest zeal for the literature to be sold in train cars 'in order to discipline or direct the people's culture'.⁶ He was in charge of the mission of sending ambulatory teachers across the country, establishing libraries stocked with editions of clas-

---

3 Fidel Dávalos, department head, to VLT, Mexico City, 21 May 1920; Gilberto Valenzuela to VLT, Mexico City, 24 June 1920; Federal District Governor to VLT, Mexico City, 30 October 1920, FHLT, file 10; VLT, 'El reparto de tierras a los pobres no se opone a las enseñanzas de nuestro Señor Jesucristo y de la Santa Iglesia. El pueblo mexicano peleó y sufrió diez años queriendo hallar la palabra de nuestro Señor Jesucristo', manifesto in favour of Constitutional Article 27, 1921, pp. 117–33; 'El eterno problema del bien', pp. 111–15, 1920; *Ética*, March 1922, in *Obra*, I/1, 1917–1923, pp. 137–83.
4 VLT, 'Los enemigos de la reforma agraria', p. 131; VLT, *Definiciones sobre el derecho público*, Cultura, Mexico City, 1922, in *Obra*, I/1, 1917–1923, pp. 187–213.
5 VLT to the Governor of the Federal District, Mexico City, 23 November 1921, FHLT, file 14; 'Proyecto de la misión del maestro ambulante', 5 December 1921, FHLT, file 15.
6 VLT to Agustín Loera y Chávez, Mexico City, 27 January 1922; VLT to the general director of Ferrocarriles Nacionales de México, Mexico City, 28 January 1922, FHLT, file 17; Cosío Villegas 1977, p. 9; Loyo 1999, pp. 248–56; Vaughan 1982, pp. 140–6.

sical works of literature as had been done with popular education in the Soviet Union and Italy.[7] Education was a mission.

Pedro Henríquez Ureña was impressed by the industriousness of the 'boy with character, intelligent and active, my ex-disciple'. Lombardo Toledano was 'one of the most worthy men in Mexico'.[8] Such was his reputation that the venerable professor Antonio Caso recommended him to José Vasconcelos for the position of director of the National Preparatory School to replace the minister who had occupied the post. Vasconcelos would regret that appointment for the rest of his life.

The meagre salary of 18 pesos a day as director forced Lombardo to occupy an apartment in the housing of the Preparatory School, which was authorised by Vasconcelos. 'And I told him when I put him in charge of the school: I'm giving you six months to do what you want, request the resources that you might need, and develop your programme; I am confident in your success', Vasconcelos expounded.[9]

Lombardo Toledano found the school in chaos. The old-fashioned teachers missed classes and students ended their academic career without having fulfilled all the course requirements. He insisted that the encyclopedic teaching methodology that the school provided should give way to practical instruction. Lombardo recommended to the teachers that 'each high-school diploma that you issue, you should be sure is accompanied by a diploma for a master shoemaker or carpenter'. The number of subjects should be reduced to improve their quality. The teachers had to submit to competitive examinations to be the head or chair of a department. Henríquez Ureña was amazed at the change: 'His most noteworthy measure at the Preparatory School, thus far, has been to impose fines for transgressions, and now no teacher misses class'.[10]

In March 1922 Rosa María was born, Lombardo Toledano and Rosa María Otero's first daughter, and in the same year his first influential treatise was published. The story writer Catherine Ann Porter called *Ética* a sign of the intellectual rebirth of Mexico.[11] The text, an exegesis of theoretical ideas on ethics and their application to morals, was a great event for the family. The father, to whom Lombardo Toledano dedicated the book, was beaming with

---

7   VLT, 'Proyecto de la Misión del Maestro Ambulante', 5 December 1921, FHLT, file 11 and 28 May 1922, FHLT, file 22.
8   PHU to AR, 4 January 1922; 14 February 1922, in Jacobo de Lara 1983, pp. 199–200 and p. 208.
9   Vasconcelos 1993, p. 146; Gómez Arias and Díaz Arciniegas 1990, p. 90.
10 Interview with VLT, *La Tribuna*, Mexico City, 1 March 1922, FHLT, file 18; PHU to AR, 9 April 1922, in Jacobo de Lara 1983, pp. 215–16.
11 Catherine Ann Porter to VLT, New York, 9 July 1922, FHLT, file 27.

pride due to his son's success, which contrasted with his unhappiness over the misfortune into which the family had fallen. Nostalgically he recalled his own father, Vincenzo, who hoped that it would be his son Pedro who would write a book, because it would have been 'the biggest satisfaction as well as one of the greatest triumphs of man in all human activities that life provides with the most glory and brilliance'.[12]

Ética, which was intended as a book for teaching morality in schools, was more than that. Permeated with Christian ethics, it offered a review of the philosophical currents from Aristotle to Nietzsche, a reaffirmation of what Lombardo Toledano believed about will, desire, suffering, seen through the lens of idealist philosophy and as a metaphysical experience. Human existence was mysterious, 'the spirit cannot be explained by physics and by false materialistic theories'.[13]

Lombardo Toledano maintained a close relationship with Pedro Henríquez Ureña, even though they were of different outlooks. He was active in the Mexican Regional Workers Confederation (CROM), created in 1918 as the first attempt at a single national labour confederation and was not interested in forming part of a select literary circle that at Henríquez Ureña's initiative met at Café Tacuba.[14] Their relationship became more intense when Pedro met Isabel, Vicente's sister, in Chapala, where the family maintained a remnant of its previous wealth.[15] Verging on 40 years of age, Henríquez Ureña returned all excited. 'It's possible that I indeed might get married', he confided in Alfonso Reyes,

> The thing is somewhat crazy because the girl is nineteen years younger than me; but I like her too much to let that be an objection. Her name is Isabel Lombardo Toledano … she's twenty-one years old. She is one of the prettiest girls in Mexico; she doesn't have the shyness of the plateau, but the liveliness of one who was born on the warm earth, in the soft Teziutlán mist.[16]

Teacher and pupil tied the knot in 1923 when Isabel married Henríquez Ureña in a 'scandalously' simple wedding at the civil registrar's office with Pepe Vas-

---

12 VL to VLT, Mexico City, 10 March 1922, FHLT, file 20.
13 VLT, *Ética*, in *Obra*, I/1, 1917–1923, p. 161 and p. 171.
14 PHU to AR, Mexico City, 27 April 1922, in Jacobo de Lara 1983, p. 217; Vasconcelos 1993, p. 142.
15 Henríquez Ureña de Hlito 1993, p. 90.
16 PHU to AR, Mexico City, 27 April 1922, in Jacobo de Lara 1983, p. 217; 12 August 1922, p. 227; 29 May 1923, p. 244.

concelos as their witness, although their relations had become strained. The best men in the church of San Cosme were Lombardo Toledano and Rosa María Otero.[17] The wedding was unadorned and without music. The party at the house of the best men was lively until at 5pm when the married couple bid its farewells and took the train to San Luis Potosí to observe the solar eclipse. 'Three and a half minutes of darkness; blue shadows and silver horizons; swallows frightened'. From San Luís Potosí they went to Ocotlan on the banks of Lake Chapala where 'I met Isabel' and where, contemplatively, Henríquez Ureña wrote: 'The lake is sad, but every lake puts the landscape and spirit at rest'.[18]

2 The Break

The relationship between the director of the Preparatory School and the minister was tense. Vasconcelos chafed at what he called the workerism of the director in bringing elite students into contact with workers. 'The Preparatory School began to become a centre of agitation' directed from the offices of the Mexican Regional Workers Confederation of which Lombardo Toledano was a recent recruit and in which, according Vasconcelos, he was scoring points. 'Impose discipline, I occasionally begged them to do',[19] since in addition to his activism, the enmity of some of the students toward Lombardo Toledano turned the school into a battleground complete with exploding firecrackers that at any hour profaned the dour building of the enlightenment.[20] What most tried the patience of Vasconcelos, a faithful follower of Álvaro Obregón, hoping that the president would not view positively the presidential ambition of his Interior Minister Plutarco Elías Calles, was that the director used the school as a means to promote such a campaign.

The straw that broke the camel's back and incensed Vasconcelos was a student poster pasted on the wall of the school, a strident broadsheet that also scandalised some students for being 'a true affront to the culture and morality of an educational institution such as the National Preparatory School', a dirty and immoral lampoon. Lombardo Toledano was not bothered by the jocular allusions of the poster to his style of teaching. Vasconcelos had prohibited such expressions, but his anger and its after-effects brought some stu-

17 Henríquez Ureña de Hlito 1993, p. 94.
18 PHU to AR, Mexico City, 29 May 1923, in Jacobo de Lara 1983, p. 244.
19 Vasconcelos 1993, p. 146.
20 Dromundo 1956, pp. 171–6.

dents closer to Lombardo Toledano and in favour of Calles's presidential campaign. The minister expelled those who signed the broadsheet for eight days, bypassing the school authorities, which enraged the preparatory school students.

Their passions whipped up by several teachers, students 'launched furious accusations against me'. Vasconcelos expelled them as well because 'kindness is weakness' and it was 'not the time to forgive', but rather to impose order. Among those expelled was Alfonso Caso, brother of the rector of the National University of Mexico, Antonio Caso, and Lombardo Toledano's brother-in-law. The expulsions exacerbated the atmosphere. When Vasconcelos appeared in the school building, he faced chants of 'Down with Vasconcelos!', 'Death to Vasconcelos!', 'Kill him', and when amid the shouting he ordered the students to return to class, clear the courtyard or 'I'll clear it', the chants continued and rocks flew. Vasconcelos, who knew that in the eyes of the students he was a tyrant, would not negotiate. If Lombardo Toledano wanted to 'conquer the schools for the Calles movement, he had failed'.[21]

The indignant students asked Vasconcelos to rescind the expulsions and for Antonio Caso to mediate the conflict. The latter did not agree to do so, annoyed by the firing of his brother. The conflict escalated and a fracas ensued. An aggressive policeman intervened, injuring several students who responded with blows, stones and shots. Lombardo Toledano resigned in August 1923 with the terse declaration that he no longer wished to be at the forefront of an institution, 'for which greater qualities than I possess are needed, but above all, because I no longer wish to continue working with a person such as the Public Education Minister with whom I have not been able to reach an understanding'.[22]

President Obregón firmly supported his minister, according to Vasconcelos, who was satisfied with the outcome of the conflict, even though he was hurt by the resignation of Antonio Caso as the dean of the university. Vasconcelos remained confident that President Obregón would not support Calles, until a few months later he realised that 'it was Obregón who moved the whole set-up' of the selection of the Interior Minister.[23] His relationship with the president was also damaged beyond repair.

Lombardo Toledano defended academic freedom as 'one of the most important aspects of the constitutional guarantee of freedom of thought'. He criticised the 'shameful tyranny' of the Education Minister, defended the change in the

---

21   Vasconcelos 1993, pp. 148–57; Gómez Arias and Díaz Arciniegas 1990, p. 95.
22   VLT to the rector of the UNM, Mexico City, 17 August 1923, FHLT, file 39.
23   Vasconcelos 1993, pp. 161–97.

teaching curriculum that he had introduced to make it less scholastic and more practical, the implementation of the extension of university education and social service on the part of students in local and working-class communities, which disgusted even some students. It was as a result of this conflict that he circulated the petition for university autonomy to prevent state interference as had just occurred at the National Preparatory School. Vasconcelos was opposed to the measure.[24]

3   On the Campaign Trail

Lombardo Toledano became unemployed but he read, wrote and had time to devote to the presidential campaign of Calles, who ran as the candidate of the working class, as well as his own campaign, since he entered the ring as a candidate for federal congressional deputy for Teziutlán. He wanted to be a congressional deputy since 1922. He had the authority among his Teziuteco friends who admired him as the prodigious son of his people and followed his political alignment proposals as if they had been the product of their own sovereign will. Then, Lombardo Toledano said he was an enemy of political parties, 'these absurd groups without castes and anonymous in terms of their constitution and purpose'. He decided his timeframes, according to the circumstances: 'If I ever must go to the Chamber of Deputies it will be thanks to the free, disinterested, and spontaneous support of my people to fulfil my own social outlook'.[25]

These were noble words that clashed with the harsh reality of the country and the paternal land in which the new and old warring chiefdoms swarmed. He had rivals who intrigued against him in the National Agrarian Reform Party, akin to the government of Álvaro Obregón, and in the National Cooperativist Party, which had its own candidate: the Teziuteco teacher José Gálvez, whose aims such as equality, justice and mutual assistance were unobjectionable. Despite his professed non-partisan conviction, Lombardo had no alternative but to rely on the local Mexican Labour Party, the Mexican Regional Workers Confederation political arm, to receive support. In the July elections he was declared the winner, but the electoral board, in charge of counting the votes,

---

24   VLT, 'Mi actuación política en la Escuela Nacional Preparatoria', Mexico City, 5 September 1923; VLT to Aurelio Bueno, 7 October 1923; L. de la Rea, president of the Mexican Student Federation to Congress, 27 August 1923, FHLT, file 40.

25   VLT to Froylán Manjarrez, Mexico City, 15 June 1922, FHLT, file 26; VLT, 'A los Ciudadanos de Teziutlán y Tlatlauqui', June 1922, FHLT, file 27; Carr 1976, p. 156.

declared that Gálvez had received a majority of the ballots cast.[26] In truth, he lost because the correlation of forces in the mountain region did not favour him and votes cast in his favour were not counted.

Meanwhile Gálvez's aspirations grew and in the 1924 elections he wanted to run for governor of Puebla. On a trip through the mountains to visit schools, Vasconcelos allowed Gálvez, as adverse to the Calles candidacy as the minister himself was, to accompany him. So as not to leave anything to the spontaneity of the Teziutecos, Lombardo had to prevent Gálvez from exploiting the trip 'to engage in reprisals and dispense favours'. He asked his Teziuteco friend Florencio Cerda 'to obtain the discreet consent of the mayor, to send me a telegram which I suggest as follows'. The telegram should inform Vasconcelos of Teziutlán's real needs 'to prevent Gálvez from only doing what suits his political interests'.[27]

Vasconcelos revelled in the majestic landscape of the mountains, tasted the freshly squeezed sugar cane juice, admired the orchids and palm trees, but should not have taken the problems of the Sierra mountain region so seriously, as he compared the neglect he found Puebla mired in and the enmity between its villages with the families of Romeo and Juliet, the Montagues, and the Capulets.[28] And Gálvez should not have accumulated political capital on this trip, since he placed his bets on the losing side in the power equation. The National Cooperativist Party was on its last legs.[29]

While he was involved in both the presidential as well as his own election campaign, Lombardo Toledano was appointed a member of the capital's city council. The appointment was to take effect on 1 January 1924 without much protocol, since the city government was in the hands of the Laboristas, such as himself, and the candidate Calles's political base.[30] But events moved in rapid succession and before the campaigns could take off big, until then loyal General Guadalupe Sánchez and Adolfo de la Huerta, who aspired to the presidency, revolted against the government. In December, embattled President Obregón manoeuvred in Congress to put Lombardo Toledano in charge of the govern-

---

26   *El Eco de la Sierra*, 7 July 1922, FHLT, file 27; VLT to Florencio Cerda, Mexico City, 16 October 1922, FHLT, file 29; Mac Gregor 2005, pp. 57–79; García Bonilla 2012, pp. 50–74.
27   VLT to Florencio Cerda, Mexico City, 20 March 1923, FHLT, file 38; Vasconcelos 1993, pp. 177–85.
28   Vasconcelos 1993, p. 180.
29   Rodríguez Kuri 2010, pp. 179–205.
30   Calles to VLT, Mexico City, 23 October 1923; VLT to Florencio Cerda, Mexico City, 11 November 1923; Red Student Party, Mexico City, 21 November 1923, FHLT, file 40; García Bonilla 2012, p. 86.

ment of Puebla. Calles was pleased by the appointment, since the Poblano would look after one of the political flank-guard, which was not entirely secure.

4 From the Government Palace

In taking stock of the situation, Lombardo Toledano found a bleak panorama. The state was bankrupt and he was surrounded by schemers. Local legislators declared themselves in rebellion against the government, as was the case with judges of the Supreme Court and its employees. To manage the state, Lombardo Toledano sought out government debtors and reduced operating expenses to a minimum, dismissed employees and closed public offices except schools. He could not collect taxes in parts of the state not under government control and dominated by the rebels. Without many alternatives, he extended the deadline for tax payments and unsuccessfully requested loans from the federal government. Had it not been for the early payment by US magnate William Jenkins on 1 January 1924, there would have been almost no money in the state treasury coffers. Thanks to this payment, the treasury had a meagre sum of 1,700 pesos to its name.[31]

In addition to the lack of resources, information was limited on what was happening in the military field. Lombardo Toledano did not know, for example, that the forces that claimed to protect the state, actually feigned doing so, nor that President Obregón planned an ambush against the enemy, allowing its forces to enter Puebla, and once inside, destroying them to prevent their advance on the country's capital.[32]

In several villages there were no authorities and government offices were leaderless. When Lombardo Toledano named officials to fill these slots, the proposed candidates were rejected by the military authorities or by the local population. In addition, defence squads organised by landowners or by Delahuertistas kept the population on edge. The aggressiveness of these forces, partially agitated from the capital by the opponents of the governor, could not be stopped either by the head of military operations or by the Interior Ministry. Amid the administrative chaos and political uncertainty, in which the armed bands prowled the state and demanded funds from public offices such as the post office, tax administration and revenue collection department, Lombardo Toledano took the time to lay the first cornerstone for the museum of history,

---

31 Ruiz González Almazán, State administration inspector, 'Informe confidencial al Gobernador', undated, January 1924, FHLT, file 45.
32 Plasencia de la Parra 1998, pp. 48–51.

archeology and ethnology of Puebla. These were difficult times and he was never separated from the automatic pistol he was carrying on his belt in an embroidered leather case.[33]

Lombardo Toledano ruled Puebla without the judiciary and without the legislature, which the federal government had refused to recognise due to their adherence to the Delahuertista cause. One of the many conflicts that arose concerned the appointment of municipal councils, when the elected city halls had abandoned the government. Often the governor swore in councilmen without knowing them, without consulting with local residents and without investigating the probity and administrative capacity of the people who replaced the Delahuertista councilmen. The local population did not necessarily recognise the legitimacy of the new village councils and the disputes that arose were not resolved due to the absence of the legislative branch of government. Those in disagreement took their case to the capital, they complained to the president or the Interior Minister that the governor had violated the popular vote. As a result, animosity toward the governor was also harbored in the capital, stimulated by congressional deputies from Puebla who were not pleased that Lombardo Toledano was governing their state with members of the CROM. It was rumoured that the presidential candidate would not be Calles but rather Vasconcelos, which helped weaken the governor. His timid or cautious father advised him to resign so that given his culture and prestige they would not treat him 'as any old vulgar unfaithful bastard'.[34]

Lombardo Toledano did not yield to adversity. In addition to the Delahuertistas, he faced the forces of the 'compañero general' José María Sánchez, once a Zapatista but for the circumstances under consideration, what was relevant was his cronyism with the president. Sánchez had been governor of Puebla for a few months in 1921, but due to his complicity in two assassinations and because it was feared that he was a radical agrarian activist, Congress discreetly removed him. In 1923 his army joined the fight against the Delahuertista rebels with the methods that gave results during the revolution. He and his army

---

33 José Santander, president de la municipal board to the General Secretary of the State of Puebla, Chalchicomula, 27 February 1924, FHLT, file 49; National Agrarian Reform Party (PNA) to VLT, Mexico City, 7 March 1924; VLT to Santibáñez, internal affairs secretary of the PNA, Mexico City, 10 March 1924, FHLT, file 50; VLT to Rafael Díaz, Mexico City, 29 March 1924, FHLT, file 53.

34 VLT, 'Minuta a todos los miembros del Congreso del Estado', Puebla, 13 December 1923; VLT to Celestino Gasca, Puebla, 19 December 1923; VLT to Enrique Colunga, Interior Minister, 24 December 1923, FHLT, file 41; VL to VLT, Mexico City, 29 December 1923, FHLT, file 42; R.C. Díaz, state treasurer, to VLT, 1 January 1924, FHLT, file 44; VLT to Enrique Colunga, Mexico City, 9 January 1924, FHLT, file 44; García Bonilla 2012, p. 87.

entered villages, stole horses from residents, recruited for his army, and if there were no volunteers 'he would take them by sheer force'. The population clamoured for guarantees that the governor had no way of offering them.³⁵

Friends were concerned about the vitriolic attacks in the Mexico City press and came to Lombardo Toledano's defence. The artist Guillermo Toussaint was his private secretary, Alfonso Caso offered to help in everything except in the justice system and in January Pedro Henríquez Ureña joined in to take charge of the state's educational system, 'which would seem like good news, but it is so very relatively'. Expenditures were twice as high as revenues. Everything amounted to good wishes, such as opening night schools and increasing primary schools. Furthermore 'everyone steals. Under Obregón, moralisation efforts began, but then slackened' and theft was taking place on a large-scale. To the rescue of the governor came the raucous poet Germán Liszt Arzubide and Salvador Azuela, one of those expelled from the National Preparatory School by Vasconcelos, They, too, offered their services.³⁶

As the state government's finances improved momentarily at the beginning of the New Year, it was possible to pay employees half their month's wages, including a salary to the governor corresponding to ten days of his term in office. The military situation, meanwhile, 'suddenly erupts in a bit of war, it's what we least understand ... and sometimes it doesn't let us sleep'. The Minister of War Francisco Serrano helped the governor's friends understand the situation and boost their spirits. With the intervention of Luis N. Morones, General Secretary of the CROM, members of the labour confederation held positions in the Puebla state government administration. One CROM leader entered the Labour Department and several joined municipal governments. Uncle Pedro was put in charge of inspecting the state government administration, the positions of the armies and the loyalty or disloyalty of municipal authorities. The governor had no qualms about subsidising causes that he considered worthy. Despite the state government's rickety finances, he provided money to the Mexican Revolutionary Party, a political machine of Mexico City students that participated in Calles's presidential campaign. It was no accident that, among the many rumours circulating, the name of Lombardo Toledano began to be aired for the post of Public Education Minister in the Calles cabinet.³⁷

---

35 Crescencio Flores to VLT, San Aparicio, Puebla, 11 January 1924; Teniente Coronel Felipe Escalante to Marciano García de Santa María Jonacatepec, 12 January 1924; Gregorio Pérez to VLT, San Miguel Canoa, 12 January 1924, FHLT, file 45; Keith 2003, pp. 73–4.

36 PHU to AR, Puebla, 7 January 1924, in Jacobo de Lara 1983, pp. 259–60; Dromundo 1956, p. 213.

37 Darío Rubio to Guillermo Touissant, Mexico City, 16 January 1924; Guillermo Touissant to

The political situation in Puebla had not stabilised, in part due to the effort by the state's congressional deputies in the capital to undermine the local administration, which began to tire the president. Lombardo Toledano was sent to Puebla to contribute to the pacification of the state, but the political shake-ups he undertook in the municipalities and his land distribution efforts aroused such animosity that the goal seemed to fail. The federal congressional deputies along with the local legislators continued to poison the atmosphere against the governor, accusing him of persecuting them in the state. He responded that those complaining were enemies of the federal government or that they had not been granted the positions they craved for in Puebla.[38]

In March 1924 Lombardo Toledano was removed from office. Officials that he had appointed in the municipalities and his friends who accompanied him on this mission impossible, resigned. 'In the three month period that my stint as state governor lasted I was able to achieve very little or nothing. My efforts were always subject to the evolution of the military events that provoked the rebellion'.[39] Lombardo Toledano knew that the situation was complex, but he simplified it, attributing it to corruption and disregard for the laws of the governments that preceded his brief passage in the Puebla state government administration. He never turned his fire on the federal government that had appointed him governor of Puebla at a time of crisis, more like a wildcard than investing him with power, leaving him alone to fight among many political wolves inside and outside the state. But he accepted the blows stoically, believing in the inevitable historical future development.

5 On the Road to the Chamber of Deputies

Back in the capital and after resting a few days in Cuernavaca, Lombardo Toledano assumed the post of councilman in the capital city government and resumed the presidential campaign for Calles and his own race. With the exper-

---

Darío Rubio, Puebla, 19 January 1924, FHLT, file 45; R. Cervantes Torres to VLT, Mexico City, 30 January 1924, FHLT, file 45; VLT to Cervantes Torres, Puebla, 14 March 1924, FHLT, file 51.

38   Enrique Colunga to VLT, Mexico City, 21 February 1924, VLT to Obregón, Mexico City, 21 February 1924, FHLT, file 48.

39   Eulalio Martínez to VLT, Mexico City, 20 March 1924, FHLT, file 52; VLT, 'Manifiesto a los habitantes del estado', Puebla, 20 March 1924, in *Excélsior* 21 March 1924 edition, FHLT, file 53.

ience of 1922 behind him, when he lost to the political machine of his opponent, this time he organised the campaign unequivocally with the help of the CROM's Labour Party.

He asked his friends who he had placed in the Puebla state government administration to resign, except for Benigno Campos, who he had appointed mayor of Teziutlán. Campos was key to his plans and Lombardo Toledano was confident 'that the new governor would not dare to replace you with another person ... he will not dare to declare war on me in my own district ... because he knows that I will be a congressional deputy despite everything he might have done against it'. He expressed confidence that his 'victory will be absolutely indisputable'[40] to instill optimism in his friends and encourage them to participate in his campaign with dedication.

His optimism was not justified. The state authorities did not let their hearts be tempted and the campaign for the congressional deputy seat was arduous. 'They changed the municipal government that you placed in office', his other intimate follower Florencio Cerda from Teziutlán wrote to him, but as a friend 'who loves you and sends you greetings candidly, Florencio would do whatever his friend would ask him to do'. However, seeing the difficulties, Lombardo Toledano did not trust the willingness of his friends to fight for him and negotiated the federal congressional and state legislative seats, as well as his brother Humberto's election in Teziutlán, with the Agrarian Party, with the CROM, with the Interior Minister, with the military chief of the Sierra Norte de Puebla region, with the agrarian leader Antonio Díaz Soto y Gama, and with the recently anointed Agrarista governor Alberto Guerrero. He did so despite the fact that it was Guerrero who had dismantled the municipal and town councils installed by Lombardo Toledano and even though the councilmen who were removed did not obtain jobs due to their proximity to the deposed governor.[41]

The newly appointed mayor of Teziutlán, Félix Pérez, once a Zapatista and in 1924 a slavish supporter of the governor, apparently received instructions not to register Humberto's candidacy for state legislator and to register the governor's son for the post and himself as an alternate for the same position. Lombardo Toledano called for the removal of this puppet of the governor in order to put an end to 'this irritating pantomime that requires men of good faith to withdraw from the struggle in order to leave the field open to this permanent scoundrel'. He advised his brother to withdraw from the race, since in these manoeuvres he

---

40   VLT to Benigno Campos, Mexico City, 7 April 1924, FHLT, file 53; García Bonilla 2012, p. 89.
41   Florencio Cerda to VLT, Teziutlán, 24 April 1924; VLT to Alberto Guerrero, Mexico City, 3 May 1924; Benito Flores to VLT, Atlixco, Puebla, 6 May 1924, FHLT, file 54; Henderson 1998, p. 177; García Bonilla 2012, pp. 100–1.

saw the evil hand of the National Agrarian Party with which Morones's Labour Party had secret agreements and negotiated the election of congressional deputies. Lombardo Toledano found himself in this crossfire among various groups of Obregonistas, Callistas, Agraristas and Laboristas.[42]

He knew that the selection of candidates for congressional deputy seats was not a matter of popular will, but of a calculation among the political elites of all ideological colours. Lombardo Toledano did not consult his friends in Teziutlán but made recommendations as well as the strategies to promote them, which they meekly accepted. When he saw that this or that appointment was unsuccessful, including his own, he knew how to beat a retreat, awaiting better times. The legality of some appointments was subordinated to the need for the conquest of political spaces in adverse situations. This was the case with Celestino Gasca, head of the capital city government, who was not a Poblano. Lombardo Toledano went as far as to suggest that Gasca did not have to appear in the district of Zacapoaxtla that he would represent, since 'I'll see to it to help Señor Huidobro [supposedly Gasca's alternate for the post] with everything necessary in order for your campaign to move forward'.[43] This service to Gasca and the 'cause' was in exchange for a month's paid leave of absence from his post as councilman in the capital to pursue his campaign and start the campaign on behalf of Gasca. As the environment was hostile to the Laboristas, the Poblano politician needed to prolong his leave of absence. 'It's almost certain that I cannot step back from this effort, since as Election Day approaches, the aggressiveness of my enemies intensifies and it's necessary that I be ready for anything. I await your prompt reply, because I'm really in urgent need of money'.[44] The race was expensive, since it was necessary to bring everything to Puebla from the capital, including printed campaign material, manifestos, the buttons with photos of the candidates and the car to move around the mountainous regions. And to deal with any eventuality, it was necessary to get licenses to carry weapons.

A new obstacle in Lombardo Toledano's campaign was Manuel Villavicencio Toscana, a former fellow student at the School of Law, with 'the moral stature of a cunning dog', a political chameleon, who went from being a Carrancista to

---

42 VLT to Enrique Colunga, telegram, Teziutlán, 11 May 1924; Rodrigo Gómez to Alberto Guerrero, Mexico City, 12 May 1924, FHLT, file 55; García Bonilla 2012, p. 98; Meyer, Krauze and Reyes 1981, p. 187; Clark 1984, p. 106.
43 VLT to Celestino Gasca, Teziutlán, Puebla, 9 May 1924, FHLT, file 54.
44 VLT to José López Cortés, secretary of the Mexico City municipal government, Teziutlán, Puebla, 10 June 1924; VLT to Humberto Lombardo Toledano (henceforth HLT), Teziutlán, Puebla, 11 June 1924, FHLT, file 57; García Bonilla 2012, pp. 106–7.

a Cooperatista and in 1924 from being an Obregonista to a Callista. While Lombardo Toledano put on a display of not being overly concerned, since 'I have always had more than enough soul to preach my convictions above the false revolutionaries and men of bad faith',[45] he was incensed to think that there was a hidden hand that moved the whole set-up. He suspected Interior Minister Enrique Colunga, who aspired to be governor of the state of Guanajuato and perhaps wanted to ingratiate himself with the anti-Lombardistas in Puebla and enlist their support for his plans.[46] With the representation costs assured by the government in the capital city to fund the campaign, he did not leave Teziutlán except for a few hours when he went to Perote in neighbouring Veracruz, because Calles made a campaign stop there for lunch. He returned to the Sierra with the impression that the presidential candidate was on his side and against the manoeuvre to impose Villavicencio.[47]

The 6 July 1924 elections were marked by ballot theft, the detention of his supporters, the disappearance of the voter registration lists, obstacles placed in the way of opening the polling stations, altercations to prevent the functioning of their presidents and false pretexts to collect voter registration cards. Lombardo Toledano proclaimed himself the winner, but Villavicencio was given the paperwork indicating he had received a majority of the votes cast.[48] With his usual parsimony and without allowing defeatism to overcome him, Lombardo Toledano returned to his position as councilman in the capital with a salary, car and paid gasoline. Meanwhile, in Teziutlán his supporters suffered hostility from the authorities, which did not diminish their devotion to him: 'For us, you are indispensable and we'd go with you wherever you wanted us to. We are proud that someone from this village has stood out, for his knowledge, his actions, and his honesty, and that someone is YOU, dear Vicente'.[49]

Plutarco Elías Calles was sworn in as president on 30 November 1924. But his victory at the polls did not mean the victory of the Callistas in the Chamber of Deputies, where the resolution on who won the congressional deputy races in dispute, such as the Teziutlán district in which Lombardo Toledano ran, was rejected by the opposition. While he did not lose, Lombardo did not win either.

---

45 VLT to HLT, Teziutlán, 11 June 1924; VLT to Crisóforo Ibáñez, president of the local agrarian reform commission of Puebla, Teziutlán, 12 June 1924, FHLT, file 57.
46 VLT to Enrique Colunga, telegram, Teziutlán, 13 June 1924, FHLT, file 57; VLT to José González Rejón, Teziutlán, 14 June 1924, FHLT, file 58; Clark 1984, p. 106; Meyer, Krauze and Reyes 1981, p. 99.
47 VLT to VL, Teziutlán, 18 June 1924, FHLT, file 58.
48 VLT to Obregón, Mexico City, 6 July 1924; VLT to Luis N. Morones, Mexico City, 7 July 1924, FHLT, file 60.
49 Florencio Cerda to VLT, Teziutlán, 14 September 1924, FHLT, file 65.

Guanajuatense politician Gasca was also unsuccessful in his bid for a congressional seat in Puebla, as he was disqualified by the federal congressional deputy for that same district, Zacapoaxtla. Unperturbed, Lombardo Toledano spent the December holidays in trips around Papantla and Tajín, given that he was passionate about pre-Hispanic culture and archaeological sites.[50]

He experienced the endless anxieties of post-revolutionary Mexico as a natural process of the country's growth and maturation. The regeneration of Mexico would be a long-term process and he was a disciplined man without economic ambitions. He liked living with amenities and drinking French wines,[51] but his lifestyle and way of thinking was different from most of the politicians of the time, who did not understand him either. He was convinced that he had a civilising mission and a strong will to fulfil it without measuring the costs or consequences. In the meantime, he was awaiting the congressional resolution on his deputy seat that his opponents had blocked 'and they had the unmitigated gall to send me word that I could receive the 12,000 pesos that corresponded to me for legislative expenses throughout the year that this question has been in abeyance. But they also led me to understand I need to change my mind'.[52]

Lombardo Toledano rejected the blackmail. His persistence and resistance were compensated. In September 1925 the Chamber of Deputies approved a resolution ratifying his majority vote and ballot box victory in the previous year's elections. At the age of 31, and father of his second daughter Adriana, who was born in March, he made a grand entrance into national political life. The news caused rejoicing among friends in Teziutlán who expected that their congressional deputy in the legislative chamber would protect them; and the deputy knew that it was his duty to do so. The task was arduous and more often than not it was a failure.[53]

Lombardo Toledano was in his element in Congress. His oratorical ability, physical stamina to speak for several hours, knowledge of laws like few others, persuasive style to repeat the same idea in different ways, led him to offer incisive arguments presented ironically, while he questioned and ridiculed the arguments of his opponents. He delighted in listening to positions debating the constitutionality of the Constitution and demolishing them in exchange for thunderous applause. He argued with a triumphant gesture when he linked

---

50 VLT to Benigno Campos, Mexico City, 3 December 1924, FHLT, file 66; 'Diario de Debates de la Cámara de la Unión', 18 December 1924, FHLT, file 69.
51 'Los mejores vinos de Francia, España y Alemania' to VLT, 24 October 1924, FHLT, file 65.
52 VLT to Florencio Cerda, Mexico City, 15 August 1925, FHLT, file 80.
53 Florencio Cerda to VLT, Teziutlán, 14 October 1925, FHLT, file 81.

the Irrigation Law proposed by Calles with 'the unshakable foundations for the future great socialist nation of Mexico', although he explained that 'I am not a blind follower of Marx's theory due to many ideological considerations', which he left unspecified. The crux of the success of a country was the planned and organised production of wealth.[54] Although the motions presented by his party were not adopted, the experience in the Chamber of Deputies was a great opportunity to sharpen his rhetorical weapons and crystallise his ideas.

If Alberto Guerrero was not to Lombardo's liking as his successor, Professor Claudio N. Tirado, elected governor of Puebla in 1925, was unacceptable. The deputy demanded his dismissal for tolerating corruption in his government. He called on the Teziutecos to be 'willing to give and receive punches' and not to lose heart, because the just rebellion would influence the mood of the president. But the cost was high for the Teziutecos; the unpopular impositions in town councils in local elections sparked off violence since both his friends and his opponents were armed. Tirado was not soft of heart and his supporters were repressed, with persecution and torture in prison with cold water baths, according to the complaints that flooded the office of President Calles and to which the president responded with reprimands to the governor. Tirado denied the allegations. Given the inability to reverse the course of events, Lombardo Toledano sent letters and telegrams to Calles, ending them with 'tremendous humility' and 'I dare to beg you Mr President'. The president responded with telegrams to the governor that had no effect.[55]

Lombardo Toledano, on this rare occasion, lost his patience, because he saw that the support for his rivals came from the Interior Ministry headed by Colonel Adalberto Tejeda, whose private secretary was a Poblano and agrarian reform advocate like his Veracruzano chief Tejeda and like Governor Tirado. Tejeda wanted to return to the governor's residence in Jalapa and his well-oiled ties with the Agraristas was the way to do so, while his secretary had political interests in Puebla. Tejeda assigned federal forces to Tirado so that at bayonet point they would sustain the mayor of Teziutlán, an adversary of Lombardo

---

54 'Diario de los Debates de la XXXI Legislatura', Tuesday, 3 November 1925 session, FHLT, file 82; Wednesday, 9 December 1925 session, FHLT, file 83.

55 VLT to Claudio Tirado, Mexico City, 1 December 1925; Florencio Cerda to VLT, Teziutlán, 7 December 1925, FHLT, file 83; VLT to Florencio Cerda, Mexico City, 29 December 1925, FHLT, file 84; VLT to Florencio Cerda, Mexico City, 26 January 1926, FHLT, file 86; VLT to Benigno Campos, Mexico City, 27 February 1926, FHLT, file 88; VLT to Calles, 2 May 1926; Calles to VLT, Mexico City, 3 May 1926; VLT a Calles, Mexico City, 6 May 1926, FHLT, file 90; VLT, 'En México no existe municipio libre', Chamber of Deputies, 16 November 1926, in *Obra*, I/3, 1926–1927, p. 222.

Toledano, who could do nothing to stop the violence.[56] Opponents of the state government were systematically intimidated, jailed and [o]nce inside, orders have been given that they be flogged and doused with cold water.[57]

Labour unions were the favourite target for the brutal repression unleashed by Gonzalo Pumarino, the mayor of Teziutlán, imposed by Tirado. While the Laboristas fled with their families to Cerro del Colihui, where the dense forests, the loggers and the coal miners protected them, or to Altolonga in Veracruz, Teziutlán became a bloody arena where the law of an eye for an eye prevailed. Florencio Cerda and his friends resisted. Instructed by their congressional deputy, they knew that in this whirlwind, the 'LIFE OR DEATH OF SOCIALISM' was at stake, although due to lack of jobs and money, 'we're seeing the devil through the eye of a needle'. The congressional deputy's commitment provided little comfort. Lombardo Toledano also was affected by the hostility surrounding him and for much of July and August 1926 he was ill in bed with rheumatism and nervous system fatigue, receiving medicines and injections, unable to work and with correspondence left unanswered.[58]

Tirado was removed by Congress toward the end of 1926, but the violence in Teziutlán did not abate. On Tuesday, around 7.30pm, Pumarino was in the small store located in the market square, with several parishioners playing cards and having drinks, when a stranger dressed in traditional white with huarache sandals stood at the door and looking at Pumarino told him, 'I finally found you', and emptied his magazine without killing him. The problem was not political but involved a few cows that Pumarino had refused to pay for and that the stranger had come to charge him for. In the heated climate, the Laboristas were accused of the attack.[59] The villagers who did not flee were imprisoned in the Perote, Veracruz fort, accused of being rebels. By then, every resident of the Sierra mountain range had people close to them who had been banished. In

---

56　VLT to Benjamín Aguillón Guzmán, Mexico City, 24 June 1926, FHLT, file 92; Falcón and García 1986, p. 172.
57　Luís Romero Coba to VLT, Teziutlán, 26 and 28 June 1926, FHLT, file 94.
58　VL to VLT, Mexico City, 2 July 1926, FHLT, file 94; VLT to Xavier Icaza, Mexico City, 27 July 1926, FHLT, file 95; Adela M. de Martínez to Lauro Camarillo, Puebla, 28 October 1926, FHLT, file 98; Benigno Campos to VLT, Teziutlán, 14 July 1926, FHLT, file 94; Florencio Cerda to VLT, Teziutlán, 28 July 1926, FHLT, file 95; VLT to Benigno Campos, Mexico City, 29 July 1926, FHLT, file 94; Florencio Cerda to VLT, Teziutlán, 2 August 1926, FHLT, file 95; VLT to Florencio Cerda, Mexico City, 2 October 1926, FHLT, file 98; Dr Rafael Campos, 'Teziutlán', unpublished manuscript.
59　Benigno Campos to VLT, Teziutlán, 23 November 1926; Florencio Cerda to VLT, Teziutlán, 24 November 1926, FHLT, file 100; A. Gutiérrez to Luís Huidobro, Puebla, 13 December 1926; Florencio Cerda to VLT, Teziutlán, 18 December 1926, FHLT, file 101.

this tense atmosphere, Max, the brother of Benigno Campos and compadre, or close friend, of Florencio, was killed by the Teziutlán police chief in a drunken altercation. Faced with such violence, the Teziutlán friends were discouraged, 'so much suffering for nothing'.[60] No one's life was safe, there were no laws to invoke or rules to defend.

President Calles removed Tirado and in his place as governor of Puebla appointed Manuel Montes, an Agrarista local power boss, another cacique. Calles was indebted to him, as along with José María Sánchez, Montes helped repel the Delahuertistas in a battle in Puebla in December 1923, saved the Obregón government and thus the transmission of the presidency from Obregón to Calles. Lombardo Toledano had nothing good to say about Montes. He characterised him as a 'caveman', who at will imposed municipal councils 'of his own moral and intellectual stature' and who claimed the rank of general although the congressional deputy investigated and found out that it was false.[61]

Agustín Limón Moscano was one of those close to Montes and who the governor wanted as mayor of Teziutlán. Limón arrived on the noon train on 14 February 1927. When he stepped down onto the platform, Lombardo Toledano's friends surrounded him and told him, 'return to Puebla or die, you decide'. The frightened Limón chose the first option, the Teziutecos bought him a return ticket and he boarded the train back to Puebla. Limón went 'tamely' but on 19 February returned, guarded by federal forces to take over the municipality. Benigno Campos reached the limit of his patience and endurance:

> I no longer want to continue witnessing what is occurring in my village. Those who yesterday were enemies of General Calles, now run people's lives, and those of us who helped in his election campaign are being persecuted. We are being shot at as if we were bandits. Damn politics.[62]

Benigno fled to the mountains, since his life was in danger. It was now necessary to dethrone Montes, who used Puebla as if it were his fiefdom.

In June 1927 Calles replaced Montes with General Donato Bravo Izquierdo, his follower. Even though Laboristas were named councilmen and the state

---

60   Florencio Cerda to VLT, Teziutlán, 8 January 1927; Florencio Cerda to VLT, Teziutlán, 19 January 1927, FHLT, file 106.
61   VLT to Calles, Mexico City, 7 December 1926, FHLT, file 101; VLT to Calles, Mexico City, 15 February 1927, FHLT, file 107; Brewster 2003, p. 75; Henderson 1998, pp. 153–76.
62   Benigno Campos to VLT, Teziutlán, 21 February 1927, FHLT, file 108; Florencio Cerda to VLT, Teziutlán, 15 February 1927, FHLT, file 107; Florencio Cerda to VLT, Teziutlán, 5 March 1927, FHLT, file 109; VLT to Calles, Mexico City, 17 June 1927, FHLT, file 115; Meyer, Krauze and Reyes 1981, p. 111.

Labour Department was headed by one of them, in Teziutlán the governor appointed authorities opposed to the congressional deputy.[63] In the July 1928 elections history repeated itself. Lombardo Toledano wanted to be re-elected in an environment no less hostile than he faced in 1922 and 1924. Again, the campaign was an exercise in political and sometimes physical extermination that Governor Bravo Izquierdo observed from a distance. Lombardo Toledano complained about another Poblano cacique, General Gabriel Barrios, who, with military detachments in the mountains 'made his officers pursue me and try to kill me on several occasions'. The general's soldiers 'shot at many of my compañeros; several were apprehended, and beaten'; they tore down his election campaign material and covered it with that of his rival. His supporters went into hiding, fled to neighbouring villages or to Veracruz, as in the days of Tirado and Montes. At the end of his wistful letter to General Joaquín Amaro, Minister of War, Lombardo boasted of his virtues in defence of the 'Indians and shirtless artisans' for whom he fought 'and I will fight until I die'.[64] To his followers in Teziutlán he wrote that there was no place for the faint-hearted in political work.[65]

6 The Trip

Lombardo Toledano did not seek government appointments or elected office as an end in itself but as a means to achieve the objectives that he pursued in each historical moment. He was always convinced that only the state could redeem working people from their prostration, lack of education and land, from bad politicians and rulers, and from their decrepit past. New ideas bounced around in his head. He took advantage of a trip to the International American Conference as a technical adviser to the Ministry of Industry in Havana to sort out his views. It was on this trip that he formulated that Pan-Americanism was equivalent to imperialism, the policy of US domination of the hemisphere, and that it was up to the hemisphere's governments to collaborate for the

---

63   Luís Romero Cova to VLT, Teziutlán, 23 August 1927; CROM president to General Donato Bravo Izquierdo, Mexico City, 23 August 1927, FHLT, file 119; Isaías Aguilera to VLT, Teziutlán, 27 August 1927, FHLT, file 120.

64   VLT to Joaquín Amaro, Mexico City, 27 June 1928; VLT to Bravo Izquierdo, Mexico City, 5 June 1928, FHLT, file 146; Brewster 2003, pp. 86–155; VLT to Calles, telegram, Teziutlán, 18 June 1928, FHLT, file 145; president of the counting committee to the chief of staff of the Chamber of Deputies, Teziutlán, 5 July 1928, FHLT, file 146.

65   Benigno Campos to VLT, Teziutlán, 13 May 1931, FHLT, file 181; Dr Rafael Campos, 'Teziutlán', manuscript.

material improvement of workers. It was only a matter of time and opportunity for the creation of a Latin American federation against US imperialism.⁶⁶

On his return he did not have much work, had little money and debts to pay. His family grew with the birth of his third daughter Marcela in 1926; he even thought of selling his car without doing so and in these circumstances contemplated his next steps.

Lombardo Toledano never lacked options for earning a living. At almost 35 years of age, he returned to the National School of Law and the National Preparatory School to teach ethics. The National University of Mexico's rector, Ignacio García Téllez, was pleased to give him more work and help him pay his debts.⁶⁷ Lombardo also decided to submit an essay on the indigenous languages of Puebla, ethnography of the Totonaca, Nahuatlato and Olmeca-Mexicano peoples of the mountains regions of Puebla, with drawings, photos and maps, with which he earned his doctorate at the Department of Philosophy and Letters.

The essay had educational and political objectives to fulfil. Educational, to teach the way of thinking of the indigenous population; and political, for the 'racial and social unification of Mexico – the supreme task of the state'.⁶⁸ He paid ten pesos in the university treasury to have his grades registered and he graduated. The degree went unnoticed and Lombardo Toledano continued being a lawyer or teacher for those who knew him. He wrote articles for the daily national newspaper *Excélsior* for 30 pesos each and took charge of the leaderless Central School of Fine Arts. For reasons perhaps having to do with personal affinities, the university rector preferred him over the more qualified for the job Diego Rivera, even though Lombardo Toledano missed classes, for which he was docked in pay; and left them altogether when the Foreign Affairs Ministry sent him to Montevideo in Uruguay as a government representative to the Inter-American University Congress.⁶⁹

---

66   VLT, 'Libreta de apuntes del viaje a La Habana', January 1928, FHLT, file 134; VLT, 'La Unión Panamericana y los problemas de los trabajadores'. Proposal of the Mexican delegation to the 6th Conference of the Pan-American Union, in *Obra*, I/4, 1927–1928, pp. 61–4; VLT, 'La Doctrina Monroe y el movimiento obrero', conference presented in March 1927, in *Obra*, I/3, 1926–1927, p. 337.
67   VLT to Pedro Limón, Mexico City, 30 April 1929, FHLT, file 157; Ignacio García Téllez to VLT, Mexico City, 1 August 1929, FHLT, file 159; VLT to Ignacio García Téllez, Mexico City, 12 September 1929, FHLT, file 160.
68   VLT, 'Geografía de las lenguas de la sierra de Puebla', in *Obra*, II/ 2, 1931, pp. 191–282.
69   Ignacio García Téllez to VLT, Mexico City, 15 January 1930, FHLT, file 165; José López Lira to VLT, Mexico City, 23 June 1930, FHLT, file 169; VLT to José León, Mexico City, 1 August 1930,

The trip to South America was the first of many that Lombardo Toledano would undertake in subsequent years. It was another journey of learning and for organising his ideas. It enabled him to meet left-wing activists and Argentine socialist and communist trade unionists. The newspaper *Excélsior* assigned him articles to write because it considered him qualified 'to offer opinions based on professional criteria about our problems'. Lombardo Toledano took on the task of enthusiastically studying the morphology, psychology and politics of the countries he visited, although the lectures he gave on his return concerning the innocuous aristocracy and the gentle pedantry of the Brazilian people, Uruguayan pride and Argentine vanity appear to be a list of stereotypes.

In Argentina he gave several lectures on Mexico and the CROM, which did not fully reflect the principles of the organisation that he claimed to represent: 'For the victory of socialism in the world, for an end to Yankee imperialism and for the triumph of social justice in our own home', were some of the stirring phrases in the conference he gave in Buenos Aires on the economic crisis being experienced in the United States following the stock market crash in 1929. US capitalism was a temporary phenomenon, he declared, and 'we will help free ourselves of American imperialism because in that way we will help the victory of the socialist cause in the entire world'.[70] In Buenos Aires, at a healthy distance from Mexico and the CROM, he tested oratorical devices and arguments that he would use in his subsequent polemics and for the rest of his life as a 'professional agitator'. Sometime in the mid-1920s he adopted socialism as his ideological and ethical persuasion, which led him to view the crisis of capitalism and the economic crisis of 1929 in the United States, up until then the engine of the global economy, as pointing to a collapse of the empire.

7   The Polemical Dispute

Even though the university rector put him in charge of running the National Preparatory School, Lombardo Toledano decided to found the Gabino Barreda preparatory school in a primary school on Regina Street in the heart of the city. He had no resources, but was motivated by the conviction that he had

---

FHLT, file 171; Foreign Relations Ministry to VLT, Mexico City, 21 November 1930, FHLT, file 174.

70   VLT, 'Conferencias sobre Sudamérica', 28 June 1931, FHLT, file 184; VLT, 'Situación social de los Estados Unidos de Norte América', Buenos Aires, 26 February 1931, FHLT, file 179; '7 conferencias sobre Sudamérica', Bolívar Amphitheater of the National Preparatory School, 18 June–19 July 1931, FHLT, file 183.

to give practical lessons to workers and technicians in factories, railway stations, in foundries and power plants. The principles of the school of which he was director and that he founded with the name of the famous positivist thinker and teacher were counterposed. 'Mexican schooling must be, therefore, an ideologically oriented, affirmative education, working for the acceptance and understanding of the concept of property as a social function against the individualistic theory. Such schooling will openly sustain the principles in relation to labour and agrarian questions on which the Mexican Revolution is based'. To accomplish those goals, it was necessary to achieve a single concept of life given the heterogeneity of the population, to unify education throughout the country 'with a single technical criterion and one social vision'.[71] Despite having adopted a materialistic worldview and a Marxist interpretation of history, Lombardo never became a member of the Mexican Communist Party.

His ideas scandalised groups of students when in the middle of the strike in May 1929 a debate took place on university autonomy. Students recognised Lombardo Toledano's intellectual gifts, but rejected his ideology and protested to the director of the Faculty of Law, Luis Xico Goerner, that they should continue to receive classes from someone who lambasted US culture as a tactic of imperialism to conquer the markets and consciences, and attacked the spirit of the Catholic Church.[72]

Lombardo Toledano put everything at stake in the controversy surrounding the university: 'I have an ideology, I have a creed to defend that I have adhered to since I was student'. Did he forget that in 1923 he defended academic freedom in the National Preparatory School and university autonomy against state interference? In 1931 at a session of the university council he waged a battle against those teachers and students 'who still believe that the university should be this neutral thing in relation to scientific ideas, political ideas, human ideas'. Anarchy reigned in the university, because it had no ideological principles or political definition, claimed the head teacher of philosophy at the National Preparatory School, supported by the rector Ignacio García Téllez and some students.[73] The university should be socialist to serve the working class and not

---

71 VLT, 'En torno a la universidad libre', *El Universal*, 20 February 1933, in *Obra*, II/4, 1934, pp. 25–9; VLT, 'Las conclusiones del congreso nacional de maestros', 2 October 1929, FHLT, file 160.
72 Arcadio Guevara and Antonio Damiano, president and secretary to the Student Society of the Law and Social Sciences Department, 17 July 1929; VLT to Luís Xico Goerner, Mexico City, 14 August 1929, FHLT, file 159; Cosío Villegas 1977, p. 137.
73 VLT, 'Sesión del Consejo Universitario', Mexico City, 12 September 1931, FHLT, file 186;

'an institution that teaches universal culture and that lacks ideology'. Culture had to preach, proclaim and define itself against injustice, be 'at the service of the revolution', 'the service of the socialist cause' and 'the presence of overalls at the National Autonomous University will somewhat purify our old environment'.[74]

And a year later, Lombardo was part of the organising committee of the First Congress of Mexican University Students and Teachers, which was to begin on 7 September 1933. He knew that there were teachers and students who did not share his beliefs, persuasions and ideas on education and life, but considered them backward and false; it was necessary to suppress such ideas in teaching along with the radicalism of the communists. Not long before becoming himself an ardent follower of the Soviet Union, he considered the Mexican communists mindless supporters of a foreign country.

The university should contribute to the replacement of the capitalist regime with a system that would socialise the means of production through the teaching of historical materialism to guide work in the educational, scientific and cultural fields. His stance put him at loggerheads with his teacher Antonio Caso, who in Lombardo Toledano's arguments saw the cancellation of the recently conquered university autonomy and academic freedom. The congress took place smoothly and in an atmosphere of civility, and approved the university reform, giving it an ideological orientation that Lombardo Toledano and persons close to his positions had proposed.[75]

But after the congress, events moved in rapid succession and the press happily stoked the furore. Teachers, who were silent during the discussions, raised their protest against the reform with indignant slander. Teachers and students opposed to the reform took aim against Lombardo Toledano and seized the university administration building. Lombardo Toledano would not yield to such a 'tempest in a teacup'. Knowing that he would be expelled from the university, he declared triumphantly, 'I confirm my belief in the need to give youth a sense of great human responsibility that it does not have'. It did not matter that he was to be thrown out of the classrooms in which he had taught for 15 years and that a similar fate could be faced by other teachers and students in the capital and in the provinces. He was informed by the newspapers that indeed he had been

---

Ignacio García Téllez to VLT, Mexico City, 29 January 1932; 'Maestros y alumnos al Consejo Universitario', Mexico City, 2 February 1932; Ignacio García Téllez to VLT, Mexico City, 13 February 1932, FHLT, file 195.

74 VLT, 'Discurso en el Paraninfo de la UNAM', Mexico City, 28 January 1932, FHLT, file 195.
75 Diego Valadés in Blanco 2001, pp. 141–6.

expelled. Defiantly he said: 'I continue and will continue to think of the need to provide a socialist orientation to teaching'.[76]

To provide a space to publicise his ideas, Lombardo Toledano began publishing the magazine *Futuro*, which for lack of other means was financed with advertisements of movie listings with the latest hits of Metro-Goldwyn-Mayer with actors such as Johnny Weissmuller, Clark Gable, Jean Harlow and Lee Tracy, *El compadre Mendoza*, 'the national movie of the year', and with ads for tailorshops and the El Palacio de Hierro department store.

8 Ideological Passion

In his acceptance speech as candidate of the National Revolutionary Party for president of Mexico and during his campaign, General Lázaro Cárdenas, a soldier of the revolution and former governor of Michoacán, emphasised his unconditional adherence to the revolution and its Constitution, and pledged to carry out social reforms that would spread to all corners of the country.[77] Lombardo Toledano viewed the candidate, one year his junior, as a well-intentioned man, but without a precise ideology and able to be manipulated. It was no coincidence that while Cárdenas was campaigning, Lombardo would give a speech whose thrust was that it was necessary to radicalise the revolution: 'The resistance of the ideas of the past or the strongest individual will, or political power however great they may be, can do nothing against the course of history'. The organised masses, 'collective forces that collectively produce, that live collectively, that suffer collectively want to suppress the individualistic ways of enjoying social goods'.[78] It was necessary to help quicken the rhythm of history.

That may have been the reason to submit, together with his friend, lawyer Xavier Icaza, a proposal to Cárdenas's close friend, Francisco J. Múgica, in the expectation that it would perhaps reach the presidential candidate. The government should assume greater control over the economic, political and cultural life of the country to create the State Socialist University, enforce compuls-

---

76   'A las agrupaciones de la CROM, al proletariado en general', Mexico City, 19 September 1933, FHLT, file 227; VLT, 'Mensaje a los partidarios de la reforma universitaria', Mexico City, 13 October 1933, file 228; VLT to Roberto Medellín, Mexico City, 14 October 1933, FHLT, file 228; Student Society of the National Preparatory School. 'Breve reseña del Congreso de Universitarios Mexicanos', Mexico City, October 1933, FHLT, file 229; Illades 2007, vol. 2, pp. 335–45.
77   Cárdenas 1978, pp. 109–35.
78   VLT, 'El aspecto filosófico de la doctrina marxista', 26 February 1934, in *Obra*, III/1, 1934, pp. 43–56.

ory collective bargaining agreements, facilitate the intervention of the trade unions in the reorganisation of industries, restrict employer lockouts, annul forced arbitration of strikes, establish a real minimum wage, sanction 'compulsory common labour', promote common ownership of land by peasants and the resident peons, and encourage the planning of agricultural production of the ejidos, semi-communal forms of property ownership in the countryside.

Among the reforms they proposed was the elimination of consulates and embassies as useless and irritating, because they were used for social activities and its officials were 'rootless parasites'. Their tasks could be performed 'with special envoys and by phone' and in the consulates general. Lombardo Toledano and Icaza were particularly annoyed by the press that miseducated the population and that had to be controlled:

> It is easy to take control of the media. The paper factory in San Rafael is a creditor of every newspaper. Expropriating 51% of the factory's shares, controlling it in this or that way, it would be possible to proceed against the media companies and take control of them. Once this is accomplished, newspapers independent of the government could be created, entrusted to specific persons, who, however, would have freedom of action.[79]

It was necessary to control the radio, which was 'destroying good popular taste, morality, and virility', to control cinema, and promote political and popular outdoor theatre, dance, and choruses.

At 40 years old, Lombardo Toledano was imbued with an ideological fervour that went beyond the boundaries of nationalism and was out of tune with the times of Mexico when Lázaro Cárdenas was about to guide the country, based on humanism, attachment to the soil and the demands of the flesh and blood of peasants and workers to fulfil the goals of the Mexican Revolution. Lombardo Toledano, however, was confident that the 'true government of a country lies in its educated minority',[80] a thinking elite whose role it was to show workers the way.[81] Unlike Marx, Lombardo Toledano never foresaw the disappearance of the state along with the disappearance of private property, as if the state were the highest form of human organisation and the best agent of the emancipation of the working class. He believed in the natural and inevitable progress

---

79 VLT and Xavier Icaza to General Francisco J. Múgica, Mexico City, 1 November 1934, FHLT, file 248.
80 VLT, 'Revolución y cultura', Excélsior, 4 January 1930, in Obra, II/1, 1929–1930, p. 279.
81 Vaughan 1982, pp. 239–75.

of the world, was confident in the power of reason, in material and moral progress, in the ontological process of nature and man, which provided a scientific focus to the process and made it predictable. Within this trajectory of nature and society, the outstanding individual, linked to the masses as their guide, was part of the gearshift of the motor of history.

CHAPTER 3

Exodus

September 1932 was a turning point in Vicente Lombardo Toledano's life. Although it might have appeared as a decision taken precipitously, his withdrawal from the Mexican Regional Workers Confederation after more than ten years of active membership was thought out. The humiliation that Luis N. Morones, the lifelong leader of the labour confederation, subjected Lombardo to in full view of everyone afforded him the opportunity to force the break that had been brewing for years. Morones's demeaning comment that Lombardo most disliked was that he entered the confederation 'when the table was already set', which denied his disciplined work in the organisation, as much as the reference to his daily practice between censoring and negotiating workers' demands with those in power.

The skirmish occurred in the Olimpia cinema on 18 September during the meeting of the Mexico City union that Lombardo Toledano led. He scathingly criticised the CROM and the regime which it had mimicked. In a tone of moral superiority Lombardo characterised the current period as 'dwarf neoporfirismo' and its officials as pigs stuck in mud. He denounced government corruption, the opportunism of its officials, and regretted that the working class 'pays the personal fortune of the members of the official family and the general bankruptcy of the country'. He called on the labour confederation to disassociate itself from the government and to maintain a 'pure' line of 'mass' struggle. The state was a dictatorship of a minority; 'we want a dictatorship of the majority'.[1] And with much fanfare, he proclaimed: 'I will continue dedicating my life, mystically if you will, but in accordance with the deeper meaning of my conscience, to the socialist cause'.[2] You and I, was the message to make a clear distinction between himself and Morones.

---

1 VLT, 'Mitin de la Federación de Sindicatos Obreros del D.F.', Mexico City, 18 September 1932, in *Obra*, II/3, p. 239, pp. 240–7.
2 VLT, 'Renuncia a la CROM', in *Obra*, II/3, 1932, p. 249; Córdova 1980, pp. 149–53; Marjorie Ruth Clark undertook her research when the events were occurring and noted: 'Lombardo Toledano has been waiting for years to control the CROM and destroy the Action Group, which he was never allowed to join and become part of', in Clark 1984, p. 218; Chassen de López 1977, pp. 145–51; VLT to Reynaldo Cervantes Torres, 'Carta de renuncia a la CROM', Mexico City, 19 September 1932, in *Obra*, II/3, 1932, pp. 250–2.

1   In the CROM

Lombardo Toledano joined the CROM as an intellectual and a university professor, after having been secretary of the People's University and having founded the Society of Conferences and Concerts, along with Alfonso Caso, Manuel Gomez Morín, some students and other teachers. They all wanted to promote culture beyond the narrow confines of the middle class and make contact with the workers to teach them his vision of socialism, justice, democratic institutions, popular education and labour associations.[3]

Even before he met Morones and prior to the founding of the CROM, Lombardo Toledano teamed up with Gustavo Espinosa Mireles, the Carrancista governor of Coahuila, like himself a graduate from the School of Law. On behalf of the government of the revolution Espinosa Mireles hosted the founding congress of the confederation in May 1918 in Saltillo, fulfilling a long-time aspiration of disparate labour unions to coalesce into a national entity, to receive the government's recognition in order to enforce labour rights before reluctant employers. Over a hundred delegates from 18 states gathered in Saltillo, representing industrial workers, artisans as well as peasants. In 1919 the CROM leadership added the Mexican Labour Party to their arsenal as an electoral instrument, to serve the organisation as much as to support the current and future governments.

When he was not yet a member of the CROM, Lombardo proposed to Espinosa Mireles the establishment of additional branches of the People's University, since he was convinced 'that the lack of culture of our artisans and workers results in very serious damage to the good progress in the country's economic life'.[4] He attended the congress, but extending workers' education did not go beyond good wishes until he was appointed director of the National Preparatory School in 1922 and linked the fate of the school with that of the CROM.

In July 1921 he attended the CROM's congress in Orizaba at the time in which the 'reds' of the General Confederation of Workers (CGT), supported from Moscow by the Communist International, disputed workers' adherence to the CROM.[5] Lombardo Toledano rejected anarchism and communism, and was pleased that the dispute did not disturb the running of the congress. Its sober atmosphere belied 'those who seek to inculcate in the people's mind the idea that the labour problem is a question raised by the agitators and encour-

3   Carretta Beltrán 2002, p. 13, pp. 106–12.
4   VLT to Gustavo Espinosa Míreles, Mexico City, 1 February 1918, FHLT, file 9.
5   Spenser 2009, pp. 161–96.

aged by utopian laws that instead of resolving it, have magnified it by providing it with a preferential status in the constitution that it did not deserve'.[6] But the plight of the working class did deserve such recognition.

Lombardo Toledano did not display ideological confusion, contra Morones's charge. He understood power and workers' democracy as being linked with the state, whose duty it was to serve the masses. If it failed, it would be necessary to pressure it to fulfil its mandate. Shoulder to shoulder, as he described himself, he worked with the government in rebuilding the country, in the legal protection of the trade unions and in promoting workers' education. The 1917 Constitution was revolutionary and was fulfilling its mission as defined by its content. For a brief time after finishing law school, he launched a lawyers' office and gained notoriety for guiding the workers through the intricate labour legislation to make them aware of the promises of the Constitution and the government's obligation to implement them.[7] 'The Mexican Revolution represented a return to Christian ethics, since only organising the spiritual crusade in the name of the Gospel, can evil, capitalism, sectarianism, be eliminated and this is the only way that our poor people can be freed from the absurd ideas that divert them from the correct road'.[8]

Lombardo Toledano's capacity for work and initiatives had no limits. In 1922 he created the Group in Solidarity with the Labour Movement with the hopes of establishing offices outside the capital and enlisting the best intellectual luminaries of the day to serve the 'social classes, not only workers, that need the advice of learned men' and must be rescued from their wretched condition.[9] Since its inception, the group suffered from organisational difficulties and lack of money. The government provided it with rail passes to facilitate its members' travel, but even so it only managed to establish a branch in Morelia, Michoacán, while the others remained on the level of good intentions.[10]

In addition to state intervention and enforcement of laws, the emancipation of the working class required practical and ideological education. Lombardo understood this as teaching, reading and writing to those who did not have such

---

6   VLT to Celestino Gasca, Orizaba, 7 July 1921, FHLT, file 10.
7   Miguel Alessio Robles to VLT, Mexico City, 16 April 1919, FHLT, file 9; 8 July 1920, FHLT, file 10.
8   VLT, 'La moral de la Revolución Mexicana', *El Heraldo*, 13 July 1923.
9   VLT, 'Mi actuación política en la Escuela Nacional Preparatoria', 5 September 1923, FHLT, file 40.
10 'Memorando sobre la fundación del Grupo', Mexico City, 10 February 1922; 'A los miembros del GSMO', Mexico City, 28 April 1922, FHLT, file 12; VLT to Felipe Carrillo Puerto, Mexico City, 28 February 1922, FHLT, file 12; Interview with Vicente Lombardo Toledano in *La Tribuna*, 1 March 1922, FHLT, file 12; Orozco 1945, p. 111.

skills, and as providing classes on the socialist movement, physical education, techniques for effective work and the future direction of industry, the art of speaking, leading assemblies and drafting propaganda for those interested in such cultural manifestations. Probably on his initiative, in 1922 the CROM's first labour education school was established, which in November 1924 became the education committee and workers' college. 'Existence is war', he said on one occasion, and the proletarian school should be based on a specific ideology, since 'you cannot educate without imposing one or more ideas'.[11] The secular education of the bourgeois state was also wrong, because it was 'a school without a banner' to rally behind, while the proletariat needed a socialist education that would imprint a sense of class and political activism in its consciousness.[12] With a smattering of knowledge of Marxism, Lombardo Toledano's beliefs were still a blend of Christian socialism and materialism narrowly conceived, which he applied to the analysis of contemporary society.

El Maestro, as he was referred to by his followers, was in a privileged position, because his brother Humberto was the Labour Department inspector and provided him with valuable information on the conditions of workers throughout the country.[13] One of the most serious problems was the arbitrary interpretation of Article 123 of the Constitution by state authorities, whose responsibility it was to ensure compliance with labour and social welfare regulations, adherence to the eight-hour day, prohibition of child labour, a mandatory weekly day of rest, non-detachable wages, setting the minimum wage in each region of the country, worker participation in company profit sharing, double pay for overtime, the right to organise in defence of workers' interests, the right to strike and unambiguous employer recognition of unions.[14] Humberto also reported to his brother that the trade unions that did not have the strength to negotiate with employers and the non-unionised workers turned to the CROM for support, and when they did not find it, appealed to the president as the supreme arbiter of labour disputes.[15]

---

11 VLT, 'El problema de educación en México', proposals presented to the Education Committee at the 6th convention of the CROM in Ciudad Juárez, November 1924, in *Obra*, I/2, 1923–1926, p. 141 and p. 138.
12 VLT, 'La teoría educativa de la CROM', April 1926, in *Obra*, I/2, 1923–1926, p. 297; Vaughan 1982, pp. 269–70.
13 Márquez Schiaffino, chief of staff of the Ministry of Industry, Commerce, and Labour, Mexico City, 28 March 1922, General National Archives (henceforth AGN), Department of Labour (henceforth DL), vol. 352, file 5 and file 10.
14 Gamboa Ojeda 2001, pp. 294–306.
15 Union of Free Workers of Atlixco to the president, Atlixco, Puebla, 11 May 1922, AGN, DL, vol. 445, file 3.

Unemployment was a serious issue. One of the strategies used by industrial workers to obtain employment was to be hired by companies as non-unionised individuals, and once they were working, join the union. Others did not do so for fear of losing what they had already gained. The employers took advantage of the precarious job market to weaken unions, closing factories or laying off the leaders. The lack of a government body that would defend the legality or avoid collusion between state officials and employers, contributed to the owners ignoring the workers' elected representatives, so that declaring a strike was risky, because the strikers could easily be replaced by the reserve labour force. Even skilled labourers suffered harassment from employers who transferred their jobs to non-unionised workers.[16]

Unemployment depressed wages and affected working conditions, such as the increase in the number of hours in the working day in the cotton fields of La Laguna. In the mines of Coahuila, with their unhealthy, dangerous and poorly paid labour with workers suffering from bouts of tuberculosis, accidents were frequent without the injured receiving medical care.[17] Another report filed by Humberto spoke of the decline in cigar production. Mexico had been an exporter, but subsequently had become an importer of the tobacco leaf. The industry's labour force declined from 15,000 in 1910 to a handful in 1924. The emergence of clandestine cigar production led to a loss in tax revenue for the state and a lack of even the nominal labour protection for the workers.[18]

All the information that Humberto passed on to Vicente allowed the federal congressional deputy for Teziutlán to attack the violation of the constitution from the rostrum of the Chamber of Deputies. However, using his word and his congressional seat as weapons, the deputy became more often than not the intermediary between the voters of the district he represented, the Interior Ministry and the presidency, without empowering the workers.

A few months before Lombardo's disputed election victory as congressional deputy was resolved in 1925, the Laborista government of the capital sent its

---

16 'Estanislao Juárez asked that in the street they greet each other rather than whip out their pistols and it is not known whether they subsequently decided to join together, but for the time being, no', Atlixco, 19 March 1924, FHLT, file 51.

17 Humberto Lombardo Toledano, chief inspector at the Department of Labour, Puebla, 30 May 1922, AGN, DL, vol. 445, file 3 and 26 June 1922, AGN, DL, vol. 445, file 5; San Pedro, Coahuila, 14 December 1922, AGN, DL, vol. 338, file 3; Sabinas, Coahuila, 7 January 1923, ibid.

18 Humberto Lombardo Toledano to the head of the DL, Puebla, 19 February 1924, vol. 728, file 3.

councilman to New York to a congress on urban planning. It was the first of countless trips that would position him in the international arena as a major figure in the country's labour movement. From New York he was sent to Geneva to attend a meeting of the International Labour Organization (ILO) to sound out the possibility that Mexico, which was not a member of the League of Nations, could join the ILO. He was accompanied in his travels by Rosa María Otero while his parents took care of their daughters. Through letters he learned that his uncles Alejandro and Pedro wanted to take advantage of his privileged position to obtain good jobs; that using his nephew's business cards, Alejandro appeared in offices of ministries as if it were his uncle who was requesting the job for him; Pedro bragged in public about all that his nephew had done for him; that city hall made personnel adjustments to economise and eliminated gasoline coupons for its employees. The father regretted that his son was not in Mexico to secure him the vacant post in the Agriculture and Development Ministry in the division of hunting and fishing that he so craved rather than the umpteenth change of employment, because once again the position was granted to some friend of someone with influence; he recommended that his son should go to Settimo Torinese to visit Aunt Mariana, the tomb of his father and lay a bouquet of flowers on his tomb. And if possible, buy him a half-dozen thick cotton socks. Everything was fine at home, except for 'the abusive behaviour of your uncouth moron chauffer who was using the car improperly without authorisation from anyone'. The girls were doing fine.[19] Lombardo Toledano visited Settimo Torinese and on the return trip to Mexico went to Niagara Falls, Chicago and Los Angeles. In August, he was back in his office at city hall, awaiting the outcome of the negotiations over how his disputed congressional deputy election would turn out.

The International Labour Organization commissioned Lombardo Toledano to write a book about the country's labour legislation. There was no justification for Mexico being an unknown entity after its revolution. *La libertad sindical en México*, as Lombardo Toledano called his book on labour rights in the country, sparked admiration. The American activist and academic Frank Tannenbaum, a year older than Lombardo, and interested in the Mexican labour movement until its corruption and co-optation disillusioned him and he focused his attention on the country's peasant farmers, considered it the most important book

---

19   VL to VLT, Mexico City, 9 May 1925; Isabel Lombardo to VLT, Mexico City, 20 May 1925; FHLT, file 77; Luis LT to VLT, Mexico City, 21 May 1925; Darío Rubio to VLT, Mexico City, 25 May 1925; VL to VLT, Ciudad México, 21 May 1925, FHLT, file 78.

on the results of the revolution. Xavier Icaza praised the study, because 'this balance that he achieved is simply extraordinary and reveals a political understanding very rare in Mexico'.[20]

The essay is an exegesis of Mexican jurisdiction, both historical and current, on individual rights before the revolution and collective rights after its victory, sanctioned by the 1917 Constitution. Lombardo Toledano labelled it socialist-inspired, which it was not. The bibliographical literature that he used was reduced almost exclusively to the press. He wanted to demonstrate to the world's maximum labour authorities that, thanks to the existing legislation in Mexico, there was freedom of trade union association, 'a new path created by the State for the complete emancipation of the proletariat, and for capitalism, a right limited by the defence of its material interests'. From a distance, the study does not seem as balanced as Icaza judged. In the first part of the book, Lombardo put the legislation and the reality on the same plane and in the latter part of the study counterposed the two. The result is contradictory. He hailed the CROM and the select Action Group which stood at the helm of the organisation and of which he was not a member: 'Each of them had been a prestigious local leader and then went on to cooperate in guiding the national labour organisation'. He knew better.

The Mexican Communist Party and the Soviet Union received a curt rejection as 'propaganda offices run by foreigners and sustained with foreign money' without having ties to the workers. Women and the indigenous communities each received a paragraph. In the case of women, due to their productive potential; and the indigenous peoples for their contribution to national culture, on condition that the state provided their material well-being and did not force them 'to join in a way of life that is not their own'.

The value of the book lies in the systematisation of labour legislation, without the author discussing compliance with such laws. Lombardo Toledano admitted that 'I did not take Constitutional Article 123 or labour laws as reflecting the true state of workers' rights in Mexico', but rather the experience 'outside the law' as testimony of workers' power conquered in practice. Freedom of trade union association existed to a certain degree, but given the state's and employer associations' resistance to the application of such laws and even blocking their execution, the labour movement was forcing the government to adopt federal labour legislation.[21]

---

20 Frank Tannenbaum to VLT, Washington, D.C., 10 June 1927, FHLT, file 114; Xavier Icaza to VLT, Jalapa, 23 June 1927, FHLT, file 114; Winn 2010, pp. 109–14.
21 VLT, *La libertad sindical en México*, in *Obra*, I/3, 1926–1927, pp. 1–199; quotes on pages 8, 98, 108, 160, 161.

Lombardo Toledano was satisfied with his study and expected it to be translated into several languages to reach labour leaders and the general public. He wanted the book to serve to dispel false judgements that existed 'in relation to this aspect of the Mexican Revolution, as well as concerning the real causes behind this movement'. It had taken him two months to write, but given that he was already a congressional deputy and was confronting his adversaries in Puebla, which took away time and peace-of-mind, in addition to falling ill, he wound up turning the text in late, in October 1926.[22] Quoted today, the book reveals much of what he failed to mention in order to protect the image of the revolution especially abroad.

2   Collapse

Luis N. Morones was an only child 'of parents with brown skin, steeped in hunger and misery',[23] who led the CROM directly or indirectly since the foundation of the labour confederation in 1918 until the leader's death in 1964. Morones was a shrewd man, four years older than Lombardo Toledano, but not equal to him in terms of intellectual capacity. He owed his fortune as a worker and leader to his opportune ties with the victorious revolutionaries. He and his worker cohorts helped Álvaro Obregón in 1920 to overcome Carranza's opposition to the general's desire to become president, collaborated in the suppression of Adolfo de la Huerta's rebellion in 1923 and 1924, and were the allies and instruments of Plutarco Elías Calles in clearing the road to his presidency.[24] On each occasion they were rewarded by the regime they served. The big reward they enjoyed was between 1924 and 1928, with Morones in the Ministry of Industry, Commerce and Labour and the Laboristas perched up high in the Chamber of Deputies and municipalities.

Lombardo Toledano never belonged to the CROM elite, which gathered in the Action Group, about twenty or so people loyal to Morones. He was a rare breed among the politicians of the time. He was not attached to money; he disliked extravagance and wastefulness and was aware of the Bacchanalia festivals that Morones organised in his home in the Tlalpan area of Mexico City. Although he never made any reference to what he knew, he stored such information in his memory. From one of many letters he received, he learned from

---

22   VLT to Salomón de la Selva, Mexico City, 9 June 1927, FHLT, file 114.
23   Araiza 1975, vol. 3, p. 109.
24   Retinger 1926, pp. 54–6.

a worker scandalised by one of the sumptuous parties in which the unconditional followers of the inebriated leader 'brought the woman next to him closer, with him kissing and licking her breasts, he kissed her on the mouth and for his most indecent moves, everyone cheered and chanted long live and up with Morones'.[25]

Lombardo did not publicly criticise the mandatory contributions of up to a day's pay made by government employees to the CROM, the PLM, the Federal District city government and the municipalities controlled by the CROM. He also did not publicly denounce the fraud, embezzlement of funds, intimidation and gangster practices employed against those unions that challenged the CROM, when they threatened to launch an unapproved strike or other actions independently of the labour confederation.[26]

The bonanza enjoyed by the CROM and Morones ended in 1928. If Morones believed he had the possibility of becoming president, General Obregón cut off that opportunity. The constitution was amended so that Obregón could be re-elected with the help of the Obregonistas and Laboristas in the Chamber of Deputies, which Morones approved although he would later regret his vote. The circumstances surrounding the election and then the assassination of the president in July 1928, of which Morones was accused of being the mastermind without anything definitive being proven, forced him to resign from the ministry and the CROM to be pushed to the sidelines and left to battle for survival against its eternal opponents. Emilio Portes Gil, the jack-of-all-trades in government, who detested the CROM since he was governor of Tamaulipas and pressed the federation of the capital's labour unions – comprised of unions representing milkmen, tram workers, small businessmen, gravediggers, truck and bus drivers, office workers, and in which the redoubtable Fidel Velázquez had emerged as one of the leaders – to leave the CROM when he was president in 1929 and 1930.[27]

With the CROM adrift, some unions had left the labour confederation not only for ideological, but also pragmatic reasons. The workers from the Graphic Arts Union working for the government feared losing their jobs. Several unions anticipated the advantages of the CROM's proximity to Obregón – before he was assassinated – and to the National Revolutionary Party when it was founded in 1929 as well as to state governors. In the industrial zone of Atlixco in Puebla the

---

25   Anonymous letter to Gen. Celestino Gasca, Juan Rico, VLT, undated, 1925, FHLT, file 78; Buford 1971, p. 108; Araiza 1975, vol. 4, pp. 138–9.
26   Carr 1976, pp. 160–8.
27   Portes Gil 2003, p. 490; Carr 1976, p. 254; Clark 1984, p. 114, note 27; Araiza 1975, vol. 3, p. 109, pp. 140–55; Retinger 1926, pp. 68–9; Gómez-Galvarriato 2013, pp. 172–7.

weakening of the CROM provoked violence among the unions. The Cromista leaders who controlled the local government and the police force intimidated the unions that left the CROM, forcing them back into the fold. In one case, the confrontation resulted in injuries and deaths.[28] The police and military forces that Morones used to organise the CROM, were employed against him by the authorities to destroy the confederation. Labour inspectors used their influence against the unions affiliated to the CROM to create internal opposition factions. When unions had difficulties with the employers, they were given to understand that their success depended on their withdrawing from the confederation. The pressure was so great that some unions publicly dissociated themselves from the CROM, while secretly retaining their affiliation. The CROM, meanwhile, tried to prevent such defections, putting the exclusion clause in its collective bargaining agreements into effect. Employers were forced to lay off workers who left the union holding the collective bargaining agreement, but the union did not have the support of the Conciliation and Arbitration Boards, which ruled that the workers who withdrew from the CROM had the right to reach new agreements with the employers, eliminating the confederation in the process.[29] As the influence of Morones decreased, that of Lombardo Toledano was on the rise. This was the case in Veracruz, except for Orizaba, which remained the bastion of the CROM.[30] Labour unions in Puebla, Michoacán, Sonora, Yucatán and teachers represented by the National Teachers Federation founded in 1927 remained with Lombardo.[31]

3   The Labour Law

Lombardo Toledano had unshaken faith in the progress that depended on the modernisation of industries and increased productivity through scientific organisation and management. In late 1928 he gave several lectures on the subject. The example to follow was Frederick Winslow Taylor, the American worker who became chief engineer of a company. The system that he invented, Taylorism, was the functional way to increase productivity, save energy and time to lower the cost of production and to eliminate the chaos in workplace organisation. The scientific aspect consisted of 'measuring labour time and the rational setting of wages, that is, the timing and the scientific payment

---

28   Crider 1996, pp. 208–9.
29   Clark 1984, pp. 111–13.
30   Gomez-Galvarriato 2013, pp. 175–7.
31   Chassen de López 1977, pp. 98–9.

for labour', the adaptation of the machine to the psychophysical constitution of man, everything oriented and monitored by the state so as to humanise a system criticised for being cruel. Taylorism helped overcome the economic crisis because labour power was exploited rationally in the productive process.[32] Employers and employees came together to avoid confrontations. This system was contrary to the Soviet workers' councils which, in the first years of the Bolshevik revolution, had been put in charge of running state-owned companies.

> The scientific organisation of work is leading us, therefore, as an effect that occurs in the world, to allow, from the point of view of the employer's convenience, the worker's convenience and social convenience, is leading us to allow the intervention of the working class in running companies. Not the intervention of the working class in companies to replace these technicians with the workers. We have seen the brazen failure that occurred in Russia and that had to be inevitable, as the working class is not technically qualified to run the companies by itself. The Russian experiment is eloquent because it is scandalous, and because it is, at the same time, the joint failure of an economic doctrine and a philosophical doctrine.[33]

But Taylorism was not a science of labour; it involved the control and management of alienated labour that expropriated workers' knowledge and the will to perform their duties, separating physical from mental work and the conception of the tasks at hand from their execution. Its goal was to overcome the aversion of workers to industrial discipline, the application of time, the persistence of rural and seasonal work habits, religious inhibitions and incentives to earn more. It was another way to intensify the work of the recently proletarianised rural population. Trade union organisation, strikes and sabotage resulted from the alienating work practices of this form of labour organisation.[34] But Lombardo Toledano was not advocating workers' control of production, but rather making capitalism more efficient, rational and fair. He was aware of resistance to its application in industrial corporations in the United States. In Mexico, the solution was state intervention, without having taken into account that this did not annul the system's alienating factors.

---

32 VLT, 'La organización científica del trabajo', in *Obra*, I/4, 1927–1928, p. 212 and pp. 180–1.
33 VLT, 'La organización científica del trabajo', in *Obra*, I/4, 1927–1928, pp. 214–15.
34 Vaughan 1982, pp. 146–7; Braverman 1974, pp. 90–137; Fraser 1991, pp. 187–8; Montgomery 1979, pp. 91–196.

Lombardo Toledano understood the class struggle to develop in three stages. The third, and that of his time, involved 'the participation or intervention of the working class in the running of companies'.[35] If he recalled Marx's concept of surplus value – surplus labour expropriated by capital – he did so more as part of the history of ideas than as the creator of consciousness and the driving force of the class struggle. He did not view it as an epistemological problem to explain the origin of profit. The Marxism that he professed brought together liberal humanism, trade unionism and an undefined socialism; his denunciation of capitalism was of a moral character because it was a regime based on the exploitation of labour. The solution was the organisation of the working masses under one ideological banner, since society changed to the extent that individual wishes crystallised in manifestations of collective life.

As a lawyer Lombardo Toledano had confidence in the virtues of the existing legal system, but as a politician he knew that laws were not abided by, or were complied with half-heartedly, and that to face the strength of the employers it was necessary to compensate for the weakness of legal institutions through the power of the unions and collective bargaining agreements endorsed by the state. The workers' organisations were above the law, he said, because they defended their members' interests better than the deficient laws. By union powers he understood the scaffolding that allowed unions to force compliance with laws rather than workers' democracy, understood as labour's autonomy and independence from state institutions and individual commitment derived from the debates in assemblies. He was well aware that the unions were weakened by corruption and neglect that permeated the political environment in the states and in the capital, all of which motivated him to use the levers of the state – the president, the governors and ministers – to resolve what the institutions did not have the capacity or willingness to resolve.[36]

Lombardo Toledano was familiar with the precarious conditions of the workers and had a view on how to improve their lives, but his references to the Mexican Revolution did not appear to be a guide to action; rather it was a call to adhere to the regime that emanated from the revolution. He thought he understood the world, knew the history of Mexico and labour problems, and therefore took upon himself the right to represent the workers. Several unions did give him such a role due to his knowledge of labour legislation that he helped them understand, but if a company or an employer did not recognise their union, knowledge of the law was of little use.

---

35   VLT, 'La organización científica del trabajo', in *Obra*, I/4, 1927–1928, p. 201.
36   VLT, 'El contrato sindical de trabajo', VLT, in *Obra*, I/4, 1927–1928, p. 131.

One example was the sugar workers union in Los Mochis, Sinaloa, which belonged to the CROM and that the United Sugar Companies refused to deal with. The company signed a collective bargaining agreement with a non-Cromista trade union. A labour inspector, who did not allow himself to be intimidated or bought off by the company, provided information to his superiors about irregular issues such as the high cost of water that the firm charged the residents, its tax fraud perpetrated by declaring lower sugar production than the real output, transport costs by rail that the company passed on to the cost of sugar and not the railroads, and the lack of respect for the eight-hour day, which could be extended up to 12 hours. For all these reasons, the unionised workers went on strike. In January 1930, with a group of congressional deputies and senators, Lombardo Toledano joined them 'to orient the compañeros with regard to what had to be done'. He had to borrow money to make the trip.[37]

The Ministry of Industry, Commerce and Labour asked the Central Conciliation and Arbitration Board to postpone its decision pending the report of another inspector, 'whose attitude has been partial to the company and the non-CROM workers'. The leaders met with the governor, who 'promised to collaborate within the principles of the Revolution and justice' to resolve the conflict. Meanwhile, the company hired non-CROM workers as strikebreakers.[38]

> On Sunday the 16th at one o'clock in the afternoon while we were in the middle of a demonstration attended by three thousand compañeros, we set an ultimatum of two hours for the strikebreakers to leave. This led to tremendous apprehension in the company and the federal forces, which immediately redoubled their security with orders to open fire on the strikers.[39]

The workers were not intimidated and the army did not carry out the order. The company decided to bring in 'more than twenty-five trucks with individuals who were hired and who did not know what they had been brought in for. They were deceptively brought in, and paid two or three pesos for the day to come exclusively to form the ranks of a pseudo-demonstration prepared and

---

37   VLT to HLT, Mexico City, 13 January 1930, FHLT, file 165.
38   Vidal Díaz Muñoz and José Jiménez Acevedo to VLT, Los Mochis, Sinaloa, 4 February 1930, 24 February 1930, FHLT, file 165.
39   Vidal Díaz Muñoz and José Jiménez Acevedo to VLT, Los Mochis, Sinaloa, 24 February 1930, FHLT, file 165.

directed by the Company'.⁴⁰ But the strikers convinced some of those bussed in to join them. The conflict remained at an impasse. The company had good contacts in government, which placed obstacles for the unfavourable ruling to be sanctioned against it. In the process, the company violated the legal provision that required the Conciliation and Arbitration Board to issue its decision within eight days after the parties involved filed their request. When the ruling was issued in March, the company obtained an injunction. The workers were hung out to dry, without the wages they would have accumulated for the time they were on strike in the case of a favourable ruling, while the leaders were dismissed without the severance pay they were entitled to under the law.⁴¹

By 1 April, the Los Mochis conflict was deadlocked. Having spent a week in Veracruz so that his daughters, aged four, six and nine, could recover from the effects of pertussis,⁴² Lombardo Toledano learned that the company ordered the families of the unionised compañeros to vacate the homes with which they had been provided as part of their work contract.⁴³

When a year and a half later he analysed the crisis in the sugar industry, Lombardo attributed it to overproduction amid the artificial maintenance of high prices and export losses on the part of industrialists and businessmen. The consequences were workforce unemployment and a reduction in workers' salaries. The solution would be 'the application of a programme of general organisation of production, knowledgeable, uncompromising, and honest'.⁴⁴ But that did not happen. The government intervened, as was its obligation, but not 'to prevent labour from becoming an item in the free market' or to defend the collective bargaining agreement, but to 'implacably implement the programme' that would once and for all prevent the dumping of the product or its sale at below the cost of production.⁴⁵

With the start of the New Year, the conflict continued. This time, Lombardo Toledano put the union on the sidelines, ignored the workers' mobilisation for their demands, and took his case to the governor of Sinaloa to resolve what

---

40 Ibid.
41 José Jiménez Acevedo to VLT, Culiacán, Sinaloa, 14 March and 29 March 1930, FHLT, file 167.
42 VLT to Rafael García, president de la Port of Veracruz Stevedores Union, Mexico City, 1 April 1930, FHLT, file 165.
43 Manuel Rivera and others, Los Mochis, Sinaloa, to Reynaldo Cervantes Torres, 19 April 1930, FHLT, file 165.
44 VLT, 'La crisis de nuestra industria azucarera', *El Universal*, 16 December 1931, in *Obra*, II/2, 1931, p. 292.
45 VLT, 'La crisis de nuestra industria azucarera', *El Universal*, 16 December 1931, in *Obra*, II/2, 1931, p. 295.

was not achieved via the legal route and which the union lacked the strength to impose. He pleaded with him 'to use your influence with the conciliation board that meets tomorrow on this union affair, as its chairman offered, to end once and for all this long-standing conflict'.[46] But in *El Universal* he wrote critically about the failure of the Conciliation and Arbitration Boards '[that are] subject, in practice, to the will of the government representative who intervenes in all matters. They have ceased to be an organ of the Mexican state's social policy and have become a mechanism for advancing the personal policy of the authorities who head them'. Lombardo proposed technical and organisational amendments to protect the workers, however imperfect they might have been.[47] Strengthening the efforts and autonomy of the trade unions and their leaders was not an option. The problem of the Los Mochis workers and the sugar industry remained unresolved.

Amid the economic crisis sparked by declining oil production, worrisome signs emerged such as reduced revenue due to lower taxes on foreign companies, the payment of the foreign debt, which absorbed 36% of government expenditures, declines in basic food production, the collapse of agro-mineral exports and the value of silver, which affected industrial production, the closure of mines and increased unemployment. In this context a discussion took place concerning Constitutional Article 123. The debate was a barometer for measuring the political power and union strength that the CROM and Morones had lost and also to determine how far advanced was compliance with the constitution, which had been applied more in some states than in others. There were still areas where prevailing wage levels remained unchanged since 1910 and in which the eight-hour day was a dead letter.[48]

In November 1928, Lombardo participated in the labour-management convention on behalf of the CROM to advocate the making of labour law as federal legislation and for enacting what is known as secondary legislation, further defining and amending the main laws with the aim of closing the gap between norms and reality. It was pure bravado to begin the negotiations with the challenge of 'we do not accept that the state audit the inner functioning of the unions while usurping the powers that only correspond to the members of our professional associations',[49] while at the same time he was appealing to the

---

46   VLT to General Macario Gaxiola, Mexico City, 11 January 1932, FHLT, file 194.
47   VLT, 'El fracaso de las Juntas de Conciliación', *El Universal*, 10 February 1932, in *Obra*, II/3, 1932, pp. 47–50.
48   Chassen de López 1977, pp. 115–37.
49   VLT, 'Intervenciones en la convención obrero-patronal', Mexico City, 28 November 1928, in *Obra*, I/4, 1927–1928, pp. 227–99; quote p. 271.

president and governors to settle labour disputes that unions were unable to resolve and which the government institutions such as the Conciliation and Arbitration Boards or the employers themselves obstructed.

As a tactical measure to save the weakened CROM and not lose influence in the discussions, at the December PLM convention Lombardo proposed sacrificing the labour party, because 'the CROM has been confused with a political party, whose programme should consist of the conquest of power' and 'those who seek the conquest of public power have to see our organisation as a competitor'. He believed that by suppressing the political party, the attacks on the CROM leaders would cease, because it would show that the labour confederation did not compete with the government in the political arena, but restricted its action to the union level. Most of the delegates rejected the proposal as being cowardly, contrary to Morones, and let it be understood that Lombardo Toledano did not yet have majority support in the CROM.[50]

After the first round of discussions, the CROM abandoned the session, offended since President Portes Gil hinted that the confederation did not represent the majority of the working class. The law that was passed without the CROM's participation recognised individual employment contracts and prohibited unions from participating in politics, a veiled warning against the CROM, but the Portes Gil proposal as such was not approved. The Senate returned it to the Chamber of Deputies, because the proposed law also did not satisfy foreign businessmen who opposed the obligation to employ Mexicans first and foremost.[51]

Lombardo, the lawyer, became a staunch critic of the next version of the law: 'Compañeros: The way forward today, as yesterday, as always, is to the left!'[52] He railed against the principle of the balance between capital and labour that years before he defended; they were not equivalent forces because restoring the balance meant perpetuating a poorly organised society; the balance would be achieved 'by giving the workers everything that they have the right to possess and taking away from the industrialists everything that they enjoy by force

---

[50] VLT, 'Disolución del Partido Laborista', 9 December 1928, in *Obra*, I/4, 1927–1928, pp. 301–5; Frederick Hibbard to the State Department (henceforth DS), Mexico City, 27 December 1928, National Archives and Record Administration (NARA), Record Group 59 (henceforth RG 59), file 812.504/993; Harry Pangburn, Acapulco, 2 September 1929, NARA, RG 59, file 812.504/1059; Herschel Johnson to DS, Mexico City, 24 September 1929, NARA, RG 59, file 812.504/1066; Carr 1976, pp. 239–57; Clark 1984, pp. 108–10; Chassen de López 1977, pp. 118–26.

[51] Chassen de López 1977, p. 131; Middlebrook 1995, p. 49.

[52] VLT, 'Mitin en la Alianza de ferrocarrileros mexicanos', Mexico City, 24 July 1931, in *Obra*, II/2, 1931, p. 117.

through capitalism'.[53] The new law worsened this panorama. But Labour Minister Aarón Sáenz knew that several CROM leaders had expressed their agreement with the proposed law and had even offered their collaboration in its preparation. The minister dismissed Lombardo's criticism with a sweep of a hand.[54]

The controversy over the bill was public and Lombardo Toledano's challenge brought him acclaim. The railway station porters in the capital sympathised with 'THE TEACHER OF THE WORKERS' FUTURE'.[55] Others congratulated him for that 'deserved slap in the face' administered to the 'smug and boastful' Minister Aarón Sáenz and for Lombardo's stance against 'a misguided administration'.[56]

The labour law was passed in August 1931. The CROM objected to the legislation because it restricted the right to strike by adding a clause, not included in the 1917 Constitution, declaring a strike non-existent when it was not supported by the majority of workers in a company or when the strike call filed with the labour authorities did not comply with the corresponding procedural conditions. The law empowered the Conciliation and Arbitration Boards to decide on the legality of strikes, which adversely affected workers who were at a disadvantage when dealing with the boards. The right of the trade unions to exclusively represent workers in an industry was not clearly spelled out and the rights that workers had acquired in practice were lost. The federal law instituted guardianship over and greater interference by the executive branch in labour relations and internal union affairs compared to the old state legislation. Nor did the new law prioritise collective bargaining between unions and employers or mandate obligatory union affiliation of the workforce or contain stringent stipulations governing the dismissal of employees.[57] The law did not satisfy anyone. Lombardo Toledano referred to it as fascist and set out on an offensive to restore the status that the CROM enjoyed in public life before 1928, but under a radically different banner.

He had earned a reputation of being honest, a good lawyer, who, in addition, did not charge for his services. He knew how to explain the gist of the laws and tried to ensure they were complied with, although at times and in the absence

---

53 VLT, 'Mitin en la Alianza de ferrocarrileros mexicanos', Mexico City, 24 July 1931, in *Obra*, II/2, 1931, p. 105.
54 Aarón Sáenz to VLT, telegram, Mexico City, 30 June 1931, FHLT, file 184.
55 Mauro Peña and Antonio Eufrasio García to VLT, Federal District railway station porters' union, Mexico City, 31 July 1931, FHLT, file 184.
56 Benito Castillo to VLT, Pachuca, Hidalgo, 30 July 1931; Luis Carvajal to VLT, Atlixco, Puebla, undated, FHLT, file 184.
57 Middlebrook 1995, p. 62; Meyer 1980, p. 105; Clark 1984, pp. 173–84.

of their application he often proposed waiting and negotiating in order to contain the impatience and anger of workers and before they would take the law into their own hands.

4 The Road to the Left

The letters that Lombardo Toledano received allowed him to weigh the CROM's and his own situation. From Rio Blanco, Veracruz he received a letter saying 'we sorrowfully wish to let you know that you are not well informed about all the things that are occurring with us and it is necessary that you, with that civic valour that characterises your person, make it public either in the press or at any opportunity when you take the floor, to prevent us from being exploited by unscrupulous bandits who appear among us as our leaders'.[58]

Their cooperative had been a goldmine for the leaders who charged exorbitant prices to its members; its bank was 'another den of thieves', because it charged high interest rates, dramatically eroding workers' wages. There was more: 'To be eligible to work, every week they deduct five and six percent from our salary before we receive our money'. The workers did not sign the letter for fear of being fired. Others called on Lombardo that rather than breast beating and appeals to purity, he should intervene so that those who enriched themselves such as Morones, would resign from their posts. They felt vulnerable and placed their confidence in Lombardo as someone who was not afraid of the powerful, who repudiated the state's policies and who unmercifully attacked government officials.

'My dear Pedro', Lombardo wrote to his brother-in-law after having seen him in Buenos Aires on his trip through South America. 'I received a very painful impression of my people, when I returned', they were shabbily dressed, fatigued and in a moral crisis that exceeded the economic crisis. The government was ineffective and the 'intellectuals no longer exist either as a group or as individuals'. Only the workers deserved his consideration, although they were disoriented and discontented and 'in view of the absence of ideas in general and the partial loss of enthusiasm for the struggle, I have called for a turn to the left, because I sincerely believe that is the only road possible to salvation'.[59]

---

58   'Una comisión de más de CINCUENTA que no firman por temor de ser molestados o privados de su trabajo' to VLT, Río Blanco, Veracruz, 7 October 1931, FHLT, file 187.
59   VLT to Pedro Henríquez Ureña, Mexico City, 1 August 1931, FHLT, file 185.

The working class had reached maturity he said, contradicting his previous affirmation, while the 'bourgeois' state lacked direction and leadership,[60] according to the person who negotiated with this state. In a different letter, he confided to the long-time American comrade Robert Haberman that there was 'a very strong discontent among many elements concerning the compañeros of the Action Group and a major malady among everyone'.[61] The country seemed to have fallen victim to mental and spiritual lethargy.[62] He believed himself to be the ideal person to revive the country, provide and lead it with a programmatic orientation.

If in 1928 it was advisable to dissolve the CROM's political party in order to save the labour confederation, in 1931, when the CROM was unsalvageable, Lombardo Toledano was once again extolling the labour party, since it was the only instrument that he had to consolidate his project: In contrast, the PNR was a bourgeois party 'of the worst kind ... begging and lying'. To attract the CROM audience to his side, in a stirring speech that would not leave any doubt about the historical moment marked by the most serious crisis of humanity, he charged that on the 'eve of the transformation of the bourgeois regime throughout the world ... the men of the Mexican Revolution who have power in their hands capitulate'.[63] They should resign! He expressed the hope that 'it will be our fate to witness a complete transformation of the social system worldwide', but 'those of us who have the mission of opening the road to the organised workers legions, know that a rapid transformation worldwide, a social transformation, will come to our aid'. And after an 11-page address that provoked impassioned applause, he concluded: 'We were born to take power, born to assume the reins of government, yes, to transform the Mexican social system'.[64] With the world and Mexico going through a severe economic in crisis in 1931 his words resonated among the labouring classes.

Capitalism had fulfilled its mission. It engendered the working class that was aware of its role to conquer the world. 'The road is to the left!' Lombardo Toledano declared in an assembly held at the Frontón Nacional auditorium organised by the linotype workers union, which had just settled a labour dispute with the newspaper *Excélsior*. Lombardo Toledano called for an offensive

---

60 VLT, 'México necesita un poder espiritual que lo gobierne', *El Universal*, 19 June 1931.
61 VLT to Roberto Haberman, Mexico City, 27 June 1931, FHLT, file 183.
62 VLT, 'Del patrimonio de la universidad', 8 October 1931, FHLT, file 188.
63 VLT, speech delivered in the evening event organised by the PLM, Mexico City, 21 December 1931, FHLT, file 190.
64 Ibid.

against 'the tottering capitalist regime' and 'Yankee gold' that sacrificed the workers on the pretext of saving jobs. The 'vibrant' speech was broadcast over the radio. He recommended 'something more important to do than interpreting the articles of the crooked laws, laws full of loopholes, or written agreements' because the workers had a 'revolutionary responsibility' as their destiny.[65] The only valid principle was the right of people to have the government they wanted. The road to the left meant returning to the Mexican Revolution.[66] The tactic of empowerment was more Lombardo's rallying cry than a call to action to seek new means to achieve it.

Lombardo had an agenda at which he only hinted and for which he sought massive popular support: 'The current generation is rotten and we need to prepare new people for tomorrow, when Mexico will be forced to follow the current of renewal, which will be imposed by the outside world, because I do not believe in our own Mexican renewal for many years'. He did not spell out what he meant by the outside world. With this in mind, he needed to control the CROM and destroy the Action Group, which never allowed him to join and be part of it.[67] On his trip to Buenos Aires he had met Nicholas Repetto, a socialist and several times congressional deputy to whom he wrote from Mexico, 'don't think that the teachings I received from you won't bear fruit. In two months you will receive news of how the Argentine workers have influenced their colleagues in Mexico'.[68] He was referring to his coming resignation from the CROM in September 1932.

Lombardo's defiance of the CROM on the eve of its Orizaba convention caused a furore and jubilation inside and outside the confederation. He was accused of being a communist, disruptive, ambitious, undisciplined, and a traitor. Others protested his departure from the CROM because it left the field open, which 'the enemies would take advantage of to satisfy their personal ambitions'.[69] He denied that he 'had prepared a premature defection of some elements to make me their leader and confront the rest of the organisation'. But that was his purpose: to purge the CROM of those who did not share his interpretation of the world and surround himself with those who were likely to work with him in this new crusade.[70] The CROM leadership urged him to attend the

---

65   VLT, 'El camino está a la izquierda', Mexico City, 23 June 1932, in *Obra*, II/3, 1932, pp. 182–7.
66   VLT, 'El camino está a la izquierda', Mexico City, 23 June 1932, in *Obra*, II/3, 1932, pp. 193–5.
67   Clark 1984, p. 218.
68   VLT to Alfonso Reyes, Mexico City, 5 July 1932; VLT to Nicolás Repetto, Mexico City, 25 July 1932, FHLT, file 202.
69   Miguel Gracia, general secretary of the union at the El Rosario factory, Puebla, to VLT, 23 September 1932, FHLT, file 206.
70   VLT to Herminio Pérez, Mexico City, 22 September 1932, FHLT, file 206.

convention, but he refused because he did not want the labour assembly to become an arena of insults or personal attacks.[71] Some unions asked him to show restraint, others applauded him.

His resignation opened up the cesspool to generalised discontent. Unions and leaders were freed from the silent dissatisfaction they harboured for a long time against the despotism of the Action Group and Morones. Lombardo's friends in Teziutlán assured him that in this fight he had everything going for him to win, since he had 'the sympathy and adherence not only of almost all the groups within the CROM but even those that did not belong to the confederation in and outside of Mexico'.[72] The forklift drivers and truckers from Veracruz admired the leader 'whom the handfuls of gold offered by politicians and the bourgeoisie have failed to corrupt'.[73]

Lombardo Toledano called the Cromistas to an assembly in the Díaz de León Theater in March 1933 to organise a CROM purged of the Moronistas. He wanted his speech to be heard 'by all the workers of the Republic'. Among those present were musicians and employees of the capital's movie theatres, and workers from states such as Veracruz, Durango, Zacatecas, Sonora, Sinaloa and Puebla. He promised them all a CROM purged of the judicial chicaneries that prevented the defence of the workers, free from the transactions with employers behind the backs of the workers and union advisers in cahoots with the Conciliation and Arbitration Boards, and without the Action Group. This would restore workers' democracy along with the rotation in office of the leaders of the organisation and limiting the powers of the executive committees, giving a central role to the workers' assemblies. Notwithstanding the noble aims, only those worker and peasant groups that shared Lombardo's programme were admitted.[74]

The draft on political instruction and workers' culture of the new CROM included 'Prohibition for all members of groups to intervene in religious cere-

---

71 Reynaldo Cervantes Torres to VLT, 27 September 1932, VLT to Reynaldo Cervantes Torres, 28 September 1932, FHLT, file 206.
72 Manuel Vázquez Rodríguez to VLT, Teziutlán, 15 February 1933, FHLT, file 214; VLT to Manuel Vázquez Rodríguez, Mexico City, 28 February 1933, FHLT, file 215.
73 Executive Committee of the forklift drivers, truckers, and retail trade workers union, leaflet, 3 March 1933, s.l., FHLT, file 216.
74 VLT, speech delivered to the special convention of the CROM, 12 March 1933, in *Obra*, II/4, 1933, pp. 37–9; Clark 1984, pp. 53–7; Santiago Vallejo Anaya to José Chávez, Mexico City, 19 March 1933; P. Rebolledo for the Union of Stevedores and Day Labourers to Eucario León, Veracruz, 20 March 1933; Martín Macías and Carlos Fuentes, Federation of Worker and Peasant Unions of the Lagunera Region, Gómez Palacio, Durango, 28 March 1933, FHLT, file 217; Chassen de López 1977, pp. 156–60.

monies, of any denomination or church',[75] the creation of the Karl Marx School of Higher Worker Education to teach the origin, development and the crisis of the bourgeois regime, and the means to replace this regime with the socialist system; a new magazine, *Masas de México*, that would be of 'high aesthetic value, [have] no transactions with the ideology, customs, literature or artistic taste of the bourgeoisie' such as in the case of the superficial Hollywood films, in order to achieve a cultural revolution and moral regeneration. The goal was to 'Observe a conduct of class dignity in dealing with the government and employers, without dishonest transactions or idiotic provocations'.[76] A member of the CROM could accept a public post only if the confederation gave its authorisation and he agreed that half of his salary would be earmarked to the resistance fund. A central theme was a Latin American conference 'to discuss and approve a programme of defence and action against US imperialism'.[77] This fanciful programme also proposed 'reforms of Constitutional Article 123 so that its postulates correspond to a socialist approach', mandatory collective bargaining agreements, abandonment of Taylorism, the establishment of schools to enable workers to assume the technical and economic management of industries and the application 'of the socialist doctrine in public primary, secondary and professional schools'.[78] This was a variation of the programme that Lombardo Toledano delivered in November 1934 to Francisco J. Múgica to be presented to the president elect of Mexico, General Lázaro Cárdenas.

The split in the CROM in 1933 sparked a propaganda war for the unions' affiliation to one or another confederation. The Lombardistas toured the country to attract unions to their organisation while Morones did the same, calling on them to disavow 'the mystical attorney'. There were unions that left the CROM to join the other confederation and others that did not know where to go. Unions that only operated on the level of a single company, such as the railway workers, were divided and inter-union conflicts resulted to determine who would be the party to sign the collective bargaining agreements. However, for all Lombardo Toledano did and said, he followed his rule that he established in the old CROM, to go to the country's president to settle labour disputes – in the

---

75 'Programa mínimo de acción de la CROM', special convention, Mexico City, 10–13 March 1933, FHLT, file 217 and in VLT, 'Programa mínimo de acción de la CROM', special convention, Mexico City, 10–13 March 1933, in *Obra*, II/4, 1933, p. 74.
76 VLT, 'Programa mínimo de acción de la CROM', special convention, Mexico City, 10–13 March 1933, in *Obra*, II/4, 1933, p. 76.
77 VLT, 'Programa mínimo de acción de la CROM', special convention, Mexico City, 10–13 March 1933, in *Obra*, II/4, 1933, p. 78.
78 VLT, 'Programa mínimo de acción de la CROM', special convention, Mexico City, 10–13 March 1933, in *Obra*, II/4, 1933, p. 82.

name of but behind the backs of the workers – that the institutions responsible for addressing, such as the Department of Labour and the Conciliation and Arbitration Boards, had not resolved.[79]

The CROM purged of Moronistas was a temporary organisation, which in October Lombardo Toledano – supported by various leaders and unions in the capital and in Puebla, Querétaro and Veracruz, along with the electrical workers – renamed the General Confederation of Workers and Peasants of Mexico (CGOCM) in a country that was preparing for the presidential election and in whose political future it should take part. He did not allow the communists to join. Not all the leaders who created the CGOCM agreed with Lombardo Toledano's assertion that it would be an instrument based on radical political doctrine; some favoured an organisation that would win 'certain urgent demands for the working class'. Despite the differences, the CGOCM was born as an organisation to be taken account of as the 'authentic opinion of the most important sectors of the Mexican proletariat'.[80] Its discourse was radical: it would act 'against the bourgeois regime' and for 'the disappearance of the capitalist regime'; use the weapons of revolutionary trade unionism, such as the workers' direct action in economic disputes between capital and labour, 'and in the constant opposition to all collaboration to avoid being subject to the organs of the State'. Direct action was understood 'as the removal of all intermediaries between workers and employers'.[81] This demand was also unrealistic because, when all means failed, Lombardo continued brokering agreements between workers and employers and workers and local and national authorities through the state.

The radical language found a response in the population at a time of economic crisis. Lombardo Toledano knew that workers were demanding higher wages, a reduction in working hours and taxes, but that they lacked ideological education. The Karl Marx School would correct that inadequacy. For now, it was urgent to convince them to affiliate with the new organisation amid violence between Cromistas and Lombardistas, which in Orizaba reached the point of

---

79 Fidel Vera to Abelardo Rodríguez, Orizaba, 8 April 1933, Rodolfo Vázquez, Gaspar Rodríguez, Manuel González to Abelardo Rodríguez, Fábrica La Constancia, Puebla, 21 March 1933; José Moreno to Abelardo Rodríguez, Mexicali, 17 March 1933, AGN, Ramo Abelardo Rodríguez (henceforth RAR), file 06/33; VLT to José Jiménez Acevedo, Mexico City, 28 March 1933, FHLT, file 218; VLT to Abelardo Rodríguez, Mexico City, 10 July 1933, FHLT, file 223.

80 VLT, 'La Confederación General de Obreros y Campesinos de México', *El Universal*, 8 November 1933, in *Obra*, II/4, p. 235; Middlebrook 1995, p. 358, n. 48.

81 VLT, 'Declaración de principios de la CGOCM', October 1933, in *Obra*, II/4, pp. 229 and 231–2; Chassen de López 1977, pp. 158–61.

bottles being thrown, skulls cracked open and arbitrary imprisonment of activists by the police who weighed in against Lombardistas.[82] 'You will always live poor. You should just take what you need to meet your biological requirements and to broaden your culture and feed and educate your children from the material goods that surround you. The rest belongs to those who have less than you'.[83]

Thus began the second of 18 adages with which Lombardo urged Mexican revolutionaries to eschew earthly pleasures. 'Instincts are like dogs: you can train them to bite or to remain silent'. The principles included moral purity, abnegation of one's self in favour of others, acting by way of example and humility as norms of conduct. 'Despise the bourgeois because you're convinced that his life is futile'.[84] At the same time that Lázaro Cárdenas was campaigning as the presidential candidate of the workers and peasants, Lombardo Toledano proposed a utopia for Mexico's future that fused into a single doctrine Franciscan morality with his early 1930s view of socialism.

---

82   Eduardo Vasconcelos to the governor of the State of Veracruz, Mexico City, 7 November 1933, in AGN, RAR, file 561.3/84.
83   VLT, 'Máximas para los revolucionarios mexicanos', 7 June 1934, FHLT, file 241; *El Universal*, 7 June 1934, in *Obra*, III/1, 1934, pp. 101–3.
84   Ibid.

PART 2

Crusades

∴

Russia has become a theatre of the spirit: a place where human will, human values, are incarnate. (1932)[1]

∴

Politics is not an individual thought or individual behaviour: it is always a collective judgement and also always the behaviour of the whole, of a social class that renews social relations or tries to preserve them. (1936)[2]

∴

Yes I'm sold, to my revolutionary conviction. And for that reason I will never get tired of defending the Soviet Union here and outside Mexico, anywhere in the world. (1938)[3]

∴

---

1 Frank 1932, p. 117.
2 VLT, 'Algunas reflexiones sobre el llamado "arte" de la política', *El Universal*, 15 April 1936, in *Obra*, III/4, 1936, p. 190.
3 VLT, 'Atacar a Rusia es servir al fascismo', Palacio de Bellas Artes, Mexico City, 8 November 1938, in *Obra*, III/8, 1938, p. 171.

CHAPTER 4

A Journey into the World of the Future

Interest in the Soviet Union grew when the Western world faced a bleak panorama after the 1929 economic crisis, which left millions of workers unemployed, and after Adolf Hitler took power in Germany in 1933, which was a premonition for the renewal of militarism and barbarism. Intellectuals of a broad ideological spectrum and factory workers turned their attention to the country that, for more than a decade, had carried out an experiment in building a society and an economic and social system different from that of the West and immune to economic crises. Many went there to see it with their own eyes.

When Lombardo Toledano undertook his journey, he did not take along a camera. He did not need it, because in the summer of 1935 he went to the Soviet Union not to record the reality of the country, but to extol the virtues of the socialist system, even though he had not personally witnessed them. At another time in the past, he rejected the Bolshevik Revolution as violent and intrusive in the workers' movements outside its borders. After this trip he said he had found a superior civilisation and a path forward for all humanity.

1   The Preparations

It was probably the poet Rafael Alberti and his wife, writer Teresa León, who interceded, together with Mexican communists, so that the officials of the Communist International invited Lombardo Toledano to visit the Soviet Union. They met in May 1935, when Alberti and León arrived in Mexico. 'Yo vengo desde Sevilla / desde Sevilla la roja. / Con sangre de los obreros / el Guadalquivir se moja', Alberti recited upon their arrival.[1] Spaniards, communists, defenders of the Spanish Republic and the Soviet Union, the writers made a tour of the United States, Mexico and Central America. Before packed audiences, under 'the pretext of also discussing the centennial of Lope de Vega', Alberti spoke about the situation in Spain, defended the insurrection of the Asturias miners, crushed in 1934, and for the first time recited poems written in their memory.[2]

---

1   Rafael Alberti, *Ruta*, June and July 1935, FHLT, file 264.
2   'Informe sobre el viaje de Rafael Alberti y María Teresa León por Estados Unidos, México y Centroamérica', March–October 1935, Russian State Archive of Sociopolitical History (henceforth RGASPI for its Russian-language abbreviation), book 495 (henceforth b.), registry

Mexican Communists saw Lombardo's trip to the Soviet Union as an opportunity that should not be wasted. Once there, they wrote to the leader of the labour union arm of the Communist International, 'convince him that when he talks about national unification, it is necessary to take our organisation into account'.[3] They hoped that the leaders in Moscow would influence Lombardo to adapt his politics to those of the Mexican Communist Party and strengthen its ranks. He was the undisputed leader of the General Confederation of Workers and Peasants of Mexico and the communists were the proverbial vanguard of the proletariat, but with fewer workers under their control. Moscow was the ideal setting for implementing their rapprochement.[4]

The communists were aware that on Lombardo Toledano's agenda was the construction of the great union confederation under his leadership, which would position him before the Comintern as the undisputed labour leader in Mexico. The International must have had its own reasons to agree to the trip and provide Lombardo Toledano and his travelling companions with the level of attention granted to distinguished visitors, for which they expected praise for the Soviet system when the Mexicans returned home.[5]

Before travelling to the country in which the working class was theoretically in power, Lombardo could have felt obligated to correct his image as being part of the affluent social class so as to conform to the circumstances. It did not matter that his father's lifestyle was different from what he publicly presented. The end justified the means. He wrote to the French communist novelist Henri Barbusse: 'My father was a self-taught petit bourgeois, classical liberal, anti-clerical and very sensitive to misery and injustice. He was a poor wage earner in his youth, when I was born, and through his own efforts managed to obtain capital that allowed him to live well in his golden years as a wealthy man of the provinces'.[6]

Lombardo also wanted to take advantage of the trip to rest after several months of feverish activity. It was true, since in the weeks before and after General Cárdenas took office as president at the end of 1934, Lombardo began to encourage strikes in order to display the strength of the labour movement to

---

(henceforth reg.), 79, file 231; R. Ortiz, Caribbean Secretariat on Vicente Lombardo Toledano's trip to the USSR, New York, 8 July 1935, (telegram), RGASPI, f. 534, reg. 7, file 397.

3   Jorge Fernández, organisational secretary of the United Labour Confederation of Mexico to Alexandr Lozovsky, general secretary of Red International of Labour Unions, Mexico City, 8 July 1935, RGASPI, b. 534, reg. 7, file 397.
4   No author, to Hernán Laborde, location not indicated, 16 July 1935, RGASPI, b. 495, reg. 108, file 181.
5   David-Fox 2003, pp. 300–35; David-Fox 2005, pp. 3–29.
6   VLT, 'Carta a Henri Barbusse', Mexico City, 23 June 1935, in *Obra*, III/3, 1935, p. 251.

the incoming and outgoing government and to the clergy, as well as to those opposed to trade unions and the article 3 of the Constitution, which would introduce socialist education in the nation's schools, 'thus demonstrating that there now exists true revolutionary consciousness among all the exploited of Mexico'.[7] He thought he could manipulate Lázaro Cárdenas for his own purposes, linking the power of the state to his project and shape national policy.[8] Cárdenas, a 40-year-old military official, was 'slightly romantic and naive, sincere and honest, with radical, imprecise ideas, and morally distant from the group of men unconditionally directed by Calles'. Lombardo perceived Cárdenas as well-intentioned, but without clear ideas on the way forward. He was confident that the president would lend his support to the working class, 'or at least would not make it a victim of violent repression'.[9] On his way to the USSR, he made public his vision of a future with workers, organised and led by people such as himself, with the strength to overthrow the bourgeois regime. First, however, it was necessary to create a labour confederation 'to act in the political arena'.[10] He gave the impression that he saw no limits to radical action after the victories that occurred before beginning the trip.

The workers' strikes that Lombardo and other leaders organised between 1934 and 1935 forced the split between Plutarco Elías Calles, the long-time intervener in the country's political life, and the not-at-all disingenuous President Cárdenas. In June 1935 the divided labour movement was united around the president who supported the strikes, although in some cases they were declared illegal following compulsory arbitration.[11] Lombardo Toledano emerged triumphant from this feat in which he verified the sympathy the president felt for the leading role of the workers, who once organised, declared the president, the people 'surely will not stop and will take possession of all property and everything that has been stolen from the nation'.[12] But while Lombardo Toledano believed that the dispute over the course of the nation depended on

---

7 'Convocatoria al primer congreso general de la CGOCM', Mexico City, 15 November 1934, FHLT, file 249.
8 VLT to Dr Enrique C. Enríquez, Mexico City, 27 June 1935, FHLT, file 264 and VLT to Arturo Martínez Adame, Mexico City, 9 July 1935, FHLT, file 265.
9 VLT, 'El derrumbamiento del General Plutarco Elías Calles', July 1935, FHLT, file 265.
10 'Contestación al cuestionario formulado por la revista *Americas*', New York, 26 July 1935, FHLT, file 265. In 1934, some 202 strikes occurred, while in 1935 the number increased to a 642.
11 Lázaro Cárdenas (hencefoth LC), Mexico City, 1 April 1935, in Cárdenas 1986a, p. 317.
12 VLT, 'El presidente de la república y las huelgas', *El Universal*, 30 January 1935, in *Obra*, III/3, 1935, p. 180; LC, Mexico City, 18 June 1935, in Cárdenas 1986a, p. 322.

controlling the worker and peasant movement led by himself and those like him, Lázaro Cárdenas assigned this role to the state, headed by the president.

2   The Trip

Lombardo Toledano and Victor Manuel Villaseñor, with their respective wives, left Mexico on 13 July. Thanks to Vicente having kept a detailed list of places and kilometres travelled, we know that the two couples left the capital for Monterrey by train and from there to New York went by car; and on 1 August landed in Normandy in the port of Cherbourg.

Lombardo Toledano must have chosen Villaseñor as a travelling companion due to their political affinities. From a nineteenth-century liberal family, educated as an economist in the United States, Villaseñor was also part of the radicalised post-revolutionary intellectual elite. He, too, considered himself a Marxist. Nine years younger, he held Lombardo in high esteem due to his courage in denouncing the CROM and his incisive articles in *El Universal*. Victor Manuel found in Lombardo an extraordinary and appealing personality, 'a man of fine and elegant tastes, but with the assurance of learned and seasoned maturity'. In Lombardo he foresaw 'the future mentor of the Mexican left'. He knew Marxism

> albeit in its philosophical and sociological aspects to a greater degree rather than economics, a field that he never fully mastered. The melancholy and dreamy look, the emaciated ascetic face, and the caressing tone of his suggestive verbs, led me to recall the great medieval mystics. And it seemed obvious, given the Franciscan humility that was perceived and breathed in Lombardo's home, that this encouraged an absolute contempt for all material interests.[13]

In an interview requested by a magazine in New York concerning the purpose of the trip, Lombardo Toledano said he was interested in getting to know 'the proletarian regime' whose 'methods' could not be applied in Mexico, to the extent that the same type of government did not exist there. Meanwhile, the Mexican 'proletariat' should become acquainted with the USSR in order to 'vigorously defend this system, which is unique in the world', at a time when capitalism was experiencing 'its final historical stage' and the USSR 'represents

---

13   Villaseñor 1976, vol. 1, p. 317.

the only source of the truly universal culture of the future'.[14] He planned to be outside the country for three to four months and return at the end of the year.

Formally, he made the trip on behalf of the General Confederation of Workers and Peasants of Mexico, which 'urgently ... needed to have direct information on the situation of the working class in Europe', given the increasingly serious danger of a new world war.[15] The urgency and curiosity were his own, because he wanted to meet Otto Bauer from the left-wing of the Second International in Prague, travel through the Balkans, go to Geneva to the headquarters of the International Labour Organization and hold discussions with trade unionists in Paris and Madrid.[16]

Several unions, he claimed, helped to financially cover his trip, but he did not specify names or numbers. It is most likely that given the poverty of the labour organisations, he made arrangements with his friend Xavier Icaza, a Supreme Court judge and secretary of the Gabino Barreda University, for the government to help out with his expenses. From the Ministry of the Economy he obtained 3,000 US dollars in exchange for a study on the organisation and functioning of cooperatives in the USSR and other European countries,[17] which he did not write nor perhaps was it expected of him to write.

The travellers remained in Paris for three days, met with union, socialist and communist leaders, without naming them, and took the train to the border between Poland and the USSR. They crossed the border in Nigoreloye, the only entry point that existed for entering the country by rail. The Soviet hosts organised their trip, in which the first stay was in Leningrad where they arrived on 9 August 1935. Three days later, they were escorted to Moscow, where they spent ten days accompanied by their guide. From there, in lightning trips by car, train and plane they visited Kharkov, Baku, Tbilisi, Batum, Sukhumi and Sochi in the south, industrial cities and resort towns, thousands of kilometres from Moscow. On 12 September they were back in the capital. In each of those places they remained one to four days. Villaseñor boasted that he acquired 'kaleidoscopic but accurate impressions that came together in forging my convictions'.[18] The October Revolution was violent, but such violence was justified: 'It committed errors, injustices, and even crimes, no doubt, but the prodigious rewards of this

---

14 'Contestación al cuestionario de *Americas*', New York, 26 July 1935; VLT to HLT, Mexico City, 10 July 1935, FHLT, file 265.
15 Interview for '*El Machete*', 10 July 1935, FHLT, file 265.
16 Villaseñor 1976, vol. 1, p. 325; VLT to HLT, Mexico City, 10 July 1935, FHLT, file 265.
17 Xavier Icaza to VLT, Mexico City, 31 July 1935, FHLT, file 265.
18 Villaseñor 1976, vol. 1, p. 363.

revolution ... would not have been possible without having had the five-year plans with the decisive and enthusiastic support of the great majority [of the population]'.[19]

During the trip Lombardo Toledano sent letters back to Mexico without receiving replies, but was confident that 'the liquidation of Callismo continues and that General Cárdenas maintains the same programme as ever'.[20] In his reports to the comrades on the journey he listed the places visited and the amount of kilometres travelled without giving details. As guests of the Soviet trade unions and the Red International of Labour Unions, the labour union arm of the Communist International, the visitors were able to choose the places and the issues they were interested in knowing, he reported. They chose Ukraine, the Caucasus, and the Transcaucasus to look into large-scale agriculture, to find out about the collectivisation of labour and the agricultural machinery industry in the subtropical region, the oil industry machinery and equipment, and the nationalities question. The Soviets placed at their disposal 'an intelligent, active comrade, well-versed in the general problems of the country, who spoke Spanish, and with orders to use planes, trains, cars and boats' to transport the visitors.[21]

He did not suspect that the multilingual comrades who served as guides and interpreters were undercover police agents monitoring the inquisitive foreigners so they would not depart from the selected routes and that those responding to their questions did so in accordance with the instructions given by the party.

Upon returning to Moscow on 12 September, Lombardo had hoped to meet with the top leader of the state and the Bolshevik Party, Josef Vissarionovich Stalin. Unlike the leaders of the Communist International, Stalin did not receive him. He boasted:

> I have spoken with leaders, distinguished workers, with rank-and-file workers, with intellectuals, with public officials. I have studied the peasant question extensively, and have visited several collective farms and state farms, and also have looked into several very important aspects of their organisation. I don't think that there are many who have made a trip such as ours. Everywhere I went I was spoken to with complete frankness, excess communicative spirit, true, spontaneous friendship, and a great desire to receive detailed information about our struggles. I'll wait until

---

19 Villaseñor 1976, vol. 1, pp. 364–5.
20 VLT to Tobón, Moscow, 13 September 1935, NARA, Collection of General Manuscripts, RG 238, box 15, file 598.
21 Ibid.

we meet to give a full explanation, but right now I wanted to tell you of the success of my visit, the great facilities that the unions provided me with and the distinguished status that I have been given by the representative elements of the Soviet proletariat.[22]

When Lombardo Toledano wrote this letter to the comrades of the CGOCM, he thought he would stay in Spain for a month to write a book about his trip and return to Mexico in late November. He urged them to write, letting him know what was going on with his family, because he had received only one letter and requested 'news of the Confederation, since I want to rest easily, knowing that nothing important is occurring in Mexico'. He also urged them to send him money. But if war broke out, he would return to Mexico immediately. The war would be worldwide. 'My place is in Mexico with you. The moment could be decisive for breakthroughs of the proletariat'.[23] And one last plea to give more weight to his experience:

> If you feel it to be advisable, as I believe it to be, it would be good for the National Council to issue a press release with a summary of my journey inside the Soviet Union, using data from this letter, *without saying that I have already left Russia*, simply indicating what I have thus far seen, the route travelled, the distinguished status that I have been accorded as representative of the Confederation, and adding that I am continuing on my research trip.[24]

He was ecstatic: 'It is so beautiful to see how socialism takes shape in concrete realities, which is absorbing and moving me, and making me willing to redouble my work for the proletarian revolution, with more fervour than ever, with new faith, with the encouragement given by dreams or hopes that are met. I am in the world of the future'.[25]

The travellers left the USSR on 17 September en route to Berlin and after several trips to Paris and Madrid, began the journey back home. They arrived in Mexico on 20 October.[26]

In crossing the USSR from one end to another, Lombardo was so apprehensive that his notes reach Mexico as soon as possible, that as of 11 September he

---

22   Ibid.
23   Ibid.
24   Ibid.
25   Ibid.
26   'Itinerario del viaje de los 100 días (13 de julio–20 de octubre) 1935', FHLT, file 265.

made arrangements for them to arrive at the *El Universal* daily newspaper; it is still not known how this was accomplished, considering that there was no Mexican diplomatic representation in Moscow. In comparing the observations of the trip in the newspaper with his itinerary, what is remarkable is that he made some of them from the window of the moving train or when standing in a railroad station or flying in a plane. Other articles were an exegesis of Russian history compared with the achievements of Soviet socialism, organised with military and scientific precision to achieve the perfect well-being of its population, information that he surely had culled from statistical literature and political propaganda.[27]

Lombardo and his companions travelled from the Polish border to Leningrad by train on 8 August, day and night, passing through Minsk. The lyrical article dated 18 September 1935, entitled 'Minsk-Leningrad' and published in *El Universal* begins with the following image:

> The field is covered with ripe wheat. The reapers work the harvest, opening large furrows in the sea of ears of wheat, with an ample pace of arms that seem like pendulums vitally unified with the huge scythes. In the middle of the road where the steel is doing its work, small sheaves of wheat are born, like brooms to sweep the recently discovered ground.[28]

Leningrad inspired hyperbole in Lombardo: 'Neither Paris nor Berlin or Vienna give the impression of opulence, refinement, ostentation and disparity with respect to the country that characterises Petrograd', for the city, created by and for the czars, was inhabited by citizens born in the revolution, who could enjoy its splendour like in no other imperial city.[29]

Even though 1935 was a good year to invite foreign visitors, readers of Lombardo Toledano's article were not informed about the really existing USSR. The revolution, the hardships caused by collectivisation and forced industrialisation, the massive involuntary migration undertaken by the state to dismember the pockets of insurrection against the regime, the arrests and deportations of 'class enemies' and oppositionists of the past, the cleansing of the party of

---

27 VLT, 'Itinerario del viaje de los 100 días (13 de julio–20 de octubre) 1935', in *Obra*, III/3, 1935, pp. 281–317.
28 VLT, 'Itinerario del viaje de los 100 días (13 de julio–20 de octubre) 1935', in *Obra*, III/3, 1935, p. 285.
29 VLT, 'Itinerario del viaje de los 100 días (13 de julio–20 de octubre) 1935', in *Obra*, III/3, 1935, p. 289.

'spies' and 'counter-revolutionaries' after the assassination of party secretary Sergei Kirov in Leningrad in December 1934, were hidden from the eyes of the visitors.

Life was better and happier, Josef Stalin declared, following the end of food rationing and after the markets were filled with consumer goods to satisfy the growing urban population, comprised of new technicians and bureaucrats of industries, government institutions and party. This was also after Donbas miner Alexey Stakhanov mined an amazing amount of coal and with his feat launched a movement to boost productivity in exchange for improvements in wages, housing, consumer goods and administrative positions; and after the government once again bestowed importance upon the family and private life, described as bourgeois at the beginning of the revolution, though private family life continued to be subject to public inspection. The improvements were presented as an act of kindness by Comrade Stalin, and there were parents who were so grateful for the perceived gains that they named their daughters Stalina.[30]

Wherever they went, Lombardo and Villaseñor heard praise and acclaim for the building of the USSR under strong leadership, a plan and a goal to forge a socialist culture that subordinated individual life to a collective. They absorbed the official discourse on the class struggle and the proletariat as the universal class that did not need more than a single and correct interpretation of the movement of history, embodied in the Communist Party, the vanguard of that class. According to this view, the policies of the party could change as long as they remained within the general line of Marxism-Leninism and the infallibility of historical laws. Ideology was conceived as a strategic tool to forge alliances between the people and government officials. This was also the case with the participation of the population in the construction of the socialist society, as opposed to the capitalist system, where the people were burdened by poverty, exploitation, imperialism and war. Socialism, on the other hand, provided a proud place in society to the population that would be lost if the Soviet Union were to return to capitalism.[31]

---

[30] Figes 2007, pp. 150–9; Fitzpatrick 1999, pp. 41–66; Fitzpatrick and Slezkine (eds) 2000, pp. 303–21.
[31] Kotkin 1995, pp. 151–4.

3 Different Perspectives

Those who had the possibility to visit the Soviet Union in the 1920s and return in the 1930s noticed the changes between the two periods. Walter Citrine, general secretary of the Trades Union Congress, the British labour confederation, was one of the privileged few. Before being a labour leader, Citrine was an electrician by trade. He believed that the task of the unions was to improve the workers' living conditions without overthrowing capitalism, without industrial disputes, and through the pressure of working-class organisation under a unified leadership with authority and responsibility in industrial management. His consideration of the social conditions of the day was from the standpoint of the workers, their needs and their material satisfaction with dignity.[32]

Citrine visited the Soviet Union in 1925 and again in 1935. His detailed description and photographic record provide an eloquent contrast to the claims advanced by Lombardo Toledano. He was not an impartial observer and did not go to the Soviet Union to verify any preconceived truth, despite the title of his book. He wanted to find out if the socialist system under construction outperformed the capitalist system, with the curiosity of someone who was convinced of capitalism's benefits. He was sensitive to the improvement in the lives of women, for whom the government provided childcare, maternity leave and equal wages with men, but frowned at their engaging in jobs with the same difficulty and harshness as their male co-workers. The presence of street children was a phenomenon he noted, but also the happiness of those who were in day care. The quality of daily life consumed much of his inquiries: the lack of bathrooms and hot water in homes; overcrowding in apartments previously occupied by a single family and now housing several; the supply of food seemed limited and its presentation substandard; lines in front of shops were notoriously common as were poorly dressed men, women and children.

Citrine condemned Soviet productivism and rejected the assimilation of unions to the state. His adherence to the principles of freedom of association and independent action as the basis of legitimate trade unionism made him sceptical as to whether the Soviet and British trade unions had much in common. If he included many comparisons in his book between the wages of Soviet workers and their British counterparts, it was to determine which goods could be purchased for the same hours of work. He sought hard data on the lives of

---

32 Van Goethem 2000, pp. 109–12; Citrine 1936.

workers because he wanted to know the experience of an ordinary citizen. An Englishman could buy a bicycle with 50 hours of work, for a Russian the corresponding figure was 175 hours.

His expert eye was fixed on the quality of Soviet products. Again and again he noticed the poor quality for the sake of a productivism imposed on the workers that was no different from piecework. He was impressed by production statistics, but when he looked at the workmanship of doors, furniture or buildings, he regretted that the quality of production was on the decline as the number of products increased. Citrine requested information on workplace benefits, collective bargaining agreements, income, workers' insurance and the salaries earned by officials. He was curious to know about life in the factories. He sensed that some factories seemed like national security facilities due to the strict environment that permeated the air, although he liked the well-equipped dining halls, with reasonable food for all. He noticed the libraries and rest areas. Visiting the Arbat, Moscow's main market, he noted that merchants sold shrivelled apples, which in Great Britain would be in the garbage, and women bought bruised tomatoes without complaining.[33] Citrine visited workers' homes located outside the designated route, which the guides could not deny taking the chief union leader of Great Britain to; they reluctantly answered his questions, which they perhaps thought could be explained by his capitalist mentality.

Lombardo Toledano and Citrine were in the Soviet Union at the same time, without their paths having crossed. Their outlook was diametrically different. Lombardo denied that there were food shortages; citing government statistics, he described the population's diet as being rich in meat as a sign of the citizens' well-being. Variety was a desired end, but the Soviet government 'has still not wanted to produce' extras, as long as it has 'not resolved the key problems of collective life'. In Tbilisi, the Georgian capital, Lombardo Toledano described the 'very distinguished and very elegant women' who lived 'in overabundance similar to that of the capitalist countries'. He rejected the 'superficial' commentators, the 'quaint affirmations', the 'propaganda of the capitalist press' as representing bad faith and slanders when they spoke of poor quality goods in the Soviet Union and shortages of food, housing and clothing. The Soviet system was supported by the masses, and not as the press said, imposed and manipulated from the top echelons of the state and the Communist Party, entrenched in coercive measures and intimidation.[34]

---

33   Citrine 1936, pp. 289–362; 'Visit to Russia', 14 September through 28 October 1935. Walter Citrine Archive, (henceforth WCA), series 4.
34   VLT, 'Condiciones actuales de vida del pueblo soviético', in *Obra*, III/3, 1935, pp. 354,

Lombardo did not acknowledge that housing was a problem; on the contrary, he emphasised its beauty. 'These concrete aesthetic constructions, the virile and at the same time discreet and beautiful buildings of reinforced concrete, comprise the profile of the cityscape of the new life of the USSR'.[35]

Accompanying his comments with photographs, Citrine, meanwhile, observed that 'housing in Russia is a disgrace. It is the rule rather than the exception that people have only one room per family'. Without reliable statistics, it was his view that in the cities, housing construction lagged behind population growth. The buildings 'were huge barracks, sometimes five floors, most of them without elevators. As a general rule, they do not have bathrooms. The closest bathroom can be a good distance away. There are few, if any, provisions for hanging clothes'.[36] What Citrine saw as the violation of privacy in communal apartments, in addition to poverty and ugliness, Lombardo viewed as a step forward in the collective conception of life and the liberation of women from household chores thanks to shared kitchens and laundry facilities.

The reality was not as Lombardo described it. In Moscow a person had on average 5.5 square metres of space; less in industrial districts. Most workers lived in barracks, with men and women separated, which divided families. In houses with bedrooms, couples separated their space from others with a curtain around a plank bed that hardly provided privacy. The lack of space and privacy caused tensions, frictions, disputes and scandals; residents did not talk loudly, but whispered so that no one could listen in. It was true that living space had a different connotation than in the Western countries and that communal life existed not only due to lack of construction, but also as part of an ideal of life and a place to mould people.[37]

Lombardo saw Soviet political education as 'a powerful example that we have to carefully study'; all citizens received news and commentary on world events. 'As they receive only a doctrine, they digest it, study it, and show concern; they know what attitude to take in response to any problems posed to them'.[38]

Citrine also observed this education based on a single doctrine. 'In every room we visited, there was a photograph of Stalin and I must say that this

---

      pp. 356–7. This was the second lecture, delivered in November 1935, and later published in the book *Un viaje al mundo del porvenir*.
35   Ibid.
36   Citrine, 'Visit to Russia', 27 September 1935, WCA, series 4.
37   Figes 2007, pp. 172–5; Kotkin 1995, pp. 158–60 and p. 180.
38   VLT, 'Condiciones actuales de la vida del pueblo soviético', in *Obra*, III/3, 1935, p. 375.

constant glorification of Soviet leaders was nauseating' as there was no way for people to escape from those faces.[39] And yet, although the peasants were poorly dressed, they lived in clean homes and were good-humoured; the women who selected potatoes, 'I can truthfully say, I have never seen people happier despite their abysmal poverty'.[40] As they worked, their children were well cared for in nurseries.

Where Citrine and Lombardo Toledano were in agreement was in their amazement at the new Russia as the melting pot of different nationalities. Both visited Baku, in the oil-rich Caucasus region, where the Turks lived alongside Armenians, Tatars and Russians. They differed on the quality of life of the oil workers. There were no paved roads and to reach their workplaces they had to pass through 'a mixture of mud and garbage'. Baku 'looked like a city that had been devastated by bombardments and on top of the ruins someone had the bright idea of erecting primitive homes without rhyme or reason ... Not only did these huts have dirty floors but there were huge puddles of water and gasoline mixed with mud, outside the doors'.[41]

Lombardo Toledano must have seen the same desolation, but perhaps it was no different from the conditions in the oil fields he was familiar with in Tampico and Huasteca where workers' 'cottages and barracks were built in the floodplains. That meant that heavy rainy seasons and hurricanes – simply inconvenient to those in the higher up in the labour hierarchy and the terrain – were disastrous for the Mexicans. As the rains and storms swelled the region's rivers and lagoons, Mexicans living quarters were the first to flood and be carried away in the currents'.[42]

Perhaps with this image in his memory, combined with admiration for the Soviet system, he could say that it was 'beautiful seeing the oil region, through those endless forests of towers and pumps that extracted oil from the entrails of the earth'.[43] Citrine, who saw the same 'forest of wooden towers', felt an atmosphere of helplessness.[44] Unlike Lombardo, he looked at the world from the perspective of the worker he had once been and the liberalism of an industrial power that had been unfair to its workers. His objection to the system 'was not the big financial affairs of businesses but the intimidation and small excesses

---

39　Citrine 1936, pp. 349–50.
40　Citrine 1936, p. 353.
41　Citrine, 'Visit to Russia', 16 October 1935, WCA, series 4.
42　Santiago 2006, p. 187.
43　VLT, 'Cómo resolvió el régimen soviético el problema de las nacionalidades oprimidas', in *Obra*, III/3, 1935, p. 394.
44　Citrine, 'Visit to Russia', 16 October 1935, WCA, series 4.

of authority of a foreman or a supervisor'. Workers' control was achieved by exercising it with evolutionary methods, nationalisation of industries and consumer cooperatives.[45]

Lombardo Toledano was so taken by his trip that he turned his articles and convictions into fifty 'truths about the USSR'; fifty epigrams of memorable phrases that due to their simplicity were easy to learn: 'For the generation that now has the destiny of the Soviet Union in its hands, the past can be summed up in Lenin and the future will take shape around Lenin' or 'Leningrad is to St. Petersburg what the future is to the present in the countries under the bourgeois regime'.[46] One of the phrases reads: 'In most capitalist countries we can be rest assured that almost all individuals travelling in their own cars are exploiters of others. In the USSR, for every individual who owns a car, people have a grateful smile'. Another declared that: 'In the USSR women are not protected; protecting women amounts to continuing to consider them as inferior to men: they are regarded as equals to men'. In epigram 36 he said: 'The autobiography is the brightest literary genre in the USSR, because every man and every woman should report regularly on their behaviour to the cell of the social or political organisation to which they belong'. In a fragment of another: 'Workers' housing of the past in the USSR, is workers' housing of the present in the capitalist world'; or epigram 47: 'For the new generation of the USSR, what is happening today in the capitalist world is history'. And the last: 'Travelling through space is an easy feat; travelling back in time is difficult, even as a mere act of the imagination. However, I just travelled ahead in time: the USSR is the world of the future'.[47]

4   Back in Mexico

Lombardo Toledano had planned to travel until December, but returned in October, perhaps because he felt that the rarefied political environment in Mexico and the world demanded his presence or as a result of running out of money. Italy invaded Abyssinia in October in a bid to expand its African colonies, which was a bad omen for world peace. In Mexico, tensions arose from the confrontation among anti-Cárdenas forces between the Callistas and Cromista unions that clamoured for the return of 'top leader' of the revolution, exiled in

---

45   Citrine, 'Industrial democracy', WCA, series 1.
46   VLT, 'Leningrado', *El Universal*, 30 October 1935, in *Obra*, III/3, 1935, p. 297.
47   VLT, 'Cincuenta verdades sobre la URSS', in *Obra*, III/3, 1935, pp. 425–32, quotes on pp. 427, 429, 430, 431, 432.

the United States, to save the country from communism. Amid the unrest, Lombardo arrived at the Colonia railway station on 20 October, where people on the station platforms cheered his return.[48]

As the first promotional event he brought together several organisations that belonged to the workers and peasants confederation that he created in 1933 to share his travel experiences. He described the Soviet Union as brimming with constructive enthusiasm as opposed to the Western countries with millions of unemployed. While in capitalist countries there was a surplus of labour power due to reduced production, in the USSR there was a need for more workers given the construction boom. The conclusion was clear: due to the existence of 50 million unemployed in the world, a war would necessary erupt, which the masses would take advantage of to make a social revolution. The Soviet Union must be defended 'wherever it is necessary to do so'; it was there that he experienced 'an hour in the world of the future' and where he realised 'with tremendous pleasure that in Mexico the force that will soon bring down the capitalist regime is already gestating'.[49] President Cárdenas took note of Lombardo's speeches.

At the Teatro Hidalgo, Lombardo Toledano and Villaseñor gave several 'elementary and didactic' albeit non-polemical lectures on the Soviet Union. 'Capitalist democracy leads to fascism and war; the dictatorship of the proletariat, by doing away with social classes, leads to democracy and peace'.[50] To give an immediacy and authenticity to such ideas, in his conferences Lombardo employed a rhetorical device he used to persuade his audience, interspersing dialogues with people who allegedly tried to dissuade him from making his trip, because the country he was going to visit resembled hell on earth on account of the population's persecution.[51]

Lombardo was effusive in his assertions about the Soviet population being satisfied in food, clothing and shelter. Compared to Mexico, the lives of factory workers and peasants – thanks to the services provided by the state, support for women, 'with their bodies now emancipated',[52] grandiose five-year plans, production and the magnificent construction projects – were evidence that the USSR was 'a powerful example that we have to study carefully'.[53]

---

48 Villaseñor 1976, vol. 1, pp. 366–7; Bantjes 1998, pp. 43–61; Vaughan 1997, p. 62.
49 VLT, Speech delivered in the Teatro Hidalgo, Mexico City, 7 November 1935, FHLT, file 268.
50 VLT, 'La estructura política de la URSS', in *Obra*, III/3, 1935, p. 347.
51 VLT, 'Condiciones actuales de vida del pueblo soviético', in *Obra*, III/3, 1935, p. 350 and Villaseñor 1976, vol. 1, p. 361.
52 VLT, 'Cómo resolvió el régimen soviético el problema de las nacionalidades oprimidas', in *Obra*, III/3, 1935, p. 396.
53 VLT, 'Condiciones actuales de vida del pueblo soviético', in *Obra*, III/3, 1935, p. 357.

He was not intimidated by the attacks of the press and his opponents. Lombardo continued with speeches and appeals for the unity of the proletariat in anticipation of the organisation designed to influence President Cárdenas's policies. He fulminated against his opponents, whose defeat did not depend on the government that 'is viewed as being powerless against its enemies and against the enemies of the Mexican people', and anticipated that the labour movement would join with the peasant movement so that it would be the proletariat and not 'the reaction' that would lead the country. And for resisting, he urged 'that in each union there be an armed detachment to defend it (applause), that in each peasant community there also be an armed nucleus to defend it (applause)', and that 'in the cities and the countryside, the workers, united and armed, must defend their sacred interests (applause)'.[54]

The conferences fell like a bombshell. Newspapers published editorials against the red agitation and the hand of Moscow. Undeterred, Lombardo Toledano reaffirmed that the USSR had emerged 'as an example of what the world of the future will be like'.[55] Right-wing forces unleashed their fury, friends applauded him, while some fellow labour leaders were perplexed and disavowed the propaganda that according to them he made in favour of communism. There must have been someone within the CGOCM who let it slip to *El Universal* that there was dissent in the top leadership. Lombardo called his closest allies to a meeting and possibly forced them to publish a statement denying that there were differences within the national leadership and issued orders to flood the press with telegrams supporting him. In private, and when he already knew that in a few months a new labour confederation would be launched, he identified dissent with the 'legacy of Moronismo' and the 'five little wolves'. But once the new confederation was established, he said privately, 'we must sweep away all that scum'.[56]

He was referring to Fidel Velázquez and Alfonso Sánchez Madariaga, old friends since they were retail milk distributors in the landed estates close to the capital, and united in the dairy labour union headed by Velázquez. The other three were Fernando Amilpa, Jesús Yurén and Luis Quintero, who had similar backgrounds. Amilpa was a native of Jojutla, Morelos; his passion was music, but for lack of resources he had to work in garbage collection in the capital. There he met Yurén, and together they engaged in trade union activism that led them to lose their jobs. Luis Quintero rescued them from their misfortunes

---

54 VLT, 'Discurso pronunciado en la Arena Nacional', Mexico City, 24 November 1935, FHLT, file 269.
55 Villaseñor 1976, vol. 1, p. 368.
56 Villaseñor 1976, vol. 1, p. 370.

and gave them jobs on the city bus line in the Lomas de Chapultepec neighbourhood. With numerous unions, whose pressure could affect the life of the capital, the 'five little wolves' dominated the Federal District Workers Confederation.[57] The epithet came from another labour leader who baptised them as 'five little wolves' after Morones had called them five miserable worms when in 1933 they broke away from what was once a strong bastion of the Mexican Regional Labour Confederation. Since they acted as Lombardo's allies in the CGOCM, Lombardo needed them in the construction of the proposed organisation.

In noting the disgust that his lectures caused among those close to him, Lombardo turned to the press in a less exalted tone. His propaganda in favour of the success achieved by the workers of the Soviet Union did not mean that he believed 'that the time has come in our country for the dictatorship of the proletariat'. Historical laws were above the individual will and in Mexico conditions did not exist for regime change, but at some point 'the transformation must occur despite all obstacles'.[58]

5 The President and the Leader

General Cárdenas distanced himself from the ideological and political pursuits of Lombardo Toledano. The president was concerned about the effects of Lombardo's lectures on the Soviet Union and the divisions in the leadership of the workers organisations, whose bloc had helped to strengthen his government against Calles and his lackeys in mid-1935. Cárdenas hoped to maintain the support of the labour movement during his entire six-year presidential administration in order to carry out policies that would benefit the population, such as the land reform and the defence of national sovereignty.[59]

Cárdenas was surely aware that his political project and that of Lombardo Toledano did not coincide, but trusted the good political judgement and patriotism of the labour leader as well as his sense of savvy for not opening a new front of opposition at a hectic time in the country's history. The revolu-

---

57 Araiza 1975, vol. 4, p. 155; Hernández Chávez 1979, pp. 128–53; Sánchez González 1991, pp. 36–85.

58 Benjamín Tobón and Rubén Magaña, 'Declaraciones a la prensa', Mexico City, 13 November 1935, FHLT, file 269; Villaseñor 1976, vol. 1, p. 368; VLT to *El Universal, El Nacional, Diario de Yucatán*, 28 November 1935, FHLT, file 269.

59 LC to VLT, Presidential train, from San Pedro Coahuila, telegram, 15 November 1935, FHLT, file 269; 'La agitación roja y la mano de Moscú', *El Universal*, 28 November 1935.

tion turned government ran into many obstacles to its consolidation, among them the charge that the workers' organisations were seeking 'the disintegration of the government itself'. Perhaps Cárdenas was also thinking of Lombardo Toledano when he urged organised labour to maintain its confidence in the government, the task of which was 'safeguarding the interests of the entire nation and especially the interests of the working class'.[60]

The president disarmed his critics on the left, whose support he needed to lessen the weight of his critics on the right. Teachers were right in calling for higher wages, farmers were correct in demanding the fulfilment of their rights in response to the systematic and violent opposition to agrarian reform, and 'if the opposition persists in ignoring the good faith efforts of the government, the latter will be forced to continue arming the peasants and, if necessary, the workers to guarantee land distribution and defend its use and to put the improvement in the lot of the working class into effect'.[61]

Uncertainty prevailed in the dispute over the course of the nation between Cárdenas and his opponents, linked to former president Calles. Meanwhile, the 'five little wolves' were biding their time waiting for the right moment to draw a line in the sand between themselves and Lombardo Toledano. In December 1935, Calles and Morones returned from their voluntary exile in the United States. As soon as they touched down in the capital, it was discovered that weapons and ammunition had entered Veracruz and munitions and rifles were found in Morones's home. The Senate ordered his arrest, but it was not carried out. Just as in June when Calles attacked the wave of strikes, his return in December was enough to unite the leaders, unions, ejidos, and peasant communities around Cárdenas. 'At 11 am the procession of demonstrating workers began outside the National Palace', said the president, satisfied with the massive support for the government and the call to expel Calles and Morones again 'so that right here they feel the weight of their historical responsibility'.[62]

Lombardo Toledano, intelligently, measuredly and with a sense of tactical savvy, listened to the president. The correlation of forces did not favour his project, and he knew how to adapt his strategy of building a socialist Mexico to the circumstances. Being in opposition to the existing government was not an option.

---

60   LC, 22 December 1935, in Cárdenas 1978, vol. 1, pp. 181–2.
61   LC, 'Declaraciones del presidente de la república a la prensa nacional', Tenancingo, State of Mexico, 9 December 1935, in Cárdenas 1978, vol. 1, pp. 177–8.
62   LC, Mexico City, 22 December 1935, in Cárdenas 1986a, pp. 332–3.

6   The Gide Case

One of the commitments that Lombardo Toledano must have contracted with his Russian hosts was to combat any criticism of the Soviet Union. The opportunity to demonstrate his loyalty arose when the famous French writer Andre Gide published a book with notes of his trip to the USSR. Born in 1869, at 67 years of age Gide's impressions came to light in Paris in 1936. In 1932 he wrote that in the abominable distress of the present world, Soviet economic plans seemed the salvation for which he was ready to sacrifice his life.[63] In 1933 he stated that the restricted freedom in the USSR was justified because a new society was being established. In 1935 in Paris he presided over the International Writers' Congress for the Defense of Culture. No matter how much the French communists tried, they could not prevent the case of Victor Serge from being aired. A revolutionary of Russian origin who grew up in Belgium and joined the Bolshevik Revolution shortly after it broke out, Serge became critical of Stalin while at the same time supporting the working class's aspiration to take control of the state. For opposing the regime he was deported to Siberia with his young son.[64]

Victor Serge's 'Letter from Moscow', written on 1 February 1933, circulated in France before the congress. Gide might have read the letter, in which Serge told of the unimaginable suffering and humiliation of the comrades of the anti-Stalinist opposition and their families, 'deported, imprisoned, dead, lost'; and he recounted the harassment, spying by secret police agents, and fear for one's life. He ended sombrely: 'We are increasingly facing a totalitarian, castocratic, absolutist state, drunk with its own power, in which man does not count for anything'. He expressed the hope to 'see you soon'.[65]

Gide closed the congress in which supporters and opponents of Serge attacked and counterattacked each other. After the meeting he went to see the Soviet ambassador together with the writer Romain Rolland. He managed to get Serge freed and obtained exile for him and his son Vlady in Belgium. With his fidelity apparently untainted, Gide was invited to the Soviet Union.[66] He first scheduled and then cancelled his trip due to his suspicion that his hosts would seek to woo him over with gifts as they tended to do with other visitors,

---

[63]   Ruy Sánchez 1991, p. 76.
[64]   Ruy Sánchez 1991, pp. 74–6.
[65]   Víctor Serge, 'Carta desde Moscú', 1 February 1933, in Víctor Serge papers, Bienecke Library Rare Books and Manuscripts, Yale University. I would like to thank Adolfo Gilly for providing a copy of the letter.
[66]   Ruy Sánchez 1991, pp. 77–82.

because he feared that his speeches would be distorted and given 'a meaning that I would not have wanted to give my words and the misunderstandings would grow, making me their prisoner'. Finally, he overcame his reservations and travelled in June 1936, bringing along his own interpreter, which the Soviets saw as a sign of distrust. When Serge learned of Gide's trip, he sent him a warning: to serve the working class and the USSR, his duty was to look clearly at reality and speak the truth. 'Accept that you cannot help this revolution by being silent about its illness or by covering your eyes in order not to see it'.[67]

To flatter Gide, the Soviet government printed 3,000 postcards with his photograph, published 400,000 copies of his books, and organised a royal reception, leaving nothing to chance in the refined writer's encounter with the stark reality of the USSR. Gide did not allow himself to be seduced by the attention he was receiving. He filled his notebook with comments and images depicting how children were fully enjoying life in summer camps, as well as the shortages faced by the population when they went shopping. Gide noted the authorities' disdain for popular culture, but admired the experiment in the rehabilitation of criminals imprisoned in Bolshevo near Moscow. Created at the initiative of the famed writer Maxim Gorky, this city had factories, clubs, and libraries, proving that criminality was socially induced and could also be remedied through socially oriented policies and measures. This new way of running society was in stark contrast to the misfortune of children living on the street in response to which the authorities seemed powerless. The police picked them up, but these same children or others took their place. While the Soviet Union was an unknown utopia, Gide considered it the land of development and culture, the antithesis of capitalist disorder; he travelled there to find a revolutionary society. Upon his arrival, he was mesmerised by the beauty of the Caucasian forests, by the grandeur of Leningrad and the art collection at the Hermitage Museum. He admired the sanatoriums and rest homes for workers, but was saddened when he saw the barracks inhabited by those who had built those sanatoriums.[68]

Moscow seemed to be an ugly city. Entering a store, the 'items were worse than repulsive'. The homes on a collective farm seemed to him to be 'depersonalised' with horrible furniture and with the same portrait of Stalin on all the walls. But the workers, who had no communication with the outside world, told him that the well-being of Soviet workers was superior to that of their French counterparts.

---

67 Ruy Sánchez 1991, pp. 89–93; quote on p. 112.
68 David-Fox 2003, pp. 300–35; Gide 1936, pp. 1–94; Furet 1995, pp. 328–36.

The French travellers had their own interpreter, but were accompanied by a woman who was monitoring them. Gide was disheartened because more than once he ran into sycophants of Stalin in an authoritarian atmosphere of fear and simulation, without the intellectual freedom that would allow for the creation of great literary works. What was being produced were banalities, since a work of art could not be created according to a doctrine, but by 'asking questions that anticipate the future and answering questions that have not yet been formulated'.[69]

Once his book was published, it sparked a furore, but was a commercial success thanks to Gide's fame and the curiosity of readers spurred by what was a political-literary event, *succès de scandale*. The communists accused him of prioritising the intellectual life of the USSR at the expense of everyday life and forgetting the Russian past that weighed on the present, without which current Soviet society could not be understood. In response, Gide published a postscript to the first book about his and his travelling companions' encounters with people in their daily lives. To respond to his critics, he used statistics and comments on the economy obtained from the Soviet press. Gide had read critical literature on the USSR, such as Citrine's book. He had also discussions with Victor Serge and with a worker who lived in the USSR for 11 years and published a pamphlet hostile to the workers' fatherland. He highlighted the contradiction between the intensification of production, the increase in useless products and the deplorable housing conditions for workers. One of the dramatic statistics that he cited was the elimination of women's right to abortion at the same time that the contraceptives being produced were of poor quality. He met with people who abstained from entering into romantic relationships or having a family. Gide, a homosexual, was particularly sensitive to the law condemning those who shared this sexual orientation into internal exile, accused of being counterrevolutionaries and nonconformists, and further years of deportation to Siberia if the first period of exile did not 'reform' them. He presented further data on poverty, inadequate education, children not attending school and the lack of timely payment of wages to teachers. He was prevented from seeing Nikolai Bukharin, who was already on the list of Old Bolsheviks, removed from their key party posts and subsequently shot on Stalin's orders in 1938.

It was painful to transcribe this statistical evidence, but Gide wrote his second book in protest against the blindness and bad faith of those who denied the terrible evidence of social and political life in the USSR. He added information about the show trials staged in 1936 against the Bolshevik leaders in

---

69   Gide 1937b, pp. 18–28.

Moscow and on the thousands of deportees who were accused of having ties with fabricated crimes against the Soviet leaders. Disenchanted with developments in the Soviet Union, he became sceptical of the possibility of fighting for democracy under the same banner as Josef Stalin.[70]

Lombardo did not read the sequel to Gide's first book, but the furore that the first book provoked among the communists was sufficient to make him attack the writer. In March 1937 he published a scathing article to refute the content of Gide's book, which 'has aroused great fanfare among reactionary intellectuals the world over'.[71] In Mexico three translations of the book came out. Lombardo published his article in the magazine on modern culture issued by the Workers' University for propaganda and not informational purposes. He mocked the disappointment that the famous writer felt with his visit to the USSR, reduced his book to the experience of an elegant intellectual, who when confronted with Soviet reality put out his false view of life. Lombardo compared Gide with the 'decent people' of Mexico when they had to rub shoulders with the working poor.

To refute Gide, Lombardo culled 28 quotes in total from the book, and out of context, subjected them to a devastating critique. He charged that Gide judged the USSR without a 'scientific method', in accordance with his tastes, prejudices, fears and hopes. In response to Gide's criticism of asphyxiated artistic creation in the USSR, Lombardo replied: 'Culture is not the result of individuals but of the great masses of the people who express their opinion through individuals'.[72] To Gide's bewilderment over the lack of discussion on works of art and culture following a single line of thought, Lombardo justified such phenomenon by saying that 'a country that is destroying the past and which is creating a new system needs everyone to toe the line'.[73] He disparaged the writer's comment on the lack of freedom and the vanquished, fearful and enslaved spirit, arguing that 'even the worst enemies of the Soviet Union have not dared thus far to express such an absurd judgement'. Gide did not have the ability to judge the USSR, because he lacked a 'dialectical method'.[74]

Thus culture that was not the fruit of the individual but the expression of the masses needed individuals to articulate it. Lombardo Toledano believed himself to be their spokesman and it was for them that he used to write rhetorical verses. One such poem began with:

---

70   Gide 1937a, pp. 54–79; Furet 1995, pp. 329–34.
71   VLT, 'André Gide o el sicólogo perdido en la URSS', in *Obra*, III/5, 1937, p. 57.
72   VLT, 'André Gide o el sicólogo perdido en la URSS', in *Obra*, III/5, 1937, p. 68.
73   VLT, 'André Gide o el sicólogo perdido en la URSS', in *Obra*, III/5, 1937, p. 64.
74   VLT, 'André Gide o el sicólogo perdido en la URSS', in *Obra*, III/5, 1937, p. 66.

> My machete and your hammer
> will shine in the night.
> Two beams of light that illuminate
> our search for bread.

And ended with:

> On the lips of the children
> songs will flourish,
> and they will extend their hands to us,
> not to ask for bread,
> but to give us flowers
> full of happiness.[75]

---

[75] VLT, untitled, 19 February 1936, FHLT, file 274.

CHAPTER 5

The Foundations of the Nation

In closing the founding congress of the Mexican Workers Confederation (CTM) on 24 February 1936, Lombardo Toledano took an oath: 'Comrades, don't let me keep talking; I would have nothing more to say; there are many things still beating inside my heart, but I would like to summarise them in one idea: we have to be soldiers to the end; if we do an about-face, kill us'![1] Somewhat less dramatically, days earlier, he had laid the cornerstone of the Workers' University as the other pillar that would underpin the 'definitive unity of the workers' movement' in order to cement the nation and build a new world.[2]

1   The Preparations

Even before travelling to the Soviet Union in the summer of 1935, Lombardo Toledano had contemplated the creation of a major worker and peasant confederation on a national scale. Upon his return, and with the means at his disposal, he dedicated all his efforts to achieve this goal. The CGOCM that he headed was a powerful organisation, but it did not control the Federation of Federal District Workers, which was led by the 'five little wolves'. Estimates of its numerical strength ranged wildly, from 20,000 to 200,000 members, depending on whether the statistics came from the organisation itself or the Department of Labour. Trade unions representing rail and oil workers, miners and electricians – national in scope but fragmented in regional locals – in addition to telephone workers and truck drivers, who had participated in the 1934 and 1935 strikes, represented the majority of the organised working class that Lombardo planned to unite under the same banner. On a local level, such as in Atlixco and Orizaba, the Lombardistas and Moronistas competed for the loyalty of workers in the textile industry to either dissuade or attract them to the new

---

1   'Registro estenográfico del discurso de clausura en el congreso de la CTM', 24 February 1936, AGN, Ramo Lázaro Cárdenas (henceforth RLC), vol. 481, file 437/62 and VLT, 'Discurso de clausura del congreso de unificación', Mexico City, 24 February 1936, in *Obra*, III/4, 1936, p. 102. A versión of this chapter, 'La cimentación de la Confederación de Trabajadores de México', was published in *Tzintzun*, no. 60 (July–December 2014), pp. 248–79.
2   VLT, 'La Universidad Obrera de México al servicio del proletariado', speech delivered on 8 February 1936, Mexico City, FHLT, file 275.

confederation. In Puebla, Lombardo was known for his personal attributes that contrasted with those of the notoriously corrupt Morones, but weighing against him was the radicalism that had cost the workers their jobs and even their lives in internal union struggles and confrontations with the state government and the employers.[3]

The new organisation should have the strength so that the government would recognise it as an indispensable partner in designing state policies. Lombardo distrusted the spontaneity of the masses and their capacity to understand the leader's strategy. To prepare the groundwork, to sensitise the population and the authorities about the major event and at the same time to neutralise his adversaries, Lombardo Toledano sent designated representatives to the four cardinal points of the country. However, he did not instruct nor train them to conduct organising drives among the workers.

'On our arrival at Culiacán', Enrique Mayorga and Enrique Sánchez reported by telegraph from the capital of the state of Sinaloa, 'we proceeded to have a meeting with the governor in order to reach an agreement with that government to begin the activities that we must develop in the state'. Their task was to forge alliances in accordance with the schema designed by Lombardo. The governor was attentive to the envoys and exercised his influence so that the unions belonging to the CROM 'would merge with our union with the exception of their leaders'. With their efforts concluded, they asked Lombardo 'to tell us what name should the party that we will establish in the state' have.[4] They reported that campesino groups in Mazatlán and southern Sinaloa were difficult to recruit, because they were 'agitated' by a low level military leader who in turn was under orders from a colonel 'to bring them into the PNR',[5] the National Revolutionary Party.

In other states, such as Puebla and Veracruz, Lombardo had staunch allies from when he was a union advisor, except in the cities in which the CROM dominated the labour movement. In southern Sonora he had followers after having influenced the organising drives among rural workers. In Durango, however, his name was unknown. There were groups of workers who asked to join the projected organisation so as to obtain labour protection. In Los Mochis, in the state of Sinaloa, workers agreed to join the confederation because they wanted to form a party independent of the state. There were those who offered their

---

3 Middlebrook 1995, p. 86, p. 358, n. 48; Crider 1996, pp. 318–25.
4 Ibid.
5 Enrique Mayorga and Enrique Sánchez to Vicente Lombardo Toledano, Culiacán, 1 January 1936, FHLT, file 274. PNR, National Revolutionary Party, founded in 1929, was the precursor of the Institutional Revolutionary Party (PRI), established in 1946.

talent to work with Lombardo Toledano, considered to possess 'sturdy qualities of a leader, advisor and guide' of the workers' cause. Among them were the director of the Talleres Gráficos de la Nación print shop and a group of journalists who expressed their interest in helping Lombardo produce a workers' newspaper.[6]

Organisational assistance was provided also by Witold Antonovich Lovsky. Known by his comrades as Godoy, Ambrosio, Raúl, Enrique, and in Mexico as Juan, he worked behind the scenes. A Jewish Bolshevik of Polish origin, Lovsky devoted his life to international trade union work ever since he immigrated to the Soviet Union in 1925. After a stay in Peru and Cuba between 1930 and 1934, he arrived in Mexico when government repression on the Caribbean island made his work untenable. Lovsky represented the moribund Latin American Trade Union Confederation (CSLA), founded in 1929 in Montevideo by the Red International of Labour Unions. The CSLA was created when, from Moscow, the world was viewed through the prism of the revolution and the leader of the Red International of Labour Unions, Alexandr Lozovsky, 'discovered' Latin America, as he once said. The CSLA never amounted to much. It suffered from organisational shortcomings and its activities seemed to centre in the countries of South America, with the exception of Cuba.[7]

Lovsky was under the illusion that the trade union activity in Mexico would inject life into his inactive organisation and strengthen the participation of the communists in the labour movement. He arrived in Mexico in early 1936, after spending a few days in Santiago de Chile, sowing the seed of the Latin American Workers Confederation, which was also Lombardo Toledano's hemispheric project. The same age as the Mexican, Lovsky believed himself to be endowed with the necessary experience to serve as an advisor to Lombardo in preparing the trade union congress while winning positions for the Mexican Communist Party. What was most important for Lovsky was to prepare the groundwork for the continental effort and the Mexican confederation was the indispensable first step. The impressions that he left, written in faulty Spanish, are revealing in terms of a description of the environment, the individuals and the role that Lombardo played and that he wanted him to play in the two confederations.

'LT has enormous prestige in the country', and after Cárdenas was the most popular person. But there was no love lost between the labour leaders. Among

---

6 Gustavo Ortiz Hernán to VLT, Mexico City, 23 January 1936, ibid.
7 Julio Godio 1983, pp. 171–91; Witold Antonovich Lovsky, probably Mendel Nusenovich Mijrovsky (1894–1938); Jeifets, Jeifets and Huber 2004, p. 184; Juan Alberto, 5 February 1933, RGASPI, f. 495, file 79, file 191; Tosstorff 2003, pp. 1–41.

the unions of the capital city, one of the leaders, Fernando Amilpa, 'is engaged in efforts to discredit LT'. Amilpa played dirty, defaming Lombardo for receiving money from Moscow while disqualifying him as a labour leader. Lovsky thought that he could counter these manoeuvres and brought together the top leadership of the Communist Party with Lombardo to discuss strategies such as appointing communists to the national council of the future organisation. 'There are difficulties here that are understandable',[8] referring to the enmity of the 'five little wolves' toward the communists. But there was more: 'I, who have some experience of what a congress with thousands of delegates is, fear what will happen here with this disorganisation'. Lovsky tried to help but had to act with discretion. 'Now imagine if it was discovered that someone from the CSLA was helping or intervening in this work', he wrote to a comrade in Buenos Aires, a few days before the CTM's founding congress took place.[9]

2   The First Pillar

Lombardo Toledano wanted to arrive at the founding congress of the CTM with the General Confederation of Workers and Peasants of Mexico, which he founded in 1933, in one piece and with a single idea on the way forward. Another of his goals was to prevent the new organisation from being identified with leaders hailing from the Mexican Communist Party (PCM), but without, at the same time, getting on their bad side or satisfying his anti-communist allies. He had to instil faith in the collective future and make sure that he be recognised as the indispensable leader.[10]

But in 1936, the CGOCM congress, which preceded the great event, began in disarray with a clamour of dissident voices and challenges that Lombardo was unable to lead toward a single expression and to avoid its spilling over into the new one. Delegates from different parts of the country shouted over each other to disqualify the presence of others who back home might have stepped on their toes on one or another occasion. Some called for the expropriation of agricultural estates and others created a hubbub in the congress hall, demanding a general strike. Throughout, the names of Morones and Gasca were cited as examples of the rejected past. When Lombardo Toledano took the floor, he

---

8   Lovsky, alias Godoy, to the Latin American Trade Union Confederation, Mexico City, 10 February 1936, RGASPI, f. 495, reg. 10, file 327; Campa 1985, p. 104.
9   Ibid.
10 VLT, 'Intervención en la segunda sesión del segundo congreso de la CGOCM', Mexico City, 18 February 1936, in *Obra*, III/4, 1936, p. 56; González y González 1981, pp. 66–8.

was greeted with applause as the unquestioned arbiter. On 20 February, he dissolved the organisation that he had created three years earlier in order to make way for the new labour confederation.[11]

The assembly continued with all the union currents present, minus the CROM and the CGT, about 1,500 trade unionists, who in June 1935 had closed ranks in support of General Cárdenas on the occasion of former president Calles's criticism. Present were trade unionists from large and small industries, artisans and campesinos, among them communists, syndicalists, reformists and former anarchists, representing close to half a million workers.[12]

'Comrades, today is the thirteenth anniversary of the assassination of our martyr Francisco I. Madero, so I propose a minute of silence in his memory', suggested one delegate. But he was cut short by railroad worker Juan Gutiérrez, who was chairing the session, and who argued that 'We are very respectful of the memory of Señor Madero, but the congress has many issues to deal with'. One delegate spoke for the Atlixco workers, who continued to be killed 'by the villains of the CROM', and raised the question, 'where is the boldness, where is the strength of our organisation, if we see, compañeros, that a small Moronista group appears to be winning in that region due to the single sin of our organisation of not being in collusion with Luis N. Morones ... Where is the power of our organisation?'[13]

The workers of Monterrey area companies called for increased wages; others protested the continued presence of white or company unions, clamoured for financial solidarity with striking workers and those unfairly fired, for the payment of back wages lost during strikes and against child labour. Discussion of the bylaws was postponed again and again because there were simply too many issues to be aired, too many heartaches to be shared.[14] A general strike was the collective demand of the congress delegates.

The final session of the congress was held on 24 February. The delegates had to return to their states as their funds had depleted and they had pending complaints to air. It was necessary to select the national committee and discuss the bylaws. These were major tasks, as were viewed at the time. Still to be debated was the agrarian question, which the shouting and whistles, mixed with complaints of mistreatment of workers and low wages, prevented.[15]

---

11   VLT, 'Congreso de la CGOCM', 17 February 1936 session; Stenographic version of the 20 February 1936 session, AGN, RLC, vol. 481, file 437/62.
12   Middlebrook 1995, pp. 90–1.
13   Stenographic version of the 21 February session, AGN, RLC, vol. 481, file 437/62.
14   Stenographic version of the 21 February 1936 session, ibid.
15   Stenographic version of the 24 February 1936 session, ibid.

The respected electrical workers' leader Francisco Breña Alvírez wanted to discuss the merits of whether to allow the re-election of capable and honest leaders, but his words were drowned in shouts of 'no, no, no'. That was when Lombardo took the floor. 'You have misunderstood. (Voices of no, no). You do not know what I'm going to say (the disorder grows)'. The speaker wanted to calm tempers and convince the delegates that the bylaws prevented leaders' re-election, that its spirit was anti-re-election. But the shouting increased because nowhere did the bylaws conclusively indicated that the re-election of the national committee and union leaders was prohibited. Perhaps in order to find a way out of the impasse, Lombardo declared, non-committally, 'that the principle of absolute non-re-election be established (applause)', a stance that was undercut when he also declared that 'it is not possible to establish unlimitedly the principle of no re-election, because this would go against the autonomy of the confederated organisations'. This autonomy did not exist, nor was it Lombardo's goal to put it into effect.[16]

The disorder and litany of complaints continued. The oil workers kept insisting on the call for a general strike, the declaration of which, they argued, could not be left in the hands of seven members of the national executive committee, but Lombardo silenced their proposals: 'The decision should be the responsibility of the organisation as a whole, but through representative bodies'. There was the heart of the matter as was seen when the time came to elect the national committee.

At one o'clock in the afternoon on 24 February 1936, with everyone on their feet, the founding of the new labour confederation was declared. Only then the national council was elected, with which the founding of the CTM passed into the history of anti-democratic ignominy. That Lombardo Toledano was to be elected general secretary was agreed on. The railroad worker Juan Gutiérrez was elected by majority vote to the Labour and Conflicts Commission and Pedro Morales, proposed by the communists, as head or secretary of the Campesino Action commission. Fidel Velázquez, Gustavo Ortiz Hernán, Miguel Ángel Velasco and Breña Alvírez were appointed to the Organisation and Propaganda Commission. Nobody asked the leader of the electrical workers what his opinion was, but Breña Alvírez appeared as the candidate to head two commissions. He declined both positions, declaring that 'as a representative of the Mexican Electrical Workers Union I wish to inform you that our organisation has absolutely no particular interest in having one of its members be part of the leadership of the confederation'.

---

16   Ibid.

What was important was honesty and ability. While two declined their candidacies, Velázquez from the former Lombardo-led confederation and communist militant Miguel Ángel Velasco accepted the position for which they were nominated. In the confusion over the disagreements that were aired, the chairman asked Breña Alvírez who his candidate for the post was, and he answered that it was compañero Velasco, which sparked shouts and caused disorder in the hall. Fernando Amilpa supported Velázquez. Comrade Pardo, from the rail workers union, was in favour of Velasco, since the general secretary spot was to go to someone from Lombardo's now disbanded organisation. Among the disorder and applause, the miners, Alfredo Navarrete from the National Chamber of Labour, the oil and tram workers and teachers all voted for Velasco. Amid shouting and cheers, Hernán Ortiz from the graphic arts union, the one who had declined the commission secretary slot, voted for Velasco. Lombardista stalwart Jiménez Acevedo from the sugar workers union called for order in the house, since 'there are elements here who are interested in coming to create disorder in this congress and we should not give weapons to the bourgeoisie'. The reference may have been to the communists and those who deviated from the implicit understanding that Lombardo's allies would dominate the CTM national committee.

The chairman of the session concluded that most of the votes were for Velasco. Juan Téllez from the now dissolved Lombardista confederation asked in vain that the vote be respected. With chest beating, Poblano worker Blas Chumacero scuttled the vote, accusing the National Committee for Proletarian Defense and Breña Alvírez, without explicitly mentioning his name, of erecting themselves as 'the great electors'. The accusation was painful, because the selfless performance of the electrical workers' leader was in plain sight. At that moment, Valentín Campa on behalf of the communist United Trade Union Confederation of Mexico, which with the birth of the Mexican Workers Confederation (CTM), ceased to exist, withdrew Velasco's candidacy with Breña Alvírez protesting that it was not his place to do so.[17] Then followed another vote and 'amid the disorder' 'compañero Valentín Campa's move' was approved. Velasco was named secretary of the Education Commission and Velázquez put in charge of Organisation and Propaganda, which had a decisive influence on the confederation.[18] In fact, with the proposal to withdraw Velasco's candidacy for the commission secretary spot that Velázquez aspired to occupy, Campa helped tip the balance in favour of Lombardo's followers.

---

17   Ibid, and León and Marván 1985, pp. 178–80.
18   Campa 1985, p. 119.

Villaseñor, Lombardo's travel companion to the world of the future, recalled:

> Despite finding myself upset by Lombardo's attitude in the founding assembly of the CTM, which made Fidel Velázquez's placement in the Organisation Commission possible, I continued to have faith in him and accepted his explanation that for tactical reasons he proceeded as he did, but that his aim, imitating Lenin, was to take one step backward, in order to then take two steps forward. Fidel Velázquez and company would have to be eliminated from the CTM at an opportune moment.[19]

Working-class unity was Lombardo Toledano's watchword to create an organisation that would be a bulwark against the opposition to the creation of trade unions, a strategic weapon to influence the government and employers; to project labour's strength, be recognised in the United States by the American Federation of Labor and the Congress of Industrial Organizations and in Europe by the International Federation of Trade Unions and the International Labour Organization. The times called for being vigilant. The Americas were still safe from anti-communist and anti-Soviet fascism, but Lombardo Toledano arrogated for himself the monumental task of preventing its expansion across the hemisphere. The new general secretary of the CTM now had a powerful instrument to achieve his purpose. Always the optimist, Lombardo Toledano closed the congress with incendiary speeches and incantations to unity, cleansing, loyalty and with his fist raised he intoned the workers' hymn: 'Arise ye prisoners of starvation, arise ye wretched of the Earth / For justice thunders condemnation / a better world's in birth!'[20]

3 Into Action

Lovsky was pleased, because from Moscow Alexander Lozovsky sent him and the communists a congratulatory message on the founding of the CTM, but he was also concerned because the labour confederation seemed to face the danger of disintegration. The campaign against the CTM was fierce and well-funded, in addition to problems resulting from its original dispersion and divisions. He wrote: 'LT's people went to the Unification like a forced marriage. There is no enthusiasm to put the new labour confederation into action'. The

---

19   Villaseñor 1976, vol. 1, p. 379.
20   Stenographic version of the 24 February 1936 session, AGN, RLC, vol. 481, file 437/62.

anti-communists distrusted the communists and the insolence of party general secretary Hernán Laborde did not help dispel the uneasiness. Laborde mocked Lombardo in the party newspaper and criticised the weaknesses of the CTM with which the communists claimed to collaborate. Lovsky anticipated trouble.[21]

At the same time, not all the organisations that joined the CTM dissolved as had been projected. In the capital, the 'five little wolves' were unwilling to dissolve their federation so as not to lose power, be a minority and be outvoted in the united confederation. The Bolshevik was impressed by President Cárdenas's tolerance toward the spectrum of ideas that were expressed in the street.[22]

The virulence of the attacks against Lombardo was one way to measure the hatred that the new organisation sparked in political and business circles. Physical attacks occurred as well. Despite being protected by the workers' defence guard, Lombardo's house was attacked by the paramilitary group Golden Shirts, placing a powerful bomb inside the garden. When it exploded, the bomb did considerable damage to the house. 'In LT's house was his wife, his mother and his three young daughters. The purpose was to kill everyone there'.[23]

But Lombardo did not pay much attention to this mayhem and looked at his adversaries from top to bottom. He did not resolve the complex situation in the labour movement as Lovsky thought he should, involving the party in the rank-and-file organisation and in creating 'left wing currents in the unions (I repeat, where there is a need)'.[24] The CTM had the majority of the workers, 70% nationwide, but the alliances of the union leaders with strong men in the states, 'each of whom pull another local clique to their union' prevented the organisation's unification.[25]

The other difficulty in achieving the much desired unity was the number of existing unions: if there were two or more shifts in a factory, each shift had a union; each bus line had one and each of these unions had the 'vested interests of an army of parasites, small-time lawyers, litigants, superficial legal consultants, who in the form of advisors earn their living from this separation of functions and each has its clique within the union. The Conciliation and Arbitration Boards were like anthills full of these "advisers"'.[26]

---

21 Lovsky to Tomba, Mexico City, 27 March 1936, RGASPI, f. 495, register 17, file 3.
22 Lovsky to Tomba, Mexico City, 15 March 1936, RGASPI, f. 495, register 17, file 3.
23 Ibid.
24 Lovsky, alias Godoy, to Tomba, Mexico City, 17 April 1936, RGASPI, f. 495, register 17, file 3.
25 Lovsky, alias Godoy, to the Latin American Trade Union Confederation, Mexico City, 10 April 1936, RGASPI, f. 495, register 108, file 186.
26 Ibid.

The labour law was a maze that unions, their leaders and the workers were unfamiliar with and specialists emerged to deal with the conflicts before the boards, becoming an additional obstacle for the trade unions to join together in a single confederation.[27]

The CTM was in a poor position to face this campaign, 'also due to the fact that its Executive Committee functions like a poorly oiled machine'. The organisation did not have the capacity to collect dues that the unions should pay to sustain it or 'at least maintain a newsletter'. Lombardo, who was an 'excellent speaker, brilliant journalist, a man of broad culture, however, is not a crude trade unionist who can make an organisation that is so large and with this character function properly. He remains at the head of the Workers' University, works with many cultural organisations, runs some magazines, etc., etc'.[28]

The mistrust between the leaders did not help. Lovsky wanted the communists to have a greater influence in the confederation, but 'the spectre of communism' prevented them 'from being open at work'.[29]

In May, the railroad workers strike tested the strength of the CTM and its relationship with the government. Organised in the Railroad Workers Union of the Republic since 1933, the members feared the loss of their jobs in a company that complained about having too many employees on their payroll. The communists dominated the union. The railroad workers demanded higher wages for unskilled workers, a paid day of rest, which the company was willing to grant to the workers but not to employees, claiming that the latter received monthly salaries with such payment included. The Conciliation and Arbitration Board declared the strike illegal, an attack by the government on labour legislation, wrote Lombardo. However, like Lovsky, he feared that a strike at any cost could put the president in a difficult situation, 'could push him to the right' if he did not see that he was backed against 'the tremendous imperialist pressure and right-wing sectors within the government'. However, on 18 May 'with the whistles of the locomotives blowing, the railroad workers abandoned their trains and offices'.[30]

About 10,000 workers took to the streets, calling on the CTM to declare a general strike in solidarity with the railroad workers. Communist activist Miguel Ángel Velasco as well as Lombardo had differences with the strikers. Velasco

---

27 Ibid.
28 Ibid.
29 Lovsky, alias Henri, probably to the CSLA, Mexico City, 5 May 1936, RGASPI, fond 495, register 10, file 357.
30 VLT, 'La huelga de los ferrocarrileros fue sofocada', *Futuro*, June 1936, in *Obra*, III/4, pp. 233–7; Campa 1985, pp. 121–4; León and Marván 1985, pp. 201–9; Knight 1992, p. 277.

defended President Cárdenas and even though he condemned the negative Conciliation and Arbitration Board ruling, 'all hell broke loose in the assembly'. The workers told him 'to shut up', yelled 'traitor' and 'sell out' and did not let him finish his intervention. The demonstrators felt betrayed by the CTM, by Cárdenas and by the fact that a communist member of the CTM took the side of the president, who had 'just broken the most important strike'.

Nevertheless, chronicled Lovsky, the strike committee agreed to return to work and prepare a new strategy. 'The President's prestige went to hell. A series of railroad worker organisations demanded Miguel's expulsion from the CTM', slandered Lombardo, were embittered and disillusioned. The president, on his part, believed that the CTM and the workers who had received his support, by going out on strike gave him a vote of no-confidence 'and this is being exploited by his enemies'. General Cárdenas did not remove the chairman of the conciliation board, who had declared the strike illegal, as the workers demanded. The dilemma for the party and Lombardo, as Lovsky saw it, was how to help to support Cárdenas's progressive government at the same time as defending the workers' prerogatives.[31]

The government agreed to increase wages and to pay a day of rest, but tempers did not subside. Both Lombardo as well as the party rerouted the strikers' anger toward the Conciliation and Arbitration Board. Its ruling declaring the strike illegal was an affront to the CTM and the president. To get out of the complicated situation, they proposed the establishment of a commission of experts to study the company's finances that would demonstrate that it could accede to the workers' demands without suffering economic harm, suggest a plan to improve its services, renew its equipment, cut parasitic expenditures such as the exorbitant salaries of 62 assistant administrators, eliminate payments to the different boards and improve freight policies.[32]

The outcome was a victory for Lombardo and the party, which together convinced the strikers that it was necessary to protect the president. The historical moment characterised by the rise of fascism in Europe and the hydra of right in Mexico demanded an offensive, but with the sensitivity not to strain the tolerance of the progressive president and the good neighbour policy with the United States. The general strike did not take place and the brief work stoppage did not affect the relations between the CTM and General Cárdenas.

---

31   Lovsky, alias Henry, to Tomba, Mexico City, 26 May 1936, RGASPI, fond 495, register 17, file 3.
32   Lovsky to Tombola, Mexico City, 13 May and 1 June 1936, RGASPI, f. 495, register 17, file 3.

4   The Schism

The fourth meeting of the CTM council was scheduled for April 1937. Hernán Laborde suspected that the Cetemistas organised the meeting to coincide with the communists' assembly and thereby prevent its leaders from attending the CTM gathering. But they could not miss a meeting after the communists were accused 'of wanting to take over leadership positions in the unions'. Before the council was to be held, Lombardo wrote Alexandr Lozovsky in Moscow to bring him up to date:

> I consider it to be important, not only for the current circumstances but also for the future evolution of the proletariat in Mexico and Latin America, to write you this long letter to provide information and opinions regarding the difficulties faced by the CTM, since above all, I want my personal present and future responsibility to be safeguarded from opinions arising from ignorance of the facts. I also wanted to write this document to see if it is possible that the intervention of some comrades with international prestige, such as yourself, can contribute to eliminating some of these obstacles for the sake of the interests of the Mexican workers' movement and the unity of the proletariat of the Americas.[33]

Lombardo's indignation stemmed from his conviction that the communists did not organise but rather co-opted the unions, because they 'did not represent any force of importance in the labour movement'.

> The compañeros of the Communist Party had centred their efforts on controlling posts in the leadership of the unions affiliated to the CTM. This would be legitimate and could not be subject to criticism by anyone, if it were only to strengthen the CTM and contribute to the realisation of its programme. But both the work of the communist cells that exist within the ranks of the CTM unions as well as the work of the communists who are in the leadership of the unions, consists of precipitously, publicly and noisily increasing the contingents of their party. There is almost no union membership assembly in which cards are not distributed to enrol new members in the Communist Party, or a public meeting of CTM unions in which a profession of communist faith is not made by elements of

---

33   VLT to Aleksandr Lozovsky, Mexico City, 15 April 1937, RGASPI, f. 534, register 7, file 399.

the Party holding positions in the leadership of the unions, touting these positions and exaggerating the virtues of the Party to the point of saying, for example, that thanks to the Party, the CTM exists, that thanks to the Party, General Cárdenas's government is a progressive government, etc.[34]

This was the last straw, from which followed his accusations that when the communists were not able to get themselves placed at the head of the unions, they recommended that the unions leave the CTM. The extensive letter, which dealt with details that Lozovsky had no way of understanding, perhaps sought also to neutralise or reverse the effect of the reports that the Communist Party sent to Moscow, complaining of Lombardo Toledano's reformism, the covering-up of people worse than he and of his wanting to submit the communists to his line.

In addition, Lombardo was not moved by base or personal interests, nor by the ambition 'to be the head of the labour movement in Mexico', he feigned, 'but if the Communists continued their attacks', he was willing to leave his leadership post, making the communists responsible for the division of the proletariat in Mexico that would impact the unity of the workers' movement in Latin America.[35] As a testament to his loyalty, he reminded the Soviet official that when he returned from the Soviet Union,

> I considered it my duty not to make any comments on the negative aspects of the Soviet system, just as I've never talked about the failures of the Mexican Revolution outside my country, because the proletariat must have faith in its cause and workers' leaders should never give the bourgeoisie a pretext to exploit our own confessions about errors and internal defects of the revolutionary movement, thus sowing confusion among the workers themselves, who in their large majority still remain in ignorance.[36]

Lombardo sent the letter to Moscow, perhaps through Lovsky, but he was not sure how to receive the response from New York where the Communist International should have sent their answer. So that the letter would not fall into the wrong hands, he gave the Communist Party of the United States the address of Concepción Otero, his sister-in-law, in the Colonia del Valle neighbourhood in

---

34 Ibid.
35 Ibid.
36 Ibid.

Mexico City, with instructions to insert the letter in an envelope addressed to her, and another envelope addressed to Rosa María, his wife. It was important that the letters reach their destinations before the opening of the CTM National Council meeting on 27 April 1937.[37]

The communists came to the council meeting optimistic of winning the majority and taking control of the direction of the CTM unhindered. But, reported the envoy of Earl Browder, general secretary of the Communist Party of the United States, Lombardo Toledano won each and every one of the motions he presented. His criticism that the communists were bad trade unionists, because their loyalty was divided between their party and the CTM, led to the resignation of veteran communist Miguel Ángel Velasco, campesino leader Pedro Morales and railroad worker Juan Gutiérrez. To add insult to injury, after having resigned, the CTM expelled them for being undisciplined. In their places, three of Lombardo's followers entered the executive committee.[38]

The solution to the schism in the CTM that the charges against and resignation of the communists provoked had several venues: Moscow, New York and Mexico. For being closer to where the events occurred, it is most likely that Lozovsky gave Earl Browder the responsibility to attend to the quarrel between the CTM and the communists.

Browder summoned Laborde to New York to tell him what he had to do: 'Propose immediate public statement three commission secretaries end all controversy', the admonished Laborde telegraphed his comrades in Mexico, 'ratifying willingness seek arrangement re-establish unity. Strongly suppress all written or verbal attack on our part'.[39] In the controversy, Browder supported Lombardo and bestowed on the CTM the role of leading the battered unity to fight '[the] enemies and [the] reactionaries'.[40] The enemies were real – the looming war, Morones, Hitler, national and international reaction and the rise of violent anti-Cardenista groups – but the underlying problem was sidestepped, namely the lack of union democracy. Browder demanded that the communists admit their errors and fully return to the fold, which included tolerance for the mores of the 'five little wolves' that Fidel Velázquez described graphically in an interview: 'At first, we used violence to control unions and workers, but later this was

---

37   VLT to Albert Moreaux, Mexico City, 20 April 1937, FHLT, file 295.
38   'The split in the Mexican labour movement' by S., no location indicated, 4 May 1937, Earl Browder papers, Syracuse University Library, box 11. They were Julio Batres, David Vilchis and Mariano Padilla.
39   Laborde to Rafael Carrillo, telegram, New York, 30 May 1937, FHLT, file 296.
40   Earl Browder to VLT, New York, telegram, 31 May 1937, FHLT, file 296.

no longer the case because, to begin with, the labour movement had matured and it was not necessary to employ violence to impose our will'.⁴¹

Browder forced the communists to atone for their sins which he defined as 'a certain confusion that existed concerning the characteristics and problems of the current stage of the national movement' and 'the lack of clarity on the role played by both the PNR as well as the CTM'. He forced them to accept the CTM leaders, including the right-wingers, 'with whom we must necessarily work because they are very important forces for the development of the national liberation movement'.⁴²

Laborde returned from New York repentant:

> The truth be told, comrades, is that with a series of more or less serious errors, we contributed in some way, perhaps in large part, to creating the situation that led to the division of the CTM. We have been intolerant, thoughtless, we have failed to understand the reasons why other leaders of the Mexican Workers Confederation who did not understand our ideology, acted contrary to what we thought was necessary in the CTM leadership. We wanted to move too quickly and we have not understood that the unity of the CTM in itself has a revolutionary value.⁴³

In addition to mea culpas and the willingness to sacrifice 'up to the last drop of our blood (Applause)', Laborde was full of platitudes about unity and optimism and on the popular forces that could influence the coming presidential elections. 'When the time comes, it will be the people itself who will designate this or that political *cuadillo*; it will be the people who will say what the programme of the new government should be, who will replace General Cárdenas as President of the Republic', and he ended with the call: 'For self-criticism, to victory', subjecting the party or rather its central committee, to the National Revolutionary Party, the CTM and its top leadership.⁴⁴

The key point, however, was the lack of democracy in the confederation. Laborde did not mention this, because it would involve deepening the divide

---

41   Krauze 2007, p. 170.
42   Earl Browder, 'Informe sobre el Partido Comunista de México al Sub-Comité del Partido Comunista de Estados Unidos', no location indicated, 5 May 1937, RGASPI, f. 495, register 108, file 197.
43   Hernán Laborde, 'Discurso pronunciado en el Teatro Hidalgo', Mexico City, 29 June 1937, FHLT, file 297.
44   Ibid.

between the communists and the Cetemistas. Instead, he advocated unity at all costs with the CTM, which amounted to putting 'an end to all public controversy about the Confederation's affairs ... no more attacks, no more public controversy about the causes of the division ... we will submit unconditionally to the discipline of the CTM under its national committee (Applause)', even though there might have been violations of bylaws and union democracy. The outcome of the Comintern reprimand was surrender. In Laborde's own words, 'we surrender to fraternal comrades' so as not to surrender to fascism.[45] In fact, the surrender was to Lombardo Toledano and to the leadership of the CTM, in the process strengthening the Cardenista coalition.

Neither the rank-and-file communists nor the unions suspected the role that Lombardo Toledano, with the complicity of Browder and the Communist International, played in coercing the PCM leaders to return to the fold of the CTM and assume the role of stooges of its leadership. The result was a smokescreen covering the vices that incubated in the CTM. These included in addition to the violation of its bylaws, eliminating the possibility of union democracy, the dictatorial methods of its leadership, the monopoly in union posts and commission secretaries by a closed group, the subordination of the labour unions to officials and politicians and a halt to workers' struggles.[46] All of this supposedly for the sake of the great fights against fascism, against the coming war and ultimately for socialism. Lombardo Toledano and the communists assumed as their own the international policy of the Soviet Union, which in the mid-1930s was dominated by the fear of fascism, in power in Germany, Italy and conquering Spain, as a prelude to a world war. National political and social questions were intertwined with world affairs. Mexico, a semi-colonial country dominated by imperialism, had an assigned role in world events.

5   Disunity

In 1938 the world was shaken by the defeats inflicted on the Spanish Republic by Francisco Franco and his fascist falangistas and by the dark clouds threatening democracy in Europe, when Adolf Hitler annexed Austria to Germany and when France and Britain abdicated to the Führer's appetite to take control of Czechoslovakia. In Mexico the conflict between the oil workers' union and

---

45   Ibid.
46   Vittorio Codovilla, alias Pérez, 'Informe del Pleno del CC del Partido Comunista de Méjico', no location indicated, 1 August 1937, RGASPI, f. 495, register 108, file 194; Knight 1992, p. 277.

the companies increased in intensity at the beginning of the year and ended in the bold expropriation of the oil fields from foreign hands. Mexico gained sovereignty and lost markets.

The PNR grew in line with the benefits that the population received with government reforms and it brought its ideology into line with the innovative spirit of the revolution. When the president took the decision in 1938 to transform the PNR, the party founded by former president Calles in 1929, into the Party of the Mexican Revolution, Lombardo supported the move. By adapting to the circumstances without renouncing his essential objectives, the general secretary of the CTM wanted the party of the state to become a popular class-based party and at the same time an effective electoral instrument.[47] The presidential elections were in sight, but with just two years of existence, and weakened by the loss of major unions in protest against the elementary breach of the bylaws, the CTM lacked the necessary strength to be influential, especially in the provinces.

Since January 1938, the top echelons of the CTM were seeking to remedy the confederation's organisational weaknesses in the lead up to its second congress. On 7 January, the national committee met in secret to deal with a delicate matter. At the founding congress in February 1936, Lombardo Toledano had finished his speech with a catchphrase that won a thunderous ovation. He declared 'that in no case can members occupying posts or functioning in these positions be re-elected'. In this session, whose minutes were handwritten by the general secretary, several of those present were in favour of modifying the bylaws 'just this once'. They argued that the CTM was still weak and that 'only Lombardo Toledano can sort out these problems because he has support among the various sectors'. The country's situation was serious and the CTM was not fully consolidated. The continuity of the CTM national committee was necessary for three additional years, which corresponded to the time in office of a national politician. Everyone voted in favour.[48]

To select delegates to the congress that would defend this position, the CTM top leadership took to the states. In Durango the national committee called a convention to bring together several unions under its mantle.[49] Lombardo could not go and sent Velázquez, Secretary of Organisation and Propaganda and others from the top echelon, to take charge of the task. In attendance were

---

47 Hernández 1979, pp. 181–4.
48 VLT, 'Renovación del comité nacional, sesión secreta', no location indicated, 7 January 1938, FHLT, file 306.
49 Everardo Gamiz, Director of Education of Durango to Luis Rodríguez, Durango, 26 March 1936, AGN, RLC, vol. 437, file 62.

Tomás Palomino Rojas, federal congressional deputy for the state, and Governor Enrique Calderón, who the CTM had catapulted to the post in 1936 with the support of the worker and campesino organisations.

This time the representatives from the capital broke ranks with the Durango leaders for positions in the organisation to be established. 'When several delegates and some members of the organisation from Mexico City whipped out their pistols', the meeting was suspended until the next day. It was said that the chaos ensued because Governor Calderón and congressional deputy Palomino wanted to control the convention.[50] We do not know the outcome of this political squabble, which underscored the trend of the CTM leadership from Mexico City to impose its will over that of the Cetemistas in the states. Elsewhere it happened that Lombardo appointed a CTM delegate without him being duly elected. He told his friend Adolfo Orive Alba that 'I could arrange for you to be named delegate from any other region of the Republic' if the state CTM in Northern Baja California, where Orive resided, did not select him as a delegate from one of its districts.[51]

The national congress was a success. It helped that President Cárdenas gave a speech in support of the workers and made them feel part of his larger project, expecting from them 'higher ethical values that promote respect for human life', so that the government could fulfil the monumental tasks it had charted amid powerful resistance and deadly conflicts, such as the German bombardments in Spain and the nationalists' struggle in China.[52]

Attentive to the President's message, Lombardo Toledano knew that the fate of the confederation went hand in hand with the government's popularity. He was also aware that the strength of the CTM flowed not only from the grassroots, but depended on the power of the state, even more so in those regions where local forces were opposing the labour confederation and the government. The radicalisation of the landowners following the agrarian reform and land expropriation – which the state-supported National Peasant Confederation created in August 1938 – failed to neutralise, the boycott waged by the oil companies after the industry expropriation in March, the breaking of diplomatic relations with Great Britain, opposition to the government's socialist education policies, the spectre of Callismo still lurking in the new 'party of the state', the failed rebellion of Saturnino Cedillo against the government in San Luis Potosí, the

---

50   E.W. Eaton to the State Department, Durango, 14 January 1938, NARA, RG 59, file 81.504/1702.
51   Dimas Gastón to VLT, Mexico City, 9 December 1937, FHLT, file 303; VLT to Adolfo Orive Alba, Mexico City, 14 December 1937, FHLT, file 303.
52   LC, speech delivered on 24 February 1938, in Cárdenas 1978, vol. 1, pp. 277–81.

emergence of hostile organisations of the middle classes,[53] all these developments taken as a whole forced Lombardo to recognise the untimeliness of the offensive that he had adopted at the beginning of the presidential administration.[54] Given the unexpected constellation of the different political forces and their trajectories, he had to defend the government at all costs and instead of using the labour confederation to challenge the government, he had to put it at the service of the beleaguered state.

The regional states remained the bulwark of the intricate networks of anti-CTM and anti-Cardenista interests and chiefdoms. Different factions competed for posts in municipalities, some close to a governor and others to the CTM, and bickering was poisoning the atmosphere. It was probably at Lombardo's request that Interior Minister Ignacio García Téllez went to Durango in October 1938 to intervene in the conflict between the state government and the CTM after workers accused Governor Calderón of forcing employers to fire them from their jobs. Lombardo, who wanted to control the workers of Durango and take control of the municipalities to use in his supposed presidential campaign, was a liar, the governor shot back. García Téllez appealed to the parties involved, since the breakup of the old alliance would negatively affect the federal government, and he called on the unions who had withdrawn from the CTM to return to the confederation.[55]

Another difficult case was Sonora, governed by Román Yocupicio. A native of the region and knowledgeable of its mores, a member of the state's indigenous communities and veteran of the revolution, wounded in combat and in command of troops, Yocupicio refused to recognise any outsiders. He prevented the CTM from becoming a weapon to be used against him, as a defensive weapon of the federal government and an instrument of electoral support for Cardenista candidates, as a tool to unify rural workers in the southern part of the state to push for land distribution in the Yaqui and Mayo valleys and the collective system of working the land. The governor withdrew state schools from the jurisdiction of the Education Ministry, dismissed radical teachers and created a local union. In addition, he drove the mayors who cooperated with the ministry and with the CTM from office. Given the labour authorities' collu-

---

53 Middlebrook 1995, p. 91; Pérez Montfort 1988, pp. 279–310.
54 González 1981, pp. 216–18.
55 Enrique Calderón to LC, Durango, 1 August 1938; VLT to LC, Mexico City, 6 August 1938, AGN, RLC, vol. 404/4, file 27; Agustín López, general secretary of the Durango Workers Federation to LC, Durango, 11 October 1938; Ignacio García Téllez to LC, Durango, 11 October and 13 October 1938; Godofredo Beltrán to LC, Durango, 5 November 1938; Rodolfo Piña Soria to LC, Mexico City, 25 January 1939, ibid.

sion with the factory owners and the existence of white unions it was difficult to maintain the collective bargaining agreements. Yocupicio used the Department of Labour and the Conciliation and Arbitration Board to divide the CTM unions, and provided money, gifts and job contracts to attract workers to his Sonora Workers Confederation. Opposed to collective farming of the land in ejidos, he confronted the ejidatarios in municipal elections; and there were municipalities in which the authority was exercised by the landowners and clergy. However, following the expropriation of the oil industry and the mounting opposition to his government, the president adopted a conciliatory attitude toward the Sonora state authorities, which helped alleviate the disputes between local and national labour unions and campesino organisations.[56]

Oaxaca was the other state where Lombardo and the CTM had few successes, as the organisation became a safe haven for politicians who had lost in local races to *caciques* and to politicians linked to the governments of the centre of the country and the oligarchies in the state. The Oaxaca CTM was a motley conglomeration of teachers, landowners and radicalised segments of the population who did not find a place in other political groupings. The split between communists and non-communists occurred locally, which a group of workers and peasants opposed to the communists took advantage of so that Lombardo Toledano would recognise them as the sole and legitimate Oaxaca CTM. The fragmentation and size of the state, the variety of crops and systems of production, and the working class being a minority in a sea of campesino populations of multiple ethnic identities, prevented Lombardo and the CTM from being attractive on a local level no matter how much they presented themselves as the indisputable defenders of the rights and obligations of the working class.[57]

Chiapas was divided between the Cardenistas and their implacable enemies. The unions were in their initial stage of development and every gesture of help was welcomed by what was one of the country's poorest populations. The state government had been headed by Cardenista leader Efraín Gutiérrez since 1936. It was true that he enjoyed the support of agricultural workers, some organised in unions led by communists and others from the union of indigenous work-

---

56 Jacinto López to VLT, Hermosillo, Sonora, 4 December 1937, FHLT, file 303; Bantjes 1998, p. 73, pp. 99–101, pp. 205–7; Vaughan 1997, p. 13, pp. 62–71; Aldama Bay, p. 302; pp. 350–62; Grijalba Dávila 2012, pp. 69–70, quote on p. 73; Ricardo Salazar to Guillermo Ibarra, Hermosillo, Sonora, 25 September 1937, FHLT, file 299; Gral. Felipe Dusart Quintana to Gral. LC, Hermosillo, Sonora, 5 October 1937; Reyes J. Vildósola to the Federal Attorney General, Hermosillo, Sonora, 8 October 1937, FHLT, file 299; VLT to LC, Mexico City, 14 October 1937 and VLT to LC, Mexico City, 2, 4, 6 and 13 December 1937, AGN, RLC, vol. 543.1, file 8.

57 Smith 2009, pp. 198–201; VLT to LC, Mexico City, 22 March 1937, AGN, RLC, vol. 432.3, file 217.

ers, which joined the CTM on Lombardo's initiative. There were also some farm labourers who found in the CTM a channel to voice their complaints and needs. However, the Chiapas branch of Cardenismo was weak and could achieve little against the violent opposition from growers to land distribution and union organising drives among agricultural workers employed on plantations. The official Chiapanecan political circles, especially the elite from the Los Altos highlands and the growers from Soconusco, wore down cardenismo and forced its officials to reconcile the competing interests.[58]

For reasons specific to the peninsula, the CTM failed to set up shop in Yucatán as Lombardo had wished. From an anarcho-syndicalist tradition, the workers did not sympathise with the labour confederations supported by the state that threatened their existence, and therefore they remained at arm's length so as to preserve their regional autonomy. At the same time, the clientelist relationship that existed in the henequen landed estates or haciendas was not ripe for establishing an alliance between the workers and the Cardenista government. Lombardo was opposed to anarcho-syndicalism as well as to the Socialist Party of the Southeast, which dominated the peninsula and, he said, misrepresented what socialism was all about. Independent unions also did not fit his agenda. The CTM's weakness in Yucatán diminished the influence of Cardenismo with which it was identified, but was compensated for by the land distribution, which was the prerogative and the source of the legitimacy of the president there and throughout the length and breadth of the country, and enabled the CTM to maintain a toehold in the peninsula.[59]

6   The President and the Leader

Lombardo Toledano understood the organised labour movement as an instrument to intervene in political life and in the foundation of the nation in accordance with his ideas, his ideology, national and international conditions. Initially, he conceived the labour confederation as the institution that would exercise power on par with the government of Lázaro Cárdenas. Once in 1936 he wrote to the president's private secretary on forms of collaboration between the CTM and the government for discussing and resolving the country's problems. In nineteen points he delineated his role as intermediary and participant

---

58   Lewis 2005, pp. 137–55; Benjamín 1989, p. 199; García de León 1985, vol. 2, pp. 99–218.
59   Fallaw 2001, pp. 109–15; VLT, 'El llanto del sureste', articles published in *El Universal* between 8 March and 16 May 1934, in *Obra*, III/1, 1934, pp. 57–78; Knight 1992, pp. 256–64.

in questions such as the defence of the government against its opponents and in designing economic plans. He also suggested the creation of a department or ministry to attend to press and information, asked for a building and funding to sustain the Workers' University, and in point nineteen requested 'licenses to carry weapons and annual passes on railroads and airlines for members of the CTM National Committee'.[60] He projected the confederation not only as a trade union but as a state agency, whose top level command would have the same privileges and rights as senior officials of a ministry.

However, the relationship between President Cárdenas and Lombardo Toledano was not one of equals but of strategic negotiation mediated by each one's hierarchy. The state had supreme authority over the population and territory as well as jurisdiction over its political and social rivals, who maintained a subordinate relationship. The president was the highest representative of the nation, while the labour leader symbolised one of the pillars upon which the power of the state rested. In Lombardo's way of thinking, the Marxist and liberal notions of sovereignty and the state became intertwined, interchangeable or merged, depending on the circumstances, the interlocutors, the actors and participants involved. Before the six-year presidential term began, Lombardo placed himself on the same level as the president's authority. After the first skirmishes with his authority, more verbal than real, like a field marshal, always disciplined, he stepped back from the radicalism of his discourse and the mobilisation of organisations, in accordance with existing and anticipated conditions. Lombardo recognised the limits of the government's popular policies and adapted his own to the changing 1930s. He was concerned about the security of the state in response to domestic and international challenges, advances by the right and fascism that strengthened imperialism and diminished the viability of the Mexican Revolution and the world revolution as he understood them.

Both President Cárdenas as well as Lombardo Toledano believed in socialism as a desirable vision for the world, but differed in its conception and the strategies to implement it. The collective land ownership that the president instituted in some parts of the country sought, on the one hand, to achieve a better utilisation of natural and human resources and, on the other, the dignity of the campesinos. Lombardo, however, regarded collective land ownership as the seed of the abolition of private property.

General Cárdenas pushed for the integration of the CTM into the Party of the Mexican Revolution (PRM) to ensure that the workers would be in condi-

---

60   VLT to Licenciado Luis I. Rodríguez, Mexico City, 10 October 1936, FHLT, file 283.

tions to propose people they trust to public posts and in the process consolidate their collaboration with the government, whose duty it was to protect them. He believed that it was the state that should lead the struggle and organisation of the workers, ensure that such organisational efforts would have all the necessary support so that they could improve substantially and opposition forces could not derail them.

Lombardo Toledano wanted to be the figure that would bring together the country's political forces, to form a popular front. In December 1937 he was surprised by the president's announcement of his plan to reorganise the party, which was too identified with Calles, its creator. The transformation of PNR into the Party of the Mexican Revolution in 1938 meant not only the transformation of a party of cadres, groupings and personalities into a mass party, but the convergence within its ranks of workers, campesinos, military and popular sectors and the middle class in such a way that each sector would function as a counterweight to another without any of them being able to exercise hegemony over the rest.[61]

General Cárdenas believed in labour organisation not only to provide workers with the means to defend their interests and correct the inequalities and injustices inherent in the relationship between capital and labour, but also to subject employers to a nationalist policy. In this, Lombardo did not differ from the president, but in empowering workers with his leadership and people like him, in the long run, he envisioned a shift in the correlation of forces with a view to changing the entire economic and political system. Contrary to what Lombardo expected, the expropriation of the oil industry, in which he participated with his support, and 'most of the time on issues that will never be made public', the way for workers to take power was not cleared, but rather meant the victory of the progressive wing of the state over the conservative wing and over foreign exploitation of the country's national resources.[62]

President Cárdenas had all of Mexico in mind when he governed. He expected Lombardo to lead an organisation that would contribute to the government's popular land distribution programme and would not undercut the project's advances with strikes, unless they would strengthen the government's plan or at least not negatively affect it. Cárdenas called for solidarity with the government and to 'accept a reduction in credits and wages if necessary'. The

---

61 Gilly 1994, pp. 391–470; Aziz Nassif 1989, pp. 68–79; Ashby 1967, pp. 88–92; Basurto 1983, pp. 108–11; Knight 1994, pp. 73–107; Krauze 1997a, p. 437.
62 León and Marván 1985, p. 87; Meyer 1981, pp. 343–5; VLT, 'El pueblo de México y las compañías petroleras', speech delivered at the extraordinary session of the national council of the CTM, 6 January 1938, in *Obra*, III/7, 1938, p. 7; Gilly 1994, p. 291.

president directed his efforts at the nation, whose guarantee was the institutional regime, supported by a popular programme, which for him was the same as 'respect for life, individual rights, political freedom, cancellation of privileges and better distribution of public wealth'. The entire country, including domestic and foreign businessmen and workers, should endorse the government's project, because it sought to increase the moral and economic level of all its inhabitants. The 'decorum of the country' could not be achieved if the productive factors were 'in a state of biological exhaustion with unjust inequality in the face of situations of privilege'.[63]

Lombardo had the urban and rural workers organised in the CTM in his mental horizon. Their fate depended not on the reconciliation of capital and labour, but on the class struggle and the victory of one class over the other. The two projects could be reconciled to the extent that Lombardo was convinced that Mexico and its socio-economic environment were not ripe for socialism. In the meantime, it was necessary to occupy strategic positions in the national, state and local governments at home and sow the seed of his project in the entire hemisphere.

---

63   Cárdenas, speech delivered in Cocolapam, Veracruz, 26 January 1938, in Cárdenas 1978, p. 279.

CHAPTER 6

A Continental Feat

If Witold Antonovich Lovsky had not been put before a firing squad in March 1938 by the government he loyally served, he would have seen the founding of the Latin American Workers Confederation (CTAL) as the culmination of his perseverance.[1] Lovsky had been a soldier of the world revolution, knew Latin America and was confident that Mexico, under the government run by President Cárdenas and with Lombardo Toledano's leadership, would offer the possibility of unifying the hemispheric labour movement that the communist Latin American Trade Union Confederation (CSLA) had failed to achieve. It was necessary to help them. Lovsky insisted on the task until his mission in Latin America was revoked and he disappeared into the maelstrom of the massive persecution against the 'enemies of the people', orchestrated by Stalin to intimidate, silence and eliminate any real, potential or imaginary opposition to the Soviet regime.

1 In Santiago de Chile

Lovsky took advantage of the opportunity provided by the meeting of the International Labour Organization (ILO) of the League of Nations in the Chilean capital in January 1936 to take the first step in this endeavour. Convened at the initiative of the Chilean delegate to the ILO in Geneva, it was an unprecedented meeting. Like no other, the ILO had the authority to issue opinions on working conditions, both elementary rights and those regulated by labour legislation not complied with. These included wages, the number of hours in the work day, child labour, freedom of trade union organisation, social security and healthcare. The ILO's tripartite functioning enabled employers, government officials and workers' representatives to sit facing each other as apparent equals. It gave a voice to the voiceless, promoted class collaboration and favoured workers acquiring the security and dignity that they lacked in most countries.[2]

The Latin American working class was characterised by its diverse social and occupational composition between nations and from one city to another

---

1 Jeifets, Jeifets and Huber 2004, p. 184. CSLA was created in 1929.
2 Jensen 2011, pp. 215–25; Herrera 2013a, p. 106.

within the same country. It included miners, oil industry workers, workers linked to rural communities adjacent to their places of employment, those employed in the textile industry, in ports, on railways, in ocean and river freight transportation, employees, artisans and independent workers in small manufacturing establishments, including the service sector. These divisions existing within the urban working classes were coupled with differences in their political positions with regard to the capitalist system, which some wanted to abolish and others to reform. There were also the socio-structural and ideological divisions that made organisational unity difficult. The workers understood democracy to mean more than just the right to vote and their conception included the removal of dictatorships, the realisation of favourable labour legislation and the right to independent trade union activity, all of which were judged essential so that they not be second-class citizens.

The 1929 depression changed the character of the political and economic conflicts. Reduced economic activity resulted in increased political unrest against the domination of the oligarchies. In 1935 the Communist International changed its political line from promoting a frontal confrontation with the bourgeois regime to a policy based on the creation of popular fronts, seeking collaboration with other social classes. This contributed to creating a political climate of conciliation and determined the thinking and actions of the communists, including Lovsky and his allies, among them Lombardo. In Chile, the number of independent trade unions increased; in Brazil, trade unions were created under the tutelage of the state; in Bolivia trade unionism was reborn; in Cuba, sugar workers' 'soviets' emerged. Other processes such as an incipient reconstruction of workers' organisations took place in Colombia. However, Central America continued to be the major void in the constellation of Latin American trade unionism as the region was, on par with the Dominican Republic, in the hands of ruthless dictatorships.[3]

Lombardo knew that union leaders from the CSLA would be in Santiago for the ILO meeting in November 1935. Argentine labour leader Miguel Contreras wrote Lombardo hoping that he would be with them in Santiago, 'which would facilitate the exchange of personal opinions with you' on the continental confederation.[4] But Lombardo did not put in an appearance. He mentioned to Lovsky that Emilio Portes Gil, the president of the ruling party, prevented his departure from Mexico so that he would not project a leftist image of President Cárdenas's government, which Portes Gil and other Callistas were fight-

---

3   Roxborough 1997, pp. 135–48.
4   Miguel Contreras to VLT, Montevideo, November 1935, FHLT, file 269.

ing against. As an alternative, Lombardo asked the Department of Labour to appoint a delegation, but it did not respond to his request, perhaps because Lombardo would have been an undesired delegate and sending another could be an affront to the labour leader who played such a prominent role in the workers' mobilisation.

There were also internal reasons within the labour movement. 'As LT told me, he understood very well our argument that Chile could play the historical role for Continental Unity', but seeking the success on the continental level could mean the possibility of unity in Mexico being lost.[5] With the 'five little wolves' as potential adversaries, Lombardo should not leave the country. Instead, he sent a vibrant message to the workers who met with the ILO officials, whose mission was to proclaim the virtues of labour legislation and state intervention in the economy. He presented this stance as insufficient, arguing that 'the most important problem for the working class is not the issue of social legislation, but its [working class's] effective and urgent unification'. State intervention such as in the United States under Franklin D. Roosevelt, whose slogan was the social 'new deal' and 'respect for private profit and free competition', was a failure.[6] Without clarifying what he meant, couching his message in generalities, Lombardo concealed his conviction that unity under the same banner was central to the political education and to the concerted action that the ideological diversity and dispersal of the unions hindered.

Lombardo Toledano did not disparage the usefulness of the ILO as a transnational body that studied social situations and served as a major sounding board for airing the problems of the working class in all countries. But he criticised it for not taking into account the prevalence in Latin America of Pan-Americanism, the 'economic and political dominance of the strong country over the weak countries of the continent' and where the governments presided over 'tributary peoples of its economy', namely, that of the United States.[7]

At the Santiago meeting there were worker delegates from several countries and different ideological overtones. When a communist delegate of Ecuador

---

5   Lovsky, alias Godoy, to the Latin American Trade Union Confederation, Mexico City, 10 February 1936, RGASPI, f. 495, register 10, file 327; Herrera 2013b, p. 105.
6   VLT, 'Mensaje al proletariado de la América Latina', *El Universal*, 1 January 1936, in *Obra*, III/4, 1936, pp. 1–2.
7   VLT, 'La Conferencia Internacional del Trabajo de Santiago de Chile', *El Universal*, 25 December 1935, in *Obra*, III/3, 1935, pp. 455–8; VLT, 'Intervención en la segunda sesión del segundo congreso de la CGOCM', 18 February 1936, in *Obra*, III/4, 1936, pp. 53–62; Herrera 2013a, p. 106.

took the floor he questioned 'class collaboration', since the workers had fought for the legal conquests that they paid for with their blood and the laws 'are a dead letter, are not complied with'. The jails were brimming with political prisoners who fought for the democracy that they had been denied by the native or criollo governments, subjected by imperialism and market competition. The Chilean socialist trade unionist Luis Solís Solís denounced the deplorable conditions of wage earners in a country that had social programmes for workers. He accused the Chilean authorities of ignoring treaties that they had signed with great fanfare, of opposing the unionisation of workers and appealed to the ILO for help in obtaining the freedoms due to them. Weeks later, President Arturo Alessandri, who had sponsored the meeting, arrested Solís Solís and did not allow the ILO to make inquiries into his case, arguing violation of national sovereignty.[8]

Communist trade unionists met and, without inviting those who were not of their political persuasion, signed the 'Pact for the unity of the workers of America'.[9] If this was about unity, why didn't they invite all the worker delegates from the participating countries? Lovsky was in Santiago for the first days of the event to tie up the loose ends and ensure the pact, but hastened his return to Mexico so as not to miss the preparations for the founding of the CTM and the close contact with Lombardo at a crucial moment. He had to ensure that both the new organisation as its leader did not lose sight of their continental task.

2   The Planning

The founding of the CTM in February 1936 was the occasion to call for the creation of the Latin American Workers Confederation. Lombardo denounced the paucity of workers at the ILO conference in Chile and did not mention the pact that the communist delegates signed in Santiago a few weeks before but decried 'the undeniable intervention by the government in Washington' to organise a league of American nations in anticipation of war and to open the markets for its production. Although he proposed that the nascent CTM not belong to either the Red International of Labour Unions in Moscow or the reformist International Federation of Trade Unions based in

---

8   Herrera 2013b, pp. 87–119 and Herrera 2013c, pp. 234–5.
9   Lovsky, alias Godoy, to the Latin American Trade Union Confederation, Mexico City, 10 February 1936, RGASPI, f. 495, register 10, file 327.

Amsterdam, his long-term plan was to align the Mexican and Latin American labour movement to the Soviet Union.[10]

Lovsky, who had manoeuvred so that the communists would have a prominent role in the CTM, intervened after its creation so that the confederation would have an international projection and influence in the countries in the hemisphere to both Mexico's north and south. He convinced Lombardo that an international relations commission be created that the Bolshevik could advise behind the scenes to prepare the continental congress. He insisted on the alignment of the CTM with an international confederation. The times required it. Fascism had muddied the political waters, the situation had worsened with Hitler's military campaign and invasion of the Rhineland in 1936, in the process shredding to pieces the 1919 Treaty of Versailles, which after the First World War forbade German rearmament. Meanwhile, the Argentine trade union confederation had already entered the Amsterdam-based International and the CTM could not remain in limbo. It was not advisable to join the Moscow-based labour international as doing so would provoke a split, while the Amsterdam option put the Mexicans and the Argentines on the same footing. 'I immediately consulted Alejandro on this issue and so far I have not received a reply', and without a response 'I did not risk taking a step that might not be approved by Alejandro'.[11] Lombardo was aware of Lovsky's correspondence between Mexico and Moscow and with the Red International of Labour Unions headed by Alexandr Lozovsky.

Lovsky lamented that 'the international relations commission, elected at the unity congress turned out to be a bust'. Beyond promises, nothing had been done. The comrades from South America did not answer his letters nor did they circulate Lombardo's messages about unity, the danger of native or criollo fascism, US imperialism and historical tyrannies. If the communists did not act, 'we will be wiped out as a factor, not only during the struggle for unity, but in our history, we will only go down as an insignificant episode in the past'. His hope was Lombardo and the illusion that he 'is willing to use our organisation, our contacts and our influence'.[12]

Lovsky's proposal was that the preliminary meeting to organise the Latin American confederation take place in Panama on account of it being the most centrally located venue in the hemisphere. 'We did not want to propose to the

---

10 19 and 23 February 1936 sessions, ibid.
11 Telegrams from Lovsky, alias Raúl, to Aleksandr Lozovsky, Mexico City, February–May 1936, RGASPI, f. 534, register 4, file 519; Lovsky to Tomba (alias of Miguel Contreras), Mexico City, 10 March 1936 and 13 May 1936, RGASPI, f. 495, register 17, file 3.
12 Lovsky, alias Godoy, to Tomba, Mexico City, 17 April 1936, RGASPI, f. 495, register 17, file 3.

Argentines that they come to Mexico, so as not to hurt their susceptibility and sense of rivalry'.[13] He still hoped that the congress would take place in late 1936, even though he lost contact with the signatories of the Chile pact, which was a way to revive the declining CSLA through the new organisation, without it appearing that he was 'pushing' its creation.[14]

Still pending was the international alignment of the CTM, which Lozovsky resolved in favour of Amsterdam:

> I just received a telegram from Alejandro, in which he expresses his complete agreement with our position, considering it possible that the CTM will begin negotiations with this international confederation. This response, which has been delayed, came at a very opportune time and puts clarity on such an important issue. Immediately after this, I had a long conversation with L.T. and he also expressed how pleased he was, since our point of view was accepted.[15]

After receiving the green light from Moscow, Lombardo announced the CTM's request to join the Amsterdam-based International. It did not matter that the CTM founding congress in February had considered the IFTU to be of little importance. Now it had to be glorified as a 'global organisation', given that 'the world proletariat is currently experiencing times of tremendous importance that, shortly, will lead to an organisation that unites almost the totality of the wage earners of the different nations of the earth'.[16]

In September 1936, Lombardo, 'driven by a deep sense of responsibility, as the soldier that I am for the cause of the proletariat', approached the labour confederations of Latin America. The CTM was the vanguard of the labour movement in Mexico, the continent and the entire world, which gave him moral authority in the historical moment in which 'the collapse that will mark the end of a social system that has fulfilled its mission' was in plain view.[17] The planet was divided between 'the dying world and the world that is being born … and that is an example of the world of tomorrow'.[18] The Soviet Union did not

---

13   Lovsky, alias Godoy, to Tomba, Mexico City, 12 May 1936, RGASPI, f. 495, register 17, file 3.
14   Lovsky, alías Henry, to Tomba, Mexico City, 26 May 1936, ibid.
15   Lovsky to Tómbola, 1 June 1936, ibid.
16   VLT, 'Se adhiere la CTM a la Federación Sindical Internacional', *Excélsior*, 10 June 1936, in *Obra*, III/4, 1936, p. 283.
17   VLT, 'Carta a las centrales sindicales de América Latina', September 1936, in *Obra*, III/4, 1936, pp. 347–55, quote on p. 347.
18   VLT, 'La aportación de la URSS a la civilización', *Futuro*, November 1936, in *Obra*, III/4, 1936, p. 441 and p. 442.

just represent a historic development for the proletariat; it was the 'the flesh of its flesh and the blood of its blood'.[19]

3   In the United States

President Cárdenas exiled Plutarco Elías Calles and Luis N. Morones in April 1936 to the United States for obstructing his administration's efforts. From exile the two set out to paint a picture of Mexico as communist. To neutralise the harmful propaganda against the CTM, Lovsky assumed the task of seeking allies for the plan to build the continental labour confederation. 'I worked hard in organising the CTM delegation to the May Day activities in New York'. The delegation was comprised of two members of the international relations commission and two workers from national industrial union confederations, a miner and an oil worker. The American compañeros helped a lot. 'I sent extensive explanations to the U.S. P[arty] and they appointed a special commission to attend to the delegation'. Since there were no communists in the delegation, the American comrades had to 'be very tactful, which they are doing well'.[20]

The delegation left Mexico on 27 April and arrived in New York on 1 May. It consisted of Victor Manuel Villaseñor, who spoke English and was familiar with the situation; Alejandro Carrillo, Lombardo's other right-hand man and director of the Workers' University, as well as labour leaders, miner Agustín Guzmán and oil worker Eduardo Soto Innes. In New York they were received by Alberto Moreau and Samuel Solomanick, leaders of the League Against War and Fascism, one of the front groups of the Communist Party, created by instructions of the Third International. They were not received by the American Federation of Labor, 'a reactionary fortress', which Morones plied with vicious news against Mexico, against President Cárdenas and against the CTM. Its leader William Green prepared the groundwork before the Mexicans arrived with articles on the 'destructive' policies of the Mexican government, the expulsion of Brother Morones and the persecution of the CROM.[21] With the help of the American communists, a successful effort was made to prevent Morones

---

19   VLT, 'El triunfo del proletariado soviético', unsigned editorial, *Futuro*, November 1936, p. 470.
20   Lovsky, alias Henry, to Tomba, Mexico City, 13 May 1936, RGASPI, f. 495, register 17, file 3.
21   'Green Says Mexico Hurts Labour Groups', *The New York Times*, 26 April 1936 and 'Green Protests Mexican Action Against Labour', *The Washington Post*, 26 April 1936.

from taking the floor on behalf of Mexican workers at the Madison Square Garden rally, but the CTM delegates were not able to do so either.[22]

The two labour leaders toured the country from east to west, met with their counterparts and shared their experiences insofar as their lack of English proficiency allowed them to do so, except in California, where they fraternised with the Hispanic population. They took advantage of the opportunities to lift the veil on corruption in the CROM, to discuss the origin and character of the CTM as well as the nature of President Cárdenas's administration, which was not at all communist, as it even reconciled with the Catholic Church hierarchy. The Cetemistas tour of the United States had another benefit. In dealing with influential leaders of the industrial unions, they helped underscore the diminished influence of the American Federation of Labor, which extolled Calles and Morones.[23]

In size and influence, the historic American Federation of Labor (AFL), organised in craft unions, was replaced in the 1930s by the Committee for Industrial Organization. The latter's founder and leader, John L. Lewis, once a miner, farmer and construction worker, had been, since he was 27 years old, a labour organiser, first in the AFL as president of the United Farm Workers, which in the 1920s was the largest union in the United States. Lewis, a Republican, earned the reputation as being a labour statesman. His opponents branded him autocratic and ambitious. In 1932 he joined the Democratic Party and, in cooperation with President Franklin Delano Roosevelt and his supporters, organised workers who had not previously belonged to any union as well as industrial workers. He recognised that capitalism and democracy could not be stabilised as long as the workers were not protected by the state and society, and without the social redistribution of wealth. In 1935 he left the vice presidency of the AFL, founded the Committee for Industrial Organization and gained national notoriety. The committee, which later changed its name to Congress of Industrial Organization (CIO), recruited Mexicans in the southwestern United States into ethnically and racially mixed unions, which helped them to get jobs and invited the CTM to join its work along the border to plan and carry out strikes in one or the other of the two countries.[24]

---

22   Lovsky, alías Henry, to Tomba, Mexico City, 13 May 1936, RGASPI, f. 495, register 17, file 3.
23   Luis Rodríguez, private secretary to the president, to Eduardo Hay, Mexico City, 15 May 1936, AGN, RLC, vol. 432.2, file 163.
24   Foner and Garraty (eds) 1991, p. 651; Dubofsky and Dulles 1993, pp. 255–77; Peterson 1998, pp. 21–67; Vargas 2005, pp. 117–20; C.H. Jordan to Alejandro Carrillo, San Pedro California, 19 November 1936, FHLT, file 285; Carrillo to Jordan, Mexico City, 2 December 1936 and VLT to C.H. Jordan, Mexico City, 18 December 1936, FHLT, file 285.

Lombardo was impressed by Lewis's record and wanted to win him to his causes. Following the meeting of the CTM national council in April 1937, in which Lombardo confronted the communists, he recounted the details of the division. He could have been motivated by the fear of the closeness of the Mexican communists with their American counterparts who were a major force in the CIO. The ideological brotherhood between the Mexican and US communist parties could tarnish Lombardo, who sought prominence in influential circles in the United States. His concern was that the schism in the CTM not send negative signals across the border, where he wanted to be considered and taken into account as the sole leader of the labour movement in Mexico. Lombardo presented the Mexican dilemma rhetorically in terms that resembled those used by Lewis, placing a priority on union leadership over political leadership,[25] knowing full well that they were inseparable.

'Thin, short, pale-faced, forty-two years old and with a burst of inexhaustible energy', was how one newspaper described Lombardo in June 1938 when he passed through New York on his way to Europe. On that occasion, he wanted to reach out to prominent officials of the CIO, to explain the labour panorama in Mexico, the expropriation of the oil industry, the land distribution as the Mexican version of Roosevelt's New Deal policies and the reasons behind the congresses to create the Latin American confederation. It was to his advantage to be close to a labour confederation that did not have a past in its relations with the CROM in decline.[26] Lewis welcomed and feted Lombardo in Washington with a banquet at the Carlton Hotel, because it was to his advantage to gain a foothold in Mexico given that the CIO's rival, the AFL, was trying to regain lost ground. Without boring or tiring out his audience, Lombardo reported that the Mexicans would fight the 'Nazi infection of democracy' and would inoculate the continental congress planned for September against the evil threat. The speaker left the observers perplexed. He did not want power in the government and did not want to be president; he was a socialist without belonging to the communist party and advocated the abolition of capitalism.[27]

---

25 Levenstein 1997, pp. 153 and 169, n. 21; VLT to John L. Lewis, Mexico City, 14 May 1937, FHLT, file 296.

26 The Pan-American Federation of Labor (PAFL) was created in 1918 by the leaders of the CROM and the American Federation of Labor. The PAFL held five congresses between 1918 and 1927. Following the death of Samuel Gompers, its first leader, in 1925, it began to decline.

27 Mild Speech by Mexico's 'Lewis Pleased Nervous New Deal Hosts', *New York Mirror*, 29 June 1938, FHLT, file 323; Radosh 1969, p. 356.

4   In Europe

The other scenario in which Lombardo Toledano needed to stake out his presence was in Europe through the International Labour Organization – even though he might not have believed at that time in the reconciliation of capital and labour mediated by the state – and through the International Federation of Trade Unions (IFTU). He aspired to join its board of directors, representing the Latin American workers. Membership in the IFTU had the virtue that it would position him in the milieu where the major problems of the day were being discussed and resolved.

Founded in 1919, the IFTU experienced repeated losses. In 1926 it lost the Italian labour movement after the country's unions were outlawed by the fascists. In 1933 the federation was shaken by the loss of the German trade unions, whose membership in the IFTU was banned by Hitler without the unions offering resistance. The IFTU lost about five million members and a third of its resources. Its president, Walter Citrine, who did not believe in the collapse of capitalism, sought the extension of the authority and responsibility of the unions in the field of industrial management. Citrine wanted to extend the federation's relations beyond European borders. He wanted to establish contacts in the Americas, but only the General Confederation of Labour of Argentina joined the IFTU.[28] The debacle of the German and Italian labour movement also cost the respectability of the supranational ILO, which ceased having influence on labour legislation reform in countries that dug in their heels in defence of their nationalist interests.

When Germany succumbed to Nazism, the issue of closer relations between unions in Western Europe and the USSR was again placed on the table. The tactic of the united front as an anti-fascist front won in France, where the communist and socialist unions merged in a single confederation. This international unity was discussed at the meeting of the general council of the IFTU in Copenhagen in May 1935, where French labour leader Leon Jouhaux spoke in favour of it, while Citrine rejected the alliance with the Soviets on the grounds that they could not maintain relations with those who believed in dictatorships.[29]

The AFL joined the IFTU in November 1937, after having refused to belong in order not to submit to a supranational organisation, considering its affiliation too expensive and because its decisions were politically motivated. It

---

28   Van Goethem 2000, pp. 87–145. Membership fell from 13.7 million in 1932 to 8 million in 1933.
29   Van Goethem 2000, pp. 130–1.

adopted an anti-fascist stance, but did not diminish its anti-communist feelings. It joined the IFTU, among other reasons, to isolate its rival, the CIO, from European contacts. And with the AFL in the European federation, the integration of the Soviet trade unions became impossible. For the Americans, there could be no free labour movement without a free market and where the unions were an extension of the communist party.[30]

For Lombardo Toledano, the AFL's joining the Amsterdam-based federation fell like a bucket of cold water. The CTM had just entered the IFTU as the sole representative of Mexico's organised workers, but with the AFL joining the federation, this meant that the CROM had won an ally there, even if by the back door. He found it intolerable that the organisation for which he had deep contempt would undeservedly appear on the international scene. The AFL should recognise the CTM as its partner and break relations with the CROM, which did not happen. By contrast, between the two they issued a call to resurrect the Pan-American organisation that ceased to exist in 1928, at the moment in which Lombardo and the CTM had lined up the trade unions of Cuba, Venezuela, Costa Rica, Colombia, Paraguay, Uruguay, Chile and Argentina to host the much coveted continental confederation.[31]

The war was approaching. Audacious as always, Lombardo took upon himself the role of influencing the constellation of political forces and assumed the role of Mexican proconsul whenever he was abroad. In May 1938 he was in Oslo, Norway, to attend the meeting of the council of the International Federation of Trade Unions, chaired by Citrine, and took on the task of pleading – unsuccessfully – for the affiliation of the Soviet trade unions to the IFTU. Lombardo was outraged by the federation's refusal and he charged that the IFTU was about to become 'nothing more than a political red cross'. The fight against fascism meant collaborating with the Soviet Union. Not to do so, he said sarcastically, was the equivalent of 'sending emissaries to Hitler and Mussolini pleading with them to have compassion on the proletariat and not treat it roughly'.[32]

Being in Norway, Lombardo, in another bold move, took it upon himself to sell Mexican oil. He had tried before. In the declaration on the expropri-

---

[30] Van Goethem 2000, pp. 144–5.

[31] Van Goethem 2000, p. 131; VLT to the International Federation of Trade Unions, Mexico City, 29 November 1937, FHLT, file 317.

[32] VLT in the 4th session of the International Federation of Trade Unions, Oslo, Norway, 20 May 1938, FHLT, file 319; VLT declarations on labour unity with the Soviet trade unions were reproduced in the Communist Party daily *Pravda* 'Profsoiuzi Meksiki za edinstvo' ('Mexican Unions for unity'), 3 June 1938 and in *Izvestia* 'Profsouizi Meksiki za edinstvo s sovietiskimi profsouizami' ('Mexican Unions for unity with Soviet trade unions'), 3 June FHLT, file 320.

ation, President Cárdenas said the nationalised oil should be sold to democratic countries. That included Great Britain and the United States, the two countries whose companies had been expropriated. The boycott of oil sales by the affected companies and the pressure exerted by the respective governments led Lombardo to try to resolve the problem through the CIO and Lewis in order to counteract the closure of markets for Mexican black gold. Lewis recommended that he meet with William Rhodes Davis, an independent oil magnate, who had tankers and markets. He was a supporter of Roosevelt and it was said that he was a good employer vis-à-vis his workers. Lombardo introduced him to the president, so that through him it would be possible to arrange the transportation and sale of thousands of barrels even though, painfully, it would be to undemocratic countries such as Germany and Italy. Since the expropriation of the oil industry and until the beginning of the war Germany accounted for 48% of Mexico's oil exports, Italy 17% and the United States 20%, despite the boycott that should 'drown Mexico in its own oil'.[33]

When Lombardo took the initiative to negotiate the sale of oil in Norway, it is unclear whether he had the consent of the Mexican government: 'The Nor company needs to know its price if you are willing to sell', the company's representative wrote to Lombardo in a confidential communication, with specifications on costs, transport conditions, payment and to what purposes the oil would be used. The most likely variant was that the sale did not reach fruition due to pressure from the British oil companies. However, the solidarity of the general secretary of the federation, Walter Schevenels, was beneficial to a country that by nationalising its oil took a step in favour of its workers. The support was particularly important because he himself sent recommendations to the labour confederations to circulate news favourable to Mexico and counteract the negative coverage spread by the affected oil companies.[34] The trip to Europe gave Lombardo the opportunity to invite workers' organisations to the founding congress of the CTAL in September.

5 The Founding Congress

A hemispheric confederation was the dream of trade unionists since the 1920s mostly to improve their living conditions with reforms rather than structural

---

33   VLT to LC, Mexico City, 9 April 1938, FHLT, file 316; Meyer 1991, p. 479; Meyer 1981, pp. 412–16; Levenstein 1997, pp. 155–6 and p. 170, n. 37.

34   Luis I. Rodríguez to VLT, Mexico City, 9 May 1938; Brynjolf Rjorseb to VLT, Oslo, 19 May 1938; Schevenels to VLT, Oslo, Norway, 20 May 1938, FHLT, file 319; Meyer 1981, p. 427, n. 320.

changes. However, achieving such ends involved overcoming many obstacles. The level of labour organisation differed between countries such as Argentina and Nicaragua. Countries that were exporters of raw materials had different working classes than nations with large manufacturing industries. Those with illiterate indigenous populations differed from those with European immigrants with various trades under their belt. In addition, there were also differences in terms of the relations between labour organisations and political parties and governments. Obtaining concessions from the state was so difficult and costly that in exchange the trade unions and confederations were obliged to support populist and reformist politicians. Once they were part of the reformist regime, many trade unionists preferred to remain within the system, not confronting dominant parties so as not to lose the gains that had been achieved. The governments also needed them as a counterweight to the opposition of the oligarchies, the military, and harmful outside interests, and to carry out development policies for the benefit of society, to a greater or lesser extent in an atmosphere of social peace. The conditions of the second half of the 1930s were conducive to launching a continental confederation. Once the population recovered from the economic depression, the left parties adopted the communist line of broad popular fronts and the governments committed to economic nationalism as a dike to contain domestic and foreign reactionary forces. Achieving this was a feat.[35]

While in Uruguay there was a representative democracy of traditional parties albeit without union democracy, Paraguay was engaged in a modernisation effort with land reform, agricultural credit, an eight-hour work day, mandatory medical care in factories, wage increases, union organising drives and the legalisation of a communist party. In August 1937 a military coup reversed this process and the workers' leaders were imprisoned, executed or exiled.[36] In Peru, the American Popular Revolutionary Alliance (APRA), an anti-imperialist nationalist formation, and the communist party were the organisational forces of the working class in a country where the ruling class saw the mixed-race Cholos, Indians and blacks as subjects to be overpowered and the APRA to be suppressed.[37] In Nicaragua, the workers' movement was in its initial stages, with 'the pauper' Anastasio Somoza García ruling faithfully in favour of the United States in alliance with a section of the ruling class, minimally

---

35 Kofas 1992, pp. 11–22; Keen and Haynes 2000, pp. 322–3; Bergquist 1986, pp. 138–40; Zapata 2013, pp. 17–72.
36 De Sierra 1977, vol. 1, pp. 438–9; Díaz de Arce 1977, vol. 1, pp. 347–53.
37 Cotler 1977, vol. 1, p. 386.

tolerating the mass mobilisations.[38] In Venezuela, which was recovering from the tyranny of Juan Vicente Gómez after his death in 1935, a new labour law entered into effect that allowed the existence of urban and campesino unions, but the government arrogated to itself the right to regulate their activities. As the opposition grew stronger, the government instituted repressive measures to counter its expansion, which spurred it to join with popular organisations. The government's tolerance reached its limit at the time of the strike in the oil fields in December 1936. The government unleashed such a savage persecution that the movement was forced into illegality to avoid the imprisonment of its activists.[39] In Brazil under Getulio Vargas the president conceded protective labour legislation and social security to the working class, but exerted state control over the labour movement.[40] In Cuba the unions affiliated to the labour confederation put an end to the dictatorship of Gerardo Machado, in power between 1924 and 1933, through a general strike that sparked a labour insurgency, especially in the sugar industry. The government crisis and dissatisfaction of both the Americans as well as the Cuban elite were mediated by Fulgencio Batista, establishing the *pax batistiana* that included labour reforms and the re-entry of the communist party into the political life of the island.[41]

For a sector of the labour movement and the Latin American left, Mexico was the shining light and hope for a soon-to-be-achieved liberation. The fearless voice of Lombardo Toledano spoke for many. On the occasion of the Inter-American Conference for the Maintenance of Peace held in Buenos Aires in 1936, he criticised the United States for not taking a clear stance against the Latin American right, accusing Washington of having organised the event to replace British imperialism in a region where it was at a disadvantage and not because it was concerned about peace.[42] The exiled Argentine writer Aníbal Ponce wrote to him:

> The courage with which you denounced the conspiracy of the right-wing forces can only inspire applause and respect. On the bleak map of Latin America, Mexico represents for all of us the only hope for a not too

---

38 Quintanilla Obregón 1982, pp. 72–3; Pérez Leirós 1941, p. 66; Barahona Portocarrero 1977, vol. 2, pp. 391–2.
39 Collier Berins and Collier 1991, pp. 251–4; Coronil 1997, pp. 93–111.
40 Bambirra and Dos Santos 1977, vol. 1, p. 143.
41 Pérez-Stable 1999, pp. 40–2.
42 VLT, 'Argentina en vísperas del congreso panamericano de la paz', *El Universal*, 22 April 1936, in *Obra*, III/4, 1936, pp. 191–4.

distant liberation. Your fate is, therefore, the fate of the Americas; your anguish is all of our anguish.[43]

When Lázaro Cárdenas announced the expropriation of the oil industry in March 1938, workers, students and leftist parties congratulated him from the most far-flung corners of the continent.[44] The expropriation boosted the fame of Mexico, its president and Lombardo Toledano. With the shadows of war hovering over in Spain and the threatening spread of fascism in Europe, the atmosphere was conducive for Lombardo's appeal for continental-wide workers' unity to get a hearing.

It was therefore an affront that the general secretary of the International Federation of Trade Unions, Walter Schevenels, told him that he would not attend the conference, arguing that inasmuch as neither the AFL nor the Argentina CGT, which were members of the IFTU, would be participating, he could not either, even if the CTM would be in attendance. He reasoned that since he did not know the 'nature' of the organisations that would be present, Lombardo should have reached an agreement on which organisations to invite and which organisations not to invite in order to prevent complications among the IFTU members. If the AFL did not send a delegate, it was not because they were not invited, Lombardo shot back, and the Argentines had agreed to go to Mexico. The European federation was misinformed, so as not to say that its actions in this regard had been driven by bad intentions.[45] The IFTU's absence did not overshadow the great event that reverberated throughout the country, Latin America and the United States.

Lombardo had brought prominent labour leaders of the hemisphere and Europe as well as some powerful unions that they headed to the conference. In general, the delegates were optimistic about the future following the economic crisis of the early 1930s. Adolf Staal, head of labour relations of the International Labour Organization, attended. So did the prominent socialist Francisco Pérez Leiros, steeled in the Argentine labour struggles, one of the founders of the CGT, who in Santiago de Chile in 1936 supported the creation of the Latin American trade union confederation and signed the unity pact. Cuban communist tobacco workers' leader Lázaro Peña, who became Lombardo's lifelong friend, arrived, along with leaders of several of the island's unions before the founding of a labour confederation that would bring them all together. Also

---

43 Aníbal Ponce to VLT, 9 August 1937, FHLT, file 299.
44 Kiddle 2016, pp. 109–36.
45 W. Schevenels, general secretary of the IFTU, to VLT, Paris, 11 June 1938; VLT to W. Schevenels, Mexico City, 30 July 1938, FHLT, file 324.

present was the Chilean leader Bernardo Ibáñez, who from being an enthusiastic advocate of the CTAL in the 1930s would engage in an ideological somersault against it in the 1940s. Latin American delegates arrived who represented organisations with varying degrees of influence, greater in Argentina and Chile, lesser in Bolivia, Colombia, Ecuador, Paraguay and Peru. A member of the General Union of Workers of Spain was present.[46] Brazilian legislation did not allow national federations to affiliate with international organisations except if the country's congress authorised them to do so, which led Lombardo to ridicule President Getulio Vargas for sending 'a large delegation of fake representatives of the Brazilian proletariat, to then claim it was a lie that there is a fascist regime in power in Brazil'.[47]

The jovial French socialist Leon Jouhaux of the General Confederation of Workers was a particularly welcome guest as he represented one of the most important European labour organisations. The other distinguished guest was the Dutch trade union leader Edo Fimmen. In 1919 he was general secretary of the International Federation of Trade Unions to be reconstituted after the war, and at the same time a fervent advocate of close relations with the Soviet trade unions and the Red International of Labour Unions, a proposal that since its creation in 1921 was rejected time and again. Fimmen never tired of calling for unity of the workers on one or the other side of the ideological wall given the fear of a new war and with the rise of fascism in Italy and chauvinism in Germany. The other influential invite was John Lewis. Although the CIO had not joined the CTAL, Lewis's visit had beneficial effects, since in discussing Mexico's expropriation of the oil industry, he had recognised the principle of self-determination and respect for the policies of each country. As an aside, the rivalry between the two American labour confederations now extended to Latin American unions and its weight would be felt for years to come.[48]

In Mexico City's Palacio de Bellas Artes, Lombardo, even though he was suffering from an inflamed appendix, spoke at the opening session in hyperbolic terms about continental unity, with the alternative being that 'fascism could be a victorious force in this continent'.[49] He participated in several meetings and made a dramatic appearance when he was named president of the CTAL. Lombardo arrived with his doctor and a nurse to acknowledge the hon-

---

46   VLT, 'Inauguración del Congreso Obrero Latinoamericano', in *Obra*, III/8, 1938, p. 106.
47   Elgueta and Chelén 1977, vol. 2, pp. 240–1; Echeverría 1993, pp. 102–3; Collier Berins and Collier 1991, p. 377; Tarcus 2007, pp. 503–5; Herrera 2013a, pp. 138–9.
48   Tosstorff 1998; Berger 1966, pp. 89–100.
49   Berger 1966, p. 105.

our and bent over in pain, was urgently rushed to the hospital where he was operated on for appendicitis. Pérez Leiros took his place to close the congress.⁵⁰

Staal listened carefully to the delegates. The recurring theme was the lack of freedom of trade union association, which hampered the activities of workers to obtain improvements in working conditions and to organise strikes. This concern over the right to union organisation was coupled with the growing fear of fascism, the failure to implement social legislation and the domination of American and British imperialism. The Colombian delegate was perhaps the only one who praised his government for being democratic and allowing the unions to act unrestrained. Staal did not want to get involved in debates on sensitive issues and dedicated his time to promoting the collaboration of the congress leaders with the ILO as the organisation that promised to respect labour legislation. He was pleased that most of the delegates were actual workers, with a minority being professional politicians. Staal was opposed to the delegates' expenses being covered by the CTM, that is, by the Mexican government, and in passing criticised the leaders who were government employees. He was surprised that unions did not pay fees. The ILO general secretary also noted that the CTAL did not adopt an action programme. He anticipated that its success depended on the success of the Cárdenas government and the two organisations that mattered most, the CTM and the Argentine CGT. 'Mr Lombardo Toledano enjoys high esteem, and emphasis is placed on the fact that he leads a sober life and that his integrity and that of his immediate circle is beyond doubt'. Lombardo agreed that national labour confederations join the IFTU and the ILO and participate in their regional conferences. Finally, the CTAL congress presented no grounds for the accusation that it was tied to any ideological current.⁵¹

The CTAL was the brainchild of Lombardo Toledano, the International Congress Against War that followed was a project of President Cárdenas, since 'the end of imperialist wars depends on the anti-war solidarity of the workers'.⁵² The congresses as a whole were great celebratory events, full of hope for national independence and the sovereignty of North, Central and South America, and a

---

50   VLT, 'Clausura del congreso obrero latinoamericano', newspaper article, *El Popular*, 9 September 1938, in *Obra*, III/8, 1938, pp. 113–15.
51   Adolf Staal, 'Report on a mission to Latin American Labour Congress' held in Mexico City, 5–8 September 1938, ILO Archives, Mexico Reports, series C, no. 41/1938.
52   LC, speech at the first congress of the CTM, 24 February 1938, in Cárdenas 1978, p. 280; speech at the opening of the International Congress Against War, Mexico City, 19 September 1938, Cárdenas 1978, pp. 322–6.

call for a world peace that was fading. The foreign guests in Mexico were invited to visit Teotihuacán, Xochimilco, Puebla, the sugar refinery Emiliano Zapata in Zacatepec, Morelos and view the Independence Day parade on 16 September. Lombardo considered the congresses to be a joint project of workers and the government, and he expected the latter to cover delegates' per diem and travel expenses, 158,000 pesos in total.[53]

According to Rutgers University professor and well-known commentator on Latin American working-class history, Robert Alexander, the founding of the CTAL could be attributed to a combination of factors. These included the growth of labour movements in Latin America during the 1920s and 1930s, the decline and near disappearance of anarchist influence in the workers' movement with that current's refusal to collaborate with other ideological tendencies; the change in the policy of the Communist International that placed a priority on popular front organisations, domestic and international pressure on and hostility to President Cárdenas following the implementation of the agrarian reform, the nationalisation of the railways and the expropriation of foreign-owned oil companies, which gave greater importance to labour and popular support in Mexico and beyond the country's borders. Alexander noted that the Mexican government along with some Latin American governments subsidised part of the delegates' travel expenses and hotel, food and transportation costs within Mexico.[54]

Lombardo Toledano was at the height of his notoriety, but Carter Goodrich, economics professor at Columbia University in New York and commissioned by the US government at the ILO in Geneva, did not know who he was. He asked Frank Tannenbaum, professor at the same university, a Mexican specialist and a friend of the president: what was Lombardo's role in the Mexican labour movement? How much was under his control? What opinion did his colleague have of him? How successful was he in aligning the rest of Latin America with his positions? Did Morones represent anyone?

The response from Tannenbaum, who had been disappointed in the quality of the Mexican workers' movement, reflected that feeling. Lombardo Toledano was in control of the labour movement, while Morones led a small and compact group. The Mexican labour movement was linked to politics and depended on government favours, which made it difficult to predict Lombardo's future without being able to forecast the country's future political development.

---

53   VLT to Raúl Castellanos, private secretary to the President, Mexico City, 26 August 1938, AGN, RLC, vol. 433, file 280.
54   Alexander and Parker 2009, pp. 57–60; Ashby 1967, pp. 52–3.

Lombardo Toledano is a type of Latin American who is unstable, intellectually brilliant, dynamic, ambitious, full of vague notions on the proximity of the social revolution, anti-American but sincere and personally honest. Without government support, the leadership of the Mexican labour movement would escape from his hands from one minute to the next, which is very different from the case of Morones.

I have thought more than once that Lombardo Toledano would be expelled from the leadership of the labour movement over some irrelevant issue. The current division between Communists and other labour groups may be the reason for his removal.[55]

But the CTM was an organisation with which Goodrich had to be in contact.

6   To the Attack

The founding of the CTAL in September and the prominence of Lewis in Mexico prompted the AFL into action. It sent Dr Lippschutz, who had experience living in Mexico and for a time was the liaison with the CROM, as its observer to the congress. In October, Matthew Woll, vice president of the AFL, and Chester Wright were dispatched to Mexico to assess the landscape. Woll was a member of the executive committee of the AFL and headed the international relations committee that existed since 1914. Wright had been involved in Latin American affairs since Woodrow Wilson was president in the turbulent years of the First World War and was with the Pan-American Federation of Labor after its founding in 1918. Before his trip, Wright discussed his intention to work with the conservative leadership of the CROM with State Department officials. In the executive council of the AFL in February 1939 in Miami, with Morones present, they discussed the resurrection of the Pan-American Confederation and the weakening of the 'radical' CTM and Lombardo, 'the spokesman of the Stalinists in Mexico'.[56]

Woll remained in Mexico for several months to reorganise the CROM so that it could serve to lead a Latin American organisation in opposition to the CTAL. He was willing to give a monthly sum to the CROM and, if the CROM was resurrected, significantly increase these amounts of money with a view to

---

55   Goodrich to Tannenbaum, New York, 5 August 1939; Tannenbaum to Goodrich, New York, 9 October 1939, Tannenbaum Collection, Columbia University Libraries, Manuscript Collections, box 16.
56   Levenstein 1997, pp. 160–3; Woll quoted on p. 162; Buford 1971, p. 221.

increasing its influence over the workers of South America. However, Mr Woll encountered many difficulties such as the natural suspicion against Americans.[57]

He returned disappointed, because the work did not yield results, but not resigned to cease supporting the workers of Latin America in some way and erode the influence of the AFL's rival, the Congress of Industrial Organizations, linked to Lombardo Toledano. In May 1939 the Pan-American Confederation re-emerged, but only on paper. William Green was named its president, Morones its vice president, Woll, treasurer, and Santiago Iglesias from Puerto Rico, its secretary.[58]

However, the two American federations differed on domestic issues and foreign policy. In contrast to the clumsy Monroe Doctrine, transmitted by the traditional confederation, the AFL, in its own relations, the CIO leaders called for non-intervention in the domestic and foreign affairs of Latin American unions. Congressional leaders negotiated with the leftist organisations and anticipated that the Soviet trade unions could be part of future international labour organisations. Sidney Hillman, Philip Murray, James Carey and Walter Reuther were not communists, but they were willing to work with the left if that contributed to the defeat of fascism and international collaboration among workers. Such an attitude was comparable to the feelings of European leaders of the International Federation of Trade Unions, some of whom saw the popular fronts as a weapon against fascism. The AFL, on the other hand, was entrenched in unpopular anti-communism and vehemently opposed the participation of Soviet trade unions in organisations in which the AFL was or wanted to be present.[59]

Lombardo Toledano was aware of the multiple constraints for the continental feat to prosper, but was not used to speaking about difficulties. He believed in the inexorable march of history and that natural laws would overcome all obstacles. He knew of the structural and human limitations that lay ahead, but listing them would depress the spirit, and Lombardo was an agitator who emboldened the spirits, albeit with vague promises about the bright future. He was committed to the formation of an international system and through the CTM aspired to change the balance of power between the working class and the Mexican state. Through the CTAL he sought to alter the relationship of forces both within and between states and nations, thus changing the

---

57 Wm. F. Freehoff, military attaché, Mexico City, 16 February 1939, NARA, RG 59, file 812.504/1844.
58 Buford 1971, p. 221; Levenstein 1997, pp. 156–66.
59 Fraser 1991, p. 290.

rules and ways in which states and society interact with each other. Socialism could not be built without strengthening its harbinger, the Soviet Union, its socio-political regime and state, which had to be aided in times as uncertain as the late 1930s.

PART 3

War: Threshold of a Better World?

There is not a single action that I have undertaken in my life as an activist for the proletariat, and I have dedicated my life to fight for its emancipation, which I cannot tell everyone about and of which I do not also feel satisfied, despite errors that I might have committed. (1940)[1]

∴

The power which this nation has attained – the political, the economic, the military, and above all the moral power – has brought to us the responsibility, and with it the opportunity, for leadership in the community of nations. In our best interest, in the name of peace and humanity, this nation cannot, must not, and will not shirk that responsibility. (1944)[2]

∴

Licenciado, I'm writing this with the fervour that my admiration for social problems has engendered, not just those relating to our horn-shaped wisp of land, but world problems, that you, with your absolute clarity, are resolving step by step. (1945)[3]

∴

---

1 VLT to LC, Mexico City, 13 November 1940, AGN, LC, 542.1/2415.
2 Franklin Delano Roosevelt, Manhattan, 21 October 1944, in Meacham 2003, pp. 307–8.
3 José Hernández Gutiérrez, rural teacher, to VLT, Fresnillo, Zacatecas, 1 January 1945, file 602.

CHAPTER 7

Fight Fascism!

Lombardo Toledano painted fascism with a broad brush. Everything and everyone fit into his definition. Those who opposed the labour movement were fascists; those who were against the government of President Lázaro Cárdenas and the candidacy of General Manuel Ávila Camacho were as well. Racism was tantamount to fascism, along with opposition to land distribution. It was not necessary to belong to a national-socialist, fascist or pro-Franco organisation, wear the swastika on one's arm or proclaim adherence to Adolf Hitler's racial cleansing for Lombardo to apply the fascist label. He branded Leon Trotsky, the Bolshevik leader in exile in Mexico since 1937, as fascist, along with the clerical National Synarchist Union and all opponents of Soviet communism. Fascists were those who attacked Lombardo as were the persecuted political exiles in Mexico who opposed Stalin. It was irrelevant whether they had been victims of fascism and anti-Semitism in Europe, or had suffered confinement in concentration camps. Mexico was threatened and 'the threat will grow as time passes'. It was necessary to be vigilant, because in a careless lapse, fascism could gnaw at societies in the Western Hemisphere. Italy went after Abyssinia in Africa in 1935, 'as will Germany tomorrow against the Soviet Union'.[1] War was inevitable.

In the struggle against fascism, Lombardo not only fought the totalitarian regime established in Germany since 1933, the authoritarian government of Benito Mussolini since his rise to power in Italy in 1922, and General Francisco Franco, who took up arms in 1936 to overthrow the Spanish Republic, he also fought the capitalist system. Once fascism was eliminated, the Vatican, the National Action Party, Wall Street imperialism, the Republican Party, conservatives in the Democratic Party, State Department officials and the American Federation of Labor would all be destroyed, because fascism was the war of the bourgeoisie against the proletariat and the Soviet Union, 'the worldwide vanguard of the revolution'.[2] If the First World War was the midwife of the Bolshevik Revolution, the budding Second World War would give birth to a new world.[3]

---

1 VLT, 'Congreso de la CGOCM', 19 February 1936 session, AGN, RLC, vol. 437, file 62.
2 VLT, 'El frente mundial de la barbarie', *Futuro*, February 1937, in *Obra*, III/5, 1937, p. 7.
3 Interview with foreign correspondents resident in Mexico with Vicente Lombardo Toledano, general secretary of the Mexican Workers Confederation, 23 June 1937, AGN, LCR, vol. 450, file 432.3/217.

1   The Defeat of the Spanish Republic

It was in Spain where fascism and anti-fascism faced off against each other after General Francisco Franco took up arms against the Republican government, formed following the parliamentary elections in February 1936. Military assistance in weapons and ammunition from Germany and Italy facilitated Franco's gains against Republican positions. The anti-fascist camp was comprised of the Spanish Communist Party, one of the smallest in Europe, the Republican Party and the Spanish Socialist Workers Party. Initially they were joined by the anarchists and the revolutionary Marxists of the Workers' Party of Marxist Unification (Partit Obrer D'Unificació Marxist, POUM), born in 1935 and counted on 10,000 militiamen. In the coalition there were armed workers who defended the Republican government, but some were anxious to establish 'the dictatorship of the proletariat'; there were landless peasants who saw their future in the agrarian revolution and in some regions such as Aragon and Catalonia militants of the anarchist National Confederation of Labour as well as the revolutionary Marxists, who rejected the Republican state, advocated collectivisation of land and seizure of factories. The communists seemed politically timid to them.[4]

The aid from Germany and Italy to Franco forced the Soviet Union to feel no longer bound by its initial commitment to non-intervention in the Spanish conflict, to send military experts and material, and to organise the International Brigades, with its total of 40,000 men and women combatants. Even with the military aid received, the Republican government with the Socialist Largo Caballero at its head, did not have the strength to overcome the onslaught of the better armed and organised nationalist army. The division between democrats and revolutionaries worked to the detriment of the Spanish anti-Franco forces.

Soviet aid helped the insignificant Spanish Communist Party grow from a few thousand to a quarter of a million members. But Stalin did not want the party to assume a leading role in the war; rather he wished to see it confined to strengthen the popular government without being part of it. The communists in the government could alarm the allies, France and Britain, and cause them to join Germany and Italy. If Franco were to win, the system of collective security would be weakened and the balance of forces would be altered in favour of fascism. These calculations figured decisively in the form and amount of Soviet military aid and the intervention of the Communist International in Spain to strengthen certain forces and weaken others, restrict the actions of

---

4   Rees 1998, pp. 143–67; Hobsbawm 1994, pp. 157–9; Groppo 2007, pp. 104–7.

the Republicans to the legal defence of the government against Franco and not socialise industry or expropriate the landowners. If Spain were to have its 'October' revolution, the Western countries would have been even more divided and the possibilities of reaching an understanding with the USSR further diminished.[5]

This calculation was contrary to the political line of the revolutionary Marxists and anarcho-syndicalists, who in some cities revolted against the Republican government. In the field they had successful military encounters with the nationalist army, formed revolutionary committees, took over local governments, collectivised industries and agriculture, since they believed that the civil war and the revolution were inseparable. In place of the regular army, led by the Soviet commissars, the revolutionary Marxists wanted to pursue the war with popular militias. Alarmed, the Republican government repressed them in order to count on the Soviet military support and agreed to the communists' influencing the government and the course of the war. To ensure its authority, the USSR also sent 2,000 military advisers to help the Republican government strengthen its army. Moscow also dispatched agents of the secret police and the Comintern, in order not to lose control of the communists and to repress the anarchists and POUM members, who were denounced as Trotskyists and fascists. Juan Negrín's government declared the POUM illegal and arrested its leaders. Andreu Nin, the most prominent among them was kidnapped by the Soviet secret police in Barcelona and died under torture in June 1937.[6]

In the Republican ranks the defeats and contradictions multiplied with the repression against the POUM and the murder of Nin. Friction between the International Brigades and the Republican army sparked discouragement and desertions. The outlook was grim, given the insufficient aid from the USSR, as well as from Mexico, in quantity and quality compared to what was provided by Germany and Italy to the Franco forces. By 1938, Moscow lost interest in providing further support for the popular anti-fascist coalition. In the spring of 1939 the Republic surrendered, but by then Stalin had already left it to its fate, after secretly negotiating a non-aggression pact with Hitler.[7]

Lombardo followed the developments in Spain on a daily basis and took advantage of the events to fuel his bombastic speeches on the dark future. 'We will still have to shed much blood', he said at the beginning of the war, so that the Mexican comrades not let 'the light of the Earth' be extinguished for the

---

5 Hobsbawm 1994, p. 160; Cotterill 1994, p. 114; McDermott and Agnew 1997, pp. 139–40.
6 Radosh, Habeck and Sevostianov (eds) 2001, pp. 12–14; pp. 171–210, p. 421; Rees 1998, pp. 147–8; Eley 2002, p. 273; Vaill 2014, pp. 255–6.
7 Cotterrill 1994, p. 119; Radosh, Habeck and Sevostianov (eds) 2001, pp. 431–5.

Spanish people.⁸ The civil war in Spain was an epic story that would end with 'the final blow to the adversary'. As long as this did not occur, it would be necessary to help out with money, sweaters knitted by women and toys that children should be able to do without.⁹ The bad blood and defeats on the military fronts and in the corridors of power did not make it into his speeches.

2 Exile

Since the rise of National Socialism to power in Germany, agents of the Third Reich were in Mexico active in espionage and attempting to convert the German community abroad to the ideology of the Nazi regime through the National Socialist German Workers' Party (NSDAP) to prevent its assimilation into the country's culture and make it a participant in spreading national socialist ideas about Jews and communism. But in Mexico, Nazi diplomacy did not promote grandiose dreams of domination as it did in Europe, because it came up against the economic interests of successful and acclimatised German businessmen and a population that was pro-German because it was anti-American.[10]

But throughout the war, Lombardo took advantage of the anti-fascist propaganda to draw a grim picture. With an easy and fiery oratory style that among some swept away resistance and in others led to barriers being erected, Lombardo painted a portrait of a spider's web symbolic of the fabric of Nazi-fascism in Mexico, with names and addresses. In October 1941 at the Arena Mexico in Mexico City's popular neighbourhood, he gave details of the activities of the Nazis and their Mexican collaborators with names of organisations, agents, their methods of operation and of each region in which the National Socialist Party had divided the country with its governor, Gauleiter. The information was provided by British counterintelligence services. It was necessary to stoke the fear of fascism for the population to seek safety and security in the government, its party, and leaders such as himself.[11]

It was also needed to explain who the Jews were so that, given the propensity to view them askance, the Mexicans welcomed them. Jews had given the

---

8   VLT, speech in defence of the Spanish Republic, delivered on 12 October 1936, unspecified location, in *Obra*, III/4, 1936, p. 391.
9   VLT, 'Las cuatro victorias de Teruel', editorial in *Futuro*, February 1938, in *Obra*, III/8, 1938, p. 119; 'Cómo debemos ayudar a España', leaflet, 5 December 1938, *El Popular*, 8 December, in *Obra*, III/8, 1938, pp. 301–4.
10 Miller 1995; Buchenau 2004, pp. 118–30.
11 VLT, 'Cómo actúan los Nazis en México', Mexico City, 17 October 1941, in *Obra*, IV/6, 1941, pp. 25–68; quote on p. 65; Katz 2002, p. 350.

world universal values such as monotheism and distinguished figures such as Spinoza, Marx, Bergson, Freud and Einstein. And yet they were regarded as an inferior race. Mexicans understood the Jews, because like them, they were considered inferior from birth. Lombardo wanted to touch a raw nerve in his audience at a meeting in the Palacio de Bellas Artes concert hall in August 1942 when he compared the degradation of the Jews by the Nazis with the degradation of Mexican indigenous peoples to irrational beings by the Spanish colonists.

Before a diverse audience, he offered an oratory work of propaganda and agitation, educational and forceful, to reiterate the obligation to fight for a change from the capitalist to the socialist system. His speech featured an overview of world history and the colonisation of Mexico to arrive at the assertion that there were no inferior races, only men who exploited other men, which would end once socialism was established. Lombardo knew Mexican popular culture, the primitive anti-Semitism that permeated it and that did not help the population understand the problem of the extermination of Jews in Europe. Talking before a public steeped in faith, he approached the future with biblical verses. Once men become masters of their destiny, the battle between man and nature and between man and man would come to an end, all become rich, and only then Isaiah's prophecy would be fulfilled: 'The wilderness and the dry land shall rejuvenate; the desert shall rejoice, and will blossom like the rose'.[12]

To combat fascism, Lombardo put the CTM, the newspaper *El Popular*, the magazine *Futuro*, which he had created, the Workers' University, and all his ideals, at the disposal of the anti-fascists. Since the beginning of the war, Mexico became a refuge for several dozen of these anti-fascists, who fleeing from Europe had saved their lives. They were Germans, Austrians, Swiss, Yugoslavs, Czechoslovaks, and Jews, most were intellectuals and prominent political figures in their countries. Among them were Leo Katz, Anna Seghers, Paul Merker, Otto Katz, aka Andre Simon, Otto Buhse, Hannes Meyer, Lenka Reinerová, Ludwig Renn, Alexander Abusch, Theodor Balk, Egon Erwin Kisch and Leo Zuckerman among others. Most, like Leo Katz, his wife and son Friedrich, passed through existential uncertainty for being communists, Jews, and Leo the supporter of the Republic in the Spanish Civil War before reaching the relative tranquillity of Mexico. Some who had been members of the International Brigades in Spain were locked up in internment camps in France after the defeat of the Republic, Germany's invasion of France and the latter's capit-

---

12   VLT, 'Judíos y mexicanos, ¿razas inferiores?', conference in the Palacio de Bellas Artes, Mexico City, 20 August 1942, in *Obra*, IV/9, 1942, pp. 35–64, quote on p. 64.

ulating to the Reich in 1940. The lawyer Carmen Otero, Vicente's sister-in-law, arranged visas for some refugees amid enormous bureaucratic and political difficulties to obtain them, make them valid and effective. For those who succeeded in obtaining the visas, Lombardo Toledano offered employment in the Workers' University as teachers in their fields of expertise and those with the gift of writing as journalists in *El Popular*. He collaborated with them in their cultural endeavours and ideological battles. However, with the arrival of the anti-fascists it turned out that there were not one but several varieties of anti-fascism and that they were at loggerheads with each other. Lombardo took the side of the pro-Soviet variant.[13]

In June 1939, Lombardo travelled to the port of Veracruz to welcome the first wave of refugees, 'the cream of the crop of the Spanish people',[14] whose lives were in danger if they were returned from France to Franco's Spain. In the selection process to grant the visas and to welcome them in Mexico, party affiliation or professional status should not have counted, but rather humanitarian criteria and moral responsibility.[15] Exile was a universal right:

> An exile is almost always a rebel against his country's government. He is a being who struggles for an ideal, good or bad, to which he subordinates his own life. Due to this higher moral value of the headstrong – the mediocre never revolt – the legislation that binds nations together has established the right of asylum as a human right.

Throwing 'the undesirable foreigner' out of the country was a false brand of sovereignty over which there was a higher moral precept 'that makes the world a refuge for the individual to whom the doors of his homeland are closed', without judging 'the value of his creed' and it was not granted 'in exchange for his silence'.[16]

Lombardo applied this criterion to accept the Spanish combatants and anti-fascist communists, but excluded opponents of Soviet policies from the right to exile in Mexico. He would come to the aid of the communist anti-fascists, but

---

13   Katz 2002, pp. 43–8 and Gleizer 2002, pp. 119–40; Von Hanffstengel, pp. 671–95; Leidenberger 2014, vol. 2, pp. 499–539; Jacinto 2014, pp. 159–242; Acle-Kreysing 2016, pp. 573–686.
14   VLT, 'Emocionante bienvenida se dio ayer a los refugiados españoles en Veracruz', newspaper account of the speech, Veracruz, 13 de junio 1939, *El Popular*, 14 June 1939, in *Obra*, III/9, 1939, p. 285.
15   VLT, 'No se trata de comerciar con el infortunio de los iberos', *El Popular*, 14 April 1939, in *Obra*, III/9, 1939, pp. 195–7.
16   VLT, 'México y el derecho de asilo político', in *El Universal*, 18 April 1934, in *Obra*, III/1, 1934, pp. 83–5.

would fight the anti-Stalinists.[17] This latter variant of anti-fascism was sparked by the show trials staged by the Soviet state police between 1936 and 1938 when, supervised by Stalin, the government concocted legal proceedings against the old Bolsheviks who had participated in the 1917 revolution and whose fate was the firing squad, exile or forced labour. With their physical liquidation, which shocked many communists in Western countries, Stalin wanted to erase the memory of the bond that tied them to the October Revolution and Lenin, and annul the testimony of the secondary role that he himself had played in that historic feat.

Anti-fascist refugees were grateful for the respite offered to them by Mexico. They created organisations to influence public opinion and the German colony against Nazism and to be in contact with German immigrants in Latin America and the United States. In the propaganda campaigns, they functioned as anti-fascists and not as communists, so as not to awaken anti-communist instincts in the government and segments of the population. Lombardo helped them in different ways. One was to obtain paper for their publications and low printing costs through the print shop unions.

El Libro Negro del terror Nazi en Europa: testimonios de escritores y artistas de 16 naciones (*Black Book of Nazi Terror in Europe: Testimonies from Writers and Artists of 16 Nations*) was an editorial success in terms of sales, publicity and for spreading its message. Published in April 1943 by the publishing house El Libro Libre, it was edited by the Czech communist Otto Katz, skilled in the art of propaganda.[18] It was a collaborative project of the German-speaking anti-fascists, Spanish exiles in Mexico, renowned writers such as Leon Feuchtwanger and Heinrich Mann, and French authors. A total of 56 writers contributed to the book, accompanied by Mexican graphic artists. Lombardo participated in its production, circulation, and also with an article in which he cited a supposed quote from Hitler on the perversity of the Indians and the master race's need to conquer Latin America.[19]

The book's 10,000 copy press run was financed by President Ávila Camacho's government. Swiss architect Hannes Meyer was responsible for the illustrations. Among others he included the poignant lithograph *Deportation to Death*

---

17 VLT, 'Atacar Rusia es servir al fascismo', speech, 8 November 1938, Palacio de Bellas Artes, Mexico City, *El Popular*, 8 November 1938, in *Obra*, III/8, 1938, p. 162.
18 Otto Katz/Andre Simone, 'Adolfo Hitler: la policía lo busca', *El Libro Negro del Terror Nazi en Europa*, 1943, p. 22.
19 VLT, 'Destrucción total del régimen Nazi-fascista', in *El Libro Negro del terror Nazi en Europa*, p. 277, digital version at https://archive.org/details/ElLibroNegroDelTerrorNaziEnEuropa. Accessed 4 May 2015.

by Leopoldo Méndez of the left-wing artists' workshop Taller de Gráfica Popular, in which a Nazi soldier could be seen imprisoning anguished people, squeezed into a boxcar. Other anti-fascist endeavours between 1941 and 1946 included the magazine *Freies Deutschland* (Free Germany) and the Heinrich Heine club, where the exiles performed theatre, organised lectures and concerts, and exhibited films. In doing so, they demonstrated that there was a German culture that had nothing to do with the Nazi degradation of all those 'who refused Hitler permission to rob from them the pleasure of enjoying culture'.[20]

Mexico allowed the exiles a respite from the horrors of Europe and enabled them to put their lives, and in some cases their Judaism, into perspective. The Czechoslovak journalist Egon Erwin Kisch travelled to Hidalgo, because he knew that in Venta Prieta there was a Jewish community and wrote that he had found a Sephardic adaptation to Mexican rural culture. Its description made him meditate: 'My thoughts roamed farther – to relatives, friends and enemies, sacrificed by Hitler, all entitled to be remembered in the prayer for the dead'. Killed in the gas chambers, without hope, without even the hope of revenge, of punishment for mass murder and 'as if the idea of humanity never existed, the aspiration of bringing into the world more bread, more right, more truth, more health, more wisdom, more beauty, more love, more happiness'.[21]

Kisch, among others, wanted to build a bridge between a Mexico that welcomed them and a Europe that rejected them, between peace and war, between life and death. However, the exiles also brought their ideological antagonisms to Mexico, exacerbated by the feeling of persecution, loss of family, friends, of the ideals trampled in a Europe turned into a cemetery.

3   Face to Face with Leon Trotsky

Lombardo Toledano admired the Bolshevik Revolution and knew it was inseparable from Leon Trotsky. Revolutions were not made by tyrannised peasants but by 'a group of men who dedicated their lives to meditating, to studying sci-

---

20   Egon Erwin Kisch, 'Eine Tat des kollektiven Optimismus' ('An action of collective optimism'), in Segel 1997, p. 373; Cañadas, 'El apoyo del exilio republicanos español al exilio de habla alemana en México', www.cihde.es/sites/default/files/congresos/pdf/CAÑADAS .pdf, 2014. Accessed 4 May 2015; Katz 2002, p. 45; Zogbaum 2005, pp. 1–28; Von Mentz and Radkau 1984, pp. 43–59; Barajas 2011, pp. 23–298; Merfish 2009, pp. 36–41.

21   Egon Erwin Kisch, 'Indiodorf unter dem Davidstern' translated into English as 'An Indian village under the star of David' in Segel 1997, p. 371.

entific laws as a result of which historical processes occur', trained men, 'who have, naturally, shown the road to the masses; not the masses themselves'.[22] When he delivered this speech in 1933 he recalled the revolutionary role of Trotsky who 'worked hand-in-hand with Lenin'. But when Trotsky arrived in Mexico in January 1937, Lombardo labelled him a fascist and denied him the right to seek refuge that President Cárdenas had given the Russian revolutionary to provide him a respite from the persecution of the Soviet government and political police, when no other country was willing to do so. During the three and a half years that Trotsky remained in Mexico, Lombardo dedicated his efforts to discredit him, using the CTM as the collective voice of the workers, and the press under his control, as weapons of combat to erase him from history as a collaborator of Lenin, the icon of the revolution.[23]

In his first statement against Trotsky, Lombardo made much ado about not belonging to the Communist Party, which was true, but lied when he denied having any relationship with the Communist International or that he acted with an independent mind. On the occasion of the crisis in the CTM in April 1937, he wrote to Moscow that 'through various channels I found that the decision of the President of the Republic was already taken, in the sense of giving asylum to Leon Trotsky so that it would have been futile to try to prevent his arrival'.[24]

To oppose the fait accompli, Lombardo sent a circular letter to the Cetemistas with his version of what Trotskyism was and instructions for them to demand that the president expel the exile. The PCM and Lombardo Toledano wanted to, but could not, prevent Trotsky from moving around Mexico with relative freedom.[25] Installed in the home of Diego Rivera, the Bolshevik gathered materials to refute the false and absurd allegations levelled against him during the Moscow trials, contained in the confessions extracted from the accused under torture and without proof. Trotsky presented his evidence before a tribunal of American and European intellectuals that met in Mexico and held its sessions beginning in April 1937.[26]

---

22 VLT, 'Convención extraordinaria de la CROM', 12 March 1933, *Futuro*, May 1934, in *Obra*, II/4, 1933, pp. 59–60.
23 VLT, 'El asilo de México para León Trotsky', *Futuro*, January 1937, in *Obra*, III/5, 1937, pp. 1–5; Gall 2010, pp. 367–602.
24 Vicente Lombardo Toledano to Aleksandr Lozovsky, Mexico City, 15 April 1937, RGASPI, f. 534, register 7, file 399; Kuteischikova 1998, p. 6.
25 VLT, 'Tercer Consejo Nacional de la CTM', in *Obra*, III/5, 1937, pp. 50–1; Sole Union of Agricultural Workers of the National Irrigation System # 4, Cd. Anáhuac, to the President of the Republic, Nuevo León, 25 January 1937, ibid., 79.
26 Gall 1991, pp. 93–107.

For Stalin and the Comintern officials it was unacceptable that Trotsky would have the opportunity to defend himself, to express his ideas and to continue railing against the Soviet regime. In the eyes of Moscow, the Mexican communists were responsible for Trotsky being able to breathe freely in Mexico and not be expelled. Stalin took charge of ending this insolence. Lombardo helped as well.

It was true that he did not use the virulent language of the Stalinists who called for the physical liquidation and extermination of the enemies of the people and the fascists, reducing them to decaying flesh. He had another tactic. At the CTM congress in February 1938, Lombardo attacked Trotsky as if the accusations he spit out were the opinion of the organisation. He pronounced Trotsky a danger, because he inopportunely advocated the dictatorship of the proletariat at a time in which fascism was growing and the multi-class popular fronts guaranteed peace. Lombardo may have been instructed to intensify the campaign of slander and vilification of Trotsky in the general council of the International Federation of Trade Unions held in Oslo in July 1938 in order to achieve the exile's expulsion from Mexico. In that meeting, Lombardo lobbied unsuccessfully to include the Soviet trade unions in the IFTU. Trotsky, who described the Soviet trade unions as dependent on the state and on one single man, wrote at the time that the IFTU did well in not admitting them.[27]

Trotsky was pained by the fact that Mexican workers should have thought of him what Lombardo told them, namely, that the Bolshevik leader represented reaction, fascism, the right, and that he was never a Leninist or a Marxist. Trotsky did not stop and despite having pledged to General Cárdenas's government that he would not meddle in Mexican politics, he went public to address the workers of the CTM.

> One of the most zealous and shameless of the Moscow bureaucracy's agents is Lombardo Toledano, the general-secretary of the CTM. His contemptible activity is unfolding before everyone's eyes. He defends Stalin, Stalin's violence, his betrayals, his provocateurs and his executioners. It is not the least bit surprising that Toledano should be the most avid enemy of Trotskyism; it is the gentleman's job![28]

---

27 VLT, 'La CTM y Trotski. Resolución adoptada en el Primer Congreso de la CTM el 25 de febrero 1938', in *Obra*, III/7, 1938, pp. 123–38, quote on p. 136; Olgin 1935; VLT, 'Informe acerca del viaje a Europa y a Estados Unidos ante el VIII Consejo nacional de la CTM', 14 July 1938, in *Obra*, III/7, 1938, pp. 343–4.

28 VLT, '¿Qué significa la lucha contra el "trotskismo"?' (A propósito de Lombardo Toledano y otros agentes del GPU), Coyoacán, 9 October 1938, Mexico City, Mexican section of the

If Lombardo did not want to present evidence against Trotsky, it was because 'he doesn't have a single shred of evidence to back up the slanders he repeats at Moscow's command'. When the CTM adopted a resolution against Trotskyism in February 1938, Lombardo 'was not acting in his capacity as secretary of a union, but rather as an agent of Stalin's secret police, the GPU'. Workers' democracy consisted in workers being able to form an opinion based on a clear and honest examination of the question but

> in order to serve Stalin's ends Toledano conspired against the Mexican workers. The delegates to the congress had no informational material whatsoever available to them; they were surprised by a military-like stratagem. The ignoble resolution was imposed by Toledano in the same way that Stalin, Hitler and Goebbels carry out the decisions of the 'people'.[29]

Trotsky was outraged. This method of operation indicated a 'totalitarian' scorn for the working class of a man who demanded 'that the Mexican government gags me and deprive me of the chance to defend myself against the slanders'. Lombardo was 'a treacherous liar acting in behalf of the Kremlin gang! Don't believe him'![30]

This time Lombardo's response was relentless: 'This old traitor, this old criminal suffers from delusions of persecution; He daydreams in the shadow of Stalin; he dreams in his sleep about the persecution of the Soviet government'.[31] Lombardo categorically denied that there was a plan to assassinate Trotsky. He charged that such accusations were 'phantoms created by his fevered imagination'.[32] When in May 1940 the attempt on Trotsky's life took place at his home in Coyoacán, 'a political institution and not the place of residence of a man who has come to our country to devote his life to questions outside the realm of the political struggle', Lombardo spread the story that it was a self-staged attack. Hiding behind the cover of the national committee of the CTM, Lombardo charged, Trotsky invented the story that the aim of the assault was to kill him in order to blame the Soviet secret police.[33]

4th International, 1938, Archives of the Centre for Studies of the Workers and Socialist Movement.

29 Ibid.
30 Ibid.
31 VLT, 'Atacar Rusia es servir al fascismo', speech, 8 November 1938, Palacio de Bellas Artes, Mexico City, in *Obra*, III/8, 1938, p. 162.
32 VLT, 'Atacar Rusia es servir al fascismo', speech, 8 November 1938, Palacio de Bellas Artes, Mexico City, in *Obra*, III/8, 1938, p. 163.
33 National Committee of the CTM, 'León Trotsky y la "guerra de nervios" yanqui contra Méx-

It was an attack and Lombardo must have known it. The assault squad was led by muralist David Alfaro Siqueiros, who said that he had contemplated Trotsky's death since he was a member of the International Brigades in the Spanish Civil War. According to Siqueiros's memoirs, he assumed that Trotsky 'in his tremendous theoretical confusion' had supported the Workers Party of Marxist Unification (POUM), as opposed to the communists, from 'a general command post that Trotskyism has in a Mexico City neighbourhood known as Coyoacán and which was protected by Mexican police forces'.[34] The shipment of arms to Spain and granting of asylum to Trotsky were anti-Soviet positions of President Cárdenas and represented 'a hidden ideological confusion, a political disorder on the part of General Lázaro Cárdenas', and therefore Siqueiros made the decision that 'Trotsky's general command post in Mexico should be closed, even if it means we have to find a violent way' to do so.[35] His task 'was to immobilise the outside defence squad at Trotsky's house, consisting of 35 Mexican police armed with Mausers and I adequately fulfilled that goal'.[36]

The most likely variant is that Siqueiros received instructions to carry out the assault from somewhere, and it might have been the communist militant and Comintern agent Vittorio Vidali; the rest was a smokescreen to justify it: 'We turned to Vicente Lombardo Toledano and Lombardismo. Compañero Vicente Lombardo Toledano put up the best theoretical fight against Trotsky during the time the latter was in Mexico ... There was almost not a single declaration by Trotsky that Vicente Lombardo Toledano did not completely destroy in all possible polemical styles'.[37]

But Lombardo did not polemicise with Trotsky, but discredited him. Debating his ideas would have given Trotsky the opportunity to present his critique of Stalinism, provide him with a platform, which Lombardo, following the Soviet line, wanted to prevent.

Siqueiros denied responsibility until June when his cronies betrayed him as the head of the plot.[38] In trying to avoid prison, he went on the run around the Jalisciense village of Hoxtotipaquillo where he was apprehended. In his memoirs, Siqueiros said he was in prison a year. Apparently it was six months.[39]

---

ico', Mexico City, 5 June 1940, in *Obra*, IV/2, 1940, p. 92; Trotsky to the Federal Prosecutor's Office, Chief of Police, General Núñez, Foreign Relations Ministry, Mexico City, 27 May 1940, in the Joseph Hansen collection, Hoover Institution Archive.

34 Siqueiros 1977, pp. 356–7, quote on p. 359.
35 Siqueiros 1977, pp. 361–6.
36 Siqueiros 1977, p. 369.
37 Siqueiros 1977, p. 367.
38 Dugrand 1992, p. 60.
39 Reyes Palma 1996, p. 46.

Chilean poet and consul in Mexico, Pablo Neruda, came to his rescue. Neruda vaguely recalled Siqueiros's attack, perhaps deliberately so in order not to draw attention to the Soviet secret police:

> Someone had sent him on an armed raid of Trotsky's house. I met him in prison, and outside as well, because we used to go out with Commandant Pérez Rulfo, the warden, to have a drink somewhere where we wouldn't be noticed too much. We would return late at night and I would bid David goodbye with an embrace and he would stay there behind bars.[40]

But not for long: 'During clandestine sorties from jail and conversations on every topic, Siqueiros and I planned his final deliverance' and his departure for Chile. According to Siqueiros, it was the president who unexpectedly released him, protected him against the Trotskyists who allegedly wanted to kill him and gave him safe conduct to go to Chile. Weighing in his favour was that remote attack many years earlier of the revolutionary army on Guadalajara. One night, with the soldiers hidden in a hut at the Castillo hacienda, Siqueiros opened the door to a 'chubby' lieutenant, soaked with water in search of shelter. He let him in. That night they shared a bedroll. The chubby lieutenant was the future President Manuel Ávila Camacho.[41]

Trotsky knew that Lombardo did not participate in the attack. He was a public figure to whom the secret police assigned other tasks, namely, the political assassination through verbal fire. Given that all the attempts to expel Trotsky from Mexico failed, Lombardo took this opportunity to arouse the hostility of the police against the victim of the attack, helping the aggressors and thus making it possible that he be handed over to the Soviet state police.[42]

When the predicted assassination occurred in August 1940, Lombardo condemned it as a counterrevolutionary act and declared that the CTM would cooperate with authorities in the investigation of 'the attitude assumed by provocative elements, enemies of Mexico'.[43] Lombardo probably knew where the order for the killing came from, but he had to divert attention away from

---

40 Neruda 2001, p. 214.
41 Neruda 2001, p. 215; Siqueiros 1977, pp. 379–82.
42 L. Trotsky to the Federal Attorney General, Police Chief, General Núñez, Foreign Relations Ministry, 27 May 1940; L. Trotsky, 'El diputado Toledano lanza una nueva calumnia', Coyoacán, 2 June 1940, Joseph Hansen collection, Hoover Institution Archive. Lombardo was not a congressional deputy; Trotsky might have been referring to Vicente's brother Humberto who was a local legislator.
43 VLT, 'Condena al atentado de León Trotsky', Mexico City, 21 August 1940, in *Obra*, IV/3, 1940, p. 37.

the real perpetrators toward the undefined enemies of Mexico. Thereafter, he lost interest in Trotsky as a person, but devoted himself to disprove his theory of permanent and the proletarian revolution, and to defend socialism in a single country, the Soviet Union. It might have been Lombardo who negotiated Siqueiros's departure in 1940 and his return from exile in 1943 with the President: 'You can come to Mexico as soon as you want', Lombardo wrote to him.[44] Still the president, Cárdenas's verdict on the killing of Trotsky was that the communists who were behind it on behalf of a foreign country betrayed Mexico.

4 The Pact and Its Violation

Legions of communists and sympathisers of the Soviet Union were confronted with the show trials of the old Bolsheviks, their physical liquidation and the persecution of their families. The non-aggression pact between Germany and the USSR, between Hitler and Stalin in August 1939, the raising of the German flag with the swastika at the airfield in Moscow and the Red Army band playing the Nazi Horst Wessel anthem, left the world astonished.

The pact was also an agreement for territorial division, with Poland, Finland and the Baltic States being assigned to spheres of influence. It turned out to be timely when Hitler invaded Poland in September 1939 and when Britain and France declared war on Germany, to have a neutral USSR, since the pact committed its signers to neutrality in the event that one of the two sides were to participate in war. *L'Humanité*, the organ of the French Communist Party, explained that Stalin made every effort to prevent the imperialist war. The Comintern silenced anti-fascist propaganda and presented the beginning of the war as an inter-imperialist affair. Stalin hoped the pact would leave the capitalist countries perplexed, that they would bleed themselves dry and that the war was the road to socialism.[45]

It was the end of an illusion, wrote Hungarian author Arthur Koestler, at the time a communist. Poet Octavio Paz, 25 years old, resigned from the editorial board of *El Popular*, the newspaper founded by Lombardo, 'because I do not understand anything that's happening ... I felt they had cut off not only our wings but our tongues. What could we say'?[46] The pact shattered the morale of thousands of communists and their sympathisers who could not understand

---

44 VLT to Siqueiros, Mexico City, 26 August 1943, FHLT, file 521.
45 Koestler 1991, pp. 30–2; Roberts 2006, pp. 30–60; Eley 2002, pp. 279–82.
46 Octavio Paz, cited in Domínguez Christopher 2014, p. 92.

how Stalin could team up with Hitler. Lombardo Toledano was clear. He had to defend the pact, with discretion. He knew that the deal was signed with a chancellor who had wiped out the labour unions, persecuting communists and abolishing all political parties except the national socialists. However, he defended the pact as the USSR's tactical move to gain time and prepare for war.[47]

But in June 1941 Germany unexpectedly violated the pact, attacked the Soviet Union and everything changed 'in human history'. From that point on, it was necessary to fight 'the barbaric and bloody regime of Hitler' and now cease 'raising the anti-communist argument as a smokescreen to hide a fascist agenda' because 'the moment of the supreme battle' has arrived.[48] Anti-fascism was reinstated as the policy of the Soviet state also in Lombardo's rhetoric.

In the late hours of 8 May 1943, Stalin summoned Georg Dimitrov and Dmitri Manuilsky, secretary and former secretary of the Communist International respectively, and informed them that the Comintern 'is an obstacle in today's circumstances for the independent development of the communist parties and (for them) to fulfil their special tasks'.[49] Stalin, without asking anyone's opinion, dissolved the Comintern as proof that the USSR no longer had the intention of spreading the revolution to the West.[50] Lombardo nodded in agreement that the dissolution 'will strengthen the unity of the world as an anti-fascist bloc'[51] without explaining how.

5   In Soviet Intelligence

In November 1942, Soviet secret police agent Katherine Harris, better known as Kitty, was chosen by her superiors to contact 'Shturman' (Navigator in Russian), which was the pseudonym that they had given to Lombardo Toledano. Kitty's assignment was to convince him to work with her. At that time the main task was to get Trotsky's assassin, the Spanish communist Ramón Mercader, alias

---

47   VLT, 'Intervención en la junta de orientación convocada por la CTM a propósito del estallido de la guerra', Mexico City, 8 September 1939, in *Obra*, III/10,1939, pp. 185–97; Rankin 2009, pp. 53–4.
48   VLT, 'El dilema histórico del momento actual: fascismo o antifascismo', *El Popular*, 24 June 1941, in *Obra*, IV/5, 1941, pp. 48–9.
49   Lebedeva and Narinsky 1996, cited on p. 153.
50   Banac (ed.) 2003, p. 38; Priestland 2010, p. 203; McDermott and Agnew 1997, p. 194.
51   VLT, 'La Internacional Comunista se disuelve', newspaper account, undated, in *Obra*, IV/11, 1943, p. 111.

Gnome, out of prison. Mercader, who managed to hide his true identity until 1952, was sentenced to 20 years in prison.[52]

Several individuals were connected to the effort to free Mercader from the jail. Among them were some communists, Javier Rojo Gómez, former governor of Hidalgo and mayor of Mexico City; the Spanish exile Margarita Nelken; Julio Álvarez del Vayo, former minister in the government of the Spanish Republic; Pablo Neruda and Luis Enrique Delano, who replaced him as Chilean consul in Mexico and the Chilean communist Carlos Contreras Labarca. Adolfo Orive Alba, an engineer at the National Irrigation Commission and friend of Lombardo, appeared periodically in telegrams dealing with the issue of the release of Mercader, although it has not been possible to define his role.[53] The operation was supervised from Moscow. It was not successful, because too many unreliable people were involved. Nevertheless, the prisoner lived without constraints. He had a comfortable cell and medical care from Dr Esther Chapa, former wife of communist activist Rosendo Gómez Lorenzo.[54]

The most likely variant is that Lombardo was not directly involved in that effort. He was careful in his relations with Soviet intelligence operators and put a limit to his collaboration and that of Orive de Alba with them. When the Soviet secret police, the KGB, needed to transmit money to a pair of agents illegally in the country and wanted to do so using Orive's bank account, Lombardo put a halt to the operation because Orive would not have been able to explain the origin of such a large amount of money in his account and could be accused of illicit enrichment. He helped Harris find housing and obtain passports for a pair of agents living in Mexico illegally. The relationship did not give

---

52 Jacques Monard, a Belgian citizen, was how Mercader called himself when he was apprehended.
53 'De Moscú a México', 20 February 1944, Venona, ref., no. 3/NBF/T2030. Fausto Pomar Aguilar, secretary of Friends of the USSR, possibly Rafael Carrillo, and Czech national Andre Simon were among the collaborators in this endeavour; 'De Moscú a México', 9 June 1944, Venona, ref., no. 3/NBF/T847.
54 'De México a Moscú', 31 March 1944, Venona, ref. no. 3/NBF/T988 and 'México a Moscú', 2 April 1944, ref. no. 3/NHF/T869, 'México a Moscú', 3 April 1944, ref. no. 3/NBF/T702, 'Moscú a México', 10 April 1944, Venona, ref., no. 3/NBF/T573, 'México a Moscú', 18 April 1944, ref. no. 3/NBF/T1041; 'Moscú a México', 11 May 1944, Venona, ref., no. 3/NBF/T800; 'Moscú a México', 30 May 1944, Venona, ref. no. 3/NBF/T935; 'México a Moscú', 3 June 1944, ref. no. 3/NBF/T688; 'De Bogotá a Moscú', 6 June 1944, Resent, T622; 'México a Moscú', 6 June 1944, ref. no. 3/NBF/T686; 'México a Moscú', 9 June 1944, ref. no. 3/NBF/T691; 'México a Moscú', 29 June 1944, ref. no. 3/NBF/T396; 'San Francisco a Moscú', 19 August 1944, ref. no. 3/NBF/T844; 'México a Moscú', 8 September 1944, ref. no. 3/NBF/T1731 in http://www.theblackvault.com/documents/nsa/venona/monographs/monograph-1.html.

the expected results and Kitty's superiors feared that she had fallen in love with Lombardo and instead of obtaining the information from him that they requested, she was giving him information on topics related to the USSR that he was interested in.

The secret police realised that Lombardo Toledano was not equipped for clandestine work and preferred to cultivate public relations with the Soviet ambassador Alexander Umansky since Mexico and the USSR had reopened their respective embassies in late 1942.[55] Nevertheless, it continued to report on his movements inside and outside of Mexico. When in 1944, Soviet intelligence needed a reliable person in North Africa, probably in Algeria, Lombardo named Spanish refugee Amaro del Rosal Díaz as the correspondent of *El Popular*.[56] Another service he rendered to the KGB was to recommend the Brigadier General Roberto Calvo Ramírez, alias Zapata, who served as the commander of the coastal defence forces in Baja California, and had the reputation of being an enemy of the Americans and the Church. It was said that he was to the left of Cárdenas, above succumbing to corruption and bribery, and therefore could be entrusted with the task of arranging the movement of persons illegally in Mexico across the border.[57]

Kitty Harris's mission failed because she was unable to convert Lombardo into an effective liaison between herself and the Mexican milieu to facilitate the work of Soviet espionage.[58] In the long run, Lombardo was more useful as a union and political leader than as a secret agent and more profitable for the cause as a promoter of Stalinist propaganda.

---

55 Damaskin and Elliot 2001, pp. 200–20; Haynes and Klehr 1999, pp. 283–6; Haynes, Klehr and Vassiliev 2009, pp. 406–536.
56 'Plans and financial arrangements for Kovboj's departure', 31 March 1944, Venona, 3/NBF/T988. Kovboj was identified as being Amaro del Rosal Díaz, a Spanish communist who presumably was a correspondent of *El Popular* in France and North Africa since the end of 1944. See the telegram 'México a Moscú', 3 April 1944, 3/NBF/T702; 'Sh ... to give information direct to "Redaktor"', 10 April 1944, 3/NBF/T573. 'Sh ...' corresponde a Lombardo and 'Redaktor' to Ambassador Umansky; 'De Moscú a México', telegram, 23 April 1944, 3/NBF/T927.
57 Schwartz 1997, p. 22.
58 Haynes and Klehr 1999, pp. 283–6. Damaskin and Elliot 2001, pp. 208–32; Schwartz 1997, pp. 19–25.

6 The Undesirable Anti-fascists

After the assassination of Trotsky, the attacks against anti-fascists who had once been or never were communists, and turned anti-Stalinist, did not cease. They feared that their turn would come. With frightening frequency, the cadavers of oppositionists or those who the Soviet government assumed were oppositionists would appear, as well as those who were uncomfortable witnesses of history. The latter included Soviet secret police agents Ignace Reiss, whose body was found in 1937 and Walter Krivitsky who was killed in 1941 after he published his testimony in the United States on his secret service in the Soviet intelligence apparatus. Carlo Tresca – the Italian-American journalist, labour leader and defender of the Spanish anarchists, but also a fierce critic of the Italian Mafia in the United States – showed up dead in 1943 on a street in New York. In the French countryside near Grenoble in 1940 Willi Munzenberg, a German agent and successful propagandist for Stalin in the West between the First and Second World War, was also found dead.[59]

Victor Serge, who after his expulsion from the Soviet Union settled in Belgium and then in Paris, sought a new sanctuary once France was occupied by Germany in 1940. He found it in Mexico. On the ocean voyage in 1941, he reflected:

> I believe that among our greatest mistakes and errors is, first of all, intolerance among ourselves. It comes from this feeling of possessing the truth that is at the bottom of all strong convictions, a just and necessary feeling – we possess great truths – but it also results in inquisitors and sectarians. Our salvation is in a tolerant intransigence, which consists of recognising each other's right to make mistakes, the most human of rights and the *right to think differently*, the only thing that gives meaning to the word *freedom*.[60]

But in Mexico he ran up against the inquisitors and the intolerance that he criticised, although he wrote Lázaro Cárdenas in 1942 in gratitude for the visa that his government had granted him: 'If I can now continue my task of witness and novelist in a free land, it is you to whom I largely owe it to'.[61]

Julian Gorkin, whom Serge helped along with others so that the Spaniard was released from prison in Spain, had been a communist until 1929, and later

---

59   Krivitsky 2000; McMeekin 2003, pp. 304–7; Scammell 2011, p. 105.
60   Serge quoted by Gilly, 'Victor Serge en México: el último exilio', in Gilly 2010, p. 603.
61   Gilly 2010, p. 607.

international secretary of POUM. From then onward, he dedicated his life to fighting against communism and Trotskyism, which he did not consider a rectification of Stalinism but its opponent and rival.[62] The other anti-Stalinist was the German Gustav Regler, who shared membership in the Communist Party with the Jewish anti-fascists before Hitler came to power, with the International Brigades in the trenches in Spain and at the Le Vernet concentration camp in France when Paris did not know what to do with them after the defeat of the Republic in the civil war. Like other communists, he was demoralised when Stalin allied himself with Nazi Germany, which made him leave the party. Regler's Spanish citizenship made it easier to get a visa to immigrate to Mexico. The other comrade was Marceau Pivert, a prominent French socialist and trade unionist, with political positions to the left of the party. Most of them were talented writers and firm proponents of democratic socialism. Serge, above all, influenced the political thinking of the budding poet Octavio Paz.[63]

These four, and others, were the verbal and physical target of Stalinist attacks in Mexico aimed at harassing them. The Mexican and American communist and pro-Soviet press heaped abuse against them as Trotskyite-fascists, Sinarquistas or spies. *El Popular* and *La Voz de México*, Lombardo and the communists, did not let up in attacking them as 'anarcho-Trotskyite gangsters'. They had not forgiven them for making public the KGB's effort to get Trotsky's assassin out of prison. On 29 January 1942 the communist press published a cartoon with a drawing of a tree, whose root was the skull of Trotsky and whose extending branches ended in the heads of snakes with the names of the four, plus Grandiso Muñiz, the other Spanish revolutionary socialist from the POUM.[64]

---

62 Weissman 2001, p. 177; Gorkin 1961; Claudio Albertani, '"Socialismo y Libertad" – El exilio antiautoritario de Europa en México y la lucha contra el estalinismo (1940–1950)', available at: http://www.globallabour.info/es/2008/09/socialismo_y_libertad_claudio_1html. Accessed 28 June 2017.
63 Ibid.
64 Robert G. McGregor to the State Department, Mexico City, 19 September 1940 and J. Edgar Hoover to Adolf Berle, undersecretary at the State Departament, Washington, D.C., 27 April 1944, NARA, RG 59, file 800.00B, Gorkin, Julian; Claudio Albertani, 'Vittorio Vidali, Tina Modotti, el estalinismo y la revolución', Fundación Andreu Nin at https://fundanin.net/2019/03/17/vittorio-vidali-tina-modotti/; Gustav Regler to Mauricius, Mexico City, 29 December 1941; Pivert to Regler, Mexico City, 7 May 1942; NA, KV2/3506, Gustav Regler; Otto Katz, *Novedades*, 8 February 1942; Julian Gorkin, Marceau Pivert, Victor Serge to *The Nation*, Mexico City, undated, Ralph de Toledano collection, Hoover Institution Archive; Weismann 2001, pp. 149–267; Miguel Ángel Velasco, 'En defensa de los asilados antifascistas', *La Voz de México*, 5 February 1942; Gilly 2010, p. 604; Victor Serge, 'Gorkin stabbed as Mexican C. P: Wrecks Erlich, Tresca Meeting', Mexico City, 2 April 1943. Copied from the Mexican press, without source data, in Hoover Institution Archive.

Those insulted responded:

> We sincerely regret that the noble and hospitable land of Mexico, which deserves our undying gratitude, is becoming a venue of struggles that we have neither wanted nor provoked. We feel that the right to asylum would be diminished if limited to saving our physical selves, without offering the corresponding guarantees of justice for the defence of our human dignity and our intellectual and moral selves, which for us is what counts over and above the other.[65]

The ideological quarrel between them and the other exiles demonstrated that the presence of Stalinism and anti-Stalinism weakened the common struggle against fascism and turned the European tragedy into a political weapon against some of them in the host country.

The writers Walter Benjamin, Virginia Woolf and Stefan Zweig committed suicide, not being able to bear the consequences of the global catastrophe. The exiles in Mexico, from whom the Stalinists wanted to wrest dignity and intellectual and moral freedom, who resisted amid insults, humiliation, and lack of means with which to live, continued writing about the events of the day to counter the premise that the march of history was a fatality.[66]

---

65   Victor Serge, Julián Gorkin, Marcel Pivert to the citizens and president of Mexico, to the deputies, to the Interior Minister, Mexico City, January 1942, New York Public Library, file SB p.v. 1460.
66   Serge 1984, p. 377.

CHAPTER 8

The Illusory Unity

With a dose of satisfaction Lombardo Toledano told the Wilkies, when they interviewed him in the 1960s, that 'some figures in the country's political life – important people – were thinking of my possible candidacy as successor to General Cárdenas'. But Lombardo did not accept the proposal, because 'instead of my candidacy being a factor of unity against the danger of war, it would be or could be a factor of division'. He declined, in order to 'spare my country a serious problem', because 'I have always resolved things based on the general interest and not my own'.[1] And the general interest was, at that moment in history, national unity.

1   On the Campaign Trail

Even if someone would have considered Lombardo's candidacy for the presidency, it would not have prospered, and he knew it. General Cárdenas's closest friend and the man with whom he shared ideas was his lieutenant Francisco J. Múgica, but the president did not choose him as his successor. Mexico was locked in a hostile circle due to the boycotts and insufficient markets following the nationalisation of the oil industry in March 1938. There was a malaise in the country 'with everyone tired of crazy strikes and unjustified lockouts based on workers' actions', Puebla businessman Marcos Mastretta wrote to his brother in Italy.[2] There was anxiety among workers because of rising prices, labour unrest in the oil industry as a result of periodic explosions attributable to lack of maintenance, discontent among railroad workers due to repeated accidents and deaths caused by the defective state of the railway tracks, the failure to raise wages and improve working conditions in a company that the government turned over to the workers for their own management.[3] The agrarian

---

1   Wilkie and Monzón 1995, vol. 4, pp. 226–7. These interviews have had a tremendous influence on historians and specialists, without them having been submitted to the scrutiny of what the intention was of the interviewers and interviewee. See Spenser 2016, pp. 70–87.
2   Marcos Mastretta to Carlos Mastretta, Puebla, 1 December 1938, in Mastretta (ed.) 2008, p. 126.
3   I. Ifort Rees to FO, Mexico City, 7 March 1939, FO 371/A2384/84/26; López Pardo 1997, pp. 133–44.

reform created discontent among those whose properties were expropriated and uncertainty among land owners. Meanwhile, the campesinos who received land lacked the inputs to farm it, while others waited to receive their parcel of land under the distribution programme.

Despite all the rumours, Lombardo was not a supporter of Múgica, because the Michoacano general had been one of the conduits through which Trotsky was accepted as an exile in Mexico and because his candidacy would not have brought together the fragmented society. The other unacceptable candidate was Juan Andreu Almazán, once a supporter of Victoriano Huerta after having been allied with Emiliano Zapata. He had become rich thanks to the revolution. It was also necessary to be circumspect about the electoral panorama given the sensitivities in Washington, which was not about to tolerate a hostile government right on its border when it needed its collaboration to defend the hemisphere from the much-feared fascism.[4]

In these circumstances, General Ávila Camacho, the defence minister at the time, seemed an ideal choice to lessen the acrimony of the anti-Cardenista sectors and to satisfy the campesinos and the population that hoped the reforms would continue. In this rarefied climate, there were some who associated Manuel Ávila Camacho with the 'Soviet Criollo duo' when the CTM and Lombardo Toledano endorsed him, and gladly joined the National Action Party when Manuel Gómez Morín, a kindred spirit in Lombardo's youth but now an adversary, established it in September 1939 in opposition to the government policies.[5]

Lombardo was overjoyed, since Manolo was an old friend from the days of primary school in Teziutlán. For his candidacy to succeed, he put the CTM at Ávila Camacho's disposal to promote his campaign. The organisation was already a tool that both politicians as well as union leaders used to climb the rungs of power, even though this weakened it as a labour confederation. The CTM depended on the government for resolving labour conflicts and independent forms of struggle against the employers was not its goal. In the course of its development, the confederation lost important unions that saw its bylaws systematically violated, flagrant displays of lack of democracy and dishonesty among those who comprised its national leadership. A significant number of national unions split into regional sections were, in turn, controlled by political

---

[4] Gall 1991, p. 218; Paz 1997, p. 233; Musgrave, 'Las aventuras y desventuras de Juan Andreu Almazán', available at: http://profmex.org/mexicoandtheworld/volume9/3summer04/lasaventuras_y_desenturas.htm. Accessed 14 April 2015.

[5] Marcos Mastretta to Carlos Mastretta, Puebla, 26 April 1939, in Mastretta (ed.) 2008, p. 130; Krauze 1997a, pp. 478–9.

groups: the PRM, the PCM, followers of Lombardo or of Fidel Velázquez. The oil, electrical and railway workers had sections within the CTM, some communist, others anti-communist.

Without listening to the union members, the national council meeting in February 1939 'unanimously' voted for Ávila Camacho as the CTM's presidential candidate.[6] The news sparked uncertainty and bewilderment among the rank-and-file. It was rumoured that a faction of the CTM was in favour of General Múgica, another was for Almazán, and that in the states there were not always reliable people from the national council on hand who would carry out the chosen policy.[7]

Despite what Lombardo proclaimed, he knew that the confederation was not 'indivisible'[8] and that the issue of presidential succession was ideological as much as a lever to obtain positions of power. To align the unions behind the Ávila Camacho candidacy, he and the national committee put his men in strategic places in the states, ignoring the preferences of unions whose ideas differed, even though in public he said otherwise: 'There is no CTM candidate for congressional deputy or senator who does not belong to one of the unions that comprise the confederation' or 'who is not supported by important forces in the district or state in which he is running'.[9]

Power in the state of Jalisco emanated from the governor and the top circles of the CTM and the PRM, not from the members of the Jalisco Workers Federation. The Cetemistas in the state resented such disrespect and the organisation lost members. Catalino Isaac, the federation secretary, was displeased with the national committee; people outside the unions were masquerading as leaders to get seats in congress, ignoring those who were genuine leaders. Lombardo received complaints against the ambitious 'bastards' in Hidalgo and from Yucatán he received a protest against the communists in the CTM who were campaigning in favour of Múgica.[10]

---

6   VLT, 'Ávila Camacho, precandidato de la CTM', declaration of the extraordinary meeting of the National Council of the CTM, 22 February 1939, *El Popular*, 23 February 1939, in *Obra*, III/9, 1939, p. 131.

7   I. Ifort Rees to FO, Mexico City, 18 January 1939, FO 371/A1019/84/26; Ignacio Reyes Retama to VLT, Veracruz, 27 March 1939, FHLT, file 348; Adolfo Orive Alba to VLT, Mexicali, B.C., 21 February 1939, FHLT, file 346.

8   VLT, 'Mitin en adhesión a Manuel Ávila Camacho', Mexico City, 24 July 1939, in *Obra*, III/9, 1939, p. 113.

9   VLT, 'La CTM pone en evidencia a los autores de versiones tendenciosas', *El Popular*, 27 January 1940, in *Obra*, IV/1, 1940, p. 31.

10   Catalino Isaac to the National Council of the CTM, Guadalajara, 16 February 1939, FHLT, file 346; 'El Comité Estatal del PCM saludamos a VLT y a todos los dirigentes de la CTM',

The CTM bylaws had established that the secretaries of federations and national committee members could not be candidates for elected public office, but this provision was repeatedly violated. Juan Gutiérrez was appointed and supported by the national committee when he was its member to run for governor of Nuevo León. Alejandro Carrillo was a candidate for the seventh district of the capital without being a union leader; it was enough to be friends with Lombardo, secretary of the Workers' University and director of *El Popular*. For the Celaya district in the state of Guanajuato, the designated candidate was Rafael Otero y Gama, Lombardo's brother-in-law, who without being part of the CTM, won the nomination against a union member. For a district of Campeche, the CTM supported Alberto Trueba Urbina, former president of the Board of Conciliation and Arbitration in the Federal District without being a union member.

In none of the above-mentioned cases, and others not cited, was the workers' opinion taken into account. The most famous example was that of José Jiménez Acevedo, Lombardo's private secretary. A native of Puebla, Jiménez had a bad reputation as a manager and administrator of the Ayotla sugar mill in Oaxaca; despite this, Lombardo appointed him to represent the Los Mochis district in Sinaloa.[11] In the La Laguna region in Gómez Palacio, Durango, the workers supported Maríano Padilla, but the national committee named Domingo Garibaldi. Congressional deputy Fernando Amilpa was designated as senatorial candidate for the state of Morelos without being a resident or maintaining recent ties to his home state. Luis, Lombardo's brother, after being a congressional deputy, was named a senatorial candidate for Puebla without belonging to any union. For a district in Guerrero, Arturo Martínez Adame was designated without having any greater merit in the state other than his friendship with the CTM secretary general. In Puebla, the leaders of the anti-moronista labour federation disagreed with the policy of the CTM and Lombardo's leadership, preferring the candidacy of General Almazán. Lombardo convened a 'unification' congress and manoeuvred for the creation of a new federation that would absorb all of the unions.[12]

In Sinaloa, the PRM candidate and the country's president were the arbiters over the suitability of the proposed candidates for governor, senators and congressional deputies. The general secretary of the CTM was their operator

---

Pachuca, Hidalgo, 16 February 1939, FHLT, file 346; Rubén Magaña to VLT, Mexico City, 17 April 1939, FHLT, file 350.

11 Carlos Martínez to VLT, Ingenio Central de Ayotla, Oaxaca, 16 March 1940, FHLT, file 380.
12 I. Ifort Rees a FO, Mexico City, 28 July 1939, FO 371/ A5552/84/26 and 7 August 1939, FO 371/A5708/84/26; 'Memorandum sobre la situación de la CTM', no author, date, or place of publication, November 1940, AGN, LC 433/178; Pansters 1996, pp. 58–9.

through those close to him. 'Yesterday afternoon, Compañero Lombardo Toledano gave me instructions to send you a telegram to the effect that you should no longer deal with the political question of Sinaloa', since President Cárdenas and Ávila Camacho's criterion was that 'Loaiza is not to be governor of that state, for various reasons, and they are leaning towards Colonel Leyva' to be the candidate.[13] The CTM's proposal was that the candidate would be a certain Alejandro Peña but no one contested the presidential decision.

However, Ávila Camacho changed his mind and asked the CTM to support Guillermo Liera for governor. The local CTM was divided, since several of its unions 'charged there was a lack of seriousness' involved. Others allied themselves with Liera in exchange for two federal deputies and a senate seat. At the time of the election, they obtained a seat in the Senate and one in the Chamber of Deputies for the CTM. The unions that placed their bets on the losing candidate suffered reprisals from the Conciliation and Arbitration Board, which did not resolve their cases brought before it. The campesinos from the League of Agrarian Communities of Sinaloa, which had belonged to the CTM, went with the winner in exchange for perks and privileges.[14]

In an election district in Aguascalientes, by decision of the state PRM, cetemista leader Aurelio Mercado had to step aside in favour of Benjamin Reséndiz. Resigned to the inevitable and loyal to the organisation, Reséndiz wrote: 'I am sure that the sacrifice imposed on the Cetemista organisations and members in this regard will be to the advantage of the organisation in general, because otherwise the national committee would not have allowed me to have been uselessly sacrificed'.[15]

Lombardo justified this way of proceeding because:

> Our candidates have proceeded serenely, as is the responsibility of the union delegates ... between us there is no one who is furious, no one disappointed, because no candidate of the CTM is his own personal candidate, but rather is the candidate of his organisation. And it's enough that a compañero who would not have won in the elections feel that his personal interest is above the collective interest, for him to deserve to be expelled from the CTM.[16]

---

13 José Jiménez Acevedo to Vidal Muñoz Díaz, 1 April 1939, FHLT, file 349.
14 José Jiménez Acevedo, Alejandro Peña and others to Manuel Ávila Camacho, very confidential, Mexico City, 10 August 1940, FHLT, file 392; Padilla Beltrán 2010. Accessed 10 March 2015.
15 Aurelio Mercado to VLT, Aguascalientes, 12 April 1940, FHLT, file 382.
16 VLT, 'En qué consiste mi patrimonio', speech delivered on 26 April 1940 in the Rex theatre, Mexico City, *El Popular*, 27 April 1940, in *Obra*, IV/2, 1940, p. 4.

Lombardo thought beyond individuals. The electoral process was not a 'political flea market' in a Mexico that was a link in the 'historical process [that] places the capitalist system in one of its greatest crises', and he called for 'coming to the aid of the proletariat and peoples of the destroyed Old World, to build a world truly worth living in on its ashes'. It was necessary to 'tighten the ranks'.[17] He was an example to follow 'to serve the cause of the Mexican Revolution against Mexico's traitors'. He made mistakes 'but never, I never, committed a single act contrary to the interests of my class, never!' To be in tune with his audience, Lombardo once again had to correct his past:

> When I was born, my father was a very poor wage-earner who received seventy-five centavos a day. My house was a single room in a guest-house in my village. Later on, my father, an intelligent, honourable, and hard-working man, made a small fortune, which he lent to my grandfather, who managed to raise significant capital in mines. This capital disappeared like foam with the turbulence caused by the Revolution. My father became an employee.[18]

And for the sake of transparency and scrupulousness, Lombardo presented his financial statements. He still owed thousands of pesos on his house; the garden had been arranged between himself and his wife and then with the help of his daughters. The furniture in his study 'was personally made by my wife'; the piano was a gift from the sugar workers' union and the car came from the cameramen's union. He lived from a stipend provided by the CTM and the Workers' University, which, he omitted to say, received a subsidy from government funds in the absence of union dues. He did not lead a self-indulgent life; he did not have, as he put it, 'lovers to maintain' or other commitments that prevented him from publicising what he received and how he spent it.[19]

With the upcoming elections approaching, unrest grew in different parts of the country due to the violence unleashed between the Almazanistas and their adversaries. From Orizaba, the Cetemistas called for assistance to disarm their opponents and thus avoid confrontations on election day, or acquire arms for themselves. 'Compañero Lombardo, you don't know the danger faced by our

---

17   VLT, 'En qué consiste mi patrimonio', speech delivered on 26 April 1940 in the Rex theatre, Mexico City, *El Popular*, 27 April 1940, in *Obra*, IV/2, 1940, p. 6.
18   VLT, 'En qué consiste mi patrimonio', speech delivered on 26 April 1940 in the Rex theatre, Mexico City, *El Popular*, 27 April 1940, in *Obra*, IV/2, 1940, p. 9.
19   VLT, 'En qué consiste mi patrimonio', speech delivered on 26 April 1940 in the Rex theatre, Mexico City, *El Popular*, 27 April 1940, in *Obra*, IV/2, 1940, p. 10.

representatives in the event of an armed movement and with this in mind, we are requesting instructions on what to do'.[20]

2 The Victory

'Hello America. This is Robert Frances Allen, your NBC correspondent in Mexico City', said the reporter as he began his broadcast on radio station XEW early in the morning on election day: 'unexpectedly there are few disturbances'. But at 1.30pm he reported nine dead and 27 injured, and the next day 19 dead and 259 injured.[21] The elections were violent and the results were controversial. Both Ávila Camacho as well as Almazán declared themselves the winner and both the state-party and the Republican Party of National Union published decisive numbers said to favour their respective candidates. British observers reported that between 75% and 90% of the electorate voted for Almazán and that there was intimidation before and during the election day. They also indicated that part of the CTM voted for Almazán due to the reorganisation of the railroad and oil workers' unions from above, resisted by the rank-and-file, and because state employees voted against the government that had not paid them their salaries on time.[22]

In these extraordinary national and international circumstances, the July 1940 elections were a success. General Manuel Ávila Camacho became president of a Mexico with close to 20 million inhabitants. Weighing in his favour for the end result was the blessing of the US government with which he agreed to cooperate in the hemispheric defence, although Ávila Camacho's immediate concerns were the developments in Mexico and not the distant scenario of the world war. To seal the friendship, US Vice President Henry Wallace came for the presidential inauguration in December, although the guest was received 'in a hail of stones'.[23]

The elections were a victory for the CTM and Lombardo. At the Palacio de Bellas Artes just after the elections his words 'so full of optimism, so sure and brave, so expressive' conveyed to his listeners a clear vision on the decline

---

20 Gabriel Andrade and others to VLT, Orizaba, Veracruz, 11 June 1940, FHLT, file 387.
21 'Hello America', 7 and 8 July 1940, FHLT, file 390.
22 'Votes for General Almazán in recent elections', Mexico City, 16 July 1940, FO 371/A3817/359/26; Contreras 1980, pp. 73–93; Agustín 2007, pp. 11–19.
23 I. Ifort Rees to FO, Mexico City, 27 November 1940, FO 371/A4978/359/26; Paz 1997, pp. 4–5; Schuler 1997, pp. 195–6; Taracena 1976, p. 13; Agustín 2007, p. 22.

of the capitalist system and the birth of a fairer world.²⁴ From Tampico, the semi-literate Isauro Villarreal commissioned someone to write a letter because he wanted to congratulate Lombardo: 'In my humble opinion, there are few men in our country and throughout the Americas who, like you, so dutifully deserve to be applauded by his fellow citizens' for the 'incredible energy, exemplary honesty, and admirable attributes' which have made you 'the most feared man by domestic and foreign reaction'.²⁵ From Veracruz, the veteran agrarian reform activist Manuel Almanza, who in 1940 was secretary of the state executive committee of the PRM, wrote: 'You, compañero Lombardo, have been able to interpret us' even though 'you have never spent hours and hours in front of a lathe'. Lombardo, instead of becoming wealthy, 'comes to the labour unions to feel close to our sorrows and to teach the road to liberation'.²⁶ Employees from the retail trade, industry and customs of the port of Veracruz admired Lombardo and, in appreciation of his wife who was the godmother of the union building, they implored him 'most attentively to give us the honour of obtaining a real life sculpture of her' once she had recovered from her recent surgery.²⁷

Those who expected an eclipse of Lombardo's influence in public life and in the new government were to be stripped of their illusion. Ávila Camacho might have given the impression of wanting to limit Lombardo's influence,²⁸ but real life brought them together. The 1940 elections showed that the CTM and Lombardo were indispensable as a political instrument of the state and its party. His personal attributes made him a vital link between the powerful and many of the powerless at a time when the election result provoked feelings of resentment and further defections from the CTM's ranks among those workers who due to the bribery, slanders, shenanigans and attacks aimed at favouring the PRM and CTM candidates felt cheated.²⁹ But Lombardo covered up his role

---

24 Julio Bandala to VLT, Mexico City, 18 July 1940, FHLT, file 390.
25 Isauro Villarreal Barte to VLT, Tampico, 18 July 1940, FHLT, file 390.
26 Manuel Almanza to VLT, Jalapa, 4 August 1940, FHLT, file 392.
27 Luis Gil Sequeda and Roberto J. Valle to Rosa María Otero de Lombardo, Veracruz, 5 August 1940, FHLT, file 392.
28 Loaeza 2013, p. 276.
29 Dip. Juan Pérez to the National Executive Committee of the CTM, Mexico City, 1 August 1940, FHLT, file 392; VLT to Adolfo Orive Alba, Mexico City, 21 August 1940, FHLT, file393; Adolfo Orive Alba to VLT, Tijuana, B.C., 4 September 1940, FHLT, file 395; Graciano Sánchez, Virgilio Salmerón, Magdalena Aguilar to the National Executive Committee of the CTM, Mexico City, 14 October 1940, FHLT, file 398; Congressional Deputy José Ch. Ramírez to VLT, Mexico City, 24 October 1940, FHLT, file 398; Oscar Gutiérrez to VLT, Mexicali, B.C., 20 November 1940, FHLT, file 401; Crider 1996, pp. 204–26.

in the decomposition and discontent in the ranks of the labour unions with his repeated profession of loyalty to the workers' cause.

During the six-year presidential administration Lombardo had the privilege of entering the National Palace through the front door and continued the practice of meeting with the president to discuss different types of issues, among them problems of the labour and campesino movements, personal concerns such as posts for acquaintances and friends, including the firing of his uncle and the request that he be reassigned to some new position, help for antifascists stranded in France, the problems of cooperatives, a building for the Workers' University, meetings for other people or transmission of confidential information on a variety of questions. If the matter was not resolved satisfactorily, Lombardo would schedule it for the agenda of the next meeting along with new requests for subsidies for his university or for *El Popular*.[30]

The former schoolmates knew how to take advantage of each other. Ávila Camacho counted on Lombardo and his trade union network to temper labour conflicts, as occurred in the arms factory in September 1941. The problem was the authoritarianism of its director, General Luis Bobadilla. The workers gathered in front of the presidential residence. Their tempers flared because the president would receive a delegation and not all the workers, some of whom were under the influence of alcohol. Angry, they tried to forcibly enter the premises and the officer guarding the building lost his head and ordered his men to open fire. When the smoke cleared, there were seven dead, including one union leader, and 35 wounded, two of whom subsequently died. Ávila Camacho could not punish the soldiers, but had to satisfy the relatives of the workers and the clamour in the unions to punish the guilty party. The CTM exonerated the president of any responsibility. Lombardo made an appearance at the funeral of the deceased, but the workers criticised him because he left without making any statement. The unions that wanted to march past the national palace as an act of solidarity were dissuaded by Lombardo and Velázquez from doing so, based on the argument that they shouldn't weaken national unity. The two labour officials got their way.[31]

The president rewarded his friend. In November 1941 Ávila Camacho supported the first congress of the CTAL with more than 57,000 pesos, the Workers' University with a subsidy of 250,000 pesos, and in 1942 agreed that he would provide an additional 75,000 pesos because the previous amount was

---

30   VLT, 'Asuntos para tratar con el C. Presidente de la República', Mexico City, 8 October 1941, FHLT, file 432; VLT, 'Asuntos para tratar con el C. Presidente de la República', Mexico City, November 1941, FHLT, file 436.
31   Campa 1985, pp. 169–79; Taracena 1972, pp. 436–9.

not sufficient.³² He was assigned two judicial police, for 'your immediate service', provided by the Attorney General.³³ There was nothing extraordinary in any of these acts. Lombardo was convinced that the government had a commitment to the workers and to him as the latter's personification, and he did not cease to ask for additional favours for himself and the CTM leaders.³⁴

3   The Farewell

Lombardo resigned as head of the Mexican Workers Confederation in March 1941. It was a conscious act and not the result of the loss of power or popularity as some felt or desired. Presenting the appointment of his successor, Fidel Velázquez, as unanimous and democratic was a minor simulation in the serious international circumstances to which he wanted to devote his full attention.

The transfer of power took place in the Arena Mexico in the popular neighbourhood of Mexico City. The walls of the arena were plastered with Lombardo's picture next to that of the president and Lázaro Cárdenas. A few months into his 47th year, Lombardo solemnly bid farewell to the leadership of the organisation that he had founded five years previously: 'If you don't see me, please know comrades that I will be working. We'll see each other at some point'.³⁵ The farewell was long and melodramatic according to the chronicle published in *El Popular*.³⁶ To seal his withdrawal from the CTM with the effect of his lasting presence, he remarked: 'I am leaving, pleased with having achieved two things at the time of my withdrawal, the interior unity of the CTM' and having put a line into practice, even though he knew that such unity did not exist and that the organisation adhered to several conflicting lines.

Fidel Velázquez, six years younger than Lombardo, should have calculated his first act in the position of general secretary as distancing himself from his predecessor. For the first time since its founding, the CTM leadership passed into the hands of a worker who represented the workers' consciousness. 'Manual workers such as me who have not had, due to their economic situation, the

---

32   Manuel Ávila Camacho (henceforth MAC), 'Acuerdo a la Secretaría de Hacienda y Crédito Público', Mexico City, 19 November 1941, AGN, Ramo Manuel Ávila Camacho (henceforth MAC), vol. 15, file 110.1/85 and 14 July 1942, vol. 1127, file 703.4/179.
33   Luís Aguilar y Maya to VLT, Mexico City, 22 August 1941, FHLT, file 434.
34   VLT to MAC, Mexico City, 4 December 1941, AGN, MAC, vol. 200, file 136.3/428.
35   VLT, 'Discurso al dejar la secretaría general de la CTM', Mexico City, 1 March 1941, *El Popular*, 2 March 1941, in *Obra*, IV/4, 1941, p. 261.
36   VLT, 'Discurso al dejar la secretaría general de la CTM', Mexico City, 1 March 1941, *El Popular*, 2 March 1941, in *Obra*, IV/4, 1941, p. 239 and p. 244.

economic situation of their families, the opportunity to receive an education, we cannot express ourselves in terms other than those used by the people'.[37] Velázquez also said he was a supporter of unity. Yet a month after he took office, at close to 41 years of age, strong and healthy, he reorganised the Mexico City labour federation as his own base and that of his friends with everything thrown in including a shock brigade.

Lombardo left the leadership of the CTM, because on a global scale, running the CTAL was of greater importance than leading a national organisation. Winning the war against fascism and Hitler and saving the USSR were the tasks of the moment and the others had to be subordinated to these goals. There was no sacrifice that he would not make to defend the USSR.[38]

Defending the interests of workers and the use of strikes as a weapon had to be suspended in favour of national and international unity. Lombardo promoted this policy in Mexico through Fidel Velázquez and the CTM, while the CTAL was his hemispheric instrument to ensure Latin America's economic cooperation with the US war effort, even though prices of raw materials and the profits of the countries that exported them had to be sacrificed. He transmitted this enormous power to his successor because he was confident that Velázquez would fulfil these tasks, even though he might employ different methods.[39]

Lombardo continued to be an arbiter of conflicts and disputes between some unions and state and federal authorities or among them, in order to influence their daily functioning and convince them of the tactic to attain the unity that he did not achieve as general secretary of the CTM. He strongly condemned the unions that broke away from the CTM and formed the dissenting National Proletarian Confederation. 'Only struggling within the ranks of the unions and keeping our distance from the influence of politicians can we assume the right to speak of being better union leaders'.[40] The criticism might have been directed at Fernando Amilpa, Alfonso Sánchez Madariaga and Arturo Martínez

---

37 Fidel Velázquez quoted in Aguilar García 1996, pp. 94–5; Granados Chapa 1996, pp. 56–9; Sánchez González 1991, p. 85.
38 VLT, 'Discurso al dejar la secretaría general de la CTM', in *Obra*, IV/4, 1941, p. 256.
39 VLT, 'Discurso al dejar la secretaría general de la CTM', in *Obra*, IV/4, 1941, p. 239, p. 244, p. 257.
40 Enrique Limón and Adolfo González Arellano to VLT, Veracruz, 19 August 1941, FHLT, file 426; Basurto 1984, pp. 30–4; Gerardo García, José Fernández, Sóstenes Ramírez, and Eduardo Casas Pérez, from section 20 of the Graphic Arts Union to Fernando Flores, its general secretary, Jalapa, Ver., 22 August 1941, FHLT, file 426; VLT to Oscar Gutiérrez, Mexico City, 22 August 1941, FHLT, file 426; VLT to FV, telegram, Mexico City, 15 November 1941, FHLT, file 435.

Adame who had become senators through the CTM. Unintentionally, the gap between Lombardo and Fidel Velázquez, who resented this interference in trade union affairs, widened.

Among the tasks to influence the labour movement in Mexico, Lombardo intensified the classes in Marxism at the Workers' University. His lectures and speeches could be incomprehensible for workers, but he believed firmly in the need for ideological education as the preamble to organising society in a different fashion and bringing workers closer to the Soviet way of thinking from which such a society flowed. 'If accomplishments are the definitive proof of theory, then the USSR is the greatest proof of the effectiveness of the Leninist theory', he expounded in the auditorium of the Mexican Electrical Workers Union on the anniversary of Lenin's death. The Soviet Union was the 'most faithful example of democracy, as an organ of the will of the people' and a system in which 'justice is law ... and is never violated', where employment is a right, where everyone 'contributes with their effort to work for the common good', where 'the people are happy based on their own satisfaction, infected with their own faith in the future'. Lombardo urged the workers to take a position on that system and then 'help the rest of the Mexicans to choose their place'.[41]

Although it might have lacked sufficient funds, the Workers' University was a unique institution at the time, enriched with the talent of many exiled intellectuals. Lombardo did not consider the inability of the labour movement to sustain it financially as a weakness. It was the government's duty to subsidise it. But those opposed to its ideology viewed it as a hotbed of the radical left in Mexico and an institution that wasted teaching talent, providing classes at a level unattainable for a worker, who was educated 'pedantically, with very confused ideas'. They wanted the Public Education Ministry to reorganise the Workers' University so 'that it is accessible to workers, independently of all the labour confederations' with a proper plan and managed by a board with representatives from the government and all the labour confederations.[42] They failed in such efforts. The UO, as it was known, would remain the preserve of Lombardo, his ideas, administered by his followers and his family members, from that point on. The subsidy that the UO received year after year was compensation for the faithful collaboration of its founder with the government that was

---

41   VLT, 'Lenin, el genio', conference given on 20 January 1942, in *Obra*, IV/7, 1942, p. 64, pp. 67–8, pp. 70–8; Entrevista con VLT 'La misión de la UO es señalar al proletariado su ruta histórica y su posición frente a los problemas actuales', *El Popular*, 22 February 1942, in *Obra*, IV/7, 1942, pp. 149–53.

42   'Informe de Enrique Jiménez a la OIT', Mexico City, December 1942, OIT-BIT, file 41/1942.

currently in office, and was not due to its substantive contribution to the education of the working class. Over time it has remained as a cultural centre in the heart of Mexico City.

4 The Re-election

Lombardo Toledano received regular complaints about the manipulation of votes by Fidel Velázquez in union leadership elections, but did nothing to counter what was wreaking havoc on the much-desired unity of the CTM. Nor did he broker any criticism of his successor or of the confederation. In a closed meeting in April 1942, no longer part of the leadership, he hailed Velázquez as the 'only one responsible for the progress of this magnificent labour confederation'. In the current conditions of the world at war, 'we need to work in military fashion, blindly receiving and blindly obeying orders given by the high command of the organisation'.[43] The Mexican government's declaration of a state of war in May 1942 as a result of the sinking of the Potrero del Llano and Faja de Oro oil tankers by German submarines, and the death of the sailors who manned them, put a halt to the struggles between the labour confederations – albeit only in appearance – and facilitated the defence of the homeland.

In February 1943, the general leadership of the CTM was up for election. Fidel Velázquez wanted to be re-elected. The other candidate was Celestino Gasca, veteran of the labour and political arena who fought together with Lombardo in the 1920s. Lombardo favoured Velázquez, without protesting against the gangster methods he employed to get like-minded leaderships into union offices. In addition, the CTM was divided among the unions that wanted Velázquez to continue as general secretary and those who favoured Lombardo's return to the leadership. Alejandro Carrillo, a CTM congressional deputy, was one of those who wanted to get rid of Velázquez, but it was too late. Given that Lombardo had endorsed Velázquez as the only and indispensable leader, the latter acted as if there was complete agreement with Lombardo, cautiously calculating his moves until the opportunity arrived to complete the distancing between the two.

Top-level CTM leaders toured several states 'to orient the workers on their duties to the homeland ... indicating the line of conduct that the CTM has established', although they could not visit the entire country for lack of funds. Lom-

---

43 Stenographic version of the meeting held in the Henry Barbusse room of the UO on 16 April 1942 called by the National Committee of the CTM, Mexico City, FHLT, file 455.

bardo made a four-day trip through Michoacán and Jalisco without abandoning his elegant three piece suit and tie. During the brief tour, he discussed workers' responsibilities such as increasing agricultural and industrial production, military training, monitoring the activities of the enemy like the fascist agents, but in reality all those who were not in agreement with the CTM, with the government's policies and cooperation with the authorities. It was true, the CTM conceded, the situation of the working class was precarious with increases in the prices of corn, beans, rice, tortillas, bread, meat in the order of 25%, cloth 50%, sandals 100%, hats 60%, while wages remained stagnant for four years and workers 'have been compelled to postpone their demands'.[44]

To ensure Velázquez's re-election, the top leadership of the CTM launched systematic voting fraud as well as the imposition of executive committees in the unions comprised of members who would support them. A Durango leader complained that compañeros Fidel Velázquez and Amilpa had issued instructions to their friends to work to depose the committee of the state federation in an extraordinary congress which violated the federation's bylaws. The unions would leave the CTM 'if the National Committee continues with its arbitrary extortion'.[45] In Sinaloa a congress was held, sponsored by a CTM federal congressional deputy and senator, at which those who did not support the national leadership were not invited. In Oaxaca, Velázquez imposed the general secretary of the state federation. Similar developments occurred in Michoacán, Guerrero, Nuevo León, Tamaulipas and Guanajuato, without Lombardo Toledano intervening to protest the fraudulent procedures.[46]

In Tamaulipas, the general secretary of the state employees union, with the consent of the national committee of the CTM, prevented the leadership of the state executive committee from being changed, even though this was contrary to the feeling of most Tamaulipeco unions.[47] With gangster-like methods, the CTM took over the leadership of the bakery workers' union in the capital in complicity with officials from the Mexico City government. Its leaders were kidnapped, to be replaced by others who were close to the national commit-

---

44 Basurto 1984, pp. 43–63; National Committee of the CTM to the 20th National Council assembly, Mexico City, 23 October 1942, AHSRE, III/382 (72) 11816; Trejo Delarbe and Yáñez 1976, p. 144.
45 José Reyes to VLT, Durango, 12 January 1943, FHLT, file 493.
46 Alberto Contreras and others from the new Executive Committee to MAC, Mexico City, 22 December 1942, FHLT, file 485; Alberto Contreras and others from the Executive Committee to Ignacio García Téllez, Mexico City, 8 January 1943, FHLT, file 493; Francisco Figueroa Mendoza to VLT, Hermosillo, 12 January 1943, FHLT, file 493.
47 Francisco de la Garza and Daniel Gallardo to Fidel Velázquez, Mexico City, 12 January 1943, FHLT, file 493.

tee.⁴⁸ With the unions left toothless with all these shenanigans, they went to the president as a last resort to resolve problems such as wage increases and the renewal of collective bargaining agreements.

Lombardo did not miss a beat despite the subterfuges he saw daily, because his eyes were set elsewhere on tasks for which he needed the unequivocal support of the CTM and his friend, the president. In a hurry before leaving for the United States in February 1943, he telegraphed: 'I earnestly implore you on the matter of the Workers' University', since the issue of UO's subsidy had not been resolved either in the Public Education or Finance ministries. For lack of funds, classes were being held for only seven months because it was not possible to cover teachers' salaries any longer.⁴⁹

Fidel Velázquez was re-elected, this time for four years. The Veracruz labour leaders who had gotten in his way were expelled from the CTM. At the national committee that was selected in March, Lombardo kept one foot in the door through Jacinto López in the Campesino Action Commission and with Alejandro Carrillo as secretary of the Education and Culture Commission.⁵⁰ His reputation remained untarnished.

José C. Valadés, once a communist and anarchist, did not share Lombardo's beliefs, but admired a man who defended his ideas and firmness of purpose. During an interview he conducted with Lombardo in February 1943, Valadés stared at a man with an 'extremely melancholy' look and hands that were moving 'as if they wanted to move you where he was going'. He was impressed by Lombardo's optimism, his 'faith in the perfectibility of man' and his quest to find 'the fundamental driving force of history'. President Roosevelt and vice president Wallace guaranteed that the 'old US imperialist policy would disappear after the war', Lombardo said with conviction. When Valadés asked about the CTM, he replied: 'If you're referring to some difficulties of an internal nature that exist, I must say that these difficulties will come to an end'. Did Lombardo know that many people hated him? He knew it, but that was not the issue; rather a 'more honest, balanced, and freer world, that's all that we who form the vanguard of the army of Mexican progress aspire for'.⁵¹

---

48 José Martínez to General Manuel Ávila Camacho, Mexico City, 11 March 1943, FHLT, file 500.
49 VLT to Manuel Ávila Camacho, Mexico City, 3 February 1943, AGN, MAC, file 577.1/39.
50 Sánchez González 1991, pp. 92–7; Report by Enrique Jiménez to the ILO, Mexico City, February 1943, March 1943, OIT-BIT, file 41/1943.
51 José C. Valadés, 'Lombardo Toledano ha experimentado una transformación casi increíble', *Novedades*, 10 February 1943.

5   The Elusive Unity

The CTM continued to be divided on several fronts, one of them between its executive committee and Lombardo Toledano. The unions went to Lombardo when they had disputes that the national committee either caused, covered up or failed to resolve. The antagonism intensified on the occasion of the July 1943 midterm elections, when the PRM wanted to create counterweights to the CTM and promoted the National Confederation of Popular Organisations (CNOP).[52] To avoid losing what had already been won, the CTM leaders further strengthened their ties to the state party, further stifling union democracy. Fernando Amilpa, senator at that time, obtained 'commitments' in a district that prevented the Veracruz Regional Workers Federation from choosing its candidate for the elections, since 'special circumstances preclude the CETEME from presenting candidates in the ninth district of Veracruz'. An oil workers leader from Coatzacoalcos, Veracruz, and candidate for congressional deputy, had complained that in his district there were impositions and influence over the unions from several sides, including the national committee of the CTM. He saw no chance to win unless he had its support, that of Lombardo and the president. Workers from La Laguna in Durango were merciless in their criticism of Fidel Velázquez when they learned that their choice for congressional deputy was ignored:

> As this attitude shows us your desire to harass the organisations and individuals who fought against your re-election, we want to make it clear that you are not the owner of the CTM, since we consider ourselves to be its initiators and founders and therefore the most obligated to defend it against those who are taking advantage of it to gratify their personal appetites or serve their interests alien to the programme and tactics of struggle that govern the life of our glorious Mexican Workers Confederation.[53]

The CTM unions complained that the PRM ignored the candidates who had won at the conventions in Tlapa, Guerrero, and in Minatitlán, Veracruz. In a district in the state of Mexico, the electrical workers proposed their candidates for full and alternate federal congressional deputy slots in the PRM without any oppon-

---

52   Loaeza 2013, p. 261.
53   Alejandro Nápoles and others to Fidel Velázquez, Gómez Palacio, Durango, 21 June 1943, FHLT, file 511.

ents, but 'our union is aware that the Governor of the State of Mexico intends to impose two lawyers, who are close collaborators of his, in this district'.[54]

The CTM was indebted to the Cocoyotla sugar mill of Morelos, since May 1939, when the sugar workers' union chose Eufemio Martínez as its candidate for the state legislator, but Lombardo pushed him aside:

> on that occasion you indicated, of your own spontaneous will after some points of views were aired, that we should abstain from getting involved in the elections in the state because you did not want difficulties either with the League of Agrarian Communities or the CNC and you promised us that at some point you and the national committee of the Mexican Workers Confederation would make sure that he would be nominated as a candidate for federal deputy. That that was required and therefore we disciplined ourselves on the previous occasion and complied then of course and therefore we are reminding you of your offer and now at the right time we allow ourselves to address you again in this matter.[55]

But, now, 'neither compañero Amilpa nor compañero Fidel Velázquez have taken compañero Martínez into account'. If Lombardo would have defended the Morelos trade union leader, they would 'be with you whenever you so ask'.[56] However, by this time, Lombardo probably did not have the power or interest in intervening in favour of a Zapatista campesino.

The expressions of admiration of powerless peasants and workers such as Eufemio Martínez were genuine. For a segment of the population – without being able to quantify it – Lombardo was an honest, educated, intelligent man, who treated people well, which contrasted to many lowlifes who fed off the poverty, isolation and ignorance of a helpless population. His elaborate discourse attracted even many communists who thought they could learn Marxism from him, not having other avenues of political education. Those who believed in the benefits of the unfulfilled Mexican Revolution saw its staunch defender in Lombardo. Those who admired the Soviet Union found him to be the best speaker on its history that led to its current government. For them, Lombardo was the Mexican Lenin.

---

54   Macario Pantaleón to VLT, Tlapa, Guerrero, 23 May 1943; Francisco Rincón and others to VLT, Minatitlán, Veracruz, 24 May 1943; Francisco Sánchez Garnica to VLT, Mexico City, 25 May 1943, FHLT, file 508.
55   Margarito Millán and José Estrada to VLT, Sugar Industry Workers Union, Cocoyotla sugar mill, Morelos, 17 June 1943, FHLT, file 511.
56   Ibid.

But Lombardo could do nothing to alleviate the precarious food situation of the workers and peasants. From Saltillo he received alarming news that there was no corn, that 'the people suffer because they are lined up in queues up to 10pm for half a kilo or a kilo at 0.35 and 0.40'. There was a drought and a lack of credits to finance agriculture.[57] The government had to import 100,000 tons of the grain. In December 1943 an emergency law was enacted to increase the wages of those earning 10 pesos or less per day and to prevent strikes. But employers transferred the inflation stoked by rising wages onto consumers, price controls by the government were ineffective, and strikes by miners, oil, textile and tram workers took place one after another. Given the inefficiency of the railways, management of which was in the workers' hands since 1938 as a result of a decision by General Cárdenas, President Ávila Camacho returned the industry to state control.

The economic situation remained difficult during 1944. The price of mercury, which before the war was 220–250 pesos a bottle, following the treaty between Mexico and the United States fell to 56 pesos in 1944, making its trade unprofitable. Tin, lead, antimony, copper, nickel and silver all saw price reductions due to their being strategic metals for the war effort. The Finance Ministry increased export taxes, affecting the economy of mining cooperatives. Manufacturing production volume fell; tires were acquired only on the black market and speculators took advantage of Mexico's solidarity with the nations at war.[58]

The CTM again suffered a split in 1944. Lombardo's former union allies in Durango, Tomás Palomino Rojas and Baltazar Hernández Juárez, turned politicians, formed the CTM Reclaimer Block, which Lombardo categorically rejected in a letter to none other than Fidel Velázquez:

> I have said and I will now repeat that whatever the disagreements that exist on the part of some unions and individual members of the Confederation with regard to their immediate leaders or the National Committee, should be raised within the CTM, not only for the purpose of not playing into the hands of the workers' enemies, but also in order not to detract from your authority, as General Secretary, and that of the other members of the top leadership of the Confederation.[59]

---

57   Joaquín Belloc Cuéllar to VLT, Saltillo, Coahuila, 2 September 1943, FHLT, file 522.
58   C.H. Bateman to Anthony Eden, Mexico City, 26 February 1944; Latin American Memoranda, Research Department, Foreign Office, 8 May 1944, FO371/A1953/138/26; 'Amenaza de un paro de los ferroviarios', El Universal, 30 May 1944.
59   VLT to Fidel Velázquez, Mexico City, 13 April 1944, FHLT, file 553.

Rojas Palomino proposed purging the CTM, which was in 'material and moral decay' for having fallen into the hands of Velázquez, Jesús Yurén, Fernando Amilpa, Alfonso Sánchez Madariaga and Luis Quintero, unscrupulous individuals. Without understanding Lombardo's tactic, which the latter hid, Palomino wrote that 'you inexplicably allowed these gentlemen to do what they wanted and even took their side when protests arose from sectors of the organisation, in order to persuade or subdue the protesters'.[60] The CTM was plagued by betrayals on a small and large scale. The imposition of the national committee in the second congress was ostensible and insolent, 'using clubs and gunmen'.[61]

The list of grievances over the lack of union democracy that Palomino Rojas presented to the president, and that explained most of the trade union divisions, was long. In Veracruz, Velázquez wanted to expand his control and divided the federation 'so as not to get in the way of his re-election'. In Jalisco 'dairy industry employers give the leaders headed by Ramón Hidalgo one centavo per liter of milk sold'. Where local union power eluded Velázquez, he 'had the audacity to order that a Workers' Congress be held in the State of Durango, without the participation of the Executive Committee of the state Federation'. In several places such as Sinaloa and Oaxaca, the workers elected their own leaders, preventing Velázquez's intervention but the CTM disqualified them. In Michoacán and Guerrero, Velázquez imposed malleable individuals to lead the trade unions. He was re-elected and more divisions followed such as the sugar workers' union. On that occasion, Lombardo intervened, but the workers, about 500 of them, lost their jobs 'under instructions from Fidel Velázquez' because they opposed his re-election. There was also collusion between employers and the Conciliation and Arbitration Board in Mexico City to recognise the executive committee of the bakers' union that was not elected by the workers and did nothing to ensure compliance with the collective bargaining agreement. There was more: 'Resorting to vulgar assaults, they have kidnapped workers from the above-mentioned industry, have imprisoned compañeros who to date remain in prison despite being completely innocent, because the only crime they committed was not wanting to serve as an instrument of the Cetemista leaders'.[62]

Dishonesty, shenanigans, pacts with politicians, selfishness and egoism were the school where workers in their daily lives learned how unions were run,

---

60   Tomas Palomino Rojas to Manuel Ávila Camacho, Mexico City, 14 December 1944, AGN, MAC, file 542.1/1060.
61   Ibid.
62   Ibid.

but no one explained their genesis. Part of the trade unionists succumbed to these vices, some became inactive and an independent minority remained that fought amid immense obstacles and adversities. When the unions wanted to convene a state congress, they had to request authorisation from the centre and if the centre refused, they could not hold one. In Chihuahua, the state federation was fragmented because a minority imposed its will over that of the majority. The leaders who were preferred by the national committee 'have had their reputations left in shreds to favour any chance they might have had and in which due to their abuse and piracy their terrible behaviour has become known'. The Regional Federation of Workers and Peasants of Delicias in Chihuahua requested that 'the National Confederation convene the congress of the Workers Federation of this state, as you promised us in the interview or meeting that both state committees of the Federation held in that city' in order to resolve the split in the state labour movement.[63] Probably without knowing it, the Chihuahuense trade unionists called for a solution to the problem from precisely those who had provoked it to begin with.

In Veracruz, women from the PRM left the CTM, because the executive committee 'has tried to impose in the women's section people whose behaviour is completely demeaning to a labour organisation'; it allowed 'two of our compañeras to be beaten up' without doing anything to prevent it, 'on the contrary, it hailed this act of savagery undertaken against these two comrades'.[64] Lombardo did not intervene, even though the assault on the women who until then had been Lombardistas was a covert attack on his leadership.

In July 1944 Lombardo turned 50 years old. The celebration took place at the Club France. In attendance were Cetemistas, close friends, the actress Dolores del Río, the writer Alfonso Reyes, senators, generals, congressional deputies, communists and intellectuals. Lombardo took advantage of the opportunity to pontificate on history from Mexican Independence until the present, a forward-moving process with himself as an example: 'I'm like you, a Mexican who loves his country dearly, who loves his people more than himself'.[65]

The motherland came first, he proclaimed, when the divided and weakened unions and their links to a careerist and corrupt political elite failed to solid-

---

63 Alberto M. Velázquez and Lázaro Anguiano to Fidel Velázquez, Chihuahua, 6 October 1944, FHLT, file 579; Salvador Santa Ana, general secretary and others to the National Committee of the CTM, Chihuahua, 14 October 1944, FHLT, file 580.
64 Victoria Hernández, Martina Vargas, Trinidad Erazo, and Rosa Gonzáles to the Executive Committee of the Veracruz Regional Federation of the CTM, Veracruz, 6 October 1944, FHLT, file 579.
65 Homage to VLT on his 50th birthday, Mexico City, 17 July 1944, in *Obra*, IV/14, 1944, pp. 213–21.

ify it; when Ávila Camacho amended the labour law so that workers could be fired for engaging in illegal strikes and the legal strikes could be hampered by complicated bureaucratic procedures and government control; when the work stoppages in socially important companies were prohibited and government employee unions prevented from allying with other unions and participating in solidarity strikes; when the workers were silenced and lacked independent media; when the socialist education that Lombardo had promoted at the beginning of the 1930s was sacrificed with the reintroduction of religious instruction in the schools.[66] Despite all of this, the CTM, the pillar of the nation, he said at a meeting in October 1944, brought together the 'best militants of the working class' and since the working class first came into existence it gained confidence in itself and in its destiny.[67]

In reality, the extension of government authority in the unions and the incessant manipulation of its leaders made them toothless; the corruption that was installed in the chain of command in the institutions and unions helped in the midst of a distant international crisis to cushion the social conflicts in Mexico, but at the same time contributed to the possibility that a segment of the working class lost confidence in itself and that national unity as a project of the Mexican State became an illusion.

66 Krauze 1997b, p. 53; Britton 1979, p. 689.
67 VLT, 'Un cuarto de siglo al servicio de la revolución y la patria', Mexico City, 5 October 1944, FHLT, file 579; Trejo Delarbe and Yáñez 1976, p. 144.

CHAPTER 9

The Fragile Harmony

Lombardo Toledano expected that the Latin American Trade Union Confederation (CTAL) would become the world's largest labour organisation. With his characteristic optimism, and a plan, he arrived with his wife Rosa María in Havana in November 1939 to make his mark at the conference of the International Labour Organization, he as president of the CTAL and she as the representative of women in the informal sector, ignored in the ILO's social security and healthcare policies. They were accompanied by Fidel Velázquez, who would remember the trip for the rest of his life. In Havana he met Nora Quintana Perera, his future wife.[1]

It was a feat that in the middle of the war the ILO officials could reach the shores of the Western hemisphere, but it was important to show that the organisation was still alive and determined to maintain its universal character despite the warfare ravaging Europe and its workers. The ILO sought to recruit new unions and be present in the Americas because the new economic relations determined by the war altered working conditions and it was its job to monitor them. While exports from the countries of the Western hemisphere, vital for the military effort, increased, employers and governments took advantage of the war to limit labour's rights, and without social justice for the working class, world peace was remote. The ILO conference was an opportunity to connect citizen rights and economic opportunities. This time the Mexican delegation consisted of representatives of business associations, labour unions and government delegates who were not present in Chile in 1936.[2]

Without engaging in agitation but with remarks heavy in substance, Lombardo defended the sovereignty of the Latin American countries and offered some moral judgements on US behaviour toward its neighbours to the south, whose autonomy must be respected in the spirit of cooperation. As an example, he cited 'Mexican economic democracy', referring to the country's incipient import substitution, 'which will soon necessarily lead to a strong and unshakable civic democracy'.[3] The other point he wanted to impress on the parti-

---

1 Jensen 2011, p. 227; Granados Chapa 1996, p. 53.
2 Ad. Staal, circular letter to the members of the ILO, Geneva, 29 October 1939, OIT, D2086/0/05; Herrera 2013a, pp. 256–63.
3 Second Labor Conference of the American States which are members of the ILO, Record of proceedings, Havana, Cuba, 21 November to 2 December 1939, OIT, Montreal, 1941, p. 55.

cipants was that like the CTM in Mexico, the CTAL was a bulwark against fascism in Latin America, which meant that it supported government's collaboration with the US war effort, exporting the raw materials that its industry needed and aligning the working class with this policy.[4]

1 The Latin American Panorama

Lombardo needed data on the situation of the international labour movement to make an analysis of the panorama in the hemisphere. He knew that the number of unions and members had grown but with differences from one country to another.[5] He had access to the diplomatic bag to send and receive correspondence from the confederations and unions wherever they might exist without such mail being intercepted, even though not all embassies could or wanted to collaborate. When he confidentially asked the Mexican embassy in El Salvador for information on that country's unions – their ideological orientations and ties with the government, their economic situation, sources of production, and labour legislation 'without a signature attached to avoid difficulties' – the commercial attaché at the legation did not know how to answer, since the correspondence of the diplomatic mission tended to be violated by the Salvadoran authorities.[6] In 'Honduras there are no labour organisations of any kind, since just mentioning them would be enough for the government to proceed against them with all its strength'. The mere mention 'of any group of workers or any interest shown in them, is cause for alarm by the official authorities'; therefore, the information would not be given to Lombardo so as not to cause problems for the Mexican government. In Ecuador and Paraguay, the Mexican diplomats did not hesitate to contact the unions and obtain the requested data.[7]

Lombardo had been in Cuba earlier that year also on the occasion of the unification of the different unions in a single confederation and left with a good impression. Fulgencio Batista, who ran the island, legalised the communist

---

4 'El Partido Revolucionario Mejicano se solidarizó con Toledano en La Habana', *La Prensa*, New York, 2 December 1939; Jensen 2011, pp. 226–7.
5 Roxborough 1997, p. 146. The number of unions increased from 421 in 1930 to 1880 in 1940 and the number of affiliates rose from 55,000 to 162,000.
6 Antonio Méndez Fernández to the Foreign Relations Ministry (SRE), San Salvador, 25 April 1939; Anselmo Meza to the Mexican business attaché, Mexico City, 3 May 1939, Archivo Histórico de la Secretaría de Relaciones Exteriores (henceforth AHSRE), III-2386-4.
7 Andrés Fenochio to the SRE, Tegucigalpa, 16 August 1939, AHSRE III/382 (727); Pablo Campos Ortiz, Quito, 24 November 1939, AHSRE III/113 (CTM); Salvador Navarro Aceves to VLT, Asunción, 3 November 1939, III/382 (72)/11816.

party in exchange for asking and receiving its support. The Cuban Workers Confederation, which included agricultural workers' unions, had about 400,000 members. Its general secretary was comrade Lázaro Peña, member of the political bureau of the communist party and one of the founders of the CTAL.[8]

The CTAL sought to be the leading factor in promoting class peace in Latin America during the war. Obstacles to collaboration with Lombardo's aim came not only from some authoritarian regimes, opposed to the CTAL, but also from its adversary, the AFL, and from some labour unions. The AFL still did not have the capacity to function in Latin America and the weakened CROM was not much help, but it had begun its insidious activities designed to undermine the CTAL.[9] When in April 1939, Venezuelan President General Eleazar López Contreras ordered the governor of the Federal District to dissolve the unions for adhering to the class struggle, which went against the constitution and contrary to the CTAL's tactic, this fell like a bucket of cold water. But the time was not right to protest, Lombardo warned the Venezuelans:

> for no reason would it be advisable to target the Venezuelan president with protests or any hostile demonstration that in other circumstances is what would be needed to support the workers in that country against the abuse that has made them victims ... we are sure that the dissolution of the unions is not an innate characteristic of the Venezuelan government, but is the expression of the reactionary and anti-democratic group that still collaborates with President López Contreras's administration.[10]

It was necessary to call on the president to nullify the decree dissolving the labour unions.

In June 1939, good news came with the establishment of the Paraguayan Workers' Confederation. But in June 1941, the government suspended trade union activities, restricted the freedom of maritime and port workers and eliminated union autonomy. The confederation split as a result of the renewed radicalism of the communists following the German attack on the Soviet Union in June even though it was against the Soviet line which required unity at all

---

8   Interview with the Havana newspaper, *Hoy*, 25 January 1939, in *Obra*, III/9, 1939, pp. 25–6; 'Movimiento sindical de América Latina (until september 1939)', RGASPI, fond 495, register 17, file 26.

9   Lázaro Peña and Juan Arévalo to Santiago Iglesias, Havana, 6 June 1939, FHLT, file 354; Lázaro Peña and Alfredo Patrón to W. Schewenels, Havana, 4 August 1939, FHLT, file 360.

10 VLT to the labour confederations affiliated to the CTAL, Mexico City, 18 April 1939, FHLT, file 350.

costs.[11] In Guatemala, General Jorge Ubico banned the fascist organisations, approved the right of asylum, suppressed company stores, and above all, toned down criticism of Mexico, Lombardo and President Cárdenas, even though he remained an iron dictator.[12]

Lombardo called on Peruvian President Manuel Prado to release that country's political prisoners in view of the desired 'continental solidarity' and 'the common defence of the New World', although he knew from ambassador Moisés Sáenz that the regime did not allow free trade unions or freedom of the press and the leaders of the General Confederation of Peruvian Workers (CGTP), affiliated to the CTAL, were exiled in Chile to avoid jail. The Nazi-fascist danger, Lombardo telegraphed the president, was sufficient reason to remove the Peruvian army from the border and end the territorial dispute between Peru and Ecuador.[13] In all cases, Lombardo put the fight against fascism above the struggle for trade union rights and the improvement in working conditions that had to be postponed until the Allies won the war against the Axis powers.

The most promising organisations to wage the battle for the CTAL and its line were the Argentine General Confederation of Labour and the Chilean Workers Confederation due to their organisational experience and because they represented the majority of the workers in their respective country. However, their negative side was the endless differences between the socialist and communist parties. In Chile, the dispute spread to the entire confederation and threatened the stability of a government that stemmed from the unity of the parties and unions. Similarly, in Argentina the renewed international polarisation following the German invasion of the USSR affected the CGT's unity due to the political differences among trade unionists of the radical, socialist and communist parties, some more militant than others and each assuming the right to be the vanguard of the proletariat.[14]

Compared to the conflict-ridden hemisphere, Mexico had an exemplary labour movement, Lombardo proclaimed and many Latin American leaders agreed. Seen from Caracas, it was an extraordinary development that the Mex-

---

11 José Argaña, 'La CTAL pide al gobierno del Paraguay la derogación de la ley 7389', Buenos Aires, 11 February 1941, FHLT, file 414; Francisco Gaona, general secretary of the CTP to VLT, Buenos Aires, 12 October 1941, FHLT, file 432; Soto Reyes to VLT, telegram, Asunción, 15 August 1941, FHLT, file 426.
12 (Illegible signature) to VLT, Colon, Panama, 8 July 1939, FHLT, file 357.
13 VLT to Manuel Prado, Mexico City, August 25, 1940, FHLT, file 394; VLT to Prado, telegram, January 5, 1941, FHLT, file 410.
14 Bernardo Ibáñez to VLT, Santiago de Chile, 29 December 1940, FHLT, file 405; José Argaña to VLT, Buenos Aires, 17 February 1941, FHLT, file 414; José Argaña to VLT, Buenos Aires, 23 April 1941, FHLT, file 418.

ican president would attend the congress of the CTM and 'express his agreement with the principles of labour organisation'. The Venezuelan trade unionists envied Mexico's labour legislation, the expropriation of the oil industry and what they perceived was a union democracy. When Venezuelan labour leader Augusto Malavé returned to Caracas from Mexico, in customs 'the government seized' the materials he had brought on labour and agrarian legislation. He didn't know whether he would be able to attend the CTAL congress, which Lombardo had convened for November, because the government 'has prohibited us from having international relations with other workers'. Finally the government allowed the Venezuelans to attend the congress, a gesture that Lombardo acknowledged.[15]

2 The Congress

The CTAL Congress opened on 21 November 1941 in Mexico, the oasis of freedom in Latin America. The core issues were the AFL's attempt to revive a continental labour confederation under its influence and the war.[16] Lombardo had requested the use of the Bellas Artes theatre from the Public Education Ministry to exhibit the work of B. Traven, *The Rebellion of the Hanged*, but this was vetoed by the poet and official Carlos Pellicer: 'the referred work, which is not without merit, leaves the most unfortunate feeling of horror and sadness in the mind of the spectator. Given the pain in our world today, I consider it improper to offer the Mexican public such a litany of horrors'.[17]

But that was the point. To exhibit a work on the reality of exploitation of the indigenous peoples, in this case, the Tzotzils in the Chiapas rainforest and their resistance against the overlords. The idea was to create awareness about the brutal exploitation before the exploited rebelled. Finally, the play was staged in a hall belonging to the Mexican Electrical Workers Union.

The congress showed that the CTAL displayed vitality in those countries where the unions were free to organise. In attendance were delegates from South America, the United States and Canada, as well as the Dutch labour leader from the ILO's worker relations services, Adolf Staal. Lombardo made a comparative analysis of the miserable situation of Latin America and the buoyant American economy on which it depended: while exports of raw mater-

---

15   Augusto Malavé Villalba to VLT, Caracas, 6 October 1941, FHLT, file 432; VLT to General Isaías Medina Angarita, telegram, Mexico City, 11 November 1941, FHLT, file 435.
16   VLT to Philip Murray, president of the CIO, Mexico City, 19 August 1941, FHLT, file 426.
17   Benito Coquet to VLT, Mexico City, 12 November 1941, FHLT, file 435.

ials to the United States increased due to lack of other markets and the war, their prices fell by up to 80% over previous years. Imperialism was not on the agenda, but fascism, the Spanish Falange and Hispanidad, promoted from Germany to 'isolate the United States from Latin America … to awaken again … the anti-imperialist sentiment of our masses'. The solution lay in the inter-Latin American market, economic planning, diversification of production and political freedoms in each country without political prisoners in their jails. The congress was a breath of fresh air amid the anxiety and turmoil. In concluding his long and well-documented speech, Lombardo declared with fanfare: 'I am absolutely sure that when the war is over, the painful and yet at the same time magnificent experience the proletariat of all countries of the world has had … will enable us to realise the ideal that moves all workers of all races, of all places and all latitudes: the unification proclaimed by Karl Marx almost a century ago'.[18] Lombardo's attention was set beyond the hemisphere, a region that had to be encouraged to support the Allies' objectives in the war.

With his presence, President Ávila Camacho gave the final touch to the Congress that he had supported by subsidising the transportation, lodging, personal expenses of the delegates and a banquet.[19] The visitors returned to their countries content with the hospitality and because they found in the CTAL the 'guiding light of the class struggle', even though class struggle was not on the agenda, and the congress did not provide practical help for the solution of their social, economic and political problems, only an abstract call for unity of 'all the forces concurring in their (respective) countries economies' to win the war.[20] Nevertheless, the congress sparked such enthusiasm that invitations arrived from trade unions everywhere for Lombardo to visit their nations.

3   The Celebrated Trip

The United States believed that since it was bearing the brunt of the war effort, it deserved the sacrifice of the subsidiary countries to its war economy. Behind the Good Neighbor policy under its leadership against a common enemy, there was the underlying concern that the Axis powers might disable the production and shipping of vital raw materials. Even though the Nazi spies in Latin Amer-

---

18   VLT, 'Informe al primer congreso general de la CTAL', 22 November 1941, in *Obra*, IV/6, 1941, pp. 135–77, quote on p. 156, p. 177; Herrera 2013a, pp. 181–8.
19   Jesús González Gallo, private secretary to MAC, to VLT; Francisco Pérez Leiros, Mexico City, 24 November 1941, AGN, MAC, file 432/234.
20   VLT, 'Informe al Primer Congreso de la CTAL', in *Obra*, IV/6, 1941, p. 175.

ica were insignificant for Germany's war effort, they served the US government's propaganda purposes in creating a menacing image, projected to the societies as posing the danger of an imminent invasion of the region. Washington's war machine could only operate on condition that it had access to Latin America's mineral deposits, specifically antimony, bauxite, vanadium, tin, copper, to make or strengthen other metals, in addition to oil, rubber to manufacture tires, and cinchona to produce quinine. Peru and Bolivia were its sole suppliers. Bolivia was the major exporter of tin; Chile of copper; Venezuela and Mexico of oil; Brazil of rubber. Ensuring the supply of these materials from their countries of origin – and thus the cooperation of their working classes – had to be maintained at all costs as well as their extraction and shipping.[21]

In October 1941, the Bolivian miners declared a work stoppage demanding higher wages. There was suspicion that German agents were behind the strike. It was true that the Bolivian army had been trained by German officers who had sympathies for the Nazis and the Axis powers took advantage of the workers' poor conditions to try to control the government and prevent the supply of tin to the Allies. There was also concern over possible sabotage of oil wells in Venezuela by Germans living in that country and the disruption of the flow of black gold to the United States. Chile's advantage was that the German population resided in the southern part of the country, while the copper deposits were located in the north. Argentina was a concern because nationalist sentiment ran strong and the country did not allow US interference in its internal affairs; it also had a huge German and Italian population and maintained diplomatic relations with the Axis countries.[22] Lombardo shared the concerns voiced by the United States, without whose military machine the defeat of Nazism was unthinkable. He had to convince the rest of the region on this point during his visit.

Some countries benefited from the relationship with the United States: Panama because of increased traffic on the canal; Mexico and Venezuela due to rising oil prices; Brazil, whose trade agreements with and loans from the United States drove its manufacturing industry and access to military equipment; Ecuador received military aid in exchange for allowing the Galapagos Islands to be used as an airbase; Colombia modernised its army with a view to participating in the defence of the Panama Canal as was the case with the Dominican Republic.

---

21 Friedman 2003, pp. 2–12.
22 Bratzel 2007, pp. 3–10; John Edgar Hoover, director of the FBI, 'United States dependency on South America', March 1942, in Records of the Office of Strategic Services, Intelligence Reports, NARA, RG 226, OSS 13903.

Meanwhile, Argentina and Chile received little military aid for not following American leadership and maintaining relations with the Axis countries. Peru became less important when the focus of the war changed in 1943 from the western to the eastern coast of South America. By 1943, the Pan-American Highway, which the United States built for defensive purposes, ceased to be a priority and Central America resented it. The war awakened old rivalries between countries, since with US military aid to some and not to others, the balance of power in the region was altered. Argentina, which was considered the South America leader, looked on with disfavour when Brazil acquired sophisticated weapons.[23]

This was the backdrop when Lombardo began his journey. The Brazilian, Argentine and Venezuelan governments did not grant him a visa.[24] Despite having obtained the seal with the Peruvian visa in his diplomatic passport, the Peruvian ambassador warned the Mexican Foreign Relations Ministry that Lombardo was not welcome. And without entering Peru, he could not reach Chile. Finally, the government relented, allowing Lombardo to enter the country and reach southern Peru, but without permission to return. Mexican ambassador Alfonso Cravioto in La Paz preferred that he not go to Bolivia. The Guatemalan government also denied Lombardo permission to be in the country, except for a transit visa to return to Mexico.[25]

Lombardo travelled with Rosa María, his indispensable companion. He left Mexico on 21 August for the United States and from there flew to Havana. Had it not been for an article in the Mexican newspaper *Novedades* reporting the sensational news that Lombardo had alluded to Pope Giovanni Pacelli Pius XII as the fifth column of fascism in Latin America, the visit would have proceeded without a hitch. The news was distorted deliberately, because what Lombardo actually said was that the Mexican Catholic popular, nationalist and anti-communist groups, the Sinarquistas, were fascists, led from Rome by the Church. The news raised hackles in Mexico, because the CTM felt included in the scandal, as well as in countries that Lombardo was about to visit. To remedy the damage, he called all the directors of the friendly media to declare in his defence that the account was a fabrication. The Cuban unions supported him and paid glowing tribute to the regional labour leader and a friend of Fulgencio Batista.[26]

---

23   Bratzel 2007, pp. 10–11.
24   Francisco Castillo Nájera to Oswaldo Aranha, Washington, D.C., 3 September 1942, FHLT, file 472.
25   Ezequiel Padilla to José Gorostiza, Mexico City, 27 August 1942, AHSRE, II-402-20.
26   VLT to Alejandro Carrillo, Havana, 8 September 1942, FHLT, file 472.

The scandal did not overshadow the Mexican Foreign Ministry's pleasure with the trip. Lombardo was discreet, 'only dealing with the points in national policy in which his criteria coincided with that of the Government and the labouring classes of Cuba', such as the need for national and international unity to defeat the Axis powers, 'and not directly attacking any of the governments of the Americas when referring to the precarious situation of the proletariat in some of the countries'.[27]

From Cuba Lombardo flew to Barranquilla. A Colombian admirer wrote a poem praising the labour leader: 'But you, together with us Comrade / Lombardo Toledano, / will forge under the skies of the Americas / An armoured landscape' until 'the sinister madness / of the barbarians will be shattered'.[28] Less enthusiastic was the Bogota daily *El Siglo*, which announced that with Lombardo's arrival comes 'communist violence'.[29] In the capital he was hailed as 'the condor of Latin American trade unionism', while his critics denounced him as an omen of bad luck. The municipal committee of the communist party in Natagaima, on the banks of the Magdalena River, sent him a telegram declaring that just like 'Stalin with the Red Army, you with workers of the Americas, will liquidate the sadistic hordes of Nazi-fascism and Falangismo'.[30] For the Cali city council, Lombardo was the representative of 'Aztec democracy'. His lecture on the Mexican Revolution at the Teatro Colón left a deep impression on Marco Antonio Rojas of Tolima, who wrote to him that 'that was the lesson that I should embrace to understand the true substance of democracy and human justice'.[31] And a few days earlier, Lombardo received a melancholy letter from Mexico: 'Thirty days of your absence cannot pass if not with the greatest spiritual and emotional nostalgia. Only the consideration that other peoples and other individuals will receive the benefits of your presence makes it possible, albeit partially to a certain extent, that resignation will follow the sadness caused by your being away'.[32]

Lombardo arrived in Lima on 15 October. The communist party organised a massive welcome at the airport and Ambassador Adalberto Tejeda came to shake his hand. A troubadour by the name of Ru. Ben. Pacheco composed the

---

27 José Gorostiza to the SRE, Havana, 21 September 1942, AHDSRE, III/551.1/11686.
28 Francisco Gaviria, Barranquilla, Colombia, 19 September 1942, FHLT, file 473.
29 'La llegada de Lombardo Toledano agita la costa', *El Siglo*, 21 September 1942, FHLT, file 473.
30 *El Tiempo* and *El Siglo*, respectively, Bogota, 24 September 1942, FHLT, file 474; Municipal committee of the Communist Party, Natagaima, Colombia, 26 September 1942, FHLT, file 475.
31 Marco Antonio Rojas to VLT, Bogota, 24 October 1942, FHLT, file 479.32.
32 O. Berra to VLT, Mexico City, 27 September 1942, FHLT, file 475.

'Song of the Americas for Lombardo Toledano', in which 'you will chart the path / and open the trail for us, / and tune the guitar of the Americas / for our song'.[33] Lombardo spoke with President Prado and labour leaders. The president invited him to the national palace for a banquet. He was pleased that Lombardo criticised the APRA, which was anti-imperialist when it shouldn't be, and thus seemed to justify the government's disarming an opposition party.[34]

The US embassies informed the FBI about Lombardo's movements and pronouncements. In Lima 'he emphasised that domestic problems were of secondary importance at this time and that the main question was the struggle against fascism'. In an evening gala organised by the writers' association, which was attended by important literary figures, some 500 in total, Lombardo received applause when he mentioned that in Mexico one of the achievements of the revolution was that the Church no longer had a say in education and that foreign capital respected national legislation and the state. In his more than two-hour long speech against the war, Hitler and fascism, Lombardo repeated his message that this was not the time to fight against imperialism and launch strikes, but rather to cooperate with the employers.

But also present were workers from Cerro de Pasco and Talavera, employed in American companies, whose wages barely allowed them to survive, without security or protective measures, and who were denied the right of trade union association and assembly. 'The workers wonder how they can enthusiastically work for Mr Roosevelt when his local representatives adopt a fascist attitude'. The workers spoke of strikes that the communist leaders tried to prevent. It was ironic that Interior Minister Dr De la Puente would deny permission for a demonstration, featuring Lombardo, for fear of disorder; meetings with workers were held but indoors. The right wing, no matter how hard they looked, could find nothing subversive in Lombardo's speeches to the point that the conservative press labelled him a pro-Yankee propagandist.[35]

On 21 October, Lombardo travelled to Chile and it was the occasion for another party. In Santiago he was handed a telegram from Alejandro Carrillo to return to Mexico for the meeting of the National Council of the CTM.[36] In addition, the celebration of the October Revolution should not be left in the hands of the CTM and the PRM, and therefore it was 'urgent send cable through me

---

33 VLT to Alejandro Carrillo, telegram, Lima, 20 October 1942, FHLT, file 478.
34 Juan P. Luna to Luís López Aliaga, Lima, 20 October 1942, FHLT, file 478.
35 J. Edgar Hoover, Federal Bureau of Investigation, Department of Justice, Washington, 28 December 1942, NARA, RG 59, file 823.00B/118 PS/TL.
36 Alejandro Carrillo to VLT, telegram, Mexico City, 23 October 1942, FHLT, file 479.

extensive greeting grandiose rally homage Russia'.³⁷ The national council meeting must have been organised to take advantage of Lombardo's absence. But to make himself heard without being present, Lombardo sent a bombastic telegram to Fidel Velázquez, saying that the unity of the workers and peoples of Latin America with Mexico made him feel as 'proud as ever to be a member of the CTM and a Mexican, son of the revolution'.³⁸

When passing through Valdivia, a Chilean troubadour composed a poem on behalf of Valdivia's teachers to 'the great Mexican' with whom 'they will be fighting'.³⁹ He visited the mining towns of Rancagua, Colla, Caletones, Teniente, Chillan, Concepción, Talcahuano and Lota. The US consul reported from Antofagasta: 'Observers here believe that the visit of this well-known international leader has had a positive impact on the recent understanding of the significance of the war, especially among the working class. The visitor's personality and his oratorical skills seem to have favourably impressed people of all classes'.⁴⁰ The issue of US imperialism did not appear in his speeches and 'his vigorous and unequivocal pronouncements have practically been a model of propaganda for our cause'.⁴¹ The pro-German right, which did not look fondly on hemispheric solidarity with the United States and calls to break relations with the Axis countries, had to invent arguments to slander Lombardo.

Entering Ecuador through Tulcan, Lombardo sent a telegram from the first post office he encountered to President Carlos Arroyo River, suspecting, perhaps, that the government 'harbored misgivings about this visit given the flammable political atmosphere here' and that his presence 'could lead to an explosion'. On the way to the capital, workers cheered him, although shouts were heard against the 'false democracies of the Americas'. Workers gathered in Quito, 'hoping to hear some suggestions from him that would show them the road to follow to achieve their improvement'. Perhaps to ensure the workers' prudence and Lombardo's discretion, the government 'decided to contribute to the expenses required to attend to Lombardo Toledano'. Although a worker here and there called for Lombardo to 'tell us what the Ecuadorian people should do to free itself from the current domestic situation', he retorted that this

---

37   Alejandro Carrillo to VLT, telegram, Mexico City, 4 November 1942, FHLT, file 480.
38   VLT to Guillermo Rodríguez, Colombian vice-president of the CTAL, Santiago de Chile, 26 October 1942; VLT to FV, Santiago de Chile, 26 October 1942, FHLT, file 479.
39   Fabián Morales Figueroa to Vicente Lombardo Toledano, when he passed through Valdivia, 30 October 1942, FHLT, file 479.
40   Samuel A. McIlhenny Jr. to the State Department, Antofagasta, Chile, 13 November 1942, NARA, RG 59, file 810.504/208.
41   Claude G. Bowers to the State Department, Santiago de Chile, 30 October 1942, NARA, RG 226, OSS 24797–24798.

was not the purpose of his visit. In Guayaquil he expounded on this point: 'with all the respect that the opinion of the Ecuadorian workers deserve, I would like to tell them that it's not by obstructing the work of the president that they're going to achieve their class demands ... an impossible wall to scale ... especially in these difficult times that the entire world is going through', and the reason for which it was necessary to 'applaud the positive actions of the government and refrain from very harshly or publicly censoring its negative acts', so that the government felt that it was supported by the popular classes and that it 'is a popular government'. The attitude of the 'perfidious' Lombardo was so unexpected that it was necessary to invent secret meetings after the public activities in which he allegedly announced that communism was on the horizon and the postwar chaos would be the grave of capitalism.[42]

The trip was impressive and Lombardo was cheered in the mass rallies wherever they were held. He was elated, but time was starting to run out and there was still a large part of the region left to visit. In Bolivia he visited the indigenous villages of Titicaca and the mining region, and gave a speech against the Hispanidad that the Spanish Republicans of La Paz thanked him for.[43] The next reception, at the airport in San José, Costa Rica, was tumultuous, with about 9,000 people from the trade unions on hand. The names of Mexico, Lázaro Cárdenas and Ávila Camacho were all applauded. The 'warehouses, factories and workshops closed their facilities so that the people could go outside to greet him'. His speeches impressed the diplomats for being so pro-American that 'rumours abounded that he was on the payroll of the United States'.[44]

On 27 November Lombardo arrived in Managua where at 4pm he met with Anastasio Somoza, his wife and daughter. The president got him into his car to show the visitor the Pan-American highway, still under construction by the United States, and the beautiful scenery of its surroundings; the next day 'he received the finest attention, with (the president) personally taking him in his car to the local rally' with workers.[45] The mass rallies in the streets were combined with the banquets at the presidential palace. While on the whole Lombardo's pronouncements caused a good impression, his reference to 'Yankee imperialism' and the American intervention in Nicaragua as remnants of the past were uncomfortable for Somoza. He did not like such comments because

---

42   Boaz Long to the State Department, Quito, 20 October 1942, NARA, RG 59, file 810.504/194.
43   V. Burgaleta to VLT, La Paz, 14 November 1942, FHLT, file 480.
44   VLT to Alejandro Carrillo, La Paz, 14 November 1942, FHLT, file 480; Romeo Ortega to the SRE, San José, 24 and 26 November 1942, AHSRE, III/551.1/11686; Scotten to the State Department, San José, 26 November 1942, NARA, RG 59, file 810.504/209.
45   Vicente L. Benéitez to the SRE, Managua, 4 December 1942, AHSRE, III/551.1/11686.

he felt they complicated his relations with the United States and diminished his stature as president,[46] in power since 1937 with the help of US marines.

Somoza wanted to present Lombardo at an anti-fascist rally. When the secretary of the Nicaraguan Trade Union Confederation found out, he warned Lombardo that it would be inadvisable: 'Since you know perfectly well who Somoza is, the trade unions are sure that you will refrain from taking part in this activity, which is part of the farce that President Somoza has been staging'.[47] If you participate, 'this will discredit you before the Nicaraguan workers represented by this Confederation'.[48] Lombardo did participate and his presence did not seem to cause the anticipated damage. Another Nicaraguan handed him a long letter, 'in handwriting that is not my own', that summed up life under Somoza as 'a life worse than that of the peoples under Hitler'. He asked Lombardo to transmit the contents of the letter to the US ambassador in Mexico, 'the most democratic country in Latin America thanks to you', and then burn it.[49]

The remarkable trip ended with an anticlimactic arrival in Guatemala. The government granted Lombardo a transit visa for an overnight stay in the capital. Sheltered by the Mexican embassy, Lombardo and his wife slept under the Guatemalan sky from one first to second of December 1942 before taking the flight back, without the possibility of meeting with the leaders of the country's weak labour movement. In Mexico, the CTM organised a welcoming committee and he continued to receive a flood of congratulatory letters for the triumphant journey.[50]

However, the amenities, cocktails, receptions with the presidents and rallies in which Lombardo was cheered in halls crowded with listeners hid the divisions within and between the unions and the gap that existed between the political and economic power elites and the world of labour. Despite the enormous obstacles the trade unions encountered to merely exist, despite the difficult living conditions of the workers, especially the miners, Lombardo's speeches were a ray of light that inspired them. While in Colombia, the Segovia miners had already been on strike for 50 days and neither the British company nor the government were trying to settle the conflict. Lombardo's speeches

---

46   Stewart to the State Department, Managua, 28 November 1942, NARA, RG 59, file 810.504/210 and 29 November 1942, NARA, RG 59, file 810.504/212.
47   L.C. Gómez to VLT, Managua, 27 November 1942, FHLT, file 482.
48   Ibid.
49   VLT to Alejandro Carrillo, Managua, 27 November 1942; Leandro Sampobeda to VLT, Managua, 27 November 1942, FHLT, file 482.
50   VLT, 'Prolegómenos para una nueva América', Bellas Artes, 29 December 1942, in *Obra*, IV/9, 1942, pp. 207–84; Kawage Rami 1943.

were a soothing balm 'to encourage the fighters for social causes' and for the labour movement to become 'a decisive factor' in the country 'despite the persecution that it may face'.[51]

4 The Catavi Massacre

Shortly after Lombardo returned to Mexico, the press was filled with news from Bolivia: 'On 21 December 1942, from ten in the morning until three in the afternoon, a Bolivian army force poured a deadly fire with a trench mortar, machine guns, and rifles upon a defenceless crowd of eight thousand men, women and children hemmed in a hollow called La Pampa'.[52] La Pampa was a village situated between two mountains and two tin mines at 4,000 metres above sea level, Llallagua and Twentieth Century, owned by Patiño Mines and Enterprises Consolidated. At the time of the shooting, the striking miners, who demanded an increase in their wages and food rations, were approaching the company offices.[53]

After the Japanese seized what is now Malaysia at the beginning of 1942, which was home to the world's largest tin deposits, Bolivia was the only source for this mineral. The president was General Enrique Peñaranda and the US Ambassador Pierre Boal, who successfully lobbied so that the labour code, enacted in the 1930s but never put into effect and which included collective bargaining, would be neither applied nor even discussed in Congress that month, because 'the workers are deliberately paid late to force them to work' until the following month and so on. Tin production could not be interrupted so as not to 'harm hemispheric security'. Nor was there a need for a collective bargaining agreement, because it did not ensure increased production.[54]

The workers lived under military control in barracks and were forced to buy food at company stores, called pulperías. They were not paid their full wages so as to put them in debt to the company. The price of tin rose between 1940 and 1941, but the workers did not benefit from the increases and their living costs became more expensive. For one hour of work, a Bolivian miner could buy 392 grams of bread, while the corresponding figure for his Amer-

---

51 Argemiro Monroy to VLT, Bogotá, 14 November 1942, FHLT, file 480.
52 Beals 1943, p. 213.
53 Nash 1979, pp. 41–4.
54 Beals 1943, p. 213.

ican counterpart was 7,823 grams.[55] Miners protested against such conditions and for an increase in wages given the exorbitant growth in prices of consumer products. Contrary to expectations, tin production by the enslaved labour force declined due to the miners' passive resistance or because the workers were fleeing their intolerable living conditions. Bringing down Hitler was not an incentive without a corresponding compensation in terms of well-being and democracy.[56]

Bolivia was hurting. During his visit Lombardo did not mention the bad conditions in which the miners lived, which were worse than in other countries, because the purpose of the trip was to build bridges between the population and their government. The Catavi massacre demonstrated the impossibility of such a proposal, but in conditions of war there was no room for a confrontation between employers, the government and the miners; what was needed was the will to remedy the ills and diplomacy so that tin production would not be interrupted. 'I have confidence in attitude President Bolivia, General Peñaranda consider him honest, patriotic, and well-meaning', Lombardo wired to Henry Wallace, chairman of the board in charge of the US war economy, with a copy to the Bolivian president. Ultimately, throughout his trip, 'I had to consider the urgent need to avoid any fissures in the block of continental unity that all our peoples are forging with great difficulties, because many of them still resent the criminal exploitation by imperialist companies of the United States and Great Britain, of which they have been victims'.[57] The living conditions of the Bolivian miners and other workers in the region had to be subordinated to the fight against Nazi fascism.

But the enemy in Latin America was not Hitler and his subordinates; the enemies were the traditional upper classes and the new rich, associated with multinational companies such as Simon Patiño in Bolivia. By attacking a target that was non-existent or of secondary importance, Lombardo, the communists, and the CTAL covered up the real adversary of the workers, the Latin American oligarchies, which this ideologically oriented offensive did not weaken.

---

55 Harold D. Finley to the State Department, Mexico City, 8 January 1943, NARA, RG 59, file 810.504/226.
56 Berger 1966, pp. 202–6; Ernesto Galarza to Juan Arévalo of the Cuban CTC, Washington, D.C., 1 February 1943, FHLT, file 496; Beals 1943, pp. 217–21.
57 VLT, 'Bolivia mártir', 1 May 1943, in *Obra*, IV/10, 1943, pp. 301–68.

5 Coups and Blows

In 1943 blows followed blows against the labour unions and the CTAL, and coup d'états launched that unmasked the deficiencies in the hemispheric harmony. The Paraguayan Workers Confederation was reduced to its minimum expression by General Higinio Morínigo and no amount of polite appeals from the CTAL would make him change his position: 'Señor Presidente, we are receiving requests from your countrymen' for you to please allow the workers' organisations to exercise their legal right of association.[58]

The Colombian labour leader Guillermo Rodríguez, vice president of the CTAL, who the previous November had accompanied Lombardo during his visit without being hindered, was arrested and expelled by the Ecuadorian government when he wanted to attend a labour congress, which the Archbishop of Quito, the Catholic unions and a conservative newspaper saw as the preparation for the 'communist revolution in the Americas'. In fact, the government wanted to hold the congress under its mantle to prevent the creation of an autonomous confederation with majority support in the organised working class. Rodríguez asked the police chief Commander Carvo Paredes the reason for his detention as he did not violate the law. 'I obey government orders', replied the top policeman, 'and in addition, the President of the Republic and his agents are not willing to tolerate workers' involvement in political affairs, because that brings unrest to the country'.[59] But the labour movement was hobbled by its anti-fascist commitment and could not adopt a combative stance against the government, limiting itself to demanding 'the application of democratic and progressive measures'.[60] The congress was held in Quito during the month of March under police surveillance. In the end, the authorities' concern was not Nazism, the Falange and the fifth column, but workers organising independently.

In Argentina, the executive committee of the CGT was divided into two opposing factions. José Domenech, its secretary general, and his deputy secretary Camilo Almarza were alarmed over how the communists wanted to take over the leadership. In the period that transpired between the Soviet-German

---

58   Francisco Pérez Leiros and José Argaña to General Higinio Morinigo, Buenos Aires, 10 February 1943, FHLT, file 497.
59   Guillermo Rodríguez to VLT, 'Informe al presidente de la CTAL sobre los sucesos del congreso de unificación de los trabajadores ecuatorianos', held on 18 March 1943, Bogota, April 1943, FHLT, file 508.
60   Pedro A. Saad, in prison, to VLT, Guayaquil, 7 April 1943, FHLT, file 503; Martínez Mercado to the SRE, Quito, 16 February 1943, AHSRE, III/551.1/11686; 'Labour Leader arrested', *The New York Times*, 18 March 1943.

non-aggression pact of August 1939 and June 1941, the communists kept a low profile, but when the Soviet Union was attacked in 1941 they resumed their aggressive pro-Soviet and anti-fascist stance and wanted the CGT to adopt the same approach. Pérez Leiros, Ángel Borlenghi and José María Argaña, close to Lombardo and the communist group, provoked a split in the CGT and were expelled in June. With their expulsion, CTAL lost a foothold in the Argentine confederation.[61]

The coup d'état in Argentina in June 1943, which overthrew the president and was endorsed by the US government, came as a surprise to Lombardo. The United Officers Group, comprised of nationalist and anti-communist military officials, sought to make Buenos Aires into the commercial and political centre of South America. Juan Domingo Perón was one of them. The communist party was outlawed. While Perón was pro-worker, he gave assurances to the 'señores capitalistas' that the state would make sure that there was no anti-capitalist revolution or 'rebellion of the masses' after the war. As the 'number one Argentine worker', Perón was determined to raise railroad workers' wages, implement social security and healthcare, and work with leaders who would cooperate with the government.[62]

Lombardo was concerned about the emergence of a pro-labour government in Latin America opposed to the CTAL, which he considered fascist because it refused to break diplomatic relations with the Axis powers. In late July 1943 the general staff of the CTAL met in Havana to discuss the deteriorating trade union situation in the hemisphere. In the entourage were Lombardo's wife, his daughter Marcela, Fidel Velázquez, Chilean labour leader Salvador Ocampo, commissioned by the CTAL in Mexico, the Argentine communist Isaac Libenson, exiled in Mexico, and the Czech communist journalist Otto Katz. Their transportation was paid by the presidency, which considered the trip as official business. The Mexican government also feared that the Argentine stance in favour of the Axis would spill over to the other South American republics. President Fulgencio Batista, 'in his capacity as leader of the people', hosted and opened the meeting, and contributed 5,000 dollars and the hotel for the 35 delegates.[63]

---

61   José Doménech and Camilo Almarza to VLT, Buenos Aires, 28 April 1943, FHLT, file 505; Camilo Almarza and José Doménech to VLT, Buenos Aires, 28 June 1943, FHLT, file 513.
62   Rock 1987, pp. 247–57.
63   Palacios 2011, pp. 345–9; 'Comisión de prioridades para transporte aéreo', 15 July 1943, AGN, MAC, vol. 109, file 121.1/281; VLT, 'Inauguración del segundo consejo de la CTAL', Havana, Cuba, 28 July 1943, in *Obra*, IV/12, 1943, pp. 273–88.

It was necessary to reactivate the fear of war, 'even though our men have not given their blood on the battlefields'.[64] It was urgent that the second front be opened in Europe to relieve the burden of the German onslaught against the USSR and cooperation on this side of the planet. It was vital to increase material, intellectual and moral effort to boost the production of strategic materials and be 'willing to refrain from sharpening the class struggle as long as the war continues. We are willing not to employ strikes as a normal weapon for resolving labour-management conflicts as long as the war continues'.[65]

And with the repeated invocation of 'we are willing ... as long as the war continues', Lombardo sought to convince the assembled delegates that the war was not alien to the region, but was its concern as well. Meat was scarce, the black market made it unaffordable for most of the working population, there was speculation and profiteering, but the solution, according to Lombardo, was the unity of the working class and between the working class and its own government.[66]

However, not long after, the fear that Argentine 'fascism' would cross the border and expand throughout South America drove Lombardo once again to head south. In Argentina, the unions were shut down, their leaders jailed, the workers' press banned, and the government was installing a new military caste.[67] In Colombia there was danger of a coup d'état. In Costa Rica, where President Dr Rafael Ángel Calderón Guardia enacted social legislation with the approval of Archbishop Monsignor Sanabria, in a volte-face Lombardo condemned American imperialism and anticipated a bad neighbour policy after the war if all social sectors did not unite in a continental block.[68] With such unexpected onslaughts on his vision and mission of Latin America during the war and postwar, Lombardo replaced his rhetorical optimism by warning of new dangers, of 'plans for an alliance between the reactionary class of financial capital and the forces ideologically represented by the Vatican, to achieve Christianised imperialism in peacetime, based on corporativist economics and a dictatorial political regime'.[69]

---

64   Ibid.
65   Ibid.
66   VLT, 'Informe ante XXI consejo nacional ordinario de la CTM sobre el congreso del Comité Central de la CTAL en La Habana', August 1943, *El Popular*, 15 August 1943, in *Obra*, IV/12, 1943, pp. 107–22.
67   Unsigned letter to VLT, Buenos Aires, 17 October 1943, FHLT, file 526. The author could have been Pérez Leiros or José María Argaña.
68   Pablo Campos Ortiz to the SRE, San Jose, Costa Rica, 8 October 1943, AHSRE, III/551.1/11686.
69   VLT, 'Resoluciones del II Consejo del Comité Central de la CTAL', Havana, September 1943, in *Obra*, IV/12, 1943, pp. 69–97, quote on p. 71.

In the Americas the danger was in Argentina; in Europe it was in Spain. In addition, Trotskyist parties reappeared along with the idea expressed by Trotsky in 1939 on the proletarian revolution that this war could trigger. Outraged because it contradicted the Soviet line, Lombardo considered it 'a new provocation of the international reactionary forces to sabotage the efforts of the United Nations during the war and postwar period'.[70]

In addition, the anti-communist Pan-American movement sprang into action during the war, having as one of its goals to fracture the CTAL. The Catavi massacre promoted the establishment of labour attachés in US diplomatic missions to convey that Washington was concerned about the fate of the workers and to prevent the unions from taking decisions regarding those industries on which the prosecution of the war depended in the countries where it seemed that they had been empowered such as in Mexico, in Brazil by Getulio Vargas, in Argentina with Perón, and Batista in Cuba.[71]

In November 1943 an American delegation from the AFL visited several Latin American countries. Lombardo knew that the Chilean labour leader Bernardo Ibáñez, one of the founders of the confederation, was flirting with the AFL and vice versa, but presented the meeting between the Americans and Chileans – workers, government and the US ambassador – as a sign of cooperation between the peoples of the hemisphere. It was important that the multiple splits within the trade union movement, and between the unions and governments, be camouflaged under the guise of unity. From his friend and ILO official, David Efron, Lombardo knew that Ibáñez was rubbing shoulders with people close to the AFL, the Socialist Party of Norman Thomas and officials from Nelson Rockefeller's Office of the Coordinator of Inter-American Affairs. Without openly defining his political position, Ibáñez indeed came to the conviction that the future of Latin American labour movement lay in alliance with the AFL, not the CTAL and the USSR. He believed that Lombardo's position was a lost cause in the United States as well as in Mexico.[72]

The series of coup d'états ended on 20 December in Bolivia. General Peñaranda was ousted and replaced by Gualberto Villarroel, a Perón sympathiser, also a nationalist and anti-imperialist, who supported the unions and sought to improve the living conditions of the miners. The Mexican government did not recognise the military junta when it was created until it was convinced

---

70   VLT to the national labour confederations affiliated to the CTAL, Mexico City, 17 November 1943, FHLT, file 530; Alexander 1973, pp. 32–3.
71   Berger 1966, pp. 224–33.
72   David Efron to VLT, without date or location, FHLT, file 526.

that the coup government was supportive of hemispheric defence and continental unity.[73] Lombardo did the same.

6 From Montevideo to Caracas

To think of the CTAL as an instrument exclusively of trade unionism was to think like 'our grandparents'. If workers did not get involved in the solution of national and international problems they would be condemned 'to play a romantic, sad and miserable role, to be content with the crumbs thrown their way, with work contracts that within five minutes after a strike the bourgeoisie rips to shreds'.[74] Lombardo adopted a new language because the circumstances had changed. Since the heroic annihilation of the German army at Stalingrad in February 1943 the end of the war could be envisioned. However, instead of having created alliances between the governments and the trade unions under the umbrella of the CTAL, partnerships emerged that threatened them. To present the directive on the Argentine government and on the postwar world, Lombardo called the members of the confederation to an emergency meeting in Montevideo, a stone's throw from Buenos Aires, and before the ILO meeting was to take place in Philadelphia in April. The top leadership of the CTM, his mother, his mother-in-law and his three daughters saw him off at the airport.[75]

This time he was allowed to land in Rio de Janeiro. It must have been a gesture of mutual convenience that Getulio Vargas, a dictator but not a fascist according to Lombardo's criteria, allowed him to visit Brazil, publicly condemn the Argentine regime, but not to allow him to visit the communist leader Luis Carlos Prestes, 'the knight of hope', imprisoned since his ill-fated insurrection in 1935.[76]

In Montevideo, Lombardo spared no invective against the military regime in Argentina, 'inviting the workers of that country to free themselves from the pro-Nazi military caste that governs them'.[77] He labelled the Argentine government as representing home-grown fascism and not a traditional dictatorship.

---

73 Palacios 2011, p. 349.
74 VLT, 'Posición de la CTAL frente al imperialismo, al Nazifascismo y las huelgas', Montevideo, 27 February 1944, in *Obra*, IV/13, 1944, p. 82.
75 VLT, 'Partió ayer hacia la América del sur Vicente Lombardo Toledano', *El Popular*, 15 February 1944.
76 VLT, 'Acerca de la reunión de emergencia de la CTAL', Mexico City, 29 March 1944, in *Obra*, IV/13, 1944, pp. 195–204.
77 M. Armendáriz del Castillo to the SRE, Montevideo, 9 March 1944, AHSRE, III/311.1 (891)/14895.

Lombardo had reached understandings with Somoza, with Trujillo, with Vargas, but the military caste that seized the Argentine government was of a new and different type. 'Adolf Hitler has opened a second front, only for our misfortune, in Latin America'.[78] Fascist Argentina sought to build a Magna Hispano-America as part of the new Christian order, and if it were able to do so, it would attack the United States. However, this illegitimate government was about to fall, without Lombardo indicating how this would come about. He accused the Argentine military junta of wanting to create a Rio Plata Viceroyalty with Uruguay, Paraguay and Bolivia as its subjects. It was necessary to fight Argentine fascism, the monster spawn of Francisco Franco in the Americas. Monitored by the US embassies, the pro-American reputation that Lombardo had earned on the trip in the southern countries of the region in 1942 came crashing down. On that trip he had raised a smokescreen to cover up his communist convictions, was the conclusion reached by observers.[79]

From Montevideo, Lombardo flew to Caracas, which he had not been able to visit in 1942. The workers cheered him along the route from the airport. The three largest hotels in Caracas, which belonged to oil companies, denied him accommodations and he had no other choice but to 'stay in some shoddy hotel or home for the poor'. The Mexican ambassador wanted to ignore his visit so that it would not appear official, but so as to save the national honour, he was forced to provide accommodations for Lombardo and his wife in the official residence.

Lombardo paid his due homage to Simon Bolívar and met with Venezuelan President General Isaías Medina Angarita, who was backed by the communists as part of the alliance to fight fascism. A workers' demonstration was held in a bullring that for the first time in the history of the country was attended by a government representative, the Labour Minister Dr Julio Diez. The Mexican ambassador was moved by the intensity of the 'viva Mexico' chants and when Lombardo appeared 'there was again a thunderous ovation and prolonged chants hailing Mexico and the above-mentioned lawyer'. There was only room for 15,000 people in the bullring and many had to remain outside. 'Lombardo Toledano's speech was one of the most prudent, intelligent oratorical

---

78   VLT, 'Inauguración de la reunión de emergencia del comité central de la CTAL', Montevideo, 28 February 1944, in *Obra*, IV/13, 1944, pp. 93–112; quote on p. 102 and p. 103.

79   VLT before the 23rd CTM National Council meeting, 11 April 1944, FHLT, file 553; 'Statements made by Vicente Lombardo Toledano at first secret session of the CTAL conference in Montevideo on 27 February 1944' by William A. Tidwell, Infantry captain, assistant to the Military Attaché, in Dudley G. Dwyre to the State Department, Montevideo, 23 March 1944, NARA, RG 59, file 810.504/383; George S. Messersmith to the State Department, Mexico City, 11 April 1944, NARA, RG 59, file 810.50/173.

pieces for the current moment in the hemisphere'. His opponents did not find anything to accuse him of. He spoke to students about the Mexican Revolution, which usually did not cause any anguish, except among those who had been dispossessed of their properties, but the issue of the expropriation of the oil companies was an obligatory topic. Even on this occasion, 'Lombardo's speech was brilliant, discreet and cleverly developed'. The Spanish Republicans living in Caracas were also pleased with his visit.[80]

But on 24 April, without any warning, the Venezuelan government issued a decree 'dissolving 90 trade unions and also dissolving the National Workers' Convention which was meeting on that date' and to which Lombardo had been invited. According to one newspaper, the measure was designed 'to ensure public order and the exercise of individual rights'. Ambassador Vicente Benéitez was of the opinion that the dissolution of the trade unions and the workers' convention was a premeditated decision due to the pressure from the oil companies in anticipation of a labour movement split caused by Lombardo's presence; it was directed against the communist party and was due to the fear that the workers' convention would call for the breaking of diplomatic relations with Francisco Franco, a declaration of war on the Axis countries, the expropriation of their properties and the detention of their citizens resident in Venezuela. Lombardo met with President Medina the following day 'in an environment marked by the frankest cordiality' and his declarations before leaving 'caused a magnificent impression in the government as well as among all the social classes'.[81] Without referring to the blow struck against the labour unions that he had just witnessed and without echoing the workers' feelings in this regard, Lombardo departed from Venezuela.

7   From Philadelphia to Cali

Lombardo could leave the ILO conference held in Philadelphia in April satisfied, because he had Argentine delegate Luis Girola's credentials rejected as the latter did not represent a free and independent trade union organisation and as 'a moral sanction against the clerical-fascist dictatorship in Argentina'. It helped that *The New York Times* published an article on the socialist newspaper *La Vanguardia* that the government had silenced, because it was not in keeping with the spirit of what was called Argentiness, mentioned the cen-

---

80   Vicente L. Benéitez, Caracas, 3 April 1944, AHSRE, III/660/37/14964.
81   Ibid.

sorship applied to the newspapers so that they could not say anything about the ILO meeting or show any affinity with the United States.[82] Lombardo, the champion of hemispheric trade unionism, was elected to the workers' council of the ILO. His opponent was the Chilean labour leader Bernardo Ibáñez.[83] Lombardo's election represented a victory for CTAL as well as for the region, which for the first time in the history of the ILO had a representative in this commission.

The fall in May of Salvadoran dictator General Maximiliano Hernández Martínez, due to a general strike and the anti-dictatorial movements in Honduras and Nicaragua were also encouraging news. In Guatemala, the dictator Jorge Ubico fell in October although his fall was preceded by the massacre of students and the suspension of individual guarantees.[84] With Juan José Arévalo as president, democratic freedoms were restored together with the conditions created for unions to function. In Ecuador, the National Workers Congress met to establish the Ecuadoran Workers Confederation, which had been banned the previous year by the government of Arroyo del Río.

On 8 December 1944 a military aircraft, which National Defense Minister General Cárdenas put at their disposal, transported the Mexican delegates to the CTAL congress in Cali, Colombia, and brought them back on 20 December. Lombardo invited the Americans in a demonstrative gesture that the CTAL and no other confederation dominated the trade union movement and the postwar policy in the Western hemisphere, though he knew that the AFL would reject the invitation.[85]

The congress was to determine the CTAL's position on the present and the future of Latin America in the global context. The military coup in Argentina had disrupted the historical evolution that was anticipated following the destruction of fascism and had opened one of several fissures in what should

---

82 'Argentina Closes Socialist Newspaper after Warning against Supporting US', *The New York Times*, 25 April 1944, FHLT, file 554; 'Statement of Vicente Lombardo Toledano', 17 April 1944, Earl R. Browder papers, Syracuse University Library, Manuscript collections, box 16.
83 VLT, 'El rudo golpe al fascismo argentino en la XXVI conferencia de la OIT en Filadelfia', *El Popular*, 23 April 1944 and 'Los delegados de México electos a las tres comisiones del consejo de administración de la OIT', in *Obra*, IV/14, 1944, pp. 19–20.
84 Eduardo Vargas Sánchez to VLT, Tapachula, 30 June 1944, FHLT, file 560; Castillo, Toussaint and Vázquez Olivera 2011, p. 96.
85 'El Teniente Coronel Dávila Caballero, pide se gestionen ante los Gobiernos correspondientes, el permiso de vuelo', undated, AHSRE, III-313.1 (72) 15529; VLT to Salvador Ocampo, Mexico City, 19 September 1944, FHLT, file 576; VLT to William Green, Mexico City, 10 October 1944, FHLT, file 579; VLT to William Green, Mexico City, 10 October 1944, FHLT, file 579.

be a united continent. Juan Domingo Perón in the south and the AFL in the north vied with the CTAL for control of the labour unions in terms of directing their political and ideological development.[86]

With the portraits of Simon Bolívar, President Roosevelt, Marshal Stalin and Prime Minister Winston Churchill as a backdrop, Lombardo extolled the patriotic and legitimate government of Dr Alfonso López in Colombia and reiterated that 'the war forced us to make sacrifices', it was time to draw up a balance sheet of the past five years and think in terms of the world of tomorrow. This new period would involve industrial regulation 'to win national independence', not class struggle. The time for socialism had not yet arrived, but the hour of democracy had. The 13 national confederations that were present re-elected Lombardo as president of the CTAL.[87]

In Cali, oil workers from Colombia, Ecuador, Mexico, Venezuela, Peru, and O.A. Knight, the CIO's leader, met to 'exchange views' on working conditions, wages, benefits and to develop a common action plan. The reality of the workers in the industry was difficult. Peruvian union leader Domingo Coloma told the other delegates that 'in his country oil workers are not organised and the oil companies, in complicity with the government, persecute those workers who launch labour movements … in the oil fields there are appalling hygienic conditions and because of the high cost of living, the low wages are not enough to live on'.[88] The Venezuelan delegate Jesús Faría spoke of the 12 foreign companies operating in the country that 'are unfortunately pillaging the underground wealth, because without any rhyme or reason and without being concerned over the future of the country, they are extracting oil'.[89] The companies did not deal with the union leaders because they did not recognise them; they only dealt with the authorities. There was social insurance for workers but it was not available in the oil industry. The amount of taxes that the companies paid the state was pitiful. The solution was a convention of Latin American oil workers under the auspices of the CTAL. When it was his turn to speak, Mexican delegate Francisco Arechandieta told his compañeros that everything changed with the expropriation of the foreign companies. The American comrade Knight painted an idyllic picture, perhaps with the intention of highlight-

---

86   VLT to Andrei Danilov, Mexico City, 30 November 1944, FHLT, file 586.
87   'Segundo Congreso General de la CTAL', Cali, Colombia, 15 December 1944, FHLT, file 590; a different interpretation of the congress can be found in Herrera 2013a, pp. 273–81.
88   'Acta de la reunión verificada en la ciudad de Cali, Colombia', 14 December 1944, FHLT, file 592.
89   Ibid.

ing the enlightened President Roosevelt's new deal that had resulted in high production, high wages, high dividends for companies, the unions holding collective bargaining agreements that were renewed each year and in all cases with signified improvements, a 36-hour working week with payment for 52 hours of work, a high standard of living and major technical innovations on the job.[90]

On the way back, Lombardo went through Guatemala, where he was wined and dined by the country's authorities and labour unions for several days and where he gave speeches in crowded halls. He painted a portrait of a near-perfect Mexico, its ancestral problems almost resolved.[91]

8   The Elusive Harmony

A greater danger than fascism was the danger of hunger, the subordination of workers to employers and brutal labour exploitation, the lack of union democracy, no respect whatsoever for the law and limits on democratic participation in each country's political and social life. But Lombardo conceived the solution of local problems within his global strategy. The end of the war was in sight, fascism was about to be defeated and the Soviet Union, the homeland of socialism and guarantor of the future for the rest of humanity, appeared invincible. The project for the postwar period was the industrial revolution in unity with workers, farmers, industrialists, technicians and bankers. It was necessary to destroy the feudal past and 'open the doors of Latin America to foreign capital, on the condition that it be a force that could contribute to the progress of the people'. In Spain it was necessary that the Republic be restored to achieve 'the full victory of the new world'.[92]

However, at the end of the war, the decline in real wages sparked strikes demanding salary increases in Brazil, Argentina and Mexico, and pressuring the respective governments to improve the living conditions of workers and expand citizenship rights. But the working-class insurgency was contrary to what the governments and Lombardo expected for the success of the great pro-

---

90   Ibid.
91   'Acta de la reunión verificada en la ciudad de Cali, Colombia', 14 December 1944, FHLT, file 592; VLT to Francisco Pérez Iscaro, Cali, Colombia, 17 December 1944, FHLT, file 592; 'La aspiración máxima para América: una democracia económica y social', *Nuestro Diario*, 20 December 1944, AHSRE, III-313.1 (72) 15529; 'Lombardo Toledano englobó el vasto panorama revolucionario de México', *El Imparcial*, 21 December 1944.
92   VLT, 'Presente y futuro de América Latina', December 1944, in *Obra*, IV/15, 1944, pp. 253–79.

ject that depended on labour submission in order to regulate labour relations and create a friendly environment for the participation of national and foreign capital.[93]

In Mexico, W.K. Ailshie, secretary of the US embassy and a new dealer by conviction, ruminated about the postwar world. Unless we

> take a firm position in favour of democracy and liberalism everywhere, our influence will diminish and the organized workers will increasingly turn toward the Soviet Union as the protector of the rights of ordinary people. It is now our chance to convince people in Mexico and Latin America that we do not sympathize at all with fascism in any form, that we sincerely believe in democracy and human rights, and that we intend to fight oppression in the postwar period ...
>
> Lombardo Toledano is an ambitious man. Much has been said about his devotion to communism and Soviet Russia. But he fully realizes that Russia is far from Mexico while the United States is really very close. Just the facts of geography make the United States a factor that cannot be ignored under any circumstances. Lombardo Toledano is sufficiently intelligent to be on the winning side.[94]

But in February 1945, even before the death of President Roosevelt in April, the good neighbor policy was losing favour with the establishment and Ailshie was about to be recalled from his post in Mexico. The US government would return to a policy of coercion to maintain the traditional economic relationship in Latin America. The new interventionism would take the face of the cold war, which was another name for the preservation of its influence in the hemisphere. Instead of winning Lombardo to Washington's position, as Ailshie recommended, and which depended on US government assistance for the development of Latin America, American supremacy in the postwar period would make Lombardo even more combative.

---

93 Roxborough 1997, pp. 149–50.
94 W.K. Ailshie to the State Department, Mexico City, 12 February 1945, NARA, RG 59, file 812.504/2-1445.

PART 4

Animosities and Confrontations

To build a new nation! To emancipate Mexico! To emancipate Latin America! Fight so that the blood spilled in this war will flower in freedom and justice for the world! (1945)[1]

∙ ∙ ∙

I know, compañero Lombardo, that the application of Marxism-Leninism to the specific situation of our country requires us to support the government of the revolutionary bourgeoisie in power. (1946)[2]

∙ ∙ ∙

Lombardo is our country's most dangerous enemy in Mexico. As part of his Communist anti-American line, he preaches that we have become the worst imperialists in history. He fights practically all measures that would strengthen our ties with Mexico and Latin America and expounds an interpretation of world affairs favouring Russian interests. (1947)[3]

∙ ∙ ∙

Señor Don Vicente Lombardo Toledano our hopes full of faith we entrust in you, since you have entered the hearts of the poor and furthermore, you understood their plight and you hear their complaints because every time we send a letter or official communication to government offices we are answered with a little piece of paper acknowledging its receipt. This way of answering in no way remedies the ills of our brothers and compañeros. (1948)[4]

∙ ∙
∙

---

1 VLT, 'La CTAL ante la guerra y la posguerra', Esperanza Iris theatre, Mexico City, 5 August 1945 in *Obra*, IV/17, 1945, p. 161.
2 Profesor Cándido Jaramillo G. to VLT, Mexico City, 20 November 1946, FHLT, file 649.
3 Juan de Zengotita to the State Department, Mexico City, 16 May 1947, NARA, RG 59, file 812.5043/5–1647.
4 Pedro López and others. Circulo Orientador Oaxaqueño in Orizaba, Veracruz, 15 June 1948, file 731.

CHAPTER 10

For the Renewal of the Nation

The press wanted to destroy Lombardo. He used to say jokingly that he was blamed even for changes in the weather. But no amount of jeers and diatribes to demonise him for being an adventurer and impostor that the newspapers launched were able to remove him from the pedestal on which his followers had placed him. Unable to defeat him, the press caricatured him by russifying his name as Lombardovich Toledanoff.[1] His stoic resistance in the face of such insults inspired a group of writers, actors, physicists, archaeologists, musicians, politicians, economists and engineers, from different ideological backgrounds, to grant him the 'Combatant Award' for having received the largest number of invectives from 'the enemies of the Revolution'. The tribute took place at the Restaurante Chapultepec, his favourite. With apparent modesty, he thanked them for the gesture as 'a very generous compensation for the humble work I have undertaken in the service of the working class and my people'.[2]

Luis N. Morones also inflamed the press with insults directed at Lombardo, forecasting his political demise. He knew that in terms of national and international popularity and success he could not measure up against his former compañero in the CROM. As he lacked arguments to diminish Lombardo Toledano's stature, Morones chose to compare himself to him on the level of machismo: 'We are not castrated; we are perfectly healthy men'. The gentleman knew nothing about the world of work and nothing of the suffering 'in the arena where we struggle'. People like him were a bunch of 'eunuchs who lack macho attributes'.[3] But Lombardo cut into the insults with his usual sarcasm: he would not bother getting worked up over 'someone who was riffraff and could only interest the vultures of Mexican politics'.[4]

---

1 'Un estudiante bruja', popular corrido, *Últimas Noticias*, 4 June 1947, FHLT, newspaper archives, file 22.
2 VLT, speech at the ceremony for the 'Fighter Award' given to Vicente Lombardo Toledano, Mexico City, 28 February 1946, in *Obra*, IV/18, 1946, p. 175.
3 'Morones: Discurso contra Lombardo Toledano y la CTM', Mexico City, April 1945, AGN, MAC, vol. 1192, file 710.1/101–145.
4 VLT, 'Respuesta a las declaraciones de Luis N. Morones', *El Popular*, 6 April 1945, in *Obra*, IV/16, 1945, p. 195.

1   The Future

Lombardo had other concerns. *Futuro* was not only the name of the magazine he founded in 1934 and which in 1943 had to suspend publication for lack of subscribers and irregular appearance. He wanted to renew its publication, this time 'on the basis of broadening its doctrinal and cultural focus', as determined by the infallible laws of history. With the help of the expert pen of Czech communist Otto Katz/Andre Simone, before he returned to Czechoslovakia from exile in Mexico, Lombardo felt that the historical moment required that the magazine extol 'the positive work done by the country's progressive industrialists, bankers and businessmen', since Mexico's industrialisation and modernisation depended on them, as was also the case for improved living standards and the opening of new domestic and regional markets. The previous years had demonstrated the benefits derived from spending on public work projects, land reform and wage increases, measures that, taken together, tended to revive domestic demand.[5]

In the US embassy there was a sigh of relief because the labour movement did not seek the destruction of capitalism. In a conversation with the consul, Fidel Velázquez cleared away any remaining doubts: 'In theory we want to overthrow the capitalist system and establish the socialist system', but the CTM did nothing to put it into practice, 'nor has it designed a plan in terms of the route to achieving it'. The CTM's goals were social reforms, on the level of land distribution, irrigation, public education, social security and healthcare and raising workers' living standards. Lombardo also believed in such goals, but he was more calculating and sinister than the affable Velázquez, the consul feared. Could it be that the CTM or the communists and Lombardo were working together secretly? Did Lombardo lose power, or would he be a factor in the presidential campaign, in the reorganisation of the Party of the Mexican Revolution (PRM) in the making? And if he already lost control of the CTM, would he also lose the support of workers because of his affinity to the USSR or, on the contrary, will he emerge stronger than ever as a labour leader? And if his position were to be consolidated in Mexico, would he be seen as a worldwide anti-American leader?[6]

---

5   Alfonso Guillén Zelaly, César Ortiz, and Rafael Carrillo, 'Memorando sobre la revista *Futuro*', Mexico City, February 1943, FHLT, file 496; VLT to Salvador Francisco Urías, Mexico City, 29 November 1944, FHLT, file 586; B. Martha Rivero Torres 1982, p. 15; Bortz 1988, p. 150.

6   Henry F. Holland, 'Interpretative comment on labour and social development in Mexico', Mexico City, 1–31 May 1945, NARA, RG 59, file 812.504/6–1425.

Lombardo's position on the country's postwar development was demonstrated by his support for the signing of the worker-industrial pact of April 1945 to achieve the sovereignty and independence of the nation with the participation of all the factors of production and all the actors. It was viewed as the continuation of the 'cooperation' of workers and industrialists in the postwar period with the immediate goal of the control of inflation, which averaged 17.8% during the war years and the creation of an attractive environment for domestic and foreign investment. Some industrialists, such as the members of the Federation of Industrial Chambers and the Federation of Manufacturing Industries approved of the pact, while those who were opposed to Lombardo, to protectionist measures and the leading role of the state in the economy, rejected it. The embassy felt that it greatly contradicted the aspirations of free trade that the Americans defended as an absolute principle.[7]

But the pact never got off the ground. The workers did not deem the so-called anti-imperialist national bourgeoisie as a reliable partner, because its aim was not necessarily the sovereignty of the nation but profits. The businessman José Cruz y Celis, who was the president of the Confederation of Industrial Chambers and manager of the Mexican Branch of the Corn Products Corporation before becoming involved in politics, and CTM leaders Francisco Macín and Fernando Amilpa, lacked the technical capacity and knowledge to investigate the needs of companies and carry out the grandiose project. José Domingo Lavín was an engineer who made a fortune by discovering a defect in the title of Compañía Águila, which was forced to pay a fabulous sum of 15 million pesos of which Lavín received about three million. With this money he launched business ventures that did not prosper. However, he defended the pact against those who rejected it as a pernicious communist influence in Mexico. The proposal that the La Tolteca cement company put on the table offered too much protection for capital without making sufficient concessions to labour. The pact was repudiated by labour unions opposed to the CTM who considered Lombardo a traitor to trade union rights and the pact as a vehicle for his political ambitions. The idea of industrialisation that the pact extolled was floated as an improvisation and presented as a plank in the presidential campaign. The social pact that it promoted was inadequate for encouraging industrialisation and economic expansion with shared responsibilities between capital and labour; rather it promoted investment of private capital in private companies and government capital in infrastructure along with the policy of deficit spending.[8]

---

7 Middlebrook 1995, p. 114 and p. 213.
8 Roxborough 1992, p. 199; Basurto 1984, pp. 68–87; Henry F. Holland to the State Department,

To make the weight of the labour movement felt, the CTM, the CROM, the National Proletarian Confederation, the Confederation of Workers and Peasants of Mexico, the General Confederation of Workers and the Mexican Electrical Workers Union, former adversaries and splits from the CTM, signed the National Workers Unity Pact at the National Palace in May 1945. It included cooperation to draw up an industrialisation plan, employment for those left jobless as a result of the war, 'respect for free and genuine trade union democracy', mechanisms to reconcile labour-management conflicts, 'using strikes only as an extreme measure and in serious situations and submitting such cases to arbitration by the President of the Republic', and the defence of wages and improved working conditions. The National Workers Council would last 'until the end of the war with Japan',[9] the date of which was still not defined, and bound the signatories to a panorama marked by a far-away war that furthermore was divorced from their living conditions. The agreement was that the council presidency would rotate among the signatory member organisations and decisions would be adopted by consensus and not by majority vote. That project did not get off the ground either. The CTM was in the minority with this arrangement and perhaps for that reason abandoned the pact along with the mine workers' union. Lombardo made no comments whatsoever so as not to contradict anyone on a question that was not a priority for his strategy.

In May 1945, Lombardo would rather have been in Chihuahua when the conditions for hunting grizzly bears were at their best, because 'the mountainous region is very dry and they have to descend to the pools where there is still water and there are only a few of them'. But this was not the time to be away from the city. The agenda for the regular confidential meeting with President Ávila Camacho was long and Lombardo felt the urgent need to inform him of his analysis of Mexico and the world. To make the panorama of Central and Eastern Europe at the end of the war more relevant to the president, Lombardo wanted him to believe that the region 'is at this moment experiencing its anti-feudal revolution, like the Mexican Revolution'. Historic details mattered little, among them that some of these countries were highly industrialised such as Czechoslovakia, newly liberated from Nazi fascism and not from feudalism, and others like Hungary and Bulgaria had been allies of the Axis powers.

Mexico City, 1 June 1945, NARA, RG 59, file 812.504/6–148; Middlebrook 1995, p. 114; Torres 2005, pp. 273–300; Rivero Torres 1982, p. 150.

9 'Bases del Pacto de unidad obrera nacional', National Palace, Mexico City, 10 May 1945, file 610; 'La COCM en contra del pacto obrero patronal', Report presented to the ILO by its Mexico representative, June 1945, OIT-BIT, file 41/1945.

What also mattered was that the United States sought to abolish customs barriers in Latin America regardless of industrialisation and investment of its capital, that it supported parties, groups and individuals who were 'in agreement with the submission of our countries to the United States'; that it was vital for the Mexican presidential campaign that there be 'a single candidate within the revolutionary sector' along with the adoption 'of a single programme: the industrialisation of Mexico'. He also felt that the PRM should be reorganised and led by men with moral authority to explain its programme to the nation and to incorporate 'elements representative of the country's progressive industrialists' into its leadership. In Latin America, he added, the prestige of anti-imperialist Mexico was in crisis, which the country's diplomatic missions should remedy with proper instructions.[10] Lombardo presented himself to the president as the national conscience and the voice of the workers.

2 On the Campaign Trail

In July 1945, Vicente Lombardo Toledano turned 51 years old. Unionised teachers under the aegis of the CTM gathered to celebrate his birthday at the Restaurante Chapultepec. He used the opportunity to extol his moral record: 'I've never been to a brothel, a place, a cabaret; I've never been to a place that was demeaning for a man. I do not have mistresses or lovers'. He was invincible because he served an immortal, undying and invincible cause that lay ahead.[11]

He apologised for the crude remarks, but they were necessary to judge his ideas 'implemented here and in the whole world'. And having established his moral authority, he egged on the teachers to participate in the presidential campaign, adopting Miguel Alemán as the next presidential candidate. Even though, 'fortunately, things are going stupendously well in our country, stupendously',[12] it was necessary to ensure that there would be no other candidate but Alemán, 'the cub of the revolution', his former student at the National Preparatory School and at the School of Law and Jurisprudence. Without saying so, only Alemán he hoped could serve as an instrument for his national and global strategy.

---

10   VLT, 'C. Presidente de la República', Mexico City, 15 May 1945, file 610; Juan Manuel Terrazas to VLT, Chihuahua, 21 May 1945, FHLT, file 611.
11   VLT, 'Banquete homenaje en LI aniversario de VLT organizado por el magisterio nacional', Mexico City, 17 July 1945, in *Obra*, IV/17, 1945, p. 27.
12   VLT, 'Banquete homenaje en LI aniversario de VLT organizado por el magisterio nacional', Mexico City, 17 July 1945, in *Obra*, IV/17, 1945, pp. 79–80; 'Banquete homenaje en LI aniversario de VLT organizado por el magisterio nacional', Mexico City, 17 July 1945, in *Obra*, IV/17, 1945, p. 17, p. 27, p. 35; Krauze 1997b, pp. 88–97.

Miguel Alemán Valdés, six years his junior, governor of Veracruz between 1936 and 1939 and interior minister in the administration of President Ávila Camacho, was pleased with Lombardo Toledano's agitation in favour of his candidacy, almost a year before the election and still without campaigning underway. But Lombardo's predilection for the Soviet Union and his anti-imperialist stance were uncomfortable and could affect the credibility of Alemán's candidacy. Privately he insisted that Lombardo would have no influence in his government and that in case of a clash between the two world powers, he would be on the side of US security in the same way that General Cárdenas and President Ávila Camacho had been during the war.

Lombardo's position also gratified the American observers because it meant that there would not be a left candidate and that the left would not object to a candidate who would favour the business community and US economic interests such as markets open to its goods; that there would be a solution to the dispute over oil favourable to the companies without the need to restore the privileges that existed prior to 1938, since Petróleos Mexicanos involved massive and wasteful expenditures and Mexico needed US technical assistance to put the industry on its feet.[13]

As far as Lombardo was concerned, the other two candidates, Miguel Henríquez Guzmán and Javier Rojo Gómez, were of no concern. They were forced or asked to withdraw from the race by President Ávila Camacho. That left Ezequiel Padilla, the foreign minister, as the only challenger to Alemán.[14] When in January 1946 the Institutional Revolutionary Party (PRI) was born, Lombardo delivered a harangue in favour of Miguel Alemán as 'the only responsible candidate, not just the only revolutionary',[15] and in April 1946 began a tour in support of the presidential candidate. While his endorsement had been agreed on, it nevertheless should have come as a breather for Alemán to hear that in Monterrey Lombardo praised the industrialisation programme, the need for the country to be free and not an economic satellite of anyone, against false leftists, and 'because I am a Marxist, I know that the only thing we can propose at this time is the bourgeois revolution'.[16] As the candidates for senators and congressional deputies were concocted by the CTM and Lombardo, based

---

13 Paz 1997, pp. 240–4.
14 Jones 2014, p. 197; Loaeza 2014, available at: http://www.nexos.com.mx/?p=20010. Accessed 1 July 2017.
15 VLT, speech at the Monument to the Revolution, Mexico City, 16 December 1945, AGN, MAC, vol. 747, file 544.61/39; VLT, speech in the 'Congreso constituyente del Partido Revolucionario Institucional', Teatro Metropolitano, Mexico City, 19 January 1946, in *Obra*, IV/18, 1946, p. 70; Loaeza 2013, pp. 317–20.
16 'Informe que rinde la Oficina Internacional del Trabajo', April 1946, ILO-BIT, file 41/1946.

on individual and corporate political interests and not according to the preferences of the unions, this was also no cause for concern. It could happen, as on previous occasions that a candidate had to step aside because the CTM was indebted to another candidate who in the previous election was not favoured and was promised the seat at the next opportunity.[17] Lombardo was still the helmsman of many unions. In Chihuahua workers were 'waiting for your guiding words ... your virile words [that] reaffirm once again the defence of our highest democratic social justice aspirations, against the intolerable, subversive and traitorous attitude of the nation's enemies'.[18]

On the way back from El Paso, passing through Chihuahua, Tamaulipas and Coahuila, cheering followers lined the route. At each stop he spoke of the presidential succession in which the country's future was at stake 'because we cannot think of any historical transformation without the quality of the men who are chosen being an important consideration'. Padilla was a traitor to the nation 'for invoking communism as a danger, with which he sabotaged the modernisation measures'. The audience cheered Lombardo and shouted 'yes'.[19]

From Ciudad Juárez, Lombardo travelled to Nogales where the voice of the Padillistas dominated the political landscape and where the CTM had little influence. According to Lombardo, 'the revolutionary sector is poor and has been divided or destroyed by opportunism'. Labour leader Hermenegildo Peña, loyal to Lombardo, organised security brigades with members of the Yaqui and Mayo indigenous communities in anticipation of acts of provocation, but the villagers who had gathered were there to crown the Queen of Spring and to organise the flower festival. To avoid a noisy 'charanga fiestera', celebration before or during the rally, 'we exercised union control over the musicians'. To provide him with a decent accommodation, a private home was sought, because the local hotels were dirty, uncomfortable and insecure, and knowing that Lombardo would not have wanted to spend the night on the other side of the border. In Nogales, Lombardo realised that the PRI had its favourites and they were not his Sonoran allies Jacinto López for senator or Hermenegildo Peña for federal congressional deputy, that his speeches were insufficient and that the votes in the federal elections would be manipulated as in the past and not only there.[20]

---

17   Carlos Ramón García to Fidel Velázquez, Los Mochis, Sinaloa, 27 February 1946, FHLT, file 629.
18   Bernardino Castro, Manuel Navarro, and others to VLT, Chihuahua, 1 May 1946, file 635; VLT, 'Discurso en la Plaza de Toros', Ciudad Juárez, 1 May 1946, FHLT, file 635.
19   Ibid.
20   VLT to Alejandro Carrillo, Nogales, Sonora, 3 May 1946, FHLT, file 635; Ramos Malzárraga,

It was necessary to infiltrate the Padillista ranks to divide them from within. Raúl Murillo, a Lombardista for more than a decade, offered to be the instrument to sabotage the opposition in western Mexico. He presented himself as a Padillista in Tepic, Nayarit, to go from village to village with Salvador García, opposition precandidate for senator. On the way, he preached that the Sinarquistas and Padillistas should join forces to defeat the PRI. He suffered when he had to listen to obscenities against Alemán, against Cárdenas, 'and very particularly against el maestro. Against el Gran Maestro'. On 14 June he arrived in Guadalajara, where 'I deepened the division that I had prepared'. But Murillo was discovered as an Alemanista spy. The Padillistas ordered him to go to the Hotel Virreinal, where he was interrogated about the payments he had received. In a simulated defence, Murillo shot back: 'If Alemán had paid me I wouldn't be walking around half dead from starvation or in tatters like we hard core Padillistas are'.[21]

It was true that Murillo had no money; he didn't even have enough to return home. He wasn't spy material, he reflected, but his faith in Lombardo sustained him. He wrote that 'since I don't think Mr Lombardo was mistaken in choosing Mr Alemán I gave myself body and soul, fully aware, to work for him'. As nobody paid Murillo for the job done, 'I'm putting an end to the work entrusted to me in the offices of "El Popular"', unless he were given another assignment. There was another mission, namely, to buy arms and ammunition, the details of which were kept secret due to the obligatory discretion.[22]

Lombardo was in Moscow in an international trade union meeting when Juan Manuel Terrazas, his friend and businessman dealing in mineralised salt for cattle, along with other of his followers, still before the elections were preparing 'two or three ranches' so that Lombardo and Miguel Alemán, who had planned to go to Chihuahua to rest after the elections, could talk

> with some degree of comfort and tranquility and without being disturbed, without being completely incommunicado with the city of Chihuahua, because you will have a plane at your unconditional disposition and that can take you to the city in less than thirty minutes. If Mr Licenciado Alemán accepts, please phone me so I can prepare everything, with the utmost discretion so that no one finds out.[23]

Secretary of Education and Information of the CTM, to VLT, Nogales, Sonora, 2 May 1946, FHLT, file 635.
21   Raúl Murillo to Alejandro Carrillo, Guadalajara, Jalisco, 26 June 1946, FHLT, file 637.
22   Raúl Murillo to VLT, Mexico City, 1 July 1946, FHLT, file 638.
23   Juan Manuel Terrazas to VLT, Chihuahua, 26 June 1946, FHLT, file 637.

The elections of 7 July 1946 involved bitterly fought races for congressional deputy and senate seats. Alemán won the presidential elections and Lombardo Toledano emerged strengthened. When he requested that his book *Por un mundo mejor* be published with the cost covered by the public coffers, 3,000 copies for 22,403 pesos, it was a small price to pay for his and the CTM's support for the victorious candidate. As with the previous presidents, Lombardo established the habit of meeting with Alemán to present him with one or another problem, bring his attention to a situation involving this or that ejido, cooperative, a sugar mill that needed government intervention and he tried to schedule meetings between those with problems to be solved and the president.[24]

But just as unity was difficult to achieve in the previous period, so too was the unequivocal renewal of the nation, which was another way of describing the policy of subordinating workers' rights and interests to the state that caused endless divisions within the labour movement. There were patriots of different allegiances: Marxists, Catholics, Sinarquistas and veterans of the revolution, who were horrified by the government's tolerance of the 'poisonous' ideologies of Cárdenas, Lombardo, Bassols, Amilpa and Campa, that Stalinist gang of Mexico.[25]

Lombardo knew he had enemies on the right that he had to fight with the left. His genius lay in his ability to periodically bring together forces that would later repeatedly break apart. The Roundtable of Mexican Marxists that he organised in January 1947 and his goal to establish a People's Party were an attempt to regroup the scattered and antagonistic left forces under the same banner and make them not into an opposition to the government and the PRI, but a force with a view to growing until, in the future, it could become the dominant political current in the country. President Ávila Camacho asked Lombardo to delay the founding of the party until after the 1946 elections.[26] He obliged.

3   The Roundtable

The Mexican Communist Party split in 1940 and again in 1943 as a result of the expulsions carried out by the Communist International based on the under-

---

24   Roberto Amorós to Ramón Beteta, Mexico City, 23 April 1947, AGN, Ramo Miguel Alemán Valdés (henceforth MAV), file 568.3/72.
25   José A. Inclán to Miguel Alemán, Mexico City, 18 October 1947, AGN, MAV, vol. 567, file 544.61/5.
26   Medina 1988, pp. 118–19.

standing that purging the party would strengthen it. Lombardo gathered the fragments of the splits and in 1944 formed the Mexican Socialist League with a view to creating a new party with the main expelled leaders from the PCM, Cardenistas left out of power and with 'people who never come together to jointly fight for great political ideals'.[27] Contrary to what his intention was, Lombardo said the League was not formed 'for the purpose of intervening in the internal life of the workers, peasants or popular organisations'.[28] It would be an organisation for the study and spread of information on national and international problems, to guide the people's consciousness with theory, doctrines and principles. The stage had not come for 'the establishment of socialism in our country'.[29] But Lombardo was not interested in creating clubs for political and ideological debate; rather his goal was to set up political and ideological organisations to intervene in public life, without putting all his cards on the table.

An unexpected enemy was the appearance of Trotskyism as a school of thought that propounded the primacy of the labour movement in the restructuring of postwar society. Lombardo's point of view was that the labour movement was a subordinate partner to the state and he rejected Trotskyism as a 'theoretical deviation of Marxism' and as a provocation, because it advocated socialism in the here and now.[30] In Lombardo's view not only could socialism not be built because in the current period doing so would be contrary to the historical laws, but also because Moscow's political strategy called for a rejection of socialist revolutions that could provoke the industrialised powers against the Soviet Union. After being bled white in the war, the USSR had to build up economic and military forces before considering the seizure of power in the next stage.[31] Without saying so, Lombardo saw Mexico as a link in this process. His role was to aid in strengthening the existing political system and in weakening imperialism with the support of the labour movement. It was necessary to satisfy the vital needs of the working population, not give it power. The League did not survive its first setbacks, but Lombardo did not give up.

---

27   VLT, 'Asamblea constituyente de la Liga Socialista Mexicana', 2 September 1944, in *Obra*, IV/14, 1944, p. 322.
28   VLT, 'Asamblea constituyente de la Liga Socialista Mexicana', 2 September 1944, in *Obra*, IV/14, 1944, p. 324.
29   VLT, 'Asamblea constituyente de la Liga Socialista Mexicana', 2 September 1944, in *Obra*, IV/14, 1944, pp. 325–9.
30   VLT, 'Asamblea constituyente de la Liga Socialista Mexicana', 2 September 1944, in *Obra*, IV/14, 1944, p. 329.
31   VLT, 'Ni abolir la propiedad privada ni sovietizar', *Novedades*, 4 September 1944 and 'Quedó formada la Liga Socialista', *Novedades*, 9 September 1944.

The Roundtable of Mexican Marxists was the next attempt to regroup the scattered left, which Lombardo characterised as confused, in order to establish a political party. Its explicit aim was to 'decide on common action in the workers' movement and the revolutionary movement in general'.[32] He did not invite the unions, although eventually 'they can obtain an exact version of the discussions'.[33] He did invite left organisations 'and some people whose opinion I consider to be valuable for the stated purpose' of the event. The list of names included Agustín Guzmán, mine workers' leader and close to Lombardo and no longer tied to the CTM; Gaudencio Peraza, a teacher who adhered to and promoted Lombardo's ideas; and Juan Manuel Elizondo, miners' leader, his friend and senator. He wanted Villaseñor and Bassols, with whom he had had differences in the past because they criticised his ties with Velázquez and Amilpa, to participate in the project and mend relations with them.

Among those participating from the Marxist group of the Workers' University were his brother Humberto, his secretary Enrique Ramírez y Ramírez, his sister-in-law Carmen Otero y Gama, and as alternates his son-in-law Federico Silva, husband of his daughter Adriana, and María Teresa Puente, friend, lawyer and wife after he became a widower. The four women who were full or alternate delegates in the debates – the third was Estela Jiménez Esponda from the PCM and the fourth was Luz Salazar from the Marxist group The Insurgent – appeared as groupies of their male mentors.

Lombardo opened the debate, giving the line – 'because it corresponds to those of us who are concerned with providing political activity with a theoretical basis' – on tactics and strategy 'that the proletariat and the revolutionary sector of Mexico should adhere to in the current historical stage of the country's life'.[34] What was needed was 'a single line and common strategy and tactics'. In a turnabout from a few years before, Lombardo took the stand that the right was off the course because it proposed the development of the national economy 'with the main cooperation coming from foreign forces'. But even more dangerous was Trotskyism because it put the weight of the engine of history on the proletariat. It was plain sectarianism and opportunism that had to be fought with the theory of history by stages. Although Lombardo said that the proletariat should lead the bourgeois-democratic revolution because capitalism was progressive in relation to the slave and feudal past and 'a step toward

---

32   VLT, 'La Invitación', Mexico City, 3 January 1947, in *Mesa redonda de los marxistas mexicanos* 1982, p. 11.
33   *Mesa redonda de los marxistas mexicanos* 1982, p. 12.
34   *Mesa redonda de los marxistas mexicanos* 1982, p. 19.

socialism', the path to follow was the People's Party, because the PRI was not such a party and the PCM went from one crisis to another.[35]

Lombardo offered an interpretation of Marxism as the contradiction between the relations of production and the productive forces, between structure and superstructure, leaving outside his perspective regarding the labour necessary for the worker's reproduction and surplus labour as the origin of capital gains, which in 1919 he had dismissed as a puerile idea of Marx and then adhered to in passing after reading the latter's texts. Nor did Lombardo consider the alienation of labour, use value and exchange value, the other central points of Marxism. Labour, in which – according to Marx – the existence of the workers was embodied, was not among his concerns. This was also the case with profits as wealth not earned with labour and capital accumulation, which together with workers' unpaid work were the sources of capitalist growth. Had he been concerned with the origin, accumulation and reproduction of capital, he would have had to qualify if not reject his ideas on national unity with the propertied classes and the state, its defender. Instead, and as if it had sprung from the Soviet manuals of the era on dialectical and historical materialism, Lombardo summarised the history of humankind, 25 centuries of thesis and antithesis, from ancient times to the present day.

The participants in the roundtable had three days to consider his ideas on the transition from capitalism to socialism, on the final stage of capitalism, on imperialism, on 'capitalism in its phase of decomposition' and on how it was weakened after the war, albeit concentrated in US monopolies. In contrast, socialism was strengthened because the war consolidated the Soviet system and the 'firm and indissoluble links between the government and the people'. Soviet economic reconstruction 'is being fulfilled mathematically, as are all the tasks that the working class and the government take on',[36] he said in relation to a Soviet Union in which it was not necessary to commit an act of sabotage, but merely to tell a joke poking fun at the Communist Party or mocking the elections for a citizen to be deprived of his or her liberty and sent to a forced labour camp.[37]

David Alfaro Siqueiros, who was not invited, came on board 'as a furtive Marxist, but here I am'.[38] He forced himself to be included in the roundtable, because he represented the Spanish Republican Army fighters and 'the man in

---

35 *Mesa redonda de los marxistas mexicanos* 1982, pp. 20–2, p. 57, p. 68.
36 *Mesa redonda de los marxistas mexicanos* 1982, pp. 33–5.
37 Applebaum 2004, p. 272; Lewis 2008, p. 71.
38 *Mesa redonda de los marxistas mexicanos* 1982, p. 560.

the street',[39] to expose reality leaving no stone unturned, to speak about corruption in the CTM, in the leadership of the trade unions and about the lack of workers' democracy.

However, workers' daily lives and their organisations were not the subject of debate at the roundtable, but rather the theorisation on the historical moment to prepare the groundwork and sow the seed of the People's Party. Lombardo did not argue with the political dilettantes that he considered the other participants to be. At most, he conceded that it was necessary to do some housecleaning in the CTM to renew the confederation without destroying it. If there were discrepancies during the days of the roundtable debate it was because there was an unresolved conflict lingering in the air such as the relations between the Mexican Communist Party and Lombardo, the anti-Lombardismo of the communists and of Siqueiros, which prevented harmony among them. Lombardo reiterated that 'I will never be, nor have been, nor will I allow myself to be an instrument of the Communist Party', prompting Laborde's response, 'You should be a member of the Communist Party'.[40]

Siqueiros criticised the 'dreadful defects' of *El Popular*, which 'invariably applauds the positive aspects of government, but remains silent about its negative aspects, or does it diplomatically so that, naturally, no one can understand it'.[41] He touched on another sore point. The Workers' University dominated how the roundtable was run, deciding who would have the floor. He proposed, unsuccessfully, that the sessions be presided over by a rotating chair.

Class struggle or national unity was one of the key issues in the debate, a dilemma for several speakers. The communists wanted to strengthen their 'glorious' party, which was the vanguard of the proletariat but without ruling out the creation of the People's Party. Luis Torres from the Insurgent group spoke for all the communists when he concluded that what should come out of the roundtable is a 'determination to create the People's Party proposed by compañero Lombardo Toledano' together with 'a true Communist Party'. But Laborde, the long-time party leader expelled in 1940, feared that the communist party would be supplanted by the People's Party. He approved of the proposal but 'we want to know what is really involved'.[42] Lombardo was not interested in such a combination of parties, since he organised the event to convince others of the virtues of his own project.

---

39   *Mesa redonda de los marxistas mexicanos* 1982, p. 179, p. 563.
40   *Mesa redonda de los marxistas mexicanos* 1982, pp. 595–8.
41   *Mesa redonda de los marxistas mexicanos* 1982, p. 186.
42   *Mesa redonda de los marxistas mexicanos* 1982, p. 390, pp. 422–4 and p. 254.

What the roundtable of Mexican Marxists did not discuss was Marxism. It repeated the incantations of Lenin and Stalin as well as the scathing criticism of Trotskyism. The meeting also involved a settling of scores, a critique of the communists' submission to Lombardo in the 1930s, the line of 'unity at all costs', and an open and veiled rebuke to the leaders who had sanctioned such a policy, which ensued a confrontation between executioners and victims and the resentments of those who were expelled from the party by the next generation of orthodox purifiers. It concluded with the collective endorsement of Lombardo as the international helmsman of the organised workers, beyond any criticism, and who, for being so extraordinary, it was necessary to defend. Although for lack of time, the painter Leopoldo Méndez could not express his ardour for 'the great workers' leader and Marxist of Mexico', in the conclusions of the roundtable it was made clear that no one like Lombardo was such 'a magnificent exponent and implementer of Marxist doctrine, to demonstrate that our identification with him is not formal or determined by narrow interests, but is based on the deep conviction that his line, his theses and his conclusions are correct'.[43]

But Lombardo was not entirely satisfied with the hero worshipping bestowed on him at the roundtable. On the last day of the debates, 22 January, he again took the floor. 'I am satisfied with the development of the discussion, but not fully satisfied'.[44] He failed to convince all the participants to adopt his position 'and as long as we don't settle these theoretical differences, these divergences in the application of theory to a historical reality of the world of today, no unified conclusion can be inferred'.[45] He was offended by everything that was said about him, which he perceived as disloyal, for being treated as 'a kind of newborn baby who you do the favour of helping so as to enable him to move within the working class, preventing him from making mistakes, spanking him so that he doesn't make errors again, and so on. This is a comedy that does not respond to reality'.[46] He argued that it was not possible to reach the conclusions that he wanted due to the personal animosities that he perceived were expressed against him and the impertinent interruptions by Siqueiros.[47]

What the roundtable did achieve was to build a personality cult around Lombardo, but it also raised doubts. 'Vicente was, unquestionably, the right person

---

43   *Mesa redonda de los marxistas mexicanos* 1982, p. 525.
44   *Mesa redonda de los marxistas mexicanos* 1982, p. 579.
45   *Mesa redonda de los marxistas mexicanos* 1982, p. 580.
46   *Mesa redonda de los marxistas mexicanos* 1982, p. 599.
47   *Mesa redonda de los marxistas mexicanos* 1982, p. 600.

to promote the creation of the party, although initially he didn't reveal a precise idea about the nature of the new organisation'.[48] Bassols perceived 'accommodative tendencies' in Lombardo, but supported his initiative, because 'there will always be a door open from which to leave'.[49] He put his finger on the quandary when he revealed his doubt: 'What's going on? As we go beyond the generalities and move to action, to the concrete application of the principles, what was previously an agreement starts to reveal at least caution and reticence, what had been unanimity begins to no longer be so'.[50] When it came to interpreting the abstractions, differences arose in determining how to act. But as opposed to a Bassols who doubted even himself, there was Lombardo with his certainty to the death in defence of his incontrovertible truth of which he wanted to convince everyone else beyond a shadow of a doubt.

4   Elections in the CTM

As soon as the roundtable concluded in January 1947, he appeared at the oil workers' convention. 'I, Lombardo Toledano, do not support either Amilpa or Gómez Z.', referring to the two candidates who aspired to the CTM leadership, which was up for renewal at the union's fourth congress in March. One of the contenders was from the group of the 'five little wolves', the other was a railroad workers' leader who wanted to restore the power of their union, under attack by the government, and nationalise the company when there were opinions in favour of privatisation.[51] Lombardo was at the oil workers' convention to persuade the powerful union to return to the fold of the CTM, since in August of the previous year, 15 locals, more than half the total, split away because the confederation 'does not represent the workers' interests, and on the contrary, without examining their true feelings, has compromised them in political situations using the security forces and seriously undermining the labour movement in the process'.[52]

---

48   Villaseñor 1976, vol. 2, p. 93.
49   Villaseñor 1976, vol. 2, p. 101.
50   Villaseñor 1976, vol. 2, p. 106.
51   VLT in the 4th Extraordinary National Convention of the oil workers' union, 23 January 1947, in *Obra*, V/1, 1947, p. 131; Alegre 2013, pp. 46–54.
52   'Informe que rinde a la Oficina Internacional del Trabajo el corresponsal en México', August 1946, ILO-BIT, file 41/1946; VLT in the 4th Extraordinary National Convention of the oil workers' union, 23 January 1947, in *Obra*, V/1, 1947, p. 129.

Of indomitable energy, on 24 January Lombardo was in Puebla with textile workers to repeat the call for unity and support for the newly anointed president. He repeated that he did not care if the next general secretary of the CTM were Amilpa or Gómez Z: 'What matters to me is the future of the CTM, and that the general secretary is named by the members. What matters to me is to know that the national committee is comprised of the ablest, most responsible elements of the Cetemista workers unity'.[53] From Puebla, Lombardo quickly returned to Mexico City to attend the CTM national council at the end of the month. 'The situation that the CTM is going through is serious'. The organisation had a great responsibility, because the CTM and the Mexican Revolution were indissoluble.

In fact, what he did and said, even if he did not mean it, was to create an environment suitable for bringing the new party together, 'pure democracy', managed by its members, 'that emerges from below and not from above, not by agreement of a handful of leaders but by the real and spontaneous commitment of those who will have to comprise it'. He announced that he would crisscross the country to investigate 'ranch by ranch' the problems of each locality in order to recruit people 'to the party individually and spontaneously'. Lombardo, who had ceased to be the formal leader of the CTM, straight to the point outlined the road forward in a party 'formed by mystics – let me say – what I mean by this is, by those who are enthusiastic to the point of being delirious if necessary'.[54]

But first the CTM had to be reorganised. Lombardo proposed that the national industrial unions should have a greater weight in the leadership of the CTM than they had up until then. Without saying so, he proposed that unions from small industries as well as the craft unions cede their places to the large industrial unions. The proposal surely touched some raw nerves among the 'five little wolves' and their unconditional followers holed up in small unions in the states that had served them well as a springboard from which to reach positions in the legislature, the Conciliation and Arbitration Boards and the leadership in state federations. Lombardo proposed a revolution in the CTM along the lines of the Congress of Industrial Organizations, which had been founded in 1935 in the United States with the industrial unions and that helped democratise the sclerotic union structure traditionally dominated by the AFL. Like Morones in the CROM, Lombardo considered himself to be a lifetime leader of the CTM.

---

53   VLT in the 4th General Ordinary Congress of the Puebla Workers Federation, 24 January 1947, in *Obra*, v/1, 1947, pp. 143–4.

54   VLT, speech in the 'XXX Consejo Nacional de la CTM', Mexico City, 28 January 1947, in *Obra*, v/1, 1947, p. 148, pp. 168–9, pp. 173–4.

'Yes, my CTM, not because it belongs to me, but because the Mexican Workers Confederation is a major part of my life'.[55]

He knew there was discontent among the electrical, telephone and railroad workers, with Luis Gómez Zepeda and Valentín Campa at the head of the latter movement, and among tramway workers and blasters. Germán Lizt Arzubide from the graphic arts workers' union was one of several who pointed to the vices that had been incubating in the organisation, which included corruption, using union office to obtain employment opportunities, using the union as a springboard for public office, loss of independence, the absence of democratic voting – promoted by Fidel Velázquez and Blas Chumacero – manipulation of delegate selection and seating to fill union congresses with unconditional followers of the current leadership.[56] But the criticism also revealed that there were two parallel and competing leaderships in existence: the leadership of the CTM and that of Lombardo, who kept receiving letters from those who 'have seen the sincere advisor and authorised guide of the Mexican worker in you',[57] and others who bemoaned 'the ridicule that you have been the object of by the impositionist faction of the CTM'.[58]

The Mexican Communist Party declared that it would 'not go with Amilpa, nor Gómez Z.', but would support Lombardo for the leadership of the CTM in view of Miguel Alemán being a progressive president, the CTM being the most important labour confederation in Mexico and the CTAL in Latin America. However, the Unified Socialist Action Group, one of the splits from the communist party with Laborde as its leader, proposed Luís Gómez Zepeda for the office and called for the renewal of the entire CTM national committee.[59] The scene was set for protracted mayhem.

Before the congress took place, CTM representatives organised rallies throughout the country. Lombardo knew about them before they were held.

---

55   VLT, speech in the 'XXX Consejo Nacional de la CTM', Mexico City, 28 January 1947, in *Obra*, V/1, 1947, pp. 181–2.
56   'Carta abierta al c. Vicente L. Toledano', Mexico City, 13 February 1947, FHLT, file 667; VLT to José Vázquez, general secretary of the State of Sonora Workers Federation, Mexico City, 4 March 1947; Enrique Ramírez y Ramírez to Miguel Barrera, Nuevo Leon Federation of People's Committees, Mexico City, 4 March 1947, FHLT, file 670.
57   Homero Gautier and Leopoldo Arana Carrera to VLT, National Union of Workers of the Hydraulic Resources Ministry, Mexico City, 6 March 1947, FHLT, file 670.
58   'Contestación al compañero Lombardo Toledano y a todas las organizaciones del CTM', Mexico City, 10 February 1947, in FHLT, newspaper archives, file 22.
59   H. Laborde, 'Síntesis de la sesión de la ASU', Mexico City, 6 March 1947, FHLT, file 670; 'Declaraciones del Comité Directivo Nacional de Acción Socialista Unificada', Mexico City, 10 March 1947, FHLT, file 670.

In the capital 'on the same day, the 16, Fidel plans to hold a rally at the Monument to the Revolution or Constitution Square, on the anniversary of the oil industry expropriation, but in fact to organise a demonstration as a display of strength of the CTM in Mexico City'.[60]

Knowing that Gómez Zepeda's election would not go anywhere given the steamroller tactics of the national committee of the CTM and the manipulation of delegate registration, the railroad workers' union, oriented by Campa as its secretary of education and culture, and by Laborde, left the CTM to create the United Confederation of Labour (CUT) with important unions such as the electrical and telephone workers, in addition to the railroad workers, about 200,000 members, further weakening the CTM prior to its congress. Luis Gómez Z., – whose political line for the labour movement involved participating in industrial policy, fighting for trade union independence, for control of inflation, wage increases and access to affordable working class housing – was named the CUT's general secretary. The affiliation to the CTM of about 13,000 rural ejidatarios from Mexicali did not compensate for the loss of the railroad workers.[61]

Lombardo opened the congress praising the president without wanting to be his lackey and declared that he was his friend without wanting to be uncritical, and in the same breath said: 'We have been Alemanistas, we are Alemanistas, and we will be Alemanistas for the future'.[62] He manoeuvred so that Amilpa would be elected as general secretary, since he agreed to the CTM's affiliation to the People's Party when it would be formed. Lombardo still managed to fill the leadership positions in the national committee with his followers. These included Jacinto López, Javier Ramos Malzárraga, Leobardo Wolstano Pineda and Alfonso Palacios. He branded Campa. Laborde and Miguel Ángel Velasco, 'expelled from the Communist Party years ago' as splitters, and denied that the PRI was anti-communist, 'because it is comprised of worker and campesino organisations and these sectors are not anti-communist'. He insulted Gómez Z. as 'cunning, but he fails at this because his thinking doesn't even reach such a level', but at the same time accused the Cetemistas of irresponsibility, indolence, neglect, lethargy, forgetfulness and disrespect. 'This, comrades of the CTM, should not occur in the future'. For Amilpa he had words of praise with some condescension, saying that from being a chauffeur by trade he went so

---

60 Enrique Ramírez y Ramírez to VLT, Mexico City, 7 March 1947, FHLT, file 670.
61 Basurto 1984, pp. 124–5; Alegre 2013, pp. 56–7; Middlebrook 1995, p. 115; Krauze 1997b, p. 200; Campa 1985, pp. 197–8.
62 VLT, 'Inauguración del Cuarto Congreso de la CTM', 26 March 1947, in *Obra*, V/1, 1947, pp. 277–80, p. 281, p. 285.

far as to acquire a 'respectable (level of) culture'. The president did not attend the congress as his predecessors had, but received the delegates at the National Palace.[63]

Knowing better, Lombardo spoke of the success of the congress because it preserved the unity of the CTM despite attempts by its enemies to divide the confederation. Perhaps in return for his loyalty, in 1947 the government approved a subsidy to the Workers' University of 250,000 pesos, which if received would have allowed Lombardo to obtain a monthly salary of 1,500 pesos, Manuel Meraz his driver 330 pesos a month, translator Isabel Carvajal, wife of his friend the Italian communist Vittorio Vidali 225 pesos and the porters 150 pesos each. However, Finance Minister Ramón Beteta did not release the funds, which led to the university failing to function for part of the year.[64]

5 The Expulsion

Henry Horton, the secretary of the US embassy took advantage of a weekend getaway at the British Boat Club in Xochimilco on the outskirts of the city to discreetly sound out José Barros and Jorge Viesca, the president's secretaries. They confirmed that Alemán's policy was to strengthen other labour unions at the expense of the CTM. They also said that Lombardo was a communist and the People's Party would also be, no matter how much he claimed that it would not be an opposition party. Barros told the inquisitive Horton that General Rodolfo Sánchez Taboada, president of the PRI, had made it clear that membership in the PRI was incompatible with belonging to any other party and that the PRI was a popular party of the revolution. He noted that in early August 1947 the CTM did not send any representative to Toluca at the first meeting of the party under construction, because the subsidies the confederation received from the PRI would have been in danger.[65]

At the national council meeting of the CTM, in August, Amilpa laid the groundwork for dissociating the CTM from Lombardo, casting doubt on whether 'workers have the necessary judgemental capacity to choose their

---

63 'Entrevista a VLT', Mexico City, 28 March 1947, FHLT, file 673; Trejo Delarbe and Yáñez, 'The Mexican Labour Movement, 1917–1975', pp. 133–53.
64 Juan de Zengotita to the State Department, Mexico City, 16 July 1947, NARA, RG, 59, file 812.5043/7–1647.
65 Walter Washington to the State Department, Mexico City, 15 August 1947, ibid, file 812.5043/8–1547; Alan. R. Tennyson to FO, Mexico City, 14 October 1947, NA, FO371/AN3647/395/26.

party' and on 'the dangers that would result if the members of the CTM were left in absolute freedom' to do so. The decision, taken in March that members of the CTM could belong to the party of their choice was then left without effect. Those who belonged to the coordinating committee of the new party – Javier Ramos Malzárraga, Jacinto López and Alfonso Palacios – should resign. He called on Lombardo 'to discipline himself' and without waiting for an answer, which was known beforehand, 'the Assembly called for the immediate expulsion of all of Lombardo's people' whose 'aim is to take over the leadership of the labour movement in Mexico to put it at the orders of a rabid anti-Pan-American campaign at the service of Russia'.[66] Dual political affiliation was inadmissible because it would undermine the strength of the PRI. In reality, Amilpa knew that without the backing of the PRI, the Cetemistas would not have the opportunity to become congressional deputies and senators.[67] Breaking with Lombardo had the additional goal of encumbering his relentless interference in the affairs of the CTM.

The National Peasant Confederation, which followed the lead of the PRI, added fuel to the fire so that the new party would not obtain popular support. The ejidal commissioner of Acultsingo viewed the formation of a new political party as unpatriotic, because 'this will result in complete and direct harm to all the organisations in the country and especially for our campesinos, due to their sorry state of backwardness'. The new party's promoters were 'of communist ideas in the service of Soviet Russia, from which it can be concluded that its main objective will be to turn the party into an instrument to achieve what they have so far failed to obtain, in other words, the commitment to sovietise Mexico, and this is why they should also be considered traitors to our country'.[68]

In October, the CTM suspended three Lombardista secretaries for refusing to leave the coordinating committee of the People's Party. Frightened, some trade unionists abstained from participating in events to organise it. Amilpa awkwardly responded to his critics that 'the CTM and state federations depend economically on the governors of each state; therefore, we must blindly abide by their sovereign will'.[69] He insisted that Lombardo's obligation was to be a

---

66   'Informe que rinde a la Oficina Internacional del Trabajo el corresponsal en México', October 1947, OIT-BIT, file 41/1947.
67   Fernando Amilpa, 'La CTM y el Partido Popular', circular letter number 15, Mexico City, 26 August 1947, FHLT, newspaper archive, file 22; Juan de Zengotita to the State Department, Mexico City, 29 August and 25 September 1947, NARA, RG 59, file 812.00/8–2947.
68   Agustín Hernández and Elpido Aguirre to Miguel Alemán, Acultsingo, Veracruz, 18 October 1947, AGN, MAV, vol. 567, file 544.61/20.
69   Fernando Amilpa to VLT, Mexico City, 21 October 1947, FHLT, file 694; Oscar Gutiérrez to Fernando Amilpa, 29 November 1947, Mexico City, FHLT, file 698.

member of the PRI, but in view of 'your most fierce self-centredness and the most unjustified indiscipline, we have decided ... to suspend our relations with you in order to be in absolute freedom to defend the integrity of our organisation and to make the will of the majority be respected, whose exponent has been the so often cited National Council'.[70]

The CTM attracted more criticism and resentment for having violated its bylaws by making decisions not supported by the unions in the different parts of the country that were committed to the founding of the People's Party. The general secretary of the CTM was violating the CTM's laws by requiring that all Cetemistas had to belong to the PRI and that the council disavowed what a congress had approved.[71]

In January 1948, Lombardo was formally expelled by the CTM national council. Few delegates were on hand. The agreement on loyalty to the PRI was not accepted by some locals of the oil workers' union, a Yucatán union, another union from Baja California, and by the state federations of Sonora and Veracruz. Several locals of the Sugar Industry Workers Union met in a special session to discuss the Amilpa circular letter declaring that Lombardo was not a member of the CTM and the obligation to belong to the PRI. The union local at the La Esperanza sugar mill in Tonila, Jalisco, rejected the decisions, as was also the case with the Cocula sugar workers union that left its members free to belong to the party that best guaranteed their interests. 'The general criterion is that the CTM is dead'.[72]

The Durango teachers were indignant and they let Amilpa know about it: 'We cannot but condemn those who, like yourself, forgetting the highest duties of a Mexican and labour leader, have chained yourselves to the chariot of imperialism', using the banner of anti-communism. Some unions from Tampico belonging to the state federation left the CTM and hoped to form a new confederation. The Tamaulipecos accused the CTM leadership of the 'crime of dissolving unions, improper leadership management, and betraying the organised labour movement for personal gain to obtain government posts. We have considered these to be serious offenses to the honourable organisations of the Mexican Workers Confederation'.[73]

---

70   Fernando Amilpa to VLT, Mexico City, 13 November 1947, FHLT, file 696.
71   VLT, 'Asamblea cívica pro-formación del Partido Popular', 19 November 1947, Arena México, Mexico City, in *Obra*, V/2, 1947, p. 306.
72   Evaristo Ramírez Olivas and Hilario Moreno Aguirre to Fernando Amilpa, Durango, 15 January 1948; Isabel Vidrio and others to the National Executive Committee of the sugar workers' union, Tonilá, Jalisco, 27 January 1948, FHLT, file 710.
73   Avelino Ramírez to Enrique Ramírez y Ramírez, Tampico, 4 February 1948, FHLT, file 713; Avelino Ramírez to the CTM National Committee, Tampico, 17 February 1948, FHLT, file 714.

Fidel Velázquez reiterated that Lombardo was expelled for his divisive activities. A CTM commission adopted a resolution to boycott *El Popular*. State committees were ordered to show their political leanings and accept the obligation to 'promote activities that benefit the PRI'. The exodus from the CTM continued and Amilpa did not know how to explain it or how to get those who left to return to the fold.[74]

Even though it was the PRI that put the leaders of the CTM against the wall to reject the project of the People's Party, Lombardo was careful to exonerate the president and the PRI of any responsibility for his expulsion. The confederations belonging to the CTAL could not understand what was happening in Mexico, which for so long was considered the beacon that illuminated the road to be followed ideologically and in terms of trade union organisation in the hemisphere. Lombardo ended their consternation: 'without the slightest exaggeration, the CTM as a coherent body, as the organisation representing the majority of the Mexican proletariat, as an independent and revolutionary confederation of the working class, has ceased to exist'.[75]

6 The Crisis of the Nation

In March 1947, Daniel Cosío Villegas – economist, historian and liberal critic of developments in the country – published an essay on the demise of the original goals of the revolution, on the loss of its prestige and moral authority. He titled his essay 'Mexico's Crisis'. Cosío Villegas criticised the government for being indulgent with the workers to the extent of making their cause indefensible, if it were not first wiped clean 'of all excrescences that such a blind government policy has produced'. He railed at the government for having created an irresponsible labour organisation, without the 'feeling of independence or dependence on its own means, and not those of others'. He described the labour movement as 'a mere appendage of the government' that served as the arbitrator in the workers' struggles, and as a result the workers had stopped fighting and had become 'laudatory choir boys' for the government. Cosío Villegas did not mention any actor in that drama and Lombardo never referred to the essay. Although 'the left has become a spent force taking its programme as far as it could', the right was not the solution, the critic argued. The faint glimmer

---

74 'Informe que rinde a la Oficina Internacional del Trabajo el corresponsal en México', March 1948, OIT-BIT, file 41/1948.

75 VLT, 'A los miembros del Comité Central y centrales afiliadas de la CTAL', Mexico City, 1 February 1948, FHLT, file 714.

of hope was the reaffirmation of the principles and cleaning the house of its residents.[76] That, however, would not be the road that the CTM would take to overcome the crisis, but rather continuing to conceal it, which Cosío Villegas feared would occur.

The economic crisis affected workers' wages to such an extent that manufacturing output could not find a domestic market. Campesino-based agriculture languished and industrialisation was threatened by the onslaught of industrial imports from the United States, which Mexican industries could not compete against, often closing their doors. The lack of revenue affected construction and investment plans. A British observer noted: 'Mexico City illustrates the point with dozens of half-built office complexes and half-empty apartments, abandoned in silence by the workers'. Dollar reserves saved up in the war years were squandered in gleaming American cars, radios and refrigerators. In July, the government was forced to put a stop to lavish spending. It stopped importing luxury goods, hiked the import tax on most products and devalued the peso. The epidemic of foot and mouth disease in cattle and the compulsory sacrificing of sick animals added to the anxiety. The US border was closed to Mexican meat products and a harmful rumour circulated that the policy was imposed to help American ranchers who wanted to see the livestock industry in Mexico go under. The campesinos hid their animals and attacked the health inspection brigades with weapons. The measure was so dramatic that the government had to revoke it and in its place vaccinate and keep the livestock in isolation.[77]

However, the government's response to the labour unrest, reacting to a fragmented trade union movement, corrupt higher echelons and locals of the oil and railroad worker unions wracked by internal divisions was to impose pro-government leaders to discipline the workforce, minimise work stoppages and strikes over unmet demands, increase productivity, accelerate the pace of work without boosting wages and create an attractive labour environment for domestic and foreign investors in machinery and industrial infrastructure. *Charrismo* was the name given to the practice in labour unions of using coercion and violence to maintain discipline; the origin of the term came from the leader imposed by the government in the railway workers' union against the will of its members in 1948, Jesús Díaz de León, who liked to wear a charro, cowboy-type suit.[78]

---

76   Cosío Villegas 1947, pp. 29–51.
77   Rapp to Atlee, 'México: annual report for 1947', NA, FO371/AN274/267/26.
78   Alegre 2013, pp. 25–58; Tennyson, 'Downfall of Sr. Luis Gomez Z.', Mexico City, 4 October 1948, NA, LAB13/541; Basurto 1984, pp. 202–22.

Charrismo helped the CTM in 1948, and thereafter, impose union leaders subordinate to and at the service of the state and to function as the political instrument of the ruling party. The CTM was reduced to about 200,000 members in 1948 after losing some 600,000, who went to other labour confederations or remained as union locals without affiliation and whose insurgency would reemerge in subsequent decades.[79]

The government's labour policy was a setback for Lombardo's plans. He expected that the railroad workers would join the People's Party, but he made no statement to this effect. Now as before, he placed himself above the vices nurtured in the unions and the CTM as if they were the work of others, of those who 'speak of corruption and try to fight it with corrupted people'.[80] In his relationship with the government and the PRI, Lombardo's conviction in the indisputable role of the state as the driver of the country's affairs was paramount, along with his equally unshaken faith in the historical laws that lead to socialism in the distant future and of his own role as part of the elite of the vanguard of the proletariat that would lead to the joyous end of history.

Setbacks were part of the anticipated process, not a demonstration of its flaws. Lombardo's initiatives, supported by each of the presidential administrations, were a success and there was no reason to change strategy. He planned the creation of the CTM and in 1936 it was formed, the same with the CTAL, which was founded in 1938, and the World Federation of Trade Unions, which he helped to found in 1945. He had no doubt that the People's Party would also take shape. With patriotic rhetoric as an indispensable weapon, he continued to form new political and cultural institutions, affirming that they were 'from the people, by the people, and for the people'.[81]

---

79   Alegre 2013, p. 59.
80   VLT, 'XXX Consejo Nacional de la CTM', Mexico City, 28 January 1947, in *Obra*, V/1, 1947, p. 161.
81   VLT, 'Llamamiento a los trabajadores de México', Mexico City, 18 August 1947, p. 131; VLT, 'Asamblea constituyente del comité estudiantil pro-Partido Popular', 22 August 1947, pp. 133–49; VLT, 'Sin mujeres no hay democracia', 10 September 1947, pp. 153–64; VLT, 'Sobre la formación del PP', 25 September 1947, p. 185; VLT, 'Asamblea a favor del PP', 22 October 1947, in *Obra*, V/2, 1947, p. 208.

CHAPTER 11

For the Spilled Blood

When Lombardo Toledano arrived in London in February 1945, Europe was exhausted from the war, its cities reduced to rubble and the dead still uncounted. A few weeks before the end of the war, Lombardo participated in the preparatory meeting to establish the World Federation of Trade Unions (WFTU). He won the approval of top political circles and the leadership of the labour movement, and received enthusiastic applause lasting several minutes when he defended the universal ideological neutrality and the motion to admit the unions from the countries defeated in war to the projected federation. But Sir Walter Citrine, general secretary of the British Trades Union Congress, took away some of his thunder by opposing the admission of the Polish trade unions, which were tied to the government hatched in the Soviet Union. The year 1945 seemed like a watershed between the bloody past and a hopeful future and at the same time a battleground between the wartime allies that extended to the world of labour.

1   The Postwar Map

Ideology and security were the pillars on which the existence of the Soviet Union rested. As a European power with moral authority and military strength earned in the war, it had plans to shape the face of the world from then on. Peace was vital for strengthening the Soviet Union. So that it did not have to fear being attacked by any other country, the Europe in its immediate geographical proximity should be socialist to prevent conflicts on its borders, although such boundaries could be modified. It was also necessary to conclude mutual assistance agreements that would allow Soviet troops to pass through these countries en route to Asia in the east and Western Europe if necessary. Stalin was concerned that the United States would not get in the way of his right – given the Soviet victory in the war – to determine the fate of Europe. His foreign policy would have to lead to the creation of spheres of influence, distributed among the powers to ensure peace. This was not to be accomplished with democratic mechanisms, but through domination of the populations in their respective spheres of influence at the expense of the least possible confrontation. If necessary, military power would be used to achieve their political goals beyond the defence of their home countries.

Poland, seen as the corridor to Germany, was first on the list of countries to be subjugated. The USSR denied the legality and legitimacy of the Polish government in exile in London after the country was invaded by Germany in September 1939 and divided between the Nazis and the Soviet Union. Stalin knew that the prospects of having a friendly population there were minimal and that even though the communists had some popular support, they would not win a majority in the elections. Nor was his goal to stimulate the revolutionary seizure of power, but, on the contrary, to put a damper on the insurrectional momentum wherever it might arise. Both in Italy and in France, where strong communist parties existed, Stalin expected their respective general secretaries Palmiro Togliatti and Maurice Thorez to lead the communists toward unification with the other forces of the left, without antagonising allies and without creating obstacles to the Soviet advance in Eastern Europe.[1]

In August 1941 in London the three powers signed the Atlantic Charter as the expression of the principle of non-territorial expansion in the postwar period, which would not contradict free expression and the right of its citizens to determine their form of government or return to the government they had previously chosen as well as economic freedom. This guarantee from Roosevelt and Churchill included Poland, which was the reason for which Britain entered the war. But in the subsequent territorial arrangement and with Churchill's comment that 'I do not intend to weep over Lviv',[2] the eastern border of Poland and its adjacent territory including this ancient Polish city were transferred to the USSR.

Lombardo supported the Atlantic Charter and the restoration of sovereign rights to the countries that had lost them. But when the time came to decide whether to recognise the Polish government in exile or the government imposed by Moscow, he chose the side of the USSR and defended its intervention in neighbouring countries: 'the Soviet Union like any other country that has been attacked in the past and which has numerous enemies, has the right, the absolute right, to intervene in order that in its sphere of individual security there are no hostile governments that could serve as an instrument, as they served in the past, for other powers to be able to attack it'.[3]

---

1 Haslam 2011, pp. 29–30; Filitov 1996, pp. 3–22; Aga-Rossi and Zaslavsky 1996, pp. 162–3.
2 Eberhardt 2012, p. 16, available at: https://www.geographiapolonica.pl/article/item/7563 .html. Accessed 23 June 2015. Churchill was referring to the city of Lviv in Ukrainian; Lvov in Russian; Lwow in Polish; Lemberg in German. See https://en.wikipedia.org/wiki/Lviv. Accessed 21 August 2015.
3 VLT, 'La conferencia de San Francisco y los intereses de México y de América Latina', speech presented in the Arena México, Mexico City, 18 May 1945, *El Popular*, 24 May, in *Obra*, IV/16, 1945, p. 274.

However, in its sphere of influence the USSR would include its enemies along with its allies, whether the populations liked it or not. As the tactics of Stalin in Eastern Europe displayed the rough and brutal side of Soviet policy in subjugating these countries, the policy of the West toward the USSR hardened, in turn, resulting in an escalation of mistrust and Soviet hostility and Moscow's determination to integrate its neighbours under its domain without regard for sovereignty.[4] Churchill's speech at Westminster College in Fulton, Missouri, in March 1946 in which he declared that an 'iron curtain' had descended on Europe, was the final blow to the alliance between the powers forged during the war. In Europe the wounds inflicted by one of the greatest horrors of its history still had not healed, when the sequel came in the form of the cold war.

Soviet policy forced Lombardo to tie his national and international strategy to the needs of the historical moment at the beginning of the confrontation between the two sides of the ideological partition. The world was divided into incompatible sides that the historical laws would lead to the final outcome, but that inevitable process could be speeded up, a task that Lombardo assumed. Mexico and Latin America were at the crossroads of the ideological crossfire due to their geopolitical position, which Lombardo would use to call for being alert to and to be vigilant against the common enemy. With Germany defeated in the war, the enemy was Francisco Franco as a remnant of the fascism that poisoned the atmosphere with the propaganda that the Soviet Union was expanding toward the West and the prognosis of a new war.[5]

2   In London

During the war Walter Citrine had been the main channel for cooperation between the Trades Union Congress (TUC) and the Soviet trade unions with a view to winning the conflict in collaboration with the government to prevent the USSR and Germany from signing a separate peace accord. In addition, the British labour leaders had to contend for influence in certain unions with the communists and their enthusiasm for restoring the damaged international labour solidarity. They had to work with them and with the Soviet trade unions if they did not want to lose followers. The desired cooperation was to extend to

---

4   Di Baggio 1996, p. 216.
5   VLT, 'La causa de la paz mundial exige el derrocamiento del régimen franquista', speech delivered in the Arena México, Mexico City, 18 July 1946, *El Popular*, 25 June 1946, in *Obra*, IV/19, 1946, pp. 125–48; VLT, interview with the Italian journalist Mario Ansaldo, *Futuro*, no. 115, September 1946, in *Obra*, IV/19, 1946, pp. 239–48.

the labour movements of the three powers as the basis for a global trade union federation, but the American AFL was firm in its refusal to maintain any kind of relationship with the Soviets. Thus it was the British unions, the Soviets and the CIO, the AFL's rival, that issued the call for the preparatory meeting in London in February 1945 to establish the world federation, while the AFL launched its crusade against communism.[6]

In the seat of the municipal government opposite parliament in Westminster on the other side of the River Thames, the largest delegation that came to the meeting was from the Soviet Union. This was justified because the Soviet trade union movement represented 27.5 million workers, while the British accounted for 6.5 million and the CIO more than six million. Citrine was concerned over the numerical strength of the Soviet delegation, more than half of all the participants. Although the principle of majority rule was adopted, decisions were approved unanimously and the differences were settled in private talks between the big three.[7]

Lombardo presented the CTAL, nominally with more than four million affiliated workers, as the international labour confederation of the Western hemisphere – North, Central and South America. He opposed Citrine's motion to preserve the former International Federation of Trade Unions (IFTU) and incorporate new organisations into it. If the old were to coexist with the new, tensions would be perpetuated, the most conspicuous being between the AFL and the Soviet trade unions. The IFTU had to be dissolved in order to create a unified world organisation. However, the aggressive campaign that the AFL had already launched against the CTAL was a bad precedent when the time came to create a harmonious organisation.[8]

The much desired unity appeared to have been achieved at the meeting, and for the time being this hid the political and ideological struggle between liberal capitalism and Soviet-style socialism. Momentarily, when it came to add up the numbers, the Soviet trade unions, together with unions from Latin America and the colonial world had an overwhelming majority.

The first major debate was on the right of membership. Lombardo weighed in on the side of the unions from the enemy countries in the past war, such as Italy, Romania, Bulgaria and Finland, which were absent from the meeting. The new organisation should sweep the slate clean in relation to the past, since the trade unionists had either been cannon fodder or in opposition to fascism, and not the perpetrators of the atrocities committed during the war. The Bulgarian

---

6   Geert van Goethem 2002, pp. 156–63.
7   Schwartz 1963, p. 86.
8   VLT, 'World Labour Unity', London, 14 February 1945, FHLT, file 605.

and Italian unions were accepted. In both cases they were dominated by communist leaders such as Guiseppe di Vittorio from the Confederazione Generale Italiana del Lavoro. The Polish unions were not admitted because they were tied to a government that no power recognised except the USSR. The British would have preferred to stick to the original list of guests and not make any decision on behalf of workers before consulting with them. But no other delegate had a problem speaking in the name of those he claimed to represent or believed he represented. It was another victory for Lombardo and the Soviets, and a practice that would be applied thereafter, whereby self-appointed spokesmen of the workers supplanted collective discussions.[9]

Lombardo left an indelible impression in London, thanks to his oratorical skills and his defence of the weak and victimised unions. He was interviewed by the BBC; Labour Minister Ernest Bevin invited him to dine at the elegant Hotel Dorchester along with other delegates; the London city council and the general council of the TUC invited them to the classic match between Arsenal and Clapton Orient; the Archbishop of Westminster Abbey spoke with them; the CIO offered them a reception, and even His Majesty the King received them.[10]

Lombardo returned to Mexico in late February as the titan of the world proletariat. One poet inspired by Lombardo's feat in London awaited him with 'Cheers!, finally, Spartacus of progress,/strange gladiator'.[11] Gabriel Medina, a teacher and law clerk, offered to work for free in the mornings 'so that I can actively cooperate in the consolidation of the just and humanitarian cause of the national, Latin American and world proletariat'.[12]

3 In Paris

'The CTAL has great prestige but the organisation in each country is abandoned', reported one of the pioneers who Lombardo sent to Latin America in search of the most suitable delegates and funds for the trip and the stay in Paris for the founding congress of the World Federation of Trade Unions.[13]

---

9   VLT, 'Entrevista con la BBC', London, 17 February 1945; VLT, 'Informe sobre la Conferencia obrera mundial', March 1945, in *Obra*, IV/16, 1945, pp. 101–51; Schwartz 1963, pp. 86–103.

10 Walter Citrine to the delegates of the World Federation of Trade Unions, London, 2 February 1945, FHLT, file 604; *Ministry of War Transport* to VLT, London, 14 February 1945, FHLT, file 605.

11 Gonzalo Cárdenas Rodríguez, 'En el aeródromo', 1 March 1945, FHLT, file 607.

12 Gabriel Medina to VLT, Mexico City, 7 March 1945, FHLT, file 607.

13 Gaudencio Peraza to VLT, Santiago de Chile, 30 April 1945, FHLT, file 609.

Only governments had the capacity to subsidise the delegates. Some communist groups and organisations took up collections and held fund raising parties and dances. In Mexico, the FBI reported that Lombardo received money from the PRM and some candidates for public office. The Nicaraguans might have received money from President Somoza, the Guatemalans from their president. The Soviet embassy could have been another source of financing. Ecuadorian labour leader Pedro Saad was Lombardo's choice, but a group of workers reviled him as a 'phony', someone out for perks, 'a college graduate, nothing more'. Saad 'might be a Communist, but this is not a credential to represent the Ecuadorian workers'.[14]

To El Salvador, Lombardo sent his follower Gaudencio Peraza to ask President Salvador Castañeda Castro for financial support, which he did not obtain. But weeks later, Cuban labour leader Angel Cofiño arrived in San Salvador, witnessed an attempted coup d'état against the president and organised a campaign in the unions in his support. The grateful president promised to pay for the trip of a Salvadoran delegate to Paris, and in return he asked the international emissaries to make their friendly stance public.[15]

In late August, Lombardo was in New York before embarking on 4 September on the Queen Elizabeth to Southampton where he would arrive on the ninth and continue his trip to Paris. During his stay, the FBI tapped his telephone conversations to confirm their suspicion that he was a communist.[16] One of the conversations they heard was between Bolivian politician in exile José Antonio Arze – who they described as eternally single, an intellectual Marxist, university professor, owner of a library, heavy smoker, diabetic, in poor health due to a gunshot wound he received in 1944, and founder of the Bolivian Confederation of Workers and the Party of the Revolutionary Left (PIR) – and his girlfriend at the time Heidi Seligsohn. Arze met with Lombardo. They had much in common. Both believed that Bolivia had to make the transition from stage-to-stage before arriving at socialism, they supported the USSR when it was invaded by Hitler and when the war economy needed the workers' labour discipline.[17]

The Bolivians were divided between collaborators and enemies of the government. It was necessary to ensure that the delegates that were going to Paris

---

14   'Grupo de doce firmantes al presidente del congreso internacional de trabajadores en Paris', Guayaquil, Ecuador, 6 September 1945, FHLT, file 618.
15   Ángel Cofiño to VLT, La Habana, 10 June 1945, FHLT, file 617.
16   E.E. Conroy to Hoover, 'VLT-internal security', New York, 7 September 1945, FBI, file 100–15625.
17   Whitehead 1992, pp. 120–46.

obtain money for their tickets and not air internal disputes. Lombardo needed a delegation that was loyal to the government, which had just enacted laws liberalising labour policy and was committed to holding a congress of the Bolivian trade unions that Lombardo would chair.

On his return from the meeting with Lombardo, Arze spoke with Heidi. The FBI was listening in. 'Let me tell you, [Lombardo] spoke for two hours'. Heidi replied incredulously: 'You mean non-stop'? 'Yes', her boyfriend said. 'No!' Heidi exclaimed. Lombardo spoke in Spanish but as there were other people at the meeting who did not understand the language, he switched to rudimentary English, according to Arze. José Antonio had more delicate things to tell Heidi: 'Wait a minute, I'll close the door'.[18] As a result, the FBI learned that Lombardo wanted to prevent delegates from airing their particular problems and sought their support for his strategic positions. The Bolivians should not put radical adversaries of the government such as the mine workers' leaders Juan Lechín and Emilio Carvajal and the National Revolutionary Movement in the delegation. His candidates for delegates in Paris were Aurelio Alcoba and Donato Flores from Arze's party, the PIR. But the FBI interpreted Lombardo's influence over the delegates as part of his plan of wanting to 'perhaps be elected president of the world workers' organisation and expand the seeds of communism throughout the Americas'.[19] In the end, the Bolivians could not leave because the government did not help them and they didn't have the money to finance the trip.

Lombardo went to Paris accompanied by his wife Rosa María, Fernando Amilpa and Sánchez Madariaga, CTM senators, still a few years before becoming adversaries, and Juan Manuel Elizondo, general secretary of the mine workers' union. The meeting took place at the Palais de Chaillot in the shadow of the Eiffel Tower in a France experiencing hardships as a result of the war. It was estimated that the delegates represented 66 million workers. The British were amazed at how many new faces were present and the increase in delegates from Eastern Europe, 65 compared to 48 who were at the London meeting. Citrine ironically referred to the unions that the delegates claimed to represent 'like Phoenix risen from the ashes', unions that emerged from the rubble. He feared that they were paper organisations and insisted on examining their credentials. It was true that new unions emerged in Romania after the country was freed from the dictatorial government of Karol II, but the representatives from Africa

---

18   FBI Director, 'VLT-internal security', Washington, D.C., 7 September 1945, FBI, file 10–15625; William Nichols, La Paz, Bolivia, to Hoover, 'José Antonio Arze-security matter', 21 November 1945, FBI, file 100–4326.

19   Stanton Brown, 'VLT-security matter', San Salvador, 11 September 1945, FBI, file 100–173.

and the Middle East seemed to be more like politicians than workers. Citrine's desire to perpetuate the British Empire must have figured in his reasoning.

> Yesterday I heard a speaker [Dange from India] that his organisation was about to enter the International because his country wanted national independence and he wished to establish socialism. As commendable as these desires are, the World Federation of Trade Unions is not the means to achieve this ... [A]s soon as we get bogged down in the labyrinth of politics, and I am sure of this as I stand before you today, the International will perish. It will fragment because the different conceptions of political aspirations, methods and positions are so broad that they will divide us.[20]

These were prophetic words. The Soviet Union, Stalin, wanted to gain control of the federation to enhance further its connection with the communist parties in countries beyond its sphere of influence through the trade unions. Vasili Vasilievich Kuznetsov, an engineer who had studied at the Carnegie Institute of Technology in Pittsburgh, and chairman of the Soviet trade unions since March 1944, was the person chosen to establish the links with the unions close to the USSR in the WFTU.[21] Lombardo was also in favour of the WFTU becoming a political instrument for the reconstruction of the world in the image of the Soviet Union.

The WFTU brought together communist and non-communist unions for the lofty task of destroying fascism, expanding democratic rights, supporting employment policies that increased jobs available to workers, improved wages, establishing fair workdays, provide social security and healthcare. A nine-person executive bureau was established and Lombardo was named as one of its members. The French trade union leader Louis Saillant, 35 years of age, was elected general secretary. The WFTU estimated that it represented 66,759,348 workers from 65 national confederations, three international organisations, and 15 professional associations. During the discussions on the ways to proceed when delegations were unable to attend meetings and the WFTU had to take a position, Lombardo proposed adopting his way of operating in Mexico and Latin America. The general secretary and the bureau should take initiatives and not wait until the congress meets nor wait for the opinion of the national centres. They should suggest to the organisations the issues around which to struggle, for example, the defeat of Francisco Franco in Spain. But the British

---

20 Schwartz 1963, p. 122.
21 Schwartz 1963, p. 78.

delegate Hallsworth was against such a procedure, arguing that the national centres should not be required to carry out the decisions of the bureau, so as to prevent the creation of dictatorial climate, since not everyone shared the same point of view and ways of acting.[22]

In both London and Paris, Lombardo advocated that the national organisations of the new confederation should call on their governments to sever diplomatic and trade relations 'with the fascist government of Argentina', but his proposal failed.[23] Unexpectedly, in February 1946, Perón won the elections with the labour vote, legalised the Communist Party, acknowledged the Soviet Union as a power that strived for world peace, which facilitated the establishment of diplomatic relations between the USSR and Argentina in June of that year.[24] Lombardo had to accept the fact and reconciled with Perón, who by then had the CGT leave the Latin American confederation.

The congress was also a gala event. The French government offered the delegates a musical soiree at the Palais de Chaillot, while the Canadian government feted them with *gaspe* salmon. The Confederation Generale du Travail prepared a delicious meal at the same time that the average French citizen was still living on rationed food. There was no visible repercussion from the communique sent from Mexico's National Workers Council to Citrine – which was opposed to the CTM – disavowing Lombardo as the spokesman of the Mexican proletariat, since, it claimed, the confederation did not represent a majority of the organised working class.[25]

4   In the Other Europe

Lombardo was not a pawn of Moscow as he was portrayed in Mexico and the United States, but rather a sincere and vehement defender of the Soviet system and the countries that the USSR placed under its sphere of influence. He presented the loss of sovereignty of these countries as a popular and demo-

---

22 'Meeting of the Executive Bureau of the la WFTU', Paris, 6–9 October 1945, IISH Archive; Carew 2002, pp. 169–71.
23 VLT, 'La CTAL y el caso de la Argentina', Paris, 24 September 1945, FHLT, file 619.
24 Vacs 1984, pp. 12–13.
25 'World Trade Union Conference', Paris, 26 September 1945, International Institute of Social History Archive (henceforth IISH); 'Menú' in FHLT, file 620; 'Un succés francais Luis Saillant a été élu secrétaire général de la Féderation syndicale mondiale', *Front National*, 6 October 1945; 'Informe que rinde la Oficina Internacional del Trabajo', October 1945, ILO-BIT, 'Mexico reports', file 41/1945. In 1945 the CTM still may have had the majority of workers before the mass exodus from the organisation in 1947.

cratic achievement. The repression of the non-communist opposition, banning of the critical press and suppression of civil society organisations did not merit any comment. He ignored the show trials of the communist leaders in the 1940s and 1950s in Bulgaria, Hungary and Czechoslovakia, a repetition of the show trials of the 1930s in the Soviet Union, which ended in their physical liquidation, long prison terms or forced labour.

When the purges took place in the Czechoslovak Communist Party, which ended the life of Otto Katz/André Simon, Lombardo's friend and collaborator in *El Popular* and in the propaganda trips through Latin America in favour of the Allies, he kept a prudent silence. What would he have thought when he read in the press that the charge against Katz/Simone was that he was a bourgeois nationalist, a 'Trotskyite' and a spy at the service of British, American and French intelligence agencies, and in his confession he declared? 'Since 1941 I lived in Mexico and directed the magazine Tribuna Israelita, which served to spread Jewish nationalism and extend the enemy ideology against the workers' movement, socialism and progress'.[26] What would he have felt when he learned that before being executed in November 1952, Katz/Simone went before the Supreme Court of the Czechoslovak Republic, which was called a people's democracy, asking it to sentence him to death? 'I implore the State court to apply the strictest punishment to me', were his last words.[27]

In June 1946, Lombardo was in Prague on his way to Moscow to attend the executive bureau of the WFTU. He came the day of or perhaps shortly after the results of the national elections were released. He found a jubilant population. He attributed their happiness to the revolution and nationalisations. He likened rural Czechoslovakia and the Mexican countryside, saying that 'the peasants up until the war were semi-serfs, as in Mexico, semi-slaves, as in our country before the revolution', but by receiving government land, their psychology changed. He found a 'people drunk' with victory, 'cheering the tremendous victory of the new democracy in Czechoslovakia'. There were no longer any employers and 'the only boss in Czechoslovakia is the people themselves'.[28]

But Lombardo presented a Czechoslovakia different from what it really was. One of the most industrialised countries of Europe, whose social democratic

---

26 London 1969, p. 295, p. 308; *Proces s vedením protistátního spikleneckého centra v čele s Rudolfem Slánským*, pp. 208–29. Rudolf Slánský was the general secretary of the Communist Party of Czechoslovakia. Lombardo learned of the trial from the Italian press, which his friend, communist Vittorio Vidali, sent him.
27 Ibid.
28 VLT, 'Mitin del SNTE contra el régimen fascista en España', 31 August 1946, in *Obra*, IV/19,1946, pp. 224–5.

government in the 1930s carried out a comprehensive agrarian reform; nationalisation of the mines, industrial enterprises with more than 500 employees, the food industry, insurance companies and banks that issued equity; and in addition, practiced electoral democracy as a form of government. In 1946 it distributed more land, this time from the properties of the collaborators with the Nazi regime in the Sudetenland, the border region with Germany. It was true that the Communist Party had won 38% of the votes in the elections, but people danced in the streets because democratic elections took place, the first after the Nazi occupation in 1939, and without knowing it, the last.[29] In 1948, private property was nationalised and the state became the only employer, building a system in the image and likeness of the Soviet Union. It monopolised power and thereafter elections became a sham.

The actual chronology of events did not matter, even less the context in which they occurred. The historical truth was irrelevant when Lombardo wanted to confirm the assumption that wars produced social revolutions. Socialist Europe was 'the genuine product of the Second World War'. Tomorrow it would be Bulgaria and Romania and perhaps Austria 'will also come to have a progressive popular government that will have to be integrated into the new peoples of Europe as a whole'. And a final comment: 'It is useless for the propaganda to depict a false picture of European reality. In the long run, eventually, the propaganda will collapse on its own accord and for the future all kinds of fraudulent claims will be discredited'.[30] Exactly like those offered by Lombardo. The end justified the means.

From Prague Lombardo flew to Moscow where he met with Citrine at the meeting of the WFTU. When the plane touched down, he learned that the president of the USSR, Mikhail Kalinin, had just died at 71 years of age. For several years, Kalinin suffered from stomach cancer. Since 1938 tragedy stalked him with the imprisonment of his wife Ekaterina Ivanovna, after a hidden microphone in their flat detected a conversation about Stalin's bloodlust. She had an aggravating factor: she was Jewish.[31] Just two hours after his arrival in Moscow, 'my compañera wife and I had the privilege of seeing Marshal Stalin presiding over the funeral procession of former President Kalinin in Red Square'.

---

29   'Volby 1946-vítězství komunistů a odsun Němců' (The 1946-victory of the Communists and the evacuation of the Germans), available at: http://www.fronta.cz/dotaz/volby-1946-vitezstvi-ksc-a-odsun-nemcu; Jaroslav Fiala, personal communication; Martina Gregorová, 'Prezidentské volby 1935 až do 1946' (Presidential elections from 1935 to 1946), 2009, available at: http://www.valka.cz/clanek_13386.html. Accessed 21 August 2015.
30   VLT, 'Balance de la reunión del buró ejecutivo de la FSM celebrada en Moscú', Mexico City, press conference, 10 July 1946, *El Popular*, 11 July 1946, in *Obra*, IV/19, 1946, pp. 119–21.
31   Montefieore 2003, p. 317 and pp. 554–5; Zubok 2007, p. 56.

Lombardo was content because around him he could see material achievements and 'the stupendous internal unity that has characterised the socialist system'.[32]

Perhaps Lombardo also coincided with Citrine at the National Hotel. The Englishman, sensitive to the details of everyday life, noted in his travel diary that everything was in order in the room, except the cold water that didn't run in the bathroom and the toilet due to a plumbing problem. But he compared it with previous visits and did not have the heart to report the defects, because 'it was clear that they did the upmost for us'. To remedy the problem, he filled the bathtub with boiling water at night so as to be able to bathe in the morning. The food was superb. One of the dinners consisted of caviar, butter, white and black bread, vegetable soup, chicken, potatoes, soufflé with chocolate sauce, vodka, wine and lemonade. Wandering the streets, he noticed the change in women's clothing. Few wore hats, but none walked barefoot. Their dresses sported colours although their shoes were simple. The stores offered tempting items; there were more buses and cars. But in the side unpaved streets he was surprised by the poor quality of children's clothing. The choral concert one night and Swan Lake performed the other at the Bolshoi Theatre were admirable. At the meeting many issues were discussed in relative harmony, but the proposal by Saillant and the Soviets to impose an economic blockade on Spain did not win a majority. A stain on the congress was the censorship of *The Daily Telegraph* correspondent, who was not able to report to London on the debates at the meetings.[33]

In June 1947, Lombardo was again in Prague, accompanied by his wife and daughter Marcela, to participate in the meeting of the general council of the WFTU. He was about to turn 53 years of age with 26 years of marriage under his belt. He purchased a hunting rifle and began a correspondence with the hunters' association in Nairobi, Kenya. He dreamed of 'hunting an elephant, a lion, a rhinoceros, a buffalo and one of each animal that the law allows'.[34]

5   Confrontations

The first 18 months of the WFTU were marked by relative harmony. The federation was committed to international economic reconstruction and wanted

---

32   VLT, 'Balance de la reunión del buró ejecutivo de la FSM celebrada en Moscú', Mexico City, press conference, 10 July 1946, *El Popular*, 11 July 1946, in *Obra*, IV/19, 1946, p. 126.
33   Walter Citrine, 'Visit to Russia', June 1946, Walter Citrine Archive, box 7.
34   VLT to Capitán Murria Smith, Geneva, June 1947, FHLT, file 683.

the United Nations to take it into account and thus obtain the right to vote in the Economic and Social Council. For the Soviets, membership in and the consolidation of the WFTU in international bodies and organisations were extremely important, because it conferred recognition and made it possible for them to influence the workers' movements that due to being beyond their geographical sphere of influence remained out of reach. They took advantage of this valuable position so that through the communist parties they could engage in anti-capitalist propaganda and defend their domestic and foreign policies.

But the non-communist members of the WFTU rejected the attacks that communists directed against their respective national governments in the press. Distrust grew. Meanwhile, US and British government officials reviewed every action that the Soviet government and the communist parties undertook for signs that would allow them to prove that the USSR used the WFTU for its own political ends. They were alarmed by communist control of the WFTU press and its secretariat as well as the imbalance between the communists and non-communists in the leadership. The divisions sharpened in October 1947, when the Soviet government opposed Washington's Marshall Plan for the reconstruction of Europe, a line that all the communist parties had to go along with.[35]

The Marshall Plan was conceived as a measure to prevent the European economy from collapsing after the devastating war and to prevent the population from seeking alternatives that would erode the liberal economic system and government. Franco's Spain was included. The plan also attempted to integrate the Eastern European countries into Western Europe's economy and thus halt the expansion of the USSR. But the Soviet leaders did not distinguish the plan from the offensive designed to subvert their security, and even though they initially proposed accepting the aid to sabotage the Marshall Plan from within, Stalin cancelled the manoeuvre at the last minute. In mid-1947 the two sides abandoned hope of finding solutions involving cooperation for the reconstruction of the new political order and from then on confrontation ensued.[36]

In September 1947 in Szklarska Poreba, Poland, the Cominform (Communist Information Bureau) was formed to direct the policy of the communist parties around the world. In the communists' view, the world at that point was divided between the anti-democratic imperialist camp and anti-imperialist

---

35   Carew 1984, pp. 174–335.
36   Aga-Rossi and Zaslavsky 1996, p. 176; Parrish 1994; Gaddis 2011, p. 269.

democratic camp. Soviet foreign policy accepted the coexistence of the capitalist and socialist systems, normal relations with the Western powers, but without renouncing the ideological struggle and its expansion through open and hidden means. When at the beginning of 1949 the Western countries with the United States at the helm created the North Atlantic Treaty Organisation (NATO), the USSR saw the 'threat of war' and aggressive intentions against its influence in Eastern Europe. The practical results of the change in the climate were the complete sovietisation of Poland, Czechoslovakia, Hungary, Bulgaria and Romania; the elimination of the remnants of bourgeois democracy and capitalist property, the eradication of opposition to communist control and the party's monopolisation of power.[37]

Louis Saillant considered the Marshall Plan to be a reactionary scheme and an expression of US monopoly capital. In opposing the plan, he placed the WFTU in an awkward position, since its general secretary, that is Saillant, seemed to be against European recovery. While the Soviets were cordial in discussions with the other members of the federation, in the pages of their press they criticised the WFTU for being reformist. The CIO supported the Marshall Plan and the AFL took advantage of the trials and tribulations within the federation to influence Western European union leaders and block Soviet positions in organisations such as the ILO. Irritation grew among the British trade unionists who accused the Soviets of lack of integrity and proposed the suspension of the activities of the federation for twelve months until its future activities could be reviewed. If their proposal was not accepted, they would withdraw from the WFTU.[38]

The Soviets considered the British threat to be a hostile act and Lombardo, furious, saw it as an 'anti-democratic' procedure. The British ultimatum emerged due to 'pressure by the governments that follow a line of conduct contrary to the people's interests, to destroy one of the greatest fruits of the tremendous sacrifice represented by the Second World War'. He accused them of contempt for the bylaws of the WFTU, since a single organisation could not put an international federation in jeopardy.[39]

---

37   Parrish 1994; Di Baggio 1996, p. 210; Egorova 1996, pp. 198–9; Judt 2005, pp. 143–7.
38   'Soviet trade unions in the service of the Comintern', prepared by the AFL based on the Soviet press and sent to European trade union leaders, 16 January 1948; 'Synopsis of the proceedings of the WFTU proposal on trade union rights and the counterproposal of the AFL on the same topic', in The George Meany Memorial Archives, Jay Lovestone Files, box 66; Frank Fenton to Matthew Woll, Washington, D.C., 16 January 1948, ibid.
39   VLT, 'Opinión del vicepresidente de la FSM acerca del ultimátum enviado por el TUC de

But it was Lombardo who came into conflict with the previously mentioned bylaws. In May 1947 the bureau suspended him from the post of vice president because he had ceased to lead a national trade union confederation affiliated to the WFTU and in Mexico he was only a member of the CTM and no longer headed it. Furthermore, in January 1948 Lombardo could not be absent from Mexico to attend the meeting of the WFTU executive bureau in which he would have had to explain his situation such as his expulsion from the CTM. Neither could he leave because a confederation opposing the CTAL had been created in Lima and it was urgent to unite Latin Americans in a congress that still had to be organised. The founding of the People's Party was also underway and in addition Lombardo had a project to replace the CTM with a new confederation. He sent his right hand man Ramírez y Ramírez to Paris, with 'verbal reports concerning various issues that relate to the labour movement in Latin America' and an invitation to Saillant to attend the upcoming congress of the CTAL.[40]

For the time being, the WFTU survived the antagonisms despite the prevailing feeling that the principles that should guide it as a worldwide organisation of free nations, economically sound and with political, religious, racial and philosophical differences, were not complied with. The British and American trade unions were systematically accused of being vehicles of Wall Street, Saillant refused to discuss the Marshall Plan, while Soviet support for the communists in Greece, and British aid to the anti-communists in that country, was embarrassing when the WFTU wanted to give the impression of unity in the organisation. Furthermore, the leaders of the TUC and the CIO criticised the WFTU's administrative inefficiency. James Carey, CIO treasurer, complained that the WFTU ceased to be independent of governments and political parties, that it was paralysed by so many disagreements, and called for Saillant's salary not to be paid as long as the federation's informational bulletin continued to attack the Marshall Plan. The British trade union leader Arthur Deakin charged that in the hands of its president, the WFTU had become an instrument of Soviet policy.[41]

Lombardo was the subject of discussion in the September meeting of the WFTU executive bureau. Saillant, who had just returned from Mexico, wanted

---

la Gran Bretaña al buró ejecutivo de la FSM pidiendo que esta organización se disuelva', Mexico City, 4 January 1948, FHLT, file 708.

40 'Memorándum sobre la situación sindical en México y sus perspectivas', no author indicated, 7 January 1948, FHLT, file 709; VLT to Saillant, Mexico City, 14 January 1948, FHLT, file 710; Salvador Ocampo to VLT, Paris, 18 January 1948, FHLT, file 710.

41 Schwartz 1963, p. 312; 'The rift in world labour', *The Economist*, August 1948.

to convince the rest of the executive bureau members that Lombardo represented a new organisation, the General Union of Workers and Peasants of Mexico, which did not yet exist. Kuznetsov and his deputy Soloviev defended Lombardo's right to remain the vice president, because he represented the CTAL which Mexico's industrial unions had just entered. The discussion led to recriminations between Lombardo and Arthur Deakin, who in 1946 had replaced Citrine as the TUC's representative in the federation's executive bureau. The Lombardo case revealed the deep and possibly irreconcilable differences that existed between the various components of the WFTU. The British and the Americans complained that they were the target of criticism, while Eastern Europe and the USSR were spared from such judgements; that the discussion of controversial issues was postponed, individuals were slandered and the communists dominated the discussions that should have centred on labour policies. The TUC could not support financially an international labour confederation that did not follow its stated goal of unity.[42]

The executive bureau of the WFTU reconvened in January 1949 in Paris. Without referring to any labour conflict, Lombardo asked for help to raise the standard of living of Latin American workers, called for a strong and unambiguous stand against imperialism and domestic reaction and presented the CTAL as the only confederation in Latin America. He avoided discussing the issue of Mexico and his own status even though in the September 1948 meeting he had been asked to provide detailed information.[43] It was an acrimonious gathering in which some members denounced others as being conspirators and manipulators until the point that everyone was speaking at the same time. To silence Arthur Deakin, who could not get the proposal to suspend the federation's activities put to a vote, a desperate Kuznetsov shouted, 'This is a world federation and not a bus station'. 'Well the situation is clear', retorted Deakin, who gathered up his papers, his coat, waved his hand goodbye and left the room. Others followed. In the coming months, some thirty organisations left the WFTU.

The WFTU disintegrated, according to the Europeans, because it opposed the economic recovery of a Europe that had been bled to death in the war. It was a hostile attitude and a provocation by the colonial peoples who wanted to rise up against the Western democracies.

---

42   WFTU, 'Session of the Executive Bureau', Paris, 17–21 September 1948; Vincent Tewson, general secretary of the Trades Union Congress, 'The TUC and the WFTU', 27 October 1948, WFTU Archives, IISH; Carew, Van Goethem and Gumbrell-McCormick 2000, p. 553.

43   'Session of the Executive Bureau', FSM, Paris, 17–22 January 1949; 'Session of the Executive Committee', WFTU, Paris, 28 January to 1 February 1949, WFTU Archive, IISH.

The world federation ceased to exist. The oldest and the most experienced labour movements will be out. When they were inside, these movements had to put up with denigration and insults from the other affiliated bodies. Now that they have left, they can't expect that the propaganda will cease, but they have the power and the determination to protect their fundamental way of life and their beliefs as labour unions.[44]

The AFL executive council was delighted because the British and Dutch trade unions and the CIO left the WFTU, clearing the way for the creation of a new international labour confederation. In 1948, the Central Intelligence Agency (CIA) received money from Averell Harriman, director of the Marshall Plan, 'to break the communist influence over the largest labour federations in France and Italy with money from the plan', bribe the maritime workers in Marseille and Naples to ensure that they unload American weapons and military equipment and weaken the unions with its perks. Jay Lovestone, who had previously been behind the campaign against the CTAL, was in charge of these operations along with Irving Brown, supporting unions that were close to the Christian Democrats and the Catholic Church.[45]

Lombardo described the split in the WFTU 'as an insult and an attack ... against the democratic norms of the international labour movement' and assumed a combative stance against 'the Marshall Plan, a plan that goes against the interests of the working class of the entire world' when 'there are only two roads: either independence, freedom and peace or the exploitation of the weak peoples'.[46]

Strictly speaking, the world federation, born from the attempt to contain the unbridgeable ideological differences between the powers and let each act in accordance with what it felt it deserved due to its efforts in the war and the number of deaths suffered, collapsed, together with the illusion that the division of Europe would not spark new conflicts. Now, without protests from the other member unions of the WFTU, Lombardo was confirmed as the federation's vice-president. His role would now be liaison and coordination between the federation and the unions in Latin America organised in the

---

44 'Free Trade Unions Leave the WFTU', Paris, 17–19 January 1949, WFTU Archive, IISH; Sturmthal 1948, pp. 624–38.
45 'Next steps for free trade unions', declaration of the Executive Committee of the AFL, 4 February 1949, WFTU Archive, IISH; Carew 1998, pp. 25–42, quote on p. 29; Weiner 2007, pp. 35–6.
46 VLT, 'A propósito de los intentos de disolver la FSM', 19 January 1949, in *Obra*, V/5, 1949, pp. 12–13, p. 16.

CTAL. In this capacity he went to the next meeting of the bureau, which this time took place in China, in order to reaffirm the WFTU's truly international scope.

6   In People's China

On a bright October morning, Lombardo looked down upon the country from the airplane that was taking him to New York. 'The Valley of Mexico – the pride of my country – shines with the magnificent transparency of its autumn sky, the rich collection of its small extinct volcanoes that in other times bordered on the fresh waters of Xochimilco and Chalco, with Teutli – the lord – as insignia, and the serene majesty of its great snow covered mountains'.[47] From New York he continued his trip to Havana and then Amsterdam, where with his travel companions boarded the Czechoslovak airliner that took three hours to reach Prague.

This was the third time that Lombardo Toledano was in Prague since the war ended. 'Czechoslovakia is the only country in the Western world, highly industrialised, that is marching toward socialism by its own road', he said, almost two years after the communist party under the supervision of Soviet advisers took power over the state. He met with Katz/Simone, who he had not seen since 1946 in Mexico. Since his return from exile, Katz/Simone had been the editor-in-chief of the communist party daily newspaper *Rudé Právo* until October 1949 when he was fired. At the time that the old comrades were greeting each other, Katz/Simone was being watched by the political police, who began to tap his telephone calls and intercept his correspondence. Sparked by the fear of contagion from the Marshall Plan, Trotskyism, and the 'cosmopolitan' ideas that the exiles, mostly Jews, could have brought to the country to the detriment of steadfast loyalty to the USSR, the persecution of communist leaders and their families was now underway. Accusations were fabricated to accuse them of being traitors, and they confessed under torture; 12 of them were hanged in 1952.[48]

On this trip Lombardo could not have known the scope of the tragedy looming over Czechoslovakia. Accompanied by the Mexican ambassador, he spent time walking on the outskirts of Prague in the late autumn drizzle, when

---

47   VLT, 'Diario de un viaje a la China nueva', 25 October to 20 December 1949, in *Obra*, V/6, 1949, p. 135, pp. 142–3.
48   Miles 2010, pp. 276–9; Applebaum 2012, pp. 307–10.

the forests 'preserve the elegant beauty of the leaves that are almost dry and sport all shades of yellow, on the black background of the trunks of the trees' branches'.[49]

From Prague Lombardo flew to Moscow, which at the time boasted five million inhabitants. Its development was amazing, he said. 'Except in the main cities in the United States, nowhere else have I seen such a tremendous number of new cars', an abundance of consumer goods, well-dressed women, wine in the stores, fruits, meats and all kinds of fish, and this growth 'goes hand-in-hand with the joy of the people' satisfied 'with life'.[50]

But the reality experienced by the Muscovites differed from that description of the horn of plenty, although by 1949 there had been a substantial improvement compared to 1946. Most of the population still 'lived in shared apartments, often with two families in a single room, while tens of thousands had to settle for barracks'. Nikita Sergeievich Khrushchev, the leader of the Communist Party in Moscow since 1949, was exasperated by the poor quality of construction. When new flats were turned over to their inhabitants, often the walls were dirty with the palm prints of the workers, 'so our crime investigators were able to trace the person responsible'. It did not help that many of the bricklayers were peasants, newcomers to the city, and that the architects were reluctant to construct buildings over four stories. Agricultural production in 1950 did not reach the level prior to 1913. The peasant farmers were paid almost nothing for the obligatory supply of their crops, while the price of tractors and trucks rose several times over. To compensate for the lack of income, they cultivated small plots of land on which the government charged them taxes. While Lombardo praised the way in which agricultural production benefited from science, Khrushchev, who had an innovative spirit, was exasperated by the artisanal nature of Soviet farming. 'I've become crazy seeing how unsophisticated our farmers are', in reference to that occasion when the authorities provided them with fertilisers, the farmers did not know what they were and let them rot in the train station.[51]

On the early morning of 8 November 1949, four aircraft took off from the Sheremetyevo airport toward the east carrying labour officials, some with their wives, interpreters, a journalist, and Lombardo with Rosa María, who in her

---

49 VLT, 'Diario de un viaje a la China nueva', 25 October to 20 December 1949, in *Obra*, v/6, 1949, pp. 150–1.
50 VLT, 'Diario de un viaje a la China nueva', 25 October to 20 December 1949, in *Obra*, v/6, 1949, p. 155.
51 Talbott (ed.) 1971, pp. 103–5; Taubman 2003, pp. 226–7; Zubok 2007, p. 52.

suitcase had a supply of Coatepec coffee. The sky was blue and the temperature eight degrees below zero centigrade. Flying over Siberia in winter under the moonlight, 'studded with stars that shine like freshly washed diamonds',[52] the plane had to land in Krasnoyarsk due to bad weather. Lombardo recalled that at the time of the czars the area was used to confine political prisoners, it was where both Lenin and Stalin had been locked up and now was an industrial centre. He recalled the verses of Russian poet Alexander Pushkin: 'Then heavy chains fall by the board/then dungeons crack/and freedom's voices will greet you at the gate, rejoicing/and brothers hand to you a sword'.[53]

But the jails, labour camps and political prisoners in Krasnoyarsk were not merely an occurrence in the past. Under Stalin, there were about two million prisoners at a given time and about 18 million between 1929 and 1953. In 1948 alone, the authorities sent more than 20,000 peasant farmers to such forced labour camps without an investigation or trial, because the previous year the collective farms failed to meet the norm of mandatory working days. That year an inspector reported that the supply of clothing and shoes for the prisoners was unsatisfactory; more than half did not have shoes, so they made them out of bark from trees, rags and old tires, which made it difficult to walk in the snow and allowed icy water to pass through causing frostbite. The prisoners who died due to the inclement Arctic weather would not be found until the spring.[54]

On 12 November the leaders of the world proletariat (the term is Lombardo's) crossed the border into Manchuria in northern China by train. At breakfast, Rosa María offered each of them a cup of aromatic Mexican coffee whose smell invaded the railroad car. The first stop was the village of Manchuri where local dignitaries, workers and children awaited the visitors. They were taken to a large hall and after the welcoming ceremonies, the guests were seated at 'a long table decorated with chrysanthemums and with the dishes already laid out awaited us for lunch'. Under the watchful eyes of Marx, Engels, Lenin, Stalin, Mao Tse-tung and Chu Teh (commander-in-chief), and the slogan 'workers of the world, unite!' inscribed on red silk fabric in Chinese, Russian and English, they feasted on roast pork, hot tongue, smoked fish and fish cooked in vinegar, ham, sausage, baked pheasant, caviar, pastries, vodka, cognac, sherry, mineral water and Chinese cigarettes. The civil war was over, but during the next leg

---

52   VLT, 'Diario de un viaje a la China nueva', 25 October to 20 December 1949, in *Obra*, v/6, 1949, p. 173 and p. 176.
53   VLT, 'Diario de un viaje a la China nueva', 25 October to 20 December 1949, in *Obra*, v/6, 1949, p. 180.
54   Applebaum 2004, pp. 214–15 and p. 416.

of the journey, in order 'to prevent an act of sabotage a security train travelled ahead of ours with a well-equipped escort'.[55]

In Harbin, still in Manchuria, it was Lombardo's turn to speak. He enjoyed speaking in open spaces. 'The bigger the audience the more I understand it and I receive better feedback'. All the places in Mexico and Latin America where he spoke to large audiences came to mind, but in less inclement weather, such as on the banks of the Magdalena River in Colombia, where he had to constantly interrupt his speech 'to spit out mosquitoes that entered my mouth'. This would be the first time in a snow storm.[56]

Everywhere he went he found 'faith in the future of Chinese democracy and world democracy'. Another royal welcome took place in Mukden, the industrial centre of Manchuria. After the rally, the Pan-China Federation of Labour invited the guests to drink tea and eat shrimp, mushrooms, chicken, eggs, vegetables, beets carved in the shape of roses, rice, prawns with mushrooms, fresh water fish with a taste of almond, eel with tender bamboo, shark fin with mushrooms, chicken livers and other chicken dishes, pheasant with mushrooms, rice, asparagus with bamboo, sweet potato with honey and after the meal, more green tea. Rejoicing and abundance, music and cheers, flowers and fruits were everywhere.[57]

At last they arrived in Beijing. As soon as they were installed in the hotel, the leaders from the Pan-China Federation of Labour paid them a visit to make sure 'we were comfortable in our accommodations and if anything was missing for our comfort'. In addition to Li Li-chun as his secretary, the federation put 'a car at my disposal for my exclusive use, as well as a military aide'. More banquets followed for the delegates and protocol toasts to unity, friendship, etc.

The meetings were rich in information on the ways of life and tribulations of the peoples of Asia, some were classes in the cultural and political anthropology of Mongolia, India, Ceylon, Burma, Vietnam and Iran, which Lombardo synthesised as the rebellion of the colonial world against imperialism. The visitors received lessons on the stages of the Chinese revolution, which had just completed a massive agrarian reform with land distribution and public trials of landowners. Lombardo thought of the great men who made revolutions possible: Lenin, the genius who planned and led the revolution and established the socialist system; Stalin, 'the creator of the always valid policy of true friend-

---

55 VLT, 'Diario de un viaje a la China nueva', 25 October to 20 December 1949, in *Obra*, v/6, 1949, pp. 182–3, p. 188.
56 VLT, speech in Harbin, China, 13 November 1949, FHLT, file 783.
57 VLT, 'Diario de un viaje a la China nueva', 25 October to 20 December 1949, in *Obra*, v/6, 1949, pp. 187, p. 188, pp. 189–94.

ship'; and Mao, the driver of the greatest national anti-imperialist revolution in history. And it was true: Mao, at 56 years of age, had brought communism to a quarter of the world's population.[58]

The return trip by train was long, 15 days to Prague. Some passengers took advantage of the time to play dominoes, others to practice English, Madame Josette Saillant and Rosa María Otero to knit and talk. 'I am classifying some of the materials that I received in Beijing, to examine them in their logical order', Lombardo wrote in his diary, and also to take a break from politics. He leafed through a French magazine; 'They're still into existentialism', he wrote in contempt for the philosophical theory of the postwar period, according to him practised by illiterate intellectuals, that 'reveals the decomposition of certain sectors, horror-struck at the profound historical change that is occurring'.[59] He did not share the pessimism that the war and the Holocaust provoked in some intellectual circles on the capacity of human beings to commit such atrocities.

Lombardo did not participate in the games played by his travel companions. He did not like them because they mimicked the struggle that for him was his daily bread, though chess was better than the others, but with one caveat.

> What I find uncomfortable in chess is its archaic structure, since fighting, even if symbolically, with the institutions and social classes of the Middle Ages – kings, Church dignitaries, feudal lords, knights and servants – in the epoch of socialism, when social classes such as the bourgeoisie and the proletariat come to the fore, classes that don't exist in chess, is as childish as a treatise on magic together with modern medicine or a book on alchemy next to one on nuclear physics.[60]

Lombardo returned from the trip filled with satisfaction. On board the KLM flight from Amsterdam to New York he wrote a paean to Stalin who was about to turn 70, a name that 'sparks the renewed gratitude and admiration of millions of Latin American workers for the driver of the new world'. With a studded and irregular handwriting, perhaps due to atmospheric turbulence, he composed a rhapsody to the person whom, he believed, opened the road to freedom and indestructible socialism.[61]

---

58   VLT, 'Diario de un viaje a la China nueva', 25 October to 20 December 1949, in *Obra*, V/6, 1949, pp. 195–233; Priestland 2010, pp. 294–5.
59   VLT, 'Diario de un viaje a la China nueva', 25 October to 20 December 1949, in *Obra*, V/6, 1949, pp. 268–9.
60   VLT, 'Diario de un viaje a la China nueva', 25 October to 20 December 1949, in *Obra*, V/6, 1949, p. 272.
61   VLT, on board the KLM flight, 14 December 1949, manuscripts, 1946–1950, FHLT, file 6.

Back in Mexico, in February 1950 he gave three lectures on China at the Workers' University, based on the many pamphlets that he had received from the union officials and on the speeches and proclamations of the Chinese leaders. The third conference dealt with the popular dictatorship as a new political and legal concept that needed explaining. It was a new democracy. According to Mao Tse-tung, it was a dictatorship because the reactionaries were 'deprived of the right to express their opinion'. Only the people had such a right. It was a radical break with liberal democracy.[62] No, China did not rely on violence, he said to contradict the information that appeared in the press:

> I was in China for a few weeks and I was able to have contact with the people. I spoke freely with the old landowners, today supporters of national liberation and agrarian reform, with the workers, with the peasants, with large and small business owners, with the soldiers ... and I can say that never, in any country except the Soviet Union, has there been such strong national unity ... around their government.[63]

Lombardo did not talk about the armed resistance in the countryside nor the terror against a population defenceless due to the abolition of laws; he did not mention the massive and public executions of the nationalists and counter-revolutionaries, the purpose of which was to intimidate the population to accept the new communist discipline. Nor did he speak of the participation of Soviet experts in the creation of the forced labour camps in order not to waste a valuable source of labour for the economic construction of the new China.[64]

Lombardo Toledano collaborated in the launching of the Cold War from the position of a translator of its concepts and policies into a language and practices comprehensible in a 'semi-colonial' country, whose place on the periphery of the world system was determined by Marxist-Stalinist theory. The historical truth was secondary, since there was no place for 'theoretical and tactical differences with the leaders of the Soviet Union and the people's democracies'.[65] Mexico, ideally emulated by other countries in the hemisphere, should contribute to the creation of an anti-imperialist community in the continent. The progressive weakening of the United States on this side of the world favoured

---

62   VLT, 'La dictadura popular y las perspectivas de la República Popular China', Workers' University, Mexico City, 17 February 1950, *El Popular*, 24 March 1950, in *Obra*, V/7, 1950, pp. 102–6.
63   Ibid.
64   Chang and Halliday 2005, pp. 336–9.
65   VLT, 'Diario de un viaje a China nueva', in *Obra*, V/7, 1950, pp. 147–8.

the expansion and influence of socialism nurtured in the Soviet Union, which alongside the countries of Eastern Europe and People's China, massively boosted the percentage of the world on the non-capitalist road of development. Meanwhile, Lombardo assumed the role of expanding its sphere of influence in the Western hemisphere.

CHAPTER 12

Emancipation

Since the founding of the Latin American Labour Confederation in 1938, the AFL was determined to destroy it. This was not easy as long as President Roosevelt's good neighbour policy was in good standing and the cooperation required between the hemispheric north and south during the war were the policy of the state. But when Roosevelt's initiatives were dismantled, US policy returned to its interventionist model of the interwar period.[1] From that point on, in conjunction with the State Department, policies that were previously applied semi-secretly were now conducted in the open. When at the end of 1944, Lombardo Toledano was at the CTAL congress in Cali, the AFL treasurer and 'apostle of capitalism' George Meany arrived in Mexico. There were rumours that his mission was to revive the old style Pan-Americanism and that he suggested to Fidel Velázquez 'that the CTM leave the CTAL'. CTM officials denied the rumour and 'said that Meany had come to Mexico to rest'.[2] After the war, the AFL would openly launch its offensive.

1 Removing Obstacles

Lombardo anticipated that after the war the Latin American governments would be in conditions to control foreign economic interests, diversify trade relations and stimulate industrialisation without abandoning economic nationalism; they would carry out social reforms, spending more and protecting their countries from US subjugation.[3] But on the occasion of the Inter-American Conference on the Problems of War and Peace, held during February and March 1945 in Mexico, the State Department unveiled its economic policy as one of hemispheric integration. This meant the domination of economic interests of the hegemonic country and the cancellation of contracts for pur-

---

1 Larsen 2010, p. 383.
2 'Biographical sketch of Vicente Lombardo Toledano', Mexico City, 27 October 1944, NARA, Records of the Office of Strategic Services, RG 226, box 1420, file 124135; Report from Enrique Jiménez to the ILO, December 1944, OIT-BIT, file 41 (1944); 'George Meany en México para promover unidad sindical entre la AFL y América Latina', International Labour News Service, 16 December 1944, FHLT, file 592; Buhle 1999, p. 91.
3 Kofas 1992, pp. 273–94.

chases of raw materials that were no longer strategic as well as the intention of lowering tariffs to favour its exports. The proposal sparked outrage among Latin Americans. If the reduction of tariffs, known as the Clayton Plan – from the name of Assistant Secretary of State William Clayton – were approved, Latin American markets would be flooded with cheaper industrial products from the United States, hindering industrialisation and along with it leading to the loss of markets and revenue. This would, in turn, cause discontent among the population and a likely shift to the left. The Latin American delegates demanded that the United States continue purchasing their raw materials, increase the price of coffee and sugar and buy their cotton, even though it was also produced domestically. Cuba, Brazil and Chile expressed their concern over the unrestricted flow of capital to the region from the most development sectors of the American economy.[4]

The United States rejected these demands, characterising them as selfish, extravagant and as an expression of an unacceptable economic nationalism. It countered with the intention to promote capital investment in private companies and reduction of government interference. But the Latin American representatives argued that the invested foreign capital should ensure that domestic capital had a fair share of the same companies and their management so as not to be displaced. It was urgent that Latin America be industrialised and was willing to accept investors no matter where they came from, including if necessary from Germany. The Uruguayan delegate, abruptly and with the support of the Colombian and Brazilian representatives, argued that if the Clayton Plan on lowering import tariffs were accepted as proposed, 'Latin America could resign itself to being the pasture land for its flocks and herds'.[5] The conference was a disappointment to many Latin America countries, which hoped that their cooperation with the United States during the war would be rewarded with a new economic order.[6]

The US ambassador to Mexico George Messersmith agreed that the trend toward industrialisation was irreversible 'and that the United States could not deny this country the right to adopt policies that they themselves had applied' decades before. Instead of being a danger, industrialisation would expand markets for American production. But in reading Lombardo's speeches during the days of the conference, such principles vanished and the ambassador displayed

---

4   Bethell and Roxborough (eds) 1992, pp. 1–32; Grandin 2004, pp. 175–98.
5   Earl of Halifax to Anthony Eden, Washington, D.C., 12 March 1945, NA, FO371, file AS 1611/317/5; C.H. Bateman to Eden, Mexico City, 22 March 1945, NA, FO371, file AS1671/317/51.
6   Bulmer-Thomas 1998, p. 300, n. 57.

his propensity to see an anti-American thrust in the economic nationalism preached by Lombardo.[7] And economic nationalism was tantamount to communism.

By 1945 the State Department had judged Lombardo Toledano to be subversive. For US embassies and the FBI both his actions as well as his ideas were pegged to the spread of communism and the interests of the USSR in the region. Wherever he went, the FBI asked its agents to discreetly follow him to determine how close he was to prominent communists. The still weak Guatemalan trade unions and their entry into the CTAL had no other purpose than to 'win prestige for communism and the Soviet Union in the countries located near the Panama Canal'.[8]

When in 1946 the prospect of war breaking out between the USSR and the United States emerged as a possibility given the deterioration of relations between the former allies, Washington saw communist influence in the labour movement that could affect the acquisition of strategic raw materials as a potential threat to security in the Western hemisphere. The danger was ideological rather than military, and therefore instead of merely strengthening the military apparatus, what was required was to support civil society and liberal forces; contribute to improving the living standards, working conditions, education and health of the population, all of which according to the United States represented a wall of containment against communism. Lombardo Toledano and CTAL had to be removed. Serafino Romualdi, an Italian who was as much an anti-fascist as an anti-communist, with years of experience in the AFL, was appointed in 1946 to influence, persuade and bribe leaders of the labour movement to leave the CTAL and with CIA funds if necessary, create in Latin America an anti-communist, anti-Lombardista and pro-American confederation.[9]

---

7 G.S. Messersmith to James Clement Dunn, Assistant Secretary of State, Mexico City, 7 March 1945, NARA, RG 59, file 812.504/3–745; George S. Messersmith to the State Department, Mexico City, 23 March 1945, file 812.504/3–2345; Torres 2005, p. 191.
8 Herbert S. Bursley to John Villard Carrigan, Mexico City, 15 June 1945, NARA, RG 59, file 812.504/6–1545; John Villard Cardigan, 'CTAL supports Central American union?', State Department, Division of Mexican Affairs, 21 June 1945, NARA, RG 59, file 812.504/6–1545; Edward Martin, US Embassy, Montevideo, Uruguay, to the Director, 'Vicente Lombardo Toledano', 26 November 1945, FBI, file 100–4326500; Edgar Hoover to Jack Deal, Washington, D.C., 8 November 1946, NARA, RG 59, file 812.504/11–846; Dunkerley 1992, p. 319; Weiner 2012, pp. 138–9.
9 Romualdi 1967, pp. 1–36; Agee 1975, pp. 75, p. 136.

2   On an Inspection Tour

It must have been an insult to Lombardo that Romualdi would take advantage of the meeting of the International Labour Organization in Mexico in April 1946 to 'manoeuvre behind the scenes to win over converts to our project' and win 'allies in the very heart of the CTAL'. It had a huge psychological effect. The Spanish socialist trade unionists, exiled in Mexico after defending the Republic in the Civil War, but were anti-communist, 'had effectively helped us establish Mexican contacts', Romualdi reported.[10]

Prior to the meeting, the CIO, purged of communists after the war and now hostile to the CTAL, in alliance with the AFL invited several Latin American leaders to the United States and sent Americans on a trip through some countries in Latin America. The CIO provided money to the families of the workers selected for the trip and included women in anticipation of their increasing numerical participation in the labour market. The Americans who were to travel south of the border should speak Spanish and be empathetic with the Latin Americans 'to win the hearts and minds for the American way of labouring'.[11]

Not everything worked as planned. On their tour of Latin America, the Americans encountered resentment from their peers due to racial and religious discrimination and bitterness over the wage differentiation in US companies between imported and native workers. Some of the visitors did not understand their government's opposition to economic nationalism. After his trip, Willard Townsend, the president of the Philadelphia-based United Transport Service Employees' Union, said that he found enough evidence to 'express deep sympathy for the desire of the Latin American people to industrialise. No doubt there is a lack of many products needed for a comfortable life'. Businesses worked better between developed countries than between unequal partners. The American workers were allies of Latin American workers in the struggle for human rights and the satisfaction of human needs that bestowed dignity on individuals.[12]

---

10   Romualdi 1967, p. 39, p. 40, p. 41; 'Memorandum no. 1, Inter-American Trade Union Project', presented in the conference of the International Labour Organization, Mexico City, 1946, 1945/08–1946/06 in The George Meany Memorial Archives, box 47, file 1945/08 –1946/06.

11   Memorandum no. 1, Inter-American Trade Union Project, The George Meany Memorial Archives, ILO conference, Mexico City, 1946, box 47, file 1945/08–1946/06.

12   Willard Townsend, Mexico City, 11 April 1946, ILO conference, The George Meany Memorial Archives, International Affairs Department, box 47, file 1945/08–1946/06.

At the ILO conference, Lombardo defined the CTAL's agenda as being a 'political International' with a nationalist policy for the semi-colonial countries. The ILO should not limit itself to labour legislation and leave aside the vital questions for the independent development of the region that with the imbalances of the war deepened the gap between prices and wages, the loss of foreign markets, the lack of US aid to offset the imbalance in international trade, the primacy of commercial capital and speculation in productive capital. Industrialisation could not take place without the participation of foreign capital, but it had to be controlled by the state.[13] Lombardo must have touched a raw nerve among the delegates, since with a secret ballot he retained the presidency of the Latin American Workers Group in the ILO.

As much as he tried, Romualdi failed to get the CTM leave the CTAL. He established contacts with the CROM, the CGT, electrical workers, with the National Proletarian Confederation, the Confederation of Workers and Peasants and textile unions, all opposed to the CTM. In bidding them farewell, he believed he had prepared the groundwork for his next visit. From Mexico, he headed south.

His sought after prize was the Argentine CGT. He was concerned over Argentina's decision to establish diplomatic relations with the USSR in 1946 since, he feared, without reason, the CGT would fill up with communists. Ambassador Messersmith, who was transferred from Mexico to Buenos Aires, agreed: 'All this communist activity in the Americas is not good and we must keep our eyes open'.[14] But Perón, president since 1946 thanks to the labour vote and being 'worker number one', chose a third road for Argentine workers who could unionise, benefit from increased wages and whose movement became one of the pillars of the regime. When Romualdi arrived and sought the labour leaders, the socialist Nicolás Repetto warned him and his travel companions that 'the CGT seems appealing but you will never be able to swallow it'.[15]

Romualdi failed in his attempt to win the Argentines in the summer of 1946, and returned in January 1947 to insist on their joining the projected anti-communist labour confederation. He met with Perón, who excluded the CGT leaders from the talks with the Americans. At one point during the meeting, Perón got so upset that he showed Romualdi the door, shouting: 'The plane is ready to take you back home ... I know what your intentions are Señor Romu-

---

13   VLT in the fourth plenary session of the third conference of the International Labour Organization of the United Nations in the Alameda Hotel, Mexico City, 5 April 1946, AGN, MAC, vol. 434, file 433/588.
14   George S. Messersmith to Spruille Braden, Buenos Aires, 30 August 1946, NARA, RG 59, file 835.5043/8–3046.
15   Romualdi 1967, p. 52.

aldi'. He wanted nothing to do with organising an inter-American labour confederation in Argentina as an instrument of the imperialists.[16]

The ambassadors and labour attachés of the US embassies, in consultation with the AFL, coordinated Romualdi's visits. The results of the search for suitable adherents to the anti-communist labour organisation were mixed. Venezuelan President Rómulo Betancourt and APRA leader Victor Haya de la Torre in Peru supported the initiative along with the Chilean leader Bernardo Ibáñez. But the tense situation in Bolivia when Romualdi arrived in August 1946, a month after the ousted president Gualberto Villaroel was hanged from a lamppost, did not allow him to appear in public. He obtained the approval of some trade unionists to participate in the yet to be built confederation, but failed to convince miners' leaders Juan Lechín and Mario Torres. His mission to Ecuador was salvaged thanks to AFL pressure on President José María Velasco Ibarra's administration not to dissolve the labour confederation, the same government that in March 1946 had suspended the constitution. One labour leader confided that so as not to divide the workers' movement, the Ecuadorian confederation wanted to be part of both: the free trade unionism initiative and the CTAL. The socialists shared the leadership of the confederation with the communists and wanted to be on good terms with Romualdi without breaking with Lombardo. But this option was not feasible for Romualdi.[17]

Brazilian participation in the projected confederation was uncertain, because the unions were prohibited from joining international organisations, unless such affiliation was recommended by the president and formally authorised by congress. Cuban labour leaders Eusebio Mujal and Francisco Aguirre were willing to come on board as were the Costa Rican Catholic unions and their leader Luis Alberto Monge. In the rest of Central America, Romualdi left empty-handed, except for a vague promise from a group of Salvadoran trade unionists. From Colombia he left with a small trophy of Catholic unions.[18]

Lombardo knew that Tomás Palomino Rojas, his former ally and now the head of the trade unionists of a splinter 'cleansed' CTM maintained contact with Romualdi and was testing the waters for its entry into the 'anti-totalitarian and anti-Lombardista confederation'.[19] But the CTAL was 'indestructible', he told the CTM workers in hyperboles, despite the slanders, the money from the

---

16 Romualdi 1967, pp. 41–63; Rubens Iscaro to VLT, Buenos Aires, 6 September 1946, FHLT, file 643; Rapoport 1992, pp. 110–17.
17 Romualdi 1967, pp. 42–3.
18 Romualdi 1967, p. 68.
19 Matthew Woll to Juan Arévalo, New York, 27 June 1946; Serafíno Romualdi to Tomás Palomino Rojas, Rio de Janeiro, 30 June 1946, FHLT, file 637.

AFL, and even though 'many believe that the day Lombardo Toledano is killed, it will come to an end. How wrong they are! That day will bring victory closer to our peoples'![20]

Despite the high-sounding words, Lombardo resented the loss of the Argentine CGT; it had to be recovered, making 'any sacrifice in order to achieve the indicated goal'.[21] The other setback was the Chilean Workers Confederation's opposition to the CTAL's mediation in the political and labour conflict that finally divided the local communists and socialists. The background to the conflict between the authorities and the unions were the workers' struggles in American mining companies and a government that responded to the need for US loans. President Gabriel González Videla was elected in September 1946 and brought three communists into his cabinet. A civil war broke out in the labour movement that the president, under pressure from the State Department, took advantage of to get rid of the uncomfortable communists and in the process subdue the trade unionists.[22] Lombardo took the aggression against the Chileans communists as an attack on himself and in a sensationalist tone warned that 'we are experiencing the most difficult period since the war of independence. Our obligation is to prevent a setback', and if that is not achieved, 'I will present my resignation as president of the CTAL'.[23] But Lombardo did not step down, although the setbacks continued.

The collaboration between governments and social movements in Central America, with the CTAL serving as the liaison between the two sides, summed up what Lombardo understood as the emancipation of Latin America under the existing conditions. In El Salvador, the government made concessions to workers during the last strike and replaced three ministers. It was not tactically advisable to condemn the Salvadoran government, 'since not all the doors are closed to the workers'. The same applied to the Nicaraguan government. It was not necessary to seek the overthrow of Anastasio Somoza, but to fight for democratic rights. The radical thrust of the Central American exiles, who lacked political education, had to be tempered, since the plots they were pre-

---

20 VLT, 'Discurso en la sesión de clausura del XXIX consejo nacional de la CTM', Mexico City, 21 August 1946, FHLT, file 642.
21 VLT to Lázaro Peña, Mexico City, 3 September 1946, FHLT, file 643.
22 Bernardo Ibáñez, Carlos Godoy, Hipólito Saavedra and Isidro Godoy to VLT, Santiago de Chile, 24 December 1946, FHLT, file 653; Barnard 1992, pp. 66–91; Barnard 1981, pp. 357–74; CTCH to CTAL, Santiago de Chile, 22 October 1947, FHLT, file 694; Roxborough 1997, pp. 154–5.
23 VLT, 'Informe en la reunión inaugural del comité ejecutivo de la CTAL', San José, Costa Rica, 8 December 1946, FHLT, file 652.

paring to overthrow the dictators made the struggle difficult. This did not mean that it was necessary to help the dictators. It was a question of tactics, Lombardo declared.[24]

Lombardo was aware of the preparations to create the organisation in opposition to the CTAL. Thanks to the information furnished to him by the National Union of Detectives and Technical Police, he learned that the AFL and the 'cleansed' CTM, in collusion with officials from Miguel Alemán's government, met; that Cuban trade unionist Juan Arévalo, who lost his leadership position in the CTC elections, worked with them and received money from Romualdi;[25] that Tomás Palomino Rojas together with Mexican Finance Minister Ramón Beteta and the private secretary of Alemán, Jorge Viesca y Palma, were authorised to send three representatives from the 'cleansed' CTM and the secretary of the Jalisco Workers Federation to the United States. Viesca would take care of the tickets and the AFL 'will introduce the representatives to State Department officials in Washington to inform them of the problems of communist infiltration among Mexico's workers'. These meetings coincided with President Alemán's trip to the United States. Lombardo also knew that 'Viesca has stated that they will give the coup de grâce to communism in Mexico'.[26]

Perhaps to prepare the envoys, Romualdi arrived in Mexico on 5 May 1947. Palomino Rojas and Rangel waited for him at the airport and then met at the hotel where Romualdi was staying. They presented him to the delegate who was ready to leave for Washington 'on a confidential matter of international significance'. The delegate was Honorato González Castro from the 'cleansed' CTM in Nuevo León and was a relative of Emilio Portes Gil. Romualdi was pleased with the ideas in the speech that González Castro had prepared, because they represented the anti-communist trend pursued by the American Federation of Labor and the American industrialists, 'who wish to raise the economic level of Mexican workers'. González Castro received 1,500 pesos from the newspaper *Novedades* and 1,300 pesos from *Excélsior*, probably for articles he would write on the subject of Lombardo, the AFL and the creation of an inter-American labour confederation.[27]

---

24   'Acta no. 5 de la reunión del Comité Ejecutivo de la CTAL', San José, Costa Rica, 13 December 1946, FHLT, file 652.
25   Juan Arévalo to the 'cleansed' CTM, Havana, Cuba, 23 March 1947, FHLT, file 672.
26   'Reunión nacional de detectives y técnicos policiales', 'Relaciones entre la AFL y la CTM depurada así como altos funcionarios del gobierno del licenciado Miguel Alemán', Mexico City, 10 April 1947 and 'Memorándum confidencial para el Lic. Vicente Lombardo Toledano', 14 April 1947, FHLT, file 675.
27   Gregory Linder to Robert Reynolds, Mexico City, 1 May 1947, FHLT, file 677; 'Confidencial', unsigned, 5 May 1947, FHLT, file 678.

But González Castro never reached Washington. Lombardo was apprised of his hesitations. González Castro was against communism, Lombardo and the CTAL; he was in favour of a hemispheric labour organisation that would include Latin Americans and Americans,

> because I believed that, deep down inside, there would be a sincere desire to unite workers regardless of differences in nationality and ideology, in accordance with a programme that would be in line with the principles of continental unity, underpinned on respect for the independence of Mexico and the other Latin American peoples, free of any communist influence and from any interference discordant with the fairest hemispheric ideals.
>
> But the time came when I became clearly aware that the activities of certain leaders of the American Federation of Labor (AFL) are not moving in the direction of creating a hemispheric body, based on the principles I just mentioned. On the contrary, what is involved is serving those interests of US capital that seek to absorb the Latin American economy and forever intervene in the destiny of our peoples with serious negative consequences for the present and future independence of them all. I am a revolutionary but as a Mexican, if I have to choose between foreign capitalists and Mexican capitalists, there is no doubt that I have to defend the Mexican capitalists.[28]

González Castro could not defend the Clayton Plan as recommended by Romualdi. He saw only a sinister plan that in no way benefited Latin American workers. The attitude of the Argentine CGT and government to defend themselves from interference by foreign companies seemed to him to be correct. He also did not like the fact that Romualdi wanted the future Inter-American Confederation of Workers to be founded in Caracas, since Romualdi feared a link between President Alemán and communism. For all these reasons, González Castro concluded his collaboration with the AFL and Romualdi. He was an anti-communist, a Mexican patriot 'and see that the fate of Mexico is the fate of all Latin America'. The task he was entrusted with was nothing else but an international adventure.[29]

---

28 Honourato González Castro to Tomás Palomino Rojas, Mexico City, 13 May 1947, FHLT, file 678.
29 Ibid.

3   In Lima

Luis N. Morones also wanted to meddle in the emergence of the new hemispheric labour confederation. On 4 July 1947 he hosted a dinner for the labour attaches of several embassies in the Restaurante Astoria, his favourite. In attendance were two Argentines, Julio Caprara and Vicente Diana; Allan Tennyson from the British Embassy and Juan de Zengotita from the US diplomatic mission. According to Tennyson, the Argentines had the task of establishing Argentina as the sponsor for the creation of the international labour confederation that would be an alternative to the CTAL and also of the one which the AFL had been preparing. Morones spared nothing, offering toasts with imported champagne and crowning the dinner with Hennessy three star brandy. The Argentines let the cat out of the bag, bragging of their role in Mexico as propagandists, launching attacks on Lombardo and against the CTAL, and extolling the good relationship between Juan Domingo Perón and the workers of the CGT. During the toast, Morones referred to the USSR: 'Russia had to be crushed or it would crush us'. He had nothing good to say about Romualdi, who he characterised as 'bossy' because he told Mexicans what they had to do.[30] He so disliked Romualdi's way of behaving that when on a different occasion the president of the AFL, William Green, proposed to him that he be part of the new federation to defeat the CTAL and Lombardo, and even though he wanted to 'do the deed twenty years ago', Morones did not accept the offer. It was true that he had denounced Lombardo Toledano 'as a communist agent working at the service of a foreign power', but displacing Lombardo and putting in his place a leader 'who would emerge serving the policy of the US State Department', would not do.[31] US imperialism was as unacceptable as Russian imperialism.

Only in appearance was everything ready at the end of 1947 for the AFL, Romualdi and the leaders attracted to the proposed Inter-American Confederation of Workers (known by its Spanish initials CIT) to consummate its founding. While its explicit purpose was to combat communism, the implicit aim was to ensure a labour movement that would favour the conditions for the expansion of US capital, companies and trade, lay the groundwork for collaboration between north and south on the basis of the terms set by the United States. The mobilisation of the non-communists was incomplete and the State Department failed to convince all the governments to cooperate in the endeavour.

---

30   Allan Tennyson to H.A.N. Brown, Mexico City, 17 July 1947, NA, LAB file 13/542; Juan de Zengotita to the State Department, Mexico City, 8 July 1947, NARA, RG 59, file 812.5045/7–847.

31   *Memoria de la CROM*, Mexico City, no publishing house indicated, August 1945–July 1947, p. 242, quote on p. 243.

A number of politicians, governments and union leaders resented the blatant participation of Washington in the formation of the CIT, suspecting that its aim was to control the hemispheric labour movement. The conference took place thanks to the enormous funding from the AFL and the logistical support of US diplomats.[32]

On 10 January 1948 at the Lima municipal theatre, Chilean labour leader Bernardo Ibáñez opened the conference sessions with a salvo: 'We reject Lombardo Toledano and Stalin. We are building hemispheric unity despite them'. He acknowledged that the future of the confederation was not assured: 'We may have to struggle to organise but we are ready to struggle'. US delegate Philip Hannah from the Ohio State Federation of Labor spoke at the end of the first day. His speech in English, carefully rehearsed and translated by Romualdi during the event, filled the air with good wishes and high-sounding proclamations on 'inter-Americanism without imperialism' and the organisation as an 'impregnable bastion of human rights'; he spoke about 'social progress' and 'the true Christian civilization', causing the hall to burst into chants of 'Long live the Americas, long live the AFL, long live Hannah'. The 156 delegates – 132 according to another estimate – came from 17 countries. The largest contingents arrived from Chile and Peru, but also in attendance were Brazilian trade unionists, workers from the Venezuelan confederation, Cubans, Costa Ricans, Puerto Ricans, Colombians, some trade unionists from Bolivia and El Salvador and Leo Eliézer, acclaimed trade unionist from the Dutch colony of Surinam. The conference was covered by journalists from *The New York Times, The Chicago Tribune* and *Time*. On the night of 12 January the new confederation was born, 'for the express purpose of rooting out the communists from the Latin American labour movement'.[33]

The CIT included several unions from the United States and Canada, rejected the communists, but accepted the socialists because they were anti-communist. Peru was not the best place to organise a democratic confederation because the American Popular Revolutionary Alliance (APRA) and Haya de la Torre, who were anti-communist and against the CTAL, supported workers' strikes for increased wages that were directed against the government.[34] Morones was in Lima, but not to support the creation of the confederation. He questioned the absence of the Argentine CGT, which the AFL had not invited on the grounds that it was an instrument of the Perón dictatorship, and accused Romualdi of being an agent of the State Department, of manipulating the congress and of

---

32   Kofas 1992, p. 315.
33   Romualdi 1967, p. 76; Holmes 1948; Alexander and Parker 2009, p. 100.
34   Haworth 1992, pp. 184–6.

having bribed the trade unionists. Romualdi denied the charges, and supported by many delegates, demanded that Morones present evidence, which he could not or would not provide. Morones left the conference and went to Buenos Aires where the CGT gave him a grand welcome at Luna Park and Perón granted him a private meeting.[35]

In addition to Morones, also present in Lima were Enrique Rangel from the National Proletarian Confederation and Tomás Palomino Rojas, who according to the US embassy did not represent anyone regardless of how anti-communist, anti-Lombardista, anti-CTAL and anti-Soviet he might be. Rangel was elected as one of the vice presidents of the CIT and Bernardo Ibáñez its general secretary.[36]

Upon returning to Mexico, Morones asked to talk to an official from the US Embassy. Not satisfied with the result of the conversation, he decided to travel to the United States to personally complain to Green: 'He wanted to go, he said, to warn him that Romualdi was a dangerous man, and of the mistakes that the AFL had committed in Latin America'.[37] He went to Washington, convinced of his own importance, to ask Green to remove Romualdi. The AFL president dismissed Morones's charge with a sweep of a hand, denied any link between its representative in Latin America and the State Department from which, he said, Romualdi only requested visas for AFL representatives.[38]

4 The Third Congress

The next CTAL congress had been scheduled to take place in Santiago de Chile for January 1948. However, the division of the Chilean confederation between communists and anti-communists, repression used against the miners and the creation of the Inter-American Confederation of Workers in Lima, in which the Chileans played a dominant role, made holding the congress unfeasible. In several countries the labour movement was in precarious conditions for economic reasons, internal divisions and repression; in others such as Venezuela and Peru mobilising workers for higher wages created political tension and in

---

35 Romualdi 1967, pp. 76–8; Alexander and Parker 2009, p. 101.
36 Dwight Dickinson to the Secretary of State, Mexico City, 12 January 1948, NARA, RG 59, file 810.5043/1–1248.
37 Dwight Dickinson, 'Statements of Luis Morones Concerning Serafino Romualdi', Mexico City, 24 March 1948, NARA, RG 59, file 810.5043/3–2448.
38 Dwight Dickinson, 'Luis Morones and William Green', Mexico City, 27 May 1948, NARA, RG 59, file 810.5043/5–2748.

still others the increase in the number of industrial workers was coupled with the corporativist control of their trade unions by the state as in Brazil, Mexico and Argentina, which resulted in labour compliance at the expense of trade union autonomy.[39]

The congress was held in Mexico in March with about 5,000 participants in attendance. The Mexican capital was always the easy logistical alternative that Lombardo could help arrange. Delegates arrived from countries with large and politically important labour movements while others represented only part of the organised working class. This was the case of Brazil, Venezuela and Peru. Absent from the congress were the Argentines, Bolivians, Paraguayans, Nicaraguans and Dominicans. Salvador Ocampo, Chilean senator and prominent member of the CTAL, wanted to go to talk with the Argentines before the congress, but he was denied a visa. Louis Saillant, general secretary of the World Federation of Trade Unions, was a guest of particular importance.[40]

O.A. Knight, president of the Oil Workers International Union attended in the name of the CIO in order not to lose contact with the CTAL and to defend the Marshall Plan. He was also interested in meeting with representatives of Petróleos Mexicanos to discuss the CIO's dealings with the US government to assure the supply of steel to Mexico to manufacture drill pipes for wells and help increase production 'in the event that the supply (of oil) is necessary for a third world war'.[41]

President Miguel Alemán opened the conference at the Palacio de Bellas Artes, where the CTAL had been founded almost ten years previously. The opening ceremony starred both the president and Lombardo. Before 7:45pm, President Alemán, accompanied by Lombardo, met with the leaders of the other labour confederations. Once inside he sat in the middle of the presidium, with Lombardo on his right and flanked by Labour Minister Ramírez Vázquez and Saillant on his left. Lombardo arranged the seating so that his seat was higher than that of the president, which gave the effect, according to the report by the American consul, of looking at him from the top down. During the sessions, Lombardo was constantly leaning toward the president, who was forced

---

39 Roxborough 1997, pp. 154–63.
40 Salvador Ocampo to VLT, La Paz, Bolivia, 21 February 1948, FHLT, file 714; Herrera 2013a, pp. 304–5.
41 Jacob Potofsky, president of the CIO Committee on Latin American Affairs, to O.A. Knight, 30 January 1948; VLT to Philip Murray, Mexico City, 5 February 1948; O.A. Knight, to Jacob Potofsky, Fort Worth, Texas, 9 April 1948, in The George Meany Memorial Archives, Congress of Industrial Organizations, International Affairs Department (1945–1955), box 34.

to look at him from the bottom up. 'It is no exaggeration to say that Lombardo looked like the cat that ate the canary, or was about to do so, while the President, without a smile, looked very uncomfortable and unhappy about the whole situation'.[42]

Lombardo's inaugural speech was in no way embarrassing for the president, but when he mentioned Lázaro Cárdenas the audience burst into applause. The class struggle was unproductive in the transition from capitalism passing through imperialism to socialism. 'We are builders, we are not destroyers', said Lombardo. Mexico was an example of a democratic system, worthy of being emulated by a Latin America that has suffered tyrannies. He called the Clayton Plan 'economic fascism' and a 'diabolical plan' by the United States to subjugate Latin America.[43]

Saillant was one of the keynote speakers. He condemned the British and American corporations as obstacles to industrialisation and condemned the Lima congress. He also aimed his criticism at the Marshall Plan and the Clayton Plan that would destroy many of the emerging Latin American industries, subordinate the Latin American armies to the US military and use Latin American resources against the democratic forces in some Latin American countries under the banner of the fight against communism.[44]

Saillant later tried to promote reconciliation between the CTM and Lombardo. He met with Amilpa, who he had heard behaved like a dictator, was seeking personal enrichment and had ignored the workers' well-being. A commission was created to meet with him, but the leadership of the CTM decided to leave the CTAL and there was nothing to discuss with an organisation that they had broken ties with.[45]

The parting of the CTM from CTAL was offset by the entry of unions representing mineworkers, metalworkers, oil and railroad workers. The labour confederation (CUT) directed by Luis Gómez and Valentín Campa, joined the CTAL, even though shortly beforehand Lombardo had vilified it. The Workers and Peasants Alliance of Mexico, the forerunner of the General Union of

---

42 Dwight Dickinson to the State Department, 'Inauguration of Third CTAL Congress', Mexico City, 23 March 1948, NARA, RG 59, file 810.5043 – Mexico City/3–2348.

43 VLT, 'Informe del presidente de la CTAL', Mexico City, 22 March 1948, p. 131, p. 149; VLT, 'III congreso general de la CTAL. Discurso inaugural', Mexico City, 22 March 1948, p. 105; 'Resoluciones del congreso', pp. 173–225, quote on p. 198, in *Obra*, V/3, 198.

44 Frances Borden, *Allied Labor News*, New York, 30 March 1948, in The George Meany Memorial Archives, Congress of Industrial Organizations, International Affairs Department (1945–1955), box 34.

45 'Informe de la comisión especial designada por el III congreso de la CTAL para estudiar la situación del movimiento sindical de México', Mexico City, 26 March 1948, FHLT, file 722.

Workers and Peasants of Mexico (UGOCM) about to be founded as an alternative to the CTM, also joined.[46]

The British Embassy's Labour Attache Allan Tennyson was present in all the sessions of the congress. He informed His Majesty that in a long speech Lombardo denounced imperialism and praised the reconstruction of the USSR and the new world by the people's governments of Czechoslovakia, Yugoslavia and Poland; Tennyson confirmed that behind the scenes Saillant wanted a reconciliation between Lombardo and the CTM to ensure that Lombardo could continue in the executive bureau of the WFTU.[47] But Saillant was unsuccessful and returned to Paris with the commitment that an organisation, the UGOCM, would be created, as indeed occurred in 1949. By then, the statutory complexities had disappeared and Saillant, Lombardo as well as the Soviets were indisputably at the head of the WFTU.

Delegates aired their problems such as loss of rights won during the war and the deteriorating working conditions imposed by US companies that bribed labour leaders and governments. Salvador Ocampo presented an overview of repression against the communists and the labour movement in Chile, which President Gabriel González Videla justified, based on the argument that war would soon break out between the United States and the USSR, and the Chileans had to demonstrate support for Washington. Repression, Ocampo explained, occurred in areas in which American companies extracted raw materials.[48]

The news from Ecuador was not encouraging. In eleven single-spaced pages, delegates presented the details on the repressive government of President Velasco Ibarra. In terms of the economy 'we're going from bad to worse', while agriculture was constrained by the concentration of land, with 20% in the hands of 189 owners. Among the many impediments to a sovereign economic life, Ecuadorians detailed the harmful trade treaties thanks to US monopolies and foreign exchange control imposed by Washington. The large foreign exchange reserves that had been accumulated during the war had been squandered on unnecessary consumer items after the United States had refused to sell Ecuador machinery with which to help its industrialisation.[49] However, the Ecuadorian Workers Confederation had not split as had occurred with the

---

46 'Informe que rinde a la Organización Internacional del Trabajo el corresponsal en México', April 1948, OIT-BIT, file 41/1948.
47 Allan Tennyson, 'III congress of the CTAL', Mexico City, 22–28 March 1948, NA, LAB13/542.
48 Salvador Ocampo, 'Extracto del informe de la CTCH al III congreso de la CTAL', FHLT, file 721.
49 Primitivo Barreto and others, 'Informe de la delegación de la CTE', Mexico City, 24 March 1948, FHLT, file 722.

other labour organisations and had remained faithful to the CTAL and the WFTU. The Bolivian delegate could not attend despite having received money for his transportation expenses from the CTAL because the funds did not arrive on time.

While the congress was in session, a civil war broke out in Costa Rica, spurred by the confrontation between the modernising elite and the anti-communist coffee oligarchy, even though the country did not have an important communist party. The unions affiliated to CTAL and at the same time to the communist party, with Manuel Mora at the helm, took the side of the modernising elite and the anti-imperialist, nationalist, liberal, but also anti-communist José Figueres Ferrer. They urgently needed weapons that the government of Costa Rica, under attack, had solicited from the Mexican government and asked Lombardo for assistance, because 'you can give us decisive help by accelerating the paperwork'.[50] The outcome of his efforts is unknown.

The arrival from Moscow of US Ambassador Nathaniel Davis, considered an expert on communism, the civil war and the cold war, created an environment hostile to organised labour and to the communist party. Rodolfo Guzmán, the general secretary of the Costa Rican Workers Confederation, was jailed along with hundreds of workers. The workers who belonged to the party lost their jobs and Lombardo and the CTAL lost a key member organisation in Central America.[51]

Despite all the attacks in the previous months and contrary to what many expected and wanted, Lombardo emerged from the congress strengthened. As seen by the comrades, his speeches were eloquent, clear and gave hope in a difficult time. The illusions of a better world were not met after the war; the workers' sacrifice for the Allies had not been repaid. The congress was not a panacea, but the delegates were able to share experiences, feel a continental brotherhood and there was 'the orientation of compañero Lombardo Toledano, who demonstrated in his interventions and his report to be one of the men who best knows the problems of the Americas and who, in my opinion, has good formulas for resolving them'.[52] Despite Lombardo's failing to propose concrete solutions to hard-pressing problems, his speeches were soothing. Nevertheless, for the diplomats he was a communist and nothing else.[53]

---

50   Miller 1993, pp. 515–41; Cerdas Cruz 1992, pp. 280–99; Manuel Mora to VLT, Costa Rica, 25 March 1948, FHLT, file 722.
51   VLT to Adolfo Ruiz Cortines, Mexico City, 27 September 1948, file 742.
52   Mauricio Báez to Valentín Tejeda and to Chabán Morell, Mexico City, 1 April 1948, FHLT, file 725.
53   José Adame Esparza, 'Corrido Vicente Lombardo Toledano', Mexico City, May 1948, FHLT, file 730; T.C. Rapp to Bevin, Mexico City, 9 April 1948, NA, FO371/AS2730/973/51.

Lombardo's future in Mexico, and before the WFTU's fragmentation in 1949, depended on his capacity to organise a new national labour confederation and preserve his leadership in CTAL. The CTAL itself was facing significant losses, partly due to the new hemispheric organisation, but also due to the purge that Lombardo applied to those national federations that attended the Lima congress because they wanted to be members of both simultaneously.[54] Many labour unions did not share the growing and irreconcilable ideological divide between communists and non-communists that the leader required them to follow.

5 The Oil Workers

The international secretariats or commissions of the unions were a useful organisational mechanism for transnational collaboration and solidarity since the founding of the Second International in 1889 that spurred their creation. In their meetings, union leaders from different countries and trades could discuss issues of common concern, focusing on the economic problems of this or that industry. From these meetings the International Federation of Trade Unions was established in 1913 of which they were a part, but within which they could also act autonomously.[55]

The meeting of the leaders of the oil industry and their labour unions, organised by Lombardo, was inspired by these secretariats. The Latin American Oil Workers Congress was held in Tampico in September 1948. The agenda of the congress was determined by the environment of the postwar period and as a result turned into a meeting with a strong anti-imperialist ideological content that overshadowed its central goal. Once again, Mexico was the only place where it was possible to hold the congress. Lombardo would have preferred that it take place in Venezuela, but the oil companies pressured President Betancourt to prevent the gathering. Mexico did not have private oil companies to pressure its government, but did have a belligerent US embassy that could not

---

54 'The CTAL convention in Mexico: an analysis', in The George Meany Archive, International Affairs Department, Jay Lovestone files, 1939–1974, box 43; Dwight Dickinson, 'Discussion of Marshall Plan in CTAL Congress by American Knight and Goldblatt', Mexico City, 26 April 1948, NARA, RG 59, file 810.5043 Mexico City/4–2648; O.A. Knight, 'Report on the Third General Congress of the CTAL', Mexico City, 9 April 1948, The George Meany Memorial archive, International Affairs Department (CIO), Director's Files, 1945–1955, box 34.

55 Van der Linden 2008, pp. 273–7.

prevent it. As an act of revenge, the embassy denied Lombardo a visa to attend the Mexican Independence Day commemoration in Los Angeles organised by the CIO. The congress in Mexico was attended by leaders from Venezuela – albeit not from the most important union, the Venezuelan Oil Workers Federation – from Colombia, Ecuador and Peru, although the latter delegates arrived late. All had few funds, which the Mexican Oil Workers Union supplemented with money borrowed from Pemex.

Lombardo pronounced passionate speeches on the need to destroy the imperialist and capitalist companies to prevent their oil from being used in an attack on the USSR. Jaime Rubio from Colombia reported that the country's oil workers were ready for a general strike in October because the company, Tropical Oil, refused to comply with the collective bargaining agreement, but the ultimate goal was to expropriate the company. Manuel Taborda of Venezuela pledged that Venezuelans would not provide their oil to the imperialists for a new war; Porfirio Alver from the Maritime Oil Workers Union spoke of the need to gather economic strength and political support for the revolution, described the popular anger against the leaders who had signed unpopular collective bargaining agreements; he expected the help of Mexicans whose conditions were better than those of the Venezuelans and had greater experience to assist them. Mexican labour leader Bernardo Calzada said that as long as there were workers in Latin America who 'suffered the lashes of the blond beasts of the north' the Latin American labour movement would have no salvation. Mexican union leader and conference organiser Francisco Arechandieta announced that the aspiration should be the nationalisation of the oil industry in Latin America.[56]

The press railed against the congress, labelling it as communist and criticised the general director of Pemex and the president's representative for attending the event. The fact that Lombardo was staying in Pemex hospitality lodging instead of at the hotel with other delegates made a bad impression on the participants. The absence of delegates from the United States was a surprise and it was not until the third day of the congress that a telegram arrived reporting that their trip was stopped by a strike on the Pacific coast, which no one believed. Lombardo said that the American delegates did not come because of pressure from the US government. He did not mention that there had been a split between the CTAL and the CIO for several reasons, the most important of

---

56   VLT, 'Convocatoria al primer congreso latinoamericano de trabajadores petroleros', in *Obra*, v/4, 1948, p. 179; VLT, inaugural address to the Latin Americano Oil Workers' Congress, Tampico, Tamaulipas, 22 September 1948, pp. 187–209; quote on p. 195.

which was the CTAL's opposition to the Marshall Plan, which the oil workers' union leader O.A. Knight had defended in the third congress of the CTAL.[57]

At the congress problems were aired, there was an exchange of experiences, but the gathering was not able to consolidate a programme to defend the interests of the workers on a continental level. Oil, as strategic as it might be for its producers, was not a good shared by all, but rather by a group of countries. The Tampico congress represented the sector of the labour movement affiliated to the CTAL, anti-American, anti-capitalist, close to the USSR and its political and economic system, in an industry that was indispensable for the US economy. The congress was the first and last of its kind.

6 Failed Emancipation

The Inter-American Confederation of Workers (CIT) claimed to be committed to democracy, but the events that accompanied its birth and its first steps as an organisation clouded that purpose. Political questions and the persecution of trade unionists by several governments came to permeate the organisation and made the trade unionists' aspirations incompatible with the promises of democracy and freedom of action in the new organisation.

Following its establishment in Lima, the Peruvian government prohibited it from operating in its territory because of the dispute it had with the APRA representative in the CIT concerning the labour mobilisation for higher wages. The headquarters of the CIT was moved to Santiago de Chile for the facilities offered by Bernardo Ibáñez, its general secretary. In April 1948, the ninth Pan-American Conference was held in Bogotá to create the Organisation of American States (OAS), with US Secretary of State George Marshall as the harbinger of the policies of modernisation, collective security and anti-communism. Bernardo Ibáñez, one of the invited guests, arranged a meeting with Jorge Eliécer Gaitán to discuss union affairs and communism. Gaitán, a 47-year-old Colombian lawyer and leader of the Liberal Party, committed to economic redistribution and political participation, was not invited to the conference because he defended the Colombia of the masses which the municipality of Bogota just cleaned up the city of before the arrival of the diplomats. A few hours before the appointment with Ibáñez, Gaitán was killed by a hit man. The furious wit-

---

57 Tennyson, 'First Congress of Oil Workers of Latin America', Tampico, México, 22–26 September 1948, NA, LAB13/541; Dwight Dickinson, 'Transmitting Stenographic Notes of Sessions of First Congress of Latin American Petroleum Workers', Mexico City, 28 January 1949, NARA, RG 59, file 810.5043 Tampico/12849.

nesses to what occurred in broad daylight on the street attacked and beat the killer. Bogota descended into pandemonium and Colombia into a decade of violence.[58]

The assassinations of both communist labour leaders and opposition figures became all too frequent. The Cuban Workers Confederation was an example of what was happening. To attract it to the CIT, the AFL cultivated Juan Arévalo of the National Federation of Maritime Workers for general secretary of the CTC. At the convention, however, communist militant Lázaro Peña won the vote. The government of Ramón Grau San Martin refused to recognise his election, stripped the CTC of its legal status and dismissed its leaders despite the workers voting in their favour.

In this environment, Jesús Menéndez, the general secretary of the National Federation of Sugar Workers of Cuba was assassinated. Menéndez fought for increasing wages by the same percentage as the growth in prices of basic necessities that Cuba imported from the United States. Because of this clause in the collective bargaining agreement, sugar workers obtained a wage increase of 13.42 % in 1947. Menéndez was assassinated in January 1948 by an army captain, who wanted to apprehend him even though the sugar workers' leader enjoyed immunity as a congressman, when he turned his back on the killer. On 17 October, Aracelio Iglesias, secretary of the Maritime Workers Federation of the port of Havana was killed, when he was meeting with other port leaders in the union headquarters. This assassination joined the list of others, which included the killing of Manuel Montoro, tram workers' leader; Rafael Lazcano, bus workers' leader; Miguel Fernández Roig, leader of the tobacco workers of Havana; Felipe Navarro, sugar workers' leader; Héctor Cabrera, tram workers' leader; and Carlos Febles, who was killed when 'he fell asleep travelling on a bus heading home'. This scenario emboldened the employers who were preparing to lower wages in the next harvest. The decline in living standards would affect not only the population, but trade relations involving imports and exports to and from the United States. On 28 November 1948 the police raided the union headquarters, which had become the workers' meeting place.[59]

In Chile the communist leader Bernardo Araya was imprisoned. Brazilian activist Roberto Moreno, on a propaganda tour for peace and democracy prior

---

58   Hawortth 1992, pp. 184–6; Romualdi, 'CIT gets down to business', *AFL's Federationist*, May 1948, FHLT, file 730; Romualdi 1967, pp. 82–8; Sánchez 1992, pp. 76–81.

59   Jesús Menéndez, available at: https://es.wikipedia.org/wiki/Jesús_Menéndez. Accessed 8 August 2015; Lázaro Peña to VLT, Havana, Cuba, 18 October 1948; Lázaro Peña to the CIO, Havana, Cuba, 8 November 1948, FHLT, file 746; Lázaro Peña to VLT, Havana, Cuba, 30 November 1948, file 749.

to the Continental Congress for Peace, sponsored by the USSR, was arrested in Venezuela and expelled. When he was in Colombia, he was stripped of his belongings and deported to Ecuador. The leaders of Chilean unions representing workers from the copper, nitrate and coal mines were jailed and held in Pisagua prison. The poet Pablo Neruda was deprived of his post as senator for being a communist.[60]

Lombardo was not prepared for the changes in the political configuration that were occurring in Latin America. With the exception of Guatemala, the rest of the region moved away from the ideal of a hemisphere united under one banner to control the economic forces adverse to the workers in accordance with his plan. The war, he believed, had been an opportunity to unify the region behind a global anti-fascist project that he expected was to take a giant step forward toward nationalisation of the economies in the postwar period as the preamble to the next stage. But this was not happening. The ILO established relations with the WFTU as one of its regional organisations at the same time that it admitted the Inter-American Confederation of Workers and the International Federation of Christian Trade Unions. Their admission was voted and accepted because several governments and labour confederations, including that of Colombia and Cuba, sent delegates they considered reliable. To add salt to the wound, at the ILO meeting in San Francisco in June, Lombardo was replaced by Ibáñez as the labour advisor. He didn't even run for re-election because he knew he would have lost. The Mexican delegate was his nemesis, Fernando Amilpa. Salvador Ocampo, secretary of the CTAL, could not attend because he was denied a visa. Most of the worker delegates disagreed with the appointment, but the voice of governments and the employers dominated the session. It could have been, as Lombardo charged, a demand from and a concession to the AFL. When the meeting was over, he sent circular letters to all the confederations affiliated to the CTAL, asking whether relations should be maintained with the ILO.[61]

---

60   Víctor Julio Silva to VLT, Bogota, 4 November 1948; Rodolfo Morena to Filiberto Velázquez Trejo, Secretary to VLT, Guayaquil, 4 November 1948, file 746; Morena, general secretary of the Brazilian Workers Confederation; National Committee of Resistance, Santiago de Chile, 11 November 1948, file 746.

61   VLT and others, 'A las centrales nacionales y agrupaciones afiliadas a la CTAL', Mexico City, 6 August 1948, FHLT, file 740; Colombian Workers Confederation, resolution no. 13, Bogota, 19 July 1948, file 732; Barría to Salvador Ocampo, San Francisco, California, 20 June 1948, file 732; VLT and Salvador Ocampo to the national confederations and groups affiliated to the CTAL, Mexico City, 14 October 1948, file 744.

Free trade unionism was one of the conditions that the AFL promised and needed in order to prove its superiority over the CTAL and to neutralise the anti-American approach of its opponents. But in October 1948 in Peru and in November in Venezuela, legitimate governments and reliable US allies were overthrown in two military coups without President Harry Truman's administration making any gesture conducive to the preservation of democracy. The Peruvian government accused Arturo Sabroso, president of the Peruvian Confederation of Labour and vice-president of the CIT of launching a violent revolt of naval and military forces in Callao, and he was imprisoned along with other leaders who could not be accused of being communists. The military junta annulled the right to trade union organisation throughout the country. After the coup against Rómulo Gallegos in Venezuela, oil workers' leader A. Malavé Villalba went into exile in Cuba, unions were dissolved and their finances frozen. The AFL condemned the anti-worker reprisals, but without dissuading the military junta that had seized power. It protested the military coup in Peru to the Secretary General of the United Nations in December 1948, but because it coincided with the complaint presented by the WFTU against governments that used the anti-communist banner against their population, the motion did not proceed.[62]

'Dear Serafino', wrote Jay Lovestone, one of the masterminds of the new confederation and whose anti-communist credentials were impeccable, to Romualdi:

> The events in Venezuela, following on the heels of the tragedy of Peru, demand, in my opinion, immediate action by the International Confederation of Labor.
>
> From the little I know, it would seem to me that the hands of our oil companies are not entirely clean in this business. Furthermore, I think our government in recognizing the Peruvian putsch and in keeping silent about it and planning to recognize the Venezuelan putsch is playing a part which deserves the most vigorous condemnation by the free trade union movement.
>
> It is not an accident that these two military putsches came as heavy blows against the most strongly developed and stable genuine democratic

---

62 Romualdi, 'De la CIT para la prensa', Washington, D.C., 28 October 1948; Lovestone to Romualdi, 6 December 1948, The George Meany Memorial Archive, International Affairs Department, country files, 1945–1971, box 22; Democratic Action Committee, 'Boletín informativo', Havana, Cuba, 5 March 1949, file 764; Schwartzberg 1997, pp. 653–66.

forces in Latin America. Without the support of these forces there will never be a trade union movement in our sister Republics.[63]

With these precedents, it was not possible to build a democratic trade union movement. While the United States did not participate in the coups, it did nothing to foster democracy. The change in labour relations in the United States also influenced this panorama. The Taft-Hartley Act, enacted in 1947, eliminated the gains that the unions had won through the Wagner Act of 1935. It restricted unions' freedom to declare strikes, forced labour leaders to swear under oath that they were not communists and reaffirmed management prerogatives over trade union rights.[64] The Inter-American Confederation of Workers achieved its goal of establishing an anti-communist labour movement to reduce the role of CTAL, but did not make a convincing case of its good democratic intentions.

In order that tyranny was not perpetuated in the rest of Latin America, Mexico must not 'lose its physiognomy', Lombardo declared. The only strategy for labour was to wager its bets on the government, 'regardless of its mistakes that can constantly be overcome'.[65] He truly believed that the Mexican Revolution and the government that had emanated from it had to remain firm because it existed in a hostile environment and was, albeit imperfect, a beacon of hemispheric democracy. The CTAL was the organisation that he assigned the task of integrating the labour movement of Mexico and Latin America in the global movement. Based on its strength, he expected that it would tip the balance of international relations toward ideological, political and economic positions in line with those of the Soviet Union and contrary to the world dominated by the United States.

---

63 Jay Lovestone to Serafino Romualdi, Washington, D.C., 6 December 1948, The George Meany Memorial Archive, International Affairs Department, Jay Lovestone files, 1939–1974, box 43.
64 Romualdi 1967, pp. 89–90; Foner and Garraty (eds) 1991, p. 105; McPherson 2006, p. 21.
65 VLT to Gilberto Bosques, Mexico City, 4 January 1948, FHLT, file 708.

PART 5

On the Fronts of the Cold Peace

Some accuse me of having been inconsistent because I have changed tactics on many occasions. But those who accuse me of being a zigzagging man or intractable or an individual difficult to understand due to the changes in my activity unfortunately confuse principles with tactics. (1950)¹

• • •

Yes, it is true that I have been a manoeuvrer all my life, I confess, a manoeuvrer in the sense of a man that makes manoeuvres and also an inveterate manoeuvrer because I'll keep doing so until I die. (1955)²

• • •

I will not withdraw from the fight, today or tomorrow, and I will keep fighting until the last moment of my existence. Because I am a revolutionary who can only think one way, and can only live one way. I think in terms of the abolition of the capitalist system and I contribute my share for the arrival of socialism in the shortest period of time. (1956)³

---

1 Interview with VLT by Carlos Argüelles, *Mañana*, 6 May 1950.
2 VLT, 'Intervención de inicio del debate sobre la tesis de orientación ideológica y educación política del Partido Popular', 21 November 1955, in *Obra*, V/22, 1955, p. 40.
3 VLT, speech delivered in the Restaurante Chapultepec, Mexico City, 27 July 1956, FHLT, file 1024.

CHAPTER 13

Rearmament

The fiery rhetoric and sharp pen were part of Lombardo's arsenal. Oratory skills, he once said, were 'a weapon of the people against their oppressors and also serves to guide the lower classes'.[1] His language was not always easy to understand, but repeating an idea could turn it into a spell. He had charisma and a soft and warm voice. The historical moment demanded that he energise his followers so that they would not lose heart in a Mexico that was not the sovereign country of their dreams. The Yankees dominated the country, but the popular forces, no matter how confused and disorganised they might be, rejected 'the imperialist and reactionary offensive', seeking instead to 'ensure a new development of the democratic revolution'.[2] Lombardo had no doubt that 'Mexico will be a socialist country, as will all countries of the world, without exception'. There was no other road, predicted one who described himself as 'a believer in Mexico and humanity'.[3]

1 The People's Party

Founding the party in 1948, usually referred to as PP, was a bold step after the initiative was attacked by the press, the government, some trade unions, campesino organisations and employers' associations, at a time in which the PRI, the CTM and the National Peasant Federation (CNC) feared the loss of their members. The organisers who travelled the country to recruit members suffered all sorts of harassment, persecution and attacks by thugs. Amilpa and Velázquez offered perks and patronage to dissuade Cetemistas from entering the party. The railroad workers, an important reserve of potential adherents, were divided between those who ignored Amilpa's warning that they would suf-

---

1 Apolinar Ruiz Espínosa, agent 52 to the Federal Security Directorate (DFS), VLT, 'El orador y el expositor del Partido Popular', Mexico City, 22 November 1948, AGN, Federal Security Directorate (henceforth DFS), People's Socialist Party (henceforth PPS), vol. 1, 1947–1950, file 11-20-48; Krauze 1997b, p. 220.
2 'La situación política de México', Mexico City, 2 December 1948, FHLT, file 749. No author indicated, but Lombardo's authorship can be deduced from the style and content of the speech.
3 VLT, 'La perspectiva de México, una democracia del pueblo. Informe ante el Noveno Consejo del PP', 5 April 1955, in *Obra*, V/20, 1955, p. 146.

fer reprisals if they entered the party and those who joined anyway. In Mazatlán, Sinaloa, the Cetemistas remained firmly on the side of their national leadership and with the PRI, because the posts of councilman and mayor of the port city were at stake. In Tijuana, Baja California, party organisers were persecuted and in Tlacotalpan, Veracruz, they were jailed. The oil workers from various union locals adhered to the proposal to create the party because Lombardo promised them that what the revolution offered, such as the popular representation that was taken away from them by the CTM and the PRI, would be fulfilled and the government would ensure that prices would not keep rising faster than wages.[4]

In the telephone workers' union hall, where one of several assemblies to establish the party was held, the speakers couldn't be heard because of the clamour. But one union representative managed to hear Lombardo say that 'only an idiot' could assert that the party was Soviet-inspired. The new organisation would not be an opposition party, but 'an arm of Mexico's democratic revolution'. A long-standing Cromista asked 'if this time you'll decide to take things to the end'. Lombardo replied without entering into details that 'that there be will such a decision. I would ask the compañero to renew his lost faith and join the Popular Party'.[5]

No, it would not be an opposition party. In a promotional tour through northern Mexico, Lombardo declared that the new party would not fight against the PRI but against poverty, ignorance and imperialism, serve the Mexican Revolution and the homeland: 'The People's Party was born to help Alemán be a great president but it will be independent of Alemán'.[6] But it would not be. Before launching the campaign to organise it, Antonio Bermúdez, general director of Pemex, handed Lombardo a cheque for 20,000 pesos to subsidise the Workers' University campus in Tampico.[7]

---

4 Miguel Barrera to VLT, Monterrey, 20 November 1947, FHLT, file 697; Guillermo Ibáñez López to VLT, Mazatlán, Sinaloa, 2 December 1947, FHLT, file 698; VLT to the Interior Ministry, Mexico City, 15 December 1947, FHLT, file 700; Report presented to the International Labour Organization by its representative in Mexico, October 1947, OIT-BIT, file 41/1947.

5 VLT, 'Discursos pronunciados en la asamblea política organizada por los trabajadores petroleros de la zona centro, pro Partido Popular', Mexico City, 22 October 1947, FHLT, file 694; Luís García Rojas Sánchez, agent 49, to the DFS, Mexico City, 26 April 1948 and Francisco García Márquez, agent 32, to the DFS, Mexico City, 30 May 1948, DFS, AGN, PPS, vol. 1, file 11-20-48.

6 VLT, 'Acto proselitista a favor del Partido Popular en Torreón, Coahuila', 30 May 1948, in *Obra*, V/3 1948, p. 330.

7 VLT to Manuel Gual Vidal, Public Education Minister and VLT to Bermúdez, 12 January 1948, FHLT, file 709. The cheque was dated 17 January 1948, FHLT, file 710.

One of the trips to recruit members for the party took Lombardo to Uruapan, Michoacán. He was with his friend Victor Manuel Villaseñor. There he visited General Cárdenas to discuss issues related to the party. Lombardo complained about the lack of money and the PRI's campaign against it. Cárdenas later recalled that at that meeting he 'spoke to me about accepting the leadership of the Party and I let him know my decision not to participate in it'.[8] Lombardo must have anticipated that the former president would not accept. Did he want to take advantage of the general's prestige to give a Cardenista veneer to the party he himself wanted to lead? Had he hoped to receive financial support? He must have known that Lázaro Cárdenas as a party chairman would have caused a scandal among the new generation of government officials whose goal was to diminish the stature and popularity of the former president.

In his memoirs, Villaseñor did not mention this meeting with General Cárdenas and perhaps did not know that Lombardo offered him the post of party chairman. Bassols also visited General Cárdenas to express his concern because individuals contrary to the principles of the revolution had been admitted and that the party had little chance to remain afloat if it had not been for 'the funds personally delivered by Toledano, which we now know were provided by MAC',[9] Manuel Ávila Camacho.

The founding assembly of the party was held on 20 and 21 June. The delegates learned of and received a written copy of the programme and the statement of principles the same day as they were called to vote on them, which disturbed Pedro Mireles Malpica from Monterrey. He did not conceive the party as left-wing, 'a tendency that for years we have been fighting against', but as a national front. The PP calling for prohibiting the clergy from teaching, Mireles argued, 'runs the risk of offending the religious sentiments of large sectors of the population that we plan to win to the Party'.[10]

A campesino challenged the constitutional amendment introduced by President Alemán that under the injunction law shielded landowners from the implementation of agrarian reform. Diego Rivera, who joined the party and withdrew his application for readmission to the Communist Party, proposed that the PP object to the amendment. Faced with the danger that the programme would not be approved, the question was put to a vote. Voting was

---

8   LC, Uruapan, Michoacan, 17 April 1948, in Cárdenas 1973, pp. 286–7.
9   Villaseñor 1976, vol. 2, pp. 118–21; LC, Villa Obregón, 30 May 1948, in Cárdenas 1973, vol. 2, p. 292.
10 Pedro Mireles Malpica to VLT, strictly confidential, Mexico City, 21 June 1948, FHLT, file 732.

by state and the motion supported by the campesinos and Rivera lost.[11] But for most participants, the founding of the party was cause for a popular celebration. One afternoon they took the bus or tram to Rancho del Artista on Avenida Coyoacán 957 in the Colonia del Valle neighbourhood, where Lombardo invited them all to an outdoor lunch. 'Until next time, comrades. See you soon', he said bidding them farewell, 'as far as our faith, our strength, our life, serving the People's Party and the Mexican nation take us'.[12]

The party was registered in July. It claimed to have 358,000 members. On Sunday, 25 July, Lombardo called the executive committee to an urgent meeting at ten o'clock in the morning at his home. Writer and chronicler of national events, Salvador Novo, was one of those invited. It was necessary to take a position on the peso devaluation that had just occurred. At 11 o'clock there were so many people present that they no longer fitted on the terrace of Lombardo's home. He distributed copies of a statement he had drafted. Everyone wanted to speak. From the meeting came a document for the press in which it stated that the PP was not an opposition party, but had to take a stand because it was a party based on the popular classes and the devaluation was the result of the mistaken economic policy of the government that negatively affected the living standards of wage earners, distribution of wealth, credit for production, it encouraged hoarding, speculation and waste. A few days later, Lombardo met with the president, who he exonerated of any responsibility, although this was not the case with the finance and national economy ministers or the director of the Bank of Mexico. Based on the several hour long meeting with Miguel Alemán, Lombardo came away convinced that the president would take action so that the population's conditions would improve, the cost of living would stop increasing, and usurers and speculators would stop engaging in such practices.[13]

The birth of the People's Party put the intelligence agencies into high gear. Agent 62 of the Federal Security Directorate detected supposed meetings between Lázaro Cárdenas and Lombardo that 'aim to prepare a coup d'état to overthrow the current system of government' with the participation of milit-

---

11 T.C. Rapp to Ernest Bevin, Mexico City, 22 June 1948, NA, FO371/AN2885/267/26.
12 VLT, 'Informe a la Asamblea Constituyente del Partido Popular', Mexico City, 20 June 1948, in *Obra*, V/4, 1948, pp. 1–23; VLT, 'Discurso de clausura', 21 June 1948, in *Obra*, V/4, 1948, p. 32, p. 45.
13 The statistic is unreliable and the membership figures could be exaggerated. Carr 1992, p. 200; Novo 1994, pp. 174–5; PP National Executive Committee, 'La devaluación del peso mexicano significa el fracaso de la política económica de gobierno', in *El Popular*, 26 July 1948, in *Obra*, V/4, 1948, pp. 101–5; VLT to Lázaro Peña, Mexico City, 10 August 1948, FHLT, file 737.

ary officials and the heads of the presidential guards.[14] Secret agents and uniformed police officers followed Lombardo wherever he went and monitored party activities. One night they followed him to the Bottoms Up restaurant on the corner of Lerma and Melchor Ocampo streets, where he went by car 'in order to have a secret meeting'. When those who were scheduled to be at the meeting arrived, Apolinar Ruiz, Agent 52 informed, 'they closed the folding doors, isolating themselves from the rest of the reserved (section of the restaurant)'. He was unable to fulfil his mission; he stayed in the restaurant for a while but left because he could not hear anything.[15]

The emergence of the party aroused both enthusiasm and negative feelings in the capital and in the states. The Marxist writer José Revueltas, who recognised in Lombardo the 'beloved and respected leader of Marxism in Mexico',[16] doubted that the party and the 'national bourgeois' could form a bloc to deepen the revolution because 'the bourgeoisie did not need allies from the popular classes since it is finding better allies outside of Mexico in North American imperialism'. Instead, Revueltas proposed the creation of a Marxist party of the proletariat and 'submitting its activity to the most honest and rigorous self-criticism'.[17] But Lombardo's overall strategy went beyond the People's Party and he was not interested in discussing or sharing his ideas with those with whom he was building it as means to an undisclosed end.

The July 1949 midterm elections tested the democratic inclination of the party. Lombardo was in charge of nominating the candidates for the elected office in the states. Vicente Padilla, mayor of Ciudad Obregón in Sonora was pushed aside in the race, replaced by Francisco Figueroa Mendoza, a workers' leader, after he was informed of 'the opinion expressed by our dear leader compañero Lombardo Toledano in relation to the problem of the federal deputies'. Padilla did not want to obstruct the road chartered by Lombardo, because his sole purpose was 'to continue to serve my party'.[18] To encourage the voters to do

---

14   Arturo Schick to the DFS, Mexico City, 6 August 1948, AGN, DGS, Lombardo Toledano Vicente, public version (henceforth VLT, vp), 1/9, 21-22-48. The AGN organised the public version of the VLT documents in nine volumes, which are quoted in that order.

15   Gen. Brigadier Marcelino Inurreta, Memorandum, Mexico City, 3 November 1948, DFS, AGN, PPS/I, 11-20-48; Apolinar Ruiz Espinosa to the DFS, Mexico City, 9 December 1948, AGN, DFS, VLT, vp 1/9, 11-20-48.

16   José Revueltas to VLT, Mexico City, 17 February 1949, FHLT, file 762.

17   José Revueltas, 'Memorándum sobre la situación del país y las tareas del movimiento marxista en México (1949)', Mexico City, February 1949, FHLT, file 762; Luna Cárdenas 2007, pp. 129–32.

18   Vicente Padilla to Jacinto López, Ciudad Obregón, Sonora, 22 March 1949, FHLT, file 765; VLT, 'Discurso en el mitin del PP en Morelos', 12 June 1949, in *Obra*, V/5, 1949, p. 173.

as told, Lombardo expressed the unlikely view that the PRI was 'in liquidation' and that the National Confederation of Popular Organisations (CNOP) was 'the sort of mass grave where anonymous bones are scattered that have no owner and no one to gather them up'.[19] He was referring to the pipe dream concocted by President Ávila Camacho in 1943 with the unorganised sectors such as the military, professionals and the rising middle class, against which he did not say anything at the time. The PAN was the puppet of the PRI, because its candidates were also candidates of the party to which it was opposed.[20]

The elections were fraudulent. The PRI changed the location of the polling stations from where they were supposed to be installed to places far from the villages to make it difficult for voters to cast their ballots. In addition, voters were intimidated, told how to vote and killings were reported.[21] Alfonso Sánchez Madariaga of the CTM was challenged by Victor Manuel Villaseñor of the People's Party in an election district of the capital. Villaseñor knew that electoral fraud was being prepared against him, but could do nothing except write a letter to his friend, the president.

> In señor Jesús Yurén's offices on Avenida Juárez # 60 it was discovered that more than 70 percent of the voter identification cards issued were fraudulent. Plus, there were trade unionists from the CTM bussed in to vote with fake voter identification cards in several polling stations. The concluding incident in this farce was that the presidents of several polling stations refused to tally up the vote and proceeded to steal the ballot boxes and documents.[22]

Revueltas was one of the other candidates who lost. Together with his friends, they publicised his candidacy through street theatre in tents and the plazas until they found premises, which the PRI took away from them.[23]

Jacinto López, at 43 years of age, a worker, a leader of many agrarian and union conflicts, registered as the party's candidate for governor of Sonora. His campaign found an echo among the population, including the indigenous communities, but was hampered in many ways up to the point of a physical attack

---

19 VLT, 'Asamblea electoral del Partido Popular. Discurso pronunciado en el acto para iniciar la campaña del PP', 17 June 1949, Mexico City, in *Obra*, V/5, 1949, p. 195.
20 Loaeza 1988, pp. 253–4.
21 Lt. Coronel Manuel Mayoral García to the DFS, Mexico City, 18 August 1949, AGN, DFS, VLT, vp 1/9, 11-20-49; Luna Cárdenas 2007, pp. 165–9.
22 Villaseñor to Miguel Alemán, Mexico City, 16 June 1949, FHLT, file 771.
23 Ruiz Abreu 1992, pp. 214–15.

against him in Empalme by a group of drunken Priistas. In the municipalities, only local government employees or persons designated by the PRI were registered by the state government to vote. Campesinos that were members of the PP were ignored. As part of its manoeuvre, the Priistas hid the ballots marked in favour of the PP candidates and altered the minutes containing the final vote count. The military presence with propaganda in favour of the PRI candidate in Guyamas 'caused panic among the voters'.[24] In such an electoral climate, the People's Party failed to get its candidates elected.

Ignacio Soto, president of the Sonora Chamber of Industries, was the candidate of General Abelardo Rodríguez, former president and his business partner. He was proclaimed the state governor, but Jacinto López declared himself the legitimate winner. He mobilised the party members to protest the imposition of Soto and with his followers created the people's assembly. From the awning of a truck in the Francisco I. Madero park in Hermosillo, López was sworn in before the assembly as governor of Sonora, named his team and promptly began to enact laws and outline government plans.[25]

It was possibly President Alemán who pressured Lombardo to demobilise the PP's followers in Sonora. The state was a sensitive point, with high unemployment as a result of layoffs of workers in the mining and packing companies and the return of braceros from the United States to Hermosillo. Lombardo disavowed the legitimacy of the popular assembly as a provocation of the military and ended the mobilisation. Without consulting anyone, Lombardo negotiated the stolen governorship for a seat in Congress and the promise of freedom for political prisoners. He even got the protest against this transaction to end.[26]

The 3 July 1949 elections were fraudulent, said the PP in a press release, but the fraud did not weaken the party, rather it damaged the PRI and the government and 'has shown that the Revolution continues to have a fruitful

---

24 Grijalba Dávila 2012, pp. 90–4; Vicente Padilla to Miguel Alemán Valdés (henceforth MAV), Ciudad Obregón, 13 July 1949, FHLT, file 773; Ramírez y Ramírez to MAV, telegram, Mexico City, 20 July 1949, FHLT, file 774; VLT to Adolfo Ruiz Cortines, Mexico City, 10 August 1949, FHLT, file 776; VLT and Victoriano Anguiano to the Electoral College of the Chamber of Deputies, Mexico City, 15 August 1949, AGN, Ramo MAV, file 544.4.
25 Luna Cárdenas 2007, pp. 159–69; Grijalba Dávila 2012, pp. 96–9.
26 VLT, 'La actualidad política en México', interview with *El Popular*, 25 June 1949, in *Obra*, V/5, 1949, p. 215; VLT, 'II Consejo Nacional ordinario del PP', Mexico City, 18 October 1949, in *Obra*, V/6, 1949, pp. 73–8 and p. 85; Jacinto López to the inhabitants of Hermosillo, Sonora, 8 September 1949, FHLT, file 778; 'Political developments in Mexico from August 16 to October 15, 1949', NARA, RG 59, file 812.00/10–2049.

programme capable of igniting the people's civic enthusiasm'.[27] The party leadership decided not to defend any of the races it had lost in the elections due to its distrust of the board of elections and as a sign of protest, Lombardo said aloud. More important was his intention not to appear as an opposition party and not to contribute to the possible destabilisation of the system. As an olive branch, the PRI gave the PP a seat in a district in Sonora, which a candidate by the name Ignacio Pesqueira accepted, but Bassols and Villaseñor expelled him from the party. Lombardo was in Milan at the time. When he returned to Mexico, he said that the PP would accept the seat and Pesqueira returned to the party.[28]

Their decisions rejected, Bassols and Villaseñor resigned and subjected Lombardo to scathing criticism. Lombardo 'had managed to consolidate a system based on the centralisation of functions, exemplarily anti-democratic ... a totalitarian concentration of activities'. He eluded criticising the government and the president, since the villains were the 'dissidents of the Revolution'. He foiled the opportunity to create a progressive party, achieved the depoliticisation of the population and the containment of the left that was independent of the state.[29]

Lombardo did not heed criticisms. Years later, when he recapitulated his life, he referred to them: 'If some people have abandoned me in the course of my life, it was not me who they left, but the cause that I serve'.[30] In truth, he had a gift that others lacked. Those who were no longer with him took refuge in their private or professional lives, while he followed the path he had chartered, surrounded by his unconditional secretaries, his daughters, son-in-laws, grandchildren when they grew up, and all those who did not have ambitions of being part of the leadership or who hid such aspirations waiting for their opportunity to arrive. He had followers among campesinos, workers and leaders who were attracted by his demeanour, discourse and ability to mediate. He drew close to or moved away from the communists, in their different parties and groups, depending on whether or not they served his purposes.

Lombardo shared the leadership of the party in pyramid fashion with himself on top and from there on down to the servants, as he called the people

---

27 VLT to Alfredo del Mazo, 20 July 1949, FHLT, file 774; PP, 'Boletín de prensa, manifiesto al pueblo de México', Mexico City, 10 August 1949, FHLT, file 776.
28 'Political developments in Mexico from August 16 to October 15, 1949', NARA, RG 59, file 812.00/10–2049.
29 Villaseñor 1976, vol. 2, pp. 136–88; Julio Scherer García, 'Diego hace cisco a Lombardo Toledano', *Últimas Noticias*, 20 October 1949, FHLT, file 782.
30 VLT, 'Discurso pronunciado en el Restaurante Chapultepec', Mexico City, 27 July 1956, FHLT, file 1024.

who he had in his service. This generated frustration and a feeling of abandonment in the party, but no one was his equal in terms of their ability to create political and cultural organisations. Bassols and Villaseñor were men of ideas, but except in newspapers and magazines, they did not have a platform to put them into action. Lombardo did, making it available to those who shared his ideas and those who followed him, and denying it to those who competed with him in strategy such as the communists, Villaseñor, Bassols, Revueltas, Campa and many others. The plurality of opinions got in his way, since he was clear on the way forward and needed his ideas to be put into practice, even if that might asphyxiate the initiative of others. His tactic was to allow discussion and participation and then do what he thought fit.

Imperialist penetration was the primary enemy and it was necessary to ensure that the so-called national front for the country's independence would not break apart. This was the reason why Lombardo could not openly recognise the PRI's electoral fraud or the defeat of the People's Party. On the contrary, party members should abandon impatience, defeatism, opportunism and violent actions to avoid any semblance of belonging to an opposition party.[31]

With the elections over, Lombardo was 'materially crushed with excessive work'. He needed rest and was planning to spend a week in Chihuahua to go bear hunting before embarking on his next trips.[32]

2 UGOCM

Before the elections and his trip to Milan for the WFTU meeting in July 1949, Lombardo oversaw the founding of the General Union of Workers and Peasants of Mexico (UGOCM). This was his other instrument to counter his loss of influence in the CTM and the country's trade unions that were its members, to gain control over a labour confederation that would legitimise his vice presidency in the WFTU and to ensure popular support for the party. Perhaps he expected to build the new confederation with the same ease with which he founded the CGOCM in 1933 on the ruins of the CROM, and the CTM in 1936 with the support of President Cárdenas. But the late 1940s were different. The corporativist practices of the CTM and the CNC had been institutionalised, although there was a

---

31 VLT, 'II Consejo Nacional ordinario del PP', Mexico City, 18 October 1949, in *Obra*, V/6, 1949, p. 85.

32 VLT to Margarita Lombardo Toledano, Mexico City, 19 August 1949; VLT to Lorenzo Zelaya, Mexico City, 19 August 1949, FHLT, file 776.

reservoir of labour and agricultural workers' unions that were independent or dissatisfied with their current predicament.³³

The situation in the labour movement was volatile. Unions changed alliances according to the possibilities of achieving better wages and working conditions, to defend their organisations or what remained of their internal democracy. Several unions that had joined the dissenting confederation led by Campa, in 1949 returned to the CTM as their membership in the CUT had failed to result in higher income for their ranks. Since the government intervention in the railroad workers' union in 1948, Lombardo lost an important base of support. The oil workers were divided between his followers and opponents, who returned to the CTM, which was strengthened furthermore by having brought Conciliation and Arbitration Boards under its influence. The telephone workers and taxi drivers also announced their return. The CUT, according to the British Embassy's labour attaché Tennyson, was nothing more than an empty shell. Last but not least, the CTM left the CTAL, more for being anti-Lombardista than anti-communist, but did not enter the confederation controlled by the AFL.³⁴

The UGOCM came out of the Workers and Peasants' Alliance of Mexico, founded in March 1948 as a temporary organisation on the road to creating the new confederation. The founding congress of the new workers' and peasants' organisation took place from 20 to 22 June 1949 at the Teatro Abreu, with delegates representing a million and a half workers, according to a figure given by its organisers. Among the participating organisations were locals of the mine workers' union, more than half of the members of the oil workers' union, the tramway, construction and sugar industry workers, agrarian committees, agricultural colonies and rural cooperatives. The majority, 70%, were peasants, 30% were workers and small businessmen. The UGOCM was established as a confederation with 'absolute' independence from the state. Lombardo should not appear as the person running the organisation. He was there on the first day and flew to Milan where he expected, as agreed beforehand, the UGOCM to be accepted as a member of the WFTU.³⁵

---

33   Candelario Contreras to VLT, Mazatlán, Sinaloa, 17 June 1949, FHLT, file 731. Throughout this book I have tried to qualify the categorical affirmations on the defeats and decomposition of Lombardo and Lombardismo such as those expressed by Víctor Manuel Durand Ponte, 'La descomposición política del lombardismo', in Loyola (ed.) 1986, pp. 163–92 or Rivera Flores 1984.

34   Tennyson, 'Survey of Labour Affairs in Mexico in the period November 1948–mid-March 1949', Mexico City, 11 March 1949, NA, LAB13/541; Rapp to Bevin, 'Congress of the CTM', 15 April 1949, NA, FO371/AM2181/1.

35   Dwight Dickinson, 'Labour groups loyal to Lombardo Toledano form Alianza de obreros

President Alemán was represented at the conference by Adolfo Ruiz Cortines, his Interior Minister, and received the executive committee when the event was over. The well-known animosity of Labour Minister Manuel Ramírez Vázquez toward Lombardo and the workers explained his absence. The expected message from Lázaro Cárdenas never arrived. According to Lombardo's loyalist Enrique Ramírez y Ramírez, the UGOCM was 'a death blow to all our adversaries'.[36] Lombardo received the request of affiliation to the WFTU on 25 June and Antonio García Moreno, mine workers' leader, flew to Italy to formally present the application.

Due to its majority campesino composition and for being then and always an adversary, the labour minister did not register the UGOCM as a labour federation. He also refused to recognise it because several unions that said they were part of the UGOCM lacked legal status, had been dissolved or were union locals and not the union as a whole that had joined the new federation. This was the case with the oil workers. And without legal registration, unions could not negotiate collective bargaining agreements, although they could and did have the capacity to mobilise their members.

In May 1950 the mine workers' union convention was held, and was attended by workers who had not been elected as representatives in their locals, but were spurious delegates appointed by the labour ministry. Workers opposed to this manoeuvre held another convention and named the Lombardista activist García Moreno as general secretary. These dissident miners from Palau, Nueva Rosita, Parral and other coal miner union locals in Coahuila were among those who belonged to the UGOCM.[37]

The miners and metalworkers union had considerable experience with labour disputes that were resolved in their favour, often mediated by the president. As the demand for metals for industry grew and the country's industrialisation model was consolidated, the practise of negotiating between the union and the government stopped working together with its relative autonomy. The appearance of the delegates who did not represent union locals at the conven-

---

y campesinos de México', Mexico City, 10 March 1948, NARA, RG 59, file 812.5043/3–1043; Basurto 1984, pp. 135–56; Carr 1992, pp. 174–6.

36   Ramírez y Ramírez to VLT, Mexico City, 25 June 1949, FHLT, file 772; 'Comité Nacional Ejecutivo, Datos sobre la razón histórica de la UGOCM y sus relaciones internas', Mexico City, undated, FHLT, file 772; Tennyson, 'Formation of the Mexican General Union of Workers and Peasants (UGOCM)', Mexico City, 2 July 1949, NA, FO371/AN2181.

37   Tennyson to R. Turner, 3 and 6 August 1949, NA, LAB13/541; 'Mexico Reports', November 1949, ILO-BIT, 41/1949; Orlando Delgado de Garay to Lamberto Ortega Peregrina, Mexico City, 14 August 1950, AGN, Political and Social Research Department (henceforth DGIPS), box 104, file 1; Sariego 1988, pp. 233–74.

tion triggered the miners' protest. But this time, the government and companies' persecution due to the mine workers' audacity in challenging them was unprecedented. Leaders were jailed and beaten by federal soldiers. The Palau coal company suspended the supply of potable water and electricity for the population, demanded that the miners vacate company housing and the union headquarters was turned over to strikebreakers under the protection of federal troops. Some miners allowed themselves to be rehired as new workers. 'This is a movement that can be decisive to shift the course of subsequent events in favour of our line', Lombardo wrote amid a dramatic situation.[38] But in Paris a month later, he received a discouraging telegram of the desperate situation of eight thousand families without any means and in need of solidarity, caught in the middle of an unresolved conflict.[39]

In the question that he addressed to Miguel Alemán, Lombardo recognised the miners' impotence: 'Would you be so kind, Mr President, to tell me in what terms you issued the resolution on the conflict involving my striking compañeros'?[40] There was no solution and to force the situation, the strikers along with their families set off on a 1,500 kilometres march to the capital to meet with the president. After 50 days and numerous displays of solidarity along the way, the caravan reached the capital. Lombardo offered to put up some 500 miners at the Workers' University and organised solidarity among Mexico City unions, the Law School and the Faculty of Philosophy and Letters at the National University. The authorities also equipped a sports centre to provide lodging during the night. Artists organised an auction of their paintings, sketches and lithographs to support the striking miners. President Alemán did not receive them.[41]

Before embarking on their return trip, Lombardo bid farewell to the miners, congratulating them for their honesty, for their class consciousness, for having accepted the need to 'sometimes face partial defeats. But this has never discouraged the revolutionary forces, because they know that final victory awaits them'.[42] He must have been satisfied that the miners' protest did not end with the use of force, that they accepted surrendering their autonomy before the state and resigned themselves to the imposition of trade union leaders.[43] His tactic of national front triumphed over the workers' interests.

---

38 VLT to Saillant, 28 October 1950, FHLT, file 810.
39 Antonio García Moreno to VLT, Mexico City, 24 November 1950, FHLT, file 812; Basurto 1984, pp. 226–70.
40 VLT to MAV, Mexico City, 17 January 1951, FHLT, file 820.
41 Basurto 1984, p. 278.
42 VLT, 'La caravana de mineros ha dado un ejemplo a la clase trabajadora y al pueblo de México', El Popular, 21 April 1951, in Obra, V/9, 1951, pp. 239–40.
43 Sariego 1988, pp. 279–80; Rivera Flores 1984, pp. 55–108; Luna Cárdenas 2007, pp. 198–205.

In July 1951 Lombardo turned 57 years old. As before, he received dozens of telegrams and letters of congratulations and admiration. One letter from a worker said: 'Your life has followed the same path as the great champions of the transformation of the unjust world of capitalism. Your life parallels that of our teacher Karl Marx, of Lenin, and of the greatest man of our time, the great leader, teacher, and people's guide Comrade Joseph Stalin'.[44]

The British consul portrayed Lombardo as an optimist, with refined habits, and as a magnet for his followers. Furthermore,

> Lic. Lombardo relaxes as actively as he works, preferring shooting in the wilder parts of Mexico. The ceremony and entourage associated with his shooting expeditions have been likened by Mexicans to those expected of an English 'milord'. At home in Mexico City he lives comfortably, dresses well and has the unusual habit for a Mexican of preferring a pipe to cigarette or cigars. Despite his general dislike of things British, he dresses in English broadcloth, smokes John Cotton tobacco and regards *The Times* as the best newspaper in the world.[45]

3 Back on the Campaign Trail

The 1952 campaign was different from previous races. This time Lombardo decided to run for president. Mexico was in danger, he said, because it was being stalked by imperialism and because President Miguel Alemán desired to remain in office. Lombardo hinted at his intention to run for the presidency to General Cárdenas a few years before. He visited Cárdenas at the latter's home on 12 July 1950: 'He acknowledges that he will not win the elections, but it will provide a forum to demonstrate faith in the principles of the Mexican Revolution'.[46]

When Lombardo threw his hat into the ring in January 1952, General Cárdenas was of the opinion that his candidacy would divide the opposition and that: 'Acting politically based on considerations different from those of the social interests of the Revolution, is to betray the people. Political honesty and loyalty to social principles are essential qualities that must be present in every leader'.[47] Cárdenas should have detected one of the components of Lombardo's

---

44 Francisco Bernal to VLT, Mexico City, 21 July 1951, FHLT, file 833.
45 John Taylor to Mr Eden, Mexico City, 19 December 1951, NA, FO371/AM1015/9.
46 LC, Villa Obregón, 12 July 1950, in Cárdenas 1973, p. 400.
47 LC, Mexico City, 16 December 1950, in Cárdenas 1973, p. 450.

grand strategy, hidden from less expert eyes, namely, the tying of Mexico's fate to the international policy of the Soviet bloc.

Lombardo prepared the groundwork so that in December 1951 he would present his candidacy for president as the consensus of the People's Party, the communists from the PCM and the communists expelled and organised in the Mexican Workers and Peasants Party (POCM).[48] In the ceremony where Lombardo formalised his candidacy, he promised to establish a government that would intervene to create cordial and equitable treatment between employers and wage earners as well as to prevent workers from continuing to be devoured by the terrible consequences of the high cost of living.[49]

But his candidacy did not receive unanimous acceptance. Voices were raised against it on the grounds that the party did not have the required national presence. Lombardo silenced such criticism. He would have wanted a single candidate and expressed the unlikely idea that he would resign if all the candidates with similar points of view – Miguel Henríquez Guzmán, candidate of the Federation of People's Parties; Adolfo Ruiz Cortines for the PRI; and parties without ballot status such as the PCM and the POCM – were to adopt a common platform 'to save the Revolution and Mexico'.[50] Without saying so, it would have had to be his platform.

Lombardo launched his campaign on 13 January 1952 in Ixcateopan in the state of Guerrero, where the tomb with the alleged remains of Cuauhtémoc, the last, heroic and suffering Mexica emperor, had been discovered in 1949. The master of ceremonies at the campaign event introduced Lombardo as 'the reincarnation of the Great Titan of Tenochtitlan'. It did not matter that the authenticity of the bones was denied by the National Institute of Anthropology and History. Those that defended their genuineness charged that to say otherwise represented a hate campaign against Mexicans' purest traditions, against the values of national identity and for fear of Cuauhtémoc who 'embodies the rebellion of the people'.[51]

Agents from the Federal Security Directorate followed Lombardo in his campaign. In Ixcateopan 'about 250 people gathered, mostly from Mexico City, and

---

48   VLT, 'Toma de protesta como candidato del PP a la presidencia de la república', Mexico City, 16 December 1951, in *Obra*, V/9, 1951, p. 324.
49   VLT, 'Haremos un gobierno democrático, antiimperialista', *El Popular*, 21 December 1951, in *Obra*, V/9, 1951, pp. 329–30.
50   Interview with Rubén Mendoza Heredia in the magazine *ABC*, published under the title 'Yo no soy comunista, pero sí seré Presidente', *El Popular*, 7 January 1952, in *Obra*, V/11, 1952, p. 3 and p. 13; Gómez Arias with Víctor Díaz Arciniegas, p. 210, pp. 211–14, pp. 223–4; Cosío Villegas 1975, p. 54 and p. 88; Medin 1990, p. 169; Alonso 2003; Servín 2001.
51   Gillingham 2011, p. 83 and p. 189.

the rest, peasants, women and children, attended because it was market day'; more were bussed in. Lombardo arrived in his Oldsmobile, driven by Alejandro Carrillo, and accompanied by Véjar Vázquez from the PP, Dionisio Encina from the PCM and students from the National Polytechnic Institute. The first speakers were five indigenous residents who spoke in their native languages, Nahua, Maya-Quiche, Zapotec, Mixtec and Totonac. The army tried to dampen the enthusiasm of the event, but failed. Lombardo did not attack the regime, confirmed that the bones were those of Cuauhtémoc, 'the greatest man in Mexico', and prayed:

> Father Cuauhtémoc, I promise you that the People's Party will use your example to defend our territory; our land is still poor, but I promise you that I will completely replace poverty with abundance.
>
> Father Cuauhtémoc, we are with you here and I will visit you again when there is not a single Mexican who cannot read or write, when everyone has enough to eat.[52]

The indigenous participants performed traditional dances and then all were treated to a plate of barbacoa, a typical Mexican roast mutton delicacy.[53]

As with the fund raising efforts to launch the People's Party, Lombardo had donation bonds issued for his election campaign. One man gave him a portrait of his girlfriend because it was all he had, according to one account.[54] In Hermosillo, Sonora, 'the public cooperated with great enthusiasm'.[55] Careerists in search of jobs also joined in.[56] Lombardo was accompanied by communist activists and his twenty-something-year-old daughter Marcela. When she got on the dais with her father, she urged young people to vote for Lombardo to achieve prosperity and so that Mexico could rid itself of the yoke of imperialism.

Before the candidate arrived at a location, the propaganda posted by campaign workers was usually torn down or covered by publicity for another candidate and the banners destroyed by municipal authorities. Lombardo was the

---

52 General Brigadier Marcelino Inurreta, 'Memorandum', Mexico City, 13 January 1952, AGN, DGS, VLT, vp 2/9, 11-20-52.

53 VLT, 'Padre Cuauhtémoc', Ixcateopan, 13 January 1952, *El Popular*, 14 January 1952, in *Obra*, V/11, 1952, p. 28; 'Romance del peregrino', March 1952, in *Obra*, V/12, 1952, p. 47, p. 51, p. 56.

54 Interview with Luis Monter, Mexico City, 17 August 2005.

55 Marcelino Inurreta, 'Memorandum', Mexico City, 17 February 1952, AGN, DGS, VLT, vp 2/9, 11-20-52.

56 Miguel Hernández González, PP municipal organisational secretary, to VLT, Mazatlán, Sinaloa, 14 March 1952, FHLT, file 849.

candidate of the poor. His slogans consisted of attacks against Yankee domination, corrupt politicians, those responsible for starving the people and thwarting the workers' right to eat. Lombardo's language was moderate, except when he was reviled as a priest-eater. He was an atheist, but he 'would take a rifle up against a government that would suppress the freedom of thought or freedom of religion'. His audience should vote for him, because he was the best:

> I'm the best, because I know Mexico as no one can know it; its people, its problems, its historical past, its present, and I can very well interpret the wishes of the people; I'm the best because I have revolutionary ideas and because if the people elect me, I will faithfully fulfil the programme that I have presented; I'm the best because I'm not afraid of either the armed forces of our country, nor the armed forces of American imperialism. I'm the best because I have been consistent with these ideas for 30 years of my life, in accordance with the vicissitudes of each national period.[57]

Lombardo presented himself on the campaign trail as the champion of civic virtues. To make the organisation of his crusade more efficient, he relied on family ties more than on the voluble participation of citizens. Against the opposition of the PP membership in Aguascalientes and the state committee, he entrusted the campaign to Antonio Noriega, his brother-in-law. Lombardo repeatedly received complaints of Aida's husband political clumsiness, but to no avail. As a result, 'most of our grassroots activist compañeros left our ranks, deeply disturbed' by the lack of democracy in the local party.[58]

By 20 June, Lombardo had travelled 50,000 kilometres by car, 6,000 kilometres by plane and 728,000 people heard him speak in 62 public meetings.[59] He would win on 6 July 'and if not, the people would resort to a civil war if the current regime committed its usual fraud'.[60] He was unusually harsh against the outgoing president, who he had helped to catapult into office, when in the

---

57 Marcelino Inurreta, 'Memorándum', Mexico City, 17 February 1952, 11-20-5; Manuel Martínez Arellano to the DFS, Colima, 1 March 1952, 100-7-14; Marcelino Inurreta, 'Memorándum', Mexico City, 23 March 1952; Marcelino Inurreta, 'Memorándum', Mexico City, 20 April 1952, AGN, DFS, VLT, vp 2/9, 11-20-52.

58 State Leadership Committee to Enrique Ramírez y Ramírez, Aguascalientes, 21 June 1952, FHLT, file 857.

59 VLT, 'Declaraciones a José Cervantes, dirigente sinarquista', El Popular, 28 June 1952, in Obra, V/13, 1952, p. 221.

60 'Informe de Gral. de Brigada Leandro Sánchez Salazar a Miguel Alemán', Mexico City, 29 June 1952, AGN, Ramo MAV, vol. 1232, file 252/30644.

Zócalo, the capital's main square, he said that 'the current regime is a malignant oligarchy headed by an autocrat who has wielded power and violated our Constitution'; Mexico now appeared 'to be a colony intervened by the government in Washington'. Accompanied by his family, reporters, photographers and supporters, Lombardo cast his ballots 'in a burst of flash bulbs' for the Senate and Congress candidates of the People's Party.[61]

The election result was predictable: the PRI candidate Adolfo Ruiz Cortines, assisted by the CTM and the army, swept into office amid allegations of fraud. There were reports of ballot boxes being stolen and votes being tallied in the offices of the CTM. Official returns gave Ruiz Cortines 2,416,417 votes or 74.27 % of the total; Miguel Henríquez Guzmán and his organisation received 504,521 votes or 15.52 percent; Efraín González Luna of the PAN had 252,135 votes or 7.75 percent, and the People's Party and Lombardo 74,230 votes or 2.28 percent.[62] Despite its defeat, the People's Party triumphed, declared Lombardo, due to having been able to organise its forces to participate in the elections and advance a critique of the domestic and international situation.[63] He acknowledged Ruiz Cortines's victory, causing dismay among some party members who left its ranks.

4   Aftermath of Defeat

The People's Party was in tatters after the elections. In the capital, it had to close offices unable to pay rent and the PP set up its headquarters in the Workers' University or at the home of Lombardo's son-in-law Raúl Gutiérrez, activist and husband of his daughter Marcela. Humberto Lombardo Toledano had mortgaged his home to help defray the costs of his brother's campaign and lost the property. The PP had to be rebuilt with funds that it did not have.[64]

Lombardo did not win the election, but he was not defeated. He had the president and the president had him. Before travelling in February 1953, he went to the president's office to say goodbye. He was received by the secretary: 'I'm here to pay my respects, through you, to the President, to bid him farewell and to ask him for his orders because as I told him, on Friday night I'm going to Europe,

---

61   'Lombardo dice que lo de ayer fue la elección más sucia', *Excélsior*, 7 July 1952, FHLT, file 859.
62   Taylor to Eden, 'Presidential and Federal Elections', Mexico City, 30 July 1952, NA, FO371/AM1015/11.
63   VLT to WFTU, Mexico City, 18 August 1952, FHLT, file 862.
64   Interview with María Elena Lombardo, Mexico City, 1 April 2013.

to the congress of the World Federation of Trade Unions. Please tell him that I reiterate my invariable offer to collaborate in his worthy government'.⁶⁵

The collaboration that this president, and future presidents, needed from Lombardo, then and always, was the containment of popular discontent within the institutional channels. On that occasion the secretary explained that with the government having so many issues to attend to, 'I invoke your great moral authority, so that the rebellious workers would change their attitude'. The secretary was referring to the turmoil among locals of the oil workers' union that were in a dispute over job positions, wages and fulfilment of the collective bargaining agreement by the company and the threat of a strike that must be avoided. Lombardo understood and in exchange asked for help for the Workers' University and in resolving a personal problem. To cover the costs of his campaign, he mortgaged his house. To settle the mortgage he 'requested your [the president's] generosity for this assistance to be provided'.⁶⁶

Lombardo knew that the outlook for the labour movement was bleak, that white or company unions were everywhere and that his weapons – the People's Party, the UGOCM, CTAL and WFTU – were insufficient. Oratory was hollow given the deeply rooted practice of circumventing the will of the organised workers: 'the only fair way to successfully struggle is with the internal unity of the union' or the same platitude given the adverse conditions for independent organisation was that 'it be the will of the workers themselves that correct the defects or errors that have been incurred'.⁶⁷

In 1953, Lombardo resigned from the magazine *Hoy* and joined the unusually plural journal *Siempre!* From then on, the publication served Lombardo as a weekly platform from which to criticise with intelligence and good prose the country's ills as if he were a university professor, politically aseptic, without referring to his own participation in the events that led to this state of affairs. He turned an art critic and was indignant because Mexican cinema would be linked to Hollywood, which denaturalised and debilitated the country when it adopted ideas, customs and 'the way of life of the barbarians to the north'.⁶⁸

The press reported that in January 1954 Lombardo met with General Gabriel Leyva Velázquez, president of the PRI, to discuss cooperation between the

---

65 'Entrevista con el Sr. Lic. Lombardo Toledano', February 1953, AGN, Ramo Adolfo Ruiz Cortines (henceforth ARC), vol. 23, file III/1134.
66 Ibid.
67 VLT, 'Lombardo Toledano condena la labor divisionista en el Sindicato de Trabajadores de la Educación', *El Popular*, 24 September 1953, in *Obra*, V/16, 1953, p. 152.
68 VLT, 'Falso indigenismo', *Siempre!*, 13 July 1955, in *Obra*, V/20, 1955, p. 326; Krauze 1997b, p. 195.

two parties. The People's Party wanted to bank on the PRI's support, because Lombardo was afraid that the PP could not meet the membership requirements of the new electoral law. As a result of the growth in the population and women being granted the right to vote in 1953, the new electoral law now required not 30,000 but 75,000 members nationwide and 2,500 members in at least two-thirds of the states for the party to participate in the upcoming elections. The People's Party, based on the votes it received in the previous election, did not meet the minimum threshold, although it expected to reach the necessary number with the anticipated support from women.[69] General Leyva admitted that Lombardo had offered a coalition between the two parties, but the PRI rejected the proposal, suspecting a communist ploy of a united front.

The 1955 midterm elections would test the new electoral law. It was necessary to standardise the criteria for candidates for federal congressional deputies. By then Revueltas had decided to leave the PP, because it had not become a true party of the working class.[70] The party's programme required that the candidates be chosen in the localities, assemblies and municipal committees; however, the lists of candidates were centrally drawn up for the entire country 'so that the PP candidates in Sonora are known in Veracruz, those in Jalisco in the Federal District and vice versa, and so on throughout the country', based on the criteria that the congressional deputies did not represent the voters of their district or state, but rather that a deputy 'is a representative of the people as a whole'.[71] While the party thought it had Sonora guaranteed with Jacinto López as candidate for governor, from Guerrero the delegate to the National Council, Macrina Rabadán, reported on the chaotic situation and local authorities having jailed PP members to preclude their campaigning in the state; and candidates selected for congressional deputies in Mexico City, going door-to-door in the poor neighbourhoods, were mercilessly persecuted by the authorities.[72]

In the 3 July elections, the party was the target of the usual fraud. In Sonora and Nayarit, 'people abstained from voting in protest, so PRI members filled the ballot boxes as they wished'. In Guerrero, highways in poor condition as

---

69   VLT, 'Informe al Consejo Nacional del PP', Mexico City, 13 March 1954, in *Obra*, V/17, 1954, p. 87.
70   Ruiz Abreu 1992, p. 281.
71   VLT, 'A propósito de la planilla única de los candidatos del Partido Popular', April 1955, in *Obra*, V/20, 1955, pp. 181–2.
72   'Memorandum', DFS, Mexico City, 7 and 11 April 1955, AGN, ARC, vol. 860, file 544.61/7; VLT, 'Informe ante el Noveno Consejo Nacional del PP', 5 April 1955, in *Obra*, V/20, 1955, p. 145.

a result of heavy rain prevented people from voting in several villages.[73] The party charged fraud, but Adriana Lombardo Otero, president of the People's Party in the capital and heiress to the thought and work of her father, was content. 'Our party has fulfilled a new stage of its rich existence ... Compañeros, we have ahead of us a whole historical stage to consolidate'.[74] But the candidates, who were victims of the electoral fraud and went to the Chamber of Deputies to defend their cases, were expelled from the party, since in response to the fraud it was necessary to maintain decorum and not go begging for elected posts.[75] Anticipating the eruption of voter anger, Lombardo declared that 'if it were not for the existence of the People's Party, [the people] would have taken up arms a long time ago',[76] and a day later insisted that 'I firmly believe that the fraud will not reduce enthusiasm for respecting the vote'.[77]

But in Guerrero and Morelos there were incidents in which the population took up arms. So that the anger of defrauded voters would not spread to other states, the party and Lombardo himself turned into a barrier to contain the popular indignation, using the bogeyman of a US imperialist intervention with global consequences and the reaction of the clergy, which weighed more than the gangster-style tactics of the PRI. It was necessary to protect national sovereignty, the violation of which affected the international balance of forces that cost so much blood to establish during the last war. With each fraudulent election, the party and the UGOCM emerged weakened. In Puebla, the PP languished and in Michoacán it suffered desertions.[78] But Lombardo's response was to impose a new policy of pacts and alliances on the party, because to do otherwise, 'is pure childishness. It means having the conception that only the revolutionaries should join together, and that once they have come together, they must go it alone, so that they alone, confident in their exclusive forces,

---

73 Leandro Castillo Venegas to the Interior Ministry, 'Se informa en relación con el PP', Mexico City, 11 July 1955, AGN, ARC, vol. 1103, file 606.3/18.
74 Leandro Castillo Venegas, Mexico City, 7 July 1955 and 15 August 1955, AGN, DFS, PPS/1, 11-2-55.
75 VLT, 'Un frente nacional para evitar la guerra civil', *El Popular*, 15 August 1955; VLT, 'Trejo Aguilar expulsado de su partido por traidor', *El Popular*, 10 September 1955, in *Obra*, V/21, 1955, p. 113.
76 VLT, 'Reunión del Comité Central del PP sobre los resultados electorales del 3 de julio 1955', Mexico City, 7 July 1955, in *Obra*, V/20, 1955, p. 319.
77 VLT, 'Presión del monopolio político', *El Popular*, 4 July 1955, in *Obra*, V/20, 1955, p. 296.
78 Roberto Gutiérrez Armas to VLT, Uruapan, Michoacán, 29 August 1955, FHLT, file 988; VLT to Roberto Chávez and Salvador Lemus, Mexico City, 15 September 1955, FHLT, file 990.

propose carrying out the historical objectives of the working class'.⁷⁹ And to convince his audience of the gravity of the situation that Mexico faced, he boosted the tone of his invectives: 'The time has come, compañeros of the People's Party, to initiate' a holy war *'that must conclude with our victory, the victory of the people, to safeguard the independence of the Mexican nation against foreign imperialism'*, the editor of the speech and daughter of Lombardo Toledano underlined, imbued with the ideological fervour of her father.⁸⁰ From this flowed the urgent need to create a *'patriotic front'*, emphasised Marcela Lombardo, which was superior to *'national unity'*.⁸¹ 'The drums and bugles of the' holy war 'for national independence have sounded'! was Lombardo's cry, which received prolonged applause and cheers.⁸²

However, instead of unifying the party, its political line and the way it was run aroused intrigues and antagonisms. The party split into two factions and opposition against its president grew also as a result of the increase of family members' prominence in positions of leadership.⁸³ But Lombardo had no time to dwell on matters that he considered secondary. He had to prepare for the next elections. The solution to the fraud committed against the party was proportional representation and permanent and tamper-proof voter registration rolls.⁸⁴ Lombardo never considered the possibility that the low level of public participation in decision-making over issues that concerned citizens' lives was at the root of the lack of democracy. No matter how close he was to the workers, he kept them at arm's length. He was sincere when he said that his whole life was dedicated to 'serve the working class … and the great rural masses of our country and the other nations of the world'.⁸⁵ What he said and did was a reflection of his concept of ends and means. It was an aristocratic way of understanding left-wing political leadership.

79 VLT, 'Discurso del 21 de noviembre en la Segunda Asamblea Nacional del PP. Informe Político', Mexico City, 20–24 November 1955, in *Obra*, V/22, 1955, pp. 39–40, pp. 57–8; VLT, 'Intervención del 22 de noviembre 1955', in *Obra*, V/22, 1955, p. 125, and p. 139.
80 VLT, 'Discurso del 21 de noviembre en la Segunda Asamblea Nacional del PP. Informe Político', Mexico City, 20–24 November, 1955, in *Obra*, V/22, 1955, p. 9.
81 VLT, 'Discurso del 21 de noviembre en la Segunda Asamblea Nacional del PP. Informe Político', Mexico City, 20–24 November, 1955, in *Obra*, V/22, 1955, p. 17.
82 VLT, 'Discurso del 21 de noviembre en la Segunda Asamblea Nacional del PP. Informe Político', Mexico City, 20–24 November, 1955, in *Obra*, V/22, 1955, p. 7.
83 Vidal Díaz Muñoz to VLT, Mexico City, 3 November 1956; Vidal Díaz Muñoz to VLT, Mexico City, 5 December 1956, FHLT, file 1028; VLT to Alfredo Vázquez Lara, Mexico City, 4 March 1957, FHLT, file 1035.
84 Interview with VLT in *El Universal*, 6 March 1957, FHLT, file 1035.
85 VLT to Constantino Ruiz, Mexico City, 23 April 1957, FHLT, file 1037.

5 The Succession

'I just returned from the home of General Lázaro Cárdenas', Lombardo wrote at midnight on 13 June 1956, so that he was not to forget the main ideas of the conversation. A while back the two had agreed to discuss the programme and the right person for the future government and president. On the one side there was the right-wing clergy and Yankee imperialism, and on the other the popular discontent caused by the high cost of living 'that the government cannot stop because of its erroneous economic policy', the imposition of state governments, of congressional deputies and mayors 'in the most brazen manner'. And with the government not providing an outlet for this dissatisfaction, the accumulated anger 'could violently explode and be difficult to channel'. The PRI was definitively discredited. Lombardo proposed to the general that Portes Gil, Adalberto Tejeda and José Guadalupe Zuno, from the old guard of revolutionaries, some of them military officials or industrialists, could be possible allies with who to propose a new programme for the next government.[86]

Lázaro Cárdenas agreed with Lombardo's diagnosis but not with his proposal: 'The ex-presidents may not be in accord with many of the things that are happening, but all of them have large government-related business or which the government can hurt if it wanted. They express their disapproval, but that's as far as it goes'. In addition, some military officials were moved by personal ambitions and if General Cárdenas 'were to talk to them, with those who aspire to power, half an hour later the President would know about it'.[87] Lombardo insisted that there were honest men and if Cárdenas led them together with 'the proven revolutionary social and political organisations', the people would be inspired and the new programme would prevail.

The general remained sceptical. Tejeda, for example, went to see him on the occasion of the previous elections, accompanied by the interim president of the People's Party whose candidate was Lombardo, 'to ask me to accept Alemán's re-election'. Lombardo insisted: 'And the people, then, the working class, the campesinos'? The workers were indifferent or resigned to the country's situation, 'muzzled and controlled' they were inactive, replied Cárdenas.

In a last ditch effort to convince him to lead a movement in opposition to the government's enemies, Lombardo reminded Cárdenas of June 1935 as an example from the past which, simplifying history, showed that between the two

---

86   VLT, 'Cárdenas y el frente patriótico', Mexico City, 13 June 1956, FHLT, file 1021.
87   Ibid.

they were able to mobilise the population, which 'changed the situation in Mexico'. The general, aware of the power that he had and the fear that his political action sparked, concluded that it should be Lombardo and the PP that mobilise the working class. 'The only voice that remains is yours. The only struggle that exists is that of the People's Party. That's sufficient'.[88] But this time it was Lombardo who was sceptical. He did not believe in the strength of the organisation he led and feared that Mexico's weakness could lead to making it an appendage of the United States.[89] Did Lombardo seek the general to take the front line position, with emissaries from the past who Lombardo did not trust, in the hope to be followed by the mass of the people who he failed to recruit, lead it into an undefined insurrection and all together bear the responsibility for the unforeseen consequences? This proposition was uncharacteristic of Lombardo's position taken in public of not rocking the boat until the country had the strength to withstand the enemies' power.

Even though President Adolfo Ruiz Cortines was different from his predecessor, simple, honest, a good administrator, opposed to corruption and stood out as a patriot who revered the revolution,[90] Lombardo was not assuaged from his concern. In order to mobilise his followers he resorted to his oratorical skills to paint a groin picture to demonstrate that the danger from outside Mexico was gnawing at it from the inside as well. The 'federal republican system' had ceased to exist and the past, as reflected in 'the struggles of the nineteenth century undertaken by the great liberal current responsible for the autonomy of the states',[91] was no more. Instead of a constitutional and democratic state, Mexico became 'a police state'.[92] Lombardo was referring to the 1951 FBI seizure of Gus Hall, carried out with the help of the Mexican police. Hall was a worker, veteran US communist leader, deported to the United States, a country whose goal was to pit the capitalist world 'against the socialist world to destroy it' and forever preserve the capitalist system. But the laws governing society would prevent it.[93]

The PP was weak as an electoral instrument and the UGOCM had slipped out of Lombardo's hands by becoming a tool of Jacinto López to defend agrarian

---

88   Ibid.
89   Ibid.
90   Krauze 1997b, pp. 182–8.
91   VLT, 'Informe de la Dirección Nacional al Comité Nacional del PP, reunido del 14 al 17 de enero 1957', in *Obra*, V/25, 1957, p. 10; 'Llamamiento del PP a los mexicanos demócratas y progresistas', *El Popular*, 29 March 1957, in *Obra*, V/25, 1957, p. 106.
92   VLT, 'Nuestro estado policiaco', *Siempre!*, no. 208, 29 June 1957 in *Obra*, V/26, 1957, p. 13.
93   VLT, 'La sucesión presidencial', *Siempre!*, no. 211, 10 July 1957, in *Obra*, V/26, 1957, p. 25.

and land rights, denouncing the large estates and invading them if necessary.[94] For all of the above factors, it was essential to support the PRI and the government's candidate to 'rectify errors, to take advantage of experiences, to unite all patriots, to decide to fight for the cause of an independent and prosperous Mexico'.[95] The People's Party adopted Adolfo López Mateos, the Minister of Labour, as its candidate for president against the onslaught of Alemanistas, the PAN, the clergy and imperialism. To align the voters behind that option, the PP state committees presented their proposed candidates for senators and congressional deputies 'to the National Bureau for it to adopt a final decision'.[96] This policy directive worked in some villages such as Teziutlán where 'the leaf of a tree cannot move without the agreement of the leadership of the People's Party',[97] but not in Navojoa, Sonora: 'We were quite surprised that the National Assembly does not take into consideration the situation prevailing in each region in the country, and the attitude adopted in relation to the seat for the third district is having a huge negative effect. We believe that the national leadership should reconsider the fact that in this region it would be socially useful if the post were occupied by one of our own'.[98]

The electoral fraud in Sonora was flagrant. 'The army participated in the main population centres as the executor of orders from the politicians to ensure the imposition' in alliance with the governor. In one polling station tempers flared and a soldier shot a member of the People's Party. The people got angry, grabbed the soldier, disarmed him, tied him up and one of them stabbed him. When General Malaquías Medina Vallarta, commander of the Eighteenth Cavalry Regiment, saw the dead villager and the soldier who was stabbed hovering between life and death, he ordered the troops to withdraw 'even though the governor might be angry'.[99] Several cities seethed with rage and indignation.[100] Jacinto López and other UGOCM leaders who had been imprisoned because the authorities were tired of their insistence on the implementation of agrarian reform, for denouncing the establishment of new large land estates

---

94 Grijalba Davila 2012, pp. 113–21.
95 VLT, 'La sucesión presidencial 1958. El futuro de México', in *Obra*, V/26, 1957, pp. 75–7.
96 VLT 'A los comités estatales', Mexico City, 28 February 1958, FHLT, file 1057.
97 Fidel Campos to VLT, Teziutlán, Puebla, September 1958, in *Obra*, V/28, 1958, p. 114.
98 Navojoa Municipal Committee to VLT, Navojoa, Sonora, 1 September 1958, FHLT, file 1071.
99 Francisco Figueroa Mendoza and Juan de Dios Martínez Domínguez to VLT, Hermosillo, 8 July 1958, FHLT, file 1066.
100 Lázaro Rubio Félix to VLT, Ciudad Obregón, 12 July 1958, FHLT, file 1066.

and the restoration of the old ones remained in jail, even though the Cananea latifundio for which they had been fighting had been expropriated that same year.[101]

In vain, Lombardo tried to explain that the government did not recognise the victory of the party's candidates because it needed to 'assure the government of the United States that there are no left-wing sectors in Mexico', so that it would not fear for the safety of American interests, and to 'appease the right-wing clergy', even at the cost of violating the constitution. Once again he imposed the principle of not accepting 'crumbs to appease us'.[102]

But Macrina Rabadán was elected congressional deputy for the second district of Iguala in Guerrero and wanted to celebrate her victory at the Restaurante Chapultepec. She was accompanied by the anthropologist Eulalia Guzmán, the poet Renato Leduc, Alejandro Carrillo, Enrique Ramírez y Ramírez, railroad workers' leader Demetrio Vallejo, and artists Alberto Beltrán and David Alfaro Siqueiros, among others, all opposed to Lombardo. Attending the sumptuous meal were communists, Polytechnic students, employees from the social security system and Mexico City government, and leaders from the railroad and electrical workers' unions, with a congratulatory telegram to the successful candidate received from General Heriberto Jara.[103] When Lombardo found out that Rabadán had accepted the deputy seat, he expelled her from the party for violating discipline in accordance with the guidelines issued before the election and because she agreed to be the candidate of the People's Party and of the Civic Front of the People, a faction of the PRI in Guerrero. Rabadán's belonging to a faction of the PP in opposition to Lombardo, and to a minority current of the PRI in Guerrero, carried more weight than her being elected federal congressional deputy by popular vote.[104]

Despite the fraud committed in the July 1958 elections, which it denounced, the PP did not step back from its political line in favour of a patriotic front with the PRI, since it felt it was necessary to contribute to the stability of the government in response to possible threats from imperialism. Without saying so, this

---

101 'Manifiesto de la UGOCM', Mexico City, 7 August 1958, FHLT, file 1069; Lázaro Peña to the CTAL, Prague, 4 September 1958, FHLT, file 1071.
102 'Informe de la Dirección Nacional del PP al Consejo Nacional', Mexico City, 28–30 July 1958, AGN, DFS, PPS/II, 11-2-58.
103 Gilberto Suárez Torres, assistant director of the DFS, functioning as director, Mexico City, 19 September 1958, AGN, DFS, PPS/II, 11-2-58.
104 VLT, 'Por traición y desobediencia a los acuerdos de su Consejo Nacional el Partido Popular expulsa a dos elementos', El Popular, 20 September 1958, in Obra, V/28, 1958, pp. 109–12; Román Román 2003, pp. 95–103.

was considered the price that Mexico, a 'semi-colonial' country, had to pay to contribute to the strengthening of the socialist camp and the Soviet Union.

6   The Cold Peace

Mexico enjoyed remarkable growth. Not only did the population jump from 20 million in 1940 to 36 million in 1960, with an annual increase in the birth rate of 3.3 percent, but the gross national product grew between 1940 and 1960 at the equivalent of a 6.4% annual increase. Manufacturing output increased as did industrial production. The growth of the middle class was expressed in opportunities for mobility and well-being. This economic progress was coupled with an apparent political stability. But a series of problems such as the monopolisation of political power, fraudulent elections, intolerance of union democracy, land distribution proceeding at a snail's pace, the growth or concealment of large landed estates and disparities in social inequality caused by economic growth but unequal distribution, provided fertile ground for opposition to the government.[105]

In the middle of Adolfo López Mateos's presidential election campaign, the railroad workers demanded an increase in their dwindling wages. The negotiations between the salary commission and the union leadership resulted in the recommendation that wages be increased to 350 pesos a month. The union's general secretary Samuel Ortega reduced the figure to 200 pesos and the company's position was not to resolve the issue until after the July elections. In response, rank-and-file leader Demetrio Vallejo, who had been part of the above-mentioned salary commission, proposed staggered work stoppages as a protest measure. The government relented and increased the wage to 215 pesos. But the railroad workers were not satisfied. They wanted the proposed increase to 350 pesos, the restoration of union democracy violated since 1948 with the imposition of charro leaders, and Vallejo as their general secretary.[106] The professors from the teachers' colleges and telegraph employees called solidarity strikes with the railroad workers. The People's Party hailed the developments as 'an encouraging sign that these movements have emerged, even if sometimes they have not had the savvy leadership they deserved',[107] the reference being to the PP leadership.

---

105   Bethell (ed.) 1991, pp. 85–111; Loaeza 1988, pp. 119–25; Vaughan 2015, pp. 1–28.
106   Krauze 1997b, pp. 228–30; Águila 2014, chapter 8.
107   'Informe de la Dirección Nacional del PP al Consejo Nacional', Mexico City, 28–30 July 1958, AGN, DFS, PPS/II, 11-2-58; O.A. Bryer, 'Mexican Railwaymen's Union', Mexico City, 12 September 1958, NA, FO371/AM2181/8.

Vallejo, after being elected secretary general of the railroad workers' union, travelled the country, local by local, spreading a message and a programme. Workers' struggles were not won by the leaders but by workers' unity, not tied to politics or elections. He called for a reduction in union dues, the creation of cooperatives that would serve the workers, decreasing the salaries of union leaders, the right of retirees to vote in union elections, improved working conditions through a new collective bargaining agreement, thinning the company bureaucracy, increasing the rates charged for shipping minerals and fighting the high cost of living. Along the way, Vallejo uncovered countless violations of labour standards and supported requests from railroad workers to address the problems that were never attended to by the company.[108]

'What a mistake'! exclaimed General Cárdenas when he learned of the company management's malicious intention to provoke a strike if the railroad workers did not conduct their threatened work stoppages. With this manoeuvre, the company sought to replace the union leadership with one of its liking. The railroad workers' union called a strike on 27 February 1958 and the Federal Conciliation and Arbitration Board declared it illegal. In March, on the Wednesday of Holy Week, the workers again declared a strike, the labour authorities rejected the call and the union split under the weight of so many pressures. The government cracked down on the railroad workers and imprisoned Vallejo.[109]

Lombardo knew that the problem of worker discontent was charrismo, the strong-arm and anti-democratic labour bureaucracy, but he dissociated it from the regime that had generated, maintained and reaffirmed it in the railroad conflict. He judged the dispute not on the correctness of the demands raised by the workers, whose union independence was violated by the labour authorities when they refused to recognise the democratically elected leaders, but rather by the destabilising effect the conflict could have on the country.[110] The railroad workers' strike, he asserted, 'seriously endangered the democratic life of the nation' and compromised 'Mexico's international relations'. The rail conflict 'was taken advantage of by the most pernicious foreign imperialist and reactionary domestic forces to advance their plans to infiltrate the country's public life'.[111]

---

108 Águila 2014, chapter 8; Águila and Bortz 2014, p. 27.
109 LC, 25 February 1959, Guadalajara, in Cárdenas 1986b, p. 94; Agustín 2007, pp. 173–8.
110 'Acusación dolosa del Licenciado Lombardo', *El Rielero*, organ of the National Railroad Workers Council, year 1, no. 2 (6 December 1960).
111 'Declaraciones del PP ante el conflicto obrero patronal planteado por la huelga de los trabajadores ferrocarrileros', Mexico City, 2 April 1959, FHLT, file 1091; 'Secretariado de la CTAL a López Mateos', Mexico City, 30 October 1959, FHLT, file 1104; Demetrio Vallejo, Lecum-

Lombardo was sensitive to social movements that emerged as a result of years of unfulfilled demands and workers' anger over the persistent violation of their rights, but he chided them for not having made 'a serious study characterising Mexico's economic, social, and political situation or the origin and development of our bourgeois-democratic revolution'.[112] What he meant by this was that the railroad workers' movement did not act in accordance with the directives of the People's Party. The national front, which the party promoted, was unthinkable without 'the social class representing state capitalism' in power, which was not an instrument of imperialism.[113]

Yet neither Lombardo nor the government were prepared for the awakening of civil society that took place in the late 1950s after years of unfulfilled demands and violation of its rights. In addition to the railroad workers, students, many of them party members, took to the streets to protest the rising price of transportation. The army was sent in against them and occupied the installations of the National Polytechnic Institute. The government raided the headquarters of the Communist Party, destroyed its furniture and office equipment and police from the Mexico City government took its files to an unknown destination.[114] Lombardo did not like it that the movements were labelled with the epithet of communist, because it wrongly attracted the authorities' attention toward himself and the People's Party, and unthinkingly toward the Soviet Union. Intellectuals and artists lined up on the side of the workers' movement. Carlos Pellicer, Octavio Paz, Alvaro Carrillo Gil, Ali Chumacero, Abel Quesada, Carlos Fuentes, Jaime García Terrés, Fernando Benítez, Guillermo Haro, Emilio Uranga, Ricardo Martínez, Juan Soriano and Pedro Coronel urged the government 'to listen to the people'.[115] But the government turned a deaf ear.

Since the mid-1950s, a sector of teachers belonging to the National Teachers Union demanded higher wages and a change in the corrupt leadership of the organisation. Both the communists as well as the PP had members among the teachers and influenced that their trade union and economic demands

---

berri Prison, Letter to *Política*, 1 July 1960, year 1, no. 5, p. 40; Alonso 1983, pp. 156–9; Carr 1992, pp. 216–19; Campa 1985, pp. 239–51; Alegre 2013, pp. 102–75.

112   VLT, 'Informe al comité central del PP', Mexico City, 29 April 1960, in *Obra*, VI/2, 1960, pp. 40–1.

113   VLT, 'Informe al comité central del PP', Mexico City, 29 April 1960, in Obra, VI/2, 1960, p. 42.

114   VLT, 'Declaraciones de la Dirección Nacional del PP sobre la lucha de los estudiantes y los recientes movimientos de protesta popular', Mexico City, 26 August 1958, in *Obra*, V/28, 1958, pp. 87–8. These might be the documents that are housed in the Butler Library at Columbia University in New York; Agustín 2007, p. 161; Carr 1992, p. 201; Pensado 2013, pp. 86–144.

115   'Al pueblo y al gobierno', *Excélsior*, 30 August 1958, FHLT, file 1071.

were channelled through institutions recognised by the authorities. But when in 1958, local 9 of the union in the capital, headed by the popular leader Othón Salazar, founder of the Revolutionary Teachers' Movement, urged the government to 'respect their desire to choose their authentic leaders',[116] its demand was ignored and the teachers moved beyond the institutional channels.

María de Jesús Otero, a teacher and sister-in-law of Lombardo, witnessed the repression against teachers in the capital at the beginning of September, after the government refused to recognise the election of Othón Salazar as the leader of the Mexico City local of the union. The leading officer of the Interior Ministry, Gustavo Díaz Ordaz, promised the teachers that the conflict between the national committee of the union and its Mexico City local would be resolved with a new vote recount on 12 September. In return, he asked the teachers to call off the demonstration for which they had already been mobilised. They replied that this was impossible, but that the demonstration would serve to provide the teachers with the information on the resolution of the conflict. At 11pm Díaz Ordaz informed the teachers that he did not receive approval for such a solution, without providing further details. The teachers took to the streets on Saturday.[117]

A reporter from the daily *Novedades* followed the attack on the protesters minute by minute. The riot police attacked the teachers who desperately implored Captain Dehesa, who was in command: 'for the love of God, don't shoot'. The Red and Green Cross gathered up the wounded and a 16-year-old boy who was shot in the forehead. The police herded passers-by who had nothing to do with the protests and took them away along with the teachers who had regrouped in the side streets. The riot police continued dispersing the crowds with tear gas. Amid the wailing sirens of ambulances, motorcycles and patrol cars, in an atmosphere of apprehension, General Miguel Molinar ordered 'a stronger hand' from the police. Meanwhile, Dehesa prevented journalists from approaching the scene of the incidents or the doors of the Green Cross to gather information. Students who were camped out at the Cine Princesa movie theatre were evicted by the riot police.[118] Othón Salazar and Encarnación Pérez from the teachers' movement and Salvador Robles Quintero from the National Polytechnic Institute were arrested.

---

116 'Declaraciones del PP sobre la crisis del magisterio', Mexico City, 2 September 1958, FHLT, file 1071.

117 María de Jesús Otero to ARC, Mexico City, 10 September 1958, FHLT, file 1071; Hodges and Gandy 2002, pp. 66–9.

118 Adrián Fernández de Mendoza, 'Por el amor de Dios no dispare usted', *Novedades*, Mexico City, 7 September 1958, FHLT, file 1071; Pensado 2013, pp. 141–3.

The violence against the workers, against the students and against the teachers was unacceptable from the human and political point of view. The use of force worsened the social climate without resolving anything. Lombardo was clear that workers were justified in their demands in relation to their salaries and respect for their elected leaders; that landless peasants were engaged in a struggle demanding that their already recognised legal status become a reality; that the suspension of individual guarantees by the Interior Ministry usurped the powers of Congress, which was used by the rural bosses known as caciques 'to retaliate against the toiling masses and even against their political opponents'. It could be said that 'our country is in a state of emergency, disregarding the constitutional norms'.[119] And yet Lombardo had to defend the state. He was aware of the potential intervention by the US government when its interests were threatened and when it labelled the danger with the epithet of radicalism, communism and the weakness of the authorities.[120] The overthrow of the democratic government of Guatemala in June 1954 was still fresh in his memory.

119 'El PP, el PCM y el POC se dirigen al pueblo y a la nación', Mexico City, 15 October 1958, FHLT, file 1074.
120 VLT to Lázaro Peña, Mexico City, 21 October 1958, FHLT, file 1074.

CHAPTER 14

Mission Completed

At the dawn of 1949 in Paris, the World Federation of Trade Unions named Lombardo Toledano as its representative to the United Nations Economic and Social Council. When Bernardo Cobos, the CTM international relations secretary, learned of the appointment, he went to the US embassy to ask Consul Dickinson 'if the American government couldn't do anything to prevent his acceptance in that body'.[1] It could not. Dickinson would have wanted Lombardo to be denied entry to the United States, but although Lombardo lost his diplomatic passport when he was replaced by Bernardo Ibáñez in the ILO labour council, he recovered it with the new appointment. And with that distinction, the CTAL gave the impression that it had been strengthened as a solid bridge between the world and the Latin American confederation.

1   Anti-communist Liberalism

The AFL believed itself to be the archetype of democracy and the extension of the proverbial American way of life. Its role was not only to safeguard the interests of trade unionists, but to fight for good against evil and for the United States to occupy a prominent place in the world. Romualdi, its delegate for Latin America, had the task of promoting the rights of workers to organise, achieve better living standards, negotiate collectively and intervene so that unions would become independent of the state. All of this was based on the understanding that increasing the standard of living coupled with a rise in purchasing power of Latin American workers broadened the market for US goods and helped to protect jobs in Latin America and the United States.[2]

Dictatorships hindered such efforts. They violated the rights of association and the freedom to organise trade unions or to organise them independently of the state in countries such as Peru, Venezuela, the Dominican Republic,

---

[1] Dwight Dickinson, 'Lombardo Toledano as WFTU representative in ECOSOC; CTM greatly disturbed', Mexico City, 4 March 1949, NARA, RG 59, file 812.5043/3–449. A version of this chapter, entitled 'Historia, política e ideología fundidas en la vida de Vicente Lombardo Toledano', was published in *Desacatos*, no. 50, (January–April 2016), pp. 70–87.

[2] Van Goethem 2013, p. 19; Dustin Walcher, 'Reforming Latin American Labour: The AFL-CIO and Latin American Cold War', in Van Goethem 2013, pp. 123–35.

Nicaragua and Argentina. With limited resources to confront them, as a palliative the AFL helped labour leaders who were victims of dictators negotiate their freedom or go into exile. Another obstacle to extending American liberalism southward was communism, which strengthened authoritarianism. Between the two, they destroyed democratic unions. The climate of violence and terror provoked the desire for revenge and favoured the emergence of conspiratorial groups that the communists took advantage of for their own purposes. Under these conditions, Romualdi lamented, it was difficult to win the hearts and minds of the millions of workers who lived under the yoke of the ruthless military dictatorships, unless the AFL was able to demonstrate to them, in words and deeds, that it was the workers, and not their oppressors, who the American labour movement regarded as its true friends and allies.[3] Latin America was vital for the United States:

> with its 150 million people, and the store of raw materials, oil, minerals and other valuable and essential products, is slated to play an important role in the struggle we are now facing for the survival of Christian civilisation. Geographically, Latin America is out backyard, indispensable for the protection of our lines of communication and for our territorial security. We must endeavour therefore to have Latin Americans on our side as our enthusiastic partners. But the wrong way to obtain this objective would be to ignore the aspirations of the oppressed people and to be satisfied instead with superficial friendships of their dictators.[4]

But the US government did not follow the path suggested by Romualdi nor did he adhere to the principles he proclaimed. At the ILO meeting in Montevideo in April 1949, US government delegates pressured him to refrain from supporting a resolution condemning the dictatorships and only accepting an investigation into the events in Peru and Venezuela.[5]

In September, during the meeting of the Inter-American Confederation of Workers (CIT) in Havana, Romualdi again heard criticism from labour delegates from countries ruled by dictatorships against the United States for its excessive friendship with tyrannical regimes: 'I was impressed by the applause that

---

3 Romualdi, 'Report of Proceedings of the 68th Convention of the AFL', St. Paul, Minnesota, 3–10 October 1949, The Law Reporter Printing Company, Washington, D.C., 1949, p. 371.
4 Romualdi in 'Report of Proceedings of the 69th Convention of the AFL', Houston, Texas, 18–23 September 1950, The Law Reporter Printing Company, Washington, D.C., 1950, p. 467 and p. 468.
5 Romualdi 1967, pp. 92–122.

was received by the declaration of Augusto Malavé Villalba from Venezuela who, over and over again, reiterated that in case of a war between Russia and the United States, the workers of Latin America would be on the side of those who guarantee them social justice and an end to feudal military dictatorships'.[6]

The delegates also condemned racial and wage discrimination in the Panama Canal Zone, which Romualdi admitted was unacceptable and harmful for Washington's hemispheric policy and democratic trade unionism. But the funds from the north flowed south indiscriminately and by October 1949 the AFL had contributed 75,000 dollars to keep the CIT alive, while the Latin Americans supported it with the paltry sum of 5,000 dollars.[7]

At the meeting of the Inter-American Association for Democracy and Freedom, held in Havana in May 1950 at the initiative of the AFL, probably to attract the unions that had left the CTAL, a resolution was approved reiterating the demand to deny economic, financial and military aid to governments that suppressed trade union rights, because they would use the resources to repress the democratic opposition and not to defend hemispheric security.[8] One resolution declared that a government's violation of human rights threatened continental solidarity, while another reaffirmed opposition to the Francisco Franco regime and to providing assistance to any fascist government. None of this would change the AFL's institutional architecture, which linked the vigour of democratic forces and the increase in the standard of living of the people in Latin America to their struggle against communism and worldwide struggle against totalitarian aggression.[9]

---

6   Romualdi to Oldenbroek, Washington, D.C., 20 April 1950 in IISH; 'Segundo Congreso Continental de la Confederación Interamericana de Trabajadores (CIT), efectuado en La Habana La Habana (Cuba) bajo los auspicios de la Confederación de Trabajadores de Cuba (CTC) los días 7, 8, 9, 10 y 11 de septiembre de 1949, publicado por la Confederación de Trabajadores de Cuba', pamphlet, in IISH.
7   Mr Fishburn, 'Latin American Labor', Washington, D.C., 21 October 1949, NARA, RG 59, file 810.5043/10–2149.
8   'Report of the American Federation of Labor Delegation to the Inter-American Conference for Democracy and Freedom', George P. Delaney, Charles Zimmerman, Serafino Romualdi, Washington, D.C., The George Meany, International Affairs Department, Jay Lovestone files, 1939–1974, box 43.
9   Latin America, 'Report of proceedings of the 70th convention of AFL', San Francisco, California, 17–25 September 1951, The Law Reporter Printing Company, Washington, D.C., p. 71.

2 Liberal Internationalism

At the end of November 1949, delegates from north and south, east and west met in London, on the other side of the Thames River opposite Westminster Abbey for the founding congress of the International Confederation of Free Trade Unions (ICFTU). It was not enough to contest the World Federation of Trade Unions (WFTU), established in the same place in 1945, but to create an opposite pole of attraction. The ICFTU was to expand liberal democracy throughout the world with institutions that promote values such as the respect for representative democracy and the law, protect individual rights and socio-economic progress in the free market environment that best ensured economic growth, interdependence among nations and therefore peace. Regional integration projects were one of its core goals to achieve global cooperation.[10]

The AFL, which had opposed the creation of the WFTU, promoted the new confederation, which was enthusiastically received by the other labour organisations. In attendance were 261 delegates from 53 countries representing 63 unions and about 48 million workers from all continents, with the aim of creating a confederation that would not submit to any kind of oppression, referring to communist rule in Eastern Europe. While the WFTU was committed to the fight against fascism, the ICFTU declared its opposition to all forms of totalitarianism: communist, fascist, Falange, corporate or militaristic, and against forced labour.

The Latin American delegates rejected the AFL's call for an aggressive struggle against communism, since it was an argument used to justify the attacks on the working class and secondary to the existence of military dictatorships. Walter Reuther, the young leader who represented the American CIO, offered a way out of the AFL's negative anti-communism, arguing that it was necessary to fight both the right and the left, Wall Street and communism, Standard Oil and Stalin. The competition between the two systems would be determined by the success of the one that best served the workers' economic and social interests. The Latin American organisations succeeded in getting a resolution passed that condemned the 'totalitarian' conditions in Peru, Venezuela, the Dominican Republic, Nicaragua and Argentina. Mexico was not represented. Belgian labour leader Jacobus Oldenbroek was appointed general secretary and it was decided to make Brussels the headquarters of the ICFTU. The Chilean delegate Bernardo Ibáñez was elected as one of the vice presidents and Cuban labour

---

10   Rodríguez García 2010, pp. 29–33 and pp. 289–92.

leader Francisco Aguirre was designated to be part of the committee on emerging issues to deal with topics that could not wait until the following meeting of the ICFTU executive board.[11]

The ICFTU was the result of its member organisations' adherence to liberal capitalism, but it was born in the climate of the cold war, of dictatorships and the fight against them. Its hallmark was support for the regional autonomy of the trade unions, regardless of their origin. However, the Latin American leaders were wary of the Europeans, the Europeans were opposed to decolonisation, the Americans promoted a rabid anti-communism and underestimated the ability of the Latin Americans to act independently, all of which hindered ICFTU's actions. At the same time, the Europeans did not grasp the complexity of Latin American reality, the region's dependence, nationalist aspirations and their need and desire to collaborate with the Americans. The North Americans, meanwhile, preferred to keep the European social democrats at a considerable distance from the region.[12]

The non-communist or anti-communist Latin American trade unionists saw advantages in the alliance with the North Americans, who offered them financial and technical assistance, and together with Romualdi, worked to transform the Inter-American Confederation of Workers (CIT) into a regional organisation of the ICFTU.[13] The labour attachés of the US and British embassies in Mexico volunteered to assist in the organisation of the event.[14]

The ICFTU issued the call for the conference slated for January 1951 in Mexico City. From Europe, J.H. Oldenbroek and Sir J.H. Vincent Tewson came in advance to ensure the CTM's inclusion as a member of the ICFTU and Mexico as the headquarters of the Inter-American Regional Organisation of Workers (known by its Spanish language acronym, ORIT). The decision to select Mexico was an attempt at a show of force vis-à-vis the CTAL. The unions under communist influence and those controlled by nondemocratic governments such Argentina, Peru, Venezuela and the Dominican Republic were not invited. Among the delegations present were the Americans, Canadians, Chileans, Cubans, Costa Ricans, Panamanians and the CTM. Officials of the new organisation should be faithful allies of the AFL, the United States and the

---

11   'Free Trade Unions form the ICFTU', pamphlet, in IISH.
12   Carew 200b pp. 196–9; Rodriguez Garcia 2010, p. 51, pp. 73–4; French 2006, pp. 289–333; Morgan 1999, pp. 311–25.
13   Rodríguez García 2010, pp. 78–9.
14   Romualdi to Smith Simpson, Washington, D.C., 13 July 1950, NARA, RG 59, file 820.062/7-2050.

ICFTU. A total of 55 full and 23 alternate delegates and 11 observers from 29 unions in 21 countries were in attendance, representing 21,806,459 workers.[15] In the Palacio de Bellas Artes, where President Alemán spoke briefly, George Meany must have ingratiated himself with the delegates when he said: 'we believe that every country in need of capital investment from abroad has the sovereign right to fix the conditions under which such investment is to be permitted and regulated. Likewise, we believe that every country has the right to adopt its own form of economic and social organisation according to the will of its people freely expressed in a democratic way'.[16]

Fidel Velázquez chaired the congress. He could not have been in disagreement with the ORIT programme, which included salary increases, the right to rest and retirement, protection for pregnant women; and issues such as health insurance, collective bargaining agreements, the prohibition of child labour; worker training, increasing productivity and modifying outmoded forms of production. Conceptions necessary for consolidating the ORIT included friendship and solidarity, the defence of democratic governments, the elimination of monopolies, the division of large land estates, the scientific management of agriculture and livestock, transportation, credits and price controls.[17] A programme that appeared to be to everyone's liking.

But at the meeting the Mexicans could not tolerate the lukewarm attitude of some of the other participants toward the South American dictatorships, including that of Arturo Sabroso of Peru, who downplayed such regimes with the argument that the panorama was improving and that it would not be advisable to adopt a resolution condemning the governments, which could only worsen the situation. Sabroso, who had been arrested in the coup d'état that had occurred two years earlier, was released without the military government headed by General Manuel Odria freeing the more than 100 union leaders, the Apristas and many communists who were also jailed.

Velázquez and his lackeys in the CTM rejected the dominant voice of the North Americans at the expense of the Latin Americans, or actually, the Mexicans, and that he was considered only a figurehead. The Cetemistas wanted to create a Latin American bloc against the North Americans; they tried to monopolise the discussions and opposed proposals behind which they saw the

---

15 'Aspectos regionales de la CIOSL. Razón de ser de la estructura de su organización interamericana', undated, in IISH; Carew 200b, p. 222; Romualdi to Oldenbroek, Washington, D.C., 20 April 1950, in IISH; Alexander and Parker 2009, pp. 111–14.
16 Romualdi 1967, p. 113.
17 'Programa de acción y bases generales de la ORIT, miembro de la CIOSL', Mexico City, January 1951, FHLT, file 819.

dictatorship of Brussels and Oldenbroek. In their interventions, the Cetemistas pressured for Mexico to be the headquarters of the ORIT and a Mexican as president of the organisation. Velázquez became so obnoxious that the delegates united against the CTM and it was a relief when the Mexicans decided to leave the congress.

The opposition to the Argentine CGT joining the ORIT was the other apple of discord. Morones, who attended the congress as an observer, functioned as its lawyer. At one point he got up from his seat and shouted 'viva Argentina'. It caused so much animosity among the delegates that he, too, had to leave the meeting. Manuel Rivera of the National Proletarian Confederation, and a member of the CIT, remained. It was decided that the ORIT headquarters would be in Havana and the Cuban labour leader Francisco Aguirre was named its general secretary. Was it the Mexican government that decided that the CTM should take its distance from the international organisation and its desire to occupy the primary role in such efforts? According to the British Embassy labour attaché, the Alemán government was not favourably disposed to the CTM joining the ORIT, because it was subordinate to the Americans and the AFL. Mexico should be responsible for the new organisation.[18]

Lombardo was pleased by the eruption of fighting in the congress, which he characterised as 'a monstrous farce'. There were delegates, he wrote to Saillant, who agreed to come to Mexico to make contact with the CTAL. Given the failure of the congress, he conveyed, the prospects for the CTAL and the WFTU in Latin America had grown.[19]

Neither Lombardo nor anyone else suspected that Romualdi distrusted his recent creation 'in which other interests and the views of the components of the other organisations had to be taken into account'.[20] The AFL could not submit its actions to the ORIT's scrutiny. For one, in Central America, the American monopoly United Fruit Company (UFCO) was willing to negotiate with the AFL but not with Latin American unions, 'who generally had a biased hostile attitude' toward the company. Romualdi was aware of his ambiguous role, because being secretary of the ORIT he had recommended that the AFL and he himself act on the sidelines of the organisation. In his view, the hostility that there existed toward the UFCO in Central America was an expression of communism and the imperative of fighting it was more important than union democracy. He

---

18 H.G. Gee, 'International Confederation of Free Trade Unions', Mexico City, 2 February 1951, NA, FO371/A2181/2; Rodríguez García 2010, pp. 80–3; Alexander and Parker 2009, pp. 112–14.
19 VLT to Saillant, Mexico City, 8 February 1951, FHLT, file 820.
20 Romualdi to Lovestone, 15 February 1951, Hoover Institution Archives, Lovestone collection, file 342–3.

was concerned that in Guatemala the trade unions would not enter the anticommunist camp due to Lombardo's success in bringing them to the CTAL and to the WFTU. Furthermore, Romualdi was disappointed that Francisco Aguirre, the general secretary of the ORIT, did not act forcefully to counter communism in the Guatemalan unions.[21]

Seen from Europe a year after its founding, the ORIT appeared badly organised, without orientation or a work plan; it lacked leaders capable of coordinating efforts with the ICFTU and misused its financial resources.[22] From the Latin Americans' perspective, the dominant issue was the dictatorship in Venezuela and Peru, against which the ORIT did not offer decisive action to establish free trade unionism and the release of the imprisoned leaders. In Colombia, the unions had to request permission from the government to meet, making their functioning impossible. Francisco Aguirre was incompetent. Nothing was done without his supervision and since he didn't go to the office, the work did not get completed. ORIT officials were not paid regularly or not at all, its publications were not distributed on time and financial assistance to national organisations never arrived. What was the point of belonging to the ORIT?[23]

It was incomprehensible to the leaders of the outlawed unions belonging to the Venezuelan Workers Confederation and those in exile that the ICFTU and the ORIT should negotiate the release of their imprisoned leaders and the restoration of the labour movement in the country, which in any event could only be partial, with the Marcos Pérez Jiménez dictatorship. From exile, Malavé Villalba considered the labour organisations that the dictatorial regime created to be inefficient and inconsistent for focusing their struggle on anti-communism and not on union democracy. The dictatorships were as dangerous as communism; the economy might grow, new jobs might be created, investments might be made in infrastructure and in other public services, but they were poorly distributed. On top of it all, Pérez Jiménez held the ORIT in contempt for lacking the strength to defend its views. To the degree that the Venezuelan government continued displaying its nefarious side, the least that the ORIT could do was to support financially the trade unionists in exile.[24]

The ORIT's reputation deteriorated further after Fulgencio Batista seized power in Cuba in March 1952 and union leaders Eusebio Mujal and Francisco

---

21 Ibid.
22 Hermes Horne, ICFTU official, 'Informe sobre la ORIT', 18 August 1952, in IISH.
23 Robert Alexander, 'Report on Latin America', 11 September 1952, The George Meany Memorial Archives, Congress of Industrial Organisations, International Affairs Department (1945–1955), box 15, file 1.
24 Rodríguez García 2010, pp. 114–26.

Aguirre Mujal supported the regime.[25] Encouraged perhaps by the coup in Cuba, Fidel Velázquez travelled to Brussels to the headquarters of the ICFTU to complain about the ORIT's zero efforts in favour of free trade unionism in Latin America. He acknowledged that it was a mistake for the CTM not to have joined the ORIT when it was created in Mexico in 1951, but now the circumstances were conducive to moving the confederation's headquarters from Cuba to Mexico, put Mexicans in positions of importance, and as a sidebar renew contacts with the Europeans to decrease the weight of the AFL and 'its philosophy of struggle'.[26] In the second congress of the ORIT in Rio de Janeiro in December, Aguirre was removed due to the influence of Robert Alexander and replaced by the young and skilled Costa Rican leader Luis Alberto Monge in the post of general secretary.[27] The CTM entered the ORIT and the headquarters of the organisation were moved to Mexico.

Alexander, who was 34 years of age in 1952 and a professor at Rutgers University, was the eyes and ears of the AFL in Latin America, and worked with Romualdi and Lovestone. Between 1952 and 1958 he made several trips south and from each sent reports, some sounding the alarm, urging the government and the AFL to listen to the Latin Americans. The protest movement was unstoppable despite the governments' forces, but could be channelled toward democracy with the socialists, who despite having different ideas on the economy, were supporters of democracy against tyranny as were the North Americans. And yet, the US government aid was of a military nature, 'the only thing that the Latin American countries don't need', since their true defence was the United States. Helping their armies had the effect of strengthening dictatorships and betraying democracy. If the United States did not defend democracy, 'we would be weakened and we would completely weaken the cause throughout the world'.[28]

The United States was losing the cold war in Latin America not only because of the appeal of communism or Peronism, but due to animosity toward Washington's actions and American companies. The economic power was misused; the loan recently granted to Brazil was not a development credit, but a 'bait to make the Brazilians ratify a military treaty that in any event they did not want'.

25   Berger 1966, pp. 318–29.
26   'Informe sobre la visita del señor Fidel Velázquez a la CIOSL', 4 September 1952, in IISH.
27   Alexander and Parker 2009, p. 118.
28   Robert Alexander, 'Totalitarianism and democracy in Latin America', Washington dinner of the Council Against Communist Aggression, 22 April 1952, in The George Meany Memorial Archives, Congress of Industrial Organizations, International Affairs Department (1945–1955), box 15, file 1; French 2004, pp. 315–26.

It was also a mistake to award a medal to Peruvian President Odría, in power since 1948, fighting allegedly for 'security' in the hemisphere and against the enemies of democracy, as if he were not the principal violator of democratic rights. And the McCarthyite book burning in the United States was a sign that democracy there was also seriously ailing.[29]

The professor's rebukes mattered little. The AFL distributed thousands of copies of pamphlets in Spanish such as 'Who is the imperialist'?, 'Slave labour in the Soviet world' and one on communism in Guatemala. The government information service produced movies for educational purposes that in Mexico were exhibited in mobile cinema units with the support of local governments to align workers with US culture in terms of consumption patterns, technological change, productivity, social mobility, cooperation with big business, hygiene, healthcare and the environment.[30] The ORIT organised courses on labour law, political economy, collective bargaining, public speaking, the trade union movement in the United States, bookkeeping and cooperatives and distributed publications on Washington's positive role in the hemisphere without missing a beat in panegyrics to the totalitarian threat.[31]

But the balance sheet of the ORIT's work was mixed. The dictatorships persisted and new labour confederations emerged that did not affiliate to either the ORIT or the CTAL. The establishment of the Chilean Workers Confederation in 1953 with unions from different backgrounds was an enigma as was the case with the Bolivian Workers Confederation, which maintained its independence. In Uruguay and Paraguay, the Peruvian exile Arturo Jáuregui obtained affiliations to the ORIT, albeit under the watchful eye of the cruel military dictatorships of Higinio Morínigo and after 1954 of General Alfredo Stroessner.[32] In 1954 the ORIT became involved in the banana workers' strike for higher wages and better living conditions against the United Fruit Company on the northern coast of Honduras, fearing the spread of the politicisation occurring among Guatemalan workers to their Honduran counterparts. If an agreement were not reached, the communists would take advantage of the situation, Meany wrote to the company. President Juan Gálvez did not repress the strike and together

---

29 Robert J. Alexander, 'What's wrong with the US policy in Latin America?', The George Meany Memorial Archive, International Affairs Dept, Jay Lovestone Files, 1944–1973, 1953, box 3, file 5.
30 Fein 1998, pp. 400–50.
31 Alexander and Parker 2009, pp. 120–9.
32 Romualdi to Lovestone, 12 April 1954, in The George Meany Memorial Archives, Lovestone files 1945–1975, box 55, file 25; Alexander to Romualdi, New Brunswick, 18 May 1954; Romualdi to Alexander, Washington, D.C., 24 May 1954, in The George Meany Memorial Archives, Romualdi files, 1945–1961, box 3, file 16; Echeverría 1993, pp. 185–90.

with Augusto Malavé engaged in negotiations with the company on working conditions and the creation of the Honduran Workers Confederation, which joined the ORIT.[33]

Meanwhile, the State Department expected collaboration from the ORIT in denouncing the persecution of Guatemalan workers by President Jacobo Arbenz's administration when members of a small anti-government union were arrested after participating in subversive acts. But Luis Monge refused, not because he was not hostile to the Guatemalan government, which had communist officials in it, but because the public and the labour movement were unaware of the conditions in Guatemala and a condemnation would not benefit 'the free world'. The AFL was left on its own to write a public letter of concern over 'the growing influence of communist elements in Guatemala'.[34] When the democratic government of Jacobo Arbenz was overthrown in June 1954 by mercenary forces paid by the CIA, the ORIT opposed the coup and condemned the anti-labour policies of the UFCO and the interventionist stance of the US government. However, when the military government of Carlos Castillo Armas was installed, the labour confederation outlawed and trade union leaders imprisoned, exiled or assassinated, the AFL and the CIO sent their proconsuls to Guatemala to re-establish a semblance of the workers' movement.[35]

When the ORIT met again in 1955 in Costa Rica, Guatemala's Labour Minister who was invited to explain his government's labour policies, failed to convince the Uruguayan delegates, who together with Monge left the hall in protest.[36] In the Mexican Association of the Congress for Cultural Freedom in September 1956, an anti-communist advocacy group, Monge lambasted the US government which, motivated by hysterical anti-communism, supported dictators.[37] Before resigning from the leadership of the ORIT to compete for a deputy seat in Costa Rica, he summarised his experience: 'it is impossible to convince Latin Americans that they should put a priority on the struggle against the threat of totalitarian communist expansion when they are not suffering the effects of the threat, but rather the brutal oppression of their own dictators'.[38]

---

33 'AF of L activities in Latin America, Report of Proceedings of the 73rd Convention of AFL', 20–27 September 1954, Los Angeles, California, The Law Reporter Printing Company, Washington, D.C., p. 241; Alexander and Parker 2009, pp. 121–2.
34 Gleijeses 1991, pp. 258–60.
35 Alexander and Parker 2009, pp. 125–6.
36 Romualdi 1967, p. 128.
37 Iber 2015, p. 106.
38 Luis Alberto Monge to Oldenbroek, Mexico City, 23 December 1957, The George Meany

However, as of 1958 Latin America began to experience political earthquakes. In January, the Venezuelan dictatorship fell. The union leaders returned from exile and began rebuilding the labour movement that the ICFTU recognised with a financial donation.[39] Animosity toward the United States reigned in the region. Mass demonstrations by the population against the visit of Vice President and anti-communist crusader Richard Nixon in Caracas in May were cause for concern. Romualdi said in an interview with *The Machinist* magazine: 'The demonstrations against Vice-president Nixon are the harvest of the bitter fruit of years of neglect in Latin America'.[40] But when in June 1958 Cali, Colombia, was paralysed by a strike of the workers of the Croydon rubber company, with the workers declaring a hunger strike and the Socialist International announcing a consultation meeting with its members in Chile, Romualdi narrowed his previous stance to the bogeyman of communism in view of 'Russia's recent economic offensive, with its offer of trade, financial assistance, exchange of raw materials and goods, etc.'. This 'confirmed the history of economic and political imperialism always present in Russia's international relations'.[41]

The victory of the Cuban Revolution in 1959 shook the world. With the fall of the Batista dictatorship, the July 26 Movement and Fidel Castro gradually took control of the trade unions in Cuba. Romualdi arrived in Havana in February to get a feel for the terrain. The Cuban Workers Confederation financed his trip. A delegation picked him up at the airport and took him to Havana Hilton: 'I waited and waited in vain for a meeting with the leaders of the CTC'. On the first flight he could take, he returned to the United States.[42] In the following months, CTC leaders toured Latin America to invite local trade unions to leave the ORIT and form a Latin American revolutionary labour confederation, without the participation of organisations from the United States and Canada and without mentioning the role of the CTAL.[43] A new era of Latin American labour internationalism was born.

Memorial Archives, International Labour Organisation Activities, ORIT, 1951–1962, box 10, file 7.
39 Rodríguez García 2010, p. 156.
40 Romualdi 1967, p. 177.
41 Romualdi 1967, pp. 172–5; 'The Danger of Communist Infiltration in Latin America', in 'Proceedings of the Third Constitutional Convention of AFL-CIO', San Francisco, California, 17–23 September 1959, The Law Reporter Printing Company, Washington, D.C., pp. 141–2.
42 Romualdi 1967, p. 204.
43 Alexander 1961, pp. 49–52; Alexander and Parker 2009, pp. 131–4; Romualdi 1967, p. 207.

3   In Decline

After the war, the rabid prevailing anti-communism made Lombardo lose his status as intermediary with allies of weight in the North American labour movement. The labour confederations that had belonged to the CTAL such as in Chile, Peru, Venezuela, Costa Rica and Cuba, went over to the ORIT not only because they were anti-communist, but because they failed to see in the CTAL an instrument to defend their everyday interests. Some came to regard the CTAL as a sound box repeating the content of the WFTU's circular letters and slogans, with its written material later 'discarded like used paper'. The unions had real-life problems and slogans about China and instructions to celebrate its victories didn't put food on the table or prevent repression.[44] But Lombardo attributed the confederation's decline to outside factors: to the disappearance of the progressive forces and the fact that the Latin American economies served the needs of the United States and not those of their own countries. This historical configuration of relations between north and south, which he promoted during the war when it was necessary to supply the US war machine with raw materials to defeat Nazism and help the USSR win, was considered prejudicial in the new circumstances.

It was true that many of the problems that plagued the unions were linked to US companies and government repression of popular organisations. The coup in Venezuela in 1948 had eliminated the unions and the government left the field open for the FBI and CIA to eradicate communist influence in the labour movement. Jesús Faría, communist oil worker and CTAL leader, had been imprisoned. In the democratic elections in November 1952 the military government lost, but since it had the power and the weapons, it ignored the election results for the second time in four years with the consent of the United States.[45]

Violence had halted institutional life in Colombia. With conservative presidential candidate Laureano Gómez's victory in 1950, the 'inept plebs' was subjected to government terror with the cooperation of the Church and the blessing of the United States.[46] Police raided the headquarters of the communist party and arrested trade unions from the Colombian Workers Confederation, affiliated to the CTAL, who were savagely tortured. The CTAL sent letters of solidarity,

---

44   Roberto Moreno, Montevideo, 24 January 1949, FHLT, file 792.
45   Santos Yorme, 'Venezuela en el año 1950', Caracas, 11 January 1950, FHLT, file 792; Coronil 1997, pp. 154–8; pp. 183–4; Bergquist 1986, pp. 268–73.
46   Sánchez 1992, pp. 87–100.

addressed to the president and the justice minister.[47] To resist the terror and seek a way out of the situation, the population began to arm itself and wage guerrilla warfare.

In Bolivia, the unions achieved autonomy from the state. The vote of the organised miners in favour of the Revolutionary Nationalist Movement helped elect its leader Victor Paz Estenssoro as president in 1951. Eleven months after the national revolution took place, Paz Estenssoro took office, which he had not been able to do when he was elected, the government nationalised the mines, distributed land among the indigenous population and granted Indians the right to vote.[48] The influence of the CTAL in the Bolivian events was negligible. Lombardo supported the revolutionary process, but the Bolivian Workers Confederation did not join the CTAL. The economic situation of the population was precarious due to the US boycott of Bolivian tin from nationalised mines. It was important to help strengthen the Paz Estenssoro government, because it changed the balance of forces in the region. On several occasions, Lombardo recommended to President Ruiz Cortines that Mexico sell oil to Bolivia to temper the hardships of its government and the population, but the Mexican president would not entertain the suggestion.[49] Did the US government intervene to thwart the deal or did the Mexican government anticipate potential trouble or reprisals for doing so?

The Argentine unions allied to Juan Domingo Perón's government remained outside the CTAL and the ORIT's respective orbits. Perón also wanted to extend his area of international influence. With the help of labour attachés in the country's embassies, of Morones and what was left of his minions, in Mexico and not in Argentina, with the participation of minor unions from Paraguay, Peru, Cuba, Ecuador, Costa Rica and the CROM, the Peronistas created in November 1952 the Association of Unionised Latin American Workers (ATLAS), as anti-communist as it was anti-imperialist. The ATLAS was short-lived, since its role declined with the coup d'état against the Perón government in 1955. Along the way, the communist trade unionists had lost their organisations; some became Peronistas in a labour movement, strengthened by the support from the government, while others lost their freedom.[50]

---

47   Jorge Figueroa Peralta to VLT, Bogota, Colombia, 12 December 1950, FHLT, file 812.
48   Whitehead 1981, pp. 341–3; Zapata 1993, pp. 49–56; Alexander 1973, pp. 128–39.
49   'Reunión de dirigentes del movimiento obrero y cultural de México para escuchar a los delegados de Bolivia que asisten al Congreso de unidad latinoamericana', Mexico City, 24 November 1952, FHLT, file 869; VLT to Adolfo Ruiz Cortines, Mexico City, 3 June 1953, AGN, ARC, vol. 1082, file 578/4.
50   Carew 200b, pp. 224–5; Berger 1966, pp. 315–17; Bergquist 1986, pp. 182–7.

When his presidential campaign ended in 1952, Lombardo issued the call for the fourth congress of the CTAL in Quito, Ecuador, to be held in February 1953. The venue of the congress, which was to be the CTAL's last, was changed to Santiago de Chile and the event slated to take place in March. In the congress call, Lombardo denounced the dramatic imbalance between prices and wages, the poverty afflicting the campesinos, the decline in industrial production, the increasing dependence on the US market and the repercussions of Washington's aggressive foreign policy on the Latin American economies. In adopting the Soviet foreign policy line of peaceful coexistence with the West, he called on unions belonging to the ORIT, the Peronista and independent unions to join in a 'common struggle to win these demands'.[51] But despite of what he said, Lombardo did not believe in this common struggle with those who were his opponents: 'the WFTU is the true and only organisation that effectively defends, with courage and proletarian consciousness, the rights of the working class, the rights of the oppressed peoples of the world, and the interests of humanity, linked to the problem of maintaining peace among nations'.[52]

The Chilean government was aware of the preparations for the congress and at the request of the US ambassador was ready to intervene in case a strike were to erupt. And 'if the Communists engage in disturbances, the possibility has even been considered of isolating them in a concentration camp in southern Chile' where they would not be mistreated but left free to practice their utopia.[53] The State Department wanted to make it impossible for the CTAL to hold its meeting and tried to influence the different governments to refuse exit permits and visas to their citizens to prevent them from attending the congress.[54] This interference in its internal affairs was contrary to the constitution of Costa Rica. As a result, the government rejected it, although Foreign Minister Fernando Lara 'suggested as an alternative that perhaps it would be possible that the delegates be "detained" in Panama for some reason or that Panama would deny them transit visas'.[55]

---

51 VLT, 'Convocatoria al cuarto congreso de la CTAL', 20 September 1952, in *Obra*, v/14, 1952, pp. 103–5.
52 VLT, 'La situación del movimiento obrero en México y en América Latina y sus perspectivas', November 1952, FHLT, file 869; VLT, 'Hacia el cuarto congreso de la CTAL', December 1952, in *Obra*, v/14, 1952, p. 301.
53 Carlos Hall to the State Department, Santiago de Chile, 21 January 1953, NARA, RG 59, Confidential Security Information, file 398.062-SA/1–2153.
54 John Foster Dulles to American Diplomatic Officers, Washington, D.C., 12 February 1953, NARA, RG 59, Confidential Security Information, file 398.062-SA/2–1253.
55 Philip B. Fleming to the State Department, San José, Costa Rica, 17 February 1953, NARA, RG 59, Confidential Security Information, 398.062-SA/2–1753.

Honduran Foreign Minister Edgardo Valenzuela assured John Erwin of the US Embassy in Tegucigalpa that if a Honduran applied for a passport to attend the CTAL congress, the request would be rejected. The Labour Minister in Bogota implemented 'a procedure to prevent Colombian participation in any possible way'.[56] However, in democratic Guatemala in view 'of the specific local situation, the Embassy does not intend to approach the Foreign Ministry regarding this issue'. In countries such as Uruguay, it was impossible to prevent a citizen from travelling to the congress, since Uruguayans did not need a passport to travel to Chile. The Bolivians wanted to be in Santiago to denounce the US embargo on their raw materials following the nationalisation. Neither Pedro Saad of Ecuador nor Juan Lechín of Bolivia could be detained, because they were senator and minister, respectively.[57] The Cubans and Peruvians did not obtain exit permits in an attempt to keep them from reaching a congress that the State Department considered communist.

Lombardo arrived in Santiago saddened by the death of Stalin, 'one of the greatest geniuses of humanity', in early March. The working class, peace and socialism had lost their guide and 'greatest builder'[58] and a superior being 'who had spurred the evolution of human society'.[59] In Santiago, Lombardo did not mention Stalin and in addressing the delegates from several countries, perhaps not the 229 reported, he presented an overview of the plight of the workers and, despite having invited them, denounced the leaders of the ORIT and the ATLAS 'as transitory agents of the ideology of imperialism',[60] hailed the CTAL for its policy of unity and as the 'weapon of the victorious struggle against repression and misery'.[61] But call for unity sounded hollow to cure the structural social, political and economic ills, deepened and taken advantage of by the participants in the cold war.

---

56 John Edwin to the State Department, Tegucigalpa, Honduras, 17 February 1953, file 398.062-SA/2–1753; Waynick to the State Department, Bogota, Colombia, 19 February 1953, NARA, RG 59, Confidential Security Information, file 398.062-SA/2–1953.

57 Rudolf Schoenfeld to the State Department, Guatemala, 20 February 1953, NARA, RG 59, Confidential Security Information, 398.062-SA/2–1753; Edgard Rowell to the State Department, La Paz, Bolivia, 20 March 1953, NARA, RG 59, Confidential Security Information, file 398.062-SA/3–2053.

58 VLT, 'A propósito de la muerte de José Stalin', *El Popular*, 'La clase obrera pierde a su maestro y guía', 6 March 1953, in *Obra*, V/15, 1953, p. 131.

59 VLT, 'La era de Stalin', in *Obra*, V/15, 1953, p. 179.

60 VLT, 'Resoluciones del cuarto congreso general ordinario de la CTAL', in *Obra*, V/15, 1953, p. 190.

61 VLT, 'Resoluciones del cuarto congreso general ordinario de la CTAL', in *Obra*, V/15, 1953, p. 191.

The overthrow of Jacobo Arbenz in Guatemala by a military faction a year later, sponsored by the US government, was another blow to the CTAL, since it resulted in the destruction of the labour confederation Lombardo had helped to build since the fall of the General Ubico dictatorship in 1944 and Juan José Arévalo's presidency. After the coup, Lombardo aided persecuted exiles in Mexico with the dwindling financial resources that the WFTU sent to keep the CTAL alive.[62] But little could be done when the Mexican government, which reacted tepidly to the coup, stopped issuing the refugees residence permits and immigration agents sent them back from Chiapas to Guatemala.[63]

In the mid-1950s the outlook was bleak for the working class. After the labour movement in Colombia was declared illegal and the homes of trade union activists requisitioned, the CTAL's solidarity was a comfort.[64] The news coming from Peru and Ecuador was discouraging, due to the helplessness of the imprisoned trade unionists. From Chile, the comrades reported on the increase in prices and stagnation of the economy. In Honduras, the terror unleashed by Julio Lozano Díaz reigned and trade unionists were confined in the central penitentiary in Tegucigalpa 'in response to orders from the United Fruit Company'.[65] And when in the mid-1950s, coffee prices fell in the market and the United States reduced its imports from Costa Rica, the large producers laid off workers. Their alternative was to seek new markets, even behind the 'iron curtain', nationalise or expropriate land.[66] The radicalisation of the disenfranchised population was one of several responses to the unending oppression.

4 The CTAL Dies in Bucharest

The year 1956 was a turning point in the communist movement. At the twentieth Congress of the Soviet Communist Party in February, Nikita Sergeievich Khrushchev, Stalin's successor, revealed the extent of the atrocities committed by his predecessor. In the process, Khrushchev settled accounts with his rivals who were close to Stalin, but his main motivation was to restore the moral stature of the party, allegedly purifying it of the horrors of the past.[67]

---

62   VLT to Amado Zapata, Mexico City, 10 July 1954, FHLT, file 945.
63   Hilario Mancilla to VLT, Tapachula, Chiapas, 14 January 1955, FHLT, file 967; Castillo, Toussaint and Vázquez Olivera 2011, vol. 2; Mercedes de Vega in Castillo, Toussaint and Vázquez Olivera 2011, vol. 2, pp. 97–8.
64   VLT and others to Antonio Cabrera, Mexico City, 10 November 1954, FHLT, file 959.
65   Carlos Jiménez to VLT, Tegucigalpa, Honduras, 9 June 1955, FHLT, file 979.
66   Gonzalo Sierra Cantillo to the CTAL, San José, Costa Rica, 14 March 1955, FHLT, file 972.
67   Priestland 2010, p. 329.

After ten days of lectures and speeches, delegates to the congress were called to a special session. In a secret meeting on 25 February, Khrushchev detailed Stalin's responsibility in the mass arrests and deportation of thousands of people to forced labour camps in inhumane conditions, the purges in the party ranks of innocent citizens, firings from jobs, the senseless liquidation of the army officer corps in the 1930s, the deportations of entire ethnic groups to other parts of the territory of the USSR, torture and executions of honest communists without trial or investigation, which created insecurity, fear and despair in the population. For all of this, Khrushchev concluded, Stalin had betrayed Leninist principles.[68]

The Khrushchev report became known outside the Soviet Union a few weeks after having been delivered. The world was stunned, communists perplexed and numerous workers in the neighbouring countries took it seriously. The General Secretary of the Communist Party of Poland, Boleslaw Bierut died of a heart attack due to the lèse-majesté impression left by Khrushchev. In Poland, Czechoslovakia and East Germany the workers took to the streets to protest the low standard of living. In the Polish industrial city of Poznañ among the protesters there were those who condemned the exploitation by the communists as being equivalent to the previous capitalist exploitation. The workers' revolt was repressed, accompanied by the struggle between the Stalinists and reformers in the party. Khrushchev came to fear that Poland would leave the bloc. He prepared the Soviet invasion, but cancelled it in time.[69]

Demoralised, many communists resigned from their parties. The French Communist Party, led by Maurice Thorez, suffered defections. The Italian party, under Palmiro Togliatti, was divided between those who believed in national roads to socialism, an alliance with the socialist party and the orthodox Marxists. Debates emerged on the nature of the system that was capable of generating such defects. In Eastern Europe, intellectuals argued about the need to rehabilitate the good name of socialism and the leading role of the proletariat, betrayed by a state that said it represented the workers, but which exploited them and paid them poorly. For those who took Marxism seriously it was necessary to take it to the factories, so that workers could learn from the theory and acquire class consciousness in practice.[70]

The Latin American communists were among those who believed, along with Khrushchev, that it was necessary to strengthen the socialist bloc against its detractors. They took advantage of the accusations against Stalin to recover

---

68   Ibid; Taubman 2003, pp. 270–84.
69   Priestland 2010, pp. 331–4.
70   Priestland 2010, p. 337; Applebaum 2012, pp. 478–80.

the idea of the leading role of the workers' movement and of their role as its vanguard. Lombardo assumed the same commitment as the Soviet leader and the communists, in addition to minimising Khrushchev's denunciation of Stalin's crimes as 'difficulties' and 'errors that must be corrected'.[71]

It was in Sofia, Bulgaria, in October 1956, where the communists went on an offensive, subjecting the CTAL and Lombardo to an unprecedented criticism. The CTAL suffered from a confused orientation, overestimating the difficulties instigated by imperialism and reaction in Latin America and downplaying the potential forces of struggle. Even the Cuban comrade Lázaro Peña, in exile from the Batista dictatorship, criticised Lombardo for being one-sided by ignoring the possibilities of trade union work. Argentine labour leader Vicente Marischi added that Lombardo was not familiar with the struggles of the working class in the southern hemisphere, which moreover could not be run from Mexico. The leadership had to become closer to the ranks. The CTAL, Saillant said, failed to mobilise the masses. He almost apologised for taking this hard stand, but 'we should reject the method of keeping our thoughts secret for fear of not being understood'.[72] In chorus, the communist leaders from Brazil, Peru, Argentina, Cuba and Colombia, probably in harsh tones, downplayed the importance of the CTAL. Its leadership methods were bureaucratic, its circular letters were of no use, it lacked ties to the legal trade unions since it was not possible to work with the illegal unions, it was sectarian and its focus was more political than union oriented. The question that was in the air was whether it was useful to maintain the CTAL.[73]

The executive committee of the WFTU met in Prague in January 1957. There the Latin American communists, along with the leadership of the WFTU, took another decision that further weakened the CTAL. Its struggle 'against imperialism was characterised as positive', but it did not understand that 'the Communist parties are the most consistent fighters to perform this task and that they need to be at the forefront of this struggle of the broad masses of working people'. The WFTU reiterated that from Mexico the CTAL leadership did not have the capacity to connect with the southern hemisphere and therefore the WFTU established a support office in Chile.[74]

---

71   VLT, 'En torno al XX Congreso del Partido Comunista de la Unión Soviética', Mexico City, 15 June 1956, lecture given on 5 June 1956 in the PP hall, published in *El Popular* in six parts, in *Obra*, V/23, 1956, pp. 177–274, quote on p. 177 and p. 216.
72   Saillant in the joint meeting of the central committee of the CTAL and the secretariat of the WFTU, Sofía, Bulgaria, 4–6 October 1956, FHLT, file 1027.
73   Ibid.
74   'Reunión del Comité Ejecutivo de la FSM', Prague, Czechoslovakia, January 1957; 'Mater-

The leaders of the WFTU and CTAL met in Bucharest, Romania, in December 1959, 11 months after the victory of the Cuban Revolution. Lombardo knew that the CTAL was about to die and that there was a plan to create a new organisation. 'Has the time come to liquidate the CTAL'? No, he said, in answer to his own question in a futile attempt to save it, since this would leave the field clear for the ORIT and imperialism. Phrases such as that it was necessary to 'find ways for an adequate organisation' or 'not only maintaining the Latin American Workers Confederation, but strengthening it as much as possible',[75] ceased to have applicability. The CTAL, which had played an important role between 1938 and 1945, which influenced the emergence of trade unions in 11 countries with four million members and held four congresses, had lost most of its affiliated labour confederations. Its numbers plummeted to 167,000, which when coupled with the affiliates in the professional departments that existed more in name than in reality, the figure perhaps reached close to 456,000 members.

In Bucharest, several speakers delivered the epitaph for the CTAL. They recognised its constructive role in its origins, but pointed to its current stagnation. 'It has already fulfilled its historic mission and should open the way for new forms of organisation in Latin America', said the Venezuelan labour leader Eloy Torres. Oscar García of Argentina placed the CTAL 'in the past, ruminating over its glories'. The Cuban Revolution opened 'the road for the struggle of the peoples of Latin America', said Enrique Pastorino of Uruguay. Cuban union leader Lázaro Peña, also a founder of the CTAL, said the confederation was in the process of 'disappearing'. Roberto Lara of Chile called for a new democratic labour confederation and for letting the CTAL die. Gonzalo Sierra Cantillo of Costa Rica defended the CTAL, because it had provided assistance and solidarity, but that the time had come for the unification of the confederation with all other such organisations. Victor Manuel Zúñiga of Ecuador was kinder: 'We will always remember that it was the voice of Vicente Lombardo Toledano and the CTAL that made the best defence of our rights'. The Chilean labour leader Ildefonso Alemán defended the CTAL against the report presented by Saillant on its weakness in relation to the ORIT. Viktor Grishin from the Soviet Union

---

iales para la discusión sobre la situación sindical en América Latina', Executive Committee of the WFTU, Prague, Czechoslovakia, 29–31 January 1957, National Archives of the Czech Republic, box 8, file 14.

75   VLT, 'La CTAL y los problemas de organización y de lucha del movimiento sindical en la América Latina, presentado en XXXVII reunión de la FSM y el CC de la CTAL', Bucharest, Rumania, 14–17 December 1959, in *Obra*, v/30, 1959, pp. 276–8; 'Intervención de VLT en la reunión del Buró Ejecutivo de la FSM y el Comité Central de la CTAL', Bucharest, Rumania, December 1959, FHLT, manuscripts 1957–1959, file 9.

and František Zupka from Czechoslovakia said to be on the side of the independent unions, covering up in fact the true interest of the USSR, which was to extend its sphere of influence in Latin America where the Cuban Revolution, not the CTAL, broadened the anti-imperialist camp. Saillant gave the CTAL the coup de grace: 'The CTAL has lost the notion that the labour movement is run by the ranks' and not from the top.[76]

5 The CTAL Completed Its Historic Mission

Lombardo did not believe in 'the third way' that was adopted in Bandung, Indonesia, in April 1955 between newly independent Asian and African countries not aligned with any of the two blocs. Present at that conference were, among others, Gamal Abdel Nasser, president of Egypt, Jawaharlal Nehru of India and Sukarno, head of State of Indonesia, in addition to the leaders of Pakistan, Burma and Ceylon, plus 25 leaders invited to the conference for economic and cultural cooperation among Asian and African countries, unaligned, in principle, with anyone except each other.[77] His position was that it was impossible to be neutral in Latin America, dominated by imperialism, dictatorships and a weak anti-imperialist bourgeoisie, where the United States poured its capital in to control the economies and influence political life, distorting the region's culture in addition to liquidating its patriotic and democratic forces that opposed Washington's policies.[78]

However, in light of the creation of a third anti-colonial force coupled with the line of peaceful coexistence, Lombardo's dogged and one-dimensional anti-imperialism lost its validity in Soviet foreign policy, in which the WFTU was the transmission belt. Khrushchev placed his expectations in the Cuban Revolution as the glimmer of hope for socialism in Latin America. 'Castro will have to gravitate toward us as powdered iron to a magnet'.[79] With socialist Cuba, the camp expanded without resorting to war, which was the ideal form of peaceful coexistence.

The Cuban revolution also shifted the centre of gravity of the Latin American labour movement toward the unions not aligned with any international feder-

---

76 'Reunión conjunta del Buró Ejecutivo de la FSM y del Comité Central de la CTAL', Bucharest, Rumania, 13–16 December 1959, FHLT, file 1107.
77 https://es.wikipedia.org/wiki/Conferencia_de_Bandung. Accessed 25 November 2015.
78 VLT, 'Resumen de su intervención en el consejo general de la FSM', Sofía, 28 September 1956, FHLT, file 1026.
79 Pavlov 1996, p. 8.

ation, strengthened the nationalism of some trade unionists and radicalised the nationalism of others.[80] The branch of the Cuban Workers Confederation affiliated to the ORIT and committed to 'saving Cuba from the clutches of communism, albeit with a continental focus' and from Fidel Castro,[81] signed its death warrant on the island.

Lombardo was in solidarity with the revolutionary movement in Cuba even before the 1959 victory. He supported the revolution because it 'has accelerated the process of trade union unity in Latin America'.[82] He did not conceive that the revolution could have contributed to burying the CTAL. No, it was the ORIT and the US embassies in Latin American countries that 'have taken on the task of waging a systematic campaign, saying the dissolution of the CTAL is the best proof that the ORIT was right and that it is the only international confederation that exists'.[83]

In reality, it was the CTC and the communist parties, whose orientation came from the Soviet Union, which took the initiative to establish a new labour confederation that, in theory, would not be affiliated to any international organisation, but in practice would be aligned with the new path opened by the Cuban Revolution that the USSR sought to co-opt. The meeting to create it, slated for September 1962 in Santiago de Chile, was called by the Chilean labour confederation and Cuban trade unionists. According to an agent of the Federal Security Directorate, contrary to what Lombardo said in public, the CTAL leader sought help from the Cuban comrades to persuade unions in Mexico to defend the confederation in the Santiago de Chile gathering. 'Lombardo Toledano is doing everything possible so that this new labour confederation, which would put an end to the one that he leads, doesn't emerge. But it's known that this new confederation, sponsored by all the National Liberation Movements of the Latin American countries, will indeed emerge'.[84]

Lombardo went to Santiago, he said, to support the new labour unity project and when it would be created, 'I will personally come to tell you that the CTAL is dead'.[85] In Santiago the decision was taken to organise another conference

---

80 Rodríguez García 2010, pp. 158–9.
81 Eusebio Mujal Barniol to Sacha Volman, Washington, D.C., 21 May 1960, The Hoover Institution Archives, Lovestone Collection, box 342, file 3; Romualdi 1967, pp. 202–21.
82 Lombardo Toledano, 2003a; VLT to Louis Saillant, Mexico City, 2 August 1960, FHLT, file 1117.
83 VLT to Saillant, Mexico City, 10 November 1960, FHLT, file 1123.
84 Carlos Manuel Suárez and Suárez to the DFS, Mexico City, 1 August 1962, AGN, DFS, VLT, vp 6/9, 30-3-1962.
85 'La CTAL encontrará nueva vida en un movimiento amplio y poderoso', in *Obra*, VI/9, 1962,

to found the new confederation. But Lombardo argued for it to be postponed until 'a more adequate formulation is found'.[86] He still hoped to play a prominent role. That was not to be, because in 1963 the WFTU would send the last payment to support the CTAL, not enough to pay the salaries of the final three months, severance pay, the year-end bonuses for the staff working in its offices and to liquidate the 7,290 dollar debt that the confederation had with the Belgian airline Sabena.[87]

In the call for the congress in Santiago de Chile to establish the new confederation, scheduled for January 1964 in Rio de Janeiro, the authors did not mention the CTAL as the precursor of the organisation to be built. It mentioned Cuba – which 'has been fully liberated' from oppression, imperialism and the feudal castes – and declared that just as on the island, only 'deep structural changes' would liquidate imperialist domination and colonialism in Latin America.[88]

It was for that occasion that Lombardo wrote the document that announced the dissolution of the CTAL as a completed historical mission. The celebrated pamphlet was an exegesis of the history of the labour movement since the nineteenth century and the history of the CTAL, accompanied by an extensive bibliography of documents at the end of the text. With his peculiar form of argumentation, in its conclusion Lombardo contradicted what he wrote at the beginning. Unions should be inclusive of all philosophical tendencies and religious beliefs. They should not depend on any political party or any group of leaders or affiliate as an organisation to parties.[89] But the working class could not come to power without its party. Trade union autonomy was 'a useful means to achieve or maintain unity, but it should be temporary, because without the affiliation of national federations or confederations to an international grouping, the struggles will lack effective leadership, correct methods'.[90] Therefore, the new confederation should enter the WFTU and align with the pro-Soviet camp.

---

p. 25; Lt. Coronel D.E.M. Manuel Rangel Escamilla, Mexico City, 8 September 1962, AGN, DFS, VLT, vp, 6/9, 11-2-62.

86   VLT, 'Proposiciones para el congreso constituyente de la nueva central latinoamericana', in *Obra*, VI/9, 1962, p. 29.

87   Louis Saillant to VLT, Prague, 16 September 1963, FHLT, file 1169; SABENA to VLT, Mexico City, 30 January 1964, FHLT, file 1178.

88   'Convocatoria al Congreso de Unidad Sindical de los Trabajadores de América Latina', Rio de Janeiro, 24–28 January 1964, Montevideo, Uruguay, 28 July 1963, FHLT, file 1178.

89   VLT, 'La CTAL ha concluido su misión histórica', January 1964, in *Obra*, VI/14, 1964, pp. 1–24; quote on p. 18.

90   VLT, 'La CTAL ha concluido su misión histórica', January 1964, in *Obra*, VI/14, 1964, p. 19.

Lombardo did not attend the meeting in Rio, since the election campaigns had begun in Mexico and he wanted to run for congressional deputy as a candidate of his party and support the candidacy of Gustavo Díaz Ordaz for president. 'In a few months I will be 70 years old, with about 50 years of daily struggle for the rights and interests of the working class and socialism'.[91] And without putting limits on his bombast, Lombardo bid farewell to Saillant: 'I remain here in my country as a rank and file soldier of the proletariat'.[92]

It was perhaps Lombardo who wrote the unsigned article entitled 'The Trade Union Congress of Rio de Janeiro to meet 24 to 28 January 1964', in which he predicted that 'there are no conditions to create a new Latin American labour organisation'. Those who issued the call to the congress were a conglomeration of organisations and individuals who did not have a common platform. Among them were Juan Lechín, vice president of Bolivia 'and rabid anti-communist, but he is the most important of all of them, because he organises the country's miners'. To add more salt to the wound, a Chilean organiser of the Rio de Janeiro meeting had been in Mexico 'without even visiting the offices of the CTAL, making it understood that they don't want to have further relations with Lombardo Toledano in the future'. As a person with intimate knowledge of the history of the CTAL and the WFTU, the author accused the WFTU of having deprived the CTAL of political support, which meant having deprived the WFTU of worker support in Latin America. No one but Lombardo knew that the 'idea of dissolving the CTAL and creating a new Latin American trade union body had arisen from the Communist parties of South America' and the Mexican Communist Party, 'which was engaged in a huge campaign of lies aimed at removing Lombardo Toledano from the international labour movement', that had become 'a group truly dedicated to provocation without any real influence in the workers' movement or among the important democratic organisations in Mexico'. The writer dismissively referred to the Mexican delegates who were to go to Rio, campesino leaders of the UGOCM and the new organisation, the Independent Peasant Confederation (CCI), 'which represents nothing but a group of agitation in the countryside', and to the unionised teachers. The CTAL would disappear, but the new organisation had no chance of being born as long as the ORIT 'is fully committed to continue fighting the unions with progressive trends'. By dissolving it, they were 'destroying the work that the Latin American Workers Confederation managed to undertake with considerable efforts'.[93]

---

91   VLT to Saillant, Mexico City, 1 January 1964, FHLT, file 1176.
92   VLT to Saillant, Mexico City, 7 January 1964, FHLT, file 1176.
93   'El Congreso Sindical de Rio de Janeiro que se reunirá durante los días del 24 al 28 de enero de 1964', Mexico City, 7 January 1964, FHLT, file 1176.

In public, Lombardo said the closure of the CTAL was a victory because the new Latin American labour organisation to be created meant that there was 'a fierce detachment of the world proletariat'.[94] But after the Rio de Janeiro meeting and in the intimacy of friends, he regretted the decision. The ORIT endured while 'we have nothing on this continent. The Brazil meeting failed, and now after the last military coup and the things that have occurred in other Southern Hemisphere countries, the situation could not be worse'.[95]

It was true that due to a brief period of mobilisations around political and economic issues, between 1960 and 1962, the climate in Brazil allowed for the new Latin American confederation to emerge while the United States and the ORIT lost control of the organised workers movement.[96] The new organisation, Permanent Congress of Trade Union Unity of Latin American Workers (CPUSTAL), was born in Rio with headquarters in Santiago de Chile, the support of the USSR and the communist parties. Participating in its founding were the Bolivians, the Cubans, Chileans, Salvadorans, Ecuadorians and Uruguayans. The ORIT was invited with voice but no vote. But in April 1964, the government headed by Joao Goulart was overthrown, with the active assistance of the United States, and the workers' movement crushed to eliminate 'the deliberate Bolshevisation' of the nation by the president. The US position toward Brazil must have been influenced by President Goulart first having supported the United States against the Soviet Union following the discovery of nuclear weapons in Cuba in October 1962, which installed them between 1960 and 1962 on the island, and later opposed the military measures, which Washington and the Organisation of American States proposed against Cuba. The military Brazilian government prohibited the functioning of the new organisation within the country.[97]

Lombardo lamented all what had occurred in his letter to the Soviet trade union leadership, without conceiving, or perhaps knowingly, that this was where the CTAL's dissolution was floated:

> The Latin American panorama could not be worse. The Latin American Workers Confederation was dissolved at the repeated request over several years from the leaders of the Communist parties of South America, so that

---

94 'Saludos de Vicente Lombardo Toledano, presidente de la CTAL, al XIII Congreso de los Sindicatos Soviéticos', Moscow, USSR, 30 October 1963, FHLT, file 1171.
95 VLT to Vittorio Vidali, Mexico City, 18 September 1964, FHLT, file 1193.
96 Welch 1995, pp. 61–89.
97 Roxborough 1997, vol. 12, p. 169; Erickson 1977, p. 153; Alexander and Parker 2009, pp. 92–4; Keller 2014, pp. 20–7.

they could run the trade union organisation in our hemisphere, mistaking a mass organisation with a political International. When I realised that these wishes were supported by the leadership of the World Federation of Trade Unions, as you remember, I helped facilitate such a decision.[98]

Lombardo assigned the main responsibility for the dissolution of the CTAL to the AFL and imperialism. The other part of the blame was placed on the Latin American communists and to a lesser extent the World Federation of Trade Unions. He thus and forever exonerated the Soviet Union of any political move that he considered unwise.

The offensive against the CTAL had a triple origin: the new course of Soviet policy from 1956 on, the Cuban Revolution and the ORIT, which represented the non-communist and anti-communist unions and was an instrument of the AFL, although not always of the US government. The often cited slogan of 'inter-Americanism without imperialism' of the AFL representative in Latin America, Romualdi, was unconvincing in light of US government policies in the hemisphere. Sometimes the CTAL and ORIT were on the same side of the barricade, defending human rights, trade union liberties and freedom against military dictators. Even ORIT officials realised that anti-communism and democracy were antithesis, while trade unionists learned that fighting against the Soviet Union and communism did not necessarily promote democracy, hindered solidarity and regional labour unity.[99]

The Cuban Revolution became the emblem of continental liberation. Lombardo saw it as the continuation of a historical process begun by the Mexican Revolution and not as a break with the past. He hailed it because it diminished the power of the United States in the hemisphere. 'Do not extinguish the light that the people of Cuba have lit to illuminate our road. Let this flame spread to the entire continent and join the immense glow of the new dawn of the world'.[100] Lombardo, a believer in historical laws, would not allow discouragement to take over. Universal history was a chain of intertwined processes of which he was a link.

98 VLT to Viktor Grishin, Mexico City, 7 November 1964, FHLT, file 1198.
99 McPherson 2006, p. 36.
100 VLT, 'Mensaje a la juventud de la América Latina' meeting in Havana, Cuba, July 1960, *Siempre!*, no. 274, in *Obra*, VI/2, 1960, p. 188.

CHAPTER 15

The Road to 1968

The proximity to the United States was eroding Mexican traditions and customs that defined Lombardo Toledano's way of life. That men 'do the shopping' was a Yankee invention and was 'dishonourable for decent ladies', since 'it's the domestic help that does this'. Today, women 'can do whatever they want' and with the spread of 'lady's bars', cantinas are now within their reach. Another development that irritated Lombardo was the emergence of colleges, with a low cultural level, narrow philosophical outlook, oblivious to the interests of the people and the formation of national consciousness.[1] And when Lombardo didn't give the capitalist system more than a quarter century of existence, he criticised intellectuals such as the French philosopher Jean-Paul Sartre and the American novelist Howard Fast for being afflicted with an 'imbalance between reality and consciousness, between being and thinking'. They were 'subjectivists' who scorned the socialist world and the 'unsolvable antagonism between these two forms of human existence'.[2]

1   PPS

When Lombardo visited Asia, the Chinese said to him, 'Stay with us, we need you'. The Soviets also invited him to remain in their country, but despite the 'deep love for the Soviet state' he could not do so as his place was in Mexico 'where everything remains to be done', where the people were cowed, bitter, illiterate, where they 'don't laugh much', but 'fighting in such a country is very beautiful and it is a great honour'.[3]

At 66 years of age and the grandfather of several grandchildren, Lombardo believed that it was his role to show the way forward to the new generation and guide it with 'our glorious party'. Children should empathise with the life of Mexico and the lives of other children to form a kind of youth internationalism. He would accompany them on this journey of learning, beginning

---

1 VLT, 'Panorama de las universidades mexicanas', *Siempre!*, no. 238, 15 January 1958, in *Obra*, V/27, 1958, pp. 29–34.
2 VLT, 'Notas sobre el subjetivismo en política', *Siempre!*, no. 249, 2 April 1958, in *Obra*, V/27, 1958, pp. 103–6.
3 VLT, 'La unidad sindical en México', *Siempre!*, no. 344, 27 January 1960, in *Obra*, VI/1, 1960, p. 21.

with the Toltec city of Tula and then to acquire knowledge of plants, animals and societal problems of the country. In many nations there are poor children, but it was among 'the peoples who live in socialism' that poverty, ignorance and oppression have been eliminated and happy children were to be found. Mexican children should link up with youth from countries such as the USSR, Czechoslovakia, Poland, Romania, Bulgaria, Hungary, Albania and China, to learn from them how to work in order to live better.[4]

If in a baker's home, children played making bread, in the Lombardo home 'the kids played politics'.[5] Vicente Lombardo Toledano Silva, Vico as he was known at home, was his eldest grandson, predestined by his name to follow in the footsteps of his grandfather. When he was 10 years old and finished elementary school in 1957, his parents Federico and Adriana and his grandparents agreed to send him to the Soviet Union for one or two years 'mainly in order to learn the Russian language and also to have the chance to realise what its social system means and represents'. In addition to his ideological training, Vico's grandfather envisioned that in knowing Russian, he could help him with translations and reviewing documents published in Russian, 'which would also be of great value for our trade union and political work'.[6] Vicente travelled to Moscow with Lombardo, his grandmother Rosa María and Adriana. His mother accompanied him to the boarding school in Ivanovo, 300 km northeast of Moscow, and returned to Mexico.[7]

Vico learned to ice skate and was excited because he joined the ranks of the pioneers. At the same time he was interested in everything that happened in Mexico and asked for information. In January 1958 he received a long letter from Lombardo, 'the best letter I have ever received in my life', from the 'world's smartest' grandfather: 10 pages long and single-spaced about the situation in Mexico and its prospects, an analysis of the evolution of capitalism, imperialism in decline and the Bolshevik revolution, which extended social welfare and well-being to one part of the world. The letter explained the historical evolution of Mexico since the country's independence up to the 1958 presidential campaign, in which the only candidate was Adolfo López Mateos. Lombardo wrote the long letter so that Vico would understand what world he lived in and could envision the society of tomorrow, 'for which you must be decisively prepared,

---

4 VLT, 'Entender a México y amarlo; entender a la humanidad y amarla también, tarea de los pioneros del Partido Popular', speech, 5 February 1960, in *Obra*, VI/1, 1960, pp. 30–1.
5 Interview with Vicente Silva Lombardo, Amecameca, 28 October 2006.
6 VLT, 'Queridos compañeros', Mexico City, 16 April 1957, FHLT, file 1037.
7 VLT to Bedřich Pištora, Mexico City, 10 July 1957, FHLT, file 1042; Vicente (Vico) to Tata and Abuelita, Ivanovo, 3 November 1957, FHLT, file 1048.

because you'll live when the socialist system is victorious on all continents of the planet. Your duty is to educate and prepare yourself scientifically, culturally and politically, to contribute, when the time comes, to building socialism in your own country'.[8]

When he finished the school year, Vico returned to Mexico.[9] His grandfather must have thought that his education was incomplete, and in 1961 Vico returned to the Soviet Union to enrol in high school and audited courses at the University of Moscow alongside other Mexicans so that 'they will be useful afterwards for the independent development of our country, which needs both prepared cadre and a correct orientation in terms of the historical perspective'.[10]

Vico would not disappoint his Tata: he studied historical and dialectical materialism, had to read Engels's *Anti-Dühring* in Russian, although he would have preferred to do so in Spanish, as well as logic and Marx's *Capital*. He felt he was measuring up well both in Russian and political education and was proud because there was 'a very high percentage of students who politically are somewhat backward'.[11] With this knowledge, he wrote to his Tata, 'I think I can be of tremendous service to our party, although I will be of service in any event'.[12]

In October 1960, that party, on Lombardo's initiative and without any discussion among the members, added the adjective 'socialist' to its name. This did not mean that the People's Socialist Party (PPS) had been radicalised, but rather that it would be distinguished from the other left-wing groups which he believed were 'instruments of provocation and slander against the socialist countries and revolutionary activists, at the service of the police forces of the imperialist powers'. The decolonisation of Africa, Asia, and the Cuban Revolution were proof of the uprising of the peoples against imperialism.[13] There were the Soviet government production statistics which showed that the country's economy was about to outstrip that of the industrialised countries. The successful launching of the satellite Sputnik in 1957 had revealed that Soviet science and technology reached such a level 'that the capitalist

---

8   VLT to Vicente Lombardo Toledano Silva, Mexico City, 3 January 1958, FHLT, file 1054.
9   Victor Grishin to VLT, Moscow, June 1958, telegram, FHLT, file 1065; VLT to Grishin, Mexico City, 20 June 1958, FHLT, file 1065.
10 VLT to Leonid Soloviev, secretary of the Central Council of the Soviet trade unions, Mexico City, 23 October 1961, FHLT, file 1136; Interview with Rosa María Soto Lombardo, Cuernavaca, 27 July 2011.
11 Vico to Tata, Moscow, 5 September 1962, FHLT, file 1150.
12 Vico to Tata, Moscow, 25 November 1962, FHLT, file 1153.
13 'Informe de la Dirección Nacional a la III Asamblea Nacional ordinaria del PP', Mexico City, 14 October 1960, FHLT, file 1121.

countries are lagging behind its scientific and technical progress in almost all spheres of knowledge and in plans to master nature'. This certainty of the course of history inspired the party's line in Mexico, which he summed up as 'the formation of a national, patriotic and democratic front, for which the alliance of social and political forces is necessary, and not an opposition force that would make doing so impossible'.[14] In practical terms, this meant that the party would endeavour to strengthen the Mexican state through the country's economic development, unthinkable without the collaboration of the labour movement and which the class struggle and the dissident popular movements would hinder.

Within the PPS Lombardo sought to standardise ideological, political and theoretical education, which required strict discipline of its members and obedience to the organisation's single chain of command.[15] Discipline was essential to avoid opposition and discussion of alliances made in accordance with the strategy designed by the top leadership of the party. The policy of approaching the state-party and of negotiating candidacies for the Chamber of Deputies, governors and mayoral races, were not to be broached in assemblies. The UGOCM should function as the social base of the party, but the labour authorities' refusal to grant it official registration as a labour confederation prevented it from assuming such a role. In addition, the failure of land reform forced the UGOCM to become a campesino confederation, demanding land for peasant farmers and organising the seizure of plots of land and the landed estates, gradually estranging it from the party.[16] 'Better fewer but better', 'fewer but servile', were the slogans circulating to sneer at the PPS.[17]

In the 1961 midterm elections, the PPS negotiated its entry into the Chamber of Deputies with the PRI, and despite the expected fraud perpetrated against it by the state-party, it named 24 disciplined candidates for consideration.[18] Lombardo's son-in-law, Federico Silva, was a candidate in one of Mexico City's districts. Jacinto López, who in April 1961 was recovering from a stroke, was selec-

---

14 'Respuesta al cuestionario presentado to VLT para *Novedades* con motivo del 50 aniversario de la Revolución Mexicana', Mexico City, 16 November 1960, FHLT, file 1123.

15 VLT, 'La política internacional de la URSS y los países en vías de desarrollo', Mexico City, 10 November 1960, in *Obra*, VI/3, 1960, p. 254; VLT, 'Orientación general de las reformas a la declaración del principios, programmea y estatutos del Partido Popular', Mexico City, August 1960, in *Obra*, VI/3, 1960, pp. 204–7.

16 Estrada Martínez 1983, pp. 135–40; Carr 1992, p. 254.

17 Schmidt 2006, p. 378. In Spanish: 'pocos pero seguros', 'pocos pero serviles', corresponding to the party's acronym.

18 Mr Monges to the DFS, Mexico City, 1 April 1961, AGN, DFS, VLT, vp 5/9, 11-2-1961.

ted as the choice for congressional deputy from Sonora, although he aspired to the governor's spot, which he was always denied. Before the elections, Lombardo went to Hermosillo to negotiate with Jacinto and Francisco Figueroa Mendoza, as to who would be named as the candidate. No agreement was reached. Speaking before four hundred campesinos, Lombardo said that there had not been a falling out between the UGOCM and the PPS and that as candidate for governor the party should name Francisco Figueroa Mendoza, head of the PPS in Sonora. Many people attended the event, not just from the party, to hear Lombardo speak.[19]

The PPS was not well organised. The fraud was consummated as in the past and Figueroa Mendoza lost the election. The Federal Security Directorate had an infiltrator in the party from whom it knew that members from several states would be going to the capital to complain that the PPS did not run an active campaign for its candidates for congressional deputy seats, that 'some of them did not organise a single rally', did not paint slogans on walls nor paste up posters due to pressure from the authorities and the clergy's influence on Catholic voters. The 2 July fraud would be the last, Lombardo proclaimed, 'because within a few years the conditions will have changed so much in the world and therefore in Mexico, that social transformations that occur will not favour the regressive forces, but rather those who are fighting for true democracy and for the happiness of mankind'.[20]

The party had one of its candidates accepted as a congressional deputy and was to negotiate with the PRI and the government part of its political and social agenda, such as the land reform. Jilted, Jacinto López should not have given much importance to the negotiations with the head of the Agrarian Department to which Lombardo invited him in order 'to examine the reform proposals that the executive branch will immediately send to Congress'. He felt aggrieved following the recent elections and transactions with the government did not inspire confidence. Before the break between the two men occurred, Lombardo and López had differences for some time concerning agricultural policy. While López resorted to land seizures in the absence of land distribution, Lombardo appealed to the authorities, negotiating possible solutions.[21] He recognised the despair of the campesinos whose agricultural records had 'been held up for thirty years in the first level of the paperwork procedures',

---

19   Coronel D.E.M. Manuel Rangel Escamilla, DFS, Mexico City, 28 May 1961, AGN, DFS, VLT, vp 5/9, 100-24-3-61.
20   Coronel Manuel Rangel Escamilla, DFS, Mexico City, 4 July 1961 and 10 July 1961, AGN, DFS, VLT, vp 5/9, 11-2-61.
21   VLT to Jacinto López, Mexico City, 17 October 1961, FHLT, file 1136.

but felt that any subversive action that weakened Mexico 'opens the doors to a US military intervention in our domestic life' and was therefore counterrevolutionary and unpatriotic.[22]

Lombardo was referring to the abortive campesino uprising, led by the longstanding revolutionary Celestino Gasca, aimed at taking power and implementing a new agrarian programme.[23] The solution was land distribution, granting credits and providing agricultural inputs via institutional channels. The rest was anarchy that the government was right to combat.[24]

2 Against the Current

The dynamic but much harassed Cuban Revolution inspired the formation of the National Liberation Movement (MLN) in Mexico and Latin America. It emerged in August 1961, sponsored by General Cárdenas, to bring together movements and left-wingers who saw in Cuba a reflection of the revolutionary possibilities for Mexico and the rest of the hemisphere. Writer Carlos Fuentes, one of the leading lights of the MLN, summarised its programme as a need to complete the unfulfilled Mexican Revolution and democratically resolve the people's problems. That required political democracy, economic justice and planning, defence of natural resources, popular education and an independent foreign policy.[25]

Despite the similarity of their goals, the MLN and PPS were incompatible. Both claimed to defend the rights and interests of the workers and peasants, national sovereignty, economic emancipation and peace. The difference resided in what the correct method was to protect those 'so vilely despised and exploited by those who steal the fruits of their labour'. The MLN wanted to rescue the Constitution 'from the garbage heap in which it has been discarded' without compromises. The fact that Lázaro Cárdenas would lead the MLN guaranteed its fidelity to the Mexican Revolution. The movement was organised around the defence of national interests against US imperialism with individuals and organisations that might have differences among them, but which 'are convinced that there are many tasks that can be undertaken jointly and by

---

22 VLT, 'Declaraciones del PPS sobre los levantamientos armados ocurridos los días 14, 15 y 16 de septiembre 1961', *Avante*, no. 14 and no. 15, October 1961, in *Obra*, VI/6, 1961, p. 142.
23 Servín 2010, pp. 527–57.
24 Coronel Manuel Rangel Escamilla, DFS, 'Memorándum', Mexico City, 19 September 1961, AGN, DFS, VLT, vp 5/9, 11-2-61.
25 Fuentes 1980, p. 65; Zolov 2004, pp. 175–214; Keller 2015, p. 105.

mutual agreement'. The MLN decided to have its own organisation to keep its independence untainted, to prevent the autonomy of its member organisations from being affected, and so as not to become 'an instrument of this or that organisation or party'.[26] Alonso Aguilar Monteverde, one of its founders, explained the essence of its difference with the PPS, namely, the democratic centralism of the left parties as against the decentralisation, autonomy and initiative of the MLN committees, which did not seek to become a party and had no intention to participate in elections.

When the MLN arose, the PPS, Lombardo and his entourage signed the minutes of its founding meeting, but he feared that the MLN could become a left-wing party, which he deemed unnecessary, and not just a coordinating centre to fight for world peace and against imperialism, which is what he hoped it would be. There was more: the MLN did not accept members of the PPS in its leadership, except Jacinto, was dominated by communists, by the leaders of the teachers' movement headed by Othón Salazar, the journalist Jorge Carrión, Cárdenas (father and son), and the old Veracruz revolutionary Heriberto Jara.

Lombardo and the MLN engaged in mutual attacks and polemics, which reverberated among members of the UGOCM who sympathised with the movement. Among them were Arturo Orona of the La Laguna region and Ramón Danzós Palomino from the Yaqui Valley – both areas bastions of the campesino movement – who left the party and remained in the movement. PPS members closest to Lombardo accused those who wanted to belong to the MLN of dual membership, which the party prohibited. The movement leaders characterised such a proscription as a ruse, since the MLN was not a party. Finally, the fact that the PPS was fighting for socialism, which was not the goal of the MLN, made them irreconcilable.[27] The frontal attack against the MLN came in December 1962 at the congress of the UGOCM. General Cárdenas knew that the animosity did not come from Jacinto López, who proved powerless to express himself in solidarity and in fraternal terms with the MLN and most likely could not oppose orders from the leadership of the PPS.[28]

During the UGOCM congress, Lombardo disassociated the party from the movement. Intellectual and diplomat Victor Flores Olea was scathing in his

---

26   *Liberación*, organ of the MLN, Mexico City, 18 June 1962, AGN, Ramo Gustavo Díaz Ordaz (henceforth GDO), box 420, file 121/544.61/14; Alonso Aguilar in Arguedas 2014, p. 69 and pp. 70–4.
27   VLT, 'PPS y MLN', Mexico City, 9 November 1961, FHLT, file 1137; Rafael Estrada Villa to VLT, Culiacán, Sinaloa, 24 September 1962; José Jiménez Acevedo to VLT, Navojoa, Sonora, 10 October 1962, FHLT, file 1151.
28   LC, Mexico City, 14 December 1962, in Cárdenas 1986b, vol. 3, p. 317.

criticism of the decision and of Lombardo's wager in favour of the national bourgeoisie that made him an implacable judge of everything that resembled a genuine popular movement. Flores Olea charged that just as Lombardo lambasted the MLN, he had also done so previously with independent trade unions and against other left-wing organisations and autonomous popular movements. He concluded that Lombardo's 'attitude harms the Mexican anti-imperialist front, because it divides, fragments and weakens it'.[29]

President López Mateos also did not sympathise with the National Liberation Movement. 'But what are you liberating yourself from?', the president asked after General Cárdenas told him that a group of young MLN activists in Jalisco was harassed by local authorities.[30] Did López Mateos influence Lombardo to desist from collaborating with the MLN? The most likely variant is that Lombardo took his distance from the movement to the extent that he perceived it as an opposition to the PRI and the government and when Cárdenas's national and international projection remained and grew beyond what was acceptable to the president. Lombardo rejected the MLN also because whoever joined a movement and did not lead it but was at the tail end of it, in the curves, 'will crash against any obstacle'.[31] The way forward was the extension of bourgeois democracy, the only force that would enable the working class to organise to take power 'when the objective and subjective circumstances so indicate'. To proceed otherwise was anarchism and Trotskyism, 'which leads to incurable bitterness or political suicide'.[32]

It was an unpleasant surprise for Lombardo when in January 1963 the MLN and several leftist leaders created a new campesino organisation, the Independent Peasant Confederation (CCI). It represented perhaps 100,000, perhaps half a million peasant farmers, according to inaccurate data, and its aim was to enable campesinos to take control of their destiny through taking control of the land, improved access to water, credit, the unionisation of agricultural workers, better education, social security and healthcare, and to ally with the working class.[33] Lombardo rejected the CCI out of hand, 'because it is not by divid-

---

29 Flores Olea 1962, p. 11.
30 LC, Cuernavaca, 3 October 1961, in Cárdenas 1986b, vol. 3, pp. 243–4.
31 VLT, 'Mensaje al MLN a propósito de su respuesta a la invitación del PPS', 17 January 1962, *Avante*, 18–19 January 1962, in *Obra*, VI/7, 1962, p. 22; VLT, 'Reunión de los delegados del PPS al Congreso de la Paz', Mexico City, 17 June 1962, in *Obra*, VI/8, 1962, p. 76; Carr 1992, p. 233; Keller 2015, pp. 94–110.
32 VLT, 'La izquierda en la historia de México', *Siempre!*, no. 478, 22 August 1962, in *Obra*, VI/8, 1962, pp. 293–7.
33 Keller 2015, pp. 112–13; Aviña 2014, p. 93.

ing that we unify, but struggling together it is possible to achieve full unity'.[34] Lenin already said that creating pure organisations was 'childish'; that it was necessary to educate the masses. The correlation of forces and alliances were the key words in the condemnation; the communists who were behind this organisation were wrong on both counts. While Lombardo was fighting a losing battle with the communists on the international scene to save what he could of the CTAL, the formation of the Independent Peasant Confederation in Mexico, 'inspired by the old and sick sectarianism of the Communist Party and neo-Trotskyism that breathes life into the National Liberation Movement',[35] added to the division. He did not mention that General Cárdenas attended the inauguration of the CCI at the request of the campesinos, for some of whom Cárdenas was 'our Fidel'.[36] Attacks by public figures such as former President Emilio Portes Gil and Federal Attorney General Salvador Azuela against the MLN, CCI and General Cárdenas intensified because the new organisation competed with the official, PRI-affiliated CNC for the support of the peasants.

The approaching presidential succession was now his main task. Lombardo would have preferred that the PCM not have a social base and be forced to ally itself with the PPS, but in creating a peasant organisation it achieved such a base of support, weakening the UGOCM and radicalising the campesino movement. As part of his polemical attacks, Lombardo censured General Cárdenas, which angered the PPS youth, who published a pamphlet entitled *The road is to the left, compañero Lombardo*. They accused him of developing a personality cult, that changing the name of the PP to PPS was premature, took place without a discussion in the party and that the party was a front for the government.[37]

However, Lombardo was clear that the most direct path to reach his goals was through the power of the state, and at that moment through the presidential candidate Gustavo Díaz Ordaz. When they met for one hour in December 1962 they spoke of the currents opposed to Adolfo López Mateos, the MLN, the UGOCM and about the PPS, which will 'insist on the democratic and patriotic front'; they discussed the establishment of a campus of the Workers'

---

34 VLT, 'La UGOCM y el Movimiento de Liberación Nacional, resolución del congreso extraordinario de la UGOCM', December 1962, FHLT, file 1155.

35 'Declaraciones del PPS acerca de la nueva organización campesina', Mexico City, 8 January 1963, FHLT, file 1158 and in *Obra*, VI/10, 1963, pp. 13–14.

36 LC, Jiquilpan, Michoacán, 19 January 1963, in Cárdenas 1986b, vol. 3, p. 326; Pátzcuaro, 21 January 1963, in Cárdenas 1986b, vol. 3, pp. 328–31; Keller 2015, p. 113.

37 T-4, VLT, 17 January 1963, FBI file, 100-4326-1092; Lina V. de Rubio, Mexico City, 20 March 1963, FHLT, file 1161.

University in Morelia and the 'assistance offered' by the candidate; they talked about China, the railroads and the Bishop of Tehuantepec.[38]

The situation seemed to be safe for the usual transfer of power. US embassy officials could rest easy. In a conversation with attorney Pedro Reyner, married to the daughter of Emilio Portes Gil, they received valuable information so they could weigh the situation in Mexico in light of the upcoming election. López Mateos was pleased with Portes Gil's attack on Cárdenas on the occasion of the creation of the Independent Peasant Confederation, on the communist Lombardo and the PPS, which the government said to have under its control.[39]

But in April 1963 the People's Electoral Front was created. Very much feared by Lombardo as well as the government, its aim was to reorient the Mexican Revolution, defend the Cuban Revolution, and mobilise the masses against the 'traitors' to the revolution. It was endorsed by Demetrio Vallejo, Othón Salazar and the PCM. Its objectives were the same as the MLN's goals, although the movement dissociated itself from the electoral front. Its candidate was the teacher and agrarian leader Ramón Danzós Palomino, once a member of the PPS. Meanwhile, it was reassuring that General Cárdenas supported the candidacy of Díaz Ordaz. This may have contributed to the weakening of the MLN and the CCI. From then on, internal disputes would divide the campesino organisation into two irreconcilable blocs.[40]

3   On the Final Campaign Trail

Since announcing his candidacy, Lombardo knew he would be a congressional deputy. The new electoral law included proportional representation of the parties, which gave him an automatic pass to enter the Chamber of Deputies without suffering the humiliating experience of being another victim of fraud orchestrated by the PRI. The parties that obtained 2.5% of the national vote were entitled to five congressional deputies, but the goal was to get a million votes, with which the PPS would be allocated 20 deputies, 'at the head of whom I will be found'.[41]

---

38   Telegram to VLT (sender's name unintelligible), 20 November 1962, AGN, DFS, VLT, vp 6/9, 32-2-62; 'Lic. Gustavo Díaz Ordaz, apuntes para el viernes', 21 December 1962, FHLT, file 1155.
39   Irving Salert to the State Department, telegram, Mexico City, 10 April 1963, NARA, RG 59, POL 2–3 Mex.; Keller 2015, pp. 109–10.
40   Krauze 1997b, p. 265; Keller 2015, pp. 150–3; Aviña 2014, pp. 94–6; Carr 1992, p. 228.
41   VLT to Pablo González Mora, 23 January 1964, FHLT, file 1178.

The party's top brass took control over the PPS's electoral machine. All the candidates for the post of congressional deputy had to obtain the approval of the national leadership, since they did not represent the localities that they were originally from, but the national interest. Before the party assembly took place, Lombardo met with Díaz Ordaz to offer the PPS's support. The cautious Interior Minister thanked him, but told him that 'if you choose to support my candidacy, decide on how you are going to inform me of the resolution'. Díaz Ordaz gave him several options and assured him that from his perspective 'you are an important factor in the life of Mexico ... and I'd like to ask you personally to have discussions with me, as you have done with President López Mateos ... you are part of the people. I am at your service and I thank you very much for having responded to my invitation to talk this afternoon'.[42]

At the extraordinary assembly of the PPS held at the Teatro Lírico, support for Díaz Ordaz was not subject to discussion, although there were voices against such a policy. Why not have our own candidate, asked the delegate from Monterrey, while the delegate from Las Delicias, Chihuahua, questioned support for the candidate of the bourgeoisie and not one from the working class. Mexico City delegate Jesús Bernal argued that 'we cannot support a regime that violently ended the railroad strike, with so many arrests and imprisonments'. Díaz Ordaz was an unacceptable candidate.[43]

But Miguel Ángel Velasco, a former leader of the communist party and now in the national leadership of the PPS, moved to silence the criticisms, proclaiming that the PPS's position on the upcoming elections was to 'follow the strategic and tactical line dictated by Marxist dialectics'. The enemy was Yankee imperialism and then groups of the radical left with their magazines 'of the Trotskyist tendencies'. After other interventions, Lombardo took the floor in favour of Díaz Ordaz, 'a man who has led an exemplary life, of great honesty, of liberal ideas'. Lombardo also announced that he was withdrawing from his international responsibilities, without explaining the dissolution of the CTAL, and from then on he would devote his time exclusively to the PPS, which in the future will 'be in power'.[44]

Campaigning since January 1964, Lombardo took the trips necessary to achieve the one million vote goal. He was about to turn 70 and felt strong.[45]

---

42 VLT, 'Informe de la entrevista con el licenciado GDO', Mexico City, 28 November 1963, in *Obra*, VI/13, 1963, p. 135.
43 Coronel D.E.M. Manuel Rangel Escamilla, DFS, 'Se informa en relación con el Partido Popular Socialista', Mexico City, 30 November 1963, AGN, DFS, VLT, vp 6/9, 11-2-63.
44 Ibid.
45 VLT, 'Yo soy un agitador', speech delivered in Zaragoza, Puebla, 15 March 1964, FHLT, file

In Libres, Puebla, the campaign turned sour, 'idiot go home', 'traitor', 'we don't want communism in Puebla or Mexico', the villagers shouted. Undaunted, on the opposite corner from the church, Lombardo made an analogy between Francisco I. Madero and himself, travelling the country, 'speaking with the masses, knowing their problems, and seeking ways to resolve them ... Of course I will get to be a federal deputy; it's stupid and childish to think otherwise'.[46]

For some time, Rosa María Otero had been ill with cardiac decompensation, 'but she's now on the road to recovery'.[47] That day in May she saw the doctor who was pleased by the improvement in her health. But in the evening, watching television with her granddaughter Rosa María, 16 years of age, at her side, she passed away 'with a smile on her lips'.[48] Lombardo Toledano's lifelong companion had died. Rosa María had been indispensable: she organised the practical affairs of the household, looked after the family, safeguarded her husband's thoughts, did not allow others to interrupt him while he was working or sleeping, had clean and impeccable clothes and food on the table.[49] Lombardo informed his sister Margarita of his wife's death:

> Rosa María's passing away occurred on 20 May and has posed a series of problems for all of us that are easy to understand; but the most important was my own personal situation, which I have managed to overcome by intensifying my daily work, focusing on the main points in my thinking, and believing that life goes on, and I must accept it as it is and live on passionately as I have done for my entire existence.[50]

Following the funeral and burial in the Panteón de Dolores cemetery, which was attended by comrades and government officials, Lombardo continued with his campaign and that of Díaz Ordaz. Physical attacks on members of the PPS and UGOCM by armed groups of police, supported by the army in Sinaloa, Nuevo León and Puebla, did not discourage him.[51]

1181 and in *Obra*, VI/14, 1964, p. 129, pp. 130–1; VLT, speech delivered in Cuetzalan, Puebla, 29 March 1964, FHLT, file 1181.

46   Coronel D.E.M. Manuel Rangel Escamilla, DFS, 'Memorándum', Mexico City, 13 March 1964; 15 March 1964, 22 March 1964, AGN, DFS, VLT, vp 7/9, 11-3-64.
47   VLT to David Efrón, Mexico City, 15 May 1964, file 1183.
48   'Sentido sepelio de la Sra. Rosa Ma. Otero de Lombardo', *Novedades*, 22 May 1964; Interview with Rosa María Soto, Cuernavaca, 5 August 2014.
49   Interview with Marcela Lombardo Otero, Mexico City, 1 September 2005.
50   VLT to Margarita Lombardo Toledano, 18 September 1964, FHLT, file 1194.
51   Sóstenes García Cena to VLT, telegrama, Bamoa, Sinaloa, 14 June 1964, FHLT, file 1188; 'Sepultaron a la Señora Lombardo', *El Universal*, 22 May 1964.

The Federal Security Directorate knew, as did Lombardo, that a Teziuteco cattle rancher from the district in which Lombardo was a candidate, gave the presidents of the polling stations 'confidential instructions'. When the voting would end on 5 July,

> you should take the election documentation as well as the ballot boxes to your homes. Do whatever is possible to avoid furnishing the copy of the vote tally sheets for the congressional deputy elections, only turning them over if the representatives of the parties request it. If you tally up the votes, start with the election of the president, then senators and in the end the congressional deputies.
>
> If you can, it would be best to fill in the data from the vote count at your home, eliminating the votes of the candidates who it's not worthwhile counting. Once you're familiar with these instructions, destroy this piece of paper.[52]

The wind-up campaign rally took place in Teziutlán on 28 June. Lombardo praised the calm atmosphere in which it occurred, hailed the economic progress of López Mateos's six-year presidential administration and celebrated Díaz Ordaz's victory at the polls even before the elections took place.[53] Ending his speech, Lombardo predicted that he would soon be in the Chamber of Deputies. The Teziutecos were elated, erupting in cheers, applause with musical accompaniment, singing of the national anthem and they walked down the main street of the village next to the self-proclaimed soon-to-be congressional deputy.

The 5 July elections were fraudulent. Voter registration lists were falsified, PPS poll watchers were denied their right to be at the polling stations, ballot boxes were stolen, more votes were cast than registered voters, ballots were arbitrarily annulled, the PAN and PRI collaborated in several electoral districts to divide the vote between them, polling station officials received orders to prevent PPS candidates from obtaining more than 3% of the vote in order not to recognise the 20 congressional deputies claimed by the PPS under proportional representation.[54]

---

52 Coronel D.E.M. Manuel Rangel Escamilla, DFS, 'Memorándum', Mexico City, 27 June 1964, AGN, DFS, VLT, vp 7/9, 100-24-3-64.
53 VLT, 'No detener la revolución sino acelerarla', Teziutlán, Puebla, 28 June 1964, FHLT, file 1188.
54 'Declaraciones de la dirección nacional del PPS acerca de las elecciones del 5 de julio 1964', Mexico City, 21 July 1964, FHLT, file 1191.

The elections did not result in the one million votes that Lombardo expected, but his place in the Chamber of Deputies was assured. Shortly before the Chamber of Deputies' Electoral College submitted the resolution on the distribution of congressional deputy seats by party, 'I knew from a phone call that we would have deputies and who the ten would be'. The PAN objected, 'which made me laugh'. It did not matter how these congressional deputies entered the Chamber, what was important was that 'it is a great victory not only for our party but for the democratic life of Mexico'.[55] The PAN obtained 20 congressional deputy seats, and the new party of the veterans of the revolution, the Authentic Party of the Mexican Revolution (PARM), won five. Among the PPS members elected was Jacinto López, who won the district election based on simple majority vote. The other deputies which the president bestowed on the PPS corresponded to proportional representation. It is most likely that the deputy positions were negotiated in advance, regardless of the vote, whose percentage would remain a secret.[56] Officially, the PPS achieved 1.4% of the votes cast.[57] The gift from the outgoing government was the building on San Ildefonso 72 for the Workers' University, which Adriana Lombardo Otero, faithful to her father's legacy, ran for several decades.[58]

In early July, María Lombardo Toledano, Vicente's sister, writer and wife of the eminent archaeologist Alfonso Caso, passed away. Despite the two sensitive deaths, one after another, Rosa María at 66 and María at 64, Lombardo, 70 years old on 16 July, with more lines furrowing his forehead, standing straight and without losing his elegant pose, was not about to cloister himself away in mourning, but sought to embrace life.

> I have never gotten drunk, even when I drink wine, which in Mexico is difficult due to the elevation and for being expensive. Every day I do exercises, one that is mixture of Swedish and Chinese gymnastics, and strengthens the respiratory system. I walk a lot. At 70 I can climb the sides of the Popo volcano. When I can, I practice horse riding. What prolongs life is to live with euphoria, driven by the ideals and [faith in] the nature of humankind itself.[59]

---

55   VLT to Elena Lacko, Mexico City, 26 August 1964, FHLT, file 1193; VLT, 'Informe a los delegados de la reunión preparatoria del Comité Central del PPS', Mexico City, 9 January 1965, FHLT, file 1204.
56   Mabry 1974, pp. 221–33.
57   Loaeza 1999, p. 288.
58   Coronel D.E.M. Manuel Rangel Escamilla, DFS, Mexico City, 3 September 1964, AGN, DFS, VLT, vp 7/9, 44-19-64.
59   'Interview with José Natividad Rosales and Víctor Rico Galán', *Siempre!*, no. 578, 22 July 1964, in *Obra*, VI/ 15, 1964, p. 67.

On 1 August the doors to the Palacio de Bellas Artes were opened for a gala event to honour Lombardo Toledano. About 1,700 people attended, including muralist Siqueiros, who was released from prison on 13 July in a presidential amnesty after four years behind bars and who received a standing ovation when he appeared; long-standing trade unionist Jacinto Huitrón; the ambassadors of Cuba, China and the countries of the socialist camp; actor Ignacio López Tarso, the Spanish exiles, who were hissed at by the Franquistas who were present before being evicted, while messages were read from several countries in Latin America, the United States, the communist veteran Vittorio Vidali from Trieste, and other European communist friends.

It was perhaps Lombardo who wrote the chronicle of the event or at least corrected the text in his own handwriting. That afternoon a storm drenched the city, but there were hundreds of people gathered at the entrance of the Palacio de Bellas Artes waiting for the central door to open to get seats in the auditorium.[60]

> Never had such a tribute been paid to any Mexican out of power. Only a life that for over half a century was dedicated to furthering the highest human ideals could bring together so many qualities. That evening will go down in history as a testimony to the great collective sensitivity of Mexicans and their strong will to follow the path chartered since the War of Independence, which is what Vicente Lombardo Toledano has done without betrayals or hesitations.[61]

A few days later, Lombardo took office in the Chamber of Deputies and on 4 September he was present for the president's sixth state of the nation address. He hailed the country's progress and praised Adolfo López Mateos, the president who nationalised the light and power company and distributed land to the peasants, surpassed only by Lázaro Cárdenas. Even the Priistas 'were impressed by his use of the materialist dialectic and his oratory skills'.[62] His speech was received with a standing ovation by all except for the PAN legislators.[63]

---

60   'La velada en el Palacio de Bellas Artes', 2 August 1964, FHLT, file 1192. VLT corrected the chronicle in his own handwriting, which also reflected his writing style.
61   Ibid.
62   VLT, 'Diario de los Debates de la Cámara de Diputados', 4 September 1964, FHLT, file 1193; Armando Fischer S., 'Lombardo se hizo aplaudir por el PRI', Excélsior, 5 September 1964.
63   Coronel D.E.M. Manuel Rangel Escamilla, DFS, Mexico City, 4 September 1964, AGN, DFS, VLT, vp 7/9, 44-19-64.

The Chamber of Deputies was Lombardo's forum. It gave him a platform to advocate the strengthening of state capitalism and to publicise his ideas nationally, which otherwise would have remained limited to meetings, party newspapers or the magazine *Siempre!* He was a good, convincing speaker; he knew history and laws, and had a way of arranging the facts that few remembered but that were designed to persuade his audience in one or another direction. He was given the opportunity to tour the country, engage in partisan proselytising, analyse the material and moral conditions of Mexico and was allowed to narrow the distance between himself and the president.

In the Chamber of Deputies he proposed legislative motions on the financial transparency of decentralised state-owned enterprises dedicated to public investment, an initiative on broadcasting parliamentary debates on radio and television, so the population would be informed of work of the deputies; on tax increases, on reducing foreign investment and on repealing the law on the crime of social dissolution. The PRI and PAN congressional deputies supported many of his sensible motions.[64]

One of his proposals was to allow for the re-election of congressional deputies. The December legislative recess should serve 'to talk to the people to see if they want to re-elect you'.[65] The motion from committee was adopted by an overwhelming majority, including Lombardo's former colleague Enrique Ramírez y Ramírez, now a PRI congressional deputy, but caused a commotion among the public, which was against the proposal. The communists and members of the MLN anticipated that it would be a short step from allowing the re-election of congressional deputies to the re-election of the president. The Senate, that 'chamber of fossils', as Lombardo characterised it, rejected the deputies' recommendation without any argument.[66]

'Why is it that the Popular Socialist Party, instead of growing numerically, has been declining or stagnating?' was a question that Lombardo had raised

---

64   VLT, 'Respuesta al dictamen de las Comisiones de Diputados que manda al archivo la iniciativa del PPS sobre un capítulo de constitución para la economía mexicana', 20 December 1965, FHLT, file 1224.
65   VLT, 'Intervención en la Cámara de Diputados para fundamentar la iniciativa de transmitir por radio y televisión las sesiones', 16 October 1964, in *Obra*, VI/ 15, 1964, pp. 211–13; Captain Fernando Gutiérrez Barrios, DFS, Mexico City, 30 December 1964, AGN, DFS, VLT, vp 7/9, 44-19-64.
66   Coronel D.E.M. Manuel Rangel Escamilla, DFS, Mexico City, 1964, 22 September 1964, 4 December 1964 VLT, VP, DFS, 7/9, 44-19-64; Captain Fernando Gutiérrez Barrios, DFS, Mexico City, 21 Novembre 1965, AGN, DFS, VLT, vp 7/9, 11-2-65; Coronel D.E.M. Manuel Rangel Escamilla, DFS, Mexico City, 22 September 1964, 4 December 1964, AGN, DFS, VLT, vp 7/9, 44-19-64.

and which had been weighing on the minds of not a few members, creating an atmosphere of dissatisfaction. A few weeks before getting married a second time and going on his honeymoon, he answered his own question. What was important was the ideological definition of the organisation even though it might be losing members, because it was a cadre party. The cadres were the expression of the masses and without masses there were no cadres: 'the masses are the object of the application of a political theory that only the cadre can provide'.[67]

On 10 April 1965 Lombardo married the lawyer María Teresa Puente. A mutual friend introduced them in November 1932 and from then on they participated together in the courts, in the labour unions and public debates. After their house was completed, they moved into their new home on Flor de María street in Tlacopac, on the outskirts of Mexico City. One observer remarked at the time: 'The romanticism of the ideologue was without limits. At one end of the garden in the home he built a shed [and] under its protective cover planted fragrant herbs, such as orangewood, bay leaf, mint, thyme, vanilla. He went there with María Teresa Puente to transform the world in another way'.[68]

For their honeymoon they went to Europe for more than two months. While in Greece and breathing its historical magnificence, Lombardo wrote what he called 'The perfect love', unique in his literary legacy as a writer. He was not an accomplished poet, but he liked to write in verse or prose his feelings, which were inseparable from his thinking as an ideologue. On that occasion, he expressed feelings which might have been a long time in the making, as a Homeric poem, featuring a chorus of poets, the philosopher, the lover and the beloved, which in three episodes debated the arrival of perfect love, declaimed by the beloved and sublimated by the chorus as the 'symphony of the lifetime':

> My Beloved will soon arrive. I am always within him, and he is always within me. An integral magnetism attracted us since we first met. We have the same internal rhythm, identical reactions, same desires, common thoughts. We share ideals, science and culture. Our dreams symbolise the constant elevation of our inseparable life.[69]

---

67 VLT, '¿Partido de masas o partido de cuadros?', speech delivered at the plenum of the Central Committee of the PPS, Mexico City, 26 February 1965, in *Obra*, VI/17, 1965, p. 81 and p. 87.
68 Scherer García 1986, p. 51.
69 VLT, 'El perfecto amor', Greece, May 1965, FHLT, file 1213.

Upon his return to Mexico, Lombardo found the PPS in shambles, with opposition groups emboldened by his absence and with tasks left unfulfilled. In the Chamber of Deputies he was chosen to comment on the new president's first state of the nation address. The president must have pleased Lombardo when he referred to the minority parties that 'not only have the right, but also the responsibility to criticise and point out errors, omissions, corruption and abuses, and thus contribute to governance'. Lombardo responded as expected. The campesinos that had no prospects of being able to cross the border and work as braceros, to receive land and being without work 'could become a factor disrupting the normal course of the Mexican nation' but 'the greatness' of the revolutionary movement and the state with its intervention, gave Mexico 'the strength and prestige it legitimately enjoys'.[70]

In December 1966, at 72 years of age, content with the task accomplished Lombardo bade farewell to the 46th Congress. In his speech, transcribed from 21, single-spaced typewritten pages, he jokingly predicted his return to the legislature. In reality, his speech was an account of what he achieved or would like to have achieved in the Chamber of Deputies. His proposed amendments to the Constitution were important, but rejected. He was a passionate promoter of the free municipality as the primary institution in the country's political structure with its own resources. He defended the culture of the indigenous peoples and appealed, unsuccessfully, for their languages to have a written expression. He also did not succeed with his proposal to have the income tax legally codified as the means of distribution of national wealth. Lombardo failed to remove the restrictions on Constitutional Article 27, imposed by Miguel Alemán, to enable land reform to be fulfilled. He was not able to amend Article 145 of the penal code concerning the crime of social dissolution and the state's control of communications such as telephone, mail delivery and telegraph.[71] His efforts bore fruit when he fought to include the name of Francisco Villa inscribed in golden letters in the Chamber of Deputies. He argued that even though Villa 'was hard and killed without a trial', a man who 'shed tears at the tomb of Madero and a man who cries cannot be a bandit'.[72] Lombardo and the PPS's proposal for the creation of the Mexican Academy of Sciences and the cultural development of Mexico not depending on foreign funding were approved.[73]

---

70   VLT, 'La intervención del Estado ha salvado a nuestro país', notes on the President's state of the nation address, 1 September 1965, in *Obra*, VI/18, 1965, p. 41, p. 44, p. 52.
71   Ibid.
72   Captain Fernando Gutiérrez Barrios, DFS, Mexico City, 9 November 1966, AGN, DGS, VLT, vp 8/9, 44–1966.
73   Captain Fernando Gutiérrez Barrios, DFS, Mexico City, 15 December 1966, AGN, DGS, VLT, vp 8/9, 44–1966.

He left the Chamber of Deputies as jubilant as he entered; he would not return but was hopeful for the 'new Mexico'.[74]

'How is it possible that you, having always been in the opposition, have always been a friend of whoever was president at the time?' asked Lombardo the journalist Elena Poniatowska in an interview. Lombardo, who had heard this question countless times, replied in the usual way: his behaviour was governed by the 'strategic and tactical line', his alliance with the democratic sectors could be explained by the danger posed by foreign forces and his opposition was to the existing social system, not to the men in power. Poniatowska pressed him further. 'Are you not a spoiled partner of the government, the President, of all people in general?' Lombardo replied that he did not need pampering. 'What I need is to have the possibility, as I have shown, of acting and fighting at the head of my party', which still lacked the strength necessary to transform the country[75] and which, he did not say, was seething with factions that questioned his leadership.

4 Schism in the Party

The expectation that Lombardo would leave the party leadership in younger hands was repeatedly frustrated. His extended honeymoon during the months of April, May and part of June 1965 was the opportunity to replace him, but no one dared, even though in the case of Jacinto López it was not for lack of desire to do so. López was offended because prior to his trip Lombardo told the PPS cadres that there was no one who deserved to be considered his successor in case of his retirement or death. Dissident voices were heard because many of his relatives were in leadership positions. Lombardo was also criticised because, despite the new US attacks on North Vietnam, he opposed PPS members demonstrating on the street outside the embassy like the communists did. The party authorised its members to make their positions known in writing.[76] Did he fear repression by the riot police, which would have placed the party in the opposition camp to which it did not belong? To those waiting their turn, he declared that 'I think it is necessary to start replacing me. But not substitute

---

74 VLT, 'Discurso de despedida de la Cámara de Diputados', 28 December 1966, FHLT, file 1243.
75 Interview with VLT by Elena Poniatowska for *Novedades*, 20 January 1967, FHLT, file 1247.
76 Melchor Carranza Arenas to Miguel A. Velasco, Puebla, 13 November 1964, FHLT, file 1198.

me for being useless, which is different. Nobody is going to remove me from my party. It has cost me many years of my life'.⁷⁷

In mid-1966 an elite group of PPS members prepared the list of candidates for federal congressional deputies for the 1967 elections. The names were precisely those who were expected to be nominated and it was speculated that Adriana, her husband Federico, and Marcela would also be proposed. From Oaxaca there was grumbling that members who had been active for years should be taken into account and not just the 'people favoured by Vicente Lombardo Toledano'.⁷⁸

Party leader Rafael Estrada Villa, faithful to Lombardo until then, resigned from the PPS with a devastating critique and the demand for the right to criticise those in power and public officials, which Lombardo Toledano had systematically prevented, 'thinking that this helps the government, which is not true'.⁷⁹ He further accused Lombardo of receiving monetary payments from several state governments. The scandal this provoked was huge. This time Jacinto came out in defence of Lombardo, because what was happening inside the party was not a public issue or topic of discussion. Estrada Villa continued to denounce Lombardo in the press, presenting himself as being favoured by many PPS members around the country 'to remove federal congressional deputy Vicente Lombardo Toledano from the top leadership of the party'.⁸⁰

Writer José Revueltas added his critical voice in the UNAM Law School. Revueltas, who had come to adopt the thesis of the headless proletariat in Mexico, in reference to the absence of a workers' party,⁸¹ called Lombardo a 'liar and vulgar instrument of the ruling bourgeoisie' and as responsible for the crisis experienced by the PPS from which he had resigned. Disgruntled PPS members at the UNAM distributed leaflets, whose headline read 'Youth accuse Lombardo of nepotism', a situation which made change in the party leadership impossible.⁸²

---

77   VLT, '¿Partido de masas o partido de cuadros?', speech delivered in the plenary session of the Central committee of the PPS, Mexico City, 26 February 1965, in *Obra*, VI/17, 1965, p. 87.
78   Captain Fernando Gutiérrez Barrios, DFS, Mexico City, 4 June 1966, AGN, DFS, VLT, vp 8/9, 11-2-66.
79   Captain Fernando Gutiérrez Barrios, DFS, Mexico City, 29 July 1966, 1 August 1966, 19 August 1966, AGN, DFS, VLT, vp 8/9, 11-2-66.
80   Captain Fernando Gutiérrez Barrios, DFS, Mexico City DF, 15 September 1966, 3 October 1966, AGN, DFS, VLT, vp. 8/9, 11-2-66.
81   Revueltas 1987.
82   Captain Fernando Gutiérrez Barrios, DFS, Mexico City, 8 September 1966, AGN, DFS, VLT,

Dissent came out in the open in late 1967, after it became known that President Díaz Ordaz favoured the PPS with ten federal congressional deputy seats, none from the UGOCM. This time, Jacinto López expressed his views publicly. He argued that the party had abandoned the revolutionary struggle and chosen the opportunist path of collaboration with the federal government. Defying Lombardo as never before, he declared that he would not allow the PPS to intervene in campesino issues in Sonora, called for Lombardo to be disqualified as party leader because he violated its principles, and if this were not accepted, he would leave the organisation.[83] The Sonora PPS met without the knowledge of the national leadership and Lombardo, demanded a national assembly as anticipated in the bylaws in order to change the members of the leadership and the direction of the party.

The national committee met on 12 January 1968. Lombardo accused the Sonora members of deviationism and indiscipline, charged that socialism was not their goal and denigrated the UGOCM's activities as being 'mere bureaucratic paperwork procedures involving agricultural issues'. He rejected the Sonora members' allegations and called on them to 'publicly rectify their mistakes' or they would be expelled.[84] One account of Lombardo's actions argued that he was committed to the presidential candidacy of Interior Minister Luis Echeverría, while Jacinto López was in favour of presidential secretary Emilio Martínez Manautou. And 'since it is Echeverría who chooses the party's congressional deputies', Lombardo eliminated adversaries within the PPS.[85]

In June, the fourth national congress of the PPS was held in the capital, 20 years after its founding. From Sonora, a DFS agent reported, a train with 850 peasant delegates left for Mexico City, with Francisco Figueroa Mendoza at the head of the group and with 'the desire to rescue the party from the morass in which it has sunk due to its current leaders'. According to the agent's account, the Sonora delegates wanted to exercise pressure based on their membership numbers, showing that if anywhere it was in Sonora that the PPS had a social base. They wanted to purge the party of its leaders, removing Lombardo

---

vp 8/9, 44-19-1966; Agent 419, 'Memorándum Universidad', Mexico City, 12 September 1966, AGN, GDO, box 205.

83   Captain Fernando Gutiérrez Barrios, DFS, Mexico City, 21 October 1967, 26 October 1967, 14 November 1967, AGN, DFS, VLT, vp 8/9, 11-2-67; De Grammont 1989, pp. 259–60.

84   Comité Central del PPS, 'Resolución sobre la actitud del comité directivo del PPS en Sonora', 13 January 1968, FHLT, file 1250; Estrada Martínez 1983, pp. 148–51; Grijalba Dávila 2012, p. 123.

85   'La disputa de Jacinto López por el control del PPS es parte de la lucha por la sucesión presidencial', National Organisation for Revolutionary Action, Mexico City, 18 January 1968, in AGN, DFS, VLT, vp 9/9, 11-2-68.

and putting Jacinto López in his place as interim leader. In the end, about 175 campesino delegates left Sonora for the congress, but before they had time to reach Mexico City, Lombardo had dissolved their state committee and appointed another.[86]

The campesinos, headed by their leaders, reached the PPS headquarters on Avenida Morelos:

> When this was noted, the PPS members proceeded to close the doors of the building, so that the López Moreno group could not enter and disrupt the event.
> Vicente Lombardo Toledano, seeing the group, preferred not to enter the Party building so as to avoid running into López Moreno.[87]

The Sonora delegates stationed themselves at the doors to the building, so that no one could enter and the national assembly could not begin. Major Celso Zúñiga of the special services division of the Mexico City police urged the UGOCM leaders to leave along with their contingents to prevent a clash between the two sides. Jacinto López and the others protested because they were not allowed to enter, but gave up and went looking for federal authorities 'to explain the situation'. PPS's press and information secretary Manuel Stephens García brushed off the incident and told reporters that the braceros deceived by Jacinto López wanted to obstruct the work of the PPS national assembly.

Defiant, Jacinto gathered his supporters at the headquarters of the UGOCM at 29 Mesones street. If the president did not remove Lombardo from the PPS leadership, they would form the Mexican Workers and Peasants Party. But Jacinto López, ill with lung emphysema and breathing with difficulty on the high plateau of the capital, knew how the political system of Mexico worked – given that he had manoeuvred within it for decades – and of Lombardo's role in underpinning it. In the meeting, López sowed the seed of the new party, 'although this could possibly lead to our imprisonment, because perhaps the government will not allow its legal registration'.[88] But Lombardo looked down on the Sonorenses and on their leader who drove them to insub-

---

86 VLT, 'Circular a los miembros del PPS en el estado de Sonora, a propósito del legitimo órgano de dirección', 10 June 1968, in *Obra*, VI/24, 1968, pp. 53–4.
87 Captain Fernando Gutiérrez Barrios, DFS, Mexico City, 10 March 1968, 13 June 1968, June 1968, AGN, DFS, VLT, vp, 9/9, 100-17-3.
88 Captain Fernando Gutiérrez Barrios, DFS, Mexico City, June 1968, AGN, DFS, VLT, vp, 9/9, 100-17-3; Grijalba Dávila 2012, pp. 124–6.

bordination, for 'outside of a small region of the Republic no one knows who they are or has ever heard of them'.[89]

5   1968

As occurred every year, in January 1968 the PPS held its annual dinner. Lombardo spoke for about two hours, presenting a picture of the world and Mexico based on the certainty that imperialism had declined, despite the resources it had to survive, and that socialism was growing. 'Long live the socialist Mexico of tomorrow, through the road of the Mexican Revolution', he cheered. Those in attendance responded with a standing ovation.[90]

But Lombardo had no such certainty. He was concerned that ideas that were 'false' and 'treacherous to socialism' were proliferating in Eastern Europe. In Poland, students took to the streets with signs and leaflets proclaiming 'down with communism', 'let's take up arms', 'let's get rid of the Muscovite yoke'. It all began with the ban on staging at the National Theater *Forefathers' Eve* by Adam Mickiewicz, Polish playwright and an emblematic symbol of the country's romantic nationalism. The accusation was that the functions 'had become a springboard for a political demonstration of an anti-Soviet character'. Mickiewicz's work, written in 1823, was anti-Czarist, but in the Poland of 1968 verses such as 'I have to be free, yes, but I don't know where the news came from. But well I know what Muscovite freedom means. Scoundrels, to take the chains from hands and legs yet still to cramp the soul', provoked applause from the public. Quoting from the Polish Communist Party First Secretary Wladyslaw Gomulka's speech, he underlined that 'we cannot allow that, in the name of an abstract freedom and artistic creation, the anti-Czarist message of *Forefathers' Eve* be transformed into anti-Soviet weapons'.[91]

But the protests sparked by the deformations of really existing socialism took place also in Hungary and Czechoslovakia. Lombardo knew that in each of these countries, the state was forced to introduce timid reforms to address the deficient management of the economy, that there emerged Marxist criticisms of the regime that had alienated the working class and of the corruption of the ruling elite, but he euphemistically characterised the measures taken as 'adjust-

---

89   VLT, 'Circular a los miembros del PPS en el estado de Sonora a propósito de la actitud facciosa de los dirigentes de la UGOCM', Mexico City, July 1968, in *Obra*, IV/24, 1968, p. 90.
90   VLT in the PPS's New Year dinner, 13 January 1968, FHLT, file 1250.
91   'Intervención del Primer Secretario del Partido Obrero Unificado Polaco, Wladyslaw Gomulka, en la reunión del partido en Varsovia', 19 March 1968, FHLT, file 1250.

ments in the state apparatus, production methods, teaching standards, to fine tune' its functioning and accelerate the pace of socialism.[92] This was the argument he advanced until 21 August, when Soviet-led troops from the Warsaw Pact invaded Czechoslovakia to put a violent end to the Prague Spring, as the Czechs and Slovaks called their own road to 'socialism with a human face', aimed at democratising the system. When this occurred, Lombardo repeated the Soviet line that in Czechoslovakia the enemies of socialism wanted to jeopardise the country's integrity and the unity of the socialist camp.[93]

The democratisation process of Czechoslovakia undertaken by communists from the ruling party, which he put in quotation marks, was not the work of the workers, 'but of the social elements of the old system, which had remained in the dark working against socialism'. Convinced of the urgent need to defend the socialist camp from its critics, Lombardo dismissed the agony of the Czechoslovak leaders who did not want the socialist bloc to fall apart, but rather sought to improve its democratic quality, boost the standard of living of the population, to ensure that the factories be directed in accordance with elementary economic requirements and not the ideological fantasies of compliance with the five-year plans, and wished to put into practice the Marxist tenant that the emancipation of the workers was the task of the workers themselves. General Cárdenas succinctly said, referring to the invasion: 'It is a reprehensible deed that damages the principles of self-determination, and the sovereignty and integrity of nations'.[94]

With the same vehemence with which he condemned the Prague Spring, Lombardo rejected the student-worker revolt in Paris, in which barricades were erected in the streets to protest the conservative, dehumanising, consumer and capitalist order. The demonstrators also called for a better quality of existence, respect and participation in decision making and control over their daily lives. They invoked Marx and Rimbaud and painted the walls with graffiti expressing an overflow of energy: 'all power to the imagination', 'your nightmares are our dreams', 'be realistic – demand the impossible', 'revolution is the ecstasy of history'. For its participants, the French events in May and June were days of celebration.[95]

---

92   VLT, 'Lo esencial en el capitalismo y en el socialismo', 20 June, *Siempre!*, no. 784, 3 July 1968, in *Obra*, VI/24, 1968, p. 98.
93   VLT, 'La invasión de Checoslovaquia', 22 August 1968, FHLT, file 1250; VLT, 'La invasión a Checoslovaquia. El bloque socialista se adelantó a la maniobra', 4 September 1968, *Siempre!*, no. 743; Lombardo Toledano 1994a, vol. 2, p. 908.
94   LC, Ciudad Altamirano, Guerrero, 23 August 1968, in Cárdenas 1974, vol. 4, p. 99.
95   Fuentes 2005, pp. 13–14; Eley 2002, pp. 346–7.

But Lombardo wanted to see only youth manipulated by agitators of 'the forces opposed to human progress'. At the University of Paris 'extremist' students took on the challenge of leading the working class to take power. 'It's an infantile disorder that goes against the laws of history' since only the workers with their party could do so.[96] He conceded no role to the students – Trotskyist, pro-Chinese, anarchists and other professional agitators – disguised as leaders of the left and detached from the working class.[97] He could not conceive that the mobilisation was for the conquest of democratic forms of organisation, unfettered communication, collective action and even the participation of women in male-dominated groups.[98]

> I, who have been a professional agitator all my life and still am, that's my real job: to shake people up, put ideas in their head, guide men and women, make them see the situation in which they find themselves, bring light into their thinking, I cannot delude myself.[99]

Lombardo rejected the movements for democracy categorically. It was clear that the concerns of these young people for their education and professional training were minimal and that their call for the democratisation of education was false. His view was that students sharing the running of the schools with their teachers and the authorities based on the argument that they were outmoded was codified in the demand to lighten education and would result in a failure to attend classes and reduce academic standards. The global protest rejected US imperialism and 'local or circumstantial reasons should not be sought to explain the youth mobilisation'. Fighting against imperialism means fighting for democracy and that was all.[100]

Like in the Western world and Eastern Europe, there were demonstrations in the streets of Mexico City by high-school and university students, shouting slogans and carrying banners reading 'Mexico, freedom', 'books yes, bayonets no' and 'man is not to be tamed, but educated'. But Lombardo perceived

---

96 VLT 'El tumulto no corrige errores', 9 May 1968, *Siempre!*, no. 778, 22 May 1968, in Lombardo Toledano 1998a p. 75.
97 VLT, 'La crisis en Francia, otro paso adelante', *Siempre!*, no. 781, 12 June 1968, in Lombardo Toledano 1998a, pp. 79–80.
98 Gould 2009, pp. 348–75.
99 VLT, speech delivered in the 4th National Congress of the PPS youth group, the Juventud Popular Socialista, Mexico City, 16 June 1968, FHLT, file 1250.
100 VLT, 'Buscando las causas de la inquietud juvenil', *Siempre!*, no. 786, 17 July 1968, in Lombardo Toledano 2013a, pp. 97–9 and in Lombardo Toledano 1998a, p. 88.

them as no more than mimicking the European demands that had nothing in common with a "pre-industrial" country.[101] The American police and 'the forces that continue to plot against our country' financed the student movement to turn it into a political movement against the government. Outside enemies conspired to prevent the Olympic Games, to begin on 12 October, from taking place. Lombardo's theory of 'everyone is against Mexico' coincided with President Díaz Ordaz's view that there was an urgent need to save the country, which was in danger. Slogans in the street such as 'We don't want the Olympics, we want Revolution' did not help matters. On 13 September, 200,000 young people took to the streets in a silent demonstration; a few days later they held their Independence Day celebration in Ciudad Universitaria, home to the National Autonomous University of Mexico, and on 18 September, the army occupied the campus. Students regrouped in Tlatelolco, the symbolic meeting place of three cultures that comprised the history of Mexico. There they met on several occasions, the last time being on 2 October, when several hundred or perhaps thousands were killed and many taken prisoners during a premeditated ambush.[102] The PPS's newspaper account on the army's massacre, which occurred in the evening, was that in Tlatelolco a confrontation took place between provocateurs, many of them foreigners, and the armed forces, which fought to prevent a revolt and the overthrow of the government.[103]

Without mentioning the prisoners and the dead, Lombardo evaded the dishonourable reality when after the Olympics he wrote that the Mexicans realised that the Olympic Games were proof of their political maturity and of 'a political event of national importance, to represent our country as it is, without distortions, with many unsolved problems'. The people 'so beaten down in their daily battle to improve their living conditions and their chances for progress, demonstrated that it is able to close ranks in response to developments that harm and try to humiliate them'.[104]

---

101   VLT, Lecture to cadres of the JPS of the Valley of Mexico, 25 September 1968 in *Siempre!* no. 797, 2 October 1968, in Lombardo Toledano, 1998a, pp. 109–29.

102   Krauze 1997b, pp. 338–63; 'Manifiesto de la Dirección Nacional del PPS contra la provocación antinacional, unidad del pueblo', 5 August 1968, in *Escritos en Siempre!*, vol. III, vol. II, p. 860; VLT, 'Teoría y práctica del movimiento sindical', in Tavira Urióstegui 1999, pp. 149–219; VLT, '¡Todos contra México!' in *Siempre!*, no. 804, 20 November 1968, in Lombardo Toledano 1998a, pp. 131–3. Written on 7 November.

103   Condés Lara 2007, p. 121.

104   VLT, 'Balance político de la Olimpiada', 7 November 1968, FHLT, file 1251; VLT, ¡Todos contra México!, *Siempre!*, no. 804, 20 November 1968, in Lombardo Toledano 1998a, pp. 132–3.

Lombardo took on the defence of the state, whose sovereignty he believed was challenged, covering up the tragedy that engulfed Mexico in the Plaza de las Tres Culturas in Tlatelolco on 2 October 1968. That tragedy has been etched on the national memory ever since.

Epilogue: Testament and Testimonies

On the morning of 16 November, Lombardo was admitted to the Hospital Inglés. It was a Saturday. He was attended to by his family doctor and several nurses in a comfortable suite that was arranged with the donation of British philanthropist Thomas Edward. In the afternoon he went into a coma from which he never woke up. He died at 7.40pm of renal failure at 74 years of age. His body was transferred from the Gayosso funeral home on Félix Cuevas street to the Simón Bolívar Amphitheatre in the National Preparatory School, his alma mater, in downtown Mexico City. It was there that he studied, became a teacher, lived when he was the school director and had his first political skirmish with Education Minister José Vasconcelos. The grey metal coffin was covered with the dark pink coloured party flag and placed in front of *La Creación*, the mural that Diego Rivera painted when Lombardo was the school director. Manuel Gómez Morín, founder of the PAN, against which Lombardo had fought in life, stood guard at his bier; students and members of the party paid tribute at his side.[1]

A funeral chapel was set up in the family home in Tlacopac. On 17 November, he was taken to the Panteón Jardín cemetery about 750 metres from what was once his house. María Teresa preferred that the remains of her husband lay in a crypt that they would share rather than be buried in the Rotunda of Illustrious Men as the party leaders had requested. When the coffin was being lowered into the grave, she fainted. Several hundreds or thousands of people, depending on the different accounts, came to the cemetery to pay their respects. Among them were Lázaro Cárdenas, President Díaz Ordaz, the mayor of Mexico City Alfonso Corona del Rosal, mural artist David Alfaro Siqueiros, and Chile's Salvador Ocampo, his comrade from the CTAL. A representative of the WFTU also arrived, who delivered his eulogy in French and whose rendition into Spanish was broken up by the crying of the translator; Siqueiros stepped in to help finish the message. Interior Ministry agents were there to report on what General Cárdenas would say.[2]

---

1 'Murió anoche el Lic. Vicente Lombardo Toledano', in *El Universal*, 17 November 1968; 'Homenaje del Pueblo a los Restos del Lic. Vicente Lombardo Toledano', in *El Universal*, 18 November 1968.
2 Captain Fernando Gutiérrez Barrios, DFS, 'Memorándum', Mexico City, 17 November 1968, 18 November 1968, AGN, DFS, VLT, vp 9/9, 11-4-68; 'Un mal renal causó su muerte a los 74 años', in *Excélsior*, 17 November 1968; Manuel Arvizu, 'En el sepelio de Lombardo, Siqueiros pide crear otro partido de izquierda', in *Excélsior*, 19 November 1968.

The benevolent general recalled that the two had met in 1927 on a train en route to Guadalajara. Lombardo, he conveyed, did not participate 'in my political campaign for President of the Republic', but was a friend of his administration and supported it with the labour confederation he led without the government providing economic aid in return and without Lombardo requesting 'anything for his organisation, nor did he request posts for friends or union members'.[3] Cárdenas would not have recalled on that occasion their differences and Lombardo's daring attempt at sharing government responsibilities with the president. Manuel Gómez Morín recalled the time 'when Lombardo believed in God' and all were 'spiritualists'.[4]

Victor Manuel Villaseñor, with whom Lombardo travelled to the Soviet Union in 1935, was in a dilemma as to whether to attend the funeral or not:

> To attend would reveal an attitude of solidarity toward his trajectory; not showing up would be interpreted, no doubt, as a display of political recanting, since as erroneous as one might want it to be, Lombardo had died acclaimed as the greatest exponent of Marxism in Mexico. I chose to attend, but wanted to be preceded by a wreath of red carnations with a sash in front that read: IN REMEMBRANCE OF THE 1930s.[5]

A few days after his death, *Excélsior* published a cartoon in which the PPS was portrayed as a disoriented torso wandering down the street.[6] José Revueltas, after being on the run, was arrested the day that Lombardo died for his involvement in the student movement. In his cell in Lecumberri prison, Revueltas read the last speech of the 'ideologue of the bourgeois dictatorship', who legitimised in an academically polished prose 'with obsequious and gratuitous docility' the president's address to the nation, supporting one of the most 'appalling' bourgeoisie in the world, a state that wielded violence for its own preservation.[7] He once admired Lombardo as Mexico's greatest Marxist; in 1968 they were separated by an ethical and ideological wall.

What separated them was the understanding of Marxism, the nature of the Mexican state and the workers' party. Lombardo did not understand Marxism as a critique of political economy as explained in *Das Kapital*, but as 'one

---

3 LC, Mexico City, 17 November 1968, in Cárdenas 1974, vol. 4, p. 104.
4 Manuel Mejido, 'Cuando Lombardo creía en Dios', in *Excélsior*, 18 November 1968.
5 Villaseñor 1976, vol. 2, p. 183.
6 Marino, '¿Y ahora qué?', in *Excélsior*, 19 November 1968.
7 José Revueltas, 'La enajenación de la sociedad contemporánea y el canto del cisne de Lombardo Toledano', in Revueltas 1983, pp. 135–53; quote on p. 147.

of the fundamental works of culture', as the philosophy and ideology of the *Communist Manifesto*, adopted by Lenin and adapted by Stalin to the Soviet regime. Lombardo's Marxism was reduced to the unilineal development of the transitions from the slave through to the feudal, the capitalist and the socialist society. His readings were the classics: Marx, Engels, Lenin, Stalin and Mao, the Chinese writers, and then the manuals and inventions by Soviet academics, Khrushchev and the resolutions of the Communist Party of the USSR.[8] Lombardo rejected the ideas of contemporary Marxist thinkers such as Eric Hobsbawm, Perry Anderson, Herbert Marcuse and C. Wright Mills, because their analysis led to the criticisms of the Soviet system.[9]

The state was not the subject of his research nor was the historical experience of socialism. He embraced the theory of the transition from capitalism to socialism through the development of the productive forces and the inevitable advent of the proletariat, whose liberation was linked to national liberation and the anti-imperialist struggle of the Latin American peoples for their autonomy, led by the state, by the 'national' bourgeoisie and the national parties. He did not believe in the theory that held that the revolutionary action of the proletariat of the metropolis would be the axis of the world revolution, or that the oppressed masses in the dependent countries would carry out their own emancipation.[10]

Comparing Revueltas with Lombardo, a Marxist critic wrote that 'what was most tragic in the Lombardista option' was not its reformist character, but the fact that it subordinated the struggle for socialism to the development of the state and therefore eliminated the entire revolutionary potential of political democracy, that it subordinated the society to the state. The result was a complete separation between socialism and democracy, chaining the Mexican national project to the hegemonic policy of the USSR, in which was incubated 'such a deformed socialism that it is not possible to recognise it as such'.[11]

However, for Lombardo, socialism was not only an ideology and a political movement, but a transcendental moral force that would reach Mexico and Latin America as an expansive wave that radiated its strength from the Soviet Union. He had abandoned Catholicism at some point in his youth, but did not

---

8   VLT, 'Bibliografía mínima para el conocimiento del marxismo', *Avante*, no. 1, January 1961, in *Obra*, VI/4, 1961, pp. 17–23.
9   VLT, 'Judíos y mexicanos', in *Obra*, IV/9, 1942, p. 47; Van der Linden 2007, pp. 5–8.
10 Sánchez Vázquez 2011, pp. 120–7.
11 Bartra 1982, pp. 10–15; quote on p. 11.

become the atheist he claimed to be. Marxism, which would govern the new society with the great sages like torches illuminating humanity, became his secular theology.

In 1964, he finished writing SUMMA, 'a type of spiritual self-portrait'.[12] In the thin book he summarised his doctrine on the universe, love and socialism as the highest stage in the evolution of humanity. It was no coincidence that he gave it a Latin name that could evoke *Summa Theologiae*, Thomas Aquinas's opus, in which he preached the truth about God and the universe, nature and man, morality and law, virtues and sins, to educate the uninitiated. With due sense of proportion, Lombardo must have conceived the structure of SUMMA as Thomas Aquinas conceived his own everlasting work. From a discussion on the dimensions of the universe, the book moves on to considerations on the essence of man, his spirit and reason, touching the subject of sin. Stripped of religious morality and mythology, sin 'is not an offence, but the engine of history', beautiful as life itself, because it meant affective relationships and knowledge.[13] Creating a society that produced men superior to those who previously existed, with greater intelligence, will and sensitivity to grasp the harmony of the universe was the path of the ascension from depravations to perfection. 'The crises in history are the paths that man builds to establish his kingdom on earth'.[14]

SUMMA was the gospel that proclaimed socialism as the inevitable culmination of earthly fruition and evidence of man's immortality.[15] Life was a struggle between good and evil, socialism embodied redemption, the secular promise of deliverance and spiritual transcendence. A theologian of socialism, with Jesuit overtones, his life was a synthesis of ontological Marxism, purged of its critical dimensions, and the early Christianity whose existence in time and space had no limits. Lombardo Toledano went in peace, because he believed himself to be immortal.

---

12   Lombardo Toledano 1993, pp. 9–14. A sub-chapter in this and other editions of *SUMMA* is entitled 'Hunger and Love', but I think Lombardo wanted to say 'Man and Love'.
13   Lombardo Toledano 1993, pp. 40–1.
14   Lombardo Toledano 1993, p. 65 and p. 80.
15   VLT, 'Bases para una Summa Diabólica', *Siempre!*, no. 130, 21 December 1955, in *Obra*, V/22, 1955, pp. 279–86.

Bibliography and Works Cited

Archival Sources

Mexico
Archivo General de la Nación
   Departamento del Trabajo
   Dirección Federal de Seguridad
   Dirección General de Investigaciones Políticas y Sociales
   Ramo Abelardo Rodríguez
   Ramo Lázaro Cárdenas
   Ramo Manuel Ávila Camacho
   Ramo Miguel Alemán Valdés
   Ramo Adolfo Ruiz Cortines
   Ramo Adolfo López Mateos
   Ramo Gustavo Díaz Ordaz
Archivo Histórico de la Secretaría de Relaciones Exteriores
Centro de Estudios del Movimiento Obrero y Socialista
Fondo Histórico Lombardo Toledano

United States
Columbia University Libraries, Tannenbaum Collection
Federal Bureau of Investigation
Hoover Institution Archive
   Jay Lovestone Collection
   Schevenels Collection
National Archives and Record Administration
   Central Intelligence Agency
   Department of State
   Office of Strategic Services
New York Public Library
The George Meany Memorial Archives
Harvard University, Houghton Library
   Trotsky Collection

Europe
Archive of the International Labour Organization, Geneva
International Institute of Social History, Amsterdam
National Archives of the Czech Republic

Rossiiskii Gosudarstvennyi Arkhiv Sotsial'no-Politicheskoi Istorii, (RGASPI, Russian State Archive of Socio-Political History)
The National Archives, Kew Gardens, London
Walter Citrine Archives, London School of Economics, London

Newspapers and Periodicals

Mexico
El Heraldo
El Imparcial
El Machete
El Popular
El Universal
Excélsior
Futuro
Novedades
Política
Últimas Noticias

United States
Allied Labour News
Ann Arbor News
New York Mirror
The New York Times
The Washington Post

Interviews

Gutiérrez Lombardo, Raúl. Mexico City (September 1, 2005).
Lombardo Otero, Adriana. Mexico City (August 17, 2005).
Lombardo Otero, Marcela. Mexico City (September 1, 2005).
Lombardo, María Elena. Mexico City (April 1, 2013).
Monter, Luis. Mexico City (August 17, 2005).
Navarro, Laura. Mexico City (August 4, 2011).
Silva Lombardo, Vicente. Amecameca, Mexico City (October 28, 2006).
Soto Lombardo, Lili. Mexico City (August 20, 2014).
Soto Lombardo, Rosa María. Cuernavaca, Mexico City (August 5, 2014).

References

Acle-Kreysing, Andrea 2016, 'Antifascismo: un espacio de encuentro entre el exilio y la política nacional. El caso de Vicente Lombardo Toledano en México (1936–1945)', *Revista de Indias*, 76, no. 267: 573–609.

AFL *Proceedings* 1959, The Law Reporter Printing Company, Washington, D.C.

Aga-Rossi, Elena and Victor Zaslavsky 1996, 'The Soviet Union and the Italian Communist Party, 1944–8', in *The Soviet Union and Europe during the Cold War, 1943–53*, edited by Francesca Gori and Silvio Pons, New York: St. Martin's Press.

Agee, Philip 1975, *Inside the Company: CIA Diary*, New York: Stonehill.

Águila, Marcos T. 2014, 'Demetrio Vallejo: como el huizache', in *México y el mundo del trabajo: Trabajadores, líderes y gángsters*, edited by Jeffrey Bortz and Marcos T. Águila, Mexico City: CONACULTA.

Águila, Marcos T. and Jeffrey Bortz 2014, 'Con los dientes apretados: José Revueltas ante las huelgas ferrocarrileras de 1958 y 1959', in *México y el mundo del trabajo: Trabajadores, líderes y gángsters*, edited by Jeffrey Bortz and Marcos T. Águila, Mexico City: CONACULTA.

Aguilar García, Javier 1996, 'Ensayo biográfico de Fidel Velázquez Sánchez', *Espiral* 3, no. 7 (September–December): 87–105.

Aguirre Covarrubias, María Teresa 2001, 'Vicente Lombardo Toledano y la ideología de la Revolución Mexicana', unpublished PhD dissertation, Universidad Nacional Autónoma de México.

Agustín, José 2007, *Tragicomedia mexicana*, 3 vols., Mexico City: Planeta.

Albertani, Claudio, 'Vittorio Vidali, Tina Modotti, el estalinismo y la revolución', *Fundación Andreu Nin*, available at: https://fundanin.net/2019/03/17/vittorio-vidali-tina-modotti/.

Albertani, Claudio, '"Socialismo y Libertad". El exilio antiautoritario de Europa en México y la lucha contra el estalinismo (1940–1950)', available at: http://www.globallabour.info/es/2008/09/socialismo_y_libertad_claudio_1html.

Aldama Bay, Ignacio 2009, *La conexión Yocupicio. Soberanía estatal y tradición cívico-liberal en Sonora, 1913–1939*, Mexico City: El Colegio de México.

Alegre, Robert F. 2013, *Railroad Radicals in Cold War Mexico: Gender, Class, and Memory*, London and Lincoln: University of Nebraska Press.

Alexander, Robert J. 1961, 'Labour and Inter-American Relations', *Annals of the American Academy of Political and Social Science*, 334 (March): 41–53.

Alexander, Robert J. 1973, *Trotskyism in Latin America*, Stanford, CA: Hoover Institution Press.

Alexander, Robert J. and Eldon M. Parker 2009, *International Labour Organizations and Organised Labour in Latin America and the Caribbean: A History*, London: Prager.

Alonso, Antonio 1983, *El movimiento ferrocarrilero en México, 1958/1959*, Mexico City: ERA.

Alonso, Jorge 2003, *Miradas sobre la personalidad política de Efraín González Luna*, Mexico City: Universidad de Guadalajara.

Amezcua Dromundo, Cuauhtémoc 2012, *Lombardo y la* CTAL, Mexico City: Centro de Estudios Filosóficos, Políticos y Sociales 'Vicente Lombardo Toledano'.

Applebaum, Anne 2004, *Gulag: A History*, London: Penguin.

Applebaum, Anne 2012, *Iron Curtain: The Crushing of Eastern Europe, 1944–1956*, London: Penguin.

Araiza, Luis 1975, *Historia del movimiento obrero mexicano*, Mexico City: Casa del Obrero Mundial.

Arguedas, Sol 2014, *¿Qué es la izquierda mexicana?*, Mexico City: Orfila.

Ashby, Joe C. 1967, *Organized Labour and the Mexican Revolution under Lázaro Cárdenas*, Chapel Hill, NC: University of North Carolina Press.

Audirac, Augusto 1949, *Historia de un colegio*, Mexico City: SEP.

Aviña, Alexander 2014, *Specters of Revolution: Peasant Guerrillas in the Cold War Mexican Countryside*, Oxford: Oxford University Press.

Aziz Nassif, Alberto 1989, *El estado mexicano y la* CTM, Mexico City: CIESAS.

Azuela, Alicia 2005, *Arte y poder. Renacimiento artístico y revolución social. México, 1910–1945*, Mexico City: El Colegio de Michoacán and Fondo de Cultura Económica.

Bambirra, Vania and Theotonio Dos Santos 1977, 'Brasil: nacionalismo, populismo y dictadura. 50 años de crisis popular', in *América Latina: Historia de medio siglo*, vol. 1, edited by Pablo González Casanova, Mexico City: Siglo XXI.

Banac, Ivo (ed.) 2003, *The Diary of Georgi Dimitrov, 1933–1949*, New Haven, CT: Yale University Press.

Bantjes, Adrian A. 1998, *As If Jesus Walked on Earth: Cardenismo, Sonora, and the Mexican Revolution*, Wilmington, DE: Scholarly Resources.

Barahona Portocarrero, Amaru 1977, 'Estudio sobre la historia contemporánea de Nicaragua', in *América Latina: Historia de medio siglo*, vol. 2, edited by Pablo González Casanova, Mexico City: Siglo XXI.

Barajas, Rafael 2011, *Dos miradas al fascismo. Diego Rivera y Carlos Monsiváis*, Mexico City: Museo del Estanquillo.

Barnard, Andrew 1981, 'Chilean Communists, Radical Presidents and Chilean Relations with the United States, 1940–1947', *Journal of Latin American Studies*, 13, no. 2 (November): 347–74.

Barnard, Andrew 1992, 'Chile', in *Latin America Between the Second World War and the Cold War*, edited by Leslie Bethell and Ian Roxborough, New York: Cambridge University Press.

Bartra, Roger 1982, '¿Lombardo o Revueltas?', *Nexos*, 5, no. 54 (June), available at: http://www.nexos.com.mx/?p=4072.

Basurto, Jorge 1983, *Cárdenas y el poder sindical*, Mexico City: ERA.

Basurto, Jorge 1984, *La clase obrera en la historia de México. Del avilacamachismo al alemanismo, 1940–1952*, Mexico City: Siglo XXI.

Beals, Carleton 1943, 'Inside the Good Neighbour Policy: The Strange Story of Bolivian Tin', *Harpers Magazine* (August): 213–21.

Beisner, Robert L. 2009, *Dean Acheson: A Life in the Cold War*, Oxford: Oxford University Press.

Benjamín, Thomas 1989, *A Rich Land, a Poor People: Politics and Society in Modern Chiapas*, Albuquerque: University of New Mexico Press.

Berger, Henry Weinberg 1966, 'Union Diplomacy: American Labour's Foreign Policy in Latin America', unpublished PhD dissertation, University of Wisconsin.

Bergquist, Charles 1986, *Labour in Latin America: Comparative Essays on Chile, Argentina, Venezuela, and Colombia*, Stanford, CA: Stanford University Press.

Bernstein, Marvin D. 1964, *The Mexican Mining Industry, 1890–1950: A Study of the Interaction of Politics, Economics, and Technology*, Yellow Springs, OH: Antioch Press.

Bethell, Leslie 1991, 'Mexico since 1946', in *Mexico Since Independence*, edited by Leslie Bethell, Cambridge: Cambridge University Press.

Bethell, Leslie and Ian Roxborough (eds) 1992, *Latin America Between the Second World War and the Cold War, 1944–1948*, New York: Cambridge University Press.

Blanco, José (ed.) 2001, *La UNAM. Su estructura, sus aportes, su crisis, su futuro*, Mexico City: CONACULTA, CONACYT and Fondo de Cultura Económica.

Blasier, Cole 1987, *The Giant's Rival: The USSR and Latin America*, Pittsburgh: University of Pittsburgh Press.

Bolívar Meza, Rosendo 2005, *Vicente Lombardo Toledano: vida, pensamiento y obra*, Mexico City: IPN.

Bortz, Jeffrey 1988, *Los salarios industriales en la Ciudad de México, 1939–1975*, Mexico City: Fondo de Cultura Económica.

Bortz, Jeffrey 2008, *Revolution within the Revolution: Cotton Textile Workers and the Mexican Labour Regime, 1910–1923*, Stanford, CA: Stanford University Press.

Bratzel, John F. 2007, 'Introduction', in *Latin America during World War II*, edited by Thomas Leonard and John F. Bratzel, Lanham, MD: Rowman & Littlefield.

Braverman, Harry 1974, *Labour and Monopoly Capital: The Degradation of Work in the Twentieth Century*, New York: Monthly Review Press.

Britton, John A. 1979, 'Teacher Unionization and the Corporate State in Mexico, 1931–1945', *The Hispanic American Historical Review*, 59, no. 4 (November): 674–90.

Buchenau, Jurgen 2004, *Tools of Progress: A German Merchant Family in Mexico City, 1865–present*, Albuquerque: University of New Mexico Press.

Buford, Nick 1971, 'A Biography of Luis N. Morones: Mexican Labour and Political Leader', unpublished PhD dissertation, Louisiana State University and Agricultural and Mechanical College.

Buhle, Paul 1999, *Taking Care of Business: Samuel Gompers, George Meany, Lane Kirkland, and the Tragedy of American Labor*, New York: Monthly Review Press.

Bulmer-Thomas, Victor 1998 [1994], *La historia económica de América Latina desde la Independencia*, Mexico City: Fondo de Cultura Económica.
Calderón Vega, Luis 1961, *Los siete sabios de México*, Mexico City.
Campa, Valentín 1985, *Mi testimonio: memorias de un comunista mexicano*, Mexico City: Cultura Popular.
Cañadas, Teresa, 'El apoyo del exilio republicanos español al exilio de habla alemana en México', *Centro de Investigaciones Históricas de la Democracia Española*, available at: http://www.cihde.es/sites/default/files/congresos/pdf/CA%C3%91ADAS.pdf.
Carew, Anthony 1984, 'The Schism within the World Federation of Trade Unions: Government and Trade-Union Diplomacy', *International Review of Social History*, 29, no. 3 (December): 297–335.
Carew, Anthony 1998, 'The American Labor Movement in Fizzland: The Free Trade Union Committee and the CIA', *Labor History*, 39, no. 1: 25–42.
Carew, Anthony 2000a, 'The World Federation of Trade Unions 1945–1949', in *The International Confederation of Free Trade Unions*, edited by Anthony Carew and Marcel van der Linden, Vienna: Peter Lang.
Carew, Anthony 2000b, 'Towards a Free Trade Unions Centre: The International Confederation of Free Trade Unions (1949–1972)', in *The International Confederation of Free Trade Unions*, edited by Anthony Carew and Marcel van der Linden, Vienna: Peter Lang.
Carew, Anthony, Geert Van Goethem and Rebecca Gumbrell-McCormick 2000, 'Biographical Notes', in *The International Confederation of Free Trade Unions*, edited by Anthony Carew and Marcel van der Linden, Vienna: Peter Lang.
Cárdenas, Lázaro 1973, *Apuntes 1941–1956*, Mexico City: UNAM.
Cárdenas, Lázaro 1974, *Apuntes 1967–1970*, Mexico City: UNAM.
Cárdenas, Lázaro 1978, *Palabras y documentos públicos. Mensajes, discursos, declaraciones, entrevistas y otros documentos, 1928–1940*, 3 vols., Mexico City: Siglo XXI.
Cárdenas, Lázaro 1986a, *Apuntes 1913–1940*, Mexico City: UNAM.
Cárdenas, Lázaro 1986b, *Apuntes 1957–1966*, Mexico City: UNAM.
Carr, Barry 1976, *El movimiento obrero y la política en México, 1910–1929*, Mexico City: ERA.
Carr, Barry 1992, *Marxism and Communism in Twentieth-Century Mexico*, London: University of Nebraska Press.
Carretta Beltrán, Claudia 2002, 'Laberintos culturales de una institución: la Universidad Popular Mexicana, 1912–1920', unpublished Master's thesis, Centro de Investigación y Estudios Avanzados.
Carrillo Marcor, Alejandro 1989, *Apuntes y Testimonios*, Mexico City: El Nacional.
Castillo, Manuel Ángel, Mónica Toussaint and Mario Vázquez Olivera 2011, 'Siglo de cambios: acercamientos y tropiezos', in *Historia de las relaciones internacionales de México, 1821–2010. Centroamérica*, 2 vols., edited by Mercedes De Vega, Mexico City: SRE.

Ceaux, Véronique 2010, 'L'université ouvrière de Mexico, 1936–1940', unpublished PhD Master's thesis, Institut des Hautes Etudes de l'Amérique latine, Master 2 de Recherche en histoire, Paris III-Sorbonne Nouvel.

Cerdas Cruz, Rodolfo 1992, 'Costa Rica', in *Latin America Between the Second World War and the Cold War, 1944–1948*, edited by Leslie Bethell and Ian Roxborough, London: Cambridge University Press.

Chang, Jung and Jon Halliday 2005, *Mao, the Unknown Story*, London: Random House.

Chassen de López, Francie R. 1977, *Lombardo Toledano y el movimiento obrero mexicano, 1917–1940*, Mexico City: Extemporáneos.

Citrine, Sir Walter 1936, *I Search for Truth in Russia*, London: Routledge.

Clark, Marjorie Ruth 1984, *La organización obrera en México*, Mexico City: ERA.

Collier Berins, Ruth and David Collier 1991, *Shaping the Political Arena: Critical Junctures, the Labor Movement and Regime Dynamics in Latin America*, Princeton, NJ: Princeton University Press.

Condés Lara, Enrique 2007, *Represión y rebelión en México*, vol. 2, Mexico City: BUAP and Miguel Ángel Porrúa.

Contreras, Ariel José 1980, *México 1940: industrialización y crisis política*. Mexico City: Siglo XXI.

Córdova, Arnaldo 1980, *En una época de crisis, 1928–1934*, Mexico City: Siglo XXI.

Coronil, Fernando 1997, *The Magical State: Nature, Money, and Modernity in Venezuela*, Chicago: University of Chicago Press.

Cosío Villegas, Daniel 1947, 'La crisis en México', *Cuadernos Americanos XXXII* (March–April): 29–51.

Cosío Villegas, Daniel 1975, *La sucesión presidencial*, Mexico City: Joaquín Mortiz.

Cosío Villegas, Daniel 1977, *Memorias*, Mexico City: Joaquín Mortiz.

Cotler, Julio 1977, 'Perú: estado oligárquico y reformismo militar', in *América Latina: historia de medio siglo*, vol. 1, edited by Pablo González Casanova, Mexico City: Siglo XXI.

Cotterill, David (ed.) 1994, *The Serge-Trotsky Papers*, London: Pluto.

Crider, Gregory S. 1996, 'Material Struggles: Workers' Strategies During the "Institutionalization of the Revolution" in Atlixco, Puebla, Mexico, 1930–1942', unpublished PhD dissertation, University of Wisconsin-Madison.

Damaskin, Igor and Geoffrey Elliot 2001, *Kitty Harris: The Spy with Seventeen Names*, London: St. Ermin's Press.

David-Fox, Michael 2003, 'The Fellow Travelers Revisited: The "Cultured West" through Soviet Eyes', *The Journal of Modern History*, 75, no. 2 (June): 300–35.

David-Fox, Michael 2005, 'The "Heroic Life" of a Friend of Stalinism: Romain Rolland and Soviet Culture', *Slavonica*, 11, no. 1 (April): 3–29.

De Grammont, Hubert C. 1989, 'La Unión General de Obreros y Campesinos de México', in *Historia de la cuestión agraria mexicana. Política estatal y conflictos agrarios 1950–1970*, edited by Julio Moguel, Mexico City: Siglo XXI and CEHAM.

De Sierra, Gerónimo 1977, 'Consolidación y crisis del capitalismo democrático en Uruguay', in *América Latina: historia de medio siglo*, vol. 1, edited by Pablo González Casanova, Mexico City: Siglo XXI.

Di Baggio, Anna 1996, 'The Marshall Plan and the Founding of the Cominform, June–September 1947', in *The Soviet Union and Europe during the Cold War, 1943–53*, edited by Francesca Gori and Silvio Pons, New York: St. Martin's Press.

Díaz de Arce, Omar 1977, 'Paraguay contemporáneo, 1925–1975', in *América Latina: historia de medio siglo*, vol. 1, edited by Pablo González Casanova, Mexico City: Siglo XXI.

Domínguez Christopher, Michael 2014, *Octavio Paz en su siglo*, Mexico City: Aguilar.

Dromundo, Baltasar 1956, *Mi calle de San Ildefonso*, Mexico City: Guariana.

Dubofsky, Melvyn and Foster Rhea Dulles 1993, *Labour in America. A History*, (5th edn), Wheeling, IL: Harlan Davison.

Dugrand, Alain 1992, *Trotsky. México 1937–1940*, Mexico City: Siglo XXI.

Dunkerley, James 1992, 'Guatemala', in *Latin America Between the Second World War and the Cold War, 1944–1948*, edited by Leslie Bethell and Ian Roxborough, Cambridge: Cambridge University Press.

Durand, Víctor Manuel 1986, *La ruptura de la nación*, Mexico City: UNAM.

Eberhardt, Piotr 2012, 'The Curzon Line as the Eastern Boundary of Poland: The Origins and the Political Background', *Geographia Polonica*, 85, no. 1: 5–12, avaliable at: https://www.geographiapolonica.pl/article/item/7563.html.

Echeverría, Mónica 1993, *Antihistoria de un luchador. Clotario Blest*, Santiago de Chile: LOM.

Egorova, Natalia I. 1996, 'Stalin's Foreign Policy and the Cominform, 1947–1953', in *The Soviet Union and Europe during the Cold War, 1943–53*, edited by Francesca Gori and Silvio Pons, New York: St. Martin's Press.

El Libro Negro del Terror Nazi en Europa 1943, Mexico City: El Libro Libre.

Elgueta, Belarmino and Alejandro Chelén 1977, 'Breve historia de medio siglo en Chile', in *América Latina: historia de medio siglo*, vol. 1, edited by Pablo González Casanova, Mexico City: Siglo XXI.

Eley, Geoff 2002, *Forging Democracy: The History of the Left in Europe, 1850–2000*, Oxford: Oxford University Press.

Erickson, Kenneth Paul 1977, *The Brazilian Corporative State and Working Class Politics*, Berkeley, CA: University of California Press.

Estrada, Alfredo José 2007, *Havana: Autobiography of a City*, New York: Palgrave Macmillan.

Estrada Martínez, Rosa Isabel 1983, 'La Unión General de Obreros y Campesinos de México, 1949–1968', unpublished PhD thesis, Facultad Latinoamericana de Ciencias Sociales.

Falcón, Romana and Soledad García 1986, *La semilla en el surco: Adalberto Tejeda y el radicalismo en Veracruz, 1883–1960*, Mexico City: El Colegio de México and Gobierno del Estado de Veracruz.

Fallaw, Ben 2001, *Cárdenas Compromised: The Failure of Reform in Postrevolutionary Yucatán*, Durham, NC: Duke University Press.

Fein, Seth 1998, 'Film Propaganda in Cold War Mexico', in *Close Encounters of Empire: Writing the Cultural History of US-Latin American Relations*, edited by Gilbert M. Joseph, Catherine C. LeGrand and Ricardo D. Salvatore, Durham, NC: Duke University Press.

Figes, Orlando 2007, *The Whisperers: Private Life in Stalin's Russia*, London: Allen Lane.

Filitov, Aleksei M. 1996, 'Problems of Post-War Construction in Soviet Foreign Policy Conceptions during World War II', in *The Soviet Union and Europe during the Cold War, 1943–53*, edited by Francesca Gori and Silvio Pons, New York: St. Martin's Press.

Fitzpatrick, Sheila 1999, *Everyday Stalinism: Ordinary Life in Extraordinary Times: Soviet Russia in the 1930s*, Oxford: Oxford University Press.

Fitzpatrick, Sheila and Yuri Slezkine (eds) 2000, *In the Shadow of Revolution*, Princeton, NJ: Princeton University Press.

Flores Olea, Víctor 1962, 'Lombardo y la burguesía nacional', *Política*, 3, no. 52, 15 (June): 6–11.

Foner, Eric and John A. Garraty (eds) 1991, *The Reader's Companion to American History*, Boston: Houghton Mifflin.

Frank, Waldo 1932, *Dawn in Rusia, the Record of a Journey*, New York and London: Scribner's Sons.

Fraser, Steven 1991, *Labor Will Rule: Sidney Hillman and the Rise of American Labor*, Ithaca, NY: Cornell University Press.

French, John D. 2004, 'The Robert J. Alexander Interview Collection', *Hispanic American Historical Review*, 84, no. 2 (May): 315–26.

French, John D. 2006, 'The Labouring and Middle-Class Peoples of Latin America and the Caribbean: Historical Trajectories and New Research Directions', in *Global Labour History: A State of the Art*, edited by Jan Lucassen, Berlin: Peter Lang.

Friedman, Max Paul 2003, *Nazis and Good Neighbours: The United States Campaign Against the Germans of Latin America in World War II*, Cambridge: Cambridge University Press.

Fuentes, Carlos 1980, *Tiempo mexicano*, Mexico City: Joaquín Mortiz.

Fuentes, Carlos 2005, *Los 68. Paris-Praga-México*, Mexico City: Debate.

Furet, Francois 1995, *El pasado de una ilusión: ensayo sobre la idea comunista en el siglo XX*, Mexico City: Fondo de Cultura Económica.

Gaddis, Lewis 2011, *George F. Kennan: An American Life*, New York: Penguin.

Gall, Olivia 1991, *Trotsky en México y la vida política en el periodo de Cárdenas, 1937–1940*, Mexico City: ERA.

Gall, Olivia 2010, 'Trotsky, huésped del general Cárdenas: un asilo contra vientos y mareas nacionales e internacionales', in *Revolución y exilio en la historia de México. Del amor de un historiador a su patria adoptiva. Homenaje a Friedrich Katz*, edited by Javier Garciadiego and Emilio Kourí, Mexico City: El Colegio de México, Centro Katz de Estudios Mexicanos, The University of Chicago and ERA.

Gamboa Ojeda, Leticia 2001, *La urdimbre y la trama. Historia social de los obreros textiles de Atlixco, 1899–1924*, Mexico City: BUAP and FCE.

García Bonilla, Emilio 2012, 'En la tierra de Lombardo Toledano: origen y primeros años de la izquierda lombardista en Teziutlán, Puebla (Procesos electorales y conflictos políticos, 1919–1924)', unpublished PhD thesis, UAM-Iztapalapa.

García Cubas, Antonio 1959, 'Teziutlán', in *Apuntes geográficos*, edited by Luis Audirac, Mexico City: Morales hermanos.

García de León, Antonio 1985, *Resistencia y utopía. Memorial de agravios y crónica de revueltas y profecías acaecidas en la provincia de Chiapas durante los últimos quinientos años de su historia*, 2 vols., Mexico City: ERA.

Garciadiego, Javier 2000, *Rudos contra científicos. La Universidad Nacional durante la revolución mexicana*, Mexico City: El Colegio de México.

Gide, André 1936, *Back from the USSR*, London: Martin Secker and Warburg.

Gide, André 1937a, *Afterthoughts: Sequel to Back from the USSR*, London: Secker and Warburg.

Gide, André 1937b, *Return from the USSR*, translated from French by Dorothy Bussy, New York: Alfred A. Knopf.

Gillingham, Paul 2011, *Cuauhtémoc's Bones: Forging National Identity in Modern Mexico*, Albuquerque, NM: University of New Mexico Press.

Gilly, Adolfo 1977, *La revolución interrumpida*, Mexico City: El Caballito.

Gilly, Adolfo 1994, *El cardenismo. Una utopía mexicana*, Mexico City: Cal y Arena.

Gilly, Adolfo 2010, 'Víctor Serge en México: el último exilio', in *Revolución y exilio en la historia de México. Del amor de un historiador a su patria adoptiva. Homenaje a Friedrich Katz*, edited by Javier Garciadiego, and Emilio Kourí, Mexico City: El Colegio de México, Centro Katz de Estudios Mexicanos, University of Chicago and ERA.

Gleijeses, Piero 1991, *Shattered Hope: The Guatemalan Revolution and the United States, 1944–1954*, Princeton, NJ: Princeton University Press.

Gleizer, Daniela 2002, 'La política mexicana frente a la recepción de refugiados judíos (1934–1942)', in *México, país refugio. La experiencia de los exilios en el siglo XX*, edited by Pablo Yankelevich, Mexico City: Plaza y Valdés and CONACULTA-INAH.

Godio, Julio 1983, *Historia del movimiento obrero latinoamericamo. Nacionalismo y comunismo, 1918–1930*, vol. 2, Mexico City: Nueva Imagen.

Gómez Arias, Alejandro and Víctor Díaz Arciniegas 1990, *Memoria personal de un país*, Mexico City: Grijalbo.

Gómez-Galvarriato, Aurora 2013, *Industry and Revolution: Social and Economic Change in the Orizaba Valley, Mexico*, Cambridge, MA: Harvard University Press.

González y González, Luis 1981, *Los días del presidente Cárdenas*, Mexico City: El Colegio de México.

Gorkin, Julián 1961, *Cómo asesinó Stalin a Trotsky*, Mexico City: Plaza y Janés.

Gould, Jeffrey L. 2009, 'Solidarity under Siege: The Latin American Left, 1968', *American Historical Review*, 114, no. 2 (April): 348–75.

Granados Chapa, Miguel Ángel 1996, *El siglo de Fidel Velázquez*, Mexico City: Pangea.

Grandin, Greg 2004, *The Last Colonial Massacre: Latin America in the Cold War*, Chicago: University of Chicago Press.

Gregorová, Martina 2009, 'Prezidentské volby 1935 až do 1946' (The Presidential election of 1935 to 1946), available at: http://www.valka.cz/clanek_13386.html.

Grijalba Dávila, Miguel Ángel 2012, 'Jacinto López Moreno. Biografía de un agrarista sonorense', unpublished PhD thesis, El Colegio de Sonora.

Groppo, Bruno 2007, 'El antifascismo en la cultura del comunismo', in *El comunismo: otras miradas desde América Latina*, edited by Elvira Concheiro, Massimo Modonesi and Horacio Crespo, Mexico City: UNAM.

Gutiérrez Lombardo, Raúl 2010, *Lombardo mi abuelo*, Mexico City: Centro de Estudios Filosóficos, Políticos y Sociales 'Vicente Lombardo Toledano'.

Haslam, Jonathan 2011, *Russia's Cold War: From the October Revolution to the Fall of the Wall*, New Haven, CT: Yale University Press.

Haworth, Nigel 1992, 'Peru', in *Latin America Between the Second World War and the Cold War, 1944–1948*, edited by Leslie Bethell and Ian Roxborough, Cambridge: Cambridge University Press.

Haynes, John Earl and Harvey Klehr 1999, *Venona: Decoding Soviet Espionage in America*, New Haven, CT: Yale University Press.

Haynes, John Earl, Harvey Klehr and Alexander Vassiliev 2009, *Spies: The Rise and Fall of the KGB in America*, New Haven, CT: Yale University Press.

Henderson, Timothy J. 1998, *The Worm in the Wheat: Rosalie Evans and Agrarian Struggle in the Puebla-Tlaxcala Valley of Mexico, 1906–1927*, Durham, NC: Duke University Press.

Henríquez Ureña de Hlito, Sonia 1993, *Pedro Henríquez Ureña: apuntes para una biografía*, Mexico City: Siglo XXI.

Henríquez Ureña, Pedro 2013, 'La cultura de las humanidades', in *Pedro Henríquez Ureña. El hermano definidor*, edited by Berenice Villagomez and Néstor E. Rodríguez, Mexico City: El Colegio de México.

Henríquez Ureña, Pedro 2013, 'La Revolución y la cultura en México', in *Pedro Henríquez Ureña. El hermano definidor*, edited by Berenice Villagomez and Néstor E. Rodríguez, Mexico City: El Colegio de México.

Hernández Beltrán, Rosalío 2007, *Lombardo*, Mexico City: La Buena Estrella.

Hernández Chávez, Alicia 1979, *La mecánica cardenista*, Mexico City: El Colegio de México.

Hernández Soto, Ricardo, 'Descendientes de Vincenzo Lombardo Catti', available at: http://gw5.geneanet.org/sanchiz.

Herrera, Patricio 2013a, 'A favor de una patria de los trabajadores. La Confederación de Trabajadores de América Latina y su lucha por la emancipación del continente, 1938–1953', PhD dissertation, El Colegio de Michoacán.

Herrera, Patricio 2013b, 'El pacto por la unidad obrera continental: sus antecedentes en Chile y México, 1936', *Estudios de historia moderna y contemporánea de México*, 46 (July–December).

Herrera, Patricio 2013c, 'La primera conferencia regional del trabajo en América: su influencia en el movimiento obrero, 1936', in *América Latina y la Organización Internacional del Trabajo. Redes, cooperación técnica e institucionalidad social, 1919–1950*, edited by Fabián Herrera León and Patricio Herrera González, Morelia, Mexico: Universidad Michoacana de San Nicolás de Hidalgo.

Hobsbawm, Eric 1994, *The Age of Extremes*, London: Michael Joseph.

Hodges, Donald and Ross Gandy 2002, *Mexico Under Siege: Popular Resistance to Presidential Despotism*, London and New York: Zed Books.

Holmes, Olive 1948, 'New Hemisphere Labour Body Organised at Lima', *Foreign Policy Bulletin*, no. 16, 30 (January).

Hornstein, David P. 1993, *Arthur Ewert: A Life for the Comintern*, Lanham, MD: University Press of America.

Hunt, Tristram 2010, *The Frock-Coated Communist: The Revolutionary Life of Friedrich Engels*, London: Penguin.

Iber, Patrick 2015, *Neither Peace nor Freedom: The Cultural Cold War in Latin America*, Cambridge, MA: Harvard University Press.

Illades, Carlos 2007, 'La polémica Caso-Lombardo (1933–1935)', in *México en tres momentos: 1810–1910–2010*, edited by Alicia Meyer, Mexico City: UNAM.

Isaacson, Walter 2007, *Einstein: His Life and Universe*, New York: Simon & Schuster.

Jacinto, Lizette 2014, 'Desde la otra orilla: Alice Rühle-Gerstel y Otto Rühle. La experiencia del exilio político de izquierda en México 1935–1943', *Historia Mexicana*, 64, no. 1: 159–242.

Jacobo de Lara, Juan (comp.) 1983, *Pedro Henríquez Ureña y Alfonso Reyes, Epistolario íntimo (1906–1946)*, 3 vols., Santo Domingo: Universidad Nacional Pedro Henríquez Ureña.

Jeifets, Lazar, Víctor Jeifets and Peter Huber 2004, *La Internacional Comunista y América Latina, 1919–1943. Diccionario Biográfico*, Geneva: Instituto de Latinoamérica de la Academia de las Ciencias and Institut pour l'Histoire du Communisme.

Jensen, Jill 2011, 'From Geneva to the Americas: The International Labour Organization and Inter-American Social Security Standards, 1936–1948', *International Labour and Working-Class History*, 80 (Fall): 215–40.

Jones, Halbert 2014, *The War Has Brought Peace to Mexico: World War II and the Consolidation of the Post-Revolutionary State*, Albuquerque, NM: University of New Mexico Press.

Judt, Tony 2005, *Postwar: A History of Europe since 1945*, London: Penguin.
Katz, Friedrich 2002, 'El exilio centroeuropeo. Una mirada autobiográfica', in *México, país refugio. La experiencia de los exilios en el siglo XX*, edited by Pablo Yankelevich, Mexico City: Plaza y Valdés and CONACULTA-INAH.
Katz, Friedrich 2006, *Nuevos ensayos mexicanos*, Mexico City: ERA.
Kawage Rami, Alfredo 1943, *Con Lombardo Toledano. Un hombre, una nación, un continente*, Mexico City.
Keen, Benjamin and Keith Haynes 2000, *A History of Latin America, Independence to Present*, (6th edn), Boston: Houghton Mifflin.
Keith, Brewster 2003, *Militarism, Ethnicity and Politics in the Sierra Norte de Puebla, 1917–1930*, Tucson, AZ: University of Arizona Press.
Keller, Renata 2014, 'The Latin American Missile Crisis', *Diplomatic History*, 39, no. 2 (March): 195–222.
Keller, Renata 2015, *Mexico's Cold War: Cuba, the United States, and the Legacy of the Mexican Revolution*, New York: Cambridge University Press.
Kiddle, Amelia M. 2016, *Mexico's Relations with Latin America during the Cárdenas Era*, Albuquerque, NM: University of New Mexico Press.
Knight, Alan 1990, *The Mexican Revolution: Porfirians, Liberals, and Peasants*, 2 vols., Lincoln and London: University of Nebraska Press.
Knight, Alan 1992, 'The Rise and Fall of Cardenismo, c. 1930–c. 1946', in *Mexico since Independence*, edited by Leslie Bethell, Cambridge: Cambridge University Press.
Knight, Alan 1994, 'Cardenismo: Juggernaut or Jalopy?', *Journal of Latin American Studies*, 26, no. 1 (February): 73–107.
Koestler, Arthur 1991, *Scum of the Earth*, London: Eland.
Kofas, Jon V. 1992, *The Struggle for Legitimacy: Latin American Labor and the United States, 1930–1960*, Tempe, AZ: Arizona State University.
Kotkin, Stephen 1995, *Magnetic Mountain: Stalinism as a Civilization*, Berkeley, CA: University of California Press.
Krauze, Enrique 1976, *Caudillos Culturales en la Revolución Mexicana*, Mexico City: Siglo XXI.
Krauze, Enrique 1997a, *Biografía del poder. Caudillos de la Revolución Mexicana (1910–1940)*, Mexico City: Tusquets.
Krauze, Enrique 1997b, *La presidencia imperial*, Mexico City: Tusquets.
Krauze, Enrique 1999, *Pedro Henríquez Ureña*, Mexico City: CONACULTA.
Krauze, Enrique 2007, *Retratos personales*, Mexico City: Tusquets.
Krivitsky, Walter 2000, *In Stalin's Secret Service: Memoirs of the First Soviet Master Spy to Defect*, New York: Enigma.
Kuteischikova, Vera 1998, 'México, Trotsky y la Komintern (tercera parte)', *Memoria*, no. 107 (January): 6–10.
LaFrance, David G. 2003, *Revolution in Mexico's Heartland: Politics, War, and State Building in Puebla, 1913–1920*, Lanham, MD: Rowman & Littlefield.

Larsen, Neil 2010, 'Thoughts on Violence and Modernity in Latin America', in *A Century of Revolutions: Insurgent and Counterinsurgent Violence during the Latin America's Long Cold War*, edited by Greg Grandin and Gilbert M. Joseph, Durham, NC: Duke University Press.

Lebedeva, Natalia and Mijail Narinsky 1996, 'Dissolution of the Comintern in 1943', in *Centre and Periphery: The History of the Comintern in the Light of New Documents*, edited by Mijail Narinsky and Jürgen Rojahn, Amsterdam: International Institute of Social History.

Leidenberger, Georg 2014, 'Todo aquí es *vulkanisch*. El arquitecto Hannes Meyer en México, 1938–1949', in *México a la luz de sus revoluciones*, edited by Laura Rojas and Susan Deeds, Mexico City: El Colegio de México.

León, Samuel and Ignacio Marván 1985, *La clase obrera en la historia de México. En el cardenismo, 1934–1940*, Mexico City: Siglo XXI.

Levenstein, Harvey A. 1997, *Labor Organizations in the United States and México: A History of their Relations*, Greenwood, CT: Westport.

Lewis, Ben 2008, *Hammer and Tickle: A History of Communism Told Through Communist Jokes*, London: Weidenfeld & Nicolson.

Lewis, Stephen E. 2005, *The Ambivalent Revolution: Forging State and Nation in Chiapas, 1910–1945*, Albuquerque, NM: University of New Mexico Press.

Loaeza, Soledad 1988, *Clases medias y política en México: La querella escolar, 1959–1963*, Mexico City: El Colegio de México.

Loaeza, Soledad 1999, *El Partido Acción Nacional: la larga marcha, 1939–1994. Oposicion leal y partido de protesta*, Mexico City: Fondo de Cultura Económica.

Loaeza, Soledad 2013, 'La reforma política de Manuel Ávila Camacho', *Historia Mexicana*, 63, no. 1: 251–358.

Loaeza, Soledad 2014, 'El candidato gringo. Semblanza de Ezequiel Padilla', *Nexos*, 1 (April), available at: http://www.nexos.com.mx/?p=20010.

Lombardo, Marcela (ed.) 1994, *Corridos a Lombardo Toledano*, Mexico City: Centro de Estudios Filosóficos, Políticos y Sociales 'Vicente Lombardo Toledano'.

Lombardo De Caso, María 1992, *Una luz en la otra orilla*, Mexico City: Fondo de Cultura Económica.

Lombardo Toledano, Vicente 1936, *Viaje al mundo del porvenir*, Mexico City: Universidad Obrera.

Lombardo Toledano, Vicente 1993 [1969], *SUMMA*, Mexico City: Centro de Estudios Filosóficos, Políticos y Sociales 'Vicente Lombardo Toledano'.

Lombardo Toledano, Vicente 1994a, *Escritos en Siempre!*, vol. 2, Mexico City: Centro de Estudios Filosóficos, Políticos y Sociales 'Vicente Lombardo Toledano'.

Lombardo Toledano, Vicente 1994b, *1917–1928*, book I, vols. 1–4, Mexico City: Centro de Estudios Filosóficos, Políticos y Sociales 'Vicente Lombardo Toledano'.

Lombardo Toledano, Vicente 1995a, *1929–1933*, book II, vols. 1–4, Mexico City: Centro de Estudios Filosóficos, Políticos y Sociales 'Vicente Lombardo Toledano'.

Lombardo Toledano, Vicente 1995b, *1934–1935*, book III, vols. 1–3, Mexico City: Centro de Estudios Filosóficos, Políticos y Sociales 'Vicente Lombardo Toledano'.
Lombardo Toledano, Vicente 1996, *1936–1938*, book III, vols. 4–7, Mexico City: Centro de Estudios Filosóficos, Políticos y Sociales 'Vicente Lombardo Toledano'.
Lombardo Toledano, Vicente 1997, *1938–1939*, book III, vols. 8–10, Mexico City: Centro de Estudios Filosóficos, Políticos y Sociales 'Vicente Lombardo Toledano'.
Lombardo Toledano, Vicente 1998a, *Todos contra México. Escritos en torno al conflicto del 68*, Mexico City: Centro de Estudios Filosóficos, Políticos y Sociales 'Vicente Lombardo Toledano'.
Lombardo Toledano, Vicente 1998b, *1940–1943*, book IV, vols. 1–10, Mexico City: Centro de Estudios Filosóficos, Políticos y Sociales 'Vicente Lombardo Toledano'.
Lombardo Toledano, Vicente 1999, *1943–1944*, book IV, vols. 11–14, Mexico City: Centro de Estudios Filosóficos, Políticos y Sociales 'Vicente Lombardo Toledano'.
Lombardo Toledano, Vicente 2000, *1944–1946*, book IV, vols. 15–19, Mexico City: Centro de Estudios Filosóficos, Políticos y Sociales 'Vicente Lombardo Toledano'.
Lombardo Toledano, Vicente 2001, *1947–1948*, book V, vols. 1–4, Mexico City: Centro de Estudios Filosóficos, Políticos y Sociales 'Vicente Lombardo Toledano'.
Lombardo Toledano, Vicente 2002, *1949–1950*, book V, vols. 5–8, Mexico City: Centro de Estudios Filosóficos, Políticos y Sociales 'Vicente Lombardo Toledano'.
Lombardo Toledano, Vicente 2003a, *Escritos sobre Cuba. Análisis de su proceso político. 1928–1967*, Mexico City: Centro de Estudios Filosóficos, Políticos y Sociales 'Vicente Lombardo Toledano'.
Lombardo Toledano, Vicente 2003b, *1951–1952*, book V, vols. 9–12, Mexico City: Centro de Estudios Filosóficos, Políticos y Sociales 'Vicente Lombardo Toledano'.
Lombardo Toledano, Vicente 2004, *1952–1953*, book V, vols. 13–16, Mexico City: Centro de Estudios Filosóficos, Políticos y Sociales 'Vicente Lombardo Toledano'.
Lombardo Toledano, Vicente 2005, *1954–1955*, book V, vols. 17–20, Mexico City: Centro de Estudios Filosóficos, Políticos y Sociales 'Vicente Lombardo Toledano'.
Lombardo Toledano, Vicente 2006, *1955–1956*, book V, vols. 21–24, Mexico City: Centro de Estudios Filosóficos, Políticos y Sociales 'Vicente Lombardo Toledano'.
Lombardo Toledano, Vicente 2007, *1957–1958*, book V, vols. 25–28, Mexico City: Centro de Estudios Filosóficos, Políticos y Sociales 'Vicente Lombardo Toledano'.
Lombardo Toledano, Vicente 2008a, *1959*, book V, vols. 29–30, Mexico City: Centro de Estudios Filosóficos, Políticos y Sociales 'Vicente Lombardo Toledano'.
Lombardo Toledano, Vicente 2008b, *1960*, book VI, vols. 1 and 2, Mexico City: Centro de Estudios Filosóficos, Políticos y Sociales 'Vicente Lombardo Toledano'.
Lombardo Toledano, Vicente 2009, *1960–1961*, book VI, vols. 3–6, Mexico City: Centro de Estudios Filosóficos, Políticos y Sociales 'Vicente Lombardo Toledano'.
Lombardo Toledano, Vicente 2010, *1962*, book VI, vols. 7–8, Mexico City: Centro de Estudios Filosóficos, Políticos y Sociales 'Vicente Lombardo Toledano'.

Lombardo Toledano, Vicente 2011, *1962–1963*, book VI, vols. 9–12, Mexico City: Centro de Estudios Filosóficos, Políticos y Sociales 'Vicente Lombardo Toledano'.
Lombardo Toledano, Vicente 2012, *1963–1964*, book VI, vols. 13–16, Mexico City: Centro de Estudios Filosóficos, Políticos y Sociales 'Vicente Lombardo Toledano'.
Lombardo Toledano, Vicente 2013a, *Escritos a la juventud*, Mexico City: Centro de Estudios Filosóficos, Políticos y Sociales 'Vicente Lombardo Toledano'.
Lombardo Toledano, Vicente 2013, *1965–1966*, book VI, vols. 17–19, Mexico City: Centro de Estudios Filosóficos, Políticos y Sociales 'Vicente Lombardo Toledano'.
Lombardo Toledano, Vicente 2014, *1966–1967*, book VI, vols. 20–22, Mexico City: Centro de Estudios Filosóficos, Políticos y Sociales 'Vicente Lombardo Toledano'.
Lombardo Toledano, Vicente 2015, *1968*, book VI, vols. 23 and 24, Mexico City: Centro de Estudios Filosóficos, Políticos y Sociales 'Vicente Lombardo Toledano'.
London, Artur 1969 [1968], *Doznání*, Prague: Československý spisovatel.
López Pardo, Gustavo 1997, *La administración obrera de los ferrocarriles nacionales de México*, Mexico City: UNAM and El Caballito.
Loyo, Engracia 1999, 'Lectura para el pueblo', in *La educación en la historia de México*, editd by Josefina Zoraida Vázquez, Mexico City: El Colegio de México.
Loyola, Rafael (coord.) 1986, *Entre la guerra y la estabilidad política. El México de los 40*, Mexico City: CONACULTA and Grijalbo.
Luna Cárdenas, Daniel Librado 2007, 'Caminos entrelazados: el Partido Popular y la Revolución Mexicana (1944–1952)', unpublished PhD thesis, Instituto de Investigaciones Dr José María Luis Mora.
Mabry, Donald J. 1974, 'Mexico's Party Deputy System: The First Decade', *Journal of Interamerican Studies and World Affairs*, 16, no. 2 (May): 221–33.
MacGregor Campuzano, Javier 2005, 'Partidos nacionales y programas políticos en México, 1918–1928', unpublished PhD thesis, El Colegio de México.
Machorro, Ignacio 1959, 'Teziutlán de ayer', in *Apuntes geográficos e históricos*, edited by Luis Audirac, Mexico City: Morales hermanos.
Mastretta, Sergio (comp.) 2008, *Memoria y Acantilado. Carlos Mastretta Arista*, Puebla, Mexico: ACISA.
McDermott, Kevin and Jeremy Agnew 1997, *The Comintern: A History of International Communism from Lenin to Stalin*, New York: St. Martin's Press.
McMeekin, Sean 2003, *The Red Millionaire: A Political Biography of Willi Münzenberg: Moscow's Secret Propaganda Tsar in the West*, New Haven, CT: Yale University Press.
McPherson, Alan 2006, *Intimate Ties, Bitter Struggles: The United States and Latin America Since 1945*, Washington, DC: Potomac Books.
Meacham, Jon 2003, *Franklin and Winston: A Portrait of a Friendship*, London: Granta Books.
Medin, Tzvi 1990, *El sexenio alemanista. Ideología y praxis política de Miguel Alemán*, Mexico City: ERA.

Medina, Luís 1988, *Historia de la revolución mexicana. Civilismo y modernización del autoritarismo*, Mexico City: El Colegio de México.

Merfish, Beth 2009, *El Libro Negro: Mexico City at the Front of Antifascism*, New York: ArtUS.

Mesa redonda de los marxistas mexicanos 1982, Mexico City: Centro de Estudios Filosóficos, Políticos y Sociales 'Vicente Lombardo Toledano'.

Meyer, Jean, Enrique Krauze and Cayetano Reyes 1981, *Historia de la Revolución Mexicana, 1924–1928. Estado y sociedad con Calles*, Mexico City: El Colegio de México.

Meyer, Lorenzo 1980, *El conflicto social y los gobiernos del maximato*, Mexico City: El Colegio de México.

Meyer, Lorenzo 1981, *México y los Estados Unidos en el conflicto petrolero, 1917–1942*, Mexico City: El Colegio de México.

Meyer, Lorenzo 1991, *Su Majestad Británica contra la Revolución Mexicana, 1900–1950*, Mexico City: El Colegio de México.

Middlebrook, Kevin J. 1995, *The Paradox of Revolution: Labor, the State, and Authoritarianism in Mexico*, Baltimore, MD: Johns Hopkins University Press.

Miles, Jonathan 2010, *The Nine Lives of Otto Katz: The Remarkable Story of a Communist Super-Spy*, London: Bantam.

Miller, Eugene D. 1993, 'Labor and the War-Time Alliance in Costa Rica, 1943–1948', *Journal of Latin American Studies*, 25, no. 3 (October): 515–41.

Miller, Jürgen 1995, 'El NSDAP en México: historia y percepciones, 1931–1940', *Estudios Interdisciplinarios de América Latina y El Caribe*, 6, no. 2: 89–108, available at: http://eial.tau.ac.il/index.php/eial/article/view/1195/1223.

Millon, Robert P. 1964, *Lombardo: biografía intelectual de un marxista mexicano*, Mexico City: Universidad Obrera.

Montefieore, Simon Sebag 2003, *Stalin: The Court of the Red Tsar*, New York: Vintage.

Montgomery, David 1979, *Workers' Control in America: Studies in the History of Work, Technology, and Labour Struggles*, Cambridge: Cambridge University Press.

Morgan, Ted 1999, *A Covert Life: Jay Lovestone, Communist, Anti-Communist, and Spymaster*, New York: Random House.

Musgrave, Marie, 'Las aventuras y desventuras de Juan Andreu Almazán', available at: http://profmex.org/mexicoandtheworld/volume9/3summer04/lasaventuras.htm.

Nash, June 1979, *We Eat the Mines and the Mines Eat Us: Dependency and Exploitation in Bolivian Tin Mines*, New York: Columbia University Press.

Neruda, Pablo 2001, *Confieso que he vivido. Memorias*, Buenos Aires: Losada.

Novo, Salvador 1994, *La vida en México en el periodo presidencial de Miguel Alemán*, (comp. José Emilio Pacheco), Mexico City: INAH and CONACULTA.

Olcott, Jocelyn 2005, *Revolutionary Women in Postrevolutionary Mexico*, Durham, NC: Duke University Press.

Olgin, M.J. 1935, *Trotskyism: Counter-Revolution in Disguise*, New York: Workers Library Publishers.

Orozco, José Clemente 1945, *Autobiografía*, Mexico City: Occidente.

Padilla Beltrán, Francisco 2010, 'Las repercusiones políticas del cardenismo en Sinaloa, la Voz del Norte', 25 (July), available at: http://www.lavozdelnorte.com.mx/semanario/2010/07/25/las-repercusiones-politicas-del-cardenismo-en-sinaloa/.

Palacios, Guillermo 2011, 'México y América del Sur en la Segunda Guerra: ¿"El paladín del panamericanismo" o "la lengua hispánica de Estados Unidos"?', in *Historia de las relaciones internacionales de México, 1821–2010. América del Sur*, vol. 4, edited by Mercedes De Vega, Mexico City: SRE.

Pansters, Wil 1996, *Politics and Power in Puebla: The Political History of a Mexican State, 1937–1987*, Amsterdam: Centro de Estudios y Documentación Latinoamericanos.

Parrish, Scott C. 1994, 'New Evidence on the Soviet Rejection of the Marshall Plan, 1947', *Cold War International History Project*, work notebook 9 (March).

Pavlov, Yuri 1996, *Soviet-Cuban alliance, 1959–1991*, Miami: North-South Center Press.

Paxman, Andrew 2008, 'William Jenkins, Business Elites, and the Evolution of the Mexican State: 1910–1960', unpublished PhD thesis, University of Texas at Austin.

Paz, María Emilia 1997, *Strategy, Security, and Spies: Mexico and the US as Allies in World War II*, Pennsylvania: Penn State University Press.

Paz, Octavio 2014, *El peregrino en su patria. Historia y política de México*, Mexico City: Fondo de Cultura Económica.

Pensado, Jaime M. 2013, *Rebel Mexico: Student Unrest and Authoritarian Political Culture during the Long Sixties*, Stanford, CA: Stanford University Press.

Pérez Leirós, Francisco 1941, *El movimiento sindical de América Latina*, Buenos Aires: La Vanguardia.

Pérez Montfort, Ricardo 1988, '"Por la patria y por la raza". Tres movimientos nacionalistas de clase media', in *Los empresarios alemanes, el Tercer Reich y la oposición de derecha a Cárdenas*, edited by Brígida Von Mentz, Verena Radkau, Daniela Spenser and Ricardo Pérez Montfort, Mexico City: CIESAS/SEP.

Pérez-Stable, Marifeli 1999, *The Cuban Revolution, Origins, Course, and Legacy*, Oxford: Oxford University Press.

Peterson, Gigi 1998, 'Grassroots Good Neighbours: Connections between Mexican and US Labour and Civil Rights Activists, 1936–1945', unpublished PhD thesis, University of Washinghton.

Plasencia de la Parra, Enrique 1998, *Personajes y escenarios de la rebelión delahuertista, 1923–1924*, Mexico City: UNAM and Miguel Ángel Porrúa.

Pletcher, David M. 1948, 'An American Mining Company in the Mexican Revolutions of 1911–1920', *Journal of Modern History*, 20, no. 1 (March): 19–26.

Portes Gil, Emilio 2003, *Autobiografía de la Revolución*, Mexico City: INEHRM.

Proces s vedením protistátního spikleneckého centra v cele s Rudolfem Slánským ('Trial of the leadership of the conspirator centre against the state led by by Rudolf Slánský') 1953, Ministry of Justice, Prague: Orbis.

Programa de trabajos de la Universidad Popular Mexicana en el año de 1920 1920, Mexico City: Victoria.

Priestland, David 2010, *The Red Flag: Communism and the Making of the Modern World*, London: Penguin.

Quintanilla, Susana 2008, *'Nosotros'. La juventud del Ateneo de México*, Mexico City: Tusquets.

Quintanilla, Susana 2009, *A salto de mata. Martín Luis Guzmán en la Revolución mexicana*, Mexico City: Tusquets.

Quintanilla Obregón, Lourdes 1982, *Lombardismo y sindicatos en América Latina*, Mexico City: Fontamara.

Quiroga Pérez, Héctor, 'El arraigo de los artistas desarraigados, una misión del monopolismo empresarial', available at: http://cmm.cenart.gob.mx/tgd/antesala/.

Rabe, Stephen G. 1988, *Eisenhower and Latin America: The Foreign Policy of Anticommunism*, Chapel Hill, NC: University of North Carolina.

Radosh, Ronald 1969, *American Labor and United States Foreign Policy*, New York: Random House.

Radosh, Ronald, Mary R. Habeck and Grigory Sevostianov (eds) 2001, *Spain Betrayed: The Soviet Union in the Spanish Civil War*, New Haven, CT: Yale University Press.

Ramírez Cuéllar, Héctor 1992, *Lombardo, un hombre de México*, Mexico City: El Nacional.

Ramos de Guzmán, María Luisa 1978, *Memorias*, Mexico.

Rankin, Monica A. 2009, *¡México, la Patria! Propaganda and Production during World War II*, Lincoln and London: University of Nebraska Press.

Rapoport, Mario 1992, 'Argentina', in *Latin America Between the Second World War and the Cold War, 1944–1948*, edited by Leslie Bethell and Ian Roxborough, Cambridge: Cambridge University Press.

Rees, Tim 1998, 'The Highpoint of Comintern Influence? The Communist Party and the Civil War in Spain', in *International Communism and the Communist International, 1919–1943*, Manchester: Manchester University Press.

Retinger, J.H. 1926, *Morones of Mexico*, London: The Labour Publishing.

Reyes Palma, Francisco 1996, 'Cuando Coyoacán tendió su sombra sobre Paris. El caso Siqueiros', in *Otras rutas hacia Siqueiros*, edited by Oliver Debroise, Mexico City: Curare and INBA.

Revueltas, José 1983, *México: una democracia bárbara (y escritos acerca de Lombardo Toledano)*, Mexico City: ERA.

Revueltas, José 1987 [1962], *Ensayo sobre un proletariado sin cabeza*, Mexico City: ERA.

Rivera Flores, Antonio 1984, *La derrota de Lombardo Toledano y el movimiento obrero*, Querétaro, Mexico: Universidad Autónoma de Querétaro.

Rivero Torres, B. Martha 1982, 'Dos proyectos de industrialización ante la posguerra (1944–1946)', *Investigación Económica*, 41, no. 161 (July–September): 13–57.

Roberts, Goeffrey 2006, *Stalin's Wars: From World War to Cold War*, New Haven, CT: Yale University Press.

Rock, David 1987, *Argentina 1516–1987: From Spanish Colonization to Alfonsín*, Berkeley, CA: University of California Press.

Rodríguez García, Magaly 2010, *Liberal Workers of the World, Unite? The ICFTU and the Defence of Labour Liberalism in Europe and Latin America (1949–1969)*, New York: Peter Lang.

Rodríguez Kuri, Ariel 2010, *Historia del desasosiego. La revolución en la Ciudad de México, 1911–1922*, Mexico City: El Colegio de México.

Roggiano, Alfredo A. 2003, *Pedro Henríquez Ureña en México*, Mexico City: UNAM.

Román Román, Salvador 2003, *Revuelta cívica en Guerrero, 1957–1960. La democracia imposible*, Mexico City: INEHRM.

Romualdi, Serafino 1967, *Presidents and Peons: Recollections of a Labor Ambassador in Latin America*, New York: Funk & Wagnalls.

Roxborough, Ian 1992, 'Mexico', in *Latin America Between the Second World War and the Cold War, 1944–1948*, edited by Leslie Bethell and Ian Roxborough, Cambridge: Cambridge University Press.

Roxborough, Ian 1997, 'La clase trabajadora urbana y el movimiento obrero en América Latina desde 1930', in *Historia de América Latina: Política y sociedad desde 1930*, edited by Leslie Bethell, Barcelona: Grijalbo Mondadori.

Ruiz Abreu, Álvaro 1992, *José Revueltas: Los muros de la utopía*, Mexico City: Cal y Arena.

Rupprecht, Tobias 2015, *Soviet Internationalism after Stalin: Interaction and Exchange between the USSR and Latin America during the Cold War*, Cambridge: Cambridge University Press.

Ruy Sánchez, Alberto 1991, *Tristeza de la verdad. André Gide regresa de la URSS*, Mexico City: Joaquín Mortiz.

Sánchez, Gonzalo 1992, 'The Violence: An Interpretative Synthesis', in *Violence in Colombia: The Contemporary Crisis in Historical Perspective*, edited by Charles Berquist, Ricardo Peñaranda and Gonzalo Sánchez, Wilmington, DE: Scholarly Resources.

Sánchez González, Agustín 1991, *Fidel. Una historia de poder*, Mexico City: Planeta.

Sánchez Vázquez, Adolfo 2011, *De Marx al marxismo en América Latina*, Mexico City: Ithaca.

Santiago, Myrna I. 2006, *The Ecology of Oil: Environment, Labour, and the Mexican Revolution, 1900–1938*, Cambridge: Cambridge University Press.

Sariego, Juan Luis 1988, *Enclaves y minerales en el norte de México. Historia social de los mineros de Cananea y Nueva Rosita 1900–1970*, Mexico City: La Casa Chata.

Scammell, Michael 2011, *Koestler: The Indispensable Intellectual*, London: Faber and Faber.

Scherer García, Julio 1986, *Los presidentes*, Mexico City: Grijalbo.
Schmidt, Samuel 2006, *En la mira: el chiste político en México*, Mexico City: Taurus.
Schuler, Friedrich E. 1997, *Mexico Between Hitler and Roosevelt: Mexican Foreign Relations in the Age of Lázaro Cárdenas, 1934–1940*, Albuquerque, NM: University of New Mexico Press.
Schwartz, Morton 1963, 'Soviet Policy and the World Federation of Trade Unions, 1945–1949', unpublished PhD thesis, Columbia University, University Microfilms.
Schwartz, Stephen 1997, 'La Venona mexicana', *Vuelta*, no. 249 (August): 19–25.
Schwartzberg, Steven 1997, 'Rómulo Betancourt: From a Communist Anti-Imperialist to a Social Democrat with US Support', *Journal of Latin American Studies*, 29, no. 3 (October): 613–65.
Segel, Harold B. 1997, *Egon Erwin Kisch, The Raging Reporter*, West Lafayette, IN: Purdue University Press.
Serge, Victor 1984, *Memoirs of a Revolutionary*, London: Writers and Readers.
Servín, Elisa 2001, *Ruptura y oposición. El movimiento henriquista, 1945–1954*, Mexico City: Cal y Arena.
Servín, Elisa 2010, 'Reclaiming the Revolution in Light of the "Mexican Miracle": Celestino Gasca and the Federacionistas Leales Insurrection of 1961', *The Americas*, 66, no. 4 (April): 527–57.
Siqueiros, David Alfaro 1977, *Me llamaban el Coronelazo*, Mexico City: Grijalbo.
Smith, Benjamín 2009, *Pistoleros and Popular Movements. The Politics of State Formation in Postrevolutionary Oaxaca*, Lincoln, NE: University of Nebraska Press.
Spenser, Daniela 2009, *Los primeros tropiezos de la Internacional Comunista en México*, Mexico City: CIESAS.
Spenser, Daniela 2016, 'Historia, política e ideología fundidas en la vida de Vicente Lombardo Toledano', *Desacatos*, 15, no. 50 (January–April): 70–87.
Sturmthal, Adolf 1948, 'The Crisis of the WFTU', *Industrial and Labor Relations Review*, 1, no. 4 (July): 624–38.
Talbott, Strobe (ed.) 1971, *Khrushchev Remembers: The Last Testament*, London: Andre Deutsch.
Taracena, Alfonso 1972, *Historia extraoficial de la Revolución Mexicana: (desde las postrimerías del porfirismo hasta los sexenios de Echeverría y López Portillo)*, Mexico City: Jus.
Taracena, Alfonso 1976, *La vida en México bajo Ávila Camacho*, Mexico City: Jus.
Tarcus, Horacio (dir.) 2007, *Diccionario biográfico de la izquierda argentina. De los anarquistas a la 'nueva izquierda', 1870–1976*, Buenos Aires: Emecé.
Taubman, William 2003, *Khrushchev: The Man and his Era*, New York: W.W. Norton.
Tavira Urióstegui, Martín 1999, *Vicente Lombardo Toledano: acción y pensamiento*, Mexico City: Fondo de Cultura Económica.
Tibón, Gutierre 1946, *Aventuras de Gog y Magog*, Mexico City: Amexica.

Tommasi, Renzo and José Benigno Zilli Mánica 1924, 'De los italianos en México. Desde los "conquistadores" hasta los socios de la Cooperativa de emigración agrícola "San Cristóforo"', available at: http://www.oocities.org/trentinimessico/ponenciaMonte video.doc.

Torres, Blanca 2005 [1979], *México en la segunda guerra mundial*, Mexico City: El Colegio de México.

Tosstorff, Reiner 1998, 'Between Moscow and Amsterdam: The International Trade Union Movement of the 1920s Between Splits and Unity', paper presented at American Historical Association (January).

Tosstorff, Reiner 2003, 'Moscow Versus Amsterdam: Reflections on the History of the Profintern', *Labour History Review*, 68, no. 1 (April): 79–97.

Trejo Delarbe, Raúl and Aníbal Yáñez 1976, 'The Mexican Labor Movement: 1917–1975', *Latin American Perspectives*, 3, no. 1 (Winter): 133–53.

Uhthoff, Enrique 1959, 'No se me olvida', in *Apuntes geográficos e históricos*, edited by Luis Audirac, Mexico City: Morales hermanos.

Ulloa, Berta 1988, *Historia de la revolución mexicana. La Constitución de 1917*, Mexico City: El Colegio de México.

Unzueta, Gerardo 1966, *Lombardo Toledano y el marxismo-leninismo*, Mexico City: Fondo de Cultura Popular.

Vacs, Aldo César 1984, *Discreet partners. Argentina and the USSR since 1917*, Pittsburgh: University of Pittsburgh Press.

Vaill, Amanda 2014, *Hotel Florida. Verdad, amor y muerte en la Guerra Civil*, Mexico City: Turner and CONACULTA.

Van Goethem, Geert 2000, 'Conflicting Interests: The International Federation of Trade Unions, 1919–1945', in *The International Confederation of Free Trade Unions*, edited by Anthony Carew and Marcel van der Linden, Vienna: Peter Lang.

Van Goethem, Geert 2013, 'From Dollars to Deeds: Exploring the Sources of Active Interventionism, 1934–1945', in *American Labor's Global Ambassadors: The International History of the AFL-CIO during the Cold War*, edited by Robert Anthony Waters Jr. and Geert van Goethem, New York: Palgrave Macmillan.

Vargas, Zaragosa 2005, *Labour Rights are Civil Rights: Mexican American Workers in Twentieth-Century America*, Princeton, NJ: Princeton University Press.

Vasconcelos, José 1993, *Memorias. El desastre*, Mexico City: Fondo de Cultura Económica.

Vaughan, Mary Kay 1982, *The State, Education, and Social Class in Mexico, 1880–1928*, DeKalb, IL: Northern Illinois University Press.

Vaughan, Mary Kay 1997, *Cultural Politics in Revolution: Teachers, Peasants, and Schools in Mexico, 1930–1940*, Tucson, AZ: University of Arizona Press.

Vaughan, Mary Kay 2015, *Portrait of a Young Painter: Pepe Zúñiga and Mexico City's Rebel Generation*, Durham, NC: Duke University Press.

Villaseñor, Victor Manuel 1976, *Memorias de un hombre de izquierda*, 2 vols., Mexico City: Grijalbo.
Van der Linden, Marcel 2007, *Western Marxism and the Soviet Union: A Survey of Critical Theories and Debates since 1917*, Chicago, IL: Haymarket Books.
Van der Linden, Marcel 2008, *Workers of the World: Essays toward a Global Labour History*, Leiden: Brill.
'Volby 1946-vítězství komunistů a odsun Němců' ('The 1946 elections-triumph of the Communists and the evacuation of the German population'), available at: http://www.fronta.cz/dotaz/volby-1946-vitezstvi-ksc-a-odsun-nemcu.
Von Hanffstengel, Renata 2010, 'México, un exilio bien temperado para Leo Zuckermann, tanto en la guerra fría como en la de altas temperaturas', in *Revolución y exilio en la historia de México. Del amor de un historiador a su patria adoptiva. Homenaje a Friedrich Katz*, edited by Javier Garciadiego and Emilio Kourí, Mexico City: El Colegio de México, Centro Katz de Estudios Mexicanos, University of Chicago and ERA.
Von Mentz, Brigida and Verena Radkau 1984, *Fascismo y antifascismo en América Latina y México*, Mexico City: CIESAS.
Walcher, Dustin 2013, 'Reforming Latin American Labor: The AFL-CIO and Latin American Cold War', in *American Labor's Global Ambassadors: The International History of the AFL-CIO during the Cold War*, edited by Robert Anthony Waters Jr. and Geert van Goethem, New York: Palgrave Macmillan.
Weiner, Tim 2007, *Legacy of Ashes: The History of the CIA*, New York: Doubleday.
Weiner, Tim 2012, *Enemies: A History of the FBI*, New York: Random House.
Weismann, Susan 2001, *Victor Serge: The Course is Set on Hope*, London: Verso.
Welch, Cliff 1995, 'Labor Internationalism: US Involvement in Brazilian Unions, 1945–1965', *Latin American Research Review*, 30, no. 2: 61–89.
Whitehead, Laurence 1981, 'Miners as Voters: The Electoral Process in Bolivia's Mining Camps', *Journal of Latin American Studies*, 13, no. 2 (November): 313–46.
Whitehead, Laurence 1992, 'Bolivia', in *Latin America Between the Second World War and the Cold War, 1944–1948*, edited by Leslie Bethell and Ian Roxborough, Cambridge: Cambridge University Press.
Winn, Peter 2010, 'Frank Tannenbaum Reconsidered', *International Labor and Working-Class History*, no. 77 (Spring): 109–14.
Wilkie, James W. and Edna Monzón Wilkie 1969, *México visto en el siglo XX. Entrevistas de historia oral*, Mexico City: Instituto Mexicano de Investigaciones Económicas.
Wilkie, James W. and Edna Monzón Wilkie 1995, *Frente a la Revolución Mexicana, 17 protagonistas de la etapa constructiva. Entrevistas de historia oral*, 4 vols., Mexico City: UAM.
Zapata, Francisco 1993, *Autonomía y subordinación en el sindicalismo latinoamericano*, Mexico City: El Colegio de México and Fondo de Cultura Económica.

Zapata, Francisco 2013, *El sindicalismo latinoamericano*, Mexico City: El Colegio de México.

Zogbaum, Heidi 2005, 'Vicente Lombardo Toledano and the German Communist Exile in Mexico, 1940–1947', *Journal of Iberian and Latin American Studies*, 11, no. 2: 1–28.

Zolov, Eric 2004, '"¡Cuba sí, yanquis no!": el saqueo del Instituto Cultural México-Norteamericano en Morelia, Michoacán, 1961', in *Espejos de la guerra fría: México, América Central y el Caribe*, edited by Daniela Spenser, Mexico City: SRE, Miguel Ángel Porrúa and CIESAS.

Zubok, Vladislav M. 2007, *A Failed Empire: The Soviet Union in the Cold War from Stalin to Gorbachev*, Chapel Hill, NC: University of North Carolina.

Index

Abusch, Alexander   160
Action Group   62–63, 74–76, 242
Aguascalientes   180, 315
Aguilar Monteverde, Alonso   362
Aguirre, Francisco   279, 334, 336–337
Ailshie, W.K.   222
Albania   357
Alberti, Rafael   84
Alemán Valdés, Miguel   233, 242, 281, 312, 373
   and Latin American Workers Confederation (CTAL) congress   286
   and Lombardo Toledano, Vicente   231, 233, 242, 303, 311
   and Mexican Communist Party (PCM)   242
   and miners   311
   and presidential campaign   230
Alessandri, Arturo   134
Alexander, Robert   148, 338
Alemán, Ildefonso   349
Almanza, Manuel   183
Álvarez del Vayo, Julio   171
Amaro, Joaquín   48
American Federation of Labor (AFL)   114, 137–138, 156, 281–282
American Popular Revolutionary Alliance   143, 248
Amilpa, Fernando   99, 113, 234, 294, 300
   and Lombardo Toledano, Vicente   110, 240–245
   and Mexican Workers Confederation (CTM)   179, 186, 191–192, 194, 228, 256, 287
   and National Proletarian Confederation   186, 189
Amsterdam   135–136, 141, 267, 271
Anderson, Perry   385
Andreu Almazán, Juan   177
Anti-Dühring   358
Araya, Bernardo   293
Árbenz, Jacobo   340, 346
Arechandieta, Francisco   220, 291
Arévalo, Juan José   219, 281, 293, 346
Argaña, José María   213
Argentina   50, 140, 143, 200, 203–204, 221, 258, 331, 336
   and American Federation of Labor (AFL)   141, 145–146, 333
   and General Confederation of Workers (CGT)   57, 111, 145–147, 212–213, 229, 258, 278–280, 282–285, 336
   and International Confederation of Free Trade Unions (ICFTU)   334
   and Latin American Workers Confederation (CTAL)   213, 219, 283, 286, 343, 348–349
   See also Perón, Juan Domingo
Arze, José Antonio   255–256
Arroyo del Río, Carlos   207
Association of Unionised Latin American Workers   343, 345
Ateneo de México   21–22
Atlantic Charter   251
Austria   122, 260
Ávila Camacho, Manuel   156, 168, 182, 202, 208, 231, 305
   and labour conflicts   183, 193, 196
   and Lombardo Toledano, Vicente   229, 234, 302
   and Mexican Workers Confederation (CTM)   177–178, 180

Baja California Norte   124, 172, 246, 301
Baku   88, 96
Barreda, Gabino   88
Balk, Theodor   160
Barrios, Gabriel   48
Barron, George   9, 13, 16
Barron, Juan   13–14, 16
Bassols, Narciso   234, 236, 240, 302, 307–308
Batista, Fulgencio   144, 198, 215, 337, 341, 348
   and Lombardo Toledano, Vicente   204, 213
Belgium   102, 173
Beltrán, Alberto   324
Benéitez, Vicente   218
Benítez, Fernando   327
Benjamin, Walter   175
Berlin   90–91
Betancourt, Rómulo   279, 290
Beteta, Ramón   244, 281
Bevin, Ernest   254

Bierut, Boleslaw 347
Boal, Pierre 210
Bolivia 203–204, 208, 217, 255, 345, 353
   and American Federation of Labor (AFL) 279
   and Catavi Massacre 210–211, 215
   and International Labour Organization (ILO) 132, 215
   and Latin American Workers Confederation (CTAL) 146, 211, 215, 286, 289, 343
Bolivian Workers Confederation 255, 339, 343
Borlenghi, Ángel 213
Bravo Izquierdo, Donato 47–48
Brazil 132, 144, 146, 203–204, 221, 275, 286, 338, 348, 354
   and Latin American Workers Confederation (CTAL) 215–216
   See also Goulart, Joao; Prestes, Luis Carlos; Vargas, Getulio
Breña Alvírez, Francisco 112–113
Browder, Earl 120–122
Brown, Irving 266
Bucharest 346, 349
Buenos Aires 50, 73, 75, 110, 144, 213, 216, 278, 285
Buhse, Otto 160
Bukharin, Nikolai 104
Bulgaria 229, 253, 259–260, 263, 348, 357

Calderón Guardia, Rafael Ángel 124–125, 214
Calles, Plutarco Elías 33–34, 45, 47, 63, 86, 100–101, 123, 129, 137–138
   and presidential campaign 35–40, 43
Campa, Valentín 113, 234, 242–243, 287, 308, 309
Campos, Benigno 41, 47
Canada 201, 284, 341
Caracas 200–201, 216, 217, 218, 282, 341
Cárdenas, Lázaro 53–54, 77, 79, 89, 97, 111, 117, 121, 124, 127, 137, 142, 145, 147–148, 219, 233, 310, 383
   and Ávila Camacho, Manuel 180, 193, 208, 231
   and Lombardo Toledano, Vicente 79, 85–87, 98, 100–101, 109, 128–129, 131, 156, 164, 176, 185, 200, 234, 287, 302–303, 312, 321, 379, 384
   and López Mateos, Adolfo 365, 370
   and Mexican Communist Party (PCM) 109, 364–365
   and Mexican Workers Confederation (CTM) 180, 308
   and National Liberation Movement (MLN) 361–364
   and National Revolutionary Party (PRM) 53–54
   and Railroad Workers 326
   and refugees 167, 172–173
Carey, James 150, 264
Carpio, Marcelina 8, 10, 13–14
Carranza, Venustiano 17
Carrillo, Alejandro 137, 179, 188, 190, 206, 314, 324
Carrión, Jorge 362
Carter, Goodrich 148–149
Caso, Alfonso 21, 26–27, 34, 39, 57, 369
Caso, Antonio 19, 21, 23, 31, 34, 52
Castillo Armas, Carlos 340
Castro, Fidel 243, 341, 350–351, 364
Castro Leal, Antonio 21
Cedillo, Saturnino 124
Central America 84, 132, 204, 279, 280, 289, 336
Central School of Fine Arts 49
Cerda, Florencio 36, 41, 46
Chapa, Esther 171
Chiapas 126–127, 201, 346
Chihuahua 9, 195, 229, 232–233, 308, 366
Chile 136, 145, 168, 203–204, 206, 275, 288, 292–293, 341–342, 345, 348, 354
   and American Federation of Labor (AFL) 141, 215, 279, 284
   and Interamerican Confederation of Workers (CIT) 134, 285
   and International Labour Organization (ILO) 131–134, 197, 219
   and Latin American Workers Confederation (CTAL) 109, 146, 200, 213, 280, 285, 344, 346, 349, 351–353, 383
Chilean Workers Confederation 200, 280, 339
China 124, 267, 269–270, 272–273, 342, 357, 365, 370
Chumacero, Ali 327

INDEX 413

Chumacero, Blas 113, 242
Churchill, Winston 220, 251
Citrine, Walter 93–96, 140–141, 250, 252–253, 256, 258, 260–261, 265
Ciudad Juárez 232
Civic Front of the People 324
Clayton, William 275
Clayton Plan 275, 282, 287
Coahuila 57, 60, 232, 310
Cobos, Bernardo 330
Cofiño, Ángel 255
Cold War 2, 272
Coloma, Domingo 220
Colombia 132, 203, 209, 214, 270, 279, 291–292, 337, 346, 348
   and American Federation of Labor (AFL) 141, 284
   and Cali 205, 218–220, 274, 341
   and Interamerican Confederation of Workers (CIT) 284, 293
   and International Labour Organization (ILO) 147, 294
   and Latin American Workers Confederation (CTAL) 146, 212, 219–220, 342, 345
Colombian Workers Confederation 342
Colunga, Enrique 43
Communist Information Bureau (Cominform) 262
Communist International (Comintern) 85, 122, 158, 165, 167, 169–170
   See also Third International (Comintern) 137
Conciliation and Arbitration Boards 65, 70–72, 76, 78, 115, 241, 309
Confederation of Labour of Argentina (CGT) 140, 200
Confederation of Workers and Peasants of Mexico (CGOCM) 78, 85, 88, 90, 99–100, 107, 110, 229, 308
Congress for Cultural Freedom 340
Congress of Industrial Organizations (CIO) 114, 141, 146, 150, 241, 253, 254, 263–264, 266, 277, 286, 291, 333, 340
   and Committee for Industrial Organization (CIO) 138–139, 142
Constitution of 1917 21, 30, 44, 53, 58, 59, 62, 72, 86, 316, 361, 373
Contreras, Miguel 132

Contreras Labarca, Carlos 171
Corona del Rosal, Alfonso 383
Cosío Villegas, Daniel 247, 248
Costa Rica 141, 208, 214, 289, 340, 342, 343, 344, 346, 349
Cravioto, Alfonso 204
Cruz y Celis, José 228
Cuba 11, 144, 205, 337–338, 342–343, 354, 370
   and American Federation of Labor (AFL) 141, 293
   and Interamerican Confederation of Workers (CIT) 275, 293–295, 331–332, 336
   and International Labour Organization (ILO) 197–198
   and July 26 Movement 341
   and Latin American Trade Union Confederation (CSLA) 109, 132
   and Latin American Workers Confederation (CTAL) 199, 213, 215, 281, 342, 344, 348–350, 352, 355
Cuban Revolution 341, 349, 350, 351, 355, 358, 361, 365
Cuban Workers Confederation (CTC) 199, 281, 293, 341, 351
Czechoslovakia 122, 227, 229, 259, 263, 267, 288, 347, 350, 357, 378–379

Danzós Palomino, Ramón 362, 365
Davis, Nathaniel 289
Davis, William Rhodes 142
De Zengotita, Juan 283
Deakin, Arthur 264, 265
Delano, Luís Enrique 171
Del Rosal Díaz, Amaro 172
De la Huerta, Adolfo 36
Di Vittorio, Giuseppe 254
Díaz, Porfirio 10, 14
Díaz Ordaz, Gustavo 328, 353, 364, 365–367, 376, 383
Díaz Soto y Gama, Antonio 41
Dimitrov, Georg 170
Domenech, José 212
Domingo Lavín, José 228
Dominican Republic 19, 132, 203, 330, 333, 334
Durango 76, 108, 123, 124, 125, 179, 189, 191, 193, 194

El Salvador 198, 255, 280, 284
Echeverría, Luis 376
Ecuador 133, 198, 200, 203, 207, 288, 291, 294, 343, 345
  and American Federation of Labor (AFL) 279
  and International Labour Organization (ILO) 219
  and Latin American Workers Confederation (CTAL) 146, 212, 220, 344, 346, 349
Ecuadorian Workers Confederation 219, 288
Efron, David 215
Elizondo, Juan Manuel 236, 256
Encina, Dionisio 314
Engels, Friedrich 23, 269, 385
Espinosa Mireles, Gustavo 57
Estrada Villa, Rafael 375

Faculty of Philosophy and Letters 311
  See also School of Higher Education 20–21, 24
Faría, Jesús 220, 342
Fast, Howard 356
Federal District (DF) 64, 100, 107, 179, 199, 318
Federal District Federation of Labour Unions 7
Federal Security Directorate (DFS) 303, 313, 351, 360, 368
Fernández Roig, Miguel 293
Feuchtwanger, Lion 162
Figueres Ferrer, José 289
Figueroa Mendoza, Francisco 304, 360, 376
Fimmen, Edo 146
Finland 169, 253
First Congress of Mexican University Students and Teachers 52
First World War 135, 149, 156
Flores, Donato 256
Flores Olea, Víctor 362, 363
Franco, Francisco 122, 156, 157, 217, 218, 252, 257, 332
France 102, 122, 140, 157, 160–161, 169, 173–174, 184, 195, 251, 256, 266
French Communist Party 169, 347
Fuentes, Carlos 327, 361

Gabino Barreda University 88
Gaitán, Jorge Eliécer 292
Gallegos, Rómulo 295
Gálvez, José 35
García Téllez, Ignacio 49, 51, 125
García Terrés, Jaime 327
Gasca, Celestino 42, 110, 188, 361
General Confederation of Peruvian Workers (CGTP) 200
General Confederation of Workers and Peasants of Mexico (CGOCM) 78, 85, 88, 90, 99–100, 107, 110, 229, 278, 308
General Union of Workers of Spain 146
Germany 84, 122, 140, 142, 146, 156–158, 163, 169–170, 173–174, 202, 206, 251–252, 275, 347
  See also Third Reich 159, 161
Gide, André 102–105
Girola, Luis 218
Gómez, Juan Vicente 144
Gómez, Laureano 342
Gómez Lorenzo, Rosendo 171
Gómez Morín, Manuel 21, 57, 177, 383–384
Gómez Palacio 179
González Castro, Honorato 281
González Luna, Efraín 316
Gorkin, Julián 173
Gorky, Maxim 103
Goulart, Joao 354
Great Britain 94, 124, 142, 211
Green, William 137, 150, 283, 285
Grishin, Viktor 349
Group in Solidarity with the Labour Movement 30, 58
Guadalajara 12, 168, 233, 384
Guanajuato 43, 179, 189
Guatemala 209, 221, 329, 339, 345
  and American Federation of Labor (AFL) 340
  and International Labour Organization (ILO) 294
  and Latin American Workers Confederation (CTAL) 200, 219, 276, 337, 346
Guerrero 179, 189, 191, 194, 313, 318–319, 324
Guerrero, Alberto 41, 45
Gutiérrez, Efraín 126
Gutiérrez, Juan 111–112, 120, 179
Gutiérrez, Raúl 316

Gutiérrez Zamora   8
Guzmán, Agustín   137, 236
Guzmán, Eulalia   324

Haberman, Robert   74
Hall, Gus   322
Hannah, Philip   284
Haro, Guillermo   327
Harriman, Averell   266
Harris, Katherine   170
Haya de la Torre, Víctor   279, 284
Heine, Heinrich   163
Henríquez Guzmán, Miguel   231, 313, 316
Henríquez Ureña, Pedro   19–21, 29, 31–33, 39
Hidalgo   8, 163, 171, 178
Hidalgo, Ramón   194
Hillman, Sidney   150
Hitler, Adolf   84, 120, 122, 140, 141, 158, 162–163, 166, 169–170, 174, 186, 206, 209, 211, 217, 255
Hobsbawm, Eric   157n4, 158n5, 385
Honduras   198, 219, 339, 346
Honduran Workers Confederation   340
Horton, Henry   244
Huerta, Victoriano   19, 20, 177
Huitrón, Jacinto   370
Hungary   229, 259, 263, 357, 378

Ibáñez, Bernardo   146, 215, 219, 279, 284, 285, 292, 294, 330, 333
Icaza, Xavier   53, 54, 62, 88
Iglesias, Santiago   150
Independent Peasant Confederation (CCI)   353, 363–365
Institutional Revolutionary Party (PRI)   231–234, 237, 243–247, 249, 300–301, 305–307, 313, 316–319, 321, 323–324, 359–360, 363–365, 368, 371
Inter-American Association for Democracy and Freedom   332
Inter-American Conference on the Problems of War and Peace   274
Inter-American Regional Organization of Workers (ORIT)   334–342, 344–345, 349, 351, 353–355
International Confederation of Free Trade Unions (ICFTU)   333–335, 337, 338, 341
International Federation of Christian Trade Unions   294

International Federation of Trade Unions (IFTU)   114, 134, 136, 140–141, 145–147, 150, 165, 253, 290
International Labour Organization (ILO)   61, 88, 114, 131, 140, 145, 197, 277
Isaac, Catalino   178
Italy   8, 14, 31, 97, 122, 142, 146, 156–158, 176, 251, 253, 266, 310
Ivanovna, Ekaterina   260

Jalisco   178, 189, 194, 246, 281, 318, 363
Jalisco Workers Federation   178, 281
Jara, Heriberto   324, 362
Jáuregui, Arturo   339
Jenkins, William   37
Jiménez Acevedo, José   179
Jiménez Esponda, Estela   236
Jouhaux, León   140, 146

Kalinin, Mikhail   260–261
Katz, Leo   160
Katz, Otto (alias André Simone)   160, 213, 227, 259, 267
Kharkov   88
Khrushchev, Nikita Sergeievich   268, 346–347, 350, 385
Kilroe, Sidney   26
Kirov, Sergei   92
Kisch, Egon Erwin   160, 163
Knight, O.A.   220, 286, 292
Koestler, Arthur   169
Krauze, Enrique   3n6
Krivitsky, Walter   173
Kuznetsov, Vasilievich   257, 265

Laborde, Hernán   115, 118, 120–121, 238, 242, 243
Labour Department (DT)   39, 48, 59
Labour Law   65–73
Largo Caballero, Francisco   157
Latin American Workers Confederation (CTAL)   109, 131, 134, 150, 184, 186, 199, 211–213, 215–216, 242, 247, 249, 274, 283, 309, 317, 330, 332, 334, 336, 339, 364, 366, 383
   and founding of   146–148
   and First Congress   201–202
   and Second Congress   219–221
   and Third Congress   285–290

and Fourth Congress   344–345
and dissolution   348–355
League Against War and Fascism   137
League of Agrarian Communities   192
League of Nations   61, 131
Lechín, Juan   256, 279, 345, 353
Leduc, Renato   324
Lenin, Vladimir Ilyich   97, 114, 162, 164, 192, 239, 269–270, 312, 364, 385
Leningrad   88, 91–92, 97, 103
León, Teresa   84
Lewis, John L.   138–139, 142, 146, 149
Leyva Velázquez, Gabriel   317–318
Libenson, Isaac   213
Liberation Army of the South   17
Liceo Teziuteco   18
Liera, Guillermo   180
Limón Moscano, Agustín   47
Liszt Arzubide, Germán   39
Lombardo, Delfina de Jesús   14
Lombardo Catti, Vincenzo   8–10, 12–17, 32
Lombardo Carpio, Alejandro   10, 13, 61
Lombardo Carpio, Emilia   10, 13
Lombardo Carpio, Luis   10–16
Lombardo Carpio, Marcelina   10, 13
Lombardo Carpio, María   10
Lombardo Carpio, Pedro   10, 13, 14, 32, 39, 61
Lombardo Carpio, Vicente   10–18, 25–27
Lombardo Otero, Adriana   44, 369
Lombardo Otero, Marcela   3
Lombardo Toledano, Aída   10, 25
Lombardo Toledano, Elena   10, 25
Lombardo Toledano, Guillermo   10, 26
Lombardo Toledano, Humberto   10, 25
Lombardo Toledano, Isabel   10, 25
Lombardo Toledano, Luis   10, 179
Lombardo Toledano, Margarita   10, 25
Lombardo Toledano, María   10, 11, 25, 26, 27, 369
Lombardo Toledano, Vicente   56, 61, 148, 158–160, 162, 203, 210, 225, 226, 239, 250, 257–258, 274, 284, 300, 312, 315, 322, 326, 329–330, 356, 361, 363, 375, 377, 385–386
and Alemán Valdés, Miguel   231, 233–234, 286–287, 311–312
and Ávila Camacho, Manuel   231, 234, 305–306
and Biography Writing   3
and Calles, Plutarco Elías   34–36, 39, 41, 43, 45, 47, 63, 123, 128–129
and Díaz Ordaz, Gustavo   353, 364, 366, 368
and education   19–23, 30
and expulsion from CTM   246–247
and family   8, 11, 18, 25–26, 28, 314, 316, 320, 328, 357, 367, 369
and Gabino Barreda University   50, 88
and International Labour Organization (ILO)   133, 140, 142, 148, 216, 218, 219, 278, 294, 330
and Institutional Revolutionary Party (PRI)   232, 234, 244, 246–247, 249, 301, 318, 321, 363
and Latin American Workers Confederation (CTAL)   142, 146–147, 197, 201–202, 211–213, 220, 247, 253–254, 264–265, 266, 274, 276–283, 285, 287, 289–291, 294, 296, 309, 317, 330, 336, 342–344, 346, 348–355, 364
and Lázaro Cárdenas   85–86, 77, 79, 98–101, 109, 128, 131, 145, 156, 176, 200, 287, 302–303, 312, 321, 364, 379
and Mexican Communist Party (PCM)   110, 122, 164, 235–237, 313, 364
and Mexican Regional Workers Confederation (CROM)   32–33, 50, 57–59, 62, 64–65, 68–78, 108, 226, 241
and Mexican Workers Confederation (CTM)   107, 110–118, 120, 122–127, 130, 134, 136, 139, 141, 147, 149–150, 177–178, 180–183, 185–189, 191–196, 227–232, 234, 240, 242–247, 264, 279, 287–288, 309
and Oil Workers   290–291, 301
and People's University   22
and People's Socialist Party (PPS)   356, 359–360, 362, 365–367, 373–377
and presidential campaign   27, 313–316
and resignation from CTM   185–188
and Roundtable of Mexican Marxists   234–240
and Ruiz Cortines, Adolfo   310, 313, 316, 322, 343
and Trotsky, Leon   163–169, 174
and Union of Workers and Peasants of Mexico (UGOCM)   308–310, 317, 360, 362, 376–377
and Vasconcelos, José   30–35

birth of   18
death of   383
in Chamber of Deputies   40–48, 365, 368, 370–371, 374
in China   270–271, 356
in Czechoslovakia   227, 229, 259–260, 267, 288, 378
in Latin America   131–134, 144, 198–199, 204–209, 211, 214–218, 221, 255–256, 283, 345–346, 370–372, 374, 380–381
in National Preparatory School   19–20, 29, 31, 33, 49–51, 57, 383
in National Revolutionary Party (PNR)   53–54, 123
in National University   20, 34, 49, 311
in People's Party (PP)   237–238, 247, 300, 303, 304, 307, 314–319, 321–322, 324, 327
in Puebla   37–40, 241, 367
in Soviet Union   52, 84, 85, 90–97, 102, 105, 119, 135, 163–165, 170–172, 221, 223, 233, 251–252, 254, 261, 263, 268–269, 357, 384
in United States of America   87, 89, 139, 218–219, 222, 255, 267, 271, 276, 324
in Worker's University   161, 179, 184, 190, 244, 272, 301, 317
López, Jacinto   190, 232, 234, 245, 305–306, 318, 322–323, 359–360, 362, 369, 374–377
López Contreras, Eleazar   199
Los Mochis   68–70, 108, 179
Lovestone, Jay   266, 295
Lovsky, Witold Antonovich   109–110, 114–117, 119, 131–132, 134–135, 137
Lozovsky, Alexandr   85n3, 109, 114, 118–120, 135–136

Machado, Gerardo   144
Macín, Francisco   228
Madero, Francisco I.   15, 19, 111, 306, 367, 373
Madison Square Garden   138
Madrid   88, 90
Malavé Villalba, Augusto   201, 295, 332, 337, 340
Managua   208
Mann, Heinrich   162
Manuilsky, Dmitri   170
Mao Tse-Tung   269, 271–272, 385
Marcuse, Herbert   385

Marischi, Vicente   348
Marshall, George   292
Marshall Plan   262–264, 266–267, 286–287, 292
Martínez, Eufemio   192
Martínez, Ricardo   327
Martínez Adame, Arturo   179, 187
Martínez Manautou, Emilio   376
Marx, Karl   23, 54, 160, 202, 237, 269, 312, 379, 385
Marxist Group The Insurgent   236, 238
Mastretta, Marcos   176
Mayorga, Enrique   108
Meany, George   274, 335, 339
Medina Angarita, Isaías   217
Méndez, Leopoldo   163, 239
Menéndez, Jesús   293
Meraz, Manuel   244
Mercader, Ramón   170–171
Merker, Paul   160
Messersmith, George   275, 278
Mexican Academy of Sciences   373
Mexican Communist Party (PCM)   51, 62, 85, 109–110, 122, 164, 178, 234–238, 242, 313–314, 329, 353, 364–365
Mexican Electrical Workers Union   112, 187, 201, 229
Mexican Labour Party (PLM)   35, 57, 64, 71
Mexican Oil Workers Union   291
Mexican Regional Workers Confederation (CROM)   7, 32–33, 35, 38–39, 41, 50, 56–57, 59, 62–63, 68, 70–72, 74–77, 87, 108, 111, 137–139, 141, 149, 199, 226, 229, 241, 278, 308, 343
in Atlixco   64–65
in Veracruz   65, 73, 78
Mexican Revolution   2, 3, 10, 51, 54, 58, 63, 67, 74–75, 119, 123, 128, 181, 192, 205, 218, 229, 241, 296, 301, 312, 355, 361, 365, 378
Mexican Socialist League   235
Mexican Workers Confederation (CTM)   117–118, 128–130, 134–137, 141, 160, 168, 195, 198, 201, 204, 206–207, 305
and *charrismo* (bossism)   248–249
and elections   240–244
and foundation of   110–114
and Trotsky, Leon   164–168
Mexican Workers and Peasants Party   313, 377

Meyer, Hannes   160, 162
Michoacán   53, 58, 65, 189, 194, 302, 319
Mickiewicz, Adam   378
Mills, Wright   385
Mireles Malpica, Pedro   302
Monge, Luis Alberto   279, 338, 340
Monroe Doctrine   150
Montes, Manuel   47–48
Montevideo   49, 109, 216–217, 331
Mora, Manuel   289
Morales, Pedro   112, 120
Moreau, Alberto   137
Morelia   58, 365
Morelos   99, 148, 179, 192, 319, 377
Moreno, Roberto   293
Moreno Vaca, Jesús   21
Morínigo, Higinio   212, 339
Morones, Luis N.   39, 57, 65, 70–71, 73, 77, 100, 110–111, 120, 283–285, 336, 343
  and Labour Party   42, 64
  and Calles, Plutarco Elías   63, 101, 137–138
  and Ministry of Industry, Commerce and Labour   63, 68
  and Obregón, Álvaro   63–64
  and Vicente Lombardo Toledano   56–58, 71, 76, 101, 108, 148–150, 226, 241
Múgica, Francisco J.   53, 77, 176–178
Mujal, Eusebio   279, 337
Münzenberg, Willi   173
Muñiz, Grandiso   174
Murillo, Raúl   233
Murray, Philip   150
Mussolini, Benito   141, 156

Nasser, Gamal Abdel   350
National Action Party (PAN)   156, 177, 305, 316, 323, 368, 369–371, 383
National Agrarian Party (PNA)   42
National Autonomous University of Mexico (UNAM)   375, 381
National Committee for Proletarian Defense   113
National Confederation of Labour   157
National Confederation of Popular Organisations (CNOP)   191, 305
National Cooperativist Party   35–36
National Federation of Sugar Workers of Cuba   293

National Irrigation Commission   171
National Liberation Movement (MLN)   351
National Peasant Confederation (CNC)   124, 192, 245, 300, 308, 364
National Polytechnic Institute (IPN)   314, 327–328
National Preparatory School   19, 20, 29, 31, 33, 35, 39, 49–51, 57, 230, 383
National Proletarian Confederation   186, 229, 278, 285, 336
National Revolutionary Party (PNR)   53, 64, 74, 108, 121, 123, 129
National Socialist German Workers Party (NSDAP)   159
National Synarchist Union   156
National Teachers Federation   65
National Teachers' Union (SNTE)   327
National Union of Detectives and Technical Police   281
National University of Mexico   20, 34, 49, 311
Navarrete, Alfredo   113
Nayarit   233, 318
Negrín, Juan   158
Nehru, Jawaharlal   350
Nelken, Margarita   171
Neruda, Pablo   168, 171, 294
Nicaragua   143, 208, 219, 331, 333
Nicaraguan Trade Union Confederation   209
Nin, Andreu   158
Nixon, Richard   341
Nogales   232
Noriega, Antonio   315
North Atlantic Treaty Organization (NATO)   263
Norway   141–142
Novo, Salvador   303
Nuevo León   9, 179, 189, 281, 367

Oaxaca   126, 179, 189, 194, 375
Obregón, Álvaro   17, 33–37, 39, 47, 63, 64
Ocampo, Salvador   213, 286, 288, 294, 383
October Revolution   88, 162, 206
Odría, Manuel   335, 339
Office of the Coordinator of Inter-American Affairs   215
Ohio State Federation of Labor   284
Oil Fuels of Mexico   14

Oil Workers International Union 286
Oldenbroek, Jacobus 333–334, 336
Olea y Leyva, Teophilus 21, 180
Organization of American States (OAS) 292, 354
Orona, Arturo 362
Orive Alba, Adolfo 124, 171
Ortega, Samuel 325
Ortiz Hernán, Gustavo 112–113
Oslo 141, 165
Otero, Rosa María 24–25, 31, 33, 61, 120, 197, 204, 256, 268–269, 271, 367
Otero y Gama, Carmen 161, 235
Otero y Gama, Concepción 119
Otero y Gama, María de Jesús 328
Otero y Gama, Rafael 179

Padilla, Ezequiel 231–232
Padilla, Mariano 179
Padilla, Vicente 304
Palacio de Bellas Artes 146, 160, 182, 286, 335, 370
Palacios, Alfonso 243, 245
Palomino Rojas, Tomás 124, 193–194, 279, 281, 285
Pan American Federation of Labor 149
Pan-China Federation of Labour (PAFL) 149
Panama 135, 203, 344
Panama Canal 203, 276, 332
Panteón de Dolores 367
Panteón Jardín 383
Paraguay 141, 143, 146, 198, 217, 339, 343
Paraguayan Workers' Confederation 199, 212
Party of the Mexican Revolution (PRM) 123, 128–129, 178–180, 183, 191, 195, 206, 227, 230, 255
Pastorino, Enrique 349
Patiño Mines and Enterprises Consolidated 210
Patiño, Simón 211
Paz, Octavio 169, 174, 327
Paz Estenssoro, Víctor 343
Pellicer, Carlos 201, 327
Peña, Alejandro 180
Peña, Hermenegildo 232
Peña, Lázaro 145, 199, 293, 348–349
Peñaranda, Enrique 210–211, 215
Peraza, Gaudencio 236, 255

Pérez, Encarnación 328
Pérez, Félix 41
Pérez Leiros, Francisco 145, 147, 213
People's Electoral Front 365
People's Party (PP) 234, 237–238, 243–247, 249, 264, 300–301, 303–306, 308, 313–314, 316–325, 327
  See also Popular Party
People's Socialist Party (PPS) 356, 358–362, 364–369, 373–377, 384
People's University 3, 22, 30, 57, 105, 107, 116, 128, 137, 160–161, 179, 181, 184, 187, 190, 236, 238, 244, 311, 316–317, 369
  See also Workers University
Permanent Congress of Trade Union Unity of Latin American Workers (CPUSTAL) 354
Perón, Juan Domingo 213, 215, 220, 258, 278, 283–285, 343
Peru 109, 143, 146, 200, 203–204, 279, 291, 330, 335, 337, 346, 348
  and American Federation of Labor (AFL) 295
  and International Confederation of Free Trade Unions (ICFTU) 333
  and Interamerican Confederation of Workers (CIT) 284, 292, 331
  and Latin American Workers Confederation (CTAL) 220, 285–286, 334, 342–343
  and Peruvian Confederation of Labour 295
Pesqueira, Ignacio 307
Petrograd 91
Philadelphia 216, 218, 277
Pineda, Leobardo Wolstano 243
Pivert, Marceau 174
Poland 88, 169, 251, 262–263, 288, 347, 357, 378
Ponce, Aníbal 144
Poniatowska, Elena 374
Porter, Catherine Ann 31
Portes Gil, Emilio 64, 71, 132, 281, 321, 364–365
  and Labour Law 65–73
Prado, Manuel 200, 206
Prague 88, 259–261, 267, 268, 271, 348, 379
Prague Spring 379
Prestes, Luis Carlos 216
  See also Brazil

Pruneda, Alfonso   21
Public Education Ministry   30, 187, 201
Puebla   1, 8–9, 11–12, 14, 16, 17, 27, 36–45, 47, 49, 108, 148, 176, 319
  and CROM   63–65, 76, 78
  and CTM   179, 241
  and UGOCM   367
Puente, María Teresa   236, 372
Pumarino, Gonzalo   46
Pushkin, Alexandr   269

Quesada, Abel   327
Quintero, Luís   99, 194

Rabadán, Macrina   318, 324
Railroad Workers Union   116
Ramírez y Ramírez, Enrique   236, 264, 310, 324, 371
Ramírez Vázquez, Manuel   286, 310
Ramos Malzárraga, Javier   243, 245
Rangel, Enrique   281, 285
Red International of Labour Unions (Profintern)   89, 109, 134–135, 146
Regler, Gustav   174
Reinerová, Lenka   160
Reiss, Ignace   173
Renn, Ludwig   160
Repetto, Nicholas   75, 278
Reséndiz, Benjamín   180
Reuther, Walter   150, 333
Revueltas, José   304–305, 308, 318, 375, 384–385
Reyes, Alfonso   32, 195
Reyner, Pedro   365
Rivera, Diego   30, 49, 164, 302–303, 383
Rivera, Manuel   336
Rockefeller, Nelson   215
Rojo Gómez, Javier   171, 231
Rolland, Romain   102
Romania   253, 256, 260, 263, 349, 357
Romualdi, Serafino   281–285, 295, 330–332, 334, 355
  and Latin American Workers Confederation (CTAL)   276–282
Roosevelt, Franklin Delano   133, 138
Rubio, Jaime   291
Ruiz, Apolinar   304
Ruiz Cortines, Adolfo   310, 313, 316, 322, 343

Russia   66, 83, 90, 95–96, 207, 222, 245, 283, 332

Saad, Pedro   255, 345
Sabroso, Arturo   295, 335
Sáenz, Aarón   72
Sáenz, Moisés   200
Safford Towne, Robert   9
Saillant, Louis   257, 261, 263–264, 286–288, 336, 348–350, 353
Salazar, Othón   328, 362, 365
Salinas de Gortari, Carlos   1
San Luís Potosí   9, 24, 33, 124
Sánchez, Guadalupe   36
Sánchez, José María   38, 47
Sánchez Madariaga, Alfonso   99, 186, 194, 256, 305
Sánchez Taboada, Rodolfo   244
Santiago de Chile   109, 131, 145, 285, 292, 344, 351–352, 354
Sartre, Jean-Paul   356
Schevenels, Walter   142, 145
School of Law and Jurisprudence   20–22, 26, 42, 49, 51, 57, 230, 311, 375
Second International   88, 290
Second World War   2, 156, 173, 260, 263
Seghers, Anna   160
Seligsohn, Heidi   255–256
Serge, Victor   102–104, 173–174
Serrano, Francisco   39
Settimo Torinese   8, 12, 15, 17, 61
Sierra, Justo   19
Sierra Cantillo, Gonzalo   349
Silva, Federico   236, 359
Sinaloa   68–69, 76, 108, 179–180, 189, 194, 301, 367
Siqueiros, David Alfaro   167–168, 237–239, 324, 370, 383
Socialist International   341
Socialist Party of the Southeast   127
Society of Conferences and Concerts   30, 57
Solís Solís, Luis   134
Somoza García, Anastasio   143, 208–209, 217, 255, 280
Sonora   65, 76, 108, 125–126, 246, 304–307, 314, 318, 323, 360, 376–377
Sonora Workers Confederation   126
Soriano, Juan   327
Soto, Ignacio   306

INDEX   421

Soto Innes, Eduardo   137
Soviet Union   93–100, 157–158, 169–170, 172–
    173, 213, 245, 250–252, 258–261, 268,
    272–273, 276, 296, 325, 327, 347, 349,
    351, 354–355, 357–358, 384–385
    See also Moscow
    See also URSS
Spain   11, 84, 90, 122, 124, 145–146, 157–161,
    167, 173–174, 215, 221, 257, 261–262
Spanish Civil War   167
Spanish Communist Party   157
Spanish Socialist Workers Party   157
Staal, Adolf   145, 147, 201
Stalin, Josef   89–92, 95, 102–105, 156–158,
    166, 169–170, 173–174, 250–252, 257,
    262, 269–271, 284, 312, 333, 345–347,
    385
Stalingrad   216
Standard Oil   333
State of Mexico   192
Stephens García, Manuel   377
Stroessner, Alfredo   339
Sugar Industry Workers' Union   246
Supreme Court   37, 88
Szklarska Poreba   262

Taft-Hartley Act   296
Tamaulipas   25, 64, 189, 232
Tannenbaum, Frank   61, 148
Taylor, Frederick Winslow   65
Tejeda, Adalberto   45, 205, 321
Téllez, Juan   113
Tennyson, Allan   283, 288, 309
Tewson, Vincent   334
Teziutlán   8–18, 32, 35, 41–46, 368
Teziutlán Copper and Smelting company   9
Thomas, Norman   215
Thorez, Maurice   251, 347
Tirado, Claudio N.   45–48
Togliatti, Palmiro   251, 347
Toledano Silva, Vicente   357
Toledano Toledano, Isabel   11
Toussaint, Guillermo   39
Trades Union Congress (Council) (TUC)   93,
    250, 252, 254, 264–265
Traven, Bruno   201
Treaty of Versailles   135
Tresca, Carlo   173
Trotsky, Leon   156, 163–169, 173–174, 177, 215

Trueba Urbina, Alberto   179
Truman, Harry   295

Ubico, Jorge   200, 219, 346
Umansky, Alexandr   172
Unified Socialist Action Group   242
Union of Workers and Peasants of Mexico
    (UGOCM)   265, 288, 308, 309–310, 317,
    319, 322–323, 353, 359–360, 362, 364,
    367, 376–377
United Confederation of Labour (CUT)   243,
    287, 309
United Fruit Company (UFCO)   336, 339,
    340, 346
United Nations   215, 262, 295
United Nations Economic and Social Council
    330
United Officers Group   213
United Sugar Companies   68
United Transport Service Employees' Union
    277
University of Paris   380
Uranga, Emilio   327
Uruguay   49, 143, 217
    and American Federation of Labor (AFL)
        141
    and Latin American Workers Confedera-
        tion (CTAL)   339, 345, 349

Valadés, José C.   190
Valenzuela, Edgardo   345
Vallejo, Demetrio   324–326, 365
Vargas, Getulio   144, 146, 215–217
    See also Brazil
Vasconcelos, José   30, 31, 33–36, 38–39, 383
Vázquez del Mercado, Alberto   20–21, 24
Véjar Vázquez, Octavio   314
Velasco, Miguel Ángel   112–113, 116, 120, 243,
    366
Velasco Ibarra, José María   279, 288
Velázquez, Fidel   64, 99, 112, 114, 120, 178,
    185–194, 197, 207, 213, 227, 242, 247, 274,
    335, 338
Venezuela   144, 203, 218, 290–291, 294, 330,
    332
    and American Federation of Labor (AFL)
        141, 279
    and Interamerican Confederation of
        Workers (CIT)   295

and International Confederation of Free Trade Unions (ICFTU) 333–334, 337
and International Labour Organization (ILO) 331
and Latin American Workers Confederation (CTAL) 199, 201, 220, 285–286, 342
Venezuelan Oil Workers Federation 291
Veracruz Regional Workers' Federation 191
Vidali, Vittorio 167, 244, 370
Viesca y Palma, Jorge 244, 281
Villa, Francisco 17, 21, 373
Villarreal, Isauro 183
Villarroel, Gualberto 215, 279
Villaseñor, Víctor Manuel 87–88, 92, 98, 114, 137, 236, 302, 305, 307–308, 384
Villavicencio Toscana, Manuel 42–43

Wagner Act 296
Wallace, Henry 182, 190, 211
War of Independence 11, 370
Warsaw Pact 379
Washington D.C. 134, 139, 177, 281–282, 285, 316
Washington, Walter 144, 215, 276, 284, 288, 354
Waters Pierce 11

Wilkie, James and Edna Monzon 3–4
Wilson, Woodrow 149
Woll, Matthew 149–150
Woolf, Virginia 175
Workers Party of Marxist Unification (POUM) 157–158, 167, 174
World Federation of Trade Unions (WFTU) 249–250, 254, 257, 259–266, 286, 288–289, 294–295, 308–310, 317, 330, 333, 336–337, 344, 346, 348–350, 352–353, 355, 383
Wright, Chester 149, 385

Yocupicio, Román 125–126
Yugoslavia 288
Yucatán 11, 65, 127, 178, 246
Yurén, Jesús 99, 194

Zacatecas 9, 76
Zapata, Emiliano 17, 21, 148, 177
Zuckerman, Leo 160
Zuno, José Guadalupe 321
Zúñiga, Celso 377
Zúñiga, Víctor Manuel 349
Zupka, František 350
Zweig, Stefan 175

Illustrations

ILL. 1   Vicente Lombardo Toledano
SOURCE: ARCHIVE OF THE INTERNATIONAL LABOUR ORGANIZATION

ILL. 2 Vincenzo Lombardo Catti
SOURCE: ARCHIVO FOTOGRÁFICO DEL CENTRO DE ESTUDIOS FILOSÓFICOS, POLÍTICOS Y SOCIALES "VICENTE LOMBARDO TOLEDANO"

ILL. 3 Vicente Lombardo and Isabel Toledano
SOURCE: ARCHIVO FOTOGRÁFICO DEL CENTRO DE ESTUDIOS FILOSÓFICOS, POLÍTICOS Y SOCIALES "VICENTE LOMBARDO TOLEDANO"

ILL. 4   Vicente Lombardo Toledano hunting in the Sierra de Puebla. Ca. 1911
SOURCE: ARCHIVO FOTOGRÁFICO DEL CENTRO DE ESTUDIOS FILOSÓFICOS, POLÍTICOS Y SOCIALES "VICENTE LOMBARDO TOLEDANO"

ILL. 5　　Bridal photography of Vicente Lombardo Toledano and Rosa María Otero. 22 April 1921
SOURCE: ARCHIVO FOTOGRÁFICO DEL CENTRO DE ESTUDIOS FILOSÓFICOS, POLÍTICOS Y SOCIALES "VICENTE LOMBARDO TOLEDANO"

ILL. 6   Vicente Lombardo Toledano and family. Ca. 1930
SOURCE: ARCHIVO FOTOGRÁFICO DEL CENTRO DE ESTUDIOS FILOSÓFICOS, POLÍTICOS Y SOCIALES "VICENTE LOMBARDO TOLEDANO"

ILL. 7　　Vicente Lombardo Toledano sitting on the steps of an archaeological site in Yucatán. 1941
SOURCE: ARCHIVO FOTOGRÁFICO DEL CENTRO DE ESTUDIOS FILOSÓFICOS, POLÍTICOS Y SOCIALES "VICENTE LOMBARDO TOLEDANO"

ILL. 8 Vicente Lombardo Toledano and Marcela Lombardo Otero. Ca. 1946
SOURCE: ARCHIVO FOTOGRÁFICO DEL CENTRO DE ESTUDIOS FILOSÓFICOS, POLÍTICOS Y SOCIALES "VICENTE LOMBARDO TOLEDANO"

ILL. 9   Vicente Lombardo Toledano portrayed during his trip from New York to Liverpool. 1938
SOURCE: ARCHIVO FOTOGRÁFICO DEL CENTRO DE ESTUDIOS FILOSÓFICOS, POLÍTICOS Y SOCIALES "VICENTE LOMBARDO TOLEDANO".

ILL. 10 Vicente Lombardo Toledano and Fidel Velázquez in the farewell to the direction of the CTM. 1941
SOURCE: ARCHIVO FOTOGRÁFICO DEL CENTRO DE ESTUDIOS FILOSÓFICOS, POLÍTICOS Y SOCIALES "VICENTE LOMBARDO TOLEDANO"

ILL. 11 Vicente Lombardo Toledano in Yugoslavia. June–July 1947
SOURCE: ARCHIVO FOTOGRÁFICO DEL CENTRO DE ESTUDIOS FILOSÓFICOS, POLÍTICOS Y SOCIALES "VICENTE LOMBARDO TOLEDANO"

ILL. 12 María Teresa Puente delivering a speech during an assembly of the Partido Popular
SOURCE: ARCHIVO FOTOGRÁFICO DEL CENTRO DE ESTUDIOS FILOSÓFICOS, POLÍTICOS Y SOCIALES "VICENTE LOMBARDO TOLEDANO"

ILL. 13 Vicente Lombardo Toledano with the children of the workers. Ca. 1951
SOURCE: ARCHIVO FOTOGRÁFICO DEL CENTRO DE ESTUDIOS FILOSÓFICOS, POLÍTICOS Y SOCIALES "VICENTE LOMBARDO TOLEDANO"

ILL. 14   Vicente Lombardo Toledano and Cuban leader Jesús Menéndez
SOURCE: ARCHIVO FOTOGRÁFICO DEL CENTRO DE ESTUDIOS FILOSÓFICOS, POLÍTICOS Y SOCIALES "VICENTE LOMBARDO TOLEDANO"

ILL. 15 Vicente Lombardo Toledano portrayed with indigenous women from Juchitán, Oaxaca. 1952
SOURCE: ARCHIVO FOTOGRÁFICO DEL CENTRO DE ESTUDIOS FILOSÓFICOS, POLÍTICOS Y SOCIALES "VICENTE LOMBARDO TOLEDANO"

ILL. 16   Vicente Lombardo Toledano in Chihuahua, Chihuahua during his presidential campaign. 1952
SOURCE: ARCHIVO FOTOGRÁFICO DEL CENTRO DE ESTUDIOS FILOSÓFICOS, POLÍTICOS Y SOCIALES "VICENTE LOMBARDO TOLEDANO"

ILL. 17 Vicente Lombardo Toledano in the capital Zócalo. 1952
SOURCE: ARCHIVO FOTOGRÁFICO DEL CENTRO DE ESTUDIOS FILOSÓFICOS, POLÍTICOS Y SOCIALES "VICENTE LOMBARDO TOLEDANO"

ILL. 18   Vicente Lombardo Toledano leading a PPS march through the streets of Teziutlán, Puebla. 1964
SOURCE: ARCHIVO FOTOGRÁFICO DEL CENTRO DE ESTUDIOS FILOSÓFICOS, POLÍTICOS Y SOCIALES "VICENTE LOMBARDO TOLEDANO"

ILL. 19 Lázaro Cárdenas, Vicente Lombardo Toledano and Gustavo Díaz Ordaz. 1968
SOURCE: ARCHIVO FOTOGRÁFICO DEL CENTRO DE ESTUDIOS FILOSÓFICOS, POLÍTICOS Y SOCIALES "VICENTE LOMBARDO TOLEDANO"

ILL. 20 'Leon Trotsky, as he really is'
SOURCE: *FUTURO*, NO. 34, DECEMBER 1938, P. 16

ILL. 21 — 'Not even for free'
SOURCE: *EXCÉLSIOR*, 17 JUNE 1952, P. 6-A

ILL. 22 – 'I am a communist and a Marxist by conviction and as in all parts, Mexico will be completely socialist!' – Oh wow! ... He wants to be a president and a Soviet secretary?
SOURCE: *NOVEDADES*, 1 JULY 1952, P. 4

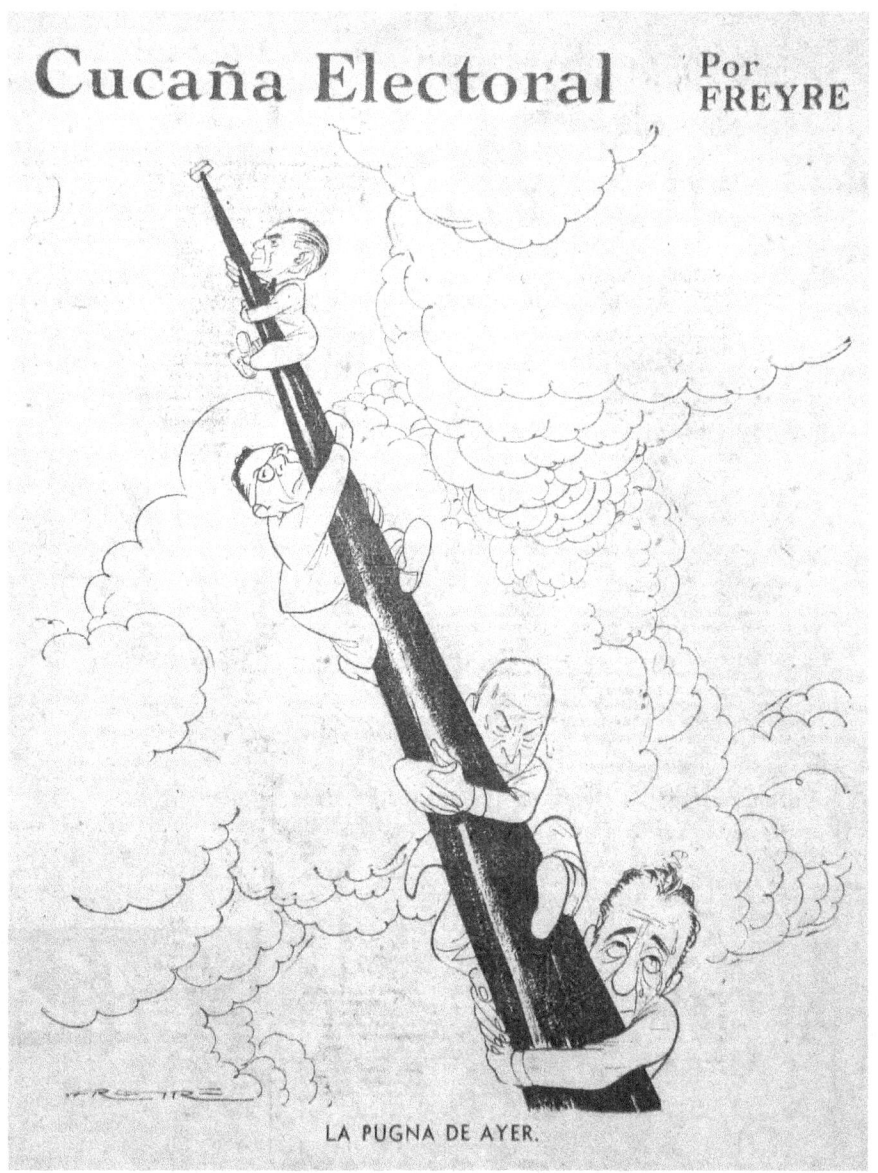

ILL. 23   'The greasy electoral pole. Yesterday's conflict'
SOURCE: *EXCÉLSIOR* BY FREYRE, 7 JULY 1952, P. 6-A

ILL. 24 'Mourning on the left'
SOURCE: *EXCÉLSIOR* BY MARINO, 18 NOVEMBER 1968, P. 6-A

ILL. 25   'And now what?'
SOURCE: *EXCÉLSIOR* BY MARINO, 19 NOVEMBER 1968, P. 6-A